Rick Steves®

BEST OF FRANCE

Rick Steves & Steve Smith

Contents

South of France

East France

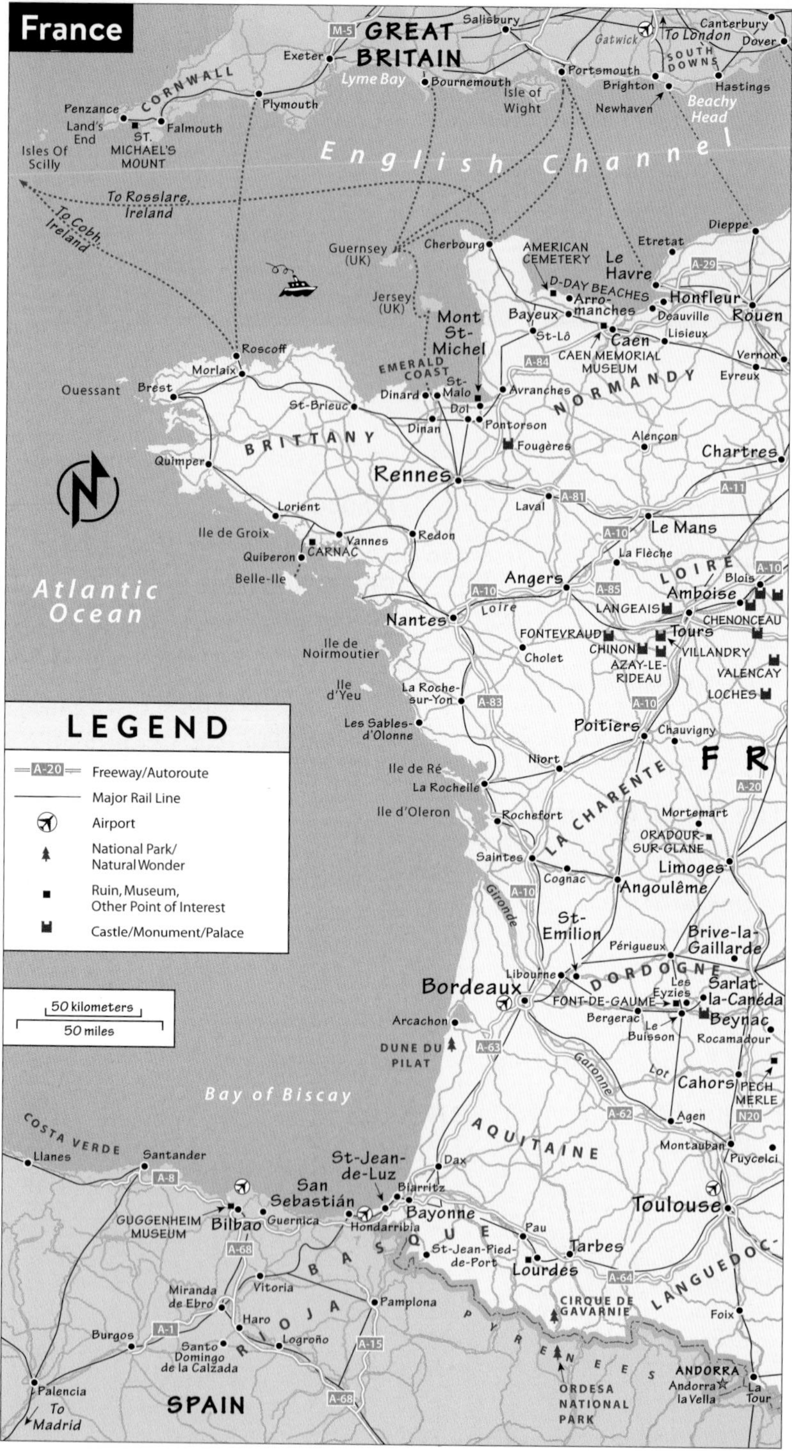
France
GREAT BRITAIN
Salisbury
Canterbury
Gatwick
To London
Dover
Exeter
CORNWALL
Lyme Bay
Bournemouth
Portsmouth
Brighton
SOUTH DOWNS
Hastings
Plymouth
Isle of Wight
Newhaven
Beachy Head
Penzance
Land's End
Falmouth
ST. MICHAEL'S MOUNT
Isles Of Scilly
English Channel
To Rosslare, Ireland
To Cobh, Ireland
Dieppe
Etretat
Guernsey (UK)
Cherbourg
AMERICAN CEMETERY
Le Havre
D-DAY BEACHES
Arromanches
Honfleur
Rouen
Jersey (UK)
Mont St-Michel
Bayeux
Deauville
St-Lô
Caen
Lisieux
CAEN MEMORIAL MUSEUM
Vernon
Roscoff
EMERALD COAST
Morlaix
NORMANDY
Evreux
Ouessant
Brest
Dinard
St-Malo
Avranches
St-Brieuc
Dol
Dinan
Pontorson
BRITTANY
Fougères
Alençon
Chartres
Quimper
Rennes
Laval
Lorient
Le Mans
Ile de Groix
Redon
Vannes
CARNAC
Quiberon
La Flèche
Belle-Ile
Angers
LOIRE
Blois
Atlantic Ocean
Amboise
Loire
LANGEAIS
CHENONCEAU
Nantes
FONTEVRAUD
Tours
Ile de Noirmoutier
Cholet
CHINON
VILLANDRY
AZAY-LE-RIDEAU
VALENCAY
Ile d'Yeu
La Roche-sur-Yon
LOCHES
Les Sables-d'Olonne
Poitiers
Chauvigny
FR
Niort
Ile de Ré
La Rochelle
LA CHARENTE
Mortemart
Ile d'Oleron
Rochefort
ORADOUR-SUR-GLANE
Saintes
Limoges
Cognac
Gironde
Angoulême
St-Emilion
Périgueux
Brive-la-Gaillarde
Libourne
DORDOGNE
Sarlat-la-Canéda
Bordeaux
FONT-DE-GAUME
Les Eyzies
Beynac
Bergerac
Le Buisson
Arcachon
Rocamadour
DUNE DU PILAT
Garonne
Lot
Cahors
PECH MERLE
Bay of Biscay
Agen
COSTA VERDE
AQUITAINE
Montauban
Puycelci
Llanes
Santander
Dax
St-Jean-de-Luz
San Sebastián
Biarritz
Toulouse
GUGGENHEIM MUSEUM
Bilbao
Guernica
Bayonne
Hondarribia
BASQUE
Pau
St-Jean-Pied-de-Port
Tarbes
Lourdes
LANGUEDOC-
Miranda de Ebro
Vitoria
Pamplona
CIRQUE DE GAVARNIE
Foix
Haro
RIOJA
Burgos
Logroño
Santo Domingo de la Calzada
PYRENEES
ANDORRA
Andorra la Vella
La Tour
ORDESA NATIONAL PARK
Palencia
To Madrid
SPAIN
M-5
A-29
A-84
A-81
A-11
A-10
A-85
A-83
A-20
A-63
A-62
N20
A-8
A-68
A-64
A-1
A-15
LEGEND
A-20 Freeway/Autoroute
Major Rail Line
Airport
National Park/ Natural Wonder
Ruin, Museum, Other Point of Interest
Castle/Monument/Palace
50 kilometers
50 miles

BELGIUM
GERMANY
LUXEMBOURG
SWITZERLAND
ITALY
ANCE
Mediterranean Sea
Channel Tunnel
Ostende
Bruges
To Amsterdam
Düsseldorf
To Berlin
Dunkerque
Antwerp
Ghent
Calais
Brussels
Cologne
Boulogne
WATERLOO
Aachen
Bonn
St-Omer
FLANDERS
Lille
Liège
Rhine
Arras
Cambrai
Namur
WALLONIE
Frankfurt
Abbeville
Aulnoye
Cochem
Mosel
Bacharach
Hahn
Amiens
ARDENNES
St-Quentin
Charleville-Mézières
LUXEMBOURG
Trier
Laon
Luxembourg City
Mannheim
Beauvais
Soissons
Longwy
Heidelberg
CHANTILLY
Senlis
Charles de Gaulle
Reims
VERDUN BATTLEFIELD
Thionville
Saarbrücken
GIVERNY
Seine
Epernay
Metz
Karlsruhe
Paris
CHAMPAGNE
Châlons
DISNEYLAND PARIS
LORRAINE
Stuttgart
Versailles
Orly
Nancy
Baden-Baden
VAUX-LE-VICOMTE
Seine
St-Dizier
Toul
Strasbourg
FONTAINEBLEAU
Moselle
ALSACE
BLACK FOREST
Troyes
Ribeauvillé
Rhein
Chaumont
Kaysersberg
LES VOSGES
Colmar
Orléans
Chablis
Laroche
Freiburg
Eguisheim
Auxerre
Culmont
Mulhouse
Loire
CHAMBORD
ABBEY OF FONTENAY
RONCHAMP
CHEVERNY
GUÉDELON
Avallon
BURGUNDY
VÉZELAY
Semur-en-Auxois
Belfort
Basel
Zürich
CENTRE
JURA MTNS.
Sancerre
Besançon
Vierzon
Dijon
Autun
Châteauneuf-en-Auxois
Bourges
Dole
Neuchâtel
Luzern
Beaune
Bern
Châteauroux
Le Creusot
LA ROCHEPOT
Chalon-sur-Saône
Frasne
Murten
Nevers
Interlaken
Moulins
Brancion
Vallorbe
Gruyères
Lausanne
BERNER OBERLAND
Gimmelwald
Cluny
Tournus
Vichy
Mâcon
Lake Geneva
Montreux
Montluçon
Bourg-en-Bresse
Geneva
Guéret
BEAUJOLAIS
Martigny
Zermatt
Lugano
Roanne
Rhône
Lago Maggiore
Annecy
Chamonix
Clermont-Ferrand
Stresa
Lyon
SAVOIE
MONT BLANC
AUVERGNE
Aosta
Malpensa
St-Etienne
Vienne
Chambéry
Bourg S.M.
Milan
Loire
PIEDMONT
Dordogne
Modane
Grenoble
Po
Turin
Le Puy-en-Velay
GOUFFRE DE PADIRAC
Lot
Valence
Briançon
Rhône
Clelles
Rodez
Mende
Montélimar
Gap
Genoa
St-Cirq-Lapopie
PROVENCE
Cuneo
GORGE DE L'ARDECHE
Vaison-la-Romaine
To Cinque Terre
GORGES DU TARN
Orange
Cordes
Tarn
Millau
Digne
PONT DU GARD
Châteauneuf-du-Pape
Avignon
Uzès
Albi
Nîmes
LES BAUX
Isle-sur-la-Sorgue
Menton
Vence
St-Rémy
Roussillon
St-Paul
Castres
MONACO
Arles
LUBERON
Grasse
Villefranche-sur-Mer
ROUSSILLON
GRAND CANYON DU VERDON
Montpellier
CAMARGUE
Caunes-Minervois
Minerve
Aix-en-Provence
Nice
Antibes
To Bastia, Corsica
AIGUES-MORTES
Cannes
Carcassonne
Béziers
Marseille
Narbonne
St-Tropez
COTE D'AZUR
LES CALANQUES
QUERIBUS & PEYREPERTUSE
Cassis
Toulon
Perpignan
To Ajaccio, Corsica
To Porto Torres, Sardinia
L'Ile-Rousse
Collioure
Port Bou
Corsica (France)
To Barcelona
Cadaqués
Figueres
E-40
E-17
E-42
E-25
A-4
A-1
A-3
A-5
A-16
A-26
A-28
A-13
A-10
A-31
A-35
A-6
A-38
A-36
A-71
A-12
A-2
A-40
A-9
A-72
A-42
A-43
A-47
A-41
A-49
A-7
A-32
A-21
A-10
A-54
A-8
N97
A-61

Introduction

France is a place of gentle beauty, where the play of light transforms the routine into the exceptional. Here, you'll discover a dizzying array of artistic and architectural wonders—soaring cathedrals, chandeliered châteaux, and museums filled with the cultural icons of the Western world. Gaze dreamy-eyed at Monet's water lilies, rejoice amid the sunflowers that so moved Van Gogh, and roam the sunny coastlines that inspired Picasso and Matisse.

There are two Frances: Paris...and the rest of the country. France's cultural energy has always been centered in Paris, resulting in an overwhelming concentration of world-class museums, cutting-edge architecture, and historic monuments. The other France venerates land, tradition, and a slower pace of life. *Le terroir* (the soil) brings the flavor to food and wine and nourishes the life the French enjoy. Although the country's brain resides in Paris, its soul lives in its villages—and that's where you'll feel the pulse of France.

L'art de vivre—the art of living—is not just a pleasing expression. France demands that you slow down and savor the finer things. Come with an appetite to understand and a willingness to experience. Linger in sidewalk cafés, make unplanned stops a habit, and surrender to the play of light as the Impressionists did.

France is Europe's most diverse, tasty, and most exciting country. *Bienvenue!* You've chosen well.

THE BEST OF FRANCE

In this selective book, I recommend France's top destinations—a mix of the most fascinating cities and intimate villages, from jet-setting beach resorts to the traditional heartland.

Paris is the queen of culture. Coastal Normandy features romantic Honfleur, historic Bayeux, the stirring D-Day beaches, and the surreal island abbey of Mont St-Michel. The lovely Loire offers *beaucoup de châteaux* in all shapes and sizes. Go back in time in the Dordogne to visit prehistoric cave art and cliff-hanging medieval castles. You won't need a year in Provence to enjoy down-to-earth Arles, elegant Avignon, and the Côtes du Rhône wine road. On the French Riviera, choose your favorite coastal resort and become an expert in the art of relaxation. Wine connoisseurs savor Burgundy.

In some cases, when there are interesting sights or towns near my top destinations, I cover these briefly (as "Near" sights), to help you enjoyably fill out a free day or a longer stay.

Beyond these top destinations, I cover the Best of the Rest—great destinations that don't quite make my top cut, but are worth seeing if you have more time or specific interests: Reims (with Champagne *caves*), Carcassonne (with medieval walls), Chamonix (with alpine wonders), and Colmar (with Germanic flair).

To help you link the best destinations, I've designed a two-week itinerary (see page 26), with tips to help you tailor it to your interests and time.

THE BEST OF PARIS

Paris is the grand-dame of art, culture, and fine living. Saunter down the Champs-Elysées, climb Notre-Dame, cruise the Seine, and zip to the top of the Eiffel Tower. Savor France's greatest selection of cuisine and save some after-dark energy for this romantic city.

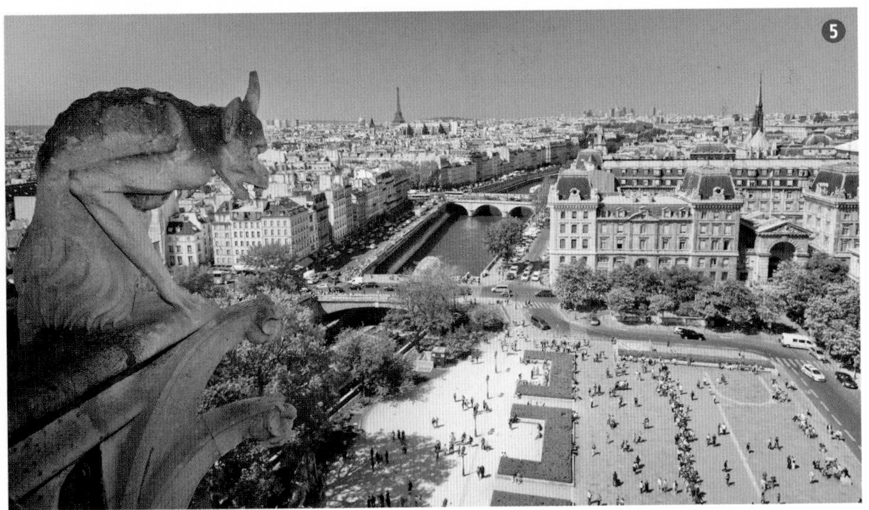

❶ ***Versailles'*** *colorful gardens lead into a vast park with ponds, fountains, and a royal retreat.*

❷ *The* ***Rodin Museum****'s iconic statue,* The Thinker, *ponders in the garden.*

❸ *The best time to enjoy a* ***Seine river-boat cruise*** *is at sunset.*

❹ *Paris' oldest and most appealing square,* ***Place des Vosges,*** *is central in the Marais district.*

❺ *The* ***grand view*** *from atop Notre-Dame Cathedral stretches from the Seine River to the Eiffel Tower.*

❻ *The* ***Eiffel Tower,*** *viewed from the Champs de Mars park, is loveliest after dark when it's floodlit.*

❼ *The* ***Louvre Museum****'s pyramid entrance, glistening at twilight, is worth a detour to see after hours.*

❽ *The west facade of* ***Notre-Dame Cathedral*** *is ground zero in Paris.*

THE BEST OF NORMANDY

Sweeping coastlines, half-timbered towns, and thatched roofs decorate the rolling green hills of Normandy. Its rugged coast harbors enchanting fishing villages like Honfleur and memories of a WWII battle that changed the course of history. And on its southern border, the island abbey of Mont St-Michel rises serene and majestic, oblivious to the tides of tourists.

❶ *Rising dramatically from the sea, **Mont St-Michel** has long attracted pilgrims and travelers.*

❷ *In picturesque **Bayeux,** a stone building on the river-bank sports an old water mill.*

❸ *In a series of scenes, the **Bayeux Tapestry** depicts William the Conqueror's victory over England in 1066.*

❹ *At **Pointe du Hoc,** US Army Rangers heroically scaled cliffs under Nazi fire on D-Day, June 6, 1944.*

❺ *The **American Cemetery,** which lies above **Omaha Beach,** makes a powerful pilgrimage.*

❻ *Creamy cheeses, including locally made **Camembert,** tempt buyers at cheese shops.*

❼ *Charming, **half-timbered buildings** dot townscapes throughout Normandy.*

❽ ***Honfleur**'s harbor is lined with skinny, soaring homes from the 16th and 17th centuries.*

4

5
JOHN R. HALE
CPL 506 PRCHT INF 101 ABN DIV
WASHINGTON JUNE 20 1944

6

7
HOTEL DU DAUPHIN

8

THE BEST OF THE LOIRE

The Loire Valley is crisscrossed by rivers, laced with rolling hills, and dotted with inviting towns like Amboise. Thanks to a strategic location, it's also home to more than a thousand castles and palaces.

Admire Chenonceau's dreamy elegance, be dazzled by the sheer scale of Chambord, and appreciate the homey intimacy of Cheverny.

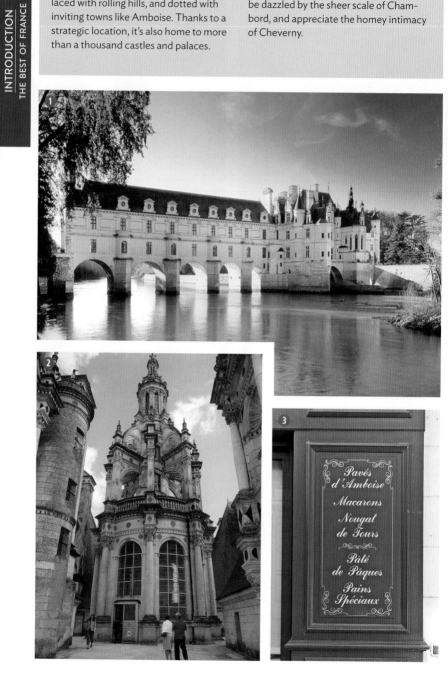

1

2

3

Pavés
d'Amboise
Macarons
Nougat
de Tours
Pâté
de Pâques
Pains
Spéciaux

❶ *Arcing over the Cher River, the graceful **Château de Chenonceau** is the toast of the Loire.*

❷ *The rooftop of massive **Château de Chambord** is a pincushion of spires and towers.*

❸ *Bigot's Patisserie and Salon de Thé offers the best chocolate and desserts in **Amboise.***

❹ *The defense-minded **Château de Chaumont** features palatial luxury, fine gardens, and state-of-the-art stables.*

❺ *The many hunting dogs at **Château de Cheverny** prove that hunting is still the rage here.*

❻ *The gardens at the **Château de Villandry** are the most elaborate and decorative in the Loire.*

THE BEST OF THE DORDOGNE

Sunflowers, walnut orchards, and tobacco plants decorate the Dordogne River Valley's floor, while stone fortresses patrol the cliffs above. The joys of the Dordogne include lazy canoe rides, thriving market towns, and mouth-watering local cuisine. But it's most famous for its cache of prehistoric cave paintings.

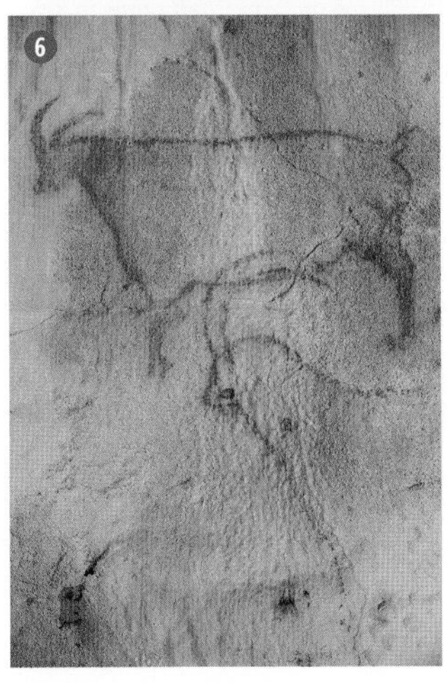

❶ *Floating down the lazy* ***Dordogne River*** *is the best way to appreciate this glorious region.*

❷ *The locally quarried stone, used here for a church in* ***Domme,*** *exudes a timeless warmth.*

❸ *In summer, radiant fields of* ***sunflowers*** *brighten large swaths of the Dordogne.*

❹ *Classic delicacies of the region are* ***patés and fois gras****—worth loosening your belt for.*

❺ *It's dinnertime on the main square of* ***Sarlat,*** *one of France's most pedestrian-friendly towns.*

❻ *Colorful paintings from* ***Grottes de Cougnac*** *are testament to the artistry of prehistoric man.*

❼ *The brooding* ***Château de Castlenaud*** *was an English stronghold during the Hundred Years' War.*

THE BEST OF PROVENCE

Provence features lively cities, adorable hill-capping villages, scenic vineyards, and some of Europe's best Roman ruins. Like Van Gogh, enjoy a starry, starry night in Arles. In Avignon, wander the brooding Palace of the Popes. Then sample the wines and splendid scenery of the Côtes du Rhône.

❶ *Fragrant samples of* ***lavender*** *are a common sight in Provence's shops and restaurants.*

❷ *In* ***Arles,*** *the Place du Forum is lined with cafés and filled with ambience.*

❸ *The* ***Pont du Gard*** *aqueduct is one of the world's most magnificent Roman monuments.*

❹ *Provençal* ***outdoor markets*** *are France's best, offering the most fun and greatest range of products.*

❺ **Boules,** *a wonderful French spectator sport, is most popular in Provence.*

❻ *The powerful* ***Palace of the Popes*** *evokes medieval memories of when the popes ruled from* ***Avignon.***

❼ *Easels featuring scenes from* ***Van Gogh****'s time in Arles illustrate the artist's unique vision.*

❽ *Provence is littered with brilliant* ***Roman structures*** *like this arena—nearly 2,000 years old—in Arles.*

4
POLICE
MUNICIPALE

5

6

7

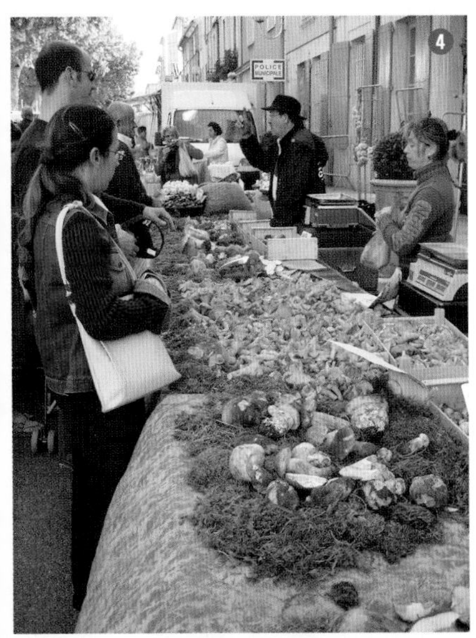

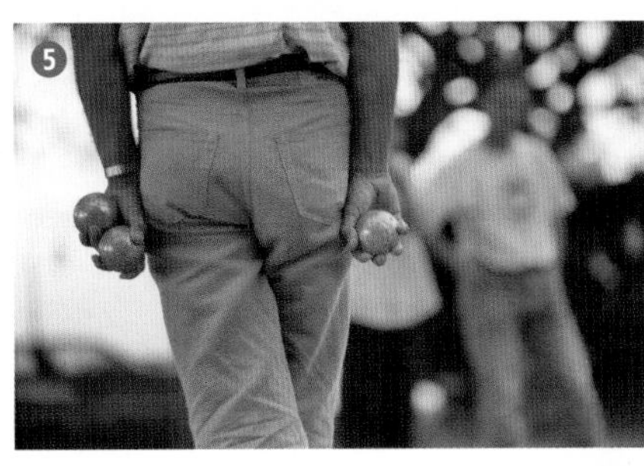

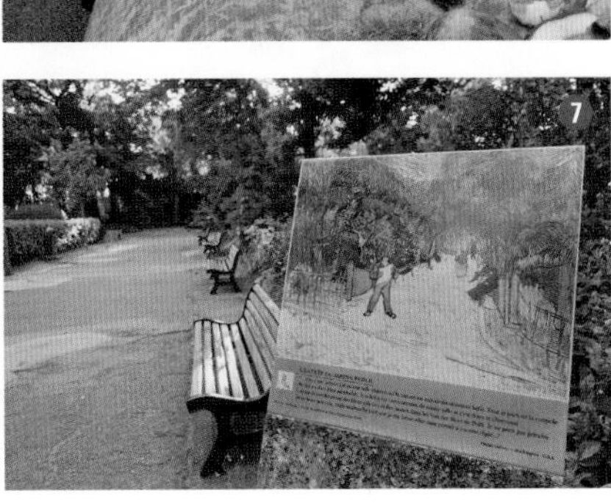

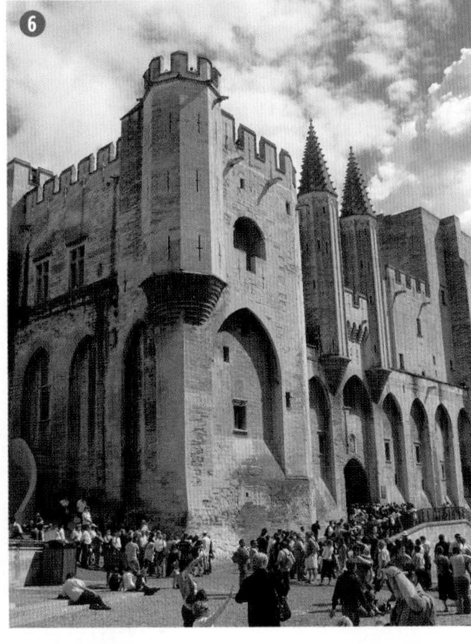

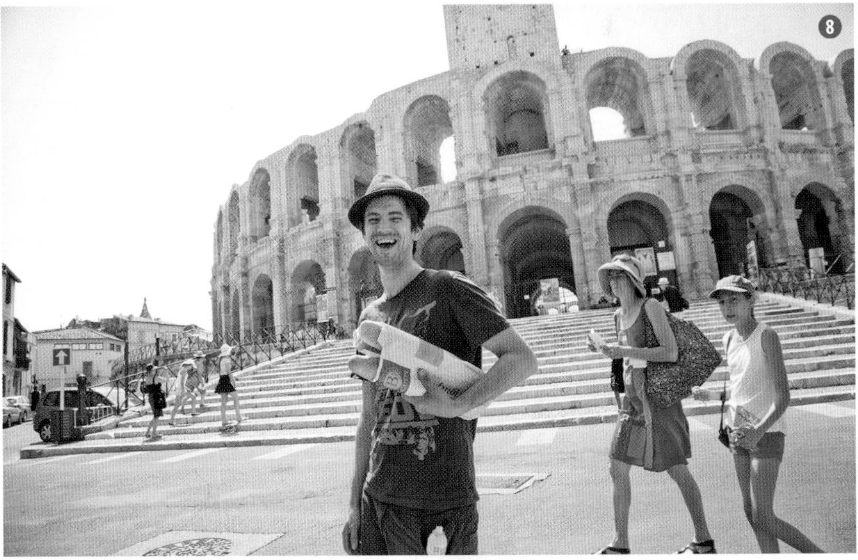

8

THE BEST OF THE FRENCH RIVIERA

Stunning beaches, appealing towns, and intriguing museums lie along the French Riviera. Seductive Nice has world-class museums and an irresistible beachfront promenade. Lovely little Villefranche-sur-Mer charms visitors, the lively port of Antibes offers silky beaches, and Monaco extends a royal welcome. Balmy evenings on the Riviera are made for strolling.

*❶ **Nice**, the Riviera's capital, offers an engaging mix of urban sightseeing and seaside relaxation.*

*❷ The French Riviera's **Italianate character** is revealed in old-town centers.*

*❸ **Monte Carlo**'s elegant casino lies between a lush park and the Mediterranean.*

*❹ A refreshing **salade niçoise** makes an ideal lunch or light dinner on warm days.*

*❺ The **Picasso Museum** in **Antibes,** housed in a fine stone building, showcases a memorable collection of his work.*

*❻ Renting a lounge chair is the perfect antidote to **Nice's rocky beaches.***

3

THE BEST OF BURGUNDY

Burgundy welcomes wine lovers with open doors and scenic drives. The compact capital of Beaune features a colorful medieval hospital, full-bodied wines, and pedestrian-friendly strolls. Exploring the nearby villages and vineyards, by car or by bike, is a delight.

❶ *The courtyard of* ***Beaune****'s medieval hospital dazzled its patients 500 years ago and dazzles travelers today.*

❷ ***Market days*** *in Burgundy offer a chance to sample what's fresh and to meet the producer.*

❸ *Traditional* ***wine tastings*** *in Burgundy come with pewter wine cups and candlelight.*

❹ *The* ***Château de la Rochepot*** *is beautifully situated in the hills above Beaune.*

❺ *Only the French can make a snail taste good. Be sure to sample* **escargots.**

THE BEST OF THE REST

With extra time, add any of these destinations to your itinerary. A short trip east of Paris, **Reims** offers a historic cathedral and dazzling champagne cellars. Farther east, Germanic Alsace is home to half-timbered buildings and the charming town of **Colmar.** A few hours southeast of Paris, **Chamonix** delivers grand alpine panoramas. Europe's greatest fortress city, **Carcassonne,** guards its perch in southern France.

❶ *The mountains just above* ***Chamonix*** *are laced with scenic hiking trails for all levels of ability.*

❷ ***Reims****' magnificent cathedral sparkles at night with 800 years of history.*

❸ *The feudal fortress of* ***Carcassonne*** *is a romantic's dream come true.*

❹ ***Colmar****'s lovely half-timbered, pastel buildings proudly show off its Germanic heritage.*

TRAVEL SMART

Approach France like a veteran traveler, even if it's your first trip. Design your itinerary, get a handle on your budget, line up your documents, and follow my travel strategies on the road.

Designing Your Itinerary

Decide when to go. Late spring and fall generally have decent weather and lighter crowds. Summer brings festivals, good weather, and tourists. Crowds hit their peak from mid-July to mid-August, but they concentrate primarily on the Alps, the Riviera, and Dordogne. June is generally quiet outside of Paris.

Winter travel is fine for Paris and Nice, but smaller cities are buttoned up tight. The weather is gray, milder in the south and wetter in the north. Sights and tourist-information offices keep shorter hours.

Choose your top destinations. My itinerary (on page 26) gives you an idea of how much you can reasonably see in 14 days, but you can adapt it to fit your timeframe and choice of destinations.

Suave, classy Paris is a must for anyone, especially for art and history lovers. WWII buffs storm the Normandy beaches while sun worshippers bask on the Riviera. Fans of opulent architecture explore luxurious Loire châteaux. Wine devotees meander along the wine roads of Provence and Burgundy. If you like your art prehistoric, linger in the Dordogne, but if it's ancient Roman ruins you're after, focus on Provence. Hikers love to go a'wandering in the French Alps, and photographers want to go everywhere.

Draft a rough itinerary. Figure out how many destinations you can comfortably fit in the time you have. Don't overdo it—few travelers wish they'd hurried more. Allow enough days per stop: Count on at least two days for major destinations. Staying in a home base—like Paris, Arles, or Nice—and making day trips can be more time-efficient than changing locations and hotels. Minimize one-night stands, especially consecutive ones; it can be worth taking a late-afternoon train ride or drive to get settled into a town for two nights.

Connect the dots. Link your destinations into a logical route. Determine which cities in Europe you'll fly into and out of. Begin your search for transatlantic flights at Kayak.com.

Even if you're flying into Paris, you

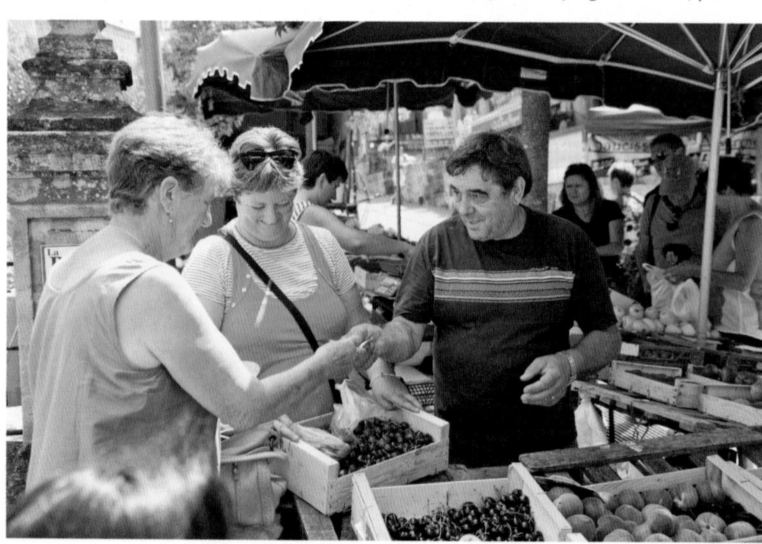

The Language Barrier and That French Attitude

You've probably heard that the French are cold and refuse to speak English. This preconception is outdated. The French are as friendly as any other people (if a bit more serious). You'll find the French more reserved in the north, more carefree in the sunny south, and everywhere more formal than you are.

The best advice? Slow down. Hurried, impatient travelers who don't understand the pleasures of people-watching from a sun-dappled café often misinterpret French attitudes. With *beaucoup* paid vacation and 35-hour workweeks, your hosts can't understand why anyone would rush through their time off. By making an effort to appreciate French culture, you're likely to have a richer experience.

The French view formality as being polite. When tourists stroll down the street with a big grin blurting "Hi!" to everyone, it's considered a little crazy rather than friendly.

Communication difficulties are exaggerated. Many French people speak English, especially those in the tourist trade and in big cities, but you'll get better treatment everywhere if you use the pleasantries. Learn these five phrases: *bonjour* (good day), pardon (pardon me), *s'il vous plaît* (please), *merci* (thank you), and *au revoir* (goodbye).

Begin every encounter (for instance, when entering a shop) with "*Bonjour, madame* (or *monsieur*)," and end every encounter with "*Au revoir, madame* (or *monsieur*)."

When you attempt to speak French, you may be politely corrected—*c'est normal* (to be expected). The French are linguistic perfectionists; they take their language (and other languages) seriously. Often they speak more English than they let on. This isn't a tourist-baiting tactic, but timidity on their part about speaking another language less than fluently. To ask a French person to speak English, say, "*Bonjour, madame* (or *monsieur*). *Parlez-vous anglais?*" They may say "*non,*" but as you struggle on, butchering their language, you'll likely soon find out they speak more English than you speak French.

Practice the French survival phrases in this book (see the Practicalities chapter), and have a translation app or a French/English dictionary handy. In transactions, a notepad and pen minimize misunderstandings; have vendors write down the price. For more tips, consider the *Rick Steves French Phrase Book & Dictionary* (available at www.ricksteves.com).

don't need to start your trip there. You could drive or take the train to Bayeux in Normandy for a gentle small-town start, and let Paris be the finale, when you're rested and ready to tackle the big city. Or you could fly into Nice and out of Paris; many find the easygoing Mediterranean city of Nice easier than Paris as a starting point.

Decide if you'll travel by car, public transportation, or a combination. Regions that are ideal to explore by car—Normandy's D-Day beaches, the Loire, the Dordogne, and Provence—usually offer minivan tours, buses, or taxis for nondrivers. Cars are useless in big cities (park it). If relying on public transportation, the bigger cities are easy to visit, well

THE BEST OF FRANCE IN 2 WEEKS

This unforgettable trip will show you the very best France has to offer. It's geared for drivers, but can be traveled by public transportation.

DAY	PLAN	SLEEP IN
	Arrive in Paris, orient to your neighborhood	Paris
1	Sightsee Paris	Paris
2	Paris	Paris
3	Drivers rent a car in Paris and head for Normandy's Bayeux (3 hours by train); stop in Honfleur en route (easier for drivers)	Bayeux
4	D-Day beaches (by car, taxi, or minivan tour)	Bayeux
5	Morning for Bayeux, afternoon travel to Mont St-Michel (2.5 hours with a train-and-bus combination)	Mont St-Michel
6	Travel to Loire Valley (5 hours by train), visit Amboise in afternoon	Amboise
7	Explore the Loire Valley (by car, shuttle bus, minivan tour, taxi, or bike)	Amboise
8	Travel to Sarlat-le-Canéda (6 hours by train); drivers visit Oradour-sur-Glane en route	Sarlat
9	Explore the Dordogne (by car, taxi, minivan tour, canoe, or bike)	Sarlat
10	More Dordogne, then travel to Carcassonne (6 hours by train)	Carcassonne
11	Travel to Arles (3 hours by train)	Arles
12	Explore Provence (by car, bus, train, minivan tour, or bike)	Arles
13	Travel to Nice (4 hours by train); drivers drop off car in Nice	Nice
14	Explore the Riviera (by train and bus)	Nice
	Fly out of Nice	

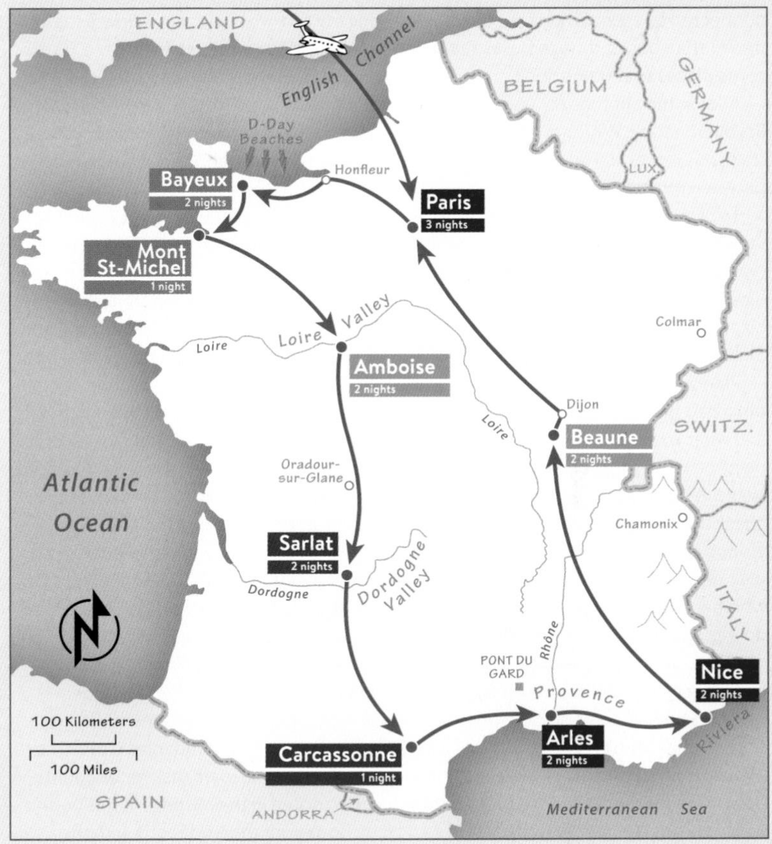

Customize this itinerary. If history doesn't interest you, neither would the D-Day beaches (skip Day 4). You could trim a day by overnighting in Arles on Day 10 rather than Carcassonne.

Adding Burgundy

Wine lovers can add this extension, and end up with a grand finale in Paris.

DAY	PLAN	SLEEP IN
15	Travel from Nice to Beaune in Burgundy (7 hours by train)	Beaune
16	Explore Beaune and nearby vineyards	Beaune
17	Return to Paris (2.5 hours by train); drivers drop off car in Dijon, then catch train	Paris
	Fly home	

connected by trains. Trains are faster and pricier than buses, though buses reach some places that trains don't.

Allot sufficient time for transportation in your itinerary. Whether you travel by train, bus, or car, it'll take a half-day to get between most destinations.

To determine approximate transportation times, research driving distances (www.viamichelin.com) or train schedules (www.sncf.com). If France is part of a bigger trip, consider budget flights; check Skyscanner.com for intra-European flights.

Plan your days. Finetune your trip; write out a day-by-day plan of where you'll be and what you want to be sure to see. To help you make the most of your time, I've suggested day-plans for destinations. But check the opening hours of sights; avoid visiting a town on the one day a week that your must-see sight is closed. Research whether any holidays or festivals will fall during your trip—these attract crowds and can close sights (for the latest, visit France's tourist website, http://us.france.fr).

Give yourself some slack. Nonstop sightseeing can turn a vacation into a blur. Every trip, and every traveler, needs downtime for doing laundry, picnic shopping, relaxing, people-watching, and so on. Pace yourself. Assume you will return.

Ready, set . . . You've designed the perfect itinerary for the trip of a lifetime.

Trip Costs

Run a reality check on your dream trip. You'll have major transportation costs in addition to daily expenses.

Airfare: A basic round-trip flight from the US to Paris or Nice can cost about $1,000 to $2,000 total, depending on where you fly from and when.

Car Rental: Figure on paying about $250 per week, not including tolls, gas, parking, and insurance. Rentals and leases (an economical way to go if you need a car for at least three weeks) are cheaper if arranged from the US.

Public Transportation: If you're following my two-week itinerary, allow $450 per person; it'd be worthwhile to buy a France Flexipass with six train days (to use for longer trips between major destinations) and purchase point-to-point tickets for short, cheap, regional trips (such as exploring the French Riviera). If you add the Burgundy-to-Paris extension, allow a total of $600 per person and get a France Flexipass for nine days for maximum coverage.

Train passes (including France rail passes) normally must be purchased outside of Europe, but aren't necessarily your best option—you may save money either by buying tickets as you go, or by getting advance-purchase discounts for long-distance trips or any TGV ride. Don't hesitate to consider flying, as budget airlines can be cheaper than taking the train. Inexpensive flights can get you between Paris and other major cities such as Nice.

Budget Tips: Cut your daily expenses (see chart on next page) by taking advantage of the deals you'll find throughout France and mentioned in this book.

Some businesses—especially hotels and walking-tour companies—offer discounts to my readers (ask for discounts when noted in their listings in this book).

Book your rooms directly with the hotel. Some hotels offer a discount if you stay three nights or more (check online or ask). Or check Airbnb-type sites for deals.

It's easy to eat cheap in France. You can get tasty, inexpensive meals at bakeries (sandwiches, quiche, and mini-pizzas), cafés, crêperies, department-store cafe-

Average Daily Expenses Per Person: $195

Cost	Category	Notes
$75	Meals	$15 for breakfast, $20 for lunch, and $40 for dinner with drinks
$75	Lodging	Based on two people splitting the cost of a $150 double room
$35	Sights and Entertainment	This daily average works for most people
$10	City Transit	Buses or Métro
$195	**Total**	Applies to most of France, allow 30% more for Paris

terias, and takeout stands. Cultivate the art of picnicking in atmospheric settings.

City transit passes (for multiple rides or all-day usage) decrease your cost per ride in Paris: Buy a *carnet* of 10 Métro tickets or a Passe Navigo (which covers Paris as well as trips to outlying châteaux and the airports). Avid sightseers buy combo-tickets or passes that cover multiple museums (like the worthwhile Paris Museum Pass). If a town doesn't offer deals, visit only the sights you most want to see, and seek out free sights and experiences (people-watching counts).

When you splurge, choose an experience you'll always remember, such as a concert in Paris' Sainte-Chapelle or an alpine lift to panoramic views. Minimize souvenir shopping— how will you get it all home? Focus instead on collecting vivid memories, wonderful stories, and new friends.

Before You Go

You'll have a smoother trip if you tackle a few things ahead of time. For more information on these topics, see the Practicalities chapter, and check www.ricksteves.com for book updates, more travel tips, and travel talks.

Make sure your passport is valid. If it's due to expire within six months of your ticketed date of return, you need to renew it. Allow up to six weeks to renew or get a passport (www.travel.state.gov).

Arrange your transportation. Book your international flights early. Figure out your main form of transportation within France: You can get a rail pass, buy train tickets as you go, rent a car, or book a cheap flight. Train travelers: You're required to make seat reservations for high-speed trains (your only option on some routes); book these as early as possible, particularly if using a rail pass, because trains can fill up and pass-holder reservations are limited.

Book rooms well in advance, especially if your trip falls during peak season or any major holidays or festivals.

Reserve or buy tickets ahead for major sights, saving you from long ticket-buying lines. Book an entry time online for the Eiffel Tower several months in advance (see Paris chapter). Some prehistoric caves in the Dordogne region take online reservations (see Dordogne chapter). If the greatest cave, Font-de-Gaume, is accepting reservations, cross your fingers and book it soon (at least six months ahead).

Hire guides in advance. Popular guides can get booked up. If you want a specific guide, reserve by email as far ahead as possible—especially important for Paris, the

D-Day beaches, Provence, and Burgundy's wine country.

Consider travel insurance. Compare the cost of the insurance to the cost of your potential loss. Check whether your existing insurance (health, homeowners, or renters) covers you and your possessions overseas.

Call your bank. Alert your bank that you'll be using your debit and credit cards in Europe. Ask about transaction fees, and get the PIN number for your credit card. You don't need to bring euros for your trip; you can withdraw euros from cash machines in Europe.

Use your smartphone smartly. Sign up for an international service plan to reduce your costs, or rely on Wi-Fi in Europe instead. Download any apps you'll want on the road, such as maps, translation, transit schedules, and Rick Steves Audio Europe (see sidebar).

Pack light. You'll walk with your luggage more than you think. Bring a single carry-on bag and a daypack. Use the packing checklist in Practicalities as a guide.

Stick This Guidebook in Your Ear!

My free Rick Steves Audio Europe app makes it easy for you to download my audio tours of many of Europe's top attractions and listen to them offline during your travels. For France, these include my Historic Paris Walk and tours of the Louvre and Orsay museums, plus my tour of Versailles Palace. Sights covered by audio tours are marked in this book with this symbol: 🎧. The app also offers insightful travel interviews from my public radio show with experts from France and around the globe. It's all free! You can download the app via Apple's App Store, Google Play, or Amazon's Appstore. For more info, see www.ricksteves.com/audioeurope.

Travel Strategies on the Road

If you have a positive attitude, equip yourself with good information (this book), and expect to travel smart, you will.

Read—and reread—this book. To have an "A" trip, be an "A" student. Note opening hours of sights, closed days, crowd-beating tips, and whether reservations are required or advisable. Check the latest at www.ricksteves.com/update.

Be your own tour guide. As you travel, get up-to-date info on sights, reserve tickets and tours, reconfirm hotels and travel arrangements, and check transit connections. Find out the latest from tourist-information offices (TIs), your hoteliers, checking online, or phoning ahead. Upon arrival in a new town, lay the groundwork for a smooth departure; confirm the train, bus, or road you'll take when you leave.

Give local tours a spin. Your appreciation of a city or region and its history can increase dramatically if you take a walking tour in any big city or even hire a private guide. If you want to learn more about any aspect of France, you're in the right place with experts happy to teach you.

Outsmart thieves. Pickpockets abound in crowded places where tourists congregate. Treat commotions as smokescreens for theft. Keep your cash, credit cards, and passport secure in a money belt tucked under your clothes; carry only a day's spending money in your front pocket. Don't set valuable items down on counters or café tabletops, where they can be quickly stolen or easily forgotten.

Minimize potential loss. Keep expensive gear to a minimum. Bring photocopies of important documents (passport and cards) to aid in replacement if the originals are lost or stolen.

Guard your time and energy. Taking

Welcome to Rick Steves' Europe

Travel is intensified living—maximum thrills per minute and one of the last great sources of legal adventure. Travel is freedom. It's recess, and we need it.

I discovered a passion for European travel as a teen and have been sharing it ever since—through my tours, public television and radio shows, and travel guidebooks. Over the years, I've taught thousands of travelers how to best enjoy Europe's blockbuster sights—and experience "Back Door" discoveries that most tourists miss.

Written with my talented co-author, Steve Smith, this book offers you a balanced mix of France's lively cities and cozy towns, from the traditional heartland to jet-setting beach resorts. It's selective: Rather than listing dozens of beautiful châteaux in the Loire region, we cover only the top five. And it's in-depth: Our self-guided museum tours, city walks, and driving tours give insight into France's vibrant history and today's living, breathing culture.

We advocate traveling simply and smartly. Take advantage of our money- and time-saving tips on sightseeing, transportation, and more. Try local, characteristic alternatives to pricey chain hotels and famous restaurants. In many ways, spending more money only builds a thicker wall between you and what you traveled so far to see.

We visit France to experience it—to become temporary locals. Thoughtful travel engages us with the world, as we learn to appreciate other cultures and new ways to measure quality of life.

Judging from the positive feedback we receive from readers, this book will help you enjoy a fun, affordable, and rewarding vacation—whether it's your first trip or your tenth.

Bon voyage! Happy travels!

Rick Steves

a taxi can be a good value if it saves you a long wait for a cheap bus or an exhausting walk across town. To avoid long lines, follow the crowd-beating tips in this book, such as making advance reservations or sightseeing early or late.

Be flexible. Even if you have a well-planned itinerary, expect changes, strikes, closures, sore feet, bad weather, and so on. Your Plan B could turn out to be even better. And when problems arise (miscommunication, a transit strike, a minuscule hotel room), keep things in perspective. You're on vacation in a beautiful country.

Attempt the language. The French appreciate your effort. If you learn even just a few phrases, you'll get more smiles and make more friends. See the sidebar on page 25 for tips.

Connect with the culture. Interacting with locals carbonates your experience. Enjoy the friendliness of the French people. Ask questions—many locals are as interested in you as you are in them. Slow down, step out of your comfort zone, and be open to unexpected experiences. When an interesting opportunity pops up, make it a habit to say "yes."

Ready to linger at a sidewalk café? Smell the fragrance of warm croissants? See the Eiffel Tower sparkling with light?

Your next stop...France!

Paris

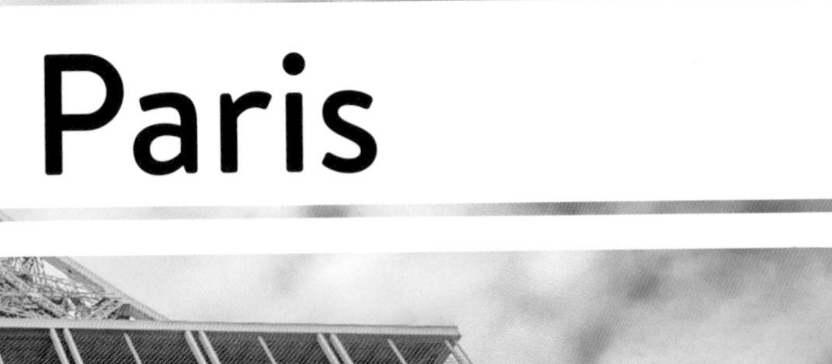

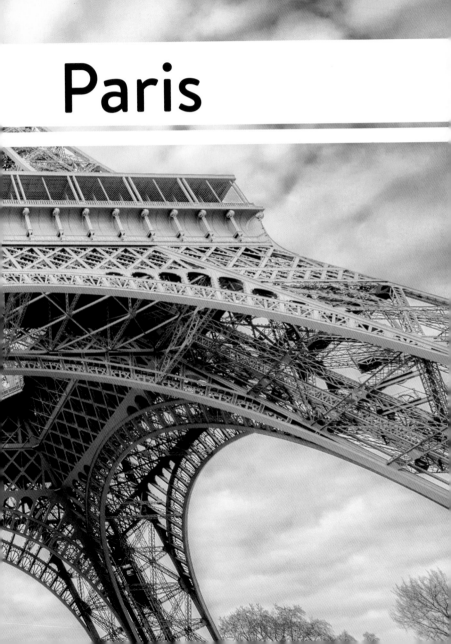

Paris has been a beacon of culture for centuries. As a world capital of art, fashion, food, literature, and ideas, it stands as a symbol of all the fine things human civilization can achieve, with a splash of romance and *joie de vivre.*

Paris offers grand boulevards, chatty crêpe stands, chic boutiques, and world-class art galleries. Sip coffee at a sidewalk café near the Eiffel Tower, then step into an Impressionist painting in a tree-lined park. Rub shoulders with the gargoyles at Notre-Dame. Master the Louvre and Orsay museums. Explore the City of Light at night, when monuments are floodlit and Paris sparkles.

PARIS IN 3 DAYS

On your first day, follow my Historic Paris Walk, featuring Ile de la Cité, Notre-Dame, the Latin Quarter, and Sainte-Chapelle. In the afternoon, tour the Louvre. Late in the day, enjoy the Place du Trocadéro scene and a twilight ride up the Eiffel Tower.

On your second day, stroll the Champs-Elysées from the Arc de Triomphe (ascend for the view) to the Tuileries Garden, then tour the Orsay and Rodin museums.

On your third day, head to Versailles. Catch Train-C by 8:00 to arrive early. Tour the palace's interior, then either visit the vast gardens, or return to Paris for more sightseeing.

On any evening: Take a nighttime tour by cruise boat, taxi, or bus. Or enjoy dinner on Ile St. Louis, then a floodlit walk by Notre-Dame. For a free skyline view, head to the rooftop of the neighboring Galeries Lafayette or Printemps department stores.

With extra time: Choose from Montmartre (Sacré-Cœur Basilica), the Army Museum and Napoleon's Tomb, the Marais neighborhood (Picasso Museum and Pompidou Center), or the Opéra Garnier (near the department stores).

ORIENTATION

Central Paris is circled by a ring road and split in half by the Seine River, which runs east-west. If you were floating downstream, the Right Bank (Rive Droite) would be on your right, and the Left Bank (Rive Gauche) on your left. The bull's-eye on your map is Notre-Dame, on an island in the middle of the Seine.

Twenty arrondissements (administrative districts) spiral out from the center, like an escargot shell. If your hotel's zip code is 75007, you know (from the last two digits) that it's in the 7th arrondissement. The city is peppered with Métro stops, and most Parisians locate addresses by the closest stop. So in Parisian jargon, the Eiffel Tower is on *la Rive Gauche* (the Left Bank) in the *7ème* (7th arrondissement), zip code 75007, Mo: Trocadéro (the nearest Métro stop).

The major sights cluster in convenient

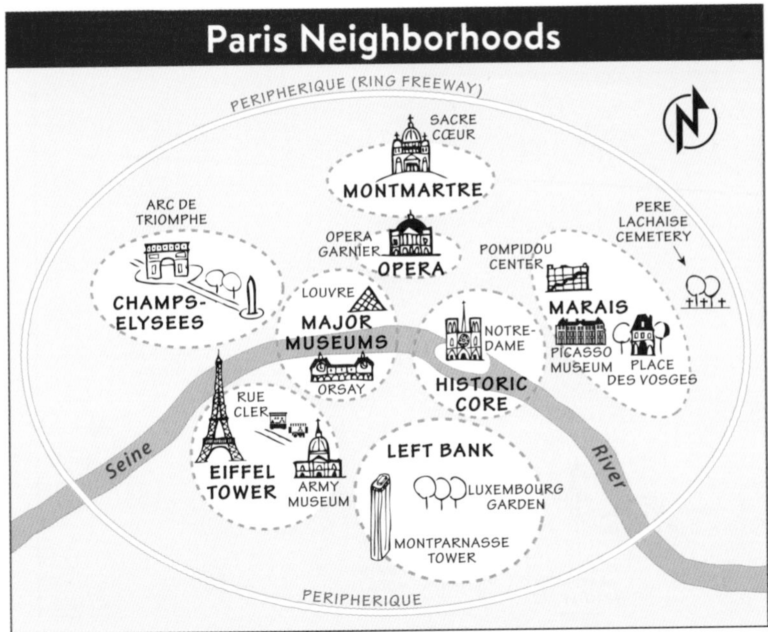

zones. Grouping your sightseeing, walks, dining, and shopping thoughtfully can save you lots of time and money.

Historic Core: This area centers on the Ile de la Cité ("Island of the City"), located in the middle of the Seine. On the Ile de la Cité, you'll find Paris' oldest sights, from Roman ruins to the medieval Notre-Dame and Sainte-Chapelle churches.

Major Museums Neighborhood: Located just west of the historic core, this is where you'll find the Louvre, Orsay, Orangerie, and Tuileries Garden.

Champs-Elysées: The greatest of the many grand, 19th-century boulevards on the Right Bank, the Champs-Elysées runs northwest from Place de la Concorde to the Arc de Triomphe.

Eiffel Tower Neighborhood: Dominated by the Eiffel Tower, this area also boasts the colorful Rue Cler, Army Museum and Napoleon's Tomb, and the Rodin Museum.

Opéra Neighborhood: Surrounding the Opéra Garnier, this area on the Right Bank is home to a series of grand boulevards and high-end shopping.

Left Bank: Anchored by the Luxembourg Garden, the Left Bank is the traditional neighborhood of Paris' intellectual, artistic, and café life.

Marais: Stretching eastward to Bastille along Rue de Rivoli/Rue St. Antoine, this neighborhood has lots of restaurants and hotels, shops, the delightful Place des Vosges, and artistic sights, such as the Pompidou Center and Picasso Museum.

Montmartre: This hill, topped by the bulbous white domes of Sacré-Cœur, hovers on the northern fringes of your Paris map.

Tourist Information

Paris' TIs can provide useful information but may have long lines (www.parisinfo.com). Most TIs sell Museum Passes and individual tickets to sights.

Paris has several TI locations, including **Pyramides** (daily May-Oct 9:00-19:00, Nov-April 10:00-19:00, 25 Rue des Pyramides—at Pyramides Métro stop), **Gare du Nord** (daily 8:00-18:00), **Gare**

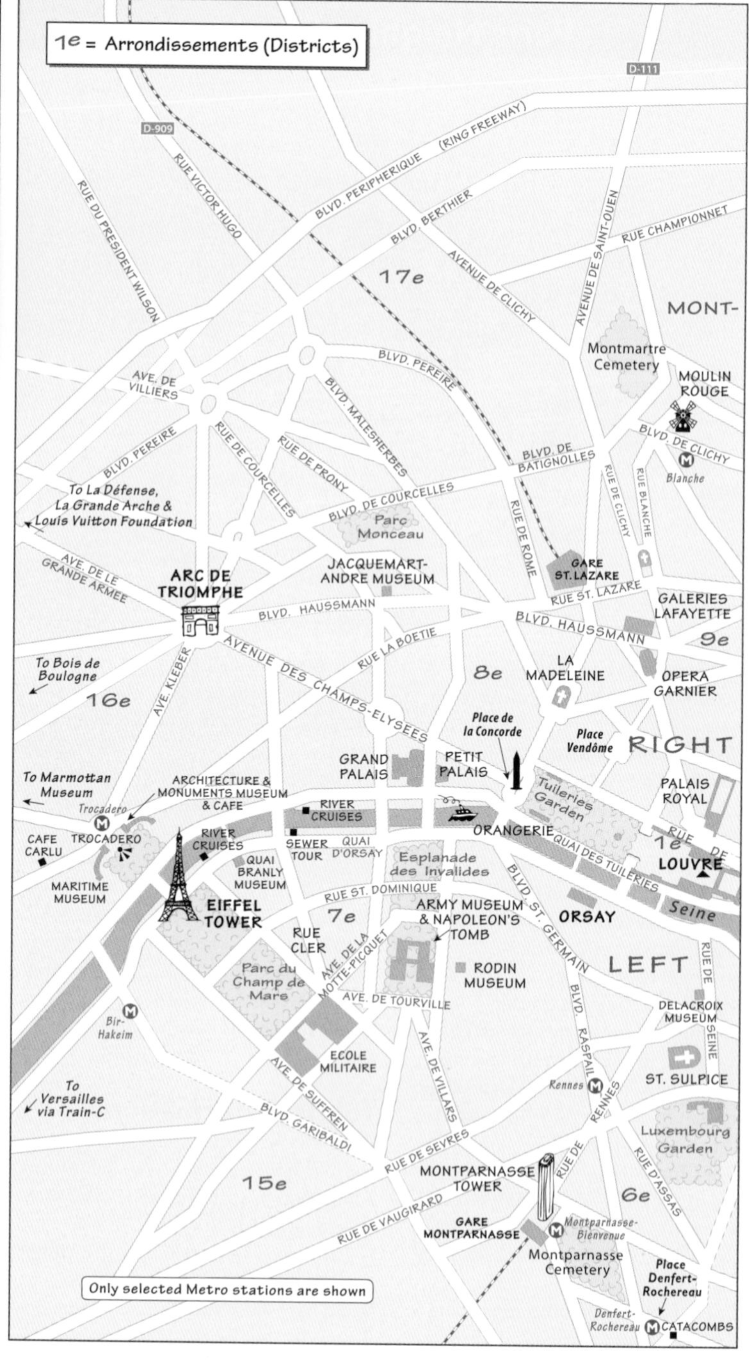

1e = Arrondissements (Districts)
D-111
D-909
BLVD. PERIPHERIQUE (RING FREEWAY)
RUE VICTOR HUGO
RUE DU PRESIDENT WILSON
BLVD. BERTHIER
AVENUE DE SAINT-OUEN
RUE CHAMPIONNET
AVENUE DE CLICHY
17e
MONT-
Montmartre Cemetery
MOULIN ROUGE
BLVD. PEREIRE
AVE. DE VILLIERS
BLVD. MALESHERBES
BLVD. DE CLICHY
Blanche
BLVD. DE BATIGNOLLES
RUE DE COURCELLES
RUE DE PRONY
RUE DE CLICHY
RUE BLANCHE
To La Défense, La Grande Arche & Louis Vuitton Foundation
BLVD. DE COURCELLES
Parc Monceau
RUE DE ROME
AVE. DE LA GRANDE ARMEE
JACQUEMART-ANDRE MUSEUM
GARE ST. LAZARE
ARC DE TRIOMPHE
RUE ST. LAZARE
GALERIES LAFAYETTE
BLVD. HAUSSMANN
9e
AVENUE DES CHAMPS-ELYSEES
RUE LA BOETIE
To Bois de Boulogne
LA MADELEINE
OPERA GARNIER
16e
AVE. KLEBER
8e
Place de la Concorde
Place Vendôme
RIGHT
GRAND PALAIS
PETIT PALAIS
To Marmottan Museum
ARCHITECTURE & MONUMENTS MUSEUM & CAFE
Tuileries Garden
PALAIS ROYAL
Trocadero
RIVER CRUISES
ORANGERIE
RUE DE
CAFE CARLU
TROCADERO
RIVER CRUISES
SEWER TOUR
QUAI D'ORSAY
QUAI DES TUILERIES
1e
LOUVRE
QUAI BRANLY MUSEUM
Esplanade des Invalides
MARITIME MUSEUM
RUE ST. DOMINIQUE
BLVD. ST. GERMAIN
Seine
EIFFEL TOWER
7e
ARMY MUSEUM & NAPOLEON'S TOMB
ORSAY
RUE CLER
AVE. DE LA MOTTE-PICQUET
LEFT
Parc du Champ de Mars
RODIN MUSEUM
RUE DE SEINE
AVE. DE TOURVILLE
DELACROIX MUSEUM
Bir-Hakeim
BLVD. RASPAIL
ECOLE MILITAIRE
AVE. DE VILLARS
ST. SULPICE
AVE. DE SUFFREN
Rennes
RUE DE RENNES
To Versailles via Train-C
BLVD. GARIBALDI
Luxembourg Garden
RUE DE SEVRES
RUE D'ASSAS
MONTPARNASSE TOWER
15e
6e
RUE DE VAUGIRARD
GARE MONTPARNASSE
Montparnasse-Bienvenue
Montparnasse Cemetery
Place Denfert-Rochereau
Only selected Metro stations are shown
Denfert-Rochereau
CATACOMBS

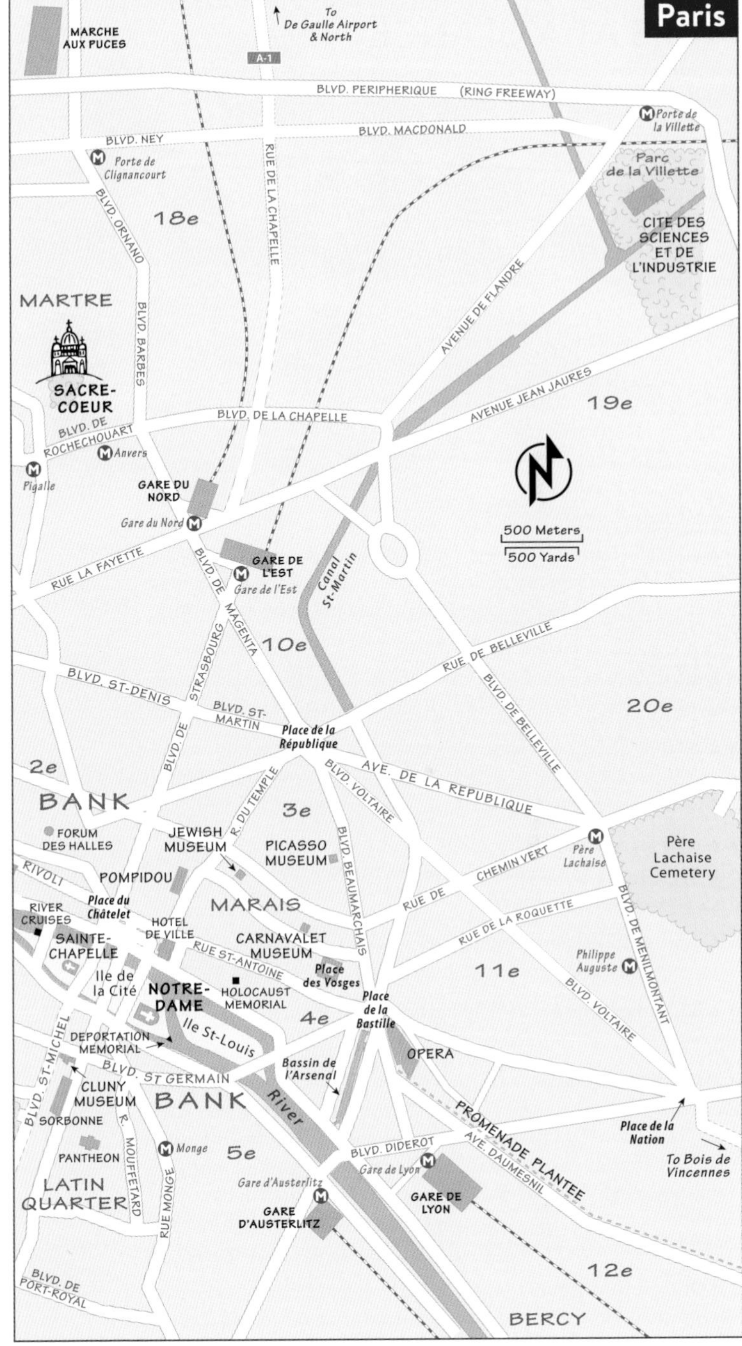
Paris
MARCHE AUX PUCES
To De Gaulle Airport & North
A-1
BLVD. PERIPHERIQUE (RING FREEWAY)
Porte de la Villette
BLVD. NEY
BLVD. MACDONALD
Porte de Clignancourt
Parc de la Villette
RUE DE LA CHAPELLE
BLVD. ORNANO
18e
CITE DES SCIENCES ET DE L'INDUSTRIE
MARTRE
BLVD. BARBES
AVENUE DE FLANDRE
SACRE-COEUR
AVENUE JEAN JAURES
19e
BLVD. DE LA CHAPELLE
BLVD. DE ROCHECHOUART
Anvers
Pigalle
GARE DU NORD
Gare du Nord
500 Meters
500 Yards
RUE LA FAYETTE
GARE DE L'EST
Gare de l'Est
BLVD. DE MAGENTA
Canal St-Martin
STRASBOURG
10e
RUE DE BELLEVILLE
BLVD. ST-DENIS
BLVD. ST-MARTIN
BLVD. DE BELLEVILLE
20e
BLVD. DE
Place de la République
2e
AVE. DE LA REPUBLIQUE
BLVD. VOLTAIRE
R. DU TEMPLE
BANK
3e
FORUM DES HALLES
JEWISH MUSEUM
PICASSO MUSEUM
BLVD. BEAUMARCHAIS
Père Lachaise
Père Lachaise Cemetery
RIVOLI
POMPIDOU
RUE DE CHEMIN VERT
Place du Châtelet
MARAIS
RIVER CRUISES
HOTEL DE VILLE
SAINTE-CHAPELLE
CARNAVALET MUSEUM
RUE DE LA ROQUETTE
RUE ST-ANTOINE
Place des Vosges
Philippe Auguste
BLVD. DE MENILMONTANT
Ile de la Cité
NOTRE-DAME
HOLOCAUST MEMORIAL
11e
Place de la Bastille
BLVD. VOLTAIRE
4e
DEPORTATION MEMORIAL
Ile St-Louis
OPERA
BLVD. ST-MICHEL
BLVD. ST GERMAIN
Bassin de l'Arsenal
CLUNY MUSEUM
BANK
River
SORBONNE
R. MOUFFETARD
PROMENADE PLANTEE
Place de la Nation
PANTHEON
Monge
5e
BLVD. DIDEROT
AVE. DAUMESNIL
To Bois de Vincennes
Gare de Lyon
LATIN QUARTER
Gare d'Austerlitz
GARE DE LYON
RUE MONGE
GARE D'AUSTERLITZ
12e
BLVD. DE PORT-ROYAL
BERCY

PARIS AT A GLANCE

▲▲▲**Notre-Dame Cathedral** Paris' most beloved church, with towers and gargoyles. **Hours:** Cathedral—daily 7:45-18:45, Sun until 19:15; Tower—daily April-Sept 10:00-18:30, Fri-Sat until 23:00 in July-Aug, Oct-March 10:00-17:30. See page 44.

▲▲▲**Sainte-Chapelle** Gothic cathedral with peerless stained glass. **Hours:** Daily April-Sept 9:00-19:00, Oct-March 9:00-17:00. See page 52.

▲▲▲**Louvre** Europe's oldest and greatest museum, starring *Mona Lisa* and *Venus de Milo*. **Hours:** Wed-Mon 9:00-18:00, Wed and Fri until 21:45, closed Tue. See page 57.

▲▲▲**Orsay Museum** Nineteenth-century art, including Europe's greatest Impressionist collection. **Hours:** Tue-Sun 9:30-18:00, Thu until 21:45, closed Mon. See page 64.

▲▲▲**Eiffel Tower** Paris' soaring exclamation point. **Hours:** Daily mid-June-Aug 9:00-24:45, Sept-mid-June 9:30-23:45. See page 71.

▲▲▲**Champs-Elysées** Paris' grand boulevard. **Hours:** Always open. See page 78.

▲▲▲**Versailles** The ultimate royal palace (Château), with a Hall of Mirrors, vast gardens, a grand canal, plus a queen's playground (Trianon Palaces and Domaine de Marie-Antoinette). **Hours:** Château—April-Oct Tue-Sun 9:00-18:30, Nov-March until 17:30; Trianon/Domaine—April-Oct Tue-Sun 12:00-18:30, Nov-March until 17:30; Gardens—generally April-Oct daily 8:00-20:30, Nov-March Tue-Sun 8:00-18:00; entire complex closed Mon year-round. See page 121.

▲▲**Orangerie Museum** Monet's water lilies and modernist classics in a lovely setting. **Hours:** Wed-Mon 9:00-18:00, closed Tue. See page 70.

▲▲**Army Museum and Napoleon's Tomb** The emperor's imposing tomb, flanked by museums of France's wars. **Hours:** Daily 10:00-18:00, July-Aug until 19:00, Nov-March until 17:00; tomb plus WWI and WWII wings open Tue until 21:00 April-Sept; museum (except for tomb) closed first Mon of month Oct-June; Charles de Gaulle exhibit closed Mon year-round. See page 74.

▲▲**Rodin Museum** Works by the greatest sculptor since Michelangelo, with many statues in a peaceful garden. **Hours:** Tue-Sun 10:00-17:45, closed Mon. See page 75.

▲▲**Cluny Museum** Medieval art with unicorn tapestries. **Hours:** Wed-Mon 9:15-17:45, closed Tue. See page 76.

▲▲**Arc de Triomphe** Triumphal arch marking start of Champs-Elysées. **Hours:** Always viewable; interior—daily April-Sept 10:00-23:00, Oct-March until 22:30. See page 80.

▲▲**Picasso Museum** World's largest collection of Picasso's works. **Hours:** Daily Tue-Fri 10:30-18:00, Sat-Sun 9:30-18:00, closed Mon. See page 83.

▲▲**Pompidou Center** Modern art in colorful building with city views. **Hours:** Wed-Mon 11:00-21:00, closed Tue. See page 88.

▲▲**Sacré-Cœur** White basilica atop Montmartre with spectacular views. **Hours:** Daily 6:00-22:30; dome climb—daily May-Sept 9:30-19:00, Oct-April 9:30-17:00. See page 90.

▲**Opéra Garnier** Grand belle époque theater with a modern ceiling by Chagall. **Hours:** Generally daily 10:00-16:30, mid-July-Aug until 18:00. See page 80.

▲**Père Lachaise Cemetery** Final home of Paris' illustrious dead. **Hours:** Mon-Fri 8:00-18:00, Sat 8:30-18:00, Sun 9:00-18:00, until 17:30 in winter. See page 89.

de Lyon (Mon-Sat 8:00-18:00, closed Sun), **Gare de l'Est** (Mon-Sat 8:00-19:00, closed Sun), and one in **Montmartre** (daily 10:00-18:00, 21 Place du Tertre—limited to Montmartre). In summer, TI kiosks may pop up in the squares in front of Notre-Dame and Hôtel de Ville. Both city **airports** have handy TIs with long hours and short lines.

Event Listings: Several French-only but easy-to-decipher periodicals list the most up-to-date museum hours, art exhibits, concerts, festivals, plays, movies, and nightclubs. The best is the weekly magazine *L'Officiel des Spectacles* (available at any newsstand). The *Paris Voice*, with snappy English-language reviews of concerts, plays, and current events, is available online only at www.parisvoice.com.

Sightseeing Pass

In Paris there are two classes of sightseers—those with a **Paris Museum Pass,** and those who stand in line. The pass admits you to many of Paris' most popular sights, and it allows you to skip ticket-buying lines. You'll save time and money by getting this pass. Pertinent details about the pass are outlined here—for more info, visit www.parismuseumpass.com.

What the Pass Covers

Here's a list of key sights and their admission prices without the pass:

- Arc de Triomphe (€9.50)
- Army Museum (€9.50)
- Cluny Museum (€8)
- Conciergerie (€8.50)
- Louvre (€12)
- Notre-Dame Tower (€8.50)
- Orangerie Museum (€9)
- Orsay Museum (€11)
- Picasso Museum (€11)
- Pompidou Center (€14)
- Rodin Museum (€10)
- Sainte-Chapelle (€8.50)
- Versailles (€25)

Notable sights that are *not* covered by the pass include the Eiffel Tower, Opéra Garnier, Notre-Dame Treasury, and Sacré-Cœur's dome.

Buying the Pass

The pass pays for itself with four key admissions in two days (for example, the Louvre, Orsay, Sainte-Chapelle, and Versailles), and it lets you skip the ticket line at most sights (2 days-€42, 4 days-€56, 6 days-€69, no youth or senior discounts). It's sold at participating museums, monuments, and TIs (even at Paris' airports). Avoid buying the pass at a major museum (such as the Louvre), where the supply can be spotty and lines long. It's not worth the cost or hassle to buy the pass online.

Rick's Tip: Don't buy the Museum Pass for kids, *as most museums are free or discounted for those under age 18 (teenagers may need to show ID as proof of age). If parents have a Museum Pass, kids can usually skip the ticket lines as well. But a few places (Arc de Triomphe, Army Museum) require everyone—even passholders—to stand in line to collect free tickets for their children.*

Using the Pass

Plan carefully to make the most of your pass. Validate it only when you're ready to tackle the covered sights on consecutive days. Activating it is simple—just write the start date you want (and your name) on the pass. But first make sure the sights you want to visit will be open (many museums are closed Mon or Tue).

The pass provides the best value on days when sights close later, letting you extend your sightseeing day. Take advantage of late hours on selected evenings or times of year at the Arc de Triomphe, Pompidou Center, Notre-Dame Tower, Sainte-Chapelle, Louvre, Orsay, Rodin Museum, and Napoleon's Tomb. On days that you don't have pass coverage, plan to visit free sights and those not covered by the pass (see page 49 for a list of free sights).

To use your pass at sights, look for signs designating the entrance for reserved ticket holders. If it's not obvious, walk to the front of the ticket line, hold up your pass, and ask the ticket taker: *"Entrez, pass?"* (ahn-tray pahs). You'll either be allowed to enter at that point, or you'll be directed to a special entrance. For major sights, such as the Louvre and Orsay museums, I've identified passholder entrances on the maps in this book. Don't be shy—some places (the Orsay and the Arc de Triomphe, in particular) have long lines in which passholders wait needlessly. At a few sights with security lines (including the Louvre), passholders can skip to the front.

Avoiding Lines Without a Pass

If you don't purchase a Paris Museum Pass, or if a sight is not covered by the pass, there are other ways to avoid long waits in ticket-buying lines.

For some sights, you can reserve **timed-entry tickets** online. This is essential at the line-plagued Eiffel Tower, and it's a big advantage at the Picasso Museum.

You can buy **advance tickets** online for many other sights (including the Louvre, Orsay, Rodin Museum, and Monet's gardens at Giverny) as well as for activities and cultural events (Bateaux-Mouches cruises, Sainte-Chapelle concerts, and performances at the Opéra Garnier). Increasingly, other Paris sights are adding this timesaving service.

TIs, FNAC department stores, and travel-services companies sell individual ***coupe-file* tickets** (pronounced "koop feel") for some sights, which allow you to use the Museum Pass entrance (worth the trouble only for sights where lines are longest). TIs sell these tickets for no extra fee, but elsewhere you can expect a surcharge of 10-20 percent. FNAC stores are everywhere, even on the Champs-Elysées (ask your hotelier for the nearest one). Despite the surcharges and often-long lines to buy them, getting *coupe-file* tickets can still be a good idea.

Some sights, such as the Louvre, have **ticket-vending machines** that save time in line. These accept cash (usually no bills larger than €20) or chip-and-PIN cards

If you buy an advance ticket for the Eiffel Tower (or take the stairs), you can avoid this line.

Daily Reminder

SUNDAY: Many sights are free on the first Sunday of the month, including the Orsay, Rodin, Cluny, Pompidou, and Picasso museums. Several sights are free on the first Sunday, but only during winter, including the Louvre and Arc de Triomphe (both Oct-March) and all the sights at Versailles (Nov-March). These free days at popular sights attract hordes of visitors. Versailles is more crowded than usual on Sunday in any season, and the garden's fountains run (April-Oct).

Most of Paris' stores are closed on Sunday, but shoppers will find relief along the Champs-Elysées, at flea markets, and in the Marais neighborhood's lively Jewish Quarter, where many boutiques are open. Many recommended restaurants in the Rue Cler neighborhood are closed for dinner.

MONDAY: These sights are closed: Orsay, Rodin, Picasso, Victor Hugo's House at Place des Vosges, Deportation Memorial, and Versailles (but the gardens are open April-Oct). The Louvre is far more crowded because of these closings. From October through June, the Army Museum is closed the first Monday of the month, though Napoleon's Tomb remains open.

Market streets such as Rue Cler and Rue Mouffetard are dead today.

TUESDAY: Many sights are closed, including the Louvre, Orangerie, Cluny, and Pompidou museums. The Orsay and Versailles are crazy busy today. The fountains at Versailles run on Tuesdays from mid-May until late June; music (no fountains) fills the gardens April-mid-May and July-October. Napoleon's Tomb and the Army Museum's WWI and WWII wings are open until 21:00 (April-Sept).

WEDNESDAY: All sights are open, and some have late hours, including the Louvre (until 21:45, last entry 21:00).

THURSDAY: All sights are open. Some sights are open late, including the Orsay (until 21:45, last entry 21:00). Some department stores are open late.

FRIDAY: All sights are open. The Louvre is open until 21:45 (last entry 21:00) and Notre-Dame's tower is open until 23:00 (July-Aug). The Picasso Museum is open until 21:00 on the third Friday of every month.

SATURDAY: All sights are open. The fountains run at Versailles (April-Oct). Notre-Dame's tower is open until 23:00 (July-Aug).

(most American credit cards won't work). And at certain sights, including the Louvre and Orsay, **nearby shops** sell tickets, allowing you to avoid the main ticket lines (for details, see the Louvre and Orsay listings).

Tours

🎧 To sightsee on your own, download my **free audio tours** that illuminate some of Paris' top sights and neighborhoods, including the Historic Paris Walk, Louvre Museum, and Orsay Museum (see sidebar on page 30 for details).

Paris Walks offers a variety of thoughtful and entertaining two-hour walks, led by British and American guides (€12-20, generally 2/day, private tours available, family guides and Louvre tours are a specialty, tel. 01 48 09 21 40, www.paris-walks.com). Reservations aren't necessary for most tours, but specialty tours—such as the Louvre, fashion, or chocolate tours—require advance reservations and prepayment with credit card (deposits are nonrefundable).

Context Travel offers "intellectual by design" walking tours geared for serious learners. The tours are led by well-versed docents (historians, architects, and academics) and cover both museums and specific neighborhoods. It's best to book in advance—groups are limited to six participants and can fill up fast (€70-105/person, admission to sights extra, generally 3 hours, tel. 09 75 18 04 15, US tel. 800-691-6036, www.contexttravel.com). They also offer private tours and excursions outside Paris.

Bike About Tours offers easygoing tours with a focus on the eastern half of the city. Their four-hour tours run daily year-round at 10:00 (also at 15:00 May-Sept). You'll meet at the statue of Charlemagne in front of Notre-Dame, then walk nearby to get your bikes. Reserve online to guarantee a spot, or show up and take your chances (€30, ask about Rick Steves discount). Their private family tours of Paris include fun activities like scavenger hunts (€200 for 2 people, €25/person after that, complimentary boat-tour tickets—a €14 value).

For many, Paris merits hiring a Parisian as a personal guide. **Thierry Gauduchon** is a terrific guide and a gifted teacher (€230/half-day, €450/day, tel. 06 19 07 30 77, tgauduchon@gmail.com). **Sylvie Moreau** also leads good tours in Paris (€200 for 3 hours, €320 for 7 hours, tel. 01 74 30 27 46, mobile 06 87 02 80 67, sylvie.ja.moreau@gmail.com). **Elisabeth Van Hest** is another likable and very capable guide (€200/half-day, tel. 01 43 41 47 31, mobile 06 77 80 19 89, elisa.guide@gmail.com).

Helpful Hints

Theft Alert: Thieves thrive near famous monuments and on Métro and train lines that serve airports and high-profile tourist sights. Beware of pickpockets working busy lines (e.g., at ticket windows at train stations). Look out for groups of young girls who swarm around you (be very firm—even forceful—and walk away). Smartphones and tablets are thief magnets anytime, so be aware whenever you're using one or holding it up to take a picture.

It's smart to wear a money belt, put your wallet in your front pocket, loop your day bag over your shoulders, and keep a tight hold on your purse or shopping bag. When wearing a daypack, don't keep valuables in the outer pockets, and don't mark yourself as a tourist by wearing it on your front.

Muggings are rare, but they do occur. If you're out late, avoid the dark riverfront embankments and any place where the lighting is dim and pedestrian activity is minimal.

Tourist Scams: Be aware of the latest

Explore Paris by bike.

Learn from an expert guide.

tricks, such as the "found ring" scam (a con artist pretends to find a "pure gold" ring on the ground and offers to sell it to you) or the "friendship bracelet" scam (a vendor asks you to help with a demo, makes a bracelet on your arm that you can't easily remove, and then asks you to pay for it).

Distractions by a stranger—often a "salesman," someone asking you to sign a petition, or someone posing as a deaf person to show you a small note to read—can all be tricks that function as a smokescreen for theft. As you try to wriggle away from the pushy stranger, an accomplice picks your pocket.

To all these scammers, simply say "no" firmly and step away purposefully. For reports from my readers on the latest scams, go to https://community.ricksteves.com/travel-forum/tourist-scams.

Medical Help: There are a variety of English-speaking resources for medical help in Paris, including doctors who will visit your hotel. Try the **American Hospital** (tel. 01 46 41 25 25, www.american-hospital.org) or **SOS Médicins** (SOS Doctors, tel. 01 47 07 77 77, www.sosmedecins.fr).

Useful Apps: Gogo Paris is an intriguing app that reviews trendy places to eat, drink, relax, and sleep in Paris (www.gogocityguides.com/paris).

🎧 For free audio versions of some of the self-guided tours in this chapter, get the **Rick Steves Audio Europe** app (for details, see page 30).

Public WCs: Most public toilets are free. If it's a pay toilet, the price will be clearly indicated. If the toilet is free but there's an attendant, it's polite to leave a tip of €0.20-0.50. Bold travelers can walk into any sidewalk café like they own the place and find the toilet downstairs or in the back. Or do as the locals do—order a shot of espresso *(un café)* while standing at the café bar (then use the WC with a clear conscience). Keep tissues with you, as some WCs are poorly stocked.

Tobacco Stands *(Tabacs)*: These little kiosks—usually just a counter inside a café—sell public-transit tickets, cards for parking meters, postage stamps (though not all sell international postage), and...oh yeah, cigarettes. Just look for a red, elongated diamond-shaped *Tabac* sign.

HISTORIC PARIS WALK

Paris has been the cultural capital of Europe for centuries. We'll start where the city did—on the Ile de la Cité—and make a foray onto the Left Bank. Along the way, we'll step into some of the city's greatest sights, including Notre-Dame and Sainte-Chapelle.

Getting There: The closest Métro stops are Cité, Hôtel de Ville, and St. Michel, each a short walk away.

Length of This Walk: Allow four hours to do justice to this three-mile self-guided walk, beginning at Notre-Dame Cathedral and ending at Pont Neuf; just follow the dotted line on the "Historic Paris Walk" map.

Tours: 🎧 Download my free Historic Paris Walk audio tour.

➔ Self-Guided Walk

• *Begin in front of Notre-Dame Cathedral, the physical and historic bull's-eye of your Paris map.*

▲▲▲*Notre-Dame Cathedral*

The church is dedicated to "Our Lady" (*Notre Dame*), Mary, the mother of Jesus. There she is, cradling God, right in the heart of the facade, surrounded by the halo of the rose window. Though the church is massive and imposing, it has always stood for the grace and compassion of Mary, the "mother of God."

Imagine the faith of the people who built this cathedral. They broke ground in 1163 with the hope that someday their great-great-great-great-great-great grandchildren might attend the dedication Mass, which finally took place two centuries later, in 1345. Look up the 200-foot-tall bell towers and imagine a tiny medieval community mustering the money and energy for construction. Master masons supervised, but the people did much of the grunt work themselves for free—hauling the huge stones from distant quarries, digging a 30-foot-deep trench to lay the foundation, and treading like rats on a wheel designed to lift the stones up, one by one. This kind of backbreaking, arduous manual labor created the real hunchbacks of Notre-Dame.

Rick's Tip: *In summer,* **sound-and-light displays** *about the history of Notre-Dame generally run twice a week (free, usually Thu and Sat at 21:00—check cathedral website or call).*

Cost and Hours: Cathedral—free, daily 7:45-18:45, Sun until 19:15; audioguide—€5, free English tours—normally Mon-Tue and Sat at 14:30, Wed-Thu at 14:00.

The cathedral hosts **Masses** several times daily. Call or check the website for a full schedule (tel. 01 42 34 56 10, www.notredamedeparis.fr).

Tower Climb: The entrance for Notre-Dame's tower climb is outside the cathedral, along the left side. You can hike to the top of the facade between the towers and then to the top of the south tower (400 steps total) for a gargoyle's-eye view of the cathedral, Seine, and city (€8.50, covered by Museum Pass but no bypass line for passholders; daily April-Sept 10:00-18:30, Fri-Sat until 23:00 in July-Aug, Oct-March 10:00-17:30, last entry 45 minutes before closing; to avoid the worst lines arrive before 10:00 or after 17:00—after 16:00 in winter; tel. 01 53 40 60 80, www.notre-dame-de-paris.monuments-nationaux.fr).

Rick's Tip: *If you're* **claustrophobic or acrophobic, skip climbing Notre-Dame's tower.** *It's a tight, crowded space—and once you start up, you're expected to finish.*

The best view of Notre-Dame is from the Left Bank.

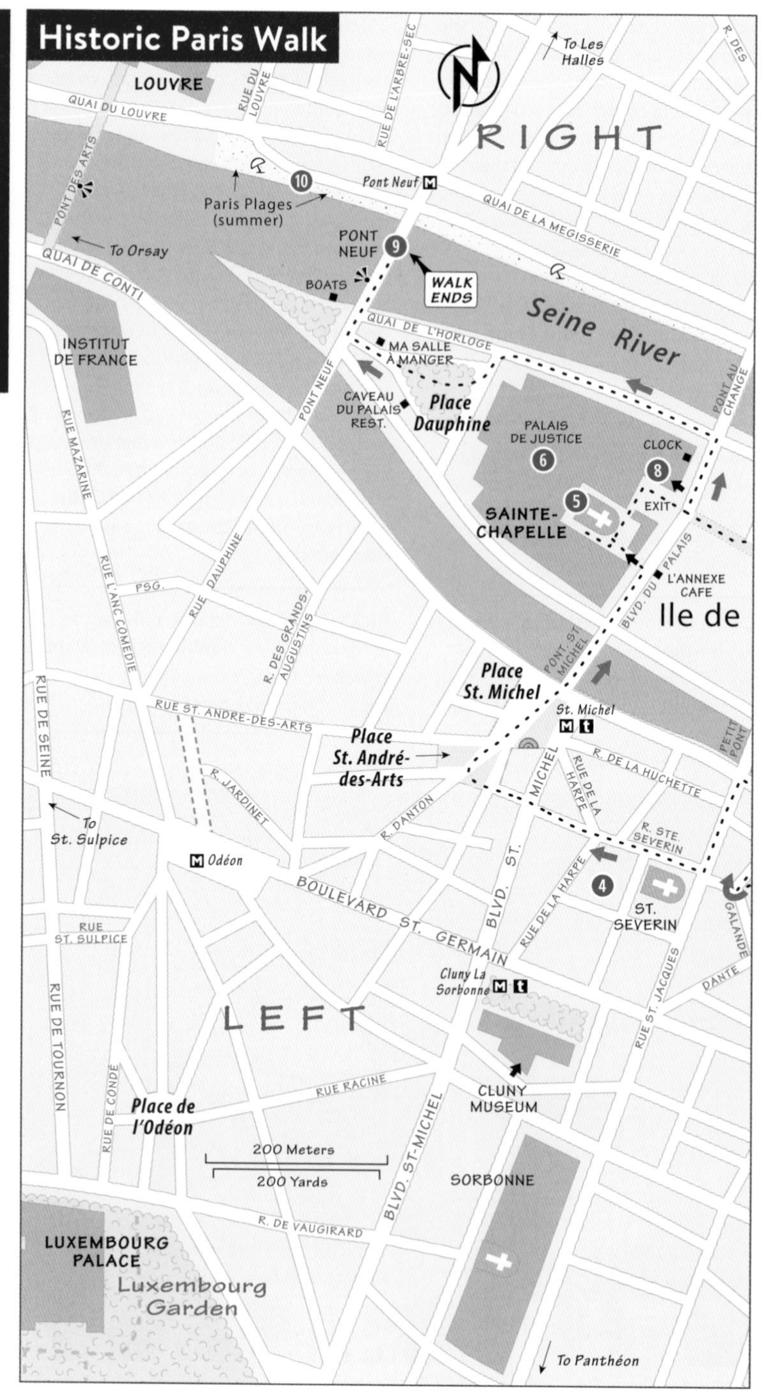
Historic Paris Walk
LOUVRE
QUAI DU LOUVRE
RUE DU LOUVRE
RUE DE L'ARBRE-SEC
To Les Halles
R. DES
RIGHT
PONT DES ARTS
Paris Plages (summer)
Pont Neuf
QUAI DE LA MEGISSERIE
To Orsay
QUAI DE CONTI
PONT NEUF
BOATS
WALK ENDS
Seine River
QUAI DE L'HORLOGE
MA SALLE À MANGER
INSTITUT DE FRANCE
CAVEAU DU PALAIS REST.
Place Dauphine
PALAIS DE JUSTICE
PONT AU CHANGE
CLOCK
SAINTE-CHAPELLE
EXIT
RUE MAZARINE
RUE DAUPHINE
PSG.
RUE L'ANC COMEDIE
R. DES GRANDS-AUGUSTINS
BLVD. DU PALAIS
L'ANNEXE CAFE
Ile de
PONT ST. MICHEL
Place St. Michel
St. Michel
RUE DE SEINE
RUE ST. ANDRE-DES-ARTS
Place St. André-des-Arts
R. DE LA HUCHETTE
RUE DE LA HARPE
PETIT PONT
R. JARDINET
R. DANTON
R. STE. SEVERIN
To St. Sulpice
Odéon
BLVD. ST. MICHEL
BOULEVARD ST. GERMAIN
RUE DE LA HARPE
ST. SEVERIN
GALANDE
RUE ST. SULPICE
Cluny La Sorbonne
RUE ST. JACQUES
DANTE
LEFT
RUE DE TOURNON
RUE RACINE
CLUNY MUSEUM
Place de l'Odéon
RUE DE CONDÉ
200 Meters
200 Yards
BLVD. ST-MICHEL
SORBONNE
R. DE VAUGIRARD
LUXEMBOURG PALACE
Luxembourg Garden
To Panthéon

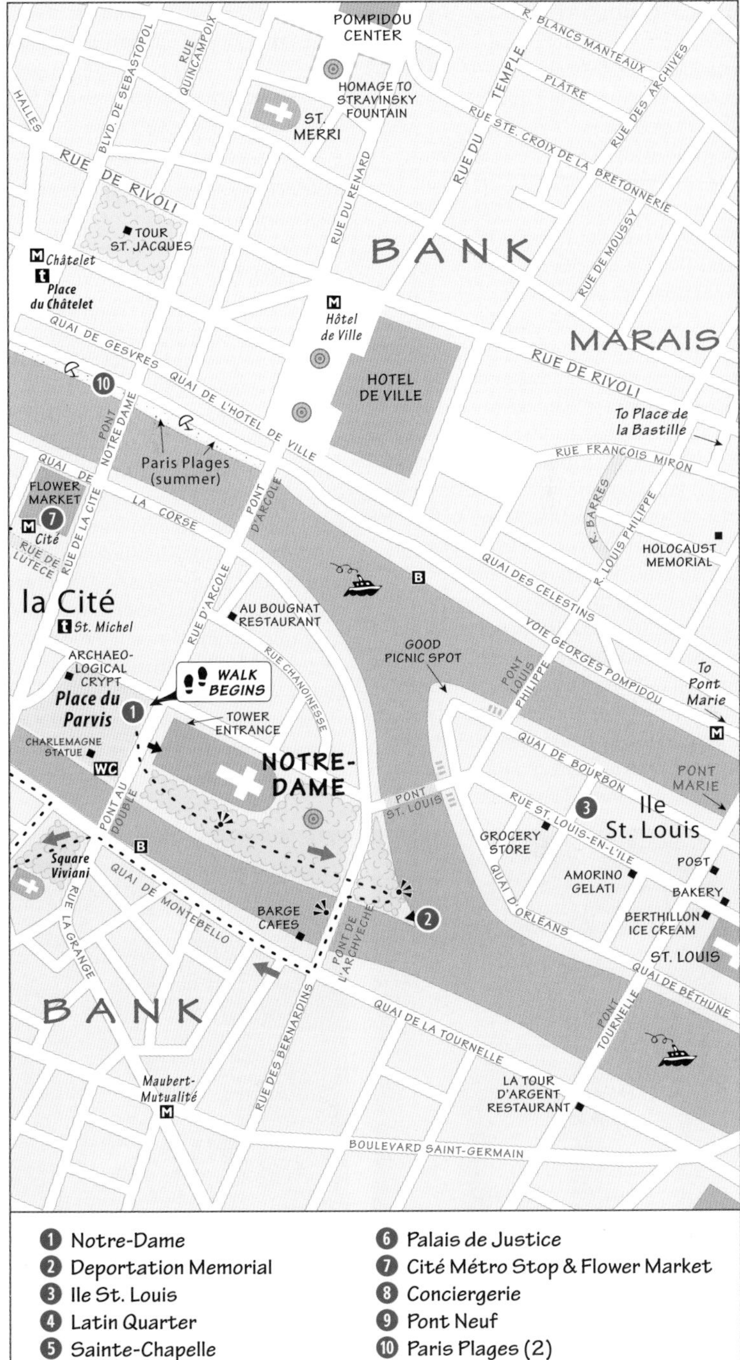
POMPIDOU CENTER
HOMAGE TO STRAVINSKY FOUNTAIN
ST. MERRI
RUE QUINCAMPOIX
BLVD. DE SEBASTOPOL
HALLES
RUE DE RIVOLI
TOUR ST. JACQUES
Châtelet
Place du Châtelet
RUE DU RENARD
RUE DU TEMPLE
R. BLANCS MANTEAUX
PLÂTRE
RUE DES ARCHIVES
RUE STE. CROIX DE LA BRETONNERIE
RUE DE MOUSSY
BANK
MARAIS
Hôtel de Ville
HOTEL DE VILLE
QUAI DE GESVRES
QUAI DE L'HOTEL DE VILLE
RUE DE RIVOLI
To Place de la Bastille
RUE FRANCOIS MIRON
PONT NOTRE DAME
Paris Plages (summer)
QUAI DE LA CORSE
FLOWER MARKET
Cité
RUE DE LUTECE
RUE DE LA CITE
PONT D'ARCOLE
R. BARRES
R. LOUIS PHILIPPE
HOLOCAUST MEMORIAL
QUAI DES CELESTINS
la Cité
St. Michel
RUE D'ARCOLE
AU BOUGNAT RESTAURANT
GOOD PICNIC SPOT
VOIE GEORGES POMPIDOU
To Pont Marie
ARCHAEO-LOGICAL CRYPT
Place du Parvis
WALK BEGINS
RUE CHANOINESSE
TOWER ENTRANCE
PONT LOUIS PHILIPPE
CHARLEMAGNE STATUE
WC
NOTRE-DAME
QUAI DE BOURBON
PONT MARIE
PONT ST. LOUIS
RUE ST. LOUIS-EN-L'ILE
Ile St. Louis
GROCERY STORE
PONT AU DOUBLE
Square Viviani
QUAI DE MONTEBELLO
AMORINO GELATI
POST
BAKERY
BARGE CAFES
QUAI D'ORLÉANS
BERTHILLON ICE CREAM
PONT DE L'ARCHEVECHE
ST. LOUIS
RUE LAGRANGE
QUAI DE BÉTHUNE
BANK
RUE DES BERNARDINS
QUAI DE LA TOURNELLE
PONT TOURNELLE
Maubert-Mutualité
LA TOUR D'ARGENT RESTAURANT
BOULEVARD SAINT-GERMAIN
1 Notre-Dame
2 Deportation Memorial
3 Ile St. Louis
4 Latin Quarter
5 Sainte-Chapelle
6 Palais de Justice
7 Cité Métro Stop & Flower Market
8 Conciergerie
9 Pont Neuf
10 Paris Plages (2)

➔ SELF-GUIDED TOUR

On the square in front of the cathedral, stand far enough back to take in the whole **facade.** Look at the left doorway, and to the left of the door, to find the statue with his head in his hands. This is **St. Denis,** the city's first bishop and patron saint. He stands among statues of other early Christians who helped turn pagan Paris into Christian Paris. Denis proved so successful at winning converts that the Romans' pagan priests got worried. Denis was beheaded as a warning to those forsaking the Roman gods. But those early Christians were hard to keep down. Denis got up, tucked his head under his arm, headed north, paused at a fountain to wash it off, and continued until he found just the right place to meet his maker: Montmartre. The Parisians were convinced by this miracle, Christianity gained ground, and a church soon replaced the pagan temple.

Find the row of 28 statues, known as the **Kings of Judah,** above the arches. In the days of the French Revolution (1789-1799), these biblical kings were mistaken for the hated French kings, and Notre-Dame represented the oppressive Catholic hierarchy. The citizens stormed the church, crying, "Off with their heads!" Plop—they lopped off the crowned heads of these kings with glee, creating a row of St. Denises that weren't repaired for decades.

Rick's Tip: *Be careful—***pickpockets** *attend church here religiously.*

Notre-Dame Interior: Enter the church at the right doorway (the line moves quickly).

Notre-Dame has the typical basilica floor plan shared by so many Catholic churches: a long central nave lined with columns and flanked by side aisles. It's designed in the shape of a cross, with the altar placed where the crossbeam intersects. The church can hold up to 10,000 faithful, and it's probably buzzing with visitors now, just as it was 600 years ago. The quiet, deserted churches we see elsewhere are in stark contrast to the busy, center-of-life places they were in the Middle Ages.

Just past the altar is the choir, the area enclosed with carved-wood walls, where more intimate services can be held in

Headless St. Denis, Paris' patron saint

Pietà *inside Notre-Dame*

Affording Paris' Sights

Paris is an expensive city, with lots of pricey sights, but—fortunately—lots of freebies, too. Smart travelers begin by buying and using the **Paris Museum Pass** (see page 40). Also consider these frugal sightseeing options.

Free (or Almost Free) Museums: Many of Paris' famous museums offer free entry on the first Sunday of the month year-round, including the Orsay, Rodin, Cluny, and Pompidou Center museums. Other sights are free on the first Sunday only in the off-season: the Louvre and Arc de Triomphe (both Oct-March) and Versailles (Nov-March). Expect big crowds on free days. You can usually visit the Orsay Museum for free right when the ticket booth stops selling tickets. For just €2, the Rodin Museum garden lets you enjoy many of his finest works in a lovely outdoor setting.

Other Freebies: There's no entry fee at Notre-Dame Cathedral, Père Lachaise Cemetery, Deportation Memorial, Paris *plages* (summers only), and Sacré-Cœur Basilica.

Reduced Prices: Several sights offer a discount if you enter later in the day, including the Orangerie and the Army Museum and Napoleon's Tomb. The Eiffel Tower costs less if you stick to the two lower levels—and even less if you use the stairs.

Free Concerts: Venues offering free or cheap (€6-8) concerts include the American Church, Army Museum, St. Sulpice Church, La Madeleine Church, and Notre-Dame Cathedral. For a listing of free concerts, check *L'Officiel des Spectacles* magazine (under the "Musique" section) and look for events marked *entrée libre*.

Good-Value Tours: At about €16, Paris Walks' tours are a good value. The €13-14 Seine River cruises, best after dark, are also worthwhile. The scenic bus route #69, which costs only the price of a transit ticket, could be the best deal of all.

Pricey...but worth it? Certain big-ticket items—primarily the top of the Eiffel Tower, the Louvre, and Versailles—are expensive and crowded, but offer once-in-a-lifetime experiences. All together they amount to less than the cost of a ticket to Disneyland—only these are real.

this spacious building. Looking past the altar to the far end of the choir (under the cross), you'll see a fine **17th-century *pietà*,** flanked by two kneeling kings: Louis XIII (1601-1643, not so famous) and his son, Louis XIV (1638-1715, very famous, also known as the Sun King).

In the right transept, a statue of **Joan of Arc** (Jeanne d'Arc, 1412-1431), dressed in armor and praying, honors the French teenager who rallied her country's soldiers to try to drive English invaders from Paris.

Join the statue in gazing up to the blue-and-purple, **rose-shaped window** in the opposite transept—with teeny green Mary and baby Jesus in the center—the only one of the three rose windows still with its original medieval glass.

The back side of the choir walls feature scenes of the **resurrected Jesus** (c. 1350) appearing to his followers, starting with Mary Magdalene. Their starry robes still gleam, thanks to a 19th-century renovation. The niches below these carvings mark the tombs of centuries of archbishops.

Notre-Dame Side View: Back outside, alongside the church, you'll notice many of the elements are Gothic: pointed arches, lacy stone tracery of the windows, pinnacles, statues on rooftops, a lead roof, and a pointed steeple covered with the prickly "flames" (Flamboyant Gothic) of the Holy Spirit. Most distinctive of all are the **flying buttresses.** These 50-foot stone "beams" that stick out of the church were the key to the complex Gothic architecture. The pointed arches we saw inside cause the weight of the roof to push outward rather than downward. The "flying" buttresses support the roof by pushing back inward.

Picture Quasimodo (the fictional hunchback) limping around along the railed balcony at the base of the roof among the **gargoyles.** These grotesque beasts sticking out from pillars and buttresses represent souls caught between heaven and earth. They also function as rainspouts (from the same French root word as "gargle") when there are no evil spirits to battle.

The Neo-Gothic 300-foot **spire** is a product of the 1860 reconstruction of the dilapidated old church. Victor Hugo's book *The Hunchback of Notre-Dame* (1831) inspired a young architecture student named Eugène-Emmanuel Viollet-le-Duc to dedicate his career to a major renovation in Gothic style. Find Viollet-le-Duc at the base of the spire among the green apostles and evangelists (visible as you approach the back end of the church). The apostles look outward, blessing the city, while the architect (at top) looks up the spire, marveling at his fine work.

• *Behind Notre-Dame, cross the street and enter through the iron gate into the park at the tip of the island. Look for the stairs and head down to reach the...*

▲*Deportation Memorial (Mémorial de la Déportation)*

This memorial to the 200,000 French victims of the Nazi concentration camps (1940-1945) draws you into their experience. France was quickly overrun by Nazi Germany, and Paris spent the war years under Nazi occupation. Jews and dissidents were rounded up and deported—many never returned.

Cost and Hours: Free, Tue-Sun 10:00-19:00, Oct-March until 17:00, closed Mon year-round; at the east tip of Ile de la Cité, behind Notre-Dame and near Ile St. Louis (Mo: Cité); www.cheminsdememoire.gouv.fr.

Visiting the Memorial: As you descend the steps, the city around you disappears. Surrounded by walls, you have become a prisoner. Your only freedom is your view of the sky and the tiny glimpse of the river below. Enter the dark, single-file chamber up ahead. Inside, the circular plaque in the floor reads, "They went to the end of the earth and did not return."

The hallway stretching in front of you is lined with 200,000 lighted crystals, one

Deportation Memorial

Shakespeare and Company bookstore

for each French citizen who died. Flickering at the far end is the eternal flame of hope. The tomb of the unknown deportee lies at your feet. Above, the inscription reads, "Dedicated to the living memory of the 200,000 French deportees shrouded by the night and the fog, exterminated in the Nazi concentration camps." The side rooms are filled with triangles—reminiscent of the identification patches inmates were forced to wear—each bearing the name of a concentration camp. Above the exit as you leave is the message you'll find at many other Holocaust sites: "Forgive, but never forget."

• *Back on street level, look across the river (north) to the island called...*

Ile St. Louis

If Ile de la Cité is a tugboat laden with the history of Paris, it's towing this classy little residential dinghy, laden only with high-rent apartments, boutiques, characteristic restaurants, and famous ice cream shops.

Ile St. Louis was developed in the 17th century, much later than Ile de la Cité. What was a swampy mess is now harmonious Parisian architecture and one of the city's most exclusive neighborhoods. If you won't have time to return here later, consider taking a brief detour across the pedestrian bridge, Pont St. Louis. It connects the two islands, leading right to Rue St. Louis-en-l'Ile. This spine of the island is lined with appealing shops, reasonably priced restaurants, and a handy grocery. A short stroll takes you to the famous Berthillon ice cream parlor at #31, which is still family-owned. The ice cream is famous not just because it's good, but because it's made right here on the island. Gelato lovers can comparison-shop by also sampling the (mass-produced-but-who's-complaining) Amorino Gelati at 47 Rue St. Louis-en-l'Ile. This walk is about as peaceful and romantic as Paris gets. When you're finished exploring, loop back to the pedestrian bridge along the parklike quays (walk north to the river and turn left).

• *From the Deportation Memorial, cross the bridge to the Left Bank. Turn right and walk along the river toward the front end of Notre-Dame. Stairs detour down to the riverbank if you need a place to picnic. This side view of the church from across the river is one of Europe's great sights and is best from river level. At times, you may find barges housing restaurants with great cathedral views docked here.*

After passing the Pont au Double (the bridge leading to the facade of Notre-Dame), watch on your left for ***Shakespeare and Company,*** *an atmospheric reincarnation of the original 1920s bookshop (open long hours daily, 37 Rue de la Bûcherie, Mo: St. Michel, tel. 01 43 25 40 93). Before returning to the island, walk a block behind Shakespeare and Company, and take a spin through the...*

▲The Latin Quarter

This area's touristy fame relates to its intriguing, artsy, bohemian character. This was perhaps Europe's leading university district in the Middle Ages, when Latin was the language of higher education. The neighborhood's main boulevards (St. Michel and St. Germain) are lined with cafés—once the haunts of great poets and philosophers, now the hangouts of tired tourists. Though still youthful

The Latin Quarter

and artsy, much of this touristy area is filled with cheap North African eateries. Exploring a few blocks up or downriver from here gives you a better chance of feeling the pulse of what survives of Paris' classic Left Bank. For colorful wandering and café-sitting, afternoons and evenings are best.

Walking along Rue St. Séverin, you can still see the shadow of the medieval sewer system. The street slopes into a central channel of bricks. In the days before plumbing and toilets, when people still went to the river or neighborhood wells for their water, flushing meant throwing it out the window. At certain times of day, maids on the fourth floor would holler, *"Garde de l'eau!"* ("Watch out for the water!") and heave it into the streets, where it would eventually wash down into the Seine.

Consider a visit to the **Cluny Museum** for its medieval art and unicorn tapestries (see page 76). The **Sorbonne**—the University of Paris' humanities department—is also nearby; visitors can ogle at the famous dome, but they are not allowed to enter the building (two blocks south of the river on Boulevard St. Michel).

Don't miss **Place St. Michel.** This square (facing Pont St. Michel) is the traditional core of the Left Bank's district of artists, poets, philosophers, winos, and *baba* cools (neo-hippies). In less commercial times, Place St. Michel was a gathering point for the city's malcontents and misfits. In 1830, 1848, and again in 1871, the citizens took the streets from the government troops, set up barricades *Les Miz*-style, and fought against royalist oppression. During World War II, the locals rose up against their Nazi oppressors (read the plaques under the dragons at the foot of the St. Michel fountain). Even today, whenever there's a student demonstration, it starts here.

• *From Place St. Michel, look across the river and find the prickly steeple of the Sainte-Chapelle church. Head toward it. Cross the river on Pont St. Michel and continue north along the Boulevard du Palais. On your left, you'll see the doorway to Sainte-Chapelle (usually with a line of people).*

▲▲▲*Sainte-Chapelle*

This triumph of Gothic church architecture is a cathedral of glass like no other. It was speedily built between 1242 and 1248 for King Louis IX—the only French king who is now a saint—to house the supposed Crown of Thorns. Its architectural harmony is due to the fact that it was completed under the direction of one architect and in only six years—unheard of in Gothic times. In contrast, Notre-Dame took over 200 years.

Cost and Hours: €8.50, €13.50 combo-ticket with Conciergerie, free for those under age 18, covered by Museum Pass; daily April-Sept 9:00-19:00, Oct-March 9:00-17:00; audioguide-€4.50, 4 Boulevard du Palais, Mo: Cité, tel. 01 53 40 60 80, www.sainte-chapelle.fr. For information on upcoming church concerts, see page 96.

Getting In: Expect long lines to get in (shortest wait first thing in the mornings and on weekends; longest on Tue and any day around 13:00-14:00). First comes the security line (all sharp objects and glass are confiscated). Once past security, you'll encounter the ticket-buying line—those with combo-tickets or Museum Passes can skip this queue.

Visiting the Church: Though the inside is beautiful, the exterior is basically functional. The muscular buttresses hold up the stone roof, so the walls are essentially there to display stained glass. The lacy spire is Neo-Gothic—added in the 19th century. Inside, the layout clearly shows an *ancien régime* approach to worship. The low-ceilinged basement was for staff and other common folks—worshipping under a sky filled with painted fleurs-de-lis, a symbol of the king. Royal Christians worshipped upstairs. The

Sainte-Chapelle

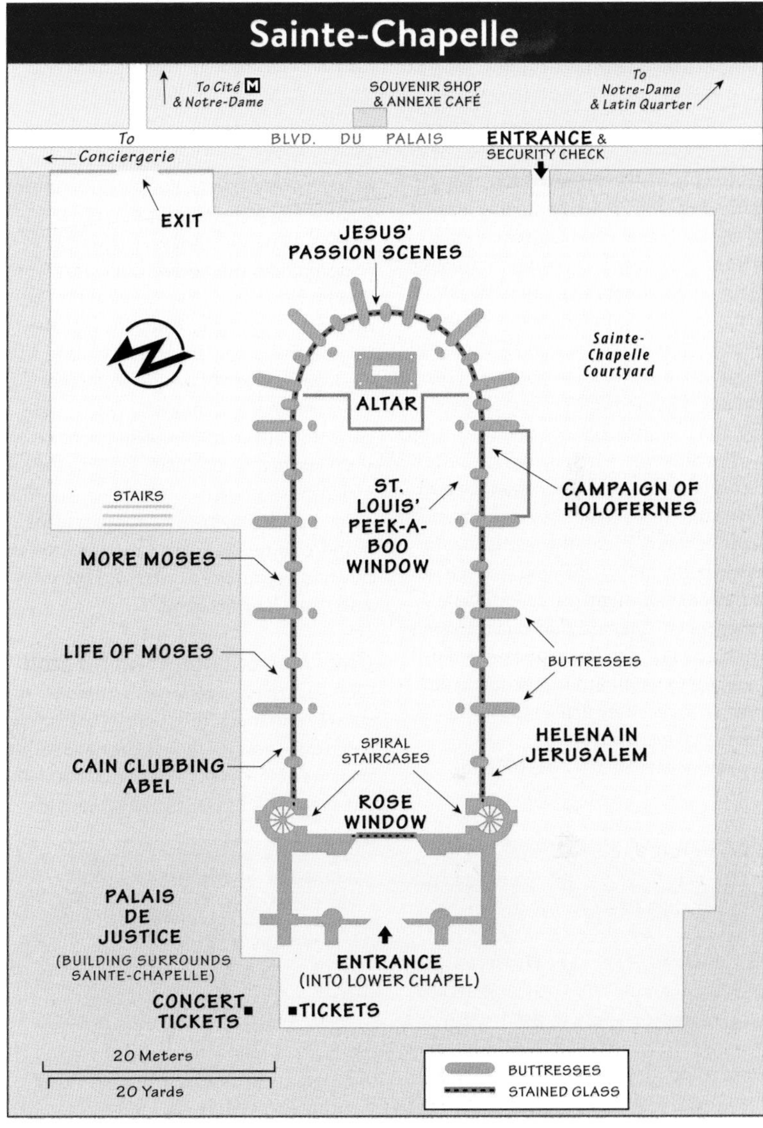

paint job, a 19th-century restoration, helps you imagine how grand this small, painted, jeweled chapel was. (Imagine Notre-Dame painted like this...) Each capital is playfully carved with a different plant's leaves.

Climb the spiral staircase to the Chapelle Haute. Fill the place with choral music, crank up the sunshine, face the top of the altar, and really believe that the Crown of Thorns is there, and this becomes one awesome space.

Fiat lux. "Let there be light." From the first page of the Bible, it's clear: Light is divine. Light shines through stained glass like God's grace shining down to earth.

Gothic architects used their new technology to turn dark stone buildings into lanterns of light. The glory of Gothic shines brighter here than in any other church.

There are 15 separate panels of **stained glass** (6,500 square feet—two thirds of it 13th-century original), with more than 1,100 different scenes, mostly from the Bible. These cover the entire Christian history of the world, from the Creation in Genesis (first window on the left, as you face the altar), to the coming of Christ (over the altar), to the end of the world (the round "rose"-shaped window at the rear of the church). Each individual scene is interesting, and the whole effect is overwhelming.

The **altar** was raised up high to better display the Crown of Thorns, which cost King Louis more than three times as much as this church. Today, the relic is kept in the treasury at Notre-Dame (though it's occasionally brought out for display).

• *Exit Sainte-Chapelle. Back outside, as you walk around the church exterior, look down to see the foundation and take note of how much Paris has risen in the 750 years since Sainte-Chapelle was built.*

Next door to Sainte-Chapelle is the...

Palais de Justice

Sainte-Chapelle sits within a huge complex of buildings that has housed the local government since ancient Roman times. It was the site of the original Gothic palace of the early kings of France. The only surviving medieval parts are Sainte-Chapelle and the Conciergerie prison.

Most of the site is now covered by the giant Palais de Justice, built in 1776, home of the French Supreme Court. The motto *Liberté, Egalité, Fraternité* over the doors is a reminder that this was also the headquarters of the Revolutionary government. Here they doled out justice, condemning many to imprisonment in the Conciergerie downstairs—or to the guillotine.

• *Now pass through the big iron gate to the noisy Boulevard du Palais. Cross the street to the wide, pedestrian-only Rue de Lutèce and walk about halfway down.*

Cité "Metropolitain" Métro Stop

Of the 141 original early-20th-century subway entrances, this is one of only a few survivors—now preserved as a national art treasure. (New York's Museum of Modern Art even exhibits one.) It marks Paris at

Sainte-Chapelle is a cathedral of stained glass like no other.

its peak in 1900—on the cutting edge of Modernism, but with an eye for beauty. The curvy, plantlike ironwork is a textbook example of Art Nouveau, the style that rebelled against the erector-set squareness of the Industrial Age. Other similar Métro stations in Paris are Abbesses and Porte Dauphine.

The flower and plant market on Place Louis Lépine is a pleasant detour. On Sundays this square flutters with a busy bird market.

• *Pause here to admire the view.*

Sainte-Chapelle is a pearl in an ugly architectural oyster. Double back to the Palais de Justice, turn right onto Boulevard du Palais, and enter the Conciergerie. It's free with the Museum Pass; passholders can sidestep the bottleneck created by the ticket-buying line.

▲*Conciergerie*

Though pretty barren inside, this former prison echoes with history. Positioned next to the courthouse, the Conciergerie was the gloomy prison famous as the last stop for 2,780 victims of the guillotine, including France's last *ancien régime* queen, Marie-Antoinette. Before then, kings had used the building to torture and execute failed assassins. (One of its towers along the river was called "The Babbler," named for the pain-induced sounds that leaked from it.) When the Revolution (1789) toppled the king, the building kept its same function, but without torture. The progressive Revolutionaries proudly unveiled a modern and more humane way to execute people—the guillotine. The Conciergerie was the epicenter of the Reign of Terror—the year-long period of the Revolution (1793-94) during which Revolutionary fervor spiraled out of control and thousands were killed. It was here at the Conciergerie that "enemies of the Revolution" were imprisoned, tried, sentenced, and marched off to Place de la Concorde for decapitation.

Cost and Hours: €8.50, €13.50 combo-ticket with Sainte-Chapelle, covered by Museum Pass, daily 9:30-18:00, 2 Boulevard du Palais, Mo: Cité, tel. 01 53 40 60 80, http://conciergerie.monuments-nationaux.fr.

Visiting the Conciergerie: Pick up a free map and breeze through the one-way circuit. See the spacious, low-ceilinged Hall of Men-at-Arms (Room 1), originally a guards' dining room, with four big fireplaces (look up the chimneys). During the Reign of Terror, this large hall served as a holding tank for the poorest prisoners. Continue to the raised area at the far end of the room (Room 4, today's bookstore). In Revolutionary days, this was notorious as the walkway of the executioner, who was known affectionately as "Monsieur de Paris."

Upstairs is a memorial room with the names of the 2,780 citizens condemned to death by the guillotine, including ex-King Louis XVI, Charlotte Corday (who murdered the Revolutionary writer

Cité Métro entrance

Conciergerie prison

Jean-Paul Marat in his bathtub), and—oh, the irony—Maximilien de Robespierre, the head rabble-rouser of the Revolution, who himself sent so many to the guillotine.

Just past the courtyard is a re-creation of Marie-Antoinette's cell. On August 12, 1793, the queen was brought here to be tried for her supposed crimes against the people. Mannequins, period furniture, and the real cell wallpaper set the scene. In the glass display case, see her actual crucifix, rug, and small water pitcher. On October 16, 1793, the queen was awakened at 4:00 in the morning and led away. She walked the corridor, stepped onto the cart, and was slowly carried to Place de la Concorde, where she had a date with "Monsieur de Paris."

• *Back outside, turn left on Boulevard du Palais, then left again onto Quai de l'Horloge and walk along the river, past "The Babbler" tower.*

The bridge up ahead is the Pont Neuf, where we'll end this walk. At the first corner, veer left into a sleepy triangular square called **Place Dauphine.** *It's amazing to find such coziness in the heart of Paris. From the equestrian statue of Henry IV, turn right onto Pont Neuf. Pause at the little nook halfway across.*

Pont Neuf and the Seine

This "new bridge" is now Paris' oldest. Built during Henry IV's reign (about 1600), its arches span the widest part of the river. Unlike other bridges, this one never had houses or buildings growing on it. The turrets were originally for vendors and street entertainers. In the days of Henry IV, who promised his peasants "a chicken in every pot every Sunday," this would have been a lively scene. From the bridge, look downstream (west) to see the next bridge, the pedestrian-only Pont des Arts. Ahead on the Right Bank is the long Louvre museum. Beyond that, on the Left Bank, is the Orsay.

• *Our walk is finished. From here, you can tour the Seine by boat (the departure point for Seine River cruises offered by Vedettes du Pont Neuf is through the park at the end of the island—see page 91), continue to the Louvre, or (if it's summer) head to the...*

Pont Neuf crosses the widest part of the Seine.

▲*Paris* Plages (*Paris Beaches*)

The Riviera it's not, but this string of fanciful faux beaches—assembled in summer along a one-mile stretch of the Right Bank of the Seine—is a fun place to stroll, play, and people-watch on a sunny day. Each summer, the Paris city government closes the embankment's highway and trucks in potted palm trees, hammocks, lounge chairs, and 2,000 tons of sand to create colorful urban beaches. You'll also find "beach cafés," climbing walls, prefab pools, trampolines, *boules*, a library, beach volleyball, badminton, and Frisbee areas.

Cost and Hours: Free, mid-July-mid-Aug daily 8:00-24:00, on Right Bank of Seine, just north of Ile de la Cité, between Pont des Arts and Pont de Sully; for information, go to www.quefaire.paris.fr/parisplages.

SIGHTS

Major Museums Neighborhood

Paris' grandest park, the Tuileries Garden, was once the private property of kings and queens. Today it links the Louvre, Orangerie, and Orsay museums, all of which are within pleasant strolling distance of one another.

▲▲▲LOUVRE (MUSEE DU LOUVRE)

This is Europe's oldest, biggest, greatest, and second-most-crowded museum (after the Vatican). Housed in a U-shaped, 16th-century palace (accentuated by a 20th-century glass pyramid), it's home to the *Mona Lisa*, *Venus de Milo*, and hall after hall of Greek and Roman masterpieces, medieval jewels,

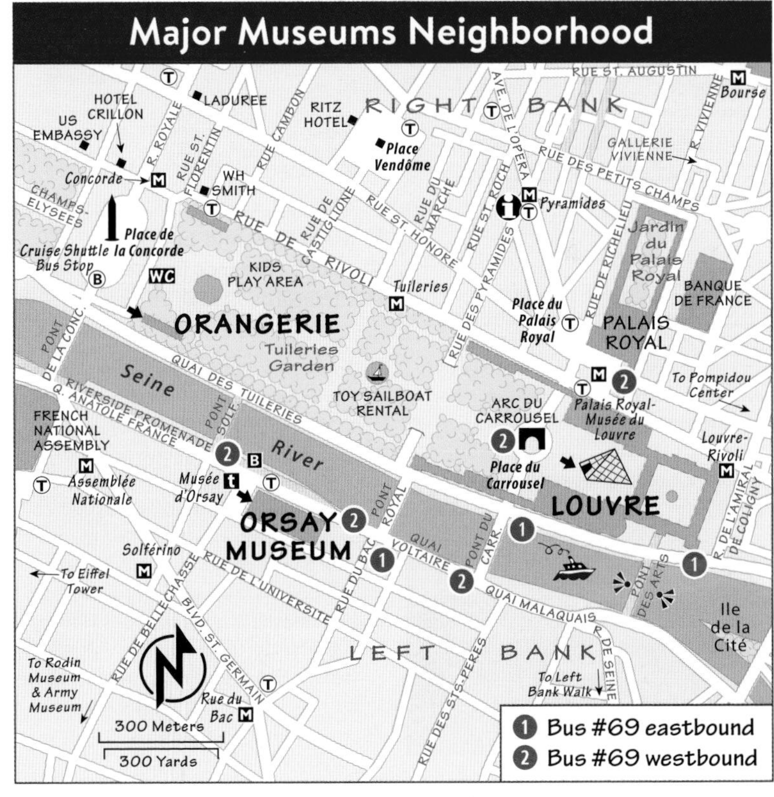

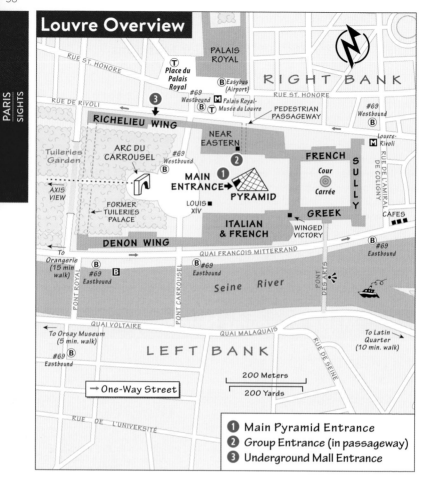

Louvre Overview

PALAIS ROYAL
RUE ST. HONORÉ
Place du Palais Royal
Easybus (Airport)
RIGHT BANK
#69 Westbound
Palais Royal-Musée du Louvre
RUE DE RIVOLI
PEDESTRIAN PASSAGEWAY
RICHELIEU WING
NEAR EASTERN
Louvre-Rivoli
Tuileries Garden
ARC DU CARROUSEL
FRENCH
Cour Carrée
SULLY
RUE DE L'AMIRAL DE COLIGNY
MAIN ENTRANCE
PYRAMID
AXIS VIEW
FORMER TUILERIES PALACE
LOUIS XIV
GREEK
CAFES
ITALIAN & FRENCH
WINGED VICTORY
DENON WING
To Orangerie (15 min walk)
QUAI FRANCOIS MITTERRAND
#69 Eastbound
PONT ROYAL
PONT CARROUSEL
PONT DES ARTS
Seine River
QUAI VOLTAIRE
QUAI MALAQUAIS
To Orsay Museum (5 min. walk)
LEFT BANK
RUE DE SEINE
To Latin Quarter (10 min. walk)
200 Meters
200 Yards
One-Way Street
RUE DE L'UNIVERSITÉ

1. Main Pyramid Entrance
2. Group Entrance (in passageway)
3. Underground Mall Entrance

Michelangelo statues, and paintings by the greatest artists from the Renaissance to the Romantics.

Under the Louvre's pyramid entrance

Touring the Louvre can be overwhelming, so be selective. Focus on the Denon wing, with Greek sculptures, Italian paintings (by Raphael and Leonardo), and—of course—French paintings (Neoclassical and Romantic), and the adjoining Sully wing, with Egyptian artifacts and more French paintings. For extra credit, tackle the Richelieu wing, displaying works from ancient Mesopotamia, as well as French, Dutch, and Northern art.

Expect Changes: The sprawling Louvre is constantly shuffling its deck. Rooms close, and pieces can be on loan or in restoration.

Cost and Hours: €12, €15 includes special exhibits, free on first Sun of month Oct-March, covered by Museum Pass, tickets good all day, reentry allowed; open Wed-Mon 9:00-18:00, Wed and Fri until 21:45 (except on holidays), closed Tue, galleries start shutting 30 minutes before closing, last entry 45 minutes before closing; videoguide-€5, several cafés, tel. 01 40 20 53 17, recorded info tel. 01 40 20 51 51, www.louvre.fr.

When to Go: Crowds are bad on Sun, Mon (the worst day), Wed, and in the morning (arrive 30 minutes before opening to secure a good place in line). Evening visits are quieter, and the glass pyramid glows after dark.

Buying Tickets: Self-serve ticket machines located under the pyramid may be faster to use than the ticket windows (machines accept euro bills, coins, and chip-and-PIN Visa cards). A shop in the underground mall sells tickets to the Louvre, Orsay, and Versailles, plus Museum Passes, for no extra charge (cash only). To find it from the Carrousel du Louvre entrance off Rue de Rivoli, turn right after the last escalator down onto Allée de France, and follow *Museum Pass* signs.

Rick's Tip: *Anyone can* **enter the Louvre from its less crowded underground entrance,** *accessed through the Carrousel du Louvre shopping mall. Enter the mall at 99 Rue de Rivoli (the door with the red awning) or directly from the Métro stop Palais Royal-Musée du Louvre (stepping off the train, take the exit to Musée du Louvre-Le Carrousel du Louvre).*

Getting There: It's at the Palais Royal-Musée du Louvre Métro stop. (The old Louvre Métro stop, called Louvre-Rivoli, is farther from the entrance.) Bus #69 also runs past the Louvre.

Getting In: There is no grander entry than through the main entrance at the **pyramid** in the central courtyard, but lines (for security reasons) can be long. Passholders should look for a queue that puts them near the head of the security line.

Tours: Ninety-minute English-

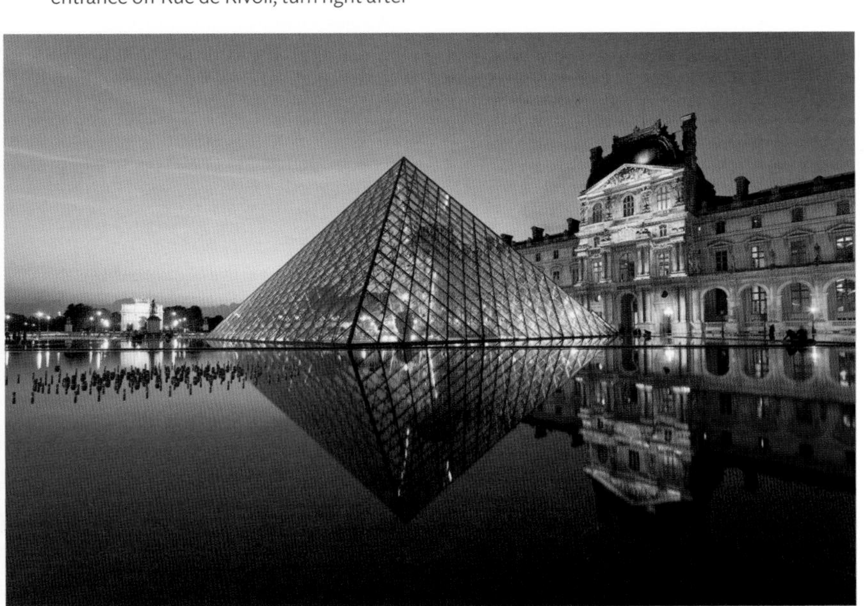

The Louvre and its pyramid glows at night.

language **guided tours** leave twice daily (except the first Sun of the month Oct-March) from the *Accueil des Groupes* area, under the pyramid (€12 plus admission, usually 11:15 and 14:00, tour tel. 01 40 20 52 63). **Videoguides** (€5) provide commentary on about 700 masterpieces.

🎧 Download my free Louvre Museum **audio tour.**

Baggage Check: The free *bagagerie* is under the pyramid, behind the Richelieu wing escalator (look for the *visiteurs individuels* sign).

➲ SELF-GUIDED TOUR

With more than 30,000 works of art, the Louvre is a full inventory of Western civilization. To cover it all in one visit is impossible. Let's focus on the Louvre's specialties—Greek sculpture, Italian painting, and French painting. If you don't find the artwork you're looking for, ask the nearest guard for its location.

• *We'll start in the Sully Wing, in Salle 16. To get there from the pyramid entrance, first enter the Denon Wing, ascend several flights of escalators, and follow the crowds—then get out your map or ask directions to the Venus de Milo.*

THE GREEKS

Venus de Milo (*Aphrodite,* late 2nd century B.C.): This goddess of love created a sensation when she was discovered in 1820 on the Greek island of Melos. The Greeks pictured their gods in human form (meaning humans are godlike), telling us they had an optimistic view of the human race. *Venus'* well-proportioned body captures the balance and orderliness of the Greek universe. The twisting pose gives a balanced S-curve to her body (especially noticeable from the back view) that Golden Age Greeks and succeeding generations found beautiful. Most "Greek" statues are actually later Roman copies; this is a rare Greek original.

Venus de Milo

• *Now head to Salle 6, behind Venus de Milo.*

Parthenon Friezes (mid-5th century B.C.): These stone fragments once decorated the exterior of the greatest Athenian temple of the Greek Golden Age. The temple glorified the city's divine protector, Athena, and the superiority of the Athenians, who were feeling especially cocky, having just crushed their archrivals, the Persians. A model of the Parthenon shows where the panels might have hung.

• *About 50 yards away, find a grand staircase. Climb it to the first floor and the...*

Winged Victory of Samothrace (c. 190 B.C.): This woman with wings, poised on the prow of a ship, once stood on an island hilltop to commemorate a naval victory. Her clothes are windblown and sea-sprayed, clinging close enough to her body to win a wet T-shirt contest. Originally, her right arm was stretched high, celebrating the victory like a Super Bowl champion, waving a "we're number one" finger. This is the *Venus de Milo* gone Hellenistic, from the time after the culture of Athens was spread around the Mediterranean by Alexander the Great (c. 325 B.C.).

• *Facing* Winged Victory, *turn right (entering the Denon Wing), and proceed to the large Salle 3.*

THE MEDIEVAL WORLD, 1200-1500

Cimabue—*The Madonna and Child in Majesty Surrounded by Angels* (c. 1280): During the Age of Faith (1200s), almost every church in Europe had a painting like this one. Mary was a cult figure—even bigger than the late-20th-century Madonna—adored and prayed to by the faithful for bringing Baby Jesus into the world. These holy figures are laid flat on a gold background like cardboard cutouts, existing in a golden never-never land, as though the faithful couldn't imagine them as flesh-and-blood humans inhabiting our dark and sinful earth.

Giotto—*St. Francis of Assisi Receiving the Stigmata* (c. 1295-1300): Francis of Assisi (c. 1181-1226), a wandering Italian monk of renowned goodness, kneels on a rocky Italian hillside, pondering the pain of Christ's torture and execution. Suddenly, he looks up, startled, to see Christ himself, with six wings, hovering above. Christ shoots lasers from his wounds to the hands, feet, and side of the empathetic monk, marking him with the stigmata. Francis' humble love of man and nature inspired artists like Giotto to portray real human beings with real emotions, living in a physical world of beauty.

• *Room 3 spills into the long Grand Gallery. Find the following paintings in the Gallery, as you make your way to the Mona Lisa (midway down the gallery, in the adjoining Salle 6—just follow the signs and the people).*

ITALIAN RENAISSANCE, 1400-1600

Andrea Mantegna—*St. Sebastian* (c. 1480): Not the patron saint of acupuncture, St. Sebastian was a Christian martyr. Notice the *contrapposto* stance (all of his weight resting on one leg) and the Greek ruins scattered around him. His executioners look like ignorant medieval brutes bewildered by this enlightened Renaissance man. Italian artists were beginning to learn how to create human realism and earthly beauty on the canvas. Let the Renaissance begin.

Leonardo da Vinci—*The Virgin and Child with St. Anne* (c. 1510): Three generations—grandmother, mother, and child—are arranged in a pyramid, with Anne's face as the peak and the lamb as the lower right corner. It's as orderly as the

A Winged Victory of Samothrace

B *Giotto,* St. Francis Receiving the Stigmata

C *Leonardo da Vinci,* Mona Lisa

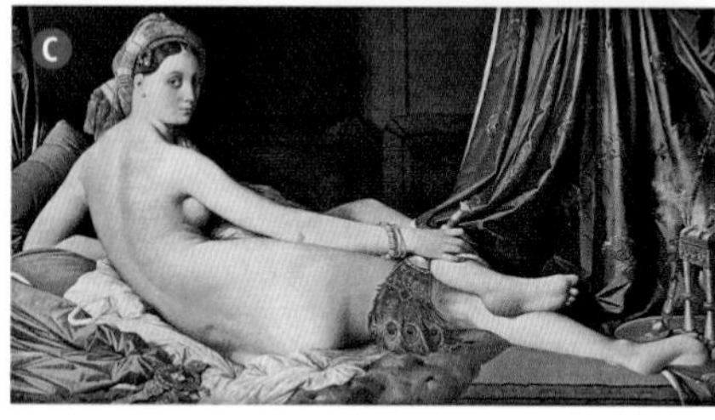

A *Raphael,* La Belle Jardinière

B *Veronese,* The Marriage at Cana

C *Ingres,* La Grande Odalisque

D *Delacroix,* Liberty Leading the People

geometrically perfect universe created by the Renaissance god. There's a psychological kidney punch in this happy painting: Jesus, the picture of childish joy, is innocently playing with a lamb—the symbol of his inevitable sacrificial death. The Louvre has the greatest collection of Leonardos in the world—five of them. Look for the neighboring *Virgin of the Rocks* and *John the Baptist*.

Raphael—*La Belle Jardinière* (c. 1507): Raphael perfected the style Leonardo pioneered. This configuration of Madonna, Child, and John the Baptist is also a balanced pyramid with hazy grace and beauty. The interplay of gestures and gazes gives the masterpiece both intimacy and cohesiveness, while Raphael's blended brushstrokes varnish the work with an iridescent smoothness. With Raphael, the Greek ideal of beauty—reborn in the Renaissance—reached its peak.

Leonardo da Vinci—*Mona Lisa* (1503-1519): When Leonardo moved to France late in life, he packed light, bringing only a few paintings with him. One was a portrait of Lisa del Giocondo, the wife of a wealthy Florentine merchant. *Mona* may disappoint you. She's smaller than you'd expect, darker, engulfed in a huge room, and hidden behind a glaring pane of glass. The famous smile attracts you first, but try as you might, you can never quite see the corners of her mouth. The overall mood is one of balance and serenity, but there's also an element of mystery. Mona's smile and long-distance beauty are subtle and elusive, tempting but always just out of reach. Mona doesn't knock your socks off, but she winks at the patient viewer.

Paolo Veronese—*The Marriage at Cana* (1563): Venetian artists like Veronese painted the good life of rich, happy-go-lucky Venetian merchants. In a spacious setting of Renaissance architecture, colorful lords and ladies, decked out in their fanciest duds, feast on a great spread of food and drink. But believe it or not, this is a religious work showing the wedding celebration in which Jesus turned water into wine. With true Renaissance optimism, Venetians pictured Christ as a party animal, someone who loved the created world as much as they did.

• *Exit behind Mona into the Salle Denon (Room 76). Turn right for French Neoclassicism (Salle Daru, David and Ingres); then backtrack through the Salle Denon for French Romanticism (Room 77, Géricault and Delacroix).*

FRENCH PAINTING, 1780-1850

Jacques-Louis David—*The Coronation of Emperor Napoleon* (1806-1807): Napoleon holds aloft an imperial crown. This common-born son of immigrants is about to be crowned emperor of a "New Rome." He has just made his wife, Josephine, the empress, and she kneels at his feet. Seated behind Napoleon is the pope, who journeyed from Rome to place the imperial crown on his head. But Napoleon feels that no one is worthy of the task. At the last moment, he shrugs the pope aside... and crowns himself.

Jean-Auguste-Dominique Ingres—*La Grande Odalisque* (1814): Take *Venus de Milo,* turn her around, lay her down, and stick a hash pipe next to her, and you have the *Grande Odalisque*. Using clean, polished, sculptural lines, Ingres exaggerates the S-curve of a standing Greek nude. As in the *Venus de Milo,* rough folds of cloth set off her smooth skin. Ingres gave the face, too, a touch of *Venus'* idealized features, taking nature and improving on it. Ingres preserves Venus' backside for posterior—I mean, posterity.

Théodore Géricault—*The Raft of the Medusa* (1819): Clinging to a raft is a tangle of bodies and lunatics sprawled over each other. The scene writhes with agitated, ominous motion—the ripple of muscles, churning clouds, and choppy seas. The bodies rise up in a pyramid of hope, culminating in a flag wave. They signal frantically, trying to catch the attention of the tiny ship on the horizon, their last desperate hope...which did finally save them. Géricault uses rippling movement and powerful colors to catch us up in the excitement. (This painting was based on the actual sinking of the ship *Medusa* off the coast of Africa in 1816.)

Eugène Delacroix—*Liberty Leading the People* (1831): The year is 1830. Parisians take to the streets to fight royalist oppressors. Leading them on through the smoke and over the dead and dying is the figure of Liberty, a strong woman waving the French flag. Does this symbol of victory look familiar? It's the *Winged Victory,* wingless and topless. To stir our emotions, Delacroix uses only three major colors—the red, white, and blue of the French flag. France is the symbol of modern democracy, and this painting has long stirred its citizens' passion for liberty.

• *Exit the room at the far end, go downstairs, where you'll bump into...*

MORE ITALIAN RENAISSANCE

Michelangelo—*Slaves* (1513-1515): These two statues by the earth's greatest sculptor are a bridge between the ancient and

Michelangelo's Slave *sculptures*

modern worlds. Michelangelo, like his fellow Renaissance artists, learned from the Greeks. The perfect anatomy, twisting poses, and idealized faces appear as if they could have been created 2,000 years earlier.

The *Dying Slave* twists listlessly against his T-shirt-like bonds, revealing his smooth skin. This is probably the most sensual nude that Michelangelo, the master of the male body, ever created. The *Rebellious Slave* fights against his bondage. His shoulders rotate one way, his head and leg turn the other. He even seems to be trying to release himself from the rock he's made of. Michelangelo said that his purpose was to carve away the marble to reveal the figures God put inside. This slave shows the agony of that process and the ecstasy of the result.

• *But, of course, there's so much more. After a break (or on a second visit), consider a stroll through a few rooms of the Richelieu wing, which contain some of the Louvre's most ancient pieces.*

Rick's Tip: *Across from the Louvre (to the north) are the lovely courtyards of the stately* **Palais Royal** *(always open and free, entrance off Rue de Rivoli). Bring a picnic and create your own* **quiet break** *amid flowers and surrounded by a serene arcade.*

▲▲▲ORSAY MUSEUM (MUSEE D'ORSAY)

The Musée d'Orsay houses French art of the 1800s and early 1900s, picking up where the Louvre's art collection leaves off. For us, that means Impressionism, the art of sun-dappled fields, bright colors, and crowded Parisian cafés. The Orsay houses the best general collection anywhere of works by Manet, Monet, Renoir, Degas, Van Gogh, Cézanne, and Gauguin.

Cost and Hours: €11, €8.50 Tue-Wed and Fri-Sun after 16:30 and Thu after 18:15, free on first Sun of month and often right when the ticket booth stops selling tickets (Tue-Wed and Fri-Sun at 17:00, Thu at 21:00; they won't let you in much after that), covered by Museum Pass, tickets valid all day, combo-ticket with Orangerie Museum (€16) or Rodin Museum (€15) valid four days. Museum open Tue-Sun 9:30-18:00, Thu until 21:45, closed Mon, last entry one hour before closing; cafés and a restaurant, tel. 01 40 49 48 14, www.musee-orsay.fr.

Avoiding Lines: You can skip long ticket-buying lines by using a Museum Pass or purchasing tickets online in advance, both of which entitle you to use a separate entrance. You can buy tickets and Museum Passes (no mark-up; tickets valid 3 months) at the newspaper kiosk just outside the Orsay entrance (along Rue de la Légion d'Honneur).

Rick's Tip: *If you're planning to* **get a combo-ticket for the Orsay Museum** *with either the Orangerie or the Rodin Museum, start at one of those museums instead, as they have shorter lines.*

Getting There: The museum, at 1 Rue de la Légion d'Honneur, sits above the Train-C stop called Musée d'Orsay; the nearest Métro stop is Solférino. Bus #69 also stops at the Orsay.

Getting In: As you face the entrance, passholders and ticket holders enter on the right (Entrance C). Ticket purchasers enter on the left (Entrance A). Security checks slow down all entrances.

Tours: Audioguides cost €5. English **guided tours** usually run daily at 11:30 (€6/1.5 hours, none on Sun, tours may also run at 14:30—inquire when you arrive).

🎧 Download my free Orsay Museum **audio tour.**

➔ SELF-GUIDED TOUR

This former train station, the Gare d'Orsay, barely escaped the wrecking ball in the 1970s, when the French realized it'd be a great place to house the enormous collections of 19th-century art scattered throughout the city.

The ground floor (level 0) houses early 19th-century art, mainly conservative art of the Academy and Salon, plus Realism. On the top floor is the core of the collection—the Impressionist rooms. If you're pressed for time, go directly there. The museum rotates its large collection often, so find the latest arrangement on your current Orsay map, and be ready to go with the flow.

CONSERVATIVE ART

In the Orsay's first few ground-floor rooms, you're surrounded by visions of idealized beauty—nude women in languid poses, Greek mythological figures, and anatomically perfect statues. This was the art adored by 19th-century French academics and the middle-class (bourgeois) public.

Jean-Auguste-Dominique Ingres' *The Source* (1856) is virtually a Greek statue on canvas. Like the Louvre's *Venus de Milo,* she's a balance of opposite motions. Alexandre **Cabanel** lays Ingres' *Source* on her back. His *Birth of Venus* (1863) is a perfect fantasy, an orgasm of beauty.

REALISM

The French Realists rejected idealized classicism and began painting what they saw in the world around them. For Honoré **Daumier,** that meant looking at the stuffy bourgeois establishment that controlled the Academy and the Salon. In the 36 bustlets of *Celebrities of the Happy Medium* (1835), Daumier, trained as a political cartoonist, exaggerates each subject's most distinct characteristic to capture with vicious precision the pomposity and self-righteousness of these self-appointed arbiters of taste.

Jean-François Millet's *The Gleaners* (1867) shows us three poor women who pick up the meager leftovers after a field has been harvested for the wealthy. Here he captures the innate dignity of these stocky, tanned women who bend their backs quietly in a large field for their small reward. This is "Realism" in two senses. It's painted "realistically," not prettified. And it's the "real" world—not the fantasy world of Greek myth, but the harsh life of the working poor.

For a Realist's take on the traditional Venus, find Edouard Manet's *Olympia* (1863). Compare this uncompromising

The Orsay Museum occupies an early-20th-century railway station.

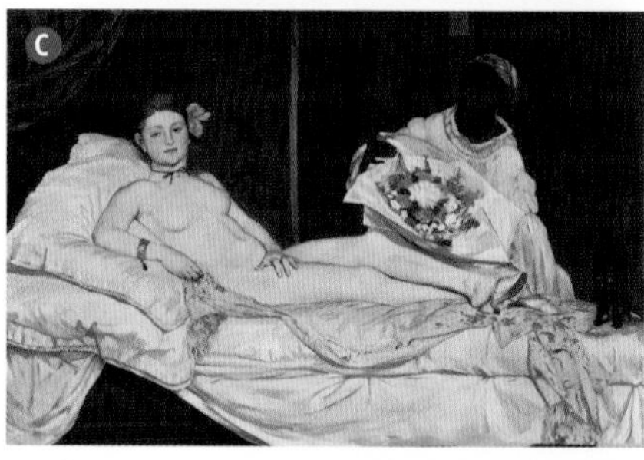

A *Cabanel,* Birth of Venus

B *Millet,* The Gleaners

C *Manet,* Olympia

D *Toulouse-Lautrec,* Jane Avril Dancing

nude with Cabanel's idealized, pastel, Vaseline-on-the-lens beauty in the *Birth of Venus*. In *Olympia*, the sharp outlines and harsh, contrasting colors are new and shocking. Manet replaced soft-core porn with hard-core art.

Gustave Courbet's *The Painter's Studio* (1855) takes us backstage, showing us the gritty reality behind the creation of pretty pictures. We see Courbet himself in his studio, working diligently on a Realistic landscape, oblivious to the confusion around him. Milling around are ordinary citizens, not Greek heroes.

TOULOUSE-LAUTREC DETOUR

The Henri **Toulouse-Lautrec** paintings tucked away on the ground floor (Room 10) rightly belong with the Post-Impressionist works on level 2, but since you're already here, enjoy his paintings, which incarnate the artist's love of nightlife and show business. Every night, Toulouse-Lautrec put on his bowler hat and visited the Moulin Rouge to draw the crowds, the can-can dancers, and the backstage action. He worked quickly, creating sketches in paint that serve as snapshots of a golden era. In *Jane Avril Dancing* (1891), he depicts the slim, graceful, elegant, and melancholy dancer, who stood out above the rabble. Her legs keep dancing while her mind is far away.

IMPRESSIONISM

The Impressionist collection is scattered randomly through Rooms 29-36, on the top floor. Look for masterworks by these artists:

In Edouard Manet's *Luncheon on the Grass* (1863), you can see that a new revolutionary movement was starting to bud—Impressionism. Notice the background: the messy brushwork of trees and leaves, the play of light on the pond, and the light that filters through the trees onto the woman who stoops in the haze. Also note the strong contrast of colors (white skin, black clothes, green grass). Let the Impressionist revolution begin!

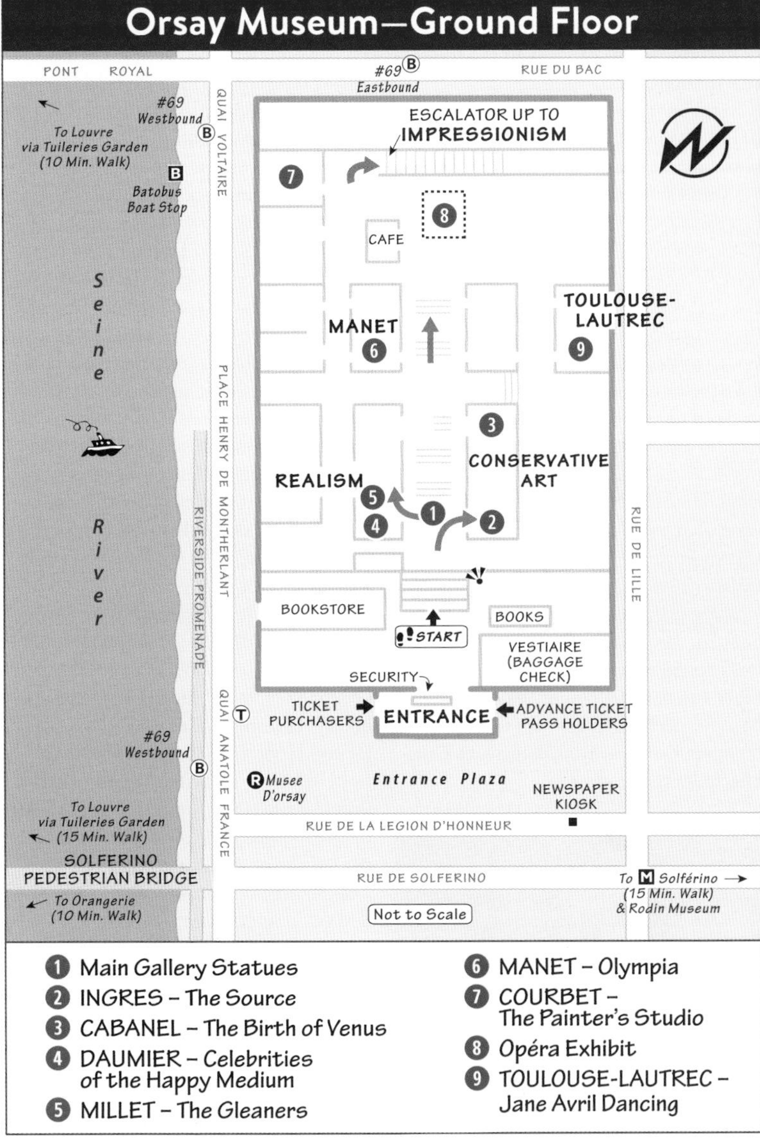

Edgar **Degas** blends classical lines and Realist subjects with Impressionist color, spontaneity, and everyday scenes from urban Paris. He loved the unposed "snapshot" effect, catching his models off guard. Dance students, women at work, and café scenes are approached from odd angles that aren't always ideal but make the scenes seem more real. He gives us the backstage view of life. For instance, a dance rehearsal let Degas capture a behind-the-scenes look at bored, tired, restless dancers (*The Dance Class*, c. 1873-1875). In the painting *In a Café* (1875-

1876), a weary lady of the evening meets morning with a last, lonely, nail-in-the-coffin drink in the glaring light of a four-in-the-morning café.

Next up is Claude **Monet,** the father of Impressionism. In the 1860s, Monet began painting landscapes in the open air. He studied optics and pigments to know just the right colors he needed to reproduce the shimmering quality of reflected light. The key was to work quickly, when the light was just right, creating a fleeting "impression" of the scene. In fact, that was the title of one of Monet's canvases; it gave the movement its name.

Pierre-Auguste **Renoir** started out as a painter of landscapes, along with Monet, but later veered from the Impressionist's philosophy and painted images that were unabashedly "pretty." His best-known work is *Dance at the Moulin de la Galette* (1876). On Sunday afternoons, working-class folk would dress up and head for the fields on Butte Montmartre (near Sacré-Cœur Basilica) to dance, drink, and eat little crêpes (galettes) till dark. Renoir liked to go there to paint the common Parisians living and loving in the afternoon sun.

Degas, The Dance Class

POST-IMPRESSIONISM

Post-Impressionism—the style that employs Impressionism's bright colors while branching out in new directions—is scattered all around the museum. You'll get a taste of the style with Paul Cézanne, on the top floor, with much more on level 2.

Paul **Cézanne** brought Impressionism into the 20th century. After the color of Monet and warmth of Renoir, Cézanne's rather impersonal canvases can be difficult to appreciate (see *The Card Players,* 1890-1895). Where the Impressionists built a figure from a mosaic of individual brushstrokes, Cézanne used blocks of paint to create a more solid, geometrical shape. These chunks are like little "cubes." It's no coincidence that his experiments in reducing forms to their geometric basics inspired the Cubists. Because of his style (not the content), he is often called the first Modern painter.

Like Michelangelo, Beethoven, Rembrandt, Wayne Newton, and a select handful of others, Vincent **van Gogh** put so much of himself into his work that art and life became one. In the Orsay's collection of paintings (level 2), you'll see both Van Gogh's painting style and his life unfold, from his early days in Paris soaking up the Impressionist style (for example, see how he might build a bristling brown beard using thick strokes of red, yellow, and green side by side) to his richly creative but wildly unstable stint in the south of France (*Van Gogh's Room at Arles,* 1889). Don't miss his final self-portrait (1889), showing a man engulfed in a confused background of brushstrokes that swirl and rave. Perhaps his troubled eyes know that in only a few months he would take a pistol and put a bullet through his chest.

Nearby are the paintings of Paul **Gauguin,** who got the travel bug early and grew up wanting to be a sailor. Instead, he became a stockbroker. At the age of 35, he got fed up with it all, quit his job, abandoned his wife (her stern portrait bust may be nearby) and family, and took refuge in his art.

Gauguin traveled to the South Seas in search of the exotic, finally settling on Tahiti. Gauguin's best-known works capture an idyllic Tahitian landscape peopled by exotic women engaged in simple tasks and making music (*Arearea*, 1892). The style is intentionally "primitive," collapsing the three-dimensional landscape into a two-dimensional pattern of bright colors. Gauguin wanted to communicate to his "civilized" colleagues back home that he'd found the paradise he'd always envisioned.

FRENCH SCULPTURE

The open-air mezzanine of level 2 is lined with statues. Stroll the mezzanine, enjoying the work of great French sculptors, including Auguste **Rodin.**

Born of working-class roots and largely self-taught, Rodin combined classical solidity with Impressionist surfaces to become the greatest sculptor since Michelangelo. Like his statue *The Walking Man* (c. 1900), Rodin had one foot in the past, while the other stepped into the future. This muscular, forcefully striding man could be a symbol of Renaissance Man with his classical power. With no mouth or hands, he speaks with his body. But get close and look at the statue's surface. This rough, "unfinished" look reflects light in the same way the rough Impressionist brushwork does, making the statue come alive, never quite at rest in the viewer's eye. Rodin created this statue in a flash of inspiration. He took two unfinished statues—torso and legs—and plunked them together at the waist. You can still see the seam. Rodin's sculptures capture the groundbreaking spirit of much of the art in the Orsay Museum. With a stable base of 19th-century stone, he launched art into the 20th century.

Ⓐ *Renoir,* Dance at the Moulin de la Galette

Ⓑ *Cézanne,* The Card Players

Ⓒ *Van Gogh,* Van Gogh's Room at Arles

Ⓓ *Gauguin,* Arearea

▲▲ORANGERIE MUSEUM (MUSEE DE L'ORANGERIE)

This Impressionist museum is as lovely as a water lily. Step out of the tree-lined, sun-dappled Impressionist painting that is the Tuileries Garden and into the Orangerie (oh-rahn-zhuh-ree), a bijou of select works by Monet, Renoir, Matisse, Picasso, and others.

Cost and Hours: €9, €6.50 after 17:00, €16 combo-ticket with Orsay Museum, covered by Museum Pass; Wed-Mon 9:00-18:00, closed Tue; audioguide-€5, English guided tours usually Mon and Thu at 14:30 and Sat at 11:00, located in Tuileries Garden near Place de la Concorde, Mo: Concorde or scenic bus #24, tel. 01 44 77 80 07, www.musee-orangerie.fr.

Visiting the Museum: On the main floor you'll find the main attraction, Monet's *Water Lilies (Nymphéas),* floating dreamily in oval rooms. These eight mammoth, curved panels immerse you in Monet's garden. We're looking at the pond in his garden at Giverny—dotted with water lilies, surrounded by foliage, and dappled by the reflections of the sky, clouds, and trees on the surface. But the true subject of these works is the play of reflected light off the surface of the pond.

Working at his home in Giverny, Monet built a special studio with skylights and wheeled easels to accommodate the canvases. For 12 years (1914-1926), Monet worked on these paintings obsessively. Monet completed all the planned canvases, but didn't live to see them installed here. In 1927, the year after his death, these rooms were completed and the canvases put in place. Some call this the first "art installation"—art displayed in a space specially designed for it in order to enhance the viewer's experience.

In the Orangerie's underground gallery are select works from the personal collection of Paris' trend-spotting art dealer of the 1920s, Paul Guillaume. These paintings—Impressionist, Fauvist, and Cubist—are a snapshot of what was hot in the world of art, circa 1920.

Monet's Water Lilies *at the Orangerie Museum*

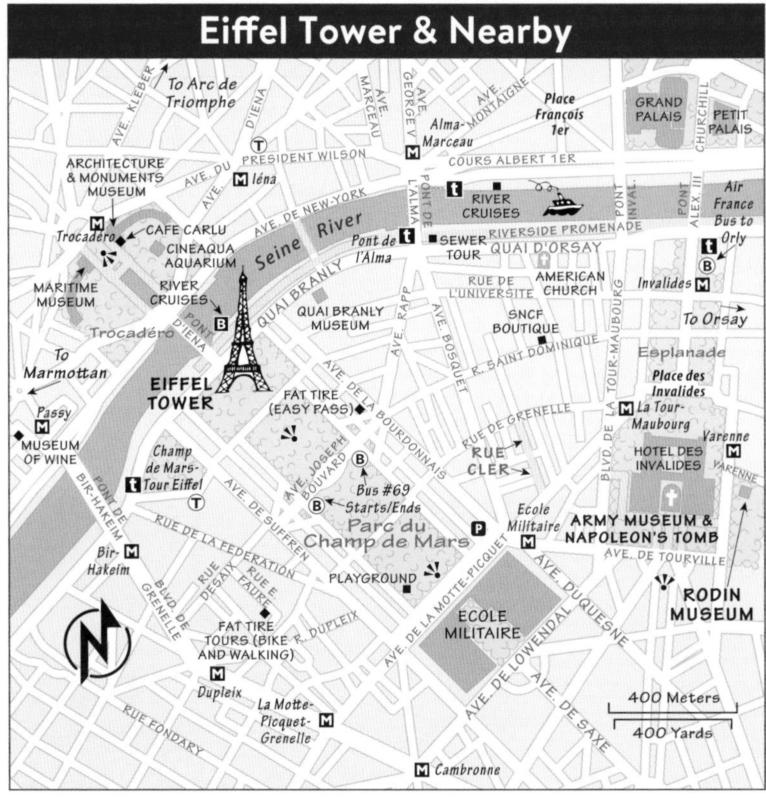

Eiffel Tower and Nearby

▲▲▲EIFFEL TOWER (LA TOUR EIFFEL)

It's crowded, expensive, and there are probably better views in Paris, but visiting this 1,000-foot-tall ornament is worth the trouble. Visitors to Paris may find the *Mona Lisa* to be less than expected, but the Eiffel Tower rarely disappoints, even in an era of skyscrapers. This is a once-in-a-lifetime, I've-been-there experience. Making the trip gives you membership in the exclusive society of the quarter of a billion other humans who have made the Eiffel Tower the most visited monument in the modern world.

Cost and Hours: €25 all the way to the top, €16 for just the two lower levels, €10 to climb the stairs to the first or second level, not covered by Museum Pass; daily mid-June-Aug 9:00-24:45, last ascent to top at 23:00 and to lower levels at 24:00 (elevator or stairs); Sept-mid-June 9:30-23:45, last ascent to top at 22:30 and to lower levels at 23:00 (elevator) or at 18:00 (stairs); cafés and great view restaurants, Mo: Bir-Hakeim or Trocadéro, Train-C: Champ de Mars-Tour Eiffel.

Reservations: You'd be crazy to show up without a reservation. At www.toureiffel.paris, you can book an entry date and time, and skip the initial entry line (the longest)—at no extra cost.

Time slots fill up months in advance (especially from April through September). Online ticket sales open up about three months before any given date (at 8:30 Paris time)—and can sell out for that day within hours. Reservations are non-refundable. When you "Choose a ticket," make sure you select "Lift entrance ticket with access to the summit" to go all the way to the top. You must create an account, with a 10-digit mobile phone number as your log-in.

If no reservation slots are available, try buying a "Lift entrance ticket with access to 2nd floor" only—you can upgrade once inside. Or, try the website again about a week before your visit—last-minute spots occasionally open up.

When to Go: For the best of all worlds, arrive with enough light to see the views, then stay as it gets dark to see the lights. The views are grand whether you ascend or not. At the top of the hour, a five-minute display features thousands of sparkling lights (best viewed from Place du Trocadéro or the grassy park below).

Rick's Tip: No reservation for the Eiffel Tower? *Get in line 30 minutes before it opens. Going late is the next-best bet (after 19:00 May-Aug). You can bypass some (but not all) lines if you have a reservation at either of the tower's view restaurants (Le Jules Verne or 58 Tour Eiffel).*

Getting In: If you have a reservation, arrive at the tower 10 minutes before your entry time, and look for either of the two entrances marked *Visiteurs avec Reservation* (Visitors with Reservation),

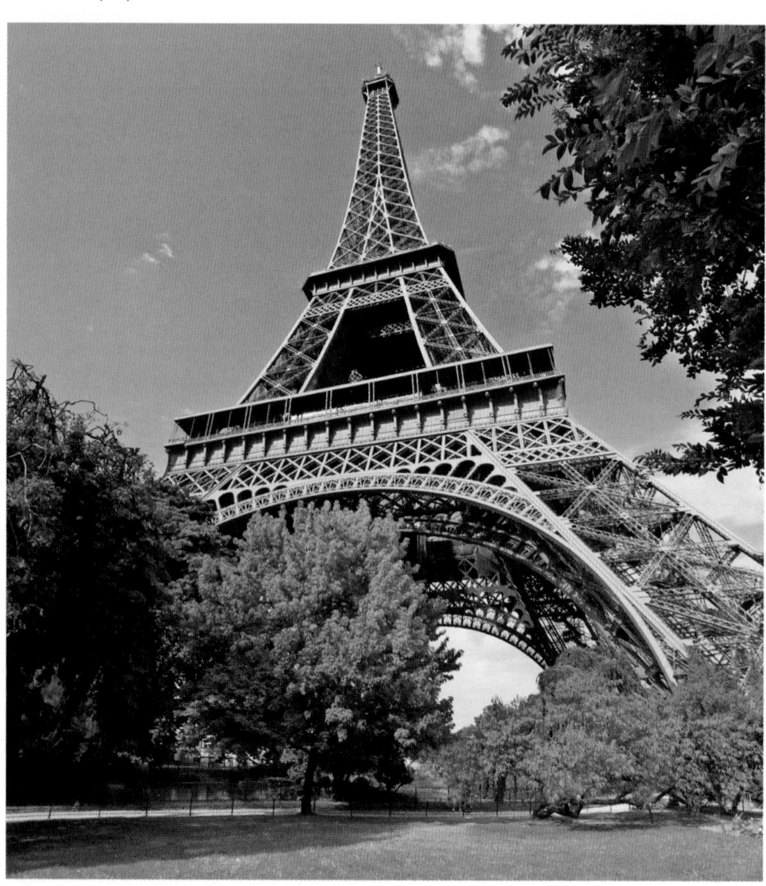

The Eiffel Tower stands more than 1,000 feet tall.

where attendants scan your ticket and put you on the first available elevator. If you don't have a reservation, follow signs for *Individuels* or *Visiteurs sans Tickets* (avoid lines selling tickets only for *Groupes*). The stairs entrance (usually a shorter line) is at the south pillar (next to Le Jules Verne restaurant entrance). When you buy tickets on-site, all members of your party must be with you. To get reduced fares for kids, bring ID.

Security Check: Bags larger than 19" × 8" × 12" inches are not allowed, but there is no baggage check. All bags are subject to a security search. No knives, glass bottles, or cans are permitted.

Rick's Tip: *Tourists in crowded elevators are like fish in a barrel for* **pickpockets**. *Beware. Thieves plunder awestruck visitors gawking below the tower. A* **police station** *is at the Jules Verne pillar.*

Background: The first visitor to the Paris World's Fair in 1889 walked beneath the "arch" formed by the newly built Eiffel Tower and entered the fairgrounds. This event celebrated both the centennial of the French Revolution and France's position as a global superpower. Bridge builder Gustave Eiffel (1832-1923) won the contest to build the fair's centerpiece by beating out rival proposals such as a giant guillotine. The tower was nothing but a showpiece, with no functional purpose except to demonstrate to the world that France had the wealth, knowledge, and can-do spirit. The original plan was to dismantle the tower as quickly as it was built after the celebration ended, but it was kept by popular demand.

The tower, including its antenna, stands 1,063 feet tall, or slightly higher than the 77-story Chrysler Building in New York. Its four support pillars straddle an area of 3.5 acres. Despite the tower's 7,300 tons of metal and 60 tons of paint, it is so well-engineered that it weighs no

Open-Air Markets

Several traffic-free street markets overflow with flowers, bakeries, produce, fish vendors, and butchers, illustrating how most Parisians shopped before there were supermarkets. Shops are open daily except Sunday afternoons, Monday, and lunchtime throughout the week. You can shop for a picnic or grab a seat at a sidewalk café to watch the action.

Rue Cler—a wonderful place to sleep and dine as well as shop—is like a refined street market, serving an upscale neighborhood near the Eiffel Tower (Mo: Ecole Militaire).

Rue Daguerre, near the Catacombs and off Avenue du Général Leclerc, is the least touristy of the street markets listed here, mixing food shops with cafés along a traffic-free street (Mo: Denfert-Rochereau).

Rue Mouffetard, on the Left Bank, is a happening market street by day and does double-duty as restaurant row at night. Hiding several blocks behind the Panthéon, it starts at Place Contrescarpe and ends below at St. Médard Church (Mo: Censier Daubenton). The upper stretch is touristic; the bottom stretch is purely Parisian.

more per square inch at its base than a linebacker on tiptoes.

VISITING THE TOWER

There are three observation platforms, at roughly 200, 400, and 900 feet. If you want to see the entire tower, from top to bottom, then see it...from top to bottom.

There isn't a single elevator straight to the top *(le sommet)*. To get there, you'll first ride an elevator to the second level. (For the hardy, there are 360 stairs to the first level and another 360 to the second.) Once on the second level, immediately line up for the next elevator, to the top. Enjoy the views, then ride back down to the second level (which has the best views). When you're ready, head to the first level via the stairs (no line and can take as little as 5 minutes) or take the elevator down (ask if it will stop on the first level—some don't). Explore the shops and exhibits on the first level and have a snack. To leave, you can line up for the elevator, but it's quickest and most memorable to take the stairs back down to earth.

For a final look at the tower, stroll across the river to Place du Trocadéro or to the end of the Champ de Mars and look back for great views. However impressive it may be by day, the tower is an awesome thing to see at twilight, when it becomes filled with light, and virile Paris lies back and lets night be on top. When darkness fully envelops the city, the tower seems to climax with a spectacular light show at the top of each hour...for five minutes.

Army Museum and Napoleon's Tomb

Near the Eiffel Tower

▲▲ARMY MUSEUM AND NAPOLEON'S TOMB (MUSEE DE L'ARMEE)

The Hôtel des Invalides—a former veterans' hospital topped by a golden dome—houses Napoleon's over-the-top-ornate tomb, as well as Europe's greatest military museum. Visiting the Army Museum's different sections, you can watch the art of war unfold from stone axes to Axis powers.

Cost and Hours: €9.50, €7.50 after 17:00, free for military personnel in uniform, free for kids but they must wait in line for ticket, covered by Museum Pass, special exhibits are extra; daily 10:00-18:00, July-Aug until 19:00, Nov-March until 17:00, tomb plus WWI and WWII wings open Tue until 21:00 April-Sept, museum (except for tomb) closed first Mon of month Oct-June, Charles de Gaulle exhibit closed Mon year-round; videoguide-€6, cafeteria, tel. 08 10 11 33 99, www.musee-armee.fr.

Getting There: The Hôtel des Invalides is at 129 Rue de Grenelle, a 10-minute walk from Rue Cler (Mo: La Tour Maubourg, Varenne, or Invalides). You can also take bus #69 (from the Marais and Rue Cler) or bus #87 (from Rue Cler and Luxembourg Garden area).

Visiting the Museum: At the center of the complex, Napoleon Bonaparte lies majestically dead inside several coffins under a grand dome—a goose-bumping pilgrimage for historians. The dome overhead glitters with 26 pounds of thinly pounded gold leaf.

Your visit continues through an impressive range of museums filled with medieval armor, cannons and muskets, Louis XIV-era uniforms and weapons, and Napoleon's horse—stuffed and mounted.

The best section is dedicated to the two World Wars. Walk chronologically through displays on the trench warfare of World War I, the victory parades, France's horrendous losses, and the humiliating Treaty of Versailles that led to World War II.

The WWII rooms use black-and-white photos, maps, videos, and artifacts to trace Hitler's rise, the Blitzkrieg that overran France, America's entry into the war, D-Day, the concentration camps, the atomic bomb, the war in the Pacific, and the eventual Allied victory. There's special insight into France's role (the French Resistance), and how it was Charles de Gaulle that actually won the war.

▲▲RODIN MUSEUM (MUSEE RODIN)

This user-friendly museum is filled with passionate works by the greatest sculptor since Michelangelo. You'll see *The Kiss, The Thinker, The Gates of Hell,* and many more.

Cost and Hours: €10 (special exhibits cost extra), free on first Sun of the month Oct-March, €4 for garden only (many important works are on display there), €15 combo-ticket with Orsay Museum, museum and garden covered by Museum Pass; Tue-Sun 10:00-17:45, closed Mon; gardens close at 18:00, Oct-March at 17:00; audioguide-€6, mandatory baggage check, self-service café in garden, 79 Rue de Varenne, Mo: Varenne, tel. 01 44 18 61 10, www.musee-rodin.fr.

Visiting the Museum: Auguste Rodin (1840-1917) was a modern Michelangelo, sculpting human figures on an epic scale, revealing through their bodies his deepest thoughts and feelings. Like many of Michelangelo's unfinished works, Rodin's statues rise from the raw stone around them, driven by the life force. With missing limbs and scarred skin, these are prefab classics, making ugliness noble. Rodin's people are always moving restlessly. Even the famous *Thinker* is moving; while he's plopped down solidly, his mind is a million miles away.

Well-displayed in the mansion where the sculptor lived and worked, exhibits

Rodin's Burghers of Calais

trace Rodin's artistic development, explain how his bronze statues were cast, and show some of the studies he created to work up to his masterpiece, the unfinished *Gates of Hell*. Learn about Rodin's tumultuous relationship with his apprentice and lover, Camille Claudel. Mull over what makes his sculptures some of the most evocative since the Renaissance. And stroll the beautiful gardens, packed with many of his greatest works (including *The Thinker*, *Balzac*, the *Burghers of Calais*, and the *Gates of Hell*) and ideal for artistic reflection.

Left Bank

Opposite Notre-Dame, on the left bank of the Seine, is the Latin Quarter. (For more about this neighborhood, see my Historic Paris Walk, earlier.)

▲▲CLUNY MUSEUM (MUSEE NATIONAL DU MOYEN AGE)

The Cluny is a treasure trove of Middle Ages (Moyen Age) art. Located on the site of a Roman bathhouse, it offers close-up looks at stained glass, Notre-Dame carvings, fine goldsmithing and jewelry, and rooms of tapestries. The highlights are several original stained-glass windows from Sainte-Chapelle and the exquisite series of six Lady and the Unicorn tapestries: A delicate, as-medieval-as-can-be noble lady introduces a delighted unicorn to the senses of taste, hearing, sight, smell, and touch.

Cost and Hours: €8, includes audioguide, free on first Sun of month, covered by Museum Pass; Wed-Mon 9:15-17:45, closed Tue, ticket office closes at 17:15; near corner of Boulevards St. Michel and St. Germain at 6 Place Paul Painlevé;

Grands Cafés Near St. Germain-des-Prés

On the Left Bank, where Boulevard St. Germain meets Rue Bonaparte, you'll find several Parisian cafés that seem like monuments to another time (all open daily, Mo: St. Germain-des-Prés; for locations, see map on page 94). Before visiting, review my tips on cafés and brasseries on page 422.

$$$ Les Deux Magots offers prime outdoor seating and a warm interior. Once a favorite of Ernest Hemingway (in *The Sun Also Rises*, Jake met Brett here) and Jean-Paul Sartre (he and Simone de Beauvoir met here), today the café is filled with international tourists (6 Place St. Germain des Prés).

$$$ Le Café de Flore, next door, feels more literary—wear your black turtleneck. Pablo Picasso was a regular (172 Boulevard St. Germain).

$ Café Bonaparte, just a block away, offers scenic outdoor seating and the same delightful view for a bit less (42 Rue Bonaparte).

$$ Café le Procope, Paris' first and most famous (1686), was a café célèbre, drawing notables such as Voltaire, Rousseau, Honoré de Balzac, Emile Zola, Maximilien de Robespierre, Victor Hugo, and two Americans, Benjamin Franklin and Thomas Jefferson (13 Rue de l'Ancienne Comédie).

Mo: Cluny-La Sorbonne, St. Michel, or Odéon; tel. 01 53 73 78 16, www.musee-moyenage.fr.

ST. GERMAIN-DES-PRES

A church was first built on this site in A.D. 558. The church you see today was constructed in 1163 and is all that's left of a once sprawling and influential monastery. The colorful interior reminds us that medieval churches were originally painted in bright colors. The surrounding area hops at night with venerable cafés, fire-eaters, mimes, and scads of artists.

Cost and Hours: Free, daily 8:00-20:00, Mo: St. Germain-des-Prés.

▲LUXEMBOURG GARDEN (JARDIN DU LUXEMBOURG)

This lovely 60-acre garden is an Impressionist painting brought to life. Slip into a green chair pondside, enjoy the radiant flower beds, go jogging, play tennis or basketball, sail a toy sailboat, or take in a chess game or puppet show. Some of the park's prettiest (and quietest) sections lie around its perimeter.

Cost and Hours: Free, daily dawn until dusk, Mo: Odéon, Train-B: Luxembourg.

Cluny Museum's Lady and the Unicorn tapestry

Luxembourg Garden

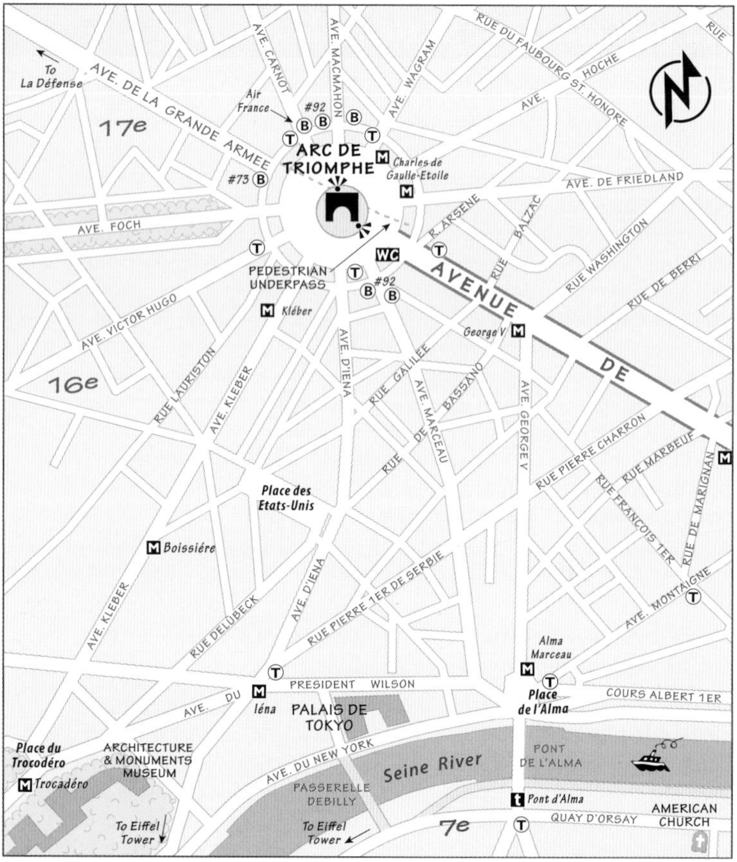

Champs-Elysées and Nearby

▲▲▲CHAMPS-ELYSEES

This famous boulevard is Paris' backbone, with its greatest concentration of traffic. From the Arc de Triomphe down Avenue des Champs-Elysées, all of France seems to converge on Place de la Concorde, the city's largest square. And though the Champs-Elysées has become as international as it is Parisian, a walk down the two-mile boulevard is still a must.

In 1667, Louis XIV opened the first section of the street, and it soon became the place to cruise in your carriage. (It still is today.) By the 1920s, this boulevard was pure elegance—fancy residences, rich hotels, and cafés. Today it's home to big business, celebrity cafés, glitzy nightclubs, high-fashion shopping, and international people-watching. People gather here to

Looking down the Champs-Elysées from the Arc de Triomphe

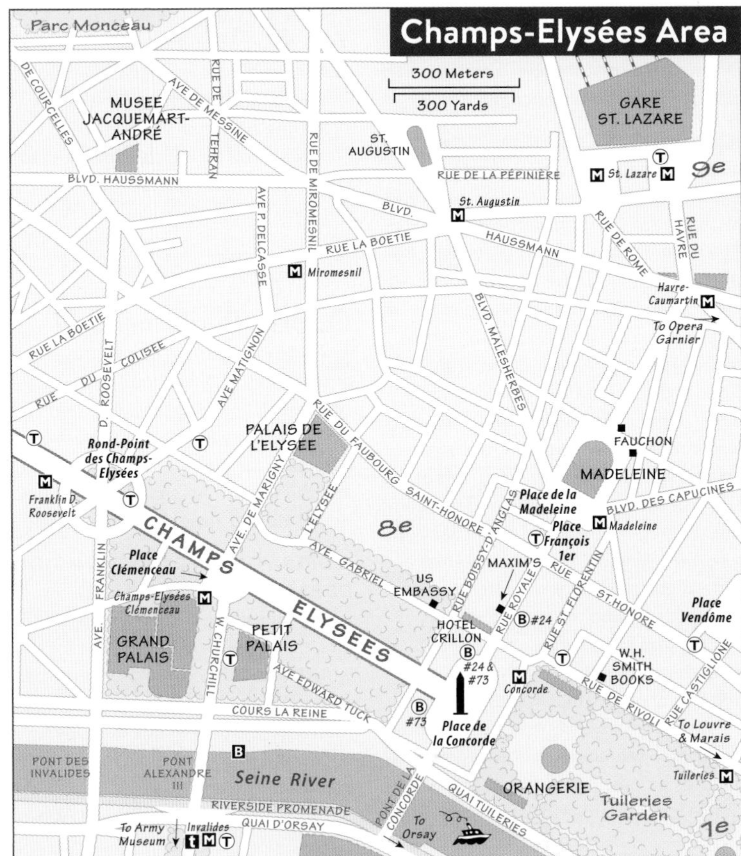

celebrate Bastille Day (July 14), World Cup triumphs, and the finale of the Tour de France.

SELF-GUIDED WALK

Start at the Arc de Triomphe (Mo: Charles de Gaulle-Etoile; if you're planning to tour the Arc, do it before starting this walk) and head downhill on the left-hand side. The arrival of McDonald's (at #140) was an unthinkable horror, but these days dining chez MacDo has become typically Parisian, and this branch is the most profitable McDonald's in the world.

Fancy car showrooms abound, including Peugeot (#136) and Renault (#53). The Lido (#116) is Paris' largest burlesque-type cabaret (and a multiplex cinema). Across the boulevard is the flagship store of leather-bag makers Louis Vuitton (#101). Fouquet's café (#99) is a popular spot for French celebrities, especially movie stars—note the names in the sidewalk in front. Enter if you dare for an €8 espresso. Ladurée café (#75) is also classy but has a welcoming and affordable takeout bakery.

Continuing on, you pass international-brand stores, such as Sephora, Virgin, Disney, and the Gap. Car buffs should park themselves at the sleek café in the Renault store (#53, open until midnight). The car exhibits change regularly, but the great tables looking down onto the Champs-Elysées are permanent.

You can end your walk at the round Rond Point intersection (Mo: Franklin D. Roosevelt) or continue to obelisk-studded Place de la Concorde.

▲▲ARC DE TRIOMPHE

Napoleon had the magnificent Arc de Triomphe commissioned to commemorate his victory at the 1805 battle of Austerlitz. The foot of the arch is a stage on which the last two centuries of Parisian history have played out—from the funeral of Napoleon to the goose-stepping arrival of the Nazis to the triumphant return of Charles de Gaulle after the Allied liberation. Examine the carvings on the pillars, featuring a mighty Napoleon and excitable Lady Liberty. Pay your respects at the Tomb of the Unknown Soldier. Then climb the 284 steps to the observation deck up top, with sweeping skyline panoramas and a mesmerizing view down onto the traffic that swirls around the arch.

Cost and Hours: Free and always viewable; steps to rooftop—€9.50, free on first Sun of month Oct-March, covered by Museum Pass; daily April-Sept 10:00-23:00, Oct-March until 22:30, last entry 45 minutes before closing; Place Charles de Gaulle, use underpass to reach arch, Mo: Charles de Gaulle-Etoile, tel. 01 55 37 73 77, http://arc-de-triomphe.monuments-nationaux.fr.

Avoiding Lines: Bypass the *slooow* ticket line with your Museum Pass (though if you have kids, you'll need to line up to get their free tickets). Expect another line (that you can't skip) at the entrance to the stairway up the arch. Lines disappear after 17:00—come for sunset.

Opéra Neighborhood

The glittering Garnier opera house anchors this neighborhood of broad boulevards and grand architecture. This area is also nirvana for high-end shoppers, with the opulent Galeries Lafayette and the sumptuous shops that line Place Vendôme and Place de la Madeleine.

▲OPERA GARNIER (OPERA NATIONAL DE PARIS—PALAIS GARNIER)

A gleaming grand theater of the belle époque, the Palais Garnier was built for Napoleon III and finished in 1875. For the best exterior view, stand in front of the Opéra Métro stop. From Avenue de l'Opéra, once lined with Paris' most fashionable haunts, the facade suggests "all power to the wealthy." And a shimmering Apollo,

Arc de Triomphe

holding his lyre high above the building, seems to declare, "This is a temple of the highest arts."

But the elitism of this place prompted former President François Mitterrand to have an opera house built for the people in the 1980s, situated symbolically on Place de la Bastille, where the French Revolution started in 1789. The smaller Opéra Garnier is now home to ballet, some opera, and other performances.

You have two choices for seeing the interior: Take a guided or self-guided tour of the public areas, or buy tickets to a performance. If you opt to tour the building, note that the auditorium is sometimes off-limits due to performances and rehearsals (you'll get your best look at the auditorium on the fully guided tour).

Cost and Hours: €11, not covered by Museum Pass, generally daily 10:00-16:30, mid-July-Aug until 18:00, 8 Rue Scribe, Mo: Opéra, Train-A: Auber, www.visitepalaisgarnier.fr.

Tours: The €5 audioguide gives a good self-guided tour. Guided tours in English run at 11:30 and 14:30 July-Aug daily, Sept-Jun Wed and Sat-Sun—call to confirm schedule (€14.50, includes entry, 1.5 hours, tel. 01 40 01 17 89 or 08 25 05 44 05).

Visiting the Theater: You'll enter around the left side of the building (as you face the front), across from American Express on Rue Scribe. As you pass the bust of the architect, Monsieur Garnier, pay your respects and check out the bronze floor plan of the complex etched below. Notice how little space is given to seating.

Rick's Tip: *Across the street from the Opéra Garnier is the illustrious* **Café de la Paix** *(on Place de l'Opéra). It's been a meeting spot for the local glitterati for generations. If you can afford the coffee, this spot offers a delightful break.*

The building is huge—though the auditorium itself seats only 2,000. The building's massive foundations straddle an underground lake (inspiring the mysterious world of the *Phantom of the Opera*). The real show was before and after the performance, when the elite of Paris—out to see and be seen—strutted their elegant stuff in the extravagant lobbies. Think of the grand marble stairway as a theater. The upstairs foyer feels more like

Opéra Garnier

Baron Georges-Eugène Haussmann

The elegantly uniform streets that make Paris so Parisian are the work of Baron Haussmann (1809-1891), who oversaw the modernization of the city in the mid-19th century. He cleared out the cramped, higgledy-piggledy, unhygienic medieval cityscape and replaced it with broad, straight boulevards lined with stately buildings and linked by modern train stations.

The quintessential view of Haussmann's work is from the pedestrian island immediately in front of the Opéra Garnier. You're surrounded by Paris, circa 1870, when it was the capital of the world. Spin slowly and find the Louvre in one direction and Place Vendôme in another. Haussmann's uniform, cohesive buildings are all five stories tall, with angled, black slate roofs and formal facades. The balconies on the second and fifth floors match those of their neighbors, creating strong lines of perspective as the buildings stretch down the boulevard. Haussmann was so intent on putting the architecture at center stage that he insisted that no trees be planted along these streets.

Chagall ceiling at the Opéra Garnier

a ballroom at Versailles. As you wander the halls and gawk at the decor, imagine this place in its heyday, filled with beautiful people sharing gossip at the Salon du Glacier.

From the uppermost floor open to the public, visitors can peek from two boxes into the actual red-velvet performance hall. Admire Marc Chagall's colorful ceiling (1964), playfully dancing around the eight-ton chandelier. The box seats next to the stage are the most expensive in the house, with an obstructed view of the stage...but just right if you're here only to be seen. Snoop about to find the side library, information panels describing costume management, and a portrait gallery of famous ballerinas and guests.

Marais Neighborhood and Nearby

Naturally, when in Paris you want to see the big sights—but to experience the city, you also need to visit a vital neighborhood. The Marais fits the bill, with hip boutiques, busy cafés, trendy art galleries, narrow streets, leafy squares, Jewish bakeries, aristocratic châteaux, nightlife, and real Parisians. It's the perfect setting to appreciate the flair of this great city.

Place des Vosges and West

▲PLACE DES VOSGES

Henry IV (r. 1589-1610) built this centerpiece of the Marais in 1605 and called it "Place Royale." As he'd hoped, it turned the Marais into Paris' most exclusive neighborhood. Walk to the center, where Louis XIII, on horseback, gestures, "Look at this wonderful square my dad built." He's surrounded by locals enjoying their community park. You'll see children frolicking in the sandbox, lovers warming benches, and pigeons guarding their fountains while trees shade this escape from the glare of the big city.

Study the architecture: nine pavilions (houses) per side. The two highest—at the front and back—were for the king and queen (but were never used). Warm red brickwork—some real, some fake—is topped with sloped slate roofs, chimneys, and another quaint relic of a bygone era: TV antennas.

The insightful writer Victor Hugo lived at #6 from 1832 to 1848. (It's at the southeast corner of the square, marked by the French flag.) This was when he wrote much of his most important work, including his biggest hit, *Les Misérables*. Inside **Victor Hugo's House,** you'll wander through eight plush rooms, enjoy a fine view of the square, and find good WCs (€8, Tue-Sun 10:00-18:00, closed Mon, http://maisonsvictorhugo.paris.fr).

Sample the upscale art galleries ringing the square (the best ones are behind Louis). Consider a daring new piece for that blank wall at home. Or consider a pleasant break at one of the eateries on the square.

▲▲PICASSO MUSEUM (MUSEE PICASSO)

Whatever you think about Picasso the man, as an artist he was unmatched in the 20th century for his daring and productivity. The Picasso Museum has the world's largest collection of his work—some 400 paintings, sculptures, sketches, and ceramics—spread across this mansion in the Marais. A visit here walks you through the full range of this complex man's life and art.

Cost and Hours: €11, covered by Museum Pass, free on first Sun of month; open Tue–Fri 10:30–18:00, Sat–Sun 9:30–18:00, closed Mon, last entry 45 minutes before closing; videoguide-€4, timed-entry tickets available via museum website; 5 Rue de Thorigny, Mo: St-Paul or Chemin Vert, tel. 01 42 71 25 21, www.musee-picasso.fr.

➲ SELF-GUIDED TOUR

The core of the museum is organized chronologically. Use this overview to trace Picasso's life and some of the themes in his work.

Early Years and Early Cubism (Floor 0): In 1900, Picasso set out from Barcelona to make his mark in Paris. The brash Spaniard quickly became a poor, homesick foreigner, absorbing the styles of many painters while searching for his own artist's voice. When his best friend committed suicide (*Death of Casagemas*, 1901), Picasso plunged into a "Blue Period," painting emaciated beggars,

Relaxing at the Place des Vosges

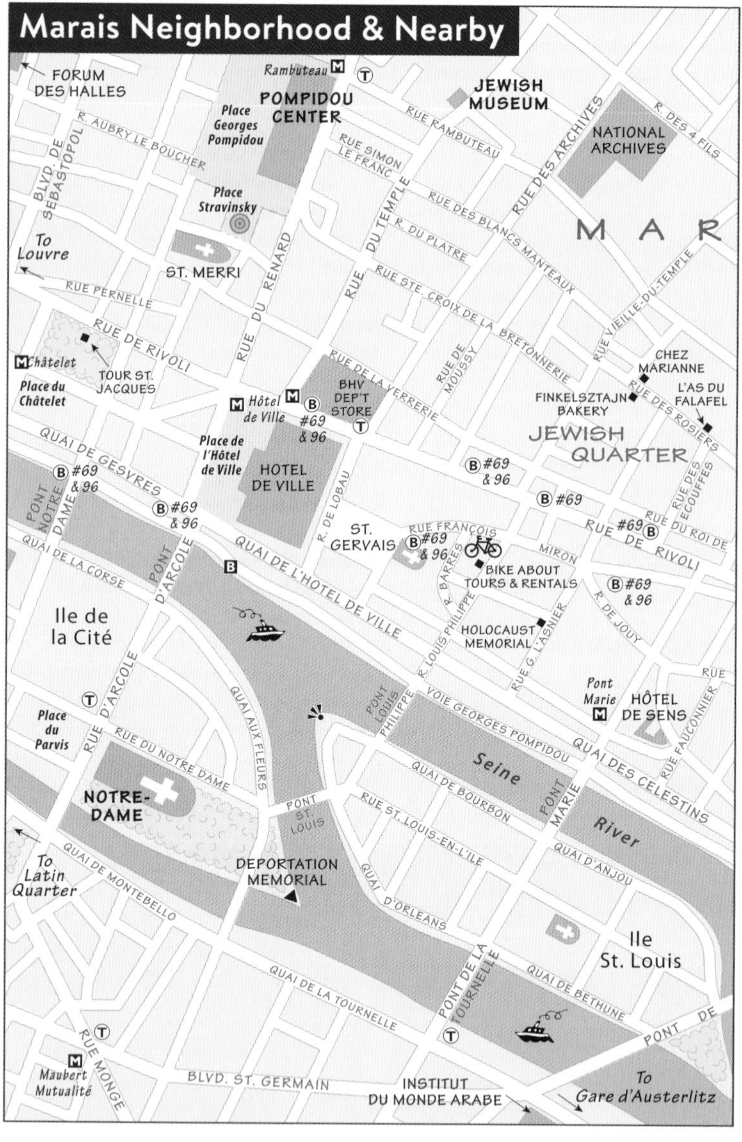
Marais Neighborhood & Nearby
FORUM DES HALLES
Rambuteau
POMPIDOU CENTER
Place Georges Pompidou
JEWISH MUSEUM
NATIONAL ARCHIVES
R. DES 4 FILS
RUE RAMBUTEAU
RUE DES ARCHIVES
R. AUBRY LE BOUCHER
BLVD. DE SEBASTOPOL
RUE SIMON LE FRANC
Place Stravinsky
RUE DES BLANCS MANTEAUX
RUE DU TEMPLE
R. DU PLATRE
MAR
To Louvre
ST. MERRI
RUE DU RENARD
RUE STE. CROIX DE LA BRETONNERIE
RUE VIEILLE-DU-TEMPLE
RUE PERNELLE
RUE DE RIVOLI
RUE DE MOUSSY
CHEZ MARIANNE
Châtelet
TOUR ST. JACQUES
Place du Châtelet
RUE DE LA VERRERIE
BHV DEP'T STORE
Hôtel de Ville
#69 & 96
FINKELSZTAJN BAKERY
L'AS DU FALAFEL
RUE DES ROSIERS
JEWISH QUARTER
QUAI DE GESVRES
Place de l'Hôtel de Ville
HOTEL DE VILLE
R. DE LOBAU
#69 & 96
#69
RUE DES ECOUFFES
RUE DU ROI DE
PONT NOTRE DAME
PONT D'ARCOLE
ST. GERVAIS
RUE FRANÇOIS MIRON
RUE DE RIVOLI
QUAI DE LA CORSE
QUAI DE L'HOTEL DE VILLE
R. BARRES
BIKE ABOUT TOURS & RENTALS
R. DE JOUY
Ile de la Cité
HOLOCAUST MEMORIAL
R. LOUIS PHILIPPE
RUE G. L'ASNIER
RUE D'ARCOLE
QUAI AUX FLEURS
PONT LOUIS PHILIPPE
VOIE GEORGES POMPIDOU
Pont Marie
HÔTEL DE SENS
RUE FAUCONNIER
Place du Parvis
RUE DU NOTRE DAME
Seine
QUAI DES CELESTINS
QUAI DE BOURBON
PONT MARIE
NOTRE-DAME
PONT ST. LOUIS
RUE ST. LOUIS-EN-L'ILE
River
QUAI D'ANJOU
To Latin Quarter
QUAI DE MONTEBELLO
DEPORTATION MEMORIAL
QUAI D'ORLEANS
Ile St. Louis
PONT DE LA TOURNELLE
QUAI DE BETHUNE
QUAI DE LA TOURNELLE
PONT DE
RUE MONGE
Maubert Mutualité
BLVD. ST. GERMAIN
INSTITUT DU MONDE ARABE
To Gare d'Austerlitz

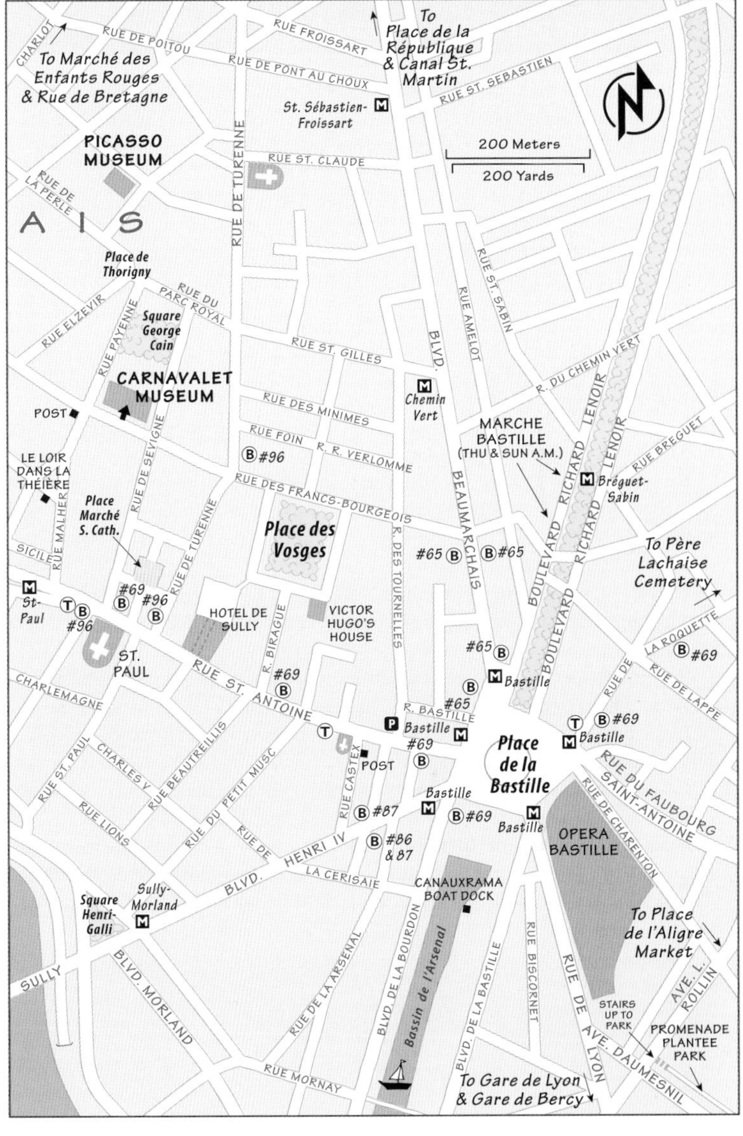
To Marché des Enfants Rouges & Rue de Bretagne
To Place de la République & Canal St. Martin
PICASSO MUSEUM
CARNAVALET MUSEUM
Place des Vosges
HOTEL DE SULLY
VICTOR HUGO'S HOUSE
ST. PAUL
MARCHE BASTILLE (THU & SUN A.M.)
Place de la Bastille
OPERA BASTILLE
To Père Lachaise Cemetery
To Place de l'Aligre Market
PROMENADE PLANTEE PARK
STAIRS UP TO PARK
CANAUXRAMA BOAT DOCK
Bassin de l'Arsenal
To Gare de Lyon & Gare de Bercy
LE LOIR DANS LA THÉIÈRE
POST
Place de Thorigny
Square George Cain
Place Marché S. Cath.
Square Henri-Galli
200 Meters
200 Yards
St. Sébastien-Froissart
Chemin Vert
Bréguet-Sabin
St-Paul
Sully-Morland
Bastille
RUE DE TURENNE
BLVD. BEAUMARCHAIS
BOULEVARD RICHARD LENOIR
RUE ST. ANTOINE
BLVD. HENRI IV
RUE DES FRANCS-BOURGEOIS
RUE DU FAUBOURG SAINT-ANTOINE
RUE DE LYON
AVE. DAUMESNIL
RUE DE CHARENTON
BLVD. DE LA BASTILLE
BLVD. DE LA BOURDON
BLVD. MORLAND

Best Views over the City of Light

The brilliance of the City of Light can only be fully appreciated by rising above it all. Many of the viewpoints I've listed are free or covered by the Museum Pass; otherwise, expect to pay €8-15. Views are best in the early morning or around sunset. Here are some prime locations:

Eiffel Tower: It's hard to find a grander view of Paris than from the tower's second level. Go around sunset and stay after dark to see the tower illuminated; or go in the early morning to avoid the midday haze and crowds (see page 71).

Arc de Triomphe: This is the perfect place to see the glamorous Champs-Elysées, if you don't mind the 284 steps (see page 80). It's great during the day, but even greater at night, when the boulevard glitters.

Notre-Dame's Tower: This viewpoint couldn't be more central—but it requires climbing 400 steps and is usually crowded with long lines (arrive early or late). You'll get an unobstructed view of gargoyles, the river, the Latin Quarter, and the Ile de la Cité (see page 45).

Steps of Sacré-Cœur: Join the party on Paris' only hilltop. Walk uphill, or take the funicular or Montmartrobus, then hunker down on Sacré-Cœur's steps to enjoy the sunset. Stay in Montmartre for dinner, then see the view again after dark (free, see page 90).

Galeries Lafayette or Printemps: Take the escalator to the top floor of either department store (they sit side by side) for a stunning overlook of the old Opéra district (free).

Pompidou Center: Take the escalator up to admire the cityscape. There may be better views over Paris, but this is the best one from a museum (see page 88).

Place du Trocadéro: Start or end your Eiffel Tower visit at Place du Trocadéro for dramatic views of the tower, particularly at night. The square itself is a happening place, with street performers, souvenir vendors, skateboarders, and pickpockets. Gawk with caution.

Arab World Institute (Institut du Monde Arabe): This building near Ile St. Louis has free views from its terrific roof terrace (Tue-Sun 10:00-18:00, closed Mon, 1 Rue des Fossés Saint-Bernard, Place Mohammed V, Mo: Jussieu, www.imarabe.org).

hard-eyed pimps, and himself, bundled up against the cold, with eyes all cried out (*Autoportrait*, 1901).

In 1904, Picasso got a steady girlfriend, and suddenly saw the world through rose-colored glasses (the Rose Period). With his next-door neighbor, Georges Braque, Picasso invented Cubism, a fragmented, "cube"-shaped style. He'd fracture a figure (such as the musician in *Man with a Mandolin*, 1911) into a barely recognizable jumble of facets. Picasso sketched reality from every angle, then pasted it all together, a composite of different views.

Cubist Experiments and *Guernica* (Floor 1): Modern art was being born. The first stage had been so-called Analytic Cubism: breaking the world down into small facets, to "analyze" the subject from every angle. Now it was time to "synthesize" it back together with the real world (Synthetic Cubism). Picasso created "constructions" that were essentially still-life paintings (a 2-D illusion) augmented with glued-on, real-life materials—wood, paper, rope, or chair caning (the real 3-D world). In a few short years, Picasso had turned painting in the direction it would go for the next 50 years.

Meanwhile, Europe was gearing up for war. From Paris, Picasso watched as his homeland of Spain erupted in a brutal civil war (1936-1939). Many canvases from this period are gray and gloomy. The most famous one—*Guernica* (1937)—captured the chaos of a Spanish village caught in an air raid (painted in Paris, but now hanging in Madrid). In 1940, Nazi tanks rolled into Paris. Picasso decided to stay for the duration and live under gray skies and gray uniforms.

The South of France and Last Years (Floor 2): At war's end, Picasso left Paris, finding fun in the sun in the south of France. Sixty-five-year-old Pablo Picasso was reborn, enjoying worldwide fame. Picasso's Riviera works set the tone for the rest of his life—sunny, light-hearted, childlike, experimenting in new media, and using motifs of the sea, Greek mythology (fauns, centaurs), and animals (birds, goats, and pregnant baboons). Picasso was fertile to the end, still painting with bright thick colors at age 91.

RUE DES ROSIERS: PARIS' JEWISH QUARTER

The intersection of Rue des Rosiers and Rue des Ecouffes marks the heart of the small neighborhood that Jews call the Pletzl ("little square"). Once the largest in Western Europe, Paris' Jewish Quarter is much smaller today but still colorful. Rue des Rosiers (named for the roses that once covered the city wall) has become the epicenter of Marais hipness and fashion. But it still features kosher *(cascher)* restaurants and fast-food places selling falafel, *shawarma, kefta,* and other Mediterranean dishes. Bakeries specialize in braided challah, bagels, and strudels. Delis offer gefilte fish, piroshkis, and blintzes.

Picasso Museum

The Jewish Quarter's Rue des Rosiers

A *Pompidou Center*

B *Otto Dix,* Portrait of Journalist Sylvia von Harden

C *Joan Miró,* Le Catalan

Art galleries exhibit Jewish-themed works, and store windows post flyers for community events.

▲▲POMPIDOU CENTER (CENTRE POMPIDOU)

One of Europe's greatest collections of far-out modern art is housed in the Musée National d'Art Moderne, on the fourth and fifth floors of this colorful exoskeletal building. Created ahead of its time, the modern and contemporary art in this collection is still waiting for the world to catch up.

The Pompidou Center and the square that fronts it are lively, with lots of people, street theater, and activity inside and out—a perpetual street fair. Kids of any age enjoy the fun, colorful fountain (called *Homage to Stravinsky*) next to the Pompidou Center.

Cost and Hours: €14, free on first Sun of month, Museum Pass covers permanent collection and escalators to sixth-floor panoramic views (but not special exhibits); Wed-Mon 11:00-21:00, closed Tue, ticket counters close at 20:00, café and pricey view restaurant, Mo: Rambuteau or Hôtel de Ville, tel. 01 44 78 12 33, www.centrepompidou.fr.

Visiting the Museum: Buy your ticket on the ground floor, then ride up the escalator (or run up the down escalator to get in the proper mood). When you see the view, your opinion of the Pompidou's exterior should improve a good 15 percent.

The Pompidou's "permanent" collection...isn't. It changes so often that a painting-by-painting tour is impossible. Generally, art from 1905 to 1980 is on the fifth floor, while the fourth floor contains more recent art. Use the museum's floor plans (posted on the wall) to find select artists. See the classics—Picasso, Matisse, Chagall, Braque, Dalí, Warhol—and leave time to browse the work of more recent artists.

As you tour, remember that most of the artists, including foreigners, spent their formative years in Paris. In the 1910s, funky Montmartre was the mecca of Modernism—the era of Picasso, Braque, and Matisse. In the 1920s the center shifted to the grand cafés of Montparnasse, where painters mingled with American expats such as Ernest Hemingway and Gertrude Stein. During World War II, it was Jean-Paul Sartre's Existentialist scene around St. Germain-des-Prés. After World War II, the global art focus moved to New York, but by the late 20th century, Paris had reemerged as a cultural touchstone for the world of Modern art.

Rick's Tip: *The sixth floor of the Pompidou has* **stunning views of the Paris cityscape.** *Your Pompidou ticket or Museum Pass gets you there, or you can buy the €3 View of Paris ticket (doesn't include museum entry).*

East of Place des Vosges

PROMENADE PLANTEE PARK (VIADUC DES ARTS)

This elevated viaduct, once used for train tracks, is now a two-mile-long, narrow garden walk and a pleasing place for a refreshing stroll or run. Botanists appreciate the well-maintained and varying vegetation.

Cost and Hours: Free, opens Mon-Fri at 8:00, Sat-Sun at 9:00, closes at sunset (17:30 in winter, 20:30 in summer). It runs from Place de la Bastille (Mo: Bastille) along Avenue Daumesnil to St. Mandé (Mo: Michel Bizot) or Porte Dorée, passing within a block of Gare de Lyon.

Getting There: To get to the park from Place de la Bastille (exit the Métro following *Sortie Rue de Lyon* signs), walk a looooong block down Rue de Lyon, hugging the Opéra on your left. Find the low-key entry and steps up the red-brick wall a block after the Opéra.

▲PERE LACHAISE CEMETERY (CIMETIERE DU PERE LACHAISE)

Lined with the tombstones of many of the city's most illustrious dead, this is your best one-stop look at Paris' fascinating, permanent residents.

Cost and Hours: Free, Mon-Fri 8:00-18:00, Sat 8:30-18:00, Sun 9:00-18:00, until 17:30 in winter; two blocks from Mo: Gambetta (do not go to Mo: Père Lachaise) and two blocks from bus #69's last stop; tel. 01 55 25 82 10, searchable map available at unofficial website: www.pere-lachaise.com.

Visiting the Cemetery: Enclosed by a massive wall and lined with 5,000 trees, the peaceful, car-free lanes and dirt paths of Père Lachaise cemetery encourage parklike meandering. Named for Father *(Père)* La Chaise, whose job was listening to Louis XIV's sins, the cemetery is relatively new, having opened in 1804 to accommodate Paris' expansion. Today, this city of the dead (pop. 70,000) still accepts new residents, but real estate prices are sky high (a 21-square-foot plot costs more than €11,000).

The 100-acre cemetery is big and confusing, with thousands of graves and tombs crammed every which way, and only a few pedestrian pathways to help you navigate. The maps available from street vendors can help guide your way. I recommend taking a one-way tour between two convenient Métro/bus stops (Gambetta and Père Lachaise),

Père Lachaise Cemetery

connecting a handful of graves from some of this necropolis' best-known residents, including Frédéric Chopin, Molière, Edith Piaf, Oscar Wilde, Gertrude Stein, Jim Morrison, Héloïse and Abélard, and more.

Rick's Tip: *To* **beat the crowds at Montmartre,** *come on a weekday or early on weekend mornings.*

Montmartre

Paris' highest hill, topped by Sacré-Cœur Basilica, is best known as the home of cabaret nightlife and bohemian artists. Struggling painters, poets, dreamers, and drunkards came here for cheap rent, untaxed booze, rustic landscapes, and the high-kicking cancan girls at the Moulin Rouge. These days, the hill is equal parts charm and kitsch—still vaguely village-like but mobbed with tourists and pickpockets on sunny weekends. Come for a bit of history, a getaway from Paris' noisy boulevards, and the view.

▲▲SACRE-CŒUR

You'll spot Sacré-Cœur, the Byzantine-looking white basilica atop Montmartre, from most viewpoints in Paris. Though only 130 years old, it's impressive and iconic, with a climbable dome.

Cost and Hours: Church—free, daily 6:00-22:30; dome—€6, not covered by Museum Pass, daily May-Sept 9:30-19:00, Oct-April 9:30-17:00; tel. 01 53 41 89 00, www.sacre-coeur-montmartre.com.

Getting There: For the location of the church, see the map on page 37. You can take the Métro to the Anvers stop (to avoid the stairs up to Sacré-Cœur, buy one more Métro ticket and ride up on the funicular). Alternatively, from Place Pigalle, you can take the "Montmartrobus," a city bus that drops you right by Sacré-Cœur (Funiculaire stop, costs one Métro ticket, 4/hour). A taxi from the Seine or the Bastille saves time and avoids sweat (about €15, €20 at night).

Visiting the Church: The Sacré-Cœur (Sacred Heart) Basilica's exterior, with its onion domes and bleached-bone pallor, looks ancient, but was finished only a century ago by Parisians humiliated by German invaders. Otto von Bismarck's Prussian army laid siege to Paris for more than four months in 1870. Things got so bad for residents that urban hunting for dinner (to cook up dogs, cats, and finally rats) became accepted behavior. Convinced they were being punished for the country's liberal sins, France's Catholics raised money to build the church as a "praise the Lord anyway" gesture.

The five-domed, Roman-Byzantine-looking basilica took 44 years to build (1875-1919). It stands on a foundation of 83 pillars sunk 130 feet deep, necessary because the ground beneath was honeycombed with gypsum mines. The exterior is laced with gypsum, which whitens with age.

Take a clockwise spin around the crowded interior to see impressive mosaics, a statue of St. Thérèse, a scale model of the church, and three stained-glass windows dedicated to Joan of Arc. Pause

Sacré-Cœur

near the Stations of the Cross mosaic to give St. Peter's bronze foot a rub. For an unobstructed panoramic view of Paris, climb 260 feet (300 steps) up the tight spiral stairs to the top of the dome.

EXPERIENCES

Seine Cruises

Several companies run boat cruises on the Seine. For the best experience, cruise at twilight or after dark. Another option is a longer dinner cruise, featuring multicourse meals and music (€100 and up, reservations required).

The companies listed below run daily one-hour sightseeing tours year-round (April-Oct 10:00-22:30, 2-3/hour; Nov-March shorter hours). On dinner cruises, proper dress is required—no denim, shorts, or sport shoes.

Bateaux-Mouches, the oldest boat company in Paris, departs from Pont de l'Alma's right bank and has the biggest open-top, double-decker boats (higher up means better views). The boats are often jammed and noisy (€13.50, kids 4-12-€5.50, Train-C: Pont de l'Alma, tel. 01 42 25 96 10, www.bateaux-mouches.fr). Dinner cruises include violin and piano music (jacket and tie required for men).

Bateaux Parisiens has smaller covered boats with handheld audioguides, fewer crowds, and only one deck. The boats leave from right in front of the Eiffel Tower (€14, kids 3-12-€5, tel. 01 76 64 14 45, www.bateauxparisiens.com). Dinner cruises feature a lively atmosphere with a singer, band, and dance floor.

Vedettes du Pont Neuf cruises start and end at Pont Neuf. The boats feature a live guide whose delivery (in English and French) is as stiff as a recorded narration—and as hard to understand, given the quality of their sound system (€14, ask about Rick Steves discount, tip requested, tel. 01 46 33 98 38, www.vedettesdupontneuf.com).

Shopping

Wandering among elegant boutiques provides a break from the heavy halls of the Louvre, and, if you approach it right, a little cultural enlightenment. Even if you don't intend to buy anything, do some window shopping, or as the French call it: *faire du lèche-vitrines* ("window licking").

Before you enter a Parisian store, remember the following points:

In small stores, always say, "*Bonjour, Madame* or *Mademoiselle* or *Monsieur*" when entering and "*Au revoir, Madame* or *Mademoiselle* or *Monsieur*" when leaving.

The customer is not always right. In fact, figure the clerk is doing you a favor by waiting on you.

Except in department stores, it's not normal for the customer to handle clothing. Ask first before you pick up an item: "*Je peux*?" (zhuh puh), meaning, "Can I?" Don't feel obliged to buy. If a shopkeeper offers assistance, just say, "*Je regarde, merci.*"

Saturday afternoons are *très* busy and not for the faint of heart.

Stores are generally closed on Sunday. Exceptions include the Carrousel du Louvre (underground shopping mall at the Louvre with a Printemps department store) and some shops near Sèvres-Babylone, along the Champs-Elysées, and in the Marais (for eclectic, avant-garde boutiques in the Marais neighborhood, peruse the artsy shops between Place des Vosges and the Pompidou Center).

For information on VAT refunds and customs regulations, see page 419.

Department Stores (Les Grands Magasins)

Parisian department stores begin with their showy perfume sections, almost always central on the ground floor. Information desks are usually located at the main entrances near the perfume section (with floor plans in English). Stores generally have affordable restaurants (some with view terraces) and a good selection of fairly priced souvenirs and toys. Shop at **Galeries Lafayette** (Mo: Chaussée d'Antin–La Fayette, Havre-Caumartin, or Opéra), **Printemps** (next door to Galeries Lafayette), and **Bon Marché** (Mo: Sèvres-Babylone). Opening hours are customarily Monday through Saturday from 10:00 to 19:00, with some open later on Thursdays. All are jammed on Saturdays and closed on Sundays (except in December, and except for the Printemps store in the Carrousel du Louvre, which is open daily year-round).

Boutique Strolls

Two very different areas to lick some windows are Place de la Madeleine to Place de l'Opéra, and Sèvres-Babylone to St. Sulpice.

➲ LA MADELEINE TO L'OPERA

The ritzy streets connecting several high-priced squares—Place de la Madeleine, Place de la Concorde, Place Vendôme, and Place de l'Opéra—form a miracle mile of gourmet food shops, glittering jewelry stores, five-star hotels, exclusive clothing boutiques, and people who spend more on clothes in one day than I do all year.

Start at Place de la Madeleine (Mo: Madeleine). In the northeast corner at #24 is the black-and-white awning of **Fauchon.** Founded on this location in 1886, this bastion of over-the-top edibles became famous around the world, catering to the refined tastes of the rich and famous. **Hédiard** (#21, northwest corner of the square) is older than Fauchon, and it's weathered the tourist mobs better. Wafting the aroma of tea and coffee, it showcases handsomely displayed produce and wines. Hédiard's small red containers—of mustards, jams, coffee, candies, and tea—make great souvenirs.

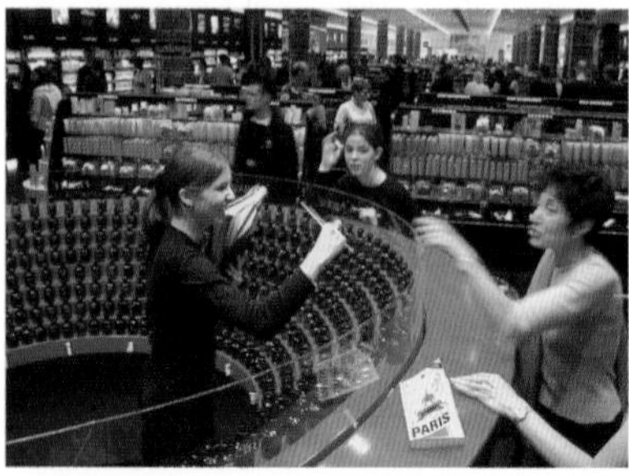

Sampling perfume

Step inside tiny **La Maison des Truffe** (#19) to get a whiff of the product—truffles, those prized edible mushrooms. Check out the tiny jars in the display case. The venerable **Mariage Frères** (#17) shop demonstrates how good tea can smell and how beautifully it can be displayed. **At Caviar Kaspia** (#16), you can add Iranian caviar, eel, and vodka to your truffle collection.

Continue along, past **Marquise de Sévígné chocolates** (#11) to the intersection with **Boulevard Malesherbes.** When the street officially opened in 1863, it ushered in the Golden Age of this neighborhood. Cross the three crosswalks traversing Boulevard Malesherbes. Straight ahead is **Patrick Roger Chocolates** (#3), famous for its chocolates, and even more so for M. Roger's huge, whimsical, 150-pound chocolate sculptures of animals and fanciful creatures.

Turn right down broad **Rue Royale.** There's Dior, Chanel, and Gucci. At Rue St. Honoré, turn left and cross Rue Royale, pausing in the middle for a great view both ways. Check out **Ladurée** (#16) for an out-of-this-world pastry break in the busy 19th-century tea salon or to just pick up some world-famous macarons. Continue east for three long blocks down **Rue St. Honoré.** The street is a parade of chic boutiques—L'Oréal cosmetics, Jimmy Choo shoes, Valentino...Looking for a €10,000 handbag? This is your spot.

Turn left on Rue de Castiglione to reach **Place Vendôme.** This octagonal square is *très* elegant—enclosed by symmetrical Mansart buildings around a 150-foot column. On the left side is the original Hôtel Ritz, opened in 1898. The square is also known for its upper-crust jewelry and designer stores—Van Cleef & Arpels, Dior,

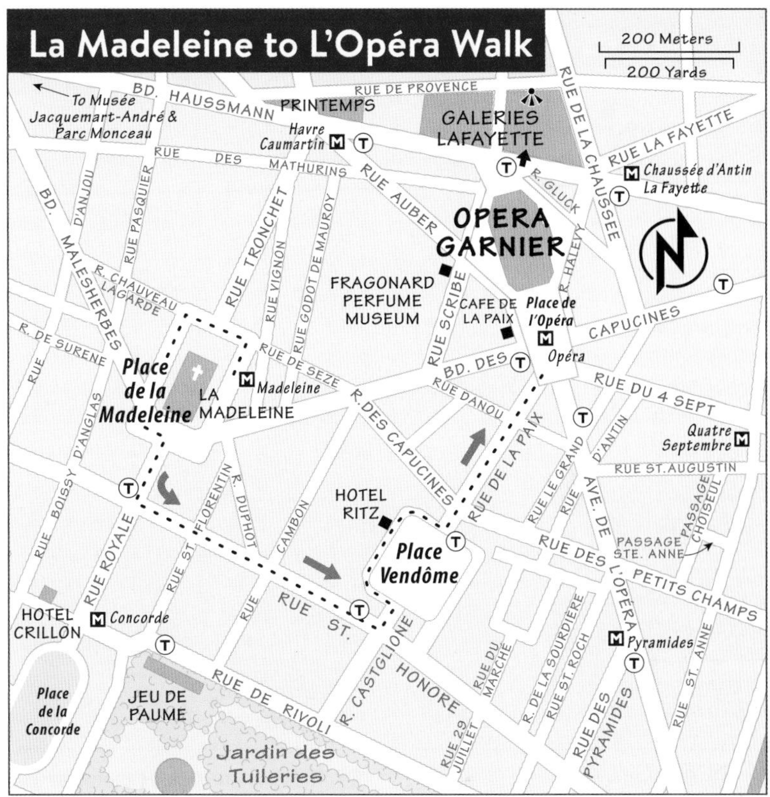

Chanel, Cartier, and others (if you have to ask how much...).

Leave Place Vendôme by continuing straight, up **Rue de la Paix**—strolling by still more jewelry, high-priced watches, and crystal—and enter **Place de l'Opéra.** Here you'll find the Opéra Garnier (described on page 80). If you're not shopped out yet, the Galeries Lafayette and Printemps department stores are located a block or two north, up Rue Halévy.

➲ SEVRES-BABYLONE TO ST. SULPICE

This Left Bank shopping stroll lets you sample smart clothing boutiques and clever window displays while enjoying one of Paris' more attractive neighborhoods. Start at the Sèvres-Babylone Métro stop (take the Métro or bus #87). You'll find the **Bon Marché** (Mo: Sèvres-Babylone), Paris' oldest department store.

From the Bon Marché, follow Rue de Sèvres, where you'll find **La Maison du Chocolat** at #19. Their mouthwatering window display will draw you helplessly inside. The shop sells handmade chocolates in exquisitely wrapped boxes and delicious ice-cream cones in season.

Lick the chocolate off your fingers before entering **Hermès** (a few doors down, at #17), famous for pricey silk scarves. Don't let the doorman intimidate you: Everyone's welcome here. This store, opened in 2011, is housed in the original Art Deco swimming pool of Hôtel Lutetia, built in 1935.

Across the street sits the old-school **Au Sauvignon Café** (open daily, 10 Rue de Sèvres). It's well situated for watching

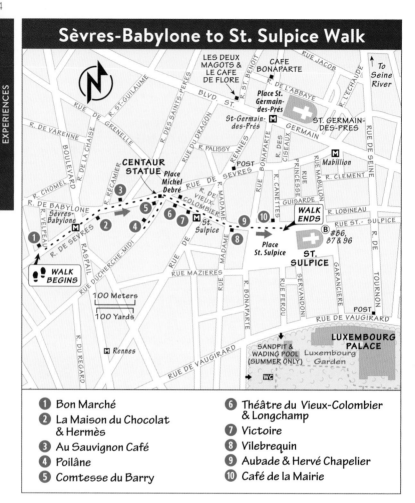

Sèvres-Babylone to St. Sulpice Walk

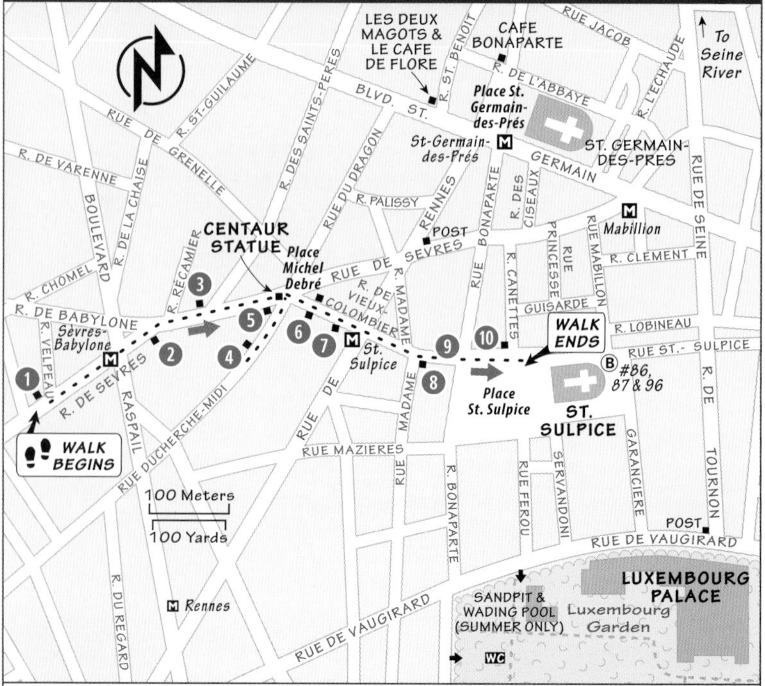

1. Bon Marché
2. La Maison du Chocolat & Hermès
3. Au Sauvignon Café
4. Poilâne
5. Comtesse du Barry
6. Théâtre du Vieux-Colombier & Longchamp
7. Victoire
8. Vilebrequin
9. Aubade & Hervé Chapelier
10. Café de la Mairie

smartly coiffed shoppers glide by. Continue a block farther down Rue de Sèvres to Place Michel Debré, a six-way intersection, where a *Centaur* statue stands guard. From here, boutique-lined streets fan out like spokes on a wheel.

Make a short detour up Rue du Cherche-Midi (follow the horse's fanny). This street offers an ever-changing but always chic selection of shoe, purse, and clothing stores. Find Paris' most celebrated bread—beautiful round loaves with designer crust—at the low-key **Poilâne** (#8). Return to the *Centaur* in Place Michel Debré. Check out the **Comtesse du Barry** pâté store, which sells small gift packs. Then turn right and head down Rue du Vieux Colombier, passing the (#6) **Théâtre du Vieux-Colombier** (1913), one of three key venues for La Comédie Française, a historic state-run troupe. At **Longchamp** (#21), you can hunt for a stylish French handbag in any color, and **Victoire** offers items for the gentleman.

Cross busy Rue de Rennes and continue down Rue du Vieux Colombier. Here you'll find more specialty boutiques.

There's **Vilebrequin** (#5) for men's swimwear, **Aubade** (#4) for lingerie, and **Hervé Chapelier** (#1) for travel totes and handbags. Spill into Place St. Sulpice, with its big, twin-tower church. **Café de la Mairie** is a great spot to sip a *café crème*, admire the lovely square, and consider your next move.

Nightlife

Paris is brilliant after dark. Save energy to experience the City of Light lit. Whether it's a concert at Sainte-Chapelle, a cruise on the Seine, a walk in Montmartre, a hike up the Arc de Triomphe, or a late-night café, you'll see Paris at its best.

Jazz and Blues Clubs

With a lively mix of American, French, and international musicians, Paris has been an internationally acclaimed jazz capital since World War II. You'll pay €12-25 to enter a jazz club (may include one drink; if not, expect to pay €5-10 per drink; beer is cheapest). See *L'Officiel des Spectacles* under "Musique" for listings, or, even better, the *Paris Voice* website. You can also check each club's website (all have English versions), or drop by the clubs to check out the calendars posted on their front doors. Music starts after 21:00 in most clubs. Some offer dinner concerts from about 20:30 on. Here are several good bets:

Caveau de la Huchette fills an ancient Latin Quarter cellar with live jazz and frenzied dancing every night (admission about €13 on weekdays, €15 on weekends, €6-8 drinks, daily 21:30-2:30 in the morning or later, no reservations needed, buy tickets at the door, 5 Rue de la Huchette, Mo: St. Michel, tel. 01 43 26 65 05, www.caveaudelahuchette.fr).

Autour de Midi et Minuit is an Old World bistro that sits at the foot of Montmartre, above a *cave à jazz*. Eat upstairs if you like, then make your way down to the basement to find bubbling jam sessions Tuesday through Thursday and concerts on Friday and Saturday nights (no cover, €5 minimum drink order Tue-Thu; €18 cover Fri-Sat includes one drink; jam sessions at 21:30, concerts usually at 22:00; no music Sun-Mon; 11 Rue Lepic, Mo: Blanche or Abbesses, tel. 01 55 79 16 48, www.autourdemidi.fr).

For a spot teeming with late-night activity and jazz, go to the two-block-long **Rue des Lombards,** at Boulevard Sébastopol, midway between the river and the Pompidou Center (Mo: Châtelet). **Au Duc des Lombards** is one of the most popular and respected jazz clubs in Paris, with concerts nightly in a plush, 110-seat theater (admission €25-40, €50-80 with dinner, buy online and arrive early for best seats, cheap drinks, shows at 20:00 and 22:00, 42 Rue des Lombards, tel. 01 42 33 22 88, www.ducdeslombards.fr). **Le Sunside,** just a block away, offers two stages: "le Sunset" on the ground floor for contemporary world jazz; and "le Sunside" downstairs for more traditional and acoustic jazz (concerts range from free to €25, check their website; 60 Rue des Lombards, tel. 01 40 26 46 60, www.sunset-sunside.com).

Old-Time Parisian Cabaret

Au Lapin Agile, a historic little cabaret on Montmartre, tries its best to maintain the atmosphere of the heady days when bohemians would gather here to enjoy wine, song, and sexy jokes. Today, you'll mix in with a few locals and many tourists for a drink and as many as 10 different performers—mostly singers with a piano. Though tourists are welcome, there's no accommodation for English speakers (except on their website), so non-French speakers will be lost. The soirée covers traditional French standards, love ballads, sea chanteys, and more (€28, €8 drinks, Tue-Sun 21:00-2:00 in the morning, closed Mon, best to reserve ahead, 22 Rue des Saules, tel. 01 46 06 85 87, www.au-lapin-agile.com).

Classical Concerts

For classical music on any night, consult *L'Officiel des Spectacles* magazine (check "Concerts Classiques" under "Musique" for listings), and look for posters at tourist-oriented churches. From March through November, these churches regularly host concerts: St. Sulpice, St. Germain-des-Prés, La Madeleine, St. Eustache, St. Julien-le-Pauvre, and Sainte-Chapelle.

At **Sainte-Chapelle,** enjoy the pleasure of hearing Mozart, Bach, or Vivaldi, surrounded by 800 years of stained glass. The acoustical quality is surprisingly good. There are usually two concerts per evening, at 19:00 and 20:30; specify which one you want when you buy or reserve your ticket. VIP tickets get you a seat in rows 3-10 (€40), Prestige tickets cover the next 15 rows (€30), and Normal tickets are the last 5 rows (€25). Seats are unassigned within each section, so arrive at least 30 minutes early to get through the security line and snare a good view. It's unheated—bring a sweater.

Book tickets at the box office, by phone, or online. Two different companies present concerts, but the schedule will tell you which one to contact for a particular performance. The small box office (with schedules and tickets) is to the left of the chapel entrance gate (8 Boulevard du Palais, Mo: Cité), or call 01 42 77 65 65 or 06 67 30 65 65 for schedules and reservations. You can leave your message in English—just speak clearly and spell your name. You can check schedules and buy your ticket at www.euromusicproductions.fr (ask about Rick Steves discount on Euromusic events—cash only at box office close to concert time).

Philharmonie de Paris, a dazzling, 2,400-seat concert hall situated in the Parc de la Villette complex, hosts world-class artists, from legends of rock and roll to string quartets to international opera stars (221 Avenue Jean-Jaurès, Mo: Porte de Pantin, tel. 01 44 84 44 84, www.philharmoniedeparis.fr).

You can also enjoy live classical **Concerts on the Seine** while cruising past Paris' iconic monuments (€30-40, summer months only, board at Vedettes du Pont Neuf, Square du Vert Galant, tel. 01 42 77 65 65, http://vedettesdupontneuf.com/concerts-en-seine). Also look for concerts in parks, such as the Luxembourg Garden, or even the Galeries Lafayette department store. Many are free *(entrée libre),* such as the Sunday atelier concert sponsored by the American Church (generally Sept-June at 17:00 but not every week and not in Dec, 65 Quai d'Orsay, Mo: Invalides, Train-C: Pont de l'Alma, tel. 01 40 62 05 00, www.acparis.org). The Army Museum offers inexpensive afternoon and evening classical music concerts year-round (for programs—in French only—see www.musee-armee.fr/programmation).

Paris churches host frequent concerts.

Extend your sightseeing into the night.

Night Walks

Go for one of these ▲▲▲ evening walks to best appreciate the City of Light. Break for ice cream, pause at a café, and enjoy the sidewalk entertainers as you participate in the post-dinner Parisian parade. Remember to exercise normal big-city caution when exploring Paris at night; avoid poorly lit areas and stick to main thoroughfares.

➲ TROCADERO AND EIFFEL TOWER

This stroll delivers one of Paris' most spectacular views at night. Take the Métro to the Trocadéro stop and join the party on Place du Trocadéro for a magnificent view of the glowing Eiffel Tower. It's a festival of hawkers, gawkers, drummers, and entertainers.

Walk down the stairs, passing the fountains and rollerbladers, then cross the river to the base of the tower, well worth the effort even if you don't go up. From the Eiffel Tower you can stroll through the Champ de Mars park past tourists and romantic couples, and take the Métro home (Ecole Militaire stop, across Avenue de la Motte-Picquet from far southeast corner of park). Or there's a handy suburban train stop (Champ de Mars-Tour Eiffel) two blocks west of the Eiffel Tower on the river.

➲ CHAMPS-ELYSEES AND THE ARC DE TRIOMPHE

The Avenue des Champs-Elysées glows after dark. Start at the Arc de Triomphe, then stroll down Paris' lively grand promenade. A right turn on Avenue George V leads to the Bateaux-Mouches river cruises. A movie on the Champs-Elysées is a fun experience (weekly listings in *L'Officiel des Spectacles* under "Cinéma"), and a drink or snack at Renault's futuristic car café is a kick (at #53).

EATING

Entire books (and lives) are dedicated to eating in Paris. Though it lacks a style of its own (only French onion soup is truly Parisian; otherwise, there is no "Parisian cuisine" to speak of), it draws from the best of France.

My recommendations center on the same great neighborhoods as my hotel listings. Serious eaters looking for even more suggestions should consult the always appetizing www.parisbymouth.com, an eating-and-drinking guide.

To save piles of euros, go to a bakery for takeout, or stop at a café for lunch. Cafés and brasseries are happy to serve a *plat du jour* (garnished plate of the day, about €12-20) or a chef-like salad (about

Restaurant Price Code

$$$$ Splurge: Most main courses over €25
$$$ Pricier: €20-25
$$ Moderate: €15-20
$ Budget: Under €15

€10-14) day or night. To save even more, consider picnics (tasty takeout dishes available at charcuteries).

Linger longer over dinner—restaurants expect you to enjoy a full meal. Most restaurants I've listed have set-price *menus* between €20 and €38. In most cases, the few extra euros you pay are well spent and open up a variety of better choices. A service charge is included in the prices (so little or no tipping is expected).

Rue Cler Area

Close to the Eiffel Tower

(Mo: Ecole Militaire)

$$$ Le Florimond is fun for a special occasion. The setting is warm and welcoming. Locals come for classic French cuisine at fair prices. Friendly English-speaking Laurent, whose playful ties change daily, gracefully serves one small room of tables and loves to give suggestions. The stuffed cabbage and the *confit de canard* are particularly tasty, and the house wine is excellent (closed Sun and first and third Sat of month, reservations encouraged, 19 Avenue de la Motte-Picquet, tel. 01 45 55 40 38, www.leflorimond.com).

$$$ Bistrot Belhara, named for a legendary 35-foot wave and surfing spot off the Basque coast, is a true French dining experience. Watch as chef Thierry peers from his kitchen window to ensure that all is well. He bases his cuisine on what's in season, but the foie gras and *riz au lait de mémé*—his grandma's rice pudding—are delicious any time of year. If you don't know French, the charming Frédéric will translate—and help you choose the perfect wine (closed Sun-Mon, reservations smart, a block off Rue Cler at 23 Rue Duvivier, tel. 01 45 51 41 77, www.bistrotbelhara.com).

$$$ La Terrasse du 7ème is a sprawling, happening café with grand outdoor seating and a living-room-like interior with comfy love seats. Located on a corner, it overlooks a busy intersection with a constant parade of people. Chairs are set up facing the street, so a meal here is like dinner theater—and the show is slice-of-life Paris (€20-25 *plats*, good €13 *salade niçoise* or Caesar salad, €8 French onion soup, tasty foie gras, no fixed-price *menu*, daily until at least 24:00, at Ecole Militaire Métro stop, tel. 01 45 55 00 02).

Between Rue de Grenelle and the River

(Mo: Ecole Militaire)

$$$$ L'Ami Jean offers authentic Basque specialties in a snug-but-fun atmosphere with red peppers and Basque stuff hanging from the ceiling. It's not cheap, but the portions are hearty and delicious, and the whole menu changes every two weeks. Parisians detour long distances to savor the gregarious chef's special cuisine and convivial atmosphere. For dinner, arrive by 19:30 or reserve ahead (€20 starters, €35 plats, €78 eight-course dinner menu, a more accessible lunch menu for €35, closed Sun-Mon, 27 Rue Malar, Mo: La Tour-Maubourg, tel. 01 47 05 86 89, www.lamijean.fr).

$$$$ La Fontaine de Mars, a longtime favorite and neighborhood institution, draws Parisians who want to be seen. It's charmingly situated on a tiny, jumbled square with tables jammed together for the serious business of eating. Reserve in advance for a table on the ground floor or on the square, and enjoy the same meal Barack Obama did. Street-level seats come with the best ambience (€20-30 plats du jour, daily, superb foie gras, superb

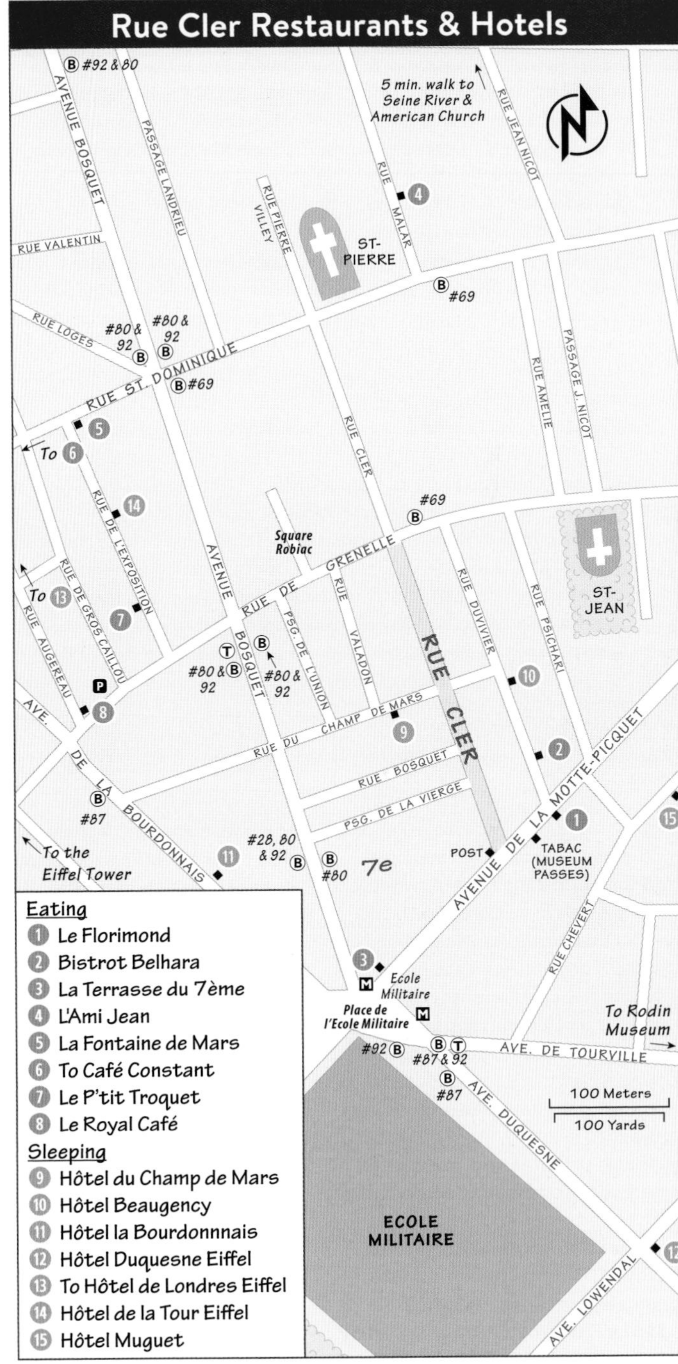
Rue Cler Restaurants & Hotels
#92 & 80
5 min. walk to Seine River & American Church
AVENUE BOSQUET
PASSAGE LANDRIEU
RUE JEAN NICOT
RUE MALAR
RUE PIERRE VILLEY
ST-PIERRE
RUE VALENTIN
#69
RUE LOGES
#80 & 92
RUE ST. DOMINIQUE
PASSAGE J. NICOT
RUE AMELIE
RUE CLER
To 6
RUE DE L'EXPOSITION
Square Robiac
RUE DE GRENELLE
AVENUE BOSQUET
RUE DE GROS CAILLOU
RUE AUGEREAU
To 13
PSG. DE L'UNION
RUE VALADON
RUE DUVIVIER
RUE PSICHARI
ST-JEAN
RUE DU CHAMP DE MARS
RUE BOSQUET
PSG. DE LA VIERGE
AVENUE DE LA MOTTE-PICQUET
AVE. DE LA BOURDONNAIS
#87
To the Eiffel Tower
#28, 80 & 92
#80
7e
POST
TABAC (MUSEUM PASSES)
RUE CHEVERT
Ecole Militaire
Place de l'Ecole Militaire
To Rodin Museum
AVE. DE TOURVILLE
#92
#87 & 92
AVE. DUQUESNE
100 Meters
100 Yards
ECOLE MILITAIRE
AVE. LOWENDAL
Eating
1 Le Florimond
2 Bistrot Belhara
3 La Terrasse du 7ème
4 L'Ami Jean
5 La Fontaine de Mars
6 To Café Constant
7 Le P'tit Troquet
8 Le Royal Café
Sleeping
9 Hôtel du Champ de Mars
10 Hôtel Beaugency
11 Hôtel la Bourdonnnais
12 Hôtel Duquesne Eiffel
13 To Hôtel de Londres Eiffel
14 Hôtel de la Tour Eiffel
15 Hôtel Muguet

Good Picnic Spots

Paris is picnic-friendly. Almost any park will do. Many have benches or grassy areas, though some lawns are off-limits—obey the signs. Parks generally close at dusk, so plan your sunset picnics carefully. Here are some especially scenic areas located near major sights:

Palais Royal: Escape to this peaceful courtyard across from the Louvre (Mo: Palais Royal-Musée du Louvre).

Place des Vosges: This exquisite grassy courtyard in the Marais is surrounded by royal buildings (Mo: Bastille).

Square du Vert-Galant: For great river views, try this little triangular park on the west tip of Ile de la Cité (Mo: Pont Neuf).

Pont des Arts: Dine at a bench on this pedestrian bridge over the Seine, near the Louvre (Mo: Pont Neuf).

Along the Seine: A grassy parkway runs along the left bank of the Seine between Les Invalides and Pont de l'Alma (Mo: Invalides, near Rue Cler).

Tuileries Garden: Have an Impressionist "Luncheon on the Grass" nestled between the Orsay and Orangerie museums (Mo: Tuileries).

Luxembourg Garden: This expansive Left Bank park is the classic Paris picnic spot (Mo: Odéon).

Les Invalides: Take a break from the Army Museum and Napoleon's Tomb in the gardens behind the complex (Mo: Varenne).

Champ de Mars: The long grassy strip below the Eiffel Tower has breathtaking views of this Paris icon. Eat along the sides of the park; the central lawn is off-limits (Mo: Ecole Militaire).

desserts, 129 Rue St. Dominique, tel. 01 47 05 46 44, www.fontainedemars.com).

$$ Café Constant is a cool, two-level place that feels more like a small bistro-wine bar than a café. Its owner, famed chef Christian Constant, has made a career of making French cuisine accessible to people like us. Delicious and fairly priced dishes are served in a snug setting to a dedicated clientele. Arrive early to get a table downstairs if you can (upstairs seating is a good fallback); the friendly staff speak English (€11 *entrées*, €16 *plats*, €7 desserts, daily, opens at 7:00 for breakfast, meals served nonstop 12:00-23:00, no reservations taken, corner of Rue Augereau and Rue St. Dominique, next to Hôtel de Londres Eiffel, tel. 01 47 53 73 34).

$$$ Le P'tit Troquet is a petite eatery taking you back to the Paris of the 1920s. Marie welcomes you warmly, and chef José cooks a delicious three-course €35 *menu* with a range of traditional choices prepared creatively. The homey charm and gourmet quality make this restaurant a favorite of connoisseurs (the same three-course *menu* is available for €25 at lunch, dinner service from 18:30, closed Sun, reservations smart, 28 Rue de l'Exposition, tel. 01 47 05 80 39).

$ Le Royal is a tiny, humble, time-warp place, with prices and decor from another era, that offers the cheapest meals in the neighborhood. Parisians dine here because "it's like eating at home." Gentle Guillaume is a fine host (€6 omelets, €9-12 *plats*, €14 for filling three-course *menu*, daily, 212 Rue de Grenelle, tel. 01 47 53 92 90).

In the Marais

On Romantic Place des Vosges

(Mo: Bastille or St-Paul)

$$$ La Place Royale has a fine location on the square with good seating inside or out. Expect a warm welcome and patient waiters, as owner Arnaud prides himself on service. The cuisine is traditional, priced well, and served nonstop all day, and the exceptional wine list is reasonable (try the Sancerre white). The €42 *menu* comes with a kir, three courses, a half-bottle of wine per person, and coffee—plenty of food to allow you to savor the setting (€26-42 *menus*, €17 lunch special, daily, 2 bis Place des Vosges, tel. 01 42 78 58 16).

$$$ Chez Janou, a Provençal bistro, tumbles out of its corner building and fills its broad sidewalk with happy eaters. Don't let the trendy and youthful crowd intimidate you: It's relaxed and charming, with helpful and calm service. The curbside tables are inviting, but I'd sit inside (with very tight seating) to immerse myself in the happy commotion. The style is French Mediterranean, with an emphasis on vegetables (daily—book ahead or arrive when it opens, 2 blocks beyond Place des Vosges at 2 Rue Roger Verlomme, tel. 01 42 72 28 41, www.chezjanou.com). They're proud of their 81 varieties of *pastis* (licorice-flavored liqueur, €4.80 each, browse the list above the bar).

$$ Café des Musées is an unspoiled bistro serving traditional meaty dishes with little fanfare. They offer a great €17 lunch special. The place is just far enough away to be overlooked by tourists, but it's packed with locals, so arrive early or book ahead (€19-26 *plats*, daily, 49 Rue de Turenne, tel. 01 42 72 96 17, www.lecafedesmusees.fr).

Near the Place de la Bastille

(Mo: Bastille)

$$ Au Temps des Cerises serves wines by the glass and meals with a smile. The woody 1950s atmosphere has tight seating and wads of character. Come for a glass of wine at the small zinc bar and say *bonjour* to Ben (try their Viognier), or stay for a tasty dinner (€11 starters, €20 *plats*, good cheap wine, daily, at the corner of Rue du Petit Musc and Rue de la Cerisaie, tel. 01 42 72 08 63).

In the Heart of the Marais

(Mo: St-Paul)

$ Breizh (Brittany) Café is worth the walk. It's a simple Breton joint serving organic crêpes and small rolls made for dipping in rich sauces and salted butter. The crêpes are the best in Paris and run the gamut from traditional ham-cheese-and-egg to Asian fusion. They also serve oysters, have a fantastic list of sweet crêpes, and talk about cider like a sommelier would talk about wine. Try a sparkling cider, a Breton cola, or my favorite—*lait ribot*, a buttermilk-like drink (€7-13 dinner crêpes, serves nonstop from 11:30 to late, closed Mon-Tue, reservations recommended for lunch and dinner, 109 Rue du Vieille du Temple, tel. 01 42 72 13 77).

$$ Chez Marianne is a Jewish Quarter fixture that blends delicious Jewish cuisine with Parisian *élan* and wonderful atmosphere. Choose from several indoor zones with a cluttered wine shop/deli feeling, or sit outside. You'll select from two dozen *Zakouski* elements to assemble your €14-18 *plat*. For takeout, pay inside first and get a ticket before you order outside. Vegetarians will find great options (€12 falafel sandwich—half that if you order it to go, long hours daily, corner of Rue des Rosiers and Rue des Hospitalières-St-Gervais, tel. 01 42 72 18 86).

$$$ Au Bourguignon du Marais is a handsome wine bar/bistro for Burgundy lovers, where excellent Burgundian wines blend with a good selection of well-designed dishes and efficient service. The *œufs en meurette* are mouthwatering, and the *bœuf bourguignon* could feed two (€11-14 starters, €20-30 *plats*, closed Sun-Mon, pleasing indoor and outdoor seating, 52 Rue François Miron, tel. 01 48 87 15 40).

On Ile St. Louis

(Mo: Pont Marie)

$$$ L'Orangerie is an inviting eatery with soft lighting and comfortable seating where diners speak in hushed voices so that everyone can appreciate the delicious cuisine and tasteful setting. Patient owner Monika speaks fluent English, and her *gratin d'aubergines* is sinfully good (€27-35 *menus*, closed Mon, 28 Rue St. Louis-en-l'Ile, tel. 01 46 33 93 98).

$ Café Med, near the pedestrian bridge to Notre-Dame, is a tiny, cheery *crêperie* with good-value salads, crêpes, and €11 *plats* (€14 and €20 *menus*, daily, 77 Rue St. Louis-en-l'Ile, tel. 01 43 29 73 17). Two similar *crêperies* are just across the street.

On the Left Bank

Near the Odéon Theater

(Mo: Odéon or Cluny-La Sorbonne)

$$$ La Méditerranée is all about seafood from the south served in a pastel and dressy setting...with similar clientele. The scene and the cuisine are sophisticated yet accessible, and the view of the Odéon is *formidable*. The sky-blue tablecloths and the lovingly presented dishes add to the romance (€29 two-course *menus*, €36 three-course *menus*, daily, reservations smart, facing the Odéon at 2 Place de l'Odéon, tel. 01 43 26 02 30, www.la-mediterranee.com).

$ L'Avant Comptoir, a stand-up-only hors d'oeuvres bar serving a delightful array of French-Basque tapas for €3-6 on a sleek zinc counter, was created to give people a sample of the cuisine from the *très* trendy Le Comptoir Restaurant next door, where the reservation wait time is four months. The menu is fun and accessible, it has a good list of wines by the glass, and crêpes are made fresh to go (daily 12:00-23:00, 9 Carrefour de l'Odéon, tel. 01 44 27 07 97).

$ Restaurant Polidor, a bare-bones neighborhood fixture since 1845, is much loved for its unpretentious quality cooking, fun old-Paris atmosphere, and fair value. Step inside to find noisy, happy diners sitting tightly at shared tables, savoring classic bourgeois *plats* from every corner of France (€12-17 *plats*, €25-35 three-course *menus*, daily 12:00-14:30 & 19:00-23:00, cash only, no reservations, 41 Rue Monsieur-le-Prince, tel. 01 43 26 95 34). Next door is the restaurant's wine shop, **Les Caves du Polidor**, where you can sip wine and nibble on cheese-and-meat plates (daily, wine and snacks served 18:00-20:00, opens earlier when weather or owner is feeling sunny).

Between the Panthéon and the Cluny Museum

(Mo: Cluny-La Sorbonne, Train-B: Luxembourg)

$$$ At **Les Papilles** you just eat what's offered—and you won't complain. It's a foodie's dream come true—one *menu*, no choices, and no regrets. Choose your wine from the shelf or ask for advice from the burly, rugby-playing owner, then relax and let the food arrive. Book this place ahead (€35 four-course *menu*, €20 daily *marmite du marché*—a.k.a. market stew, bigger and cheaper selection at lunch, closed Sun-Mon, 30 Rue Gay Lussac, tel. 01 43 25 20 79, www.lespapillesparis.fr).

$$ Le Pré Verre, a block from the Cluny Museum, is a chic wine bistro—a refreshing alternative in a part of the Latin Quarter mostly known for low-quality, tourist-trapping eateries. Offering imaginative, modern cuisine at fair prices and a good wine list, the place is packed. The astonishing bargain lunch *menu* includes a starter, main course, glass of wine, and coffee for €15. The three-course dinner *menu* at €32 is worth every *centime* (closed Sun-Mon, 8 Rue Thénard, reservations necessary, tel. 01 43 54 59 47, www.lepreverre.com).

The Paris Food Scene

To dig deeper into the food scene in Paris, take a culinary tour, cooking class, or a wine-tasting class.

Food Tours

Rosa Jackson designs personalized **"Edible Paris"** itineraries based on your interests and three-hour "food-guru" tours (unguided from €125, guided from €300, tel. 06 81 67 41 22, www.edible-paris.com).

Paris by Mouth offers more casual and frequent small group tours, with a maximum of seven foodies per group. Tours are organized by location or flavor and led by local food writers (€95/3 hours, includes tastings, www.parisbymouth.com). Sit-down cheese and wine workshops include seven wines and 14 cheeses (€95/3 hours). Given that there are 350 different types of cheese in France, you may need to take this class more than once.

Cooking Classes

At **Les Secrets Gourmands de Noémie,** Noémie shares her culinary secrets in 2.5 hours of hands-on fun in the kitchen. Thursday classes, designed for English speakers, focus on sweets; classes on other days are in French, English, or both, depending on the participants, and tackle savory dishes with the possibility of a market tour (€75-105, 92 Rue Nollet, Mo: La Fourche, tel. 06 64 17 93 32, www.lessecretsgourmandsdenoemie.com).

Cook'n with Class gets rave reviews for its convivial cooking and wine and cheese classes with a maximum of six students; tasting courses offered as well (6 Rue Baudelique, Mo: Jules Joffrin or Simplon, tel. 06 31 73 62 77, www.cooknwithclass.com).

La Cuisine Paris has a variety of classes in English, reasonable prices, and a beautiful space in central Paris (2- or 3-hour classes-€65-95, 80 Quai de l'Hôtel de Ville, tel. 01 40 51 78 18, www.lacuisineparis.com).

Susan Herrmann Loomis, an acclaimed chef and author, offers cooking courses in Paris or at her home in Normandy. Your travel buddy can skip the class but should come for the meal at a reduced "guest eater" price (www.onruetatin.com).

If you're looking for a pricey demonstration course, you'll find it at **Le Cordon Bleu** (tel. 01 53 68 22 50, www.lcbparis.com) or **Ritz Escoffier Ecole de Gastronomie** (tel. 01 43 16 30 50, www.ritzparis.com).

Wine Tasting

Olivier Magny and his team of sommeliers teach fun wine-tasting classes at the **Ô Château** wine school/bar, in the 17th-century residence of Madame de Pompadour, King Louis XV's favorite mistress. Olivier's goal is to "take the snob out of wine." Learn the basics of wine regions, the techniques of tasting, and how to read a label (68 Rue Jean-Jacques Rousseau, Mo: Louvre-Rivoli or Etienne Marcel, tel. 01 44 73 97 80, www.o-chateau.com).

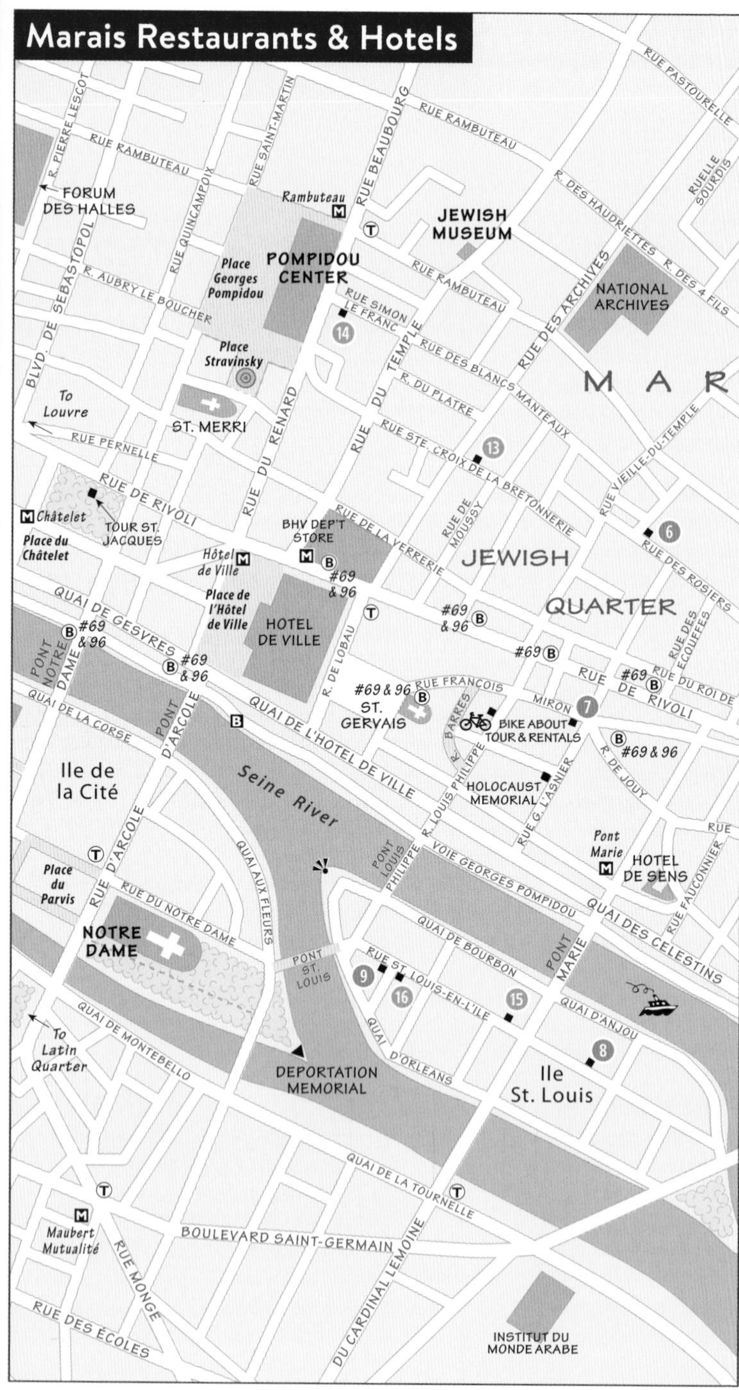
Marais Restaurants & Hotels
RUE RAMBUTEAU
FORUM DES HALLES
R. PIERRE LESCOT
RUE QUINCAMPOIX
RUE SAINT-MARTIN
RUE BEAUBOURG
Rambuteau
JEWISH MUSEUM
Place Georges Pompidou
POMPIDOU CENTER
R. AUBRY LE BOUCHER
RUE SIMON LE FRANC
Place Stravinsky
ST. MERRI
To Louvre
RUE PERNELLE
BLVD. DE SEBASTOPOL
RUE DU RENARD
RUE DU TEMPLE
RUE DES BLANCS MANTEAUX
R. DU PLATRE
RUE STE. CROIX DE LA BRETONNERIE
RUE DES ARCHIVES
NATIONAL ARCHIVES
R. DES HAUDRIETTES
R. DES 4 FILS
RUE PASTOURELLE
RUELLE SOURDIS
MAR
RUE VIEILLE-DU-TEMPLE
RUE DE RIVOLI
TOUR ST. JACQUES
Châtelet
Place du Châtelet
BHV DEP'T STORE
Hôtel de Ville
Place de l'Hôtel de Ville
HOTEL DE VILLE
RUE DE LA VERRERIE
RUE DE MOUSSY
JEWISH QUARTER
RUE DES ROSIERS
RUE DES ECOUFFES
RUE DU ROI DE
#69 & 96
QUAI DE GESVRES
PONT NOTRE DAME
QUAI DE LA CORSE
PONT D'ARCOLE
R. DE LOBAU
RUE FRANCOIS MIRON
ST. GERVAIS
BIKE ABOUT TOUR & RENTALS
R. BARRES
QUAI DE L'HOTEL DE VILLE
R. DE JOUY
HOLOCAUST MEMORIAL
R. LOUIS PHILIPPE
RUE G. L'ASNIER
Ile de la Cité
Seine River
RUE D'ARCOLE
QUAI AUX FLEURS
PONT LOUIS PHILIPPE
VOIE GEORGES POMPIDOU
Pont Marie
HOTEL DE SENS
RUE FAUCONNIER
QUAI DES CELESTINS
Place du Parvis
RUE DU NOTRE DAME
NOTRE DAME
QUAI DE BOURBON
PONT MARIE
PONT ST. LOUIS
RUE ST. LOUIS-EN-L'ILE
QUAI D'ANJOU
QUAI D'ORLEANS
To Latin Quarter
QUAI DE MONTEBELLO
DEPORTATION MEMORIAL
Ile St. Louis
QUAI DE LA TOURNELLE
Maubert Mutualité
RUE MONGE
BOULEVARD SAINT-GERMAIN
RUE DU CARDINAL LEMOINE
RUE DES ECOLES
INSTITUT DU MONDE ARABE

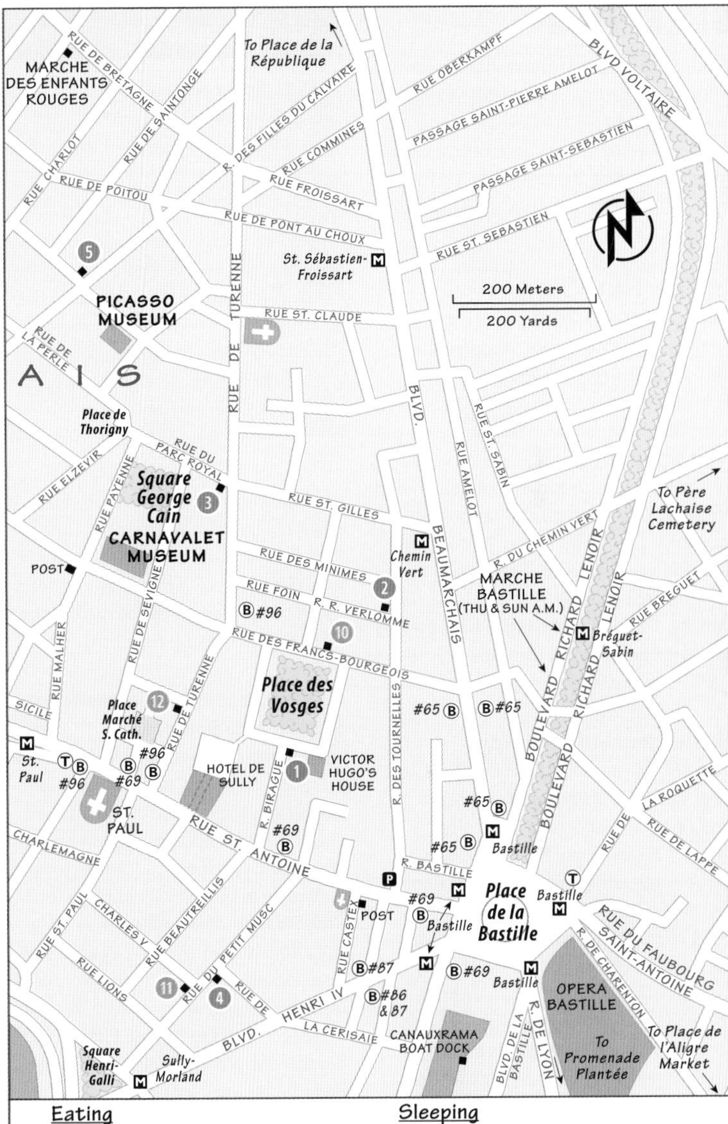

Eating

1. La Place Royale
2. Chez Janou
3. Café des Musées
4. Au Temps des Cerises
5. Breizh Café
6. Chez Marianne
7. Au Bourguignon du Marais
8. L'Orangerie
9. Café Med

Sleeping

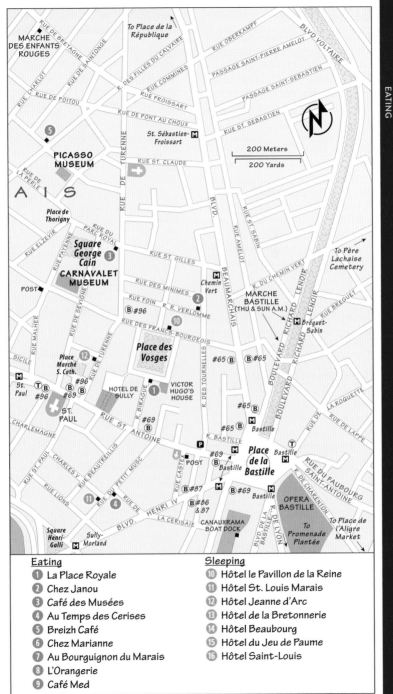

10. Hôtel le Pavillon de la Reine
11. Hôtel St. Louis Marais
12. Hôtel Jeanne d'Arc
13. Hôtel de la Bretonnerie
14. Hôtel Beaubourg
15. Hôtel du Jeu de Paume
16. Hôtel Saint-Louis

SLEEPING

I've focused my recommendations on three safe, handy, and colorful neighborhoods: the village-like Rue Cler (near the Eiffel Tower); the artsy and trendy Marais (near Place de la Bastille); and the historic island of Ile St. Louis (next door to Notre-Dame).

In the Rue Cler Neighborhood

(7th arrond., Mo: Ecole Militaire, La Tour Maubourg, or Invalides)

Rue Cler is so French that when I step out of my hotel in the morning, I feel like I must have been a poodle in a previous life. This is a neighborhood of wide, tree-lined boulevards, stately apartment buildings, and lots of Americans. Hotels here are a fair value, considering the elegance of the neighborhood. And you're within walking distance of the Eiffel Tower, Army Museum, Seine River, Champs-Elysées, and Orsay and Rodin museums.

In the Heart of Rue Cler

Many of my readers stay in the Rue Cler neighborhood. If you want to disappear into Paris, choose a hotel elsewhere. The following hotels are within Camembert-smelling distance of Rue Cler.

$$ Hôtel du Champ de Mars*** is a top choice, brilliantly located barely 10 steps off Rue Cler. This plush little hotel has a small-town feel from top to bottom. The adorable rooms are snug but lovingly kept by hands-on owners Françoise and Stéphane, and single rooms can work as tiny doubles. It's popular, so book well ahead (Sb-€150, Db-€170, no air-con, 30 yards off Rue Cler at 7 Rue du Champ de Mars, tel. 01 45 51 52 30, www.hotelduchampdemars.com, reservation@hotelduchampdemars.com).

$$ Hôtel Beaugency***, a fair value on a quieter street a short block off Rue Cler, has 30 smallish rooms and a lobby that you can stretch out in (Sb-€109-193, Db-€129-213, occasional discounts for Rick Steves readers—ask when you book, breakfast-€9.50, 21 Rue Duvivier, tel. 01 47 05 01 63, www.hotel-beaugency.com, infos@hotel-beaugency.com).

> ## *Sleep Code*
>
> **$$$$ Splurge:** Over €250
> **$$$ Pricier:** €190-250
> **$$ Moderate:** €130-190
> **$ Budget:** €70-130
> **¢ Backpacker:** Under €70
>
> Hotels are classified based on the average price of a standard double room with bath in high season. Unless otherwise noted, credit cards are accepted, breakfast is not included, hotel staff speak English, and Wi-Fi is available.

Close to Ecole Militaire Métro

$$$$ Hôtel la Bourdonnais****, near the Champs de Mars park, is upscale and tastefully designed, with comfy public spaces and rooms that blend modern and traditional accents. It's run well with American-style service (Db-€230-350, elaborate breakfast-€17 but free for Rick Steves readers, 113 Avenue de la Bourdonnais, tel. 01 47 05 45 42, www.hotellabourdonnais.fr, labourdonnais@inwood-hotels.com).

$$$$ Hôtel Duquesne Eiffel***, a few blocks farther from the action, is calm, hospitable, and very comfortable. It features handsome rooms (some with terrific Eiffel Tower views) and a welcoming lobby (Db-€249-300, Tb-€279-339, big, hot breakfast-€13 but free for Rick Steves readers, 23 Avenue Duquesne, tel. 01 44 42 09 09, www.hde.fr, contact@hde.fr).

Closer to Rue St. Dominique

$$$ Hôtel de Londres Eiffel*** is my closest listing to the Eiffel Tower and the Champ de Mars park. Here you get immaculate, warmly decorated rooms (several are connecting, for families), snazzy public spaces, and a service-oriented staff. Some rooms are pretty small—request a bigger room. It's less convenient to the Métro (10-minute walk), but very handy to buses #69, #80, #87, and #92, and to Train-C: Pont de l'Alma (Sb-€185, small Db-€235, bigger Db-€260, Db with Eiffel Tower view-€380, Tb-€360, 1 Rue Augereau, tel. 01 45 51 63 02, www.hotel-paris-londres-eiffel.com, info@londres-eiffel.com, helpful Cédric and Arnaud).

$$ Hôtel de la Tour Eiffel** is a solid two-star value on a quiet street near several of my favorite restaurants. The rooms are well-designed, well-kept, and comfortable, but they don't have air-conditioning and some have thin walls. The six sets of connecting rooms are ideal for families (snug Db-€115, bigger Db-€135-155, 17 Rue de l'Exposition, tel. 01 47 05 14 75, www.hotel-toureiffel.com, hte7@wanadoo.fr).

Near La Tour Maubourg Métro

$$$ Hôtel Muguet*** has had a full face-lift. I thought the hotel was terrific before the renovation—it's still quiet, well-located, and well-run (Db-€150-235—more with view, Tb-€235-275, strict cancellation policy, 11 Rue Chevert, tel. 01 47 05 05 93, www.hotelparismuguet.com, muguet@wanadoo.fr).

In the Marais Neighborhood

Those interested in a more central, diverse, and lively urban locale should make the Marais their Parisian home. Running from the Pompidou Center east to the Bastille (a 15-minute walk), the Marais is jumbled, medieval Paris at its finest. Classy stone mansions sit alongside trendy bars, antique shops, and fashion-conscious boutiques. The streets are an intriguing parade of artists, students, tourists, immigrants, and baguette-munching babies in strollers. The Marais is also known as a hub of the Parisian gay and lesbian scene. This area is *sans* doubt livelier and edgier than the Rue Cler area.

Near Place des Vosges

(3rd and 4th arrond., Mo: Bastille, St-Paul, or Sully-Morland)

$$$$ Hôtel le Pavillon de la Reine*****, 15 steps off the beautiful Place des Vosges, merits its stars with top service and comfort and exquisite attention to detail, from its melt-in-your-couch lobby to its luxurious rooms (Db-€350-1,000, buffet breakfast-€35, free access to spa and fitness room, free loaner bikes and parking, 28 Place des Vosges, tel. 01 40 29 19 19, www.pavillon-de-la-reine.com, contact@pavillon-de-la-reine.com).

$$$ Hôtel St. Louis Marais***, an intimate and sharp little hotel, lies on a quiet street a few blocks from the river. The handsome rooms come with character, spacious bathrooms, and reasonable rates (Db-€175-230, Tb-€245, Qb-€265, buffet breakfast-€13, 1 Rue Charles V, Mo: Sully-Morland, tel. 01 48 87 87 04, www.saintlouismarais.com, marais@saintlouis-hotels.com).

$ Hôtel Jeanne d'Arc**, a lovely small hotel with thoughtfully appointed rooms, is ideally located for (and very popular with) connoisseurs of the Marais. It's an exceptional value and worth booking way ahead. Corner rooms are wonderfully

Apartment Rentals

Intrepid travelers are accustomed to using Airbnb and VRBO when it comes to renting a vacation apartment. In Paris, you have many additional options among rental agencies; I've found the following to be the most reliable. Their websites are essential to understanding your choices. Read the rental conditions very carefully.

Paris Perfect has offices in Paris with English-speaking staff who seek the "perfect apartment" for their clients. Many units have Eiffel Tower views, and most have air-conditioning and washers and dryers (discount off regular rates for Rick Steves readers, US toll-free tel. 888-520-2087, www.parisperfect.com).

Adrian Leeds Group offers apartments owned by North Americans and is ideal for travelers looking for all the comforts, conveniences, and amenities of home (tel. 877-880-0265, ext. 701, www.adrianleeds.com).

Home Rental Service offers a big selection of apartments throughout Paris with no agency fees (120 Champs-Elysées, tel. 01 42 25 65 40, www.homerental.fr).

Haven in Paris offers exactly that—well-appointed, stylish havens for travelers looking for a temporary home. Also check out their fun blog, *Hip Paris* (tel. 617/395-4243, www.haveninparis.com).

Paris Home offers two little studios, both located on Rue Amélie in the heart of the Rue Cler area. Each has modern furnishings and laundry facilities. Friendly Slim, the owner, is the best part (no minimum stay, special rates for longer stays, free maid service, airport/train station transfers possible, mobile 06 19 03 17 55, www.parishome2000.com).

Cobblestone Paris Rentals is a small, North American-run outfit offering furnished rentals in central neighborhoods. Apartments come stocked with English-language DVDs about Paris, coffee, tea, cooking spices, basic bathroom amenities, and an English-speaking greeter who will give you the lay of the land (two free river cruises for Rick Steves readers who stay five nights or more, www.cobblestoneparis.com).

Paris for Rent, a San Francisco-based group, has been renting top-end apartments in Paris for more than a decade (US tel. 866-437-2623, www.parisforrent.com).

Cross-Pollinate is a reputable online booking agency representing B&Bs and apartments throughout Paris. Minimum stays vary from one to seven nights (US tel. 800-270-1190, France tel. 09 75 18 11 10, www.cross-pollinate.com).

bright in the City of Light but have twin beds only. Rooms on the street can be noisy until the bars close (Sb-€72-98, Db-€120, larger twin Db-€150, family rooms available, continental breakfast-€8, no air-con, 3 Rue de Jarente, Mo: St-Paul, tel. 01 48 87 62 11, www.hoteljeannedarc.com, information@hoteljeannedarc.com).

Near the Pompidou Center

(4th arrond., Mo: St-Paul, Hôtel de Ville, or Rambuteau)

$$ Hôtel de la Bretonnerie***, three blocks from Hôtel de Ville, makes a fine Marais home. It has a warm, welcoming lobby, helpful staff, and 29 well-appointed, good-value rooms with an antique, open-beam warmth (standard "classic" Db-€180, bigger "charming" Db-€220, Db suite-€250, Tb/Qb-€245, buffet breakfast-€10, no air-con, between Rue Vieille du Temple and Rue des Archives at 22 Rue Ste. Croix de la Bretonnerie, tel. 01 48 87 77 63, www.bretonnerie.com, hotel@bretonnerie.com).

$$ Hôtel Beaubourg*** is a terrific three-star value on a small street in the shadow of the Pompidou Center. The lounge is inviting, and the 28 plush and traditional rooms are quiet and thoughtfully appointed (standard Db-€135-165, bigger twin or king-size Db-€145-175 and worth the extra cost, Db suite with private patio-€190-230, continental breakfast-€9.50, 11 Rue Simon Le Franc, Mo: Rambuteau, tel. 01 42 74 34 24, www.hotelbeaubourg.com, reservation@hotelbeaubourg.com).

On Ile St. Louis

(4th arrond., Mo: Pont Marie or Sully-Morland)

The peaceful, residential character of this river-wrapped island, with its brilliant location and homemade ice cream, has drawn Americans for decades. There are no budget deals here—all the hotels are three-star or more—though prices are fair considering the level of comfort and killer location.

$$$$ Hôtel du Jeu de Paume****, occupying a 17th-century tennis center, is among the most expensive hotels I list in Paris. When you enter its magnificent lobby, you'll understand why. Greet Scoop, *le chien*, then take a spin in the glass elevator for a half-timbered-treehouse experience. The 30 rooms are carefully designed and tasteful, though not particularly spacious (you're paying for the location and public areas). Most rooms face a small garden; all are pin-drop peaceful (Sb-€195-255, standard Db-€295-360, suite Db-€450-560, apartment for up to 6-€620-900, breakfast-€18, 54 Rue St. Louis-en-l'Ile, tel. 01 43 26 14 18, www.jeudepaumehotel.com, info@jeudepaumehotel.com).

$$$ Hôtel Saint-Louis*** blends character with modern comforts. The well-maintained rooms come with cool stone floors and exposed beams. Rates are reasonable...for the location (Db-€185-225, top-floor Db with micro-balcony-€255, Tb-€295, buffet breakfast-€13, 75 Rue St. Louis-en-l'Ile, tel. 01 46 34 04 80, www.saintlouisenlisle.com, info@saintlouisenlisle.com).

TRANSPORTATION

Getting Around Paris

Paris is easy to navigate. Your basic choices are Métro (in-city subway), train (suburban rapid transit tied into the Métro system), public bus, and taxi.

You can buy tickets and passes at Métro stations and at many *tabacs*. Staffed ticket windows in stations are being phased out, so expect some stations to have only machines and an information desk. Machines accept coins, small bills of €20 or less, and chip-and-PIN cards (no American magnetic-stripe or chip-and-signature cards).

Rick's Tip: Buy Métro tickets at a *tabac* shop to avoid long lines *at the Métro station, especially at the end of the month when crowds of locals are buying next month's pass. Just look for the distinctive red* Tabac *sign.*

Public-Transit Tickets: The Métro, suburban trains (lines A-K), trams, and buses all work on the same tickets. You can make as many transfers as you need on a single ticket, except between the Métro/suburban train and the bus or tram systems (additional ticket required). A single ticket costs €1.80. To save money, buy a *carnet* (kar-nay) of 10 tickets for €14.10. *Carnets* can be shared among travelers. Kids under four ride free.

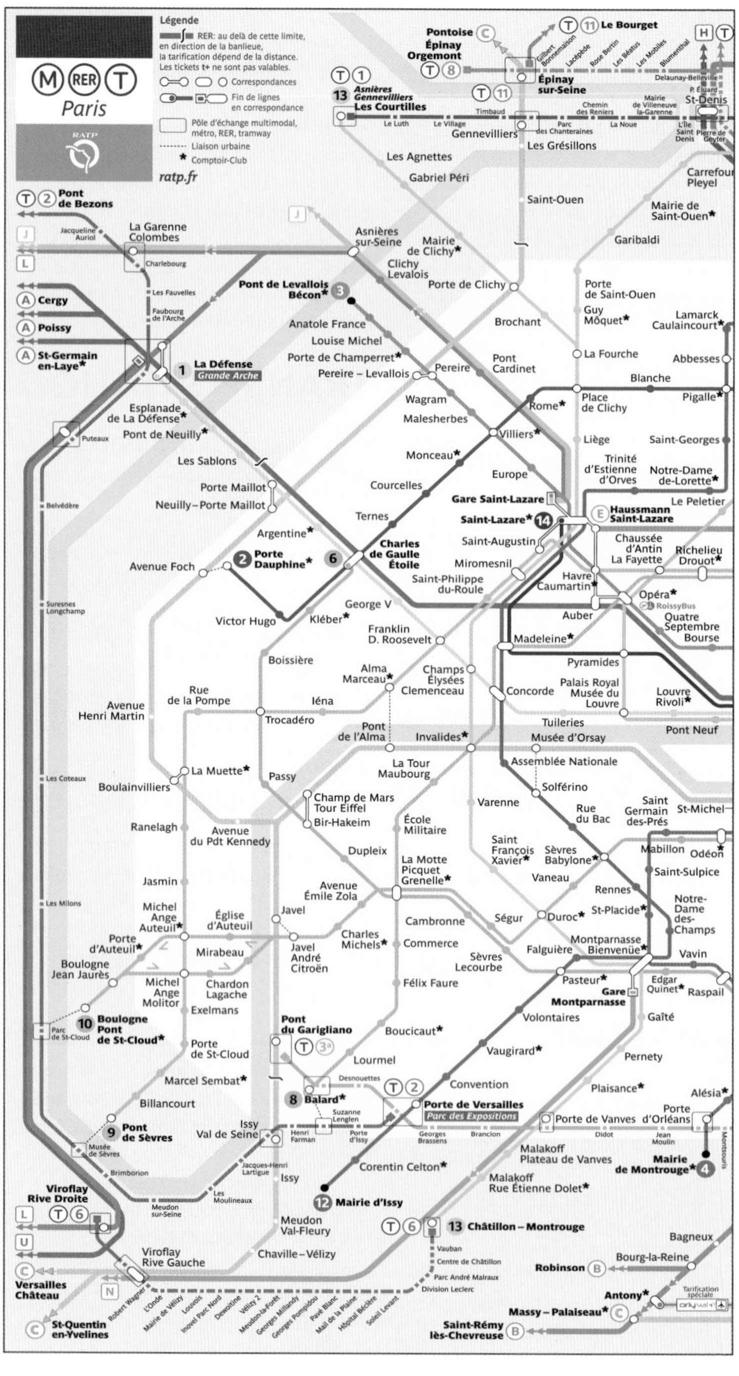
Légende
RER: au delà de cette limite, en direction de la banlieue, la tarification dépend de la distance. Les tickets t+ ne sont pas valables.
Correspondances
Fin de lignes en correspondance
Pôle d'échange multimodal, métro, RER, tramway
Liaison urbaine
Comptoir-Club
M RER T
Paris
RATP
ratp.fr
Pontoise
Épinay Orgemont
Le Bourget
Épinay sur-Seine
Asnières Gennevilliers Les Courtilles
Timbaud
Le Luth
Le Village
Gennevilliers
Les Grésillons
Delaunay-Belleville
P. Éluard
St-Denis
Les Agnettes
Gabriel Péri
Saint-Ouen
Carrefour Pleyel
Mairie de Saint-Ouen
Garibaldi
Pont de Bezons
La Garenne Colombes
Charlebourg
Les Fauvelles
Faubourg de l'Arche
Cergy
Poissy
St-Germain en-Laye
La Défense Grande Arche
Asnières sur-Seine
Mairie de Clichy
Clichy Levalois
Porte de Clichy
Pont de Levallois Bécon
Anatole France
Louise Michel
Porte de Champerret
Pereire – Levallois
Pereire
Brochant
Pont Cardinet
Porte de Saint-Ouen
Guy Môquet
La Fourche
Lamarck Caulaincourt
Abbesses
Blanche
Pigalle
Place de Clichy
Rome
Wagram
Malesherbes
Villiers
Liège
Saint-Georges
Esplanade de La Défense
Puteaux
Pont de Neuilly
Les Sablons
Monceau
Europe
Trinité d'Estienne d'Orves
Notre-Dame de-Lorette
Porte Maillot
Neuilly – Porte Maillot
Courcelles
Gare Saint-Lazare
Le Peletier
Belvédère
Ternes
Saint-Lazare
Haussmann Saint-Lazare
Argentine
Charles de Gaulle Étoile
Saint-Augustin
Chaussée d'Antin La Fayette
Richelieu Drouot
Porte Dauphine
Avenue Foch
Miromesnil
Havre Caumartin
Saint-Philippe du-Roule
Opéra
RoissyBus
Suresnes Longchamp
George V
Victor Hugo
Kléber
Auber
Quatre Septembre
Bourse
Franklin D. Roosevelt
Madeleine
Boissière
Pyramides
Alma Marceau
Champs Élysées Clemenceau
Palais Royal Musée du Louvre
Louvre Rivoli
Rue de la Pompe
Avenue Henri Martin
Iéna
Concorde
Trocadéro
Tuileries
Pont Neuf
Pont de l'Alma
Invalides
Musée d'Orsay
La Tour Maubourg
Assemblée Nationale
La Muette
Boulainvilliers
Passy
Les Coteaux
Champ de Mars Tour Eiffel
Bir-Hakeim
Varenne
Solférino
Rue du Bac
Saint Germain des-Prés
St-Michel
Ranelagh
Avenue du Pdt Kennedy
École Militaire
Saint François Xavier
Sèvres Babylone
Mabillon
Odéon
Dupleix
La Motte Picquet Grenelle
Vaneau
Saint-Sulpice
Jasmin
Avenue Émile Zola
Rennes
Notre-Dame des-Champs
Les Milons
Michel Ange Auteuil
Église d'Auteuil
Javel
Cambronne
Ségur
Duroc
St-Placide
Porte d'Auteuil
Mirabeau
Javel André Citroën
Charles Michels
Commerce
Falguière
Montparnasse Bienvenüe
Vavin
Boulogne Jean Jaurès
Michel Ange Molitor
Chardon Lagache
Sèvres Lecourbe
Félix Faure
Pasteur
Gare Montparnasse
Edgar Quinet
Raspail
Exelmans
Volontaires
Gaîté
Boulogne Pont de St-Cloud
Parc de St-Cloud
Porte de St-Cloud
Pont du Garigliano
Boucicaut
Vaugirard
Pernety
Lourmel
Marcel Sembat
Desnouettes
Convention
Plaisance
Alésia
Billancourt
Balard
Porte de Versailles Parc des Expositions
Porte de Vanves
Porte d'Orléans
Pont de Sèvres
Musée de Sèvres
Issy Val de Seine
Henri Farman
Suzanne Lenglen
Porte d'Issy
Georges Brassens
Brancion
Didot
Jean Moulin
Malakoff Plateau de Vanves
Mairie de Montrouge
Montsouris
Brimborion
Jacques-Henri Lartigue
Issy
Corentin Celton
Malakoff Rue Étienne Dolet
Viroflay Rive Droite
Meudon sur-Seine
Les Moulineaux
Mairie d'Issy
Meudon Val-Fleury
Châtillon – Montrouge
Bagneux
Vauban
Centre de Châtillon
Parc André Malraux
Division Leclerc
Viroflay Rive Gauche
Chaville – Vélizy
Bourg-la-Reine
Robinson
Versailles Château
Antony
Tarification spéciale
Massy – Palaiseau
St-Quentin en-Yvelines
Saint-Rémy lès-Chevreuse
Robert Wagner
L'Onde
Mairie de Vélizy
Louvois
Inovel Parc Nord
Dewoitine
Vélizy 2
Meudon-la-Forêt
Georges Millandy
Georges Pompidou
Pavé Blanc
Mail de la Plaine
Hôpital Béclère
Soleil Levant

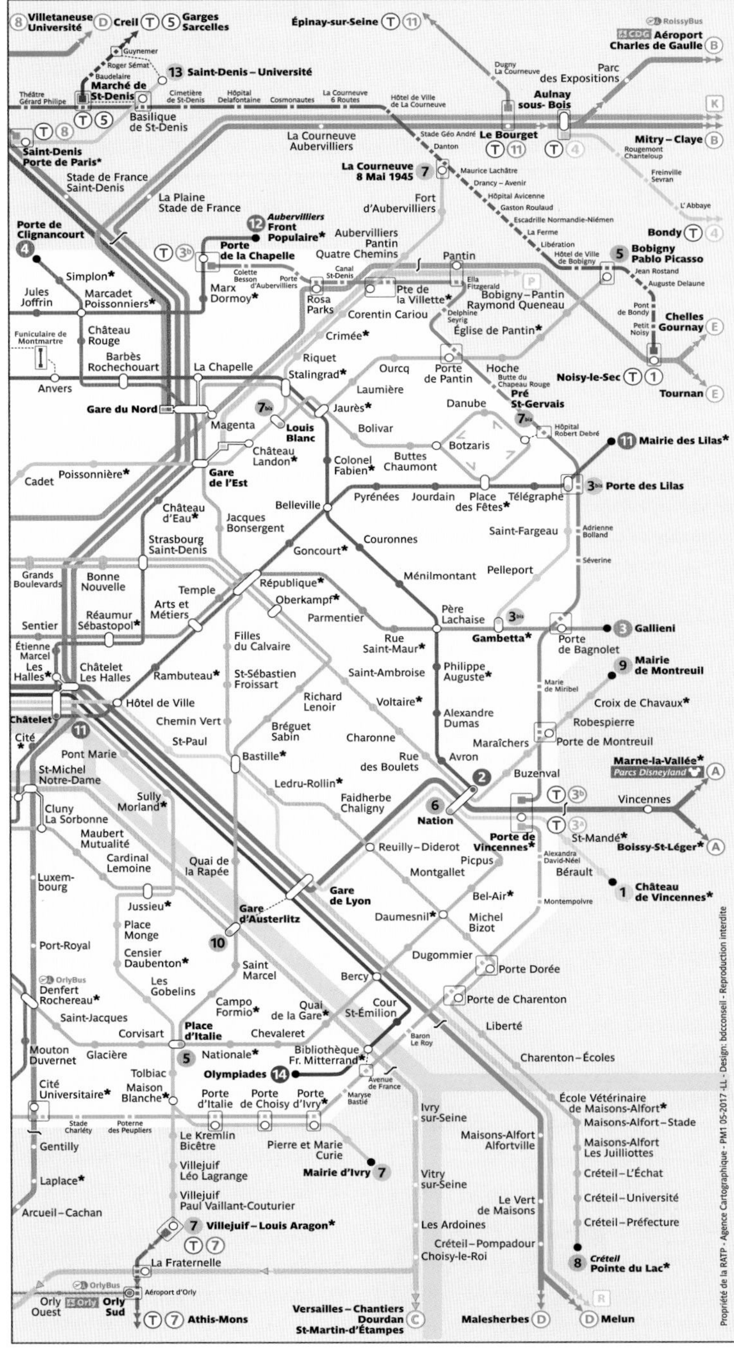
Villetaneuse Université
Creil
Garges Sarcelles
Épinay-sur-Seine
RoissyBus
Aéroport Charles de Gaulle
13 Saint-Denis – Université
Marché de St-Denis
Basilique de St-Denis
Saint-Denis Porte de Paris*
Stade de France Saint-Denis
La Plaine Stade de France
La Courneuve Aubervilliers
Parc des Expositions
Aulnay sous- Bois
Le Bourget
Mitry – Claye
La Courneuve 8 Mai 1945
Fort d'Aubervilliers
Porte de Clignancourt
Aubervilliers Front Populaire*
Porte de la Chapelle
Aubervilliers Pantin Quatre Chemins
Bondy
Bobigny Pablo Picasso
Simplon*
Jules Joffrin
Marcadet Poissonniers*
Marx Dormoy*
Rosa Parks
Pantin
Pte de la Villette*
Corentin Cariou
Bobigny–Pantin Raymond Queneau
Chelles Gournay
Château Rouge
Barbès Rochechouart
Crimée*
Église de Pantin*
Anvers
La Chapelle
Riquet
Stalingrad*
Ourcq
Porte de Pantin
Hoche
Noisy-le-Sec
Gare du Nord
Laumière
Pré St-Gervais
Tournan
Magenta
Louis Blanc
Jaurès*
Danube
Bolivar
Botzaris
11 Mairie des Lilas*
Château Landon*
Colonel Fabien*
Buttes Chaumont
Cadet
Poissonnière*
Gare de l'Est
3bis Porte des Lilas
Pyrénées
Jourdain
Place des Fêtes*
Télégraphe
Belleville
Château d'Eau*
Jacques Bonsergent
Saint-Fargeau
Couronnes
Strasbourg Saint-Denis
Goncourt*
Grands Boulevards
Bonne Nouvelle
Ménilmontant
Pelleport
Temple
République*
Arts et Métiers
Oberkampf*
Réaumur Sébastopol*
Parmentier
Père Lachaise
Gambetta*
3 Gallieni
Sentier
Filles du Calvaire
Rue Saint-Maur*
Porte de Bagnolet
Étienne Marcel
Les Halles*
Châtelet Les Halles
Rambuteau*
St-Sébastien Froissart
Saint-Ambroise
Philippe Auguste*
9 Mairie de Montreuil
Hôtel de Ville
Richard Lenoir
Voltaire*
Croix de Chavaux*
Châtelet
Chemin Vert
Alexandre Dumas
Robespierre
Cité*
St-Paul
Bréguet Sabin
Charonne
Maraîchers
Porte de Montreuil
Pont Marie
Bastille*
Rue des Boulets
Avron
Marne-la-Vallée*
Parcs Disneyland
St-Michel Notre-Dame
Ledru-Rollin*
Buzenval
Sully Morland*
Faidherbe Chaligny
Nation
Vincennes
Cluny La Sorbonne
Maubert Mutualité
Porte de Vincennes*
St-Mandé*
Boissy-St-Léger*
Reuilly – Diderot
Cardinal Lemoine
Quai de la Rapée
Picpus
Montgallet
Bérault
Luxembourg
Gare de Lyon
1 Château de Vincennes*
Jussieu*
Gare d'Austerlitz
Bel-Air*
Daumesnil*
Michel Bizot
Place Monge
Port-Royal
Censier Daubenton*
Dugommier
Saint Marcel
Porte Dorée
OrlyBus
Denfert Rochereau*
Les Gobelins
Bercy
Campo Formio*
Quai de la Gare*
Cour St-Émilion
Porte de Charenton
Saint-Jacques
Corvisart
Place d'Italie
Chevaleret
Liberté
Mouton Duvernet
Glacière
Nationale*
Bibliothèque Fr. Mitterrand*
Charenton – Écoles
Tolbiac
14 Olympiades
Cité Universitaire*
Maison Blanche*
Porte d'Italie
Porte de Choisy
Porte d'Ivry*
Ivry sur-Seine
École Vétérinaire de Maisons-Alfort*
Maisons-Alfort – Stade
Gentilly
Le Kremlin Bicêtre
Pierre et Marie Curie
Maisons-Alfort Alfortville
Maisons-Alfort Les Juilliottes
Laplace*
Villejuif Léo Lagrange
Mairie d'Ivry 7
Vitry sur-Seine
Créteil – L'Échat
Arcueil – Cachan
Villejuif Paul Vaillant-Couturier
Le Vert de Maisons
Créteil – Université
7 Villejuif – Louis Aragon*
Les Ardoines
Créteil – Préfecture
Créteil – Pompadour
Choisy-le-Roi
8 Créteil Pointe du Lac*
La Fraternelle
Orly Ouest
Orly Sud
Athis-Mons
Versailles – Chantiers Dourdan St-Martin-d'Étampes
Malesherbes
Melun

Passe Navigo: This chip-embedded card costs a one-time €5 fee (plus another €5 for the required photo; photo booths are in major Métro stations). The weekly unlimited pass (Navigo Semaine) costs €21.25 (plus the fees listed above) and covers all forms of transit from Monday to Sunday (expiring on Sunday, even if you buy it on, say, a Thursday). The pass is good for all zones in the Paris region, which means that you can travel anywhere within the city center, out to Versailles, and to Charles de Gaulle and Orly airports. To use the Navigo, touch the card to the purple pad, wait for the green validation light and the "ding," and you're on your way. You can buy your Passe Navigo at any Métro station in Paris (for more details, visit www.ratp.fr).

Navigo or *Carnet*? The Navigo covers a far greater area than *carnet* tickets, but cannot be shared, and is most worthwhile for visitors who use it for regional trips, stay a full week, and start their trip early in the week. Two 10-packs of *carnets*—enough for most travelers staying a week—cost €28.20, are shareable, don't expire, but are only valid in the center of Paris.

Other Passes: A handy one-day bus/Métro pass (called **Mobilis**) is available for €7. If you are under 26 and in Paris on a Saturday or Sunday, you can buy an unlimited daily transit pass called **Ticket Jeunes Week-end** for the unbeatable price of €3.85.

Métro ticket machines

By Métro

In Paris, you're never more than a 10-minute walk from a Métro station. Europe's best subway system allows you to hop from sight to sight quickly and cheaply (runs Sun-Thu 5:30-24:30, Fri-Sat 5:30-2:00 in the morning, www.ratp.fr).

Using the Métro System: To get to your destination, determine the closest "Mo" stop and which line or lines will get you there. The lines are color-coded and numbered, and you can tell their direction by the end-of-the-line stops. For example, the La Défense/Château de Vincennes line, also known as line 1 (yellow), runs between La Défense, on its west end, and Vincennes on its east end. Once in the Métro station, you'll see the color-coded line numbers and/or blue-and-white signs directing you to the train going in your direction (e.g., *direction: La Défense*). Insert your ticket in the automatic turnstile, reclaim your ticket, pass through, and keep it until you exit the system (some stations require you to pass your ticket through a turnstile to exit). Be warned that fare inspectors regularly check for cheaters, accept absolutely no excuses, and have portable credit-card machines to fine you on the spot: Keep that ticket or pay a minimum fine of €45.

Transfers are free and can be made wherever lines cross, provided you do so within 1.5 hours.

When you reach your destination, look for the blue-and-white *sortie* signs pointing you to the exit. Before leaving the station, check the helpful *plan du quartier* (map of the neighborhood) to get your bearings.

After you finish the entire ride and exit onto the street, toss or tear your used ticket so you don't confuse it with unused tickets.

Métro Resources: Métro maps are free at Métro stations. Several good online tools can also help you navigate the public-transit system. The website Metro.paris provides an interactive map of Paris'

Transit Basics

- The same tickets are good on the Métro, suburban trains (within the city), and city buses.
- Save money by buying a *carnet* of 10 discounted tickets or a Passe Navigo.
- Beware of pickpockets, and don't buy tickets from men roaming the stations.
- Find your train by its end-of-the-line stop.
- Insert your ticket into the turnstile, retrieve it, and keep it until the end of your journey.
- Safeguard your belongings; avoid standing near the train doors with luggage.
- At a stop, if the door doesn't open automatically, either push a square button (green or black) or lift a metal latch.
- Transfers *(correspondances)* between the Métro and suburban train system are free (but not between Métro/suburban train and bus).
- Trash or tear used tickets after you complete your ride and leave the station (not before) to avoid confusing them with fresh ones.

sights and Métro lines (www.metro.paris). The free RATP mobile app (in English, download at www.ratp.fr) and the more user-friendly Kemtro app (www.kemtro.com) can estimate Métro travel times, help you locate the best station exit, and tell you when the next bus will arrive, among other things.

By Suburban Train

The suburban train, formerly called the RER, is an arm of the Métro, serving outlying destinations such as Versailles and the airports. These routes are identified on Métro maps by the letters A-K.

Within the city center, the train works like the Métro and can be speedier if it serves your destination directly, because it makes fewer stops. Métro tickets are good on the suburban train when traveling in the city center. You can transfer between the Métro and suburban train systems with the same ticket. But to travel outside the city (to Versailles or the airport, for example), you'll need a separate, more expensive ticket (unless you're using a Passe Navigo). Unlike the Métro, not every train stops at every station along the way; check the sign over the platform to see if your destination is listed as a stop ("*toutes les gares*" means it makes all stops along the way), or confirm with a local before you board. For suburban trains, you may need to insert your ticket in a turnstile to exit the system.

By City Bus

Paris' excellent bus system is worth figuring out (www.ratp.fr). Bus stops are everywhere, and every stop comes with all the information you need: a good city bus map, route maps showing exactly where each bus goes that uses the stop, a frequency chart and schedule, a *plan du quartier* map of the immediate neighborhood, and a *soirées* map explaining night service, if available. Bus-system maps are also available in any Métro station (and in the *Paris Pratique* map book sold at newsstands).

Using the Bus System: Buses use the same tickets and passes as the Métro and suburban train. One ticket buys you a bus ride anywhere in central Paris within the freeway ring road *(le périphérique)*. Use your Métro ticket or buy one on board for €0.20 more, though note that tickets bought on board are *sans correspondance*, which means you can't use them to transfer to another bus.

Paris bus stops are getting a face-lift, and they are looking sharp; at some locations, you can charge your phone while you wait. Board your bus through the front door. Validate your ticket in the machine and reclaim it. With a Passe Navigo, scan it on the purple touchpad. Keep track of which stop is coming up next by following the on-board diagram or listening to recorded announcements. When you're ready to get off, push the red button to signal you want a stop, then exit through the central or rear door.

More Bus Tips: *Carnet* ticket holders—but not those buying individual tickets on the bus—can transfer from one bus to another on the same ticket (within 1.5 hours, revalidate ticket on next bus), but you can't do a round-trip or hop on and off on the same line. You can use the same ticket to transfer between buses and tramlines, but you can't transfer between the bus and Métro/RER systems.

By Taxi

Parisian taxis are reasonable, especially for couples and families. Fares and supplements (described in English on the rear windows) are straightforward and tightly regulated.

A taxi can fit three people comfortably. Cabbies are legally required to accept four passengers, though they don't always like it. Beyond three passengers, expect to pay €3 extra per person.

Rates: All Parisian taxis start with €2.60 on the meter and have a minimum charge of €7. A 20-minute ride (e.g., Bastille to the Eiffel Tower) costs about €25. Drivers charge higher rates at rush hour, at night, all day Sunday, for extra passengers, and to the airport. To tip, round up to the next euro (at least €0.50).

The A, B, or C lights on a taxi's rooftop sign correspond to hourly rates, which vary with the time of day and day of the week (for example, the A rate of €32.50/hour applies Mon-Sat 10:00-17:00). Tired travelers need not bother with these mostly subtle differences in fares—if you need a cab, take it.

Scenic Buses for Tourists

These scenic bus routes provide a great, cheap, and convenient introduction to the city.

Bus #69 runs east-west between the Eiffel Tower and Père Lachaise Cemetery by way of Rue Cler, Quai d'Orsay, the Louvre, and the Marais.

Bus #87 links the Marais and Rue Cler areas, but stays mostly on the Left Bank, connecting the Eiffel Tower, St. Sulpice Church, Luxembourg Garden, St. Germain-des-Prés, the Latin Quarter, the Bastille, and Gare de Lyon.

Bus #24 runs east-west along the Seine riverbank from Gare St. Lazare to Madeleine, Place de la Concorde, Orsay Museum, the Louvre, St. Michel, Notre-Dame, and Jardin des Plantes.

Bus #63 is another good east-west route, connecting Trocadéro (Eiffel Tower), Pont de l'Alma, Orsay Museum, St. Sulpice, Luxembourg Garden, Latin Quarter/Panthéon, and Gare de Lyon.

Bus #73 is one of Paris' most scenic lines, starting at the Orsay Museum and running westbound around Place de la Concorde, then up the Champs-Elysées, around the Arc de Triomphe, and down Avenue Charles de Gaulle to the La Défense business district.

How to Catch *un Taxi*: You can try waving down a taxi, but it's often easier to ask someone for the nearest taxi stand ("*Où est une station de taxi?*"; oo ay ewn stah-see-ohn duh tahk-see). Taxi stands are indicated by a circled "T" on good city maps and on many maps in this book. To order a taxi in English, call the reservation line for the G7 cab company (tel. 01 41 27 66 99), or ask your hotelier or waiter to call for you. When you summon a taxi by phone, a €4 surcharge is added to the fare (€7 if you schedule a timed pickup).

To download a taxi app, search for either "Taxi G7" or "Taxis Bleus" (the two major companies, both available in English).

If you need to catch a train or flight early in the morning, book a taxi the day before (especially for weekday departures). Some taxi companies require a €5 reservation fee by credit card for weekday morning rush-hour departures (7:00-10:00).

By Bike

Paris is surprisingly easy by bicycle. The city is flat, and riders have access to more than 370 miles of bike lanes and many of the priority lanes for buses and taxis (be careful on these). You can rent from a bike-rental shop or use the city-operated Vélib' bikes (details later). All bike-rental shops have good route suggestions. I biked along the river from Notre-Dame to the Eiffel Tower in 15 wonderfully scenic minutes. The riverside promenade between the Orsay Museum and Pont de l'Alma is magnificent for biking.

The TIs have a helpful "Paris à Vélo" map, which shows all the dedicated bike paths. Many other versions are available for sale at newsstand kiosks, some bookstores, and department stores.

Rental Bikes: **Bike About Tours** is your best bet for rental, with good information and kid-friendly solutions such as baby seats, tandem attachments, and kid-sized bikes (bike rental—€15/day during office hours, €20/24 hours, includes lock and helmet; mid-Feb-Nov Thu-Tue 9:30-17:30, closed Wed; closed Dec-mid-Feb; shop/café—called the Yellow Jersey Café—at 17 Rue du Pont Louis Philippe, Mo: Hôtel de Ville, mobile 06 18 80 84 92, www.bikeabouttours.com).

Vélib' Bikes: The city's Vélib' program (from *vélo* + *libre* = "bike freedom" or "free bike") gives residents and foreigners alike access to more than 20,000 bikes at nearly 1,500 stations scattered around the city. While the curbside stations only accept American Express or chip-and-PIN credit cards, any kind of credit card will work if you buy a subscription in advance online at http://en.velib.paris.fr. The subscription process is easy to follow; select the "Short-Term Subscription" to create a PIN, pay, and get an ID number. To pick up a bike, go to any bike rack, enter your ID number and PIN at the machine (all have English instructions), and away you go! Make sure to pick a bike in working order; if a bike has a problem, locals will

Bike tours can be fun and informative.

turn the seat backward (€1.70/1 day, €8/7 days, tel. 01 30 79 79 30).

Arriving and Departing

Whether you're aiming to catch a train or plane, budget plenty of time to reach your departure point. Paris is a big, crowded city, and getting across town on time is a goal you'll share with millions of other harried people. Factor in traffic delays and walking time through huge stations and vast terminals.

By Plane

CHARLES DE GAULLE AIRPORT

Paris' main airport (airport code: CDG) has three terminals: T-1, T-2, and T-3. Most flights from the US use T-1 or T-2 (check your ticket). You can travel between terminals on the free CDGVAL shuttle train (departs every 5 minutes, 24/7, 30 minutes).

When leaving Paris, make sure you know which terminal you are departing from (if it's T-2, you'll also need to know which hall you're leaving from—they're labeled *A* through *F*). For flight info, visit www.adp.fr.

Car-rental offices, TIs, post offices, pharmacies, and ATMs are all well-signed. All terminals have shops, cafés, and bars. T-2 has a **train station,** with suburban trains into Paris (described later), as well as longer-distance trains to the rest of France (including high-speed TGV trains).

Getting between Charles de Gaulle and Paris: Buses, airport vans, commuter trains, and taxis link the airport's terminals with central Paris. Total travel time to your hotel should be around 1.5 hours by bus and Métro, one hour by train and Métro, or 50 minutes by taxi.

By RoissyBus: The RoissyBus drops you off at the Opéra Métro stop in central Paris (€11.50, runs 6:00-23:00, 3-4/hour, 50 minutes, buy ticket at airport Paris Tourisme desk, ticket machine, or on bus, tel. 3246, www.ratp.fr/en).

Rick's Tip: *When deciding how to get from Charles de Gaulle airport into Paris, keep in mind that* **using buses and taxis requires shorter walks than taking suburban trains.** *Also remember that transfers to Métro lines often involve stairs.*

By Le Bus Direct: Several bus routes drop travelers at convenient points in and near the city (€17 one-way, €30 round-trip, runs 5:45-22:30, 2/hour, Wi-Fi and power outlets, toll tel. 08 92 35 08 20, www.lebusdirect.com). **Bus #2** goes to Porte Maillot (with connections to Beauvais Airport), the Arc de Triomphe (Etoile stop, 1 Avenue Carnot, 50 minutes), the Trocadéro (10 Place du Trocadéro, near Avenue d'Eylau), and ends near the Eiffel Tower at 20 Avenue de Suffren (1.25 hours). **Bus #4** runs to Gare de Lyon (45 minutes) and the Montparnasse Tower/train station (1.25 hours). **Bus #3** goes to Orly Airport (€21, 1.25 hours). You can book tickets online (must print out and bring with you) or pay the driver (see www.lebusdirect.com for round-trip and group discount details). All Le Bus Direct stops in Paris are identified with an airplane icon above the shelter.

From **Paris *to* the airport,** catch Le Bus Direct coaches at any of these locations: on Avenue de Suffren near the Eiffel Tower, on Place du Trocadéro, Arc de Triomphe/Etoile (on Avenue Mac Mahon—the non-Champs-Elysées side), Porte Maillot (on Boulevard Gouvion St-Cyr—east side of the Palais des Congrès), Gare Montparnasse (on Rue du Commandant René Mouchotte—facing the station with the tower behind you, it's around the left side), or Gare de Lyon (look for *Navette-Aéroport* signs, and find the stop on Boulevard Diderot across from Café Les Deux Savoies).

By Suburban Train (formerly called RER): Paris' Train-B is the fastest public-transit option for getting between the airport and the city center (€9.75, runs

5:00-24:00, 4/hour, about 35 minutes). It runs directly to well-located Train-B/Métro stations, including Gare du Nord, Châtelet-Les Halles, St. Michel, and Luxembourg. The train is handy and cheap, but it can require walking with your luggage through big, crowded stations and may include stairs. If you've been to Paris before, these trains used to be called the RER; you may see maps or websites still using the old name. For step-by-step instructions on taking the train into Paris, see www.parisbytrain.com (under "CDG Airport to Paris RER Trains").

To **return to the airport by suburban train** from central Paris, allow plenty of time to get to your departure gate. Your Métro or bus ticket is not valid on Train-B to the airport (but a Passe Navigo is); buy the ticket at any Métro or suburban train station from a clerk or the machines (bills of €20 or less, some American credit cards also work). When you catch your train, make sure the sign over the platform shows *Aéroport Roissy-Charles de Gaulle* as a stop served. (The line splits, so not every Train-B serves the airport.) If you're not clear, ask another rider, *"Air-o-por sharl duh gaul?"*

By Airport Van: Shuttle vans work best for trips from your hotel to the airport, and can be a good value for single travelers and big families (about €32 for one person, €46 for two, €58 for three; have hotelier book at least a day in advance).

By Taxi or Uber: The 50-minute trip costs about €50-65. **Taxis** are less appealing on weekday mornings as traffic into Paris can be bad—in that case, the train is likely a better option. Don't take an unauthorized taxi from cabbies greeting you on arrival. Official taxi stands are well-signed.

For trips from Paris to the airport, have your hotel arrange it. Specify that you want a real taxi (*un taxi normal*), not a more expensive limo service. For weekday morning departures (7:00-10:00), reserve at least a day ahead (€7 reservation fee payable by credit card). For more on taxis in Paris, see page 114.

Uber offers Paris airport pickup and drop-off for the same rates as taxis, but since they can't use the bus-only lanes (normal taxis can), expect some added time.

By Private Car Service: **Paris Webservices** will meet you inside the terminal and wait if you're late (€85 one-way for up to two people, about €120-225 round-trip for up to four people, tel. 01 45 56 91 67 or 09 52 06 02 59, www.pariswebservices.com).

Car Rental: Car-rental desks are well-signed from the arrival halls. Be prepared for a maze of ramps as you drive away from the lot—get directions from the rental clerks when you do the paperwork.

When **returning your car,** allow ample time to reach the drop-off lots. There are separate rental return lots depending on your T-2 departure hall—and imperfect signage can make the return lots especially confusing to navigate.

ORLY AIRPORT

This easy-to-navigate airport (airport code: ORY) feels small, but has all the services you'd expect at a major airport (www.adp.fr). Orly is good for rental-car pickup and drop-off, as it's closer to Paris and far easier to navigate than Charles de Gaulle Airport. Orly has two terminals: Ouest (west) and Sud (south). You can connect the two terminals with the free Orlyval shuttle train (well-signed) or with any of the shuttle buses that also travel into downtown Paris.

Getting between Orly and Paris: Shuttle buses *(navettes)*, suburban trains, taxis, and airport vans connect Paris with either terminal.

By Bus: Bus bays are found in the Sud terminal outside exits L and G, and in the Ouest terminal outside exit D.

Le Bus Direct route #1 runs to Gare Montparnasse, Invalides, and Etoile Métro stops. For Rue Cler hotels, take Le Bus Direct to the Eiffel Tower stop, then walk 15 minutes across the Champ de Mars park to your hotel. Buses depart from the arrivals level—Ouest exit B-C or Sud exit L—look for signs to *navettes* (€12 one-way, €20 round-trip, 4/hour, 40 minutes to the Eiffel Tower, buy ticket from driver or book online, store the ticket on your smartphone or print it out and bring your ticket with you). See www.lebusdirect.com for details on round-trip and group discounts.

For the cheapest access to the Marais area, take **tram line 7** from outside the Sud terminal (direction: Villejuif-Louis Aragon) to the Villejuif Métro station (€3.40—plus one Métro ticket, 4/hour, 45 minutes).

The next two bus options take you to the **Train-B,** with access to the Luxembourg Garden area, Notre-Dame Cathedral, handy Métro line 1 at the Châtelet stop, Gare du Nord, and Charles de Gaulle Airport. The **Orlybus** goes directly to the Denfert-Rochereau Métro and Train-B stations (€8, 3/hour, 30 minutes). The **Orlyval shuttle train** takes you to the Antony Train-B station (€12.05, 6/hour, 40 minutes, buy ticket to Paris—not just to Antony—before boarding, smart to purchase your 10-ticket *carnet* for the Métro here too). The Orlyval train leaves from the departure level at both terminals. Take Train-B in direction Mitry-Claye or Aéroport Charles de Gaulle to reach central Paris stops.

For access to Left Bank neighborhoods via **Train-C,** take the bus marked ***Go Paris*** to the Pont de Rungis station, then catch Train-C (direction: Versailles Château Rive Gauche or Pontoise) to St. Michel, Musée d'Orsay, Invalides, or Pont de l'Alma (€1.90 shuttle only, €6.25 combo-ticket includes Train-C, 4/hour, 35 minutes).

By Taxi: Taxis are outside the Ouest terminal exit B, and to the far right as you leave the Sud terminal at exit M. Allow 30 minutes for a taxi ride into central Paris (fixed fare of €30 for Left Bank, €35 for Right Bank).

BEAUVAIS AIRPORT

Budget airlines such as Ryanair use this small airport, offering cheap airfares but leaving you 50 miles north of Paris. Still, this airport has direct buses to Paris and is handy for travelers heading to Normandy or Belgium (car rental available). The airport is basic, waiting areas are crowded, and services are sparse (airport code: BVA, airport tel. 08 92 68 20 66, www.aeroportbeauvais.com).

Getting Between Beauvais and Paris: You can take a bus (1.5 hours), train (at least 2 hours), or taxi (1.5 hours).

By Bus: Buses depart from the airport when they're full (about 20 minutes after flights arrive) and take 1.5 hours to reach Paris. Buy your ticket (€17 one-way, €16 online) at the little kiosk to the right as you exit the airport. Buses arrive at Porte Maillot on the west edge of Paris (on Métro line 1 and Train-C).

Buses heading to Beauvais Airport leave from Porte Maillot about 3.5 hours before scheduled flight departures. Catch the bus in the parking lot on Boulevard Pershing next to the Hyatt Regency. Arrive with enough time to purchase your bus ticket before boarding or buy online at http://tickets.aeroportbeauvais.com.

By Train: Trains connect Beauvais' city center and Paris' Gare du Nord (20/day, 1.5 hours). To reach Beauvais' train station, take the Hôtel/Aéroport Navette shuttle or local bus #12 (each hourly, 25 minutes).

By Taxi: Taxis run from Beauvais Airport to Beauvais' train station or city center (€20), or to central Paris (allow €150 and 1.5 hours).

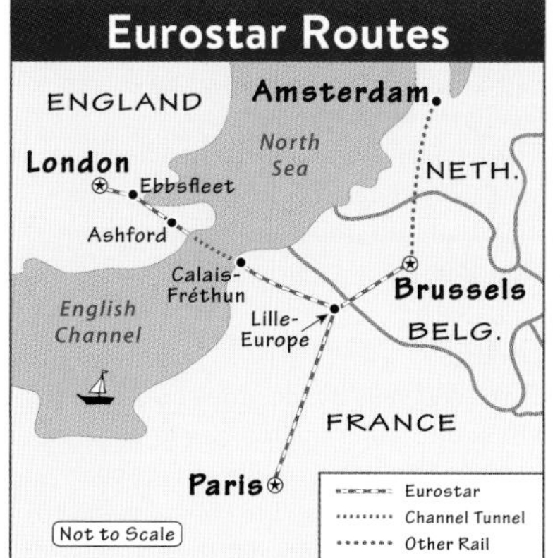

By Train

Paris is Europe's rail hub, with six major stations and one minor one:

- Gare du Nord (northbound trains)
- Gare Montparnasse (west- and southwest-bound trains)
- Gare de Lyon (southeast-bound trains)
- Gare de l'Est (eastbound trains)
- Gare St. Lazare (northwest-bound trains)
- Gare d'Austerlitz (southwest-bound trains)
- Gare de Bercy (smaller station with non-TGV southbound trains)

The main train stations have free Wi-Fi, banks or currency exchanges, ATMs, train information desks, cafés, newsstands, and clever pickpockets (pay attention in ticket lines—keep your bag firmly gripped in front of you). You'll find TIs at Gare du Nord and Gare de Lyon. Because of security concerns, not all have baggage checks. Any train station has schedule information, can make reservations, and can sell tickets for any destination.

Each station offers two types of rail service: long distance to other cities, called **Grandes Lignes** (major lines, TGV—also called "InOui"—or TER trains); and commuter service to nearby areas, called Banlieue, Transilien, or suburban trains (lines A-K, formerly called RER). When arriving by Métro, follow signs for *Grandes Lignes-SNCF* to find the main tracks. Métro and suburban train lines A-K, as well as buses and taxis, are well-marked at every station.

For clear communication at ticket/info windows, it helps to write down the date and ticket you want. For instance: "28/05 Paris-Nord→Lyon dep. 18:30." All stations have helpful information booths *(accueil);* the bigger stations have roving helpers, usually wearing red or blue vests.

GARE DU NORD

The granddaddy of Paris' train stations serves cities in northern France and international destinations north of Paris, including Copenhagen, Amsterdam, and London via the Eurostar (for more on the Eurostar, see www.ricksteves.com/eurostar).

From Gare du Nord to: Charles de Gaulle Airport (via Train-B, 4/hour, 35 minutes, track 41-44).

GARE MONTPARNASSE

This big, modern station covers three floors, serves lower Normandy and Brittany, and has TGV service to the Loire Valley and southwestern France, as well as suburban service to Chartres.

From Gare Montparnasse to: Chartres (14/day, 1 hour), **Amboise** (8/day in 1.5 hours with change in St-Pierre-des-Corps, requires TGV reservation; non-TGV trains leave from Gare d'Austerlitz), **Pontorson/Mont St-Michel** (5/day, 5.5 hours, via Rennes or Caen), and **Sarlat** (4/day, 6-6.5 hours, change in Libourne or Bordeaux).

GARE DE LYON

This huge, bewildering station offers TGV and regular service to southeastern France, Italy, Switzerland, and other international destinations. **Le Bus Direct** coaches—to Gare Montparnasse (easy transfer to Orly Airport) and direct to Charles de Gaulle Airport—stop outside the station's main entrance. They are signed *Navette-Aéroport.*

From Gare de Lyon to: Beaune (roughly hourly at rush hour but few midday, 2.5 hours, most require change in Dijon; direct trains from Paris' Bercy station take an hour longer), **Chamonix** (7/day, 5.5-7 hours, some change in Switzerland), **Avignon** (10/day direct, 2.5 hours to Avignon TGV Station, 5/day in 3.5 hours to Avignon Centre-Ville Station, more connections with change—3-4 hours), **Arles** (11/day, 2 direct TGVs—4 hours, 9 with change in Avignon—5 hours), **Nice** (hourly, 6 hours, may require change, 11.5-hour night train possible out of Gare d'Austerlitz), and **Carcassonne** (8/day, 7-8 hours, 1 change, night trains leave from Gare d'Austerlitz).

GARE DE L'EST

This two-floor station (with underground Métro) serves northeastern France and international destinations east of Paris.

From Gare de l'Est to: Colmar (12/day with TGV, 3.5 hours, change in Strasbourg) and **Reims** Centre Station (12/day with TGV, 50 minutes).

GARE ST. LAZARE

This compact station serves upper Normandy, including Rouen and Giverny.

From Gare St. Lazare to: Giverny (train to Vernon, 8/day Mon-Sat, 6/day Sun, 45 minutes), **Honfleur** (13/day, 2-3.5 hours, via Lisieux, Deauville, or Le Havre, then bus), **Bayeux** (9/day, 2.5 hours, some change in Caen), and **Pontorson/Mont St-Michel** (2/day, 4-5.5 hours, via Caen; more trains from Gare Montparnasse).

GARE D'AUSTERLITZ

This small station currently provides non-TGV service to the Loire Valley, southwestern France, and Spain.

From Gare d'Austerlitz to: Versailles (via Train-C, 4/hour, 35 minutes), **Amboise** (3/day direct in 2 hours, 5/day with transfer in Blois or Les Aubrais-Orléans; faster TGV connection from Gare Montparnasse), and **Sarlat** (1/day, 6.5 hours, requires change to bus in Souillac, 3 more/day via Gare Montparnasse).

GARE DE BERCY

This smaller station mostly handles southbound non-TGV trains, but some TGV trains do stop here in peak season (Mo: Bercy).

By Bus

Buses generally provide the cheapest—if less comfortable and more time-consuming—transportation to major European cities. The bus is also the cheapest way to cross the English Channel; book at least two days in advance for the best fares. Eurolines is the old stand-by; two relative newcomers (Ouibus and Flixbus) are cutting prices drastically for travelers and amping up onboard comfort with snacks you can purchase, Wi-Fi, and easy, online booking. These companies provide service usually between train stations and airports within France and to many international destinations.

OuiBus has routes mostly within France but serves some European cities as well (central Paris stop is at Gare de Bercy, Mo: Bercy, toll tel. 08 92 68 00 68, www.ouibus.com). **FlixBus** connects key cities within France and throughout Europe, often from secondary airports and train stations (central Paris stop is near Porte Maillot at 16 Boulevard Pershing, Mo: Porte Maillot, handy eticket system and smartphone app, tel. 01 76 36 04 12, www.flixbus.com). **Eurolines'** buses depart from Paris' Gare Routière du Paris-Gallieni in the suburb of Bagnolet (28 Avenue du Général de Gaulle, Mo: Gallieni, toll tel. 08 92 89 90 91; from the US, dial 011 33 1 41 86 24 21, www.eurolines.com).

By Car

A car is nothing but a headache in Paris: Park it and use public transportation. Street parking is generally free at night (20:00-9:00) and all day Sunday. To pay for streetside parking, you must go to a *tabac* shop and buy a parking card (*une carte de stationnement*), sold in €10 and €30 denominations (figure €4/hour in central Paris). Insert the card into the meter (chip-side in) and punch the desired amount of time, then take the receipt and display it in your windshield. Meters limit street parking to a maximum of two hours.

Underground garages are plentiful. You'll find them under Ecole Militaire, St. Sulpice Church, Les Invalides, the Bastille, and the Panthéon; all charge about €35-50/day (€66/3 days, €10/day more after that, for locations see www.vincipark.com). Some hotels offer parking for less—ask your hotelier.

For a longer stay, park for less at an airport (about €15/day) and take public transport or a taxi into the city. Orly is closer and easier for drivers to navigate than Charles de Gaulle.

NEAR PARIS

Day-trippers looking for a refreshing change from urban Paris can choose among these fascinating destinations. I've listed them in order of importance. If you have time for only one sight, visit Versailles.

The palace at Versailles, fit for a king and queen, is Europe's best. Chartres Cathedral is a Gothic masterpiece with magnificent stained glass. The city of Reims has a knockout cathedral and Champagne *caves*, too. For art lovers, Monet's flowery Giverny gardens are an Impressionist dream.

The Neptune fountain at Versailles

Versailles

Every king's dream, Versailles (vehr-"sigh") was the residence of French monarchs and the cultural heartbeat of Europe for about 100 years—until the Revolution of 1789 changed all that.

Versailles offers three ▲▲▲ blockbuster sights: The main attraction is the palace itself, the **Château,** where you'll walk through dozens of lavish, chandeliered rooms once inhabited by the Sun King Louis XIV and his successors. Next come the expansive **Gardens,** a landscaped wonderland dotted with statues and fountains. The pastoral **Trianon Palaces and Domaine de Marie-Antoinette,** designed for frolicking blue bloods and featuring several small palaces, are perfect for getting away from the mobs at the Château.

Getting There

To reach Versailles, 10 miles west of Paris, take the **Train-C** "Versailles Château Rive Gauche" (abbreviated "Versailles Chât" or "Versailles RG") from any of these Paris train stops: Gare d'Austerlitz, St. Michel, Musée d'Orsay, Invalides, Pont de l'Alma, or Champ de Mars (€7.10 round-trip, 4/hour). You can also buy train tickets at any Métro ticket window in Paris (includes connection from that Métro stop to the suburban train).

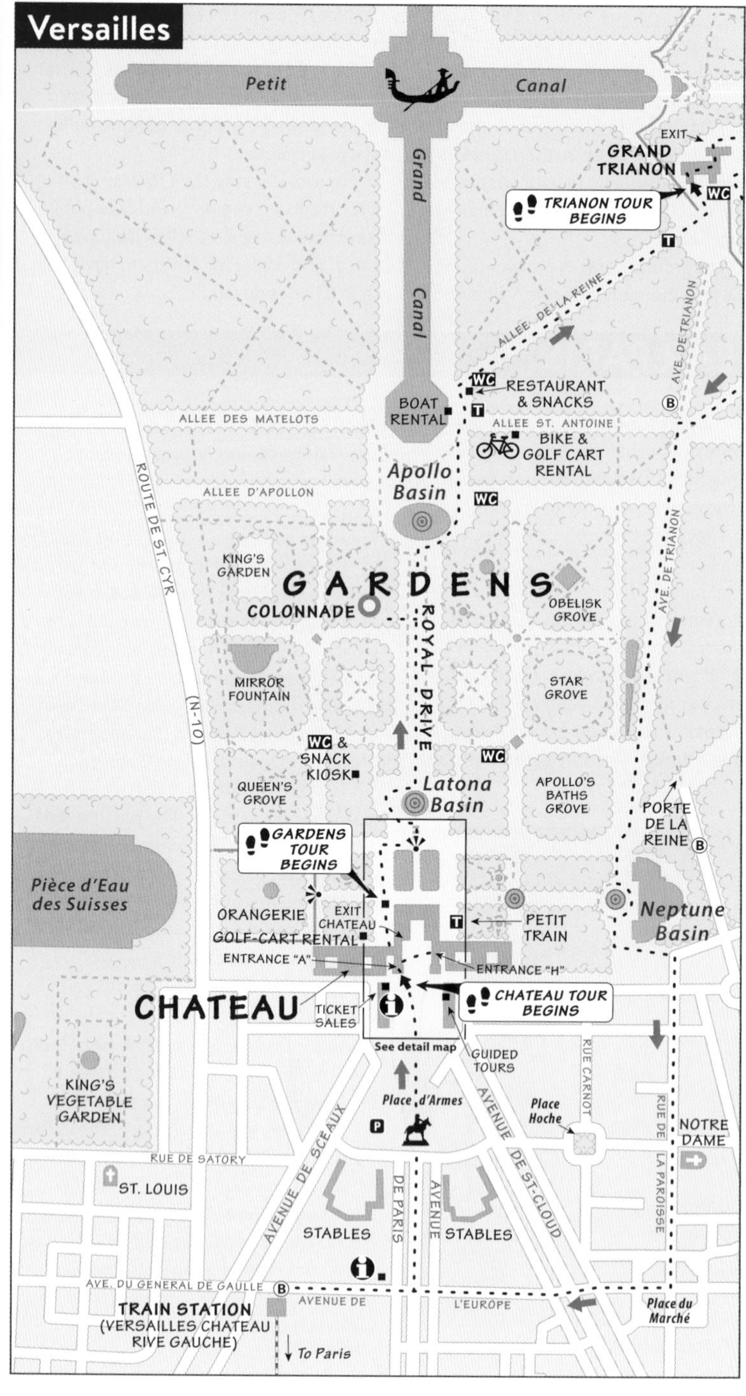
Versailles
Petit
Canal
Grand
Canal
EXIT
GRAND TRIANON
WC
TRIANON TOUR BEGINS
ALLEE DE LA REINE
AVE. DE TRIANON
RESTAURANT & SNACKS
BOAT RENTAL
ALLEE DES MATELOTS
ALLEE ST. ANTOINE
BIKE & GOLF CART RENTAL
Apollo Basin
ROUTE DE ST. CYR
(N-10)
ALLEE D'APOLLON
KING'S GARDEN
GARDENS
COLONNADE
ROYAL DRIVE
OBELISK GROVE
MIRROR FOUNTAIN
STAR GROVE
WC & SNACK KIOSK
QUEEN'S GROVE
Latona Basin
APOLLO'S BATHS GROVE
PORTE DE LA REINE
GARDENS TOUR BEGINS
Pièce d'Eau des Suisses
ORANGERIE
EXIT CHATEAU
GOLF-CART RENTAL
ENTRANCE "A"
ENTRANCE "H"
PETIT TRAIN
Neptune Basin
CHATEAU
TICKET SALES
CHATEAU TOUR BEGINS
See detail map
GUIDED TOURS
RUE CARNOT
KING'S VEGETABLE GARDEN
Place d'Armes
AVENUE DE SCEAUX
AVENUE DE ST-CLOUD
Place Hoche
RUE DE LA PAROISSE
NOTRE DAME
RUE DE SATORY
ST. LOUIS
DE PARIS
AVENUE
STABLES
STABLES
AVE. DU GENERAL DE GAULLE
TRAIN STATION (VERSAILLES CHATEAU RIVE GAUCHE)
AVENUE DE
L'EUROPE
Place du Marché
To Paris

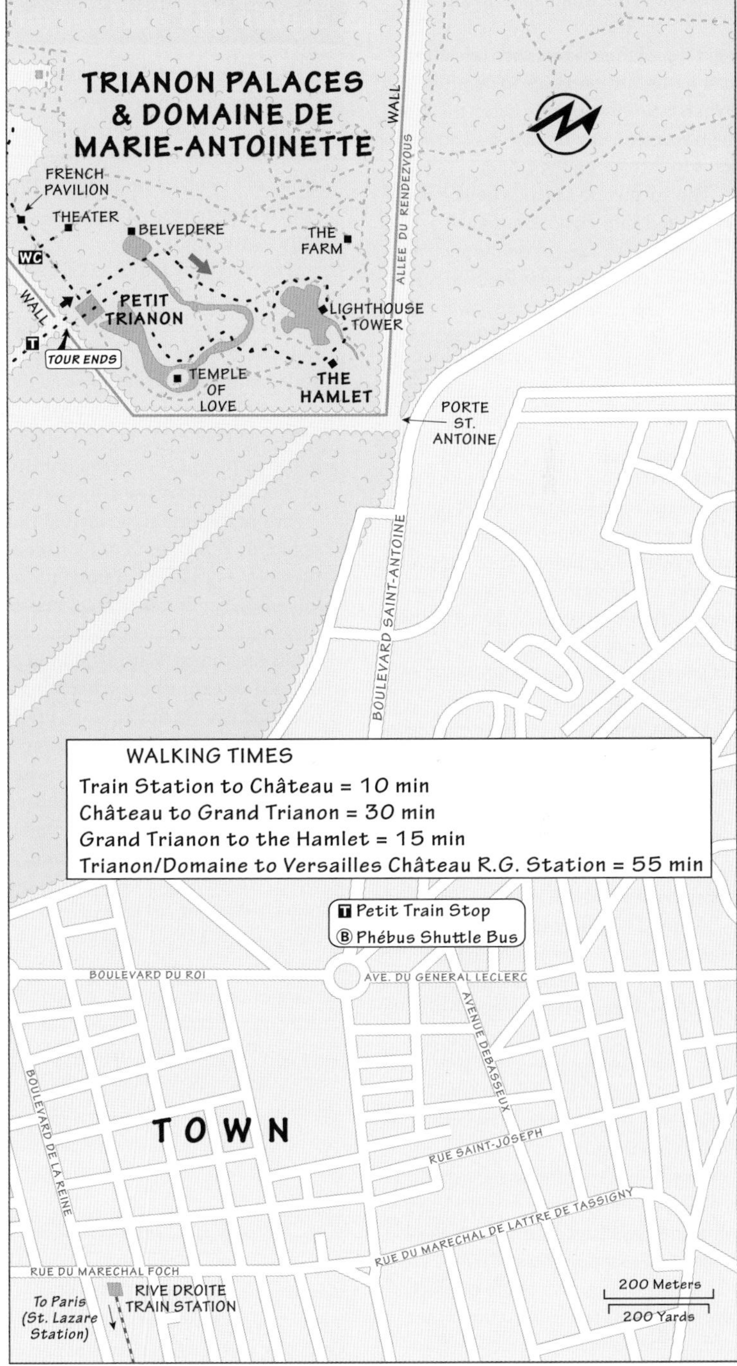
TRIANON PALACES
& DOMAINE DE
MARIE-ANTOINETTE
WALL
ALLEE DU RENDEZVOUS
FRENCH PAVILION
THEATER
BELVEDERE
THE FARM
WC
WALL
PETIT TRIANON
LIGHTHOUSE TOWER
TOUR ENDS
TEMPLE OF LOVE
THE HAMLET
PORTE ST. ANTOINE
BOULEVARD SAINT-ANTOINE
WALKING TIMES
Train Station to Château = 10 min
Château to Grand Trianon = 30 min
Grand Trianon to the Hamlet = 15 min
Trianon/Domaine to Versailles Château R.G. Station = 55 min
Petit Train Stop
Phébus Shuttle Bus
BOULEVARD DU ROI
AVE. DU GENERAL LECLERC
AVENUE DEBASSEUX
BOULEVARD DE LA REINE
TOWN
RUE SAINT-JOSEPH
RUE DU MARECHAL DE LATTRE DE TASSIGNY
RUE DU MARECHAL FOCH
RIVE DROITE TRAIN STATION
To Paris (St. Lazare Station)
200 Meters
200 Yards

To reach the Château from the Versailles train station, follow the flow: Turn right out of the station, then left at the first boulevard, and walk 10 minutes. When returning to Paris, catch the first train you see: All trains serve all downtown Paris RER stops on the C line.

The 30-minute **taxi** ride between Versailles and Paris costs about €60.

If you have a **car,** get on the *périphérique* freeway that circles Paris, and take the toll-free A-13 autoroute toward Rouen. Exit at Versailles, follow signs to *Versailles Château*, and park in the big pay lot at the foot of the Château on Place d'Armes.

Orientation

Day Plan: Versailles merits a full sightseeing day and is much more enjoyable with a relaxed, unhurried approach. Allow 1.5 hours each for the Château, Gardens, and Trianon/Domaine. Add another two hours for round-trip transit, plus another hour for lunch, and you're looking at an eight-hour day—at the very least.

Cost: Château-€15 (includes audioguide); **Trianon Palaces and Domaine de Marie-Antoinette**-€10; **Gardens**-free, except on Spectacle days, when the fountains are on and admission is €9 (weekends April-Oct plus many Tue; see "Spectacles in the Gardens," later).

Hours: The **Château** is open April-Oct Tue-Sun 9:00-18:30, Nov-March until 17:30. The **Trianon Palaces and Domaine de Marie-Antoinette** are open April-Oct Tue-Sun 12:00-18:30, Nov-March until 17:30. The **Gardens** are open April-Oct daily 8:00-20:30; Nov-March Tue-Sun 8:00-18:00. All palace buildings are closed Monday year-round.

Passes: To save money and avoid the long ticket-buying line, buy a **Paris Museum Pass** (see page 40) or a **Versailles Le Passeport Pass** (€18/one day, €25 on Spectacle days), both of which give you access to the most important parts of the complex and include the Château audioguide.

Buying Passes and Tickets: Ideally, buy your ticket or pass before arriving at Versailles from any Paris TI, FNAC department store, or www.chateauversailles.fr. In Versailles, you can buy tickets or passes

Louis XIV and Versailles

Versailles is the architectural embodiment of a time when society was divided into rulers and the ruled. To some it's the pinnacle of civilization; to others, it's a sign of a civilization in decay. Either way, it remains one of Europe's most impressive sights.

The Sun King Louis XIV (r. 1643-1715) created Versailles, spending freely from the public treasury to turn his dad's hunting lodge into a palace fit for the gods (among whom he counted himself). His reasons were partly political—at Versailles, Louis consolidated his government's scattered ministries so that he could personally control policy. More important, he invited France's nobles to Versailles in order to control them. Living a life of almost enforced idleness, the "domesticated" aristocracy couldn't interfere with the way Louis ran things. With 18 million people united under one king, a booming economy, and a powerful military, France was Europe's number-one power.

Around 1700, Versailles was the cultural heartbeat of Europe, and French culture was at its zenith. Throughout Europe, when you said "the king," you were referring to the French king—Louis XIV. Every king wanted a palace like Versailles. Everyone learned French. French taste in clothes, hairstyles, table manners, theater, music, art, and kissing spread across the Continent. That cultural dominance continued, to some extent, right up to modern times.

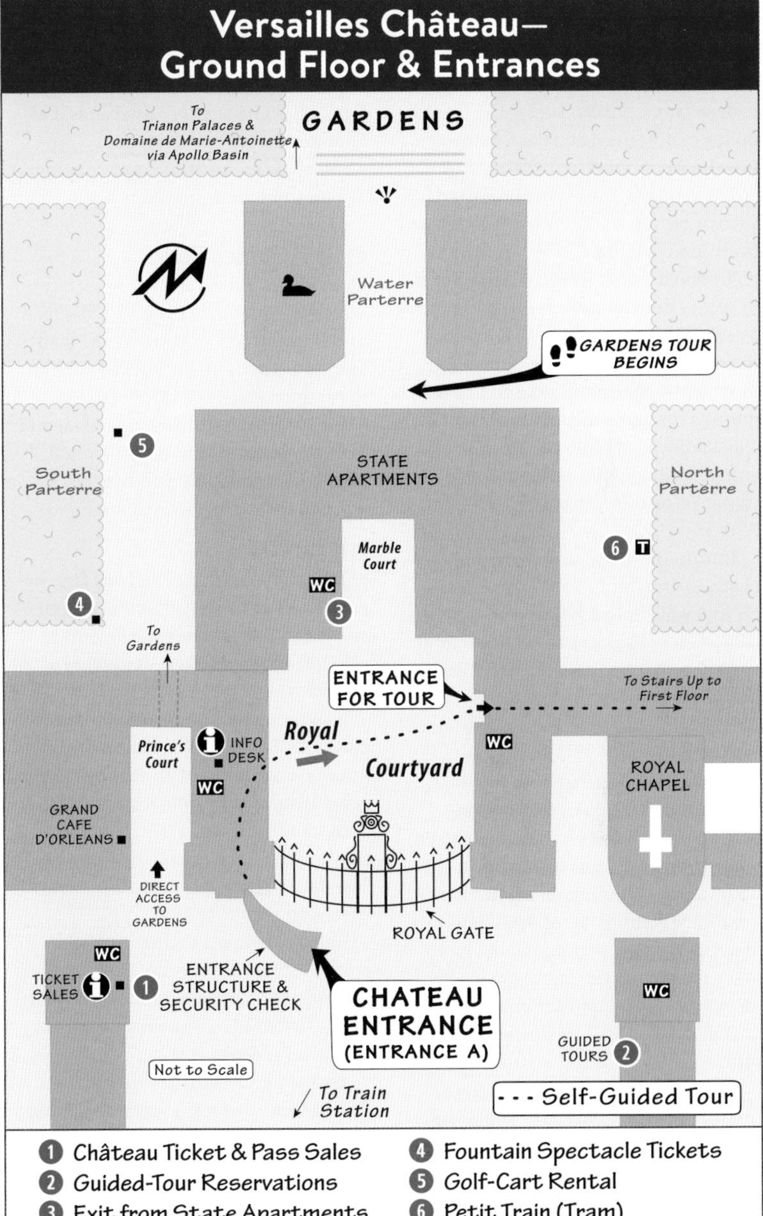

1 Château Ticket & Pass Sales
2 Guided-Tour Reservations
3 Exit from State Apartments
4 Fountain Spectacle Tickets
5 Golf-Cart Rental
6 Petit Train (Tram)

at the rarely crowded Versailles TI (see "Information," later).

Crowd-Beating Tips: Versailles is packed May-Sept 10:00-13:00, so come early or late. Consider seeing the Gardens during midmorning and the Château in the afternoon, when crowds die down. Avoid Sundays, Tuesdays, and Saturdays (in that order), when the place is jammed from open to close.

To skip ticket-buying lines, buy tickets or passes in advance (see earlier), or book a guided tour (covered below). Unfortunately, all ticket holders—including those with advance tickets and passes—must go through the often-slow security checkpoint at the Château's Royal Gate entrance (longest lines 10:00-12:00). Only by booking a tour can you skip the security line.

Information: Tel. 01 30 83 78 00, www.chateauversailles.fr. You'll pass the city TI on your walk from the train station to the palace—it's just past the Pullman Hôtel (daily 9:00-19:00, Sun until 18:00, shorter hours in winter, tel. 01 39 24 88 88). The on-site information office is to the left of the Château.

Tours: Taking the 1.5-hour English **guided tour** lets you bypass the long security check line (€22 includes palace entry; ignore the tours hawked near the train station). Book a tour in advance on the palace website, or reserve immediately upon arrival at the guided-tours office (to the right of the Château—look for yellow *Visites Conferences* signs).

🎧 Download my free Versailles **audio tour.**

Eating: The Grand Café d'Orléans, to the left of the Château's Royal Gate entrance, offers good-value self-service meals; the sandwiches are great for picnicking in the Gardens. In the Gardens, near the Latona Fountain and clustered at the Grand Canal, you'll find several cafés and snack stands with fair prices.

Spectacles in the Gardens: The fountains at Versailles come alive at selected times; check the website for current hours and prices. **Les Grandes Eaux Musicales** has 55 fountains gushing to classical music (April-Oct Sat-Sun, plus mid-May-June Tue). On some summer weekends, **Les Grandes Eaux Nocturnes** adds a fireworks show to the music-and-fountains display (mid-June-mid-Sept).

➲ *Self-Guided Tour*

On this tour, you'll see the Château (the State Apartments of the king and queen as well as the Hall of Mirrors), the landscaped Gardens in the "backyard," and the Trianon Palaces and Domaine de Marie-Antoinette, located at the far end of the Gardens. If your time is limited, skip the Trianon/Domaine, which is a 30-minute hike from the Château.

THE CHATEAU

• *Stand in the huge courtyard and face the palace. The golden Royal Gate in the center—nearly 260 feet long and decorated with 100,000 gold leaves—is a replica of the original.*

The section of the palace with the clock is the original château, where little Louis XIV spent his happiest boyhood years. Naturally, the Sun King's private bedroom (the three arched windows beneath the clock) faced the rising sun. The palace and grounds are laid out on an east-west axis.

• *Enter the Château. Continue into the reception area (bag check and WCs), where you can pick up a free map and audioguide. Follow the crowds across the courtyard to pick up an audioguide.*

On the way to the stairs up to the first floor (and our first stop), you'll pass through a dozen ground-floor rooms (the route and displays change often). Once you climb the stairs, you reach a palatial golden-brown room, with a doorway that overlooks the...

Royal Chapel: Dut-dutta-dah! Every morning at 10:00, the organist and musicians struck up the music, these big golden doors opened, and Louis XIV

Louis XIV attended Mass in Versailles' Royal Chapel.

and his family stepped onto the balcony to attend Mass. While Louis looked down on the golden altar, the lowly nobles on the ground floor knelt with their backs to the altar and looked up—worshipping Louis worshipping God.

• *Enter the next room, with a colorful painting on the ceiling.*

Hercules Drawing Room: Pleasure ruled. The main suppers, balls, and receptions were held in this room. Picture elegant partygoers in fine silks, wigs, rouge, lipstick, and fake moles (and that's just the men) as they danced to the strains of a string quartet.

• *From here on, it's a one-way tour—getting lost is not allowed.*

The King's Wing: The names of the rooms generally come from the paintings on the ceilings. For instance, the Venus room was the royal make-out space, where couples would cavort beneath the goddess of love, floating on the ceiling. In the **Diana Room,** Louis and his men played pool on a table that stood in the center of the room, while ladies sat surrounding them on Persian-carpet cushions, and music wafted in from next door.

Also known as the Guard Room (as it was the room for Louis' Swiss bodyguards), the red **Mars Room** is decorated with a military flair. The **Mercury Room** may have served as Louis' official (not actual) bedroom, where the Sun King would ritually rise each morning to warm his subjects.

The **Apollo Room** was the grand throne room. Louis held court from a 10-foot-tall, silver-and-gold, canopied throne on a raised platform placed in the center of the room. Even when the king was away, passing courtiers had to bow to the empty throne.

The final room of the King's Wing is the **War Room,** depicting Louis' victories—in marble, gilding, stucco, and paint.

• *Next you'll visit the magnificent...*

Hall of Mirrors: No one had ever seen anything like this hall when it was opened. Mirrors were still a great luxury at the time, and the number and size of these monsters were astounding. The hall is nearly 250 feet long. There are 17 arched mirrors, matched by 17 windows letting in that breathtaking view of the Gardens.

In another age altogether, this is where Germany and the Allies signed the Treaty of Versailles, ending World War I (and,

The vast painted ceiling of the Hercules Drawing Room

A *Hall of Mirrors*

B *A royal bedchamber*

C *Louis XIV, the Sun King*

D *Domaine de Marie-Antoinette*

Getting Around the Gardens

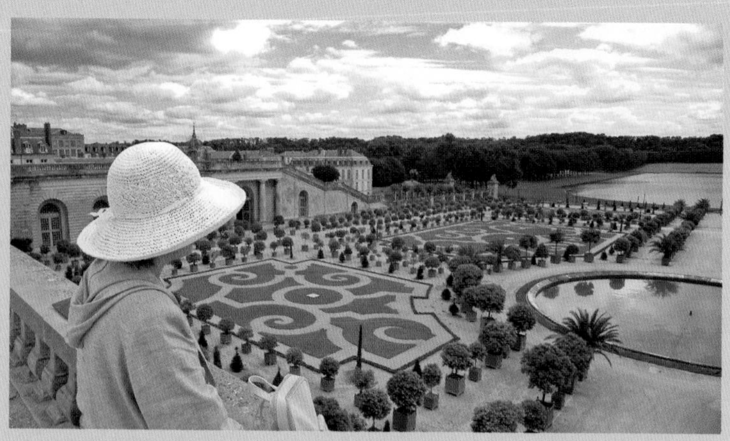

On Foot: It's a 45-minute walk from the palace and down the Grand Canal to the far end of Domaine de Marie-Antoinette. Allow more time for stops.

By Bike: You can bike through the gardens, but not inside the grounds of the Trianon/Domaine (about €7/hour or €16/half-day).

By *Petit Train:* The slow-moving tram leaves from behind the Château (north side) and makes a one-way loop, stopping at the Petit and Grand Trianons (entry points to Domaine de Marie-Antoinette), and then the Grand Canal before returning to the Château (€7.50, round-trip only, free under age 11, 4/hour, runs 10:00-18:00, 11:00-17:00 in winter). You can hop on or off the train at stops.

By Golf Cart: A cart makes for a fun drive, though it's not allowed off its circuit or in the Trianon/Domaine. Late fees are steep. To go out to the Hamlet, sightsee quickly, and return within your allotted hour, you'll need to rent a cart at the Grand Canal and put the pedal to the metal (€32/hour, €8/15 minutes after that, 4-person limit per cart, rent down by canal or just behind Château, near *petit train* stop).

By Shuttle Bus: Phébus runs an hourly TRI line shuttle bus between the Versailles Château Rive Gauche train station and the Trianon/Domaine (but doesn't stop at the Château). It works well for the end of your Versailles visit, if you want to go directly from the Trianon/Domaine to the train station (€2 or one Métro ticket, mid-April-Oct only, check schedule for "Ligne TRI" at www.phebus.tm.fr or at small Phébus office across from Versailles Château Rive Gauche train station, near McDonald's).

some say, starting World War II).

• *Next up: the queen's half of the palace.*

The Queen's Wing: The King's Wing was mostly ceremonial and used as a series of reception rooms; the Queen's Wing is more intimate.

The **Queen's Bedchamber** was where the queen rendezvoused with her husband. Two queens died here, and this is where 19 princes were born. Louis XIV made a point of sleeping with the queen as often as possible, regardless of whose tiara he tickled earlier in the evening. This room looks just like it did in the days of the last queen, Marie-Antoinette, who substantially redecorated the entire wing. That's her bust over the fireplace, and the double eagle of her native Austria in the corners.

THE GARDENS

Louis XIV was a divine-right ruler. One way he proved it was by controlling nature like a god. These lavish grounds—elaborately planned, pruned, and decorated—showed everyone that Louis was in total command. Louis loved his gardens and, until his last days, presided over their care. He personally led VIPs through them and threw his biggest parties here.

Rick's Tip: *It's fun pedaling around the greatest royal park in all of Europe. A* **bike-rental station** *is by the Grand Canal, with kid-size bikes and tandems available.*

TRIANON PALACES AND DOMAINE DE MARIE-ANTOINETTE

Versailles began as an escape from the pressures of kingship. But in a short time, the Château had become as busy as Paris ever was. Louis XIV needed an escape from his escape and built a smaller palace out in the boonies. Delicate, pink, and set amid gardens, the **Grand Trianon** was the perfect summer getaway. Nearby is the fantasy world of palaces, ponds, pavilions, and pleasure gardens called the **Domaine de Marie-Antoinette.**

Chartres

Chartres, about 50 miles southwest of Paris, gives travelers a pleasant break in a lively, midsize town with a thriving, pedestrian-friendly old center. But the big reason to come to Chartres (shar-truh) is to see its famous cathedral—arguably Europe's best example of pure Gothic.

Orientation

Day Plan: Upon arrival in Chartres, head for the cathedral. Allow an hour to savor the church on your own, then join the excellent 1.25-hour cathedral tour led by Malcolm Miller. Take another hour or two to wander the appealing old city. You can rent an audioguide from the TI, or better, just stroll. Chartres has a picnic-perfect park (behind the cathedral), peaceful lanes, and a colorful pedestrian zone.

Getting There: To come for the day, leave Paris in the morning by **train** (14/day, 1 hour, depart from Gare Montparnasse). If **driving,** you'll have fine views of the cathedral and city as you approach from the A-11 autoroute.

Chartres' old town straddles the Eure River.

Arrival in Chartres: From the train station, it's a five-minute walk up Avenue Jehan de Beauce to the cathedral, or you can take a taxi for about €7.

Tourist Information: The TI is in the historic Maison du Saumon building (Mon-Sat 9:30-18:30, Sun 10:00-17:30, shorter hours off-season, 10 Rue de la Poissonnerie, tel. 02 37 18 26 26, www.chartres-tourisme.com).

Sights

▲▲▲CHARTRES CATHEDRAL

Chartres' old church burned to the ground on June 10, 1194. Some of the children who watched its destruction were actually around to help rebuild the cathedral and attend its dedication in 1260. The cathedral has a unity of architecture that captures the spirit of the Age of Faith like no other European church.

Cost and Hours: Free, €5.50 to climb the 300-step north tower; **church** open daily 8:30-19:30 (shorter hours for tower). For daily **Mass** times, call 02 37 21 59 08 or go to www.cathedrale-chartres.org (click on "*Infos Pratiques,*" then "*Horaires des Messes*").

Tours: Historian **Malcolm Miller** gives a riveting 1.25-hour tour; no reservations needed (€10, €5 for students, Easter-mid-Oct Mon-Sat at 12:00; no tours last half of Aug, on religious holidays, or if fewer than 12 people show up). Meet inside the church at the *Visites de la Cathédrale* sign. He also offers private tours (tel. 02 37 28 15 58, millerchartres@aol.com).

You can rent **audioguides** from the gift shop inside the cathedral.

Rick's Tip: Binoculars *are a big help for studying the art and stained-glass windows in the cathedral. Bring a small pair, or rent them at souvenir shops around the cathedral.*

Visiting the Cathedral: Chartres is a picture book of the entire Christian story, told through its statues, stained glass (172 windows in all), and architecture. The complete narrative can be read—from Creation to Christ's birth (north side of church), from Christ and his followers up to the present (south entrance), and then to the end of time, when Christ returns as judge (west entrance). The remarkable cohesiveness of its architecture is due to the fact that nearly the entire church

The park behind Chartres Cathedral offers fine views.

was rebuilt in just 30 years (a blink of an eye for cathedral building). Here are the highlights:

Labyrinth: Midway up the enormous nave, find the broad, round pilgrim maze inlaid in black marble on the floor. It represents a spiritual journey: Pilgrims enter from the west rim, by foot or on their knees, and wind inward, meditating, on a metaphorical journey to Jerusalem.

Rose Windows: Stand where the nave crosses the transept to view the big, round "rose" (flower-shaped) windows. All three are predominantly blue and red, and each tells a different part of the Christian story: the birth of Jesus (north rose window), Old Testament prophecies (south rose window), and Judgment Day (west rose window).

Blue Virgin Window: This very old window (mid-12th century, south wall) was the central window behind the altar of the church that burned in 1194. It survived and was reinserted into this frame in the new church around 1230. Mary's glowing dress is an example of the famed "Chartres blue," a sumptuous glass colored with cobalt.

Mary's Veil: This veil (in the Chapel of the Sacred Heart of Mary) was supposedly worn by Mary when she gave birth to Jesus. In the frenzy surrounding the fire of 1194, the veil mysteriously disappeared, only to reappear three days later (recalling the Resurrection). This was interpreted as a sign that Mary wanted a new church, and thus the building began.

Flying Buttresses: Outside, find the flying buttresses (the arches sticking out from the upper walls) that push against the pillars lining the nave inside. These help support the heavy stone ceiling and lead-over-wood roof. The result is a tall cathedral held up by slender pillars buttressed from the outside, allowing the walls to be opened up for its stained-glass windows.

Eating

Le Bistrot de la Cathédrale has an enjoyable view terrace (closed Wed, 1 Cloître Notre-Dame); **La Picoterie** is cozy and inexpensive (36 Rue des Changes); and **Le Pichet 3,** a local-products shop and bistro, makes a fun lunch stop (19 Rue du Cheval Blanc).

Blue Virgin window

Cathedral statuary

Reims

With its Gothic cathedral, Champagne *caves*, and vibrant pedestrian zone, Reims (pronounced like "rraaaance") feels both historic and youthful. And thanks to the TGV bullet train, it's less than an hour's ride from Paris.

Orientation

Reims' hard-to-miss cathedral marks the city center and makes an easy orientation landmark.

Day Plan: You can see Reims' essential sights in an easy day, either as a side trip from Paris or as a stop en route to or from Paris.

If you're day-tripping from Paris, take a morning train and explore the cathedral and city center before lunch, then spend your afternoon below ground, in a cool, chalky Champagne cellar or *cave* (pronounced "kahv"). With extra time, stroll the busy shopping streets between the cathedral and Reims-Centre train station. Rue de Vesle, Rue Condorcet, and Place Drouet d'Erlon are most interesting. A market erupts inside the dazzling Halles Boulingrin on Wednesday, Friday, and Saturday mornings.

Getting There: From Paris' Gare de l'Est Station, take the direct **TGV train** to the Reims-Centre Station (12/day, 50 minutes). TGV trains traveling to or from points east (such as Strasbourg or Colmar) use the Champagne-Ardennes Station, five miles from the center of Reims (frequent connection by local TER train or by tramway to Reims-Centre Station). **Drivers** should follow *Cathédrale* signs, and park in metered spots on or near the street approaching the cathedral (Rue Libergier) or in the well-signed Parking Cathédrale garage.

Arrival in Reims: Most sights of interest are within a 15-minute walk from the Reims-Centre train station.

Tourist Information: The main TI is located outside the cathedral's left (north) transept (TI open Easter-Sept Mon-Sat 9:00-19:00, Sun 10:00-18:00, closes earlier in off-season, tel. 03 26 77 45 00, www.reims-tourisme.com). A smaller yet handy TI lies just outside the Reims-Centre **train station** (open daily).

Rick's Tip: *Either of Reims' TIs can book a visit to the* ***Champagne caves*** *at Mumm or Martel. They'll also call a taxi or a cheaper pedal-powered pedicab to get you to any cave. TIs also have info on* ***minivan excursions*** *into the vineyards and Champagne villages.*

Sights

▲▲▲REIMS CATHEDRAL

The cathedral of Reims is a glorious example of Gothic architecture, and one of Europe's greatest churches. Clovis, the first Christian king of the Franks, was baptized at a church on this site in A.D. 496, establishing France's Christian roots, which still hold firm today. Since Clovis'

Reims Cathedral

Palais du Tau

baptism, Reims Cathedral has served as *the* place for the coronation of 26 French kings, giving it a more important role in France's political history than Notre-Dame Cathedral in Paris.

And there's a lot more history here. A self-assured Joan of Arc led a less-assured Charles VII to be crowned here in 1429. Thanks to Joan, the French rallied around their new king to push the English out of France and finally end the Hundred Years' War. During the French Revolution, the cathedral was converted to a temple of reason (as was Paris' Notre-Dame). After the restoration of the monarchy, the cathedral hosted the crowning of Charles X in 1825—the last coronation here.

During World War I about 300 shells hit the cathedral, damaging statues and windows and destroying the roof, but the structure survived. Then, during the 1920s, it was completely rebuilt, thanks in large part to financial support from John D. Rockefeller, Jr. In 1974, a luminous set of Marc Chagall stained-glass windows was installed in the apse (east end, behind the altar).

Cost and Hours: Free, daily 7:30-19:30, helpful info boards in English throughout the church, adjacent TI rents audioguides, www.reims-cathedral.culture.fr.

Cathedral Tower: An escorted one-hour tour climbs the 250 steps of the tower to explore the rooftop and statuary (€7.50, €11 combo-ticket with Palais du Tau; tours available May-Aug Tue-Sun; off-season Sat-Sun only; no tours Nov-mid-March; get tickets and meet escort in the Palais du Tau).

Cathedral Sound and Light Show: For a memorable experience, join the crowd in front of the cathedral for a free, 25-minute sound-and-light show on most summer evenings. The show generally starts when it's dark—between 21:30 and 23:00 (nightly except Mon July-Aug, Fri-Sun only in May-June and Sept).

PALAIS DU TAU

This former Archbishop's Palace, named after the Greek letter T (*tau*) for its shape, houses artifacts from the cathedral next door and a pile of royal goodies. You'll look into the weathered eyes of original statues from the cathedral's facade, see precious tapestries, coronation jewels, and more.

Cost and Hours: €7.50, €11 combo-ticket includes cathedral tower tour, May-Aug Tue-Sun 9:30-18:30, Sept-April Tue-Sun 9:30-12:30 & 14:00-17:30, closed Mon year-round, scant English information though an audioguide is available at cathedral TI, good bookshop, tel. 03 26 47 81 79, www.palais-tau.monuments-nationaux.fr.

▲CARNEGIE LIBRARY (BIBLIOTHEQUE CARNEGIE)

The legacy of the Carnegie Library network, funded generously by the 19th-century American millionaire Andrew Carnegie and his steel fortune, extends even to Reims. Built in 1921 in the flurry of interwar reconstruction, this beautiful Art Deco building still houses the city's public library. Considering that admission is free and it's just behind the cathedral, it's worth a quick look.

Cost and Hours: Free; Tue-Wed and Fri-Sat 10:00-13:00 & 14:00-18:00, Thu 14:00-18:00, closed Sun-Mon; Place Carnegie, tel. 03 26 77 81 41.

▲MUSEUM OF THE SURRENDER (MUSEE DE LA REDDITION)

Anyone interested in World War II will enjoy visiting the place where US General

Museum of the Surrender

Dwight Eisenhower and the Allies received the unconditional surrender of all German forces on May 7, 1945. The news was announced the next day, turning May 8 into Victory in Europe (V-E) Day. The extensive collection of artifacts is fascinating, and it's thrilling to see the war room (or Signing Room), where Allied operations were managed.

Cost and Hours: €4, Wed-Mon 10:00-12:00 & 14:00-18:00, closed Tue, 12 Rue Franklin Roosevelt, tel. 03 26 47 84 19.

▲▲*Champagne Tours*

Reims, the capital of the Champagne region, offers many opportunities to visit its world-famous cellars. Most have several daily English tours and require a reservation (only Taittinger allows drop-in visits). All charge entry fees, which typically include a one-hour tour and a tasting. Call, email, or visit the website for the schedule and to secure a spot on a tour. Bring a sweater, even in summer, as the *caves* are cool and clammy.

Mumm and Cazanove are close to the city center and train station; if you don't have a car, the other cellars involve a long walk (40 minutes) or a taxi ride.

A **taxi** from either train station to the farthest Champagne *cave* will cost about €10; a **pedicab** is €6 one-way. Or ride one of the small Citadine **buses** that run loop routes (#CIT1 and #CIT2) to the farther *caves* (no Sun service).

MUMM

Mumm ("moome") is one of the easiest *caves* to visit, as it's a short walk from the central train station. Reservations are essential, especially on weekends.

Cost and Hours: €20-39 depending on tasting level; tours March-Oct daily 9:30-11:30 & 14:00-16:30, Nov-Feb Mon-Sat 9:30-11:00 & 14:00-16:00, closed Sun; 34 Rue du Champ de Mars—go to the end of the courtyard and follow *Visites des Caves* signs; tel. 03 26 49 59 70, www.mumm.com.

CHARLES DE CAZANOVE

If you're in a rush and not too concerned about quality, Cazanove is closest to the train station and has the cheapest tasting in town.

Cost and Hours: €12, daily 10:00-13:00 & 14:00-19:00, five-minute walk from the station up Boulevard Joffre to 8 Place de la République, tel. 03 26 88 53 86, www.champagnedecazanove.com.

TAITTINGER

One of the biggest, slickest, and most renowned of Reims' *caves*, Taittinger (tay-tan-zhay) runs morning and afternoon tours in English through their vast and historic cellars. Call for times; it's best to show up early. No reservation is necessary.

Cost and Hours: €17-41 depending on tasting level, April-mid-Nov daily 9:30-17:30; mid-Nov-March Mon-Fri 9:30-13:00 & 13:45-17:30, closed Sat-Sun; 9 Place St. Niçaise, tel. 03 26 85 84 33, www.taittinger.com.

MARTEL

This small operation with less extensive *caves* offers a homey contrast to Taittinger's big-business style, and it's a great deal. Call to set up a visit and expect a small group that might be yours alone. Only 20 percent of their product is exported, so you won't find much of their Champagne in the US.

Cost and Hours: €13, daily 10:00-11:30 & 14:00-17:30, reservations not required but advised, 17 Rue des Créneaux, tel. 03 26 82 70 67, www.champagnemartel.com, boutique@champagnemartel.com.

VEUVE CLICQUOT PONSARDIN

Because it's widely exported in the US, Veuve Clicquot is inundated with American travelers. Reservations are required and fill up three weeks in advance, so book early (easy via email or the website) before you start your trip.

Cost and Hours: €20, pricier options available; mid-March-mid-Nov Tue-Sat 9:30-12:30 & 13:30-17:30, closed Sun-Mon and rest of year; 1 Place des Droits de l'Homme, tel. 03 26 89 53 90, www.veuve-clicquot.com.

Eating and Sleeping

The informal **$ Bistrot du Forum** has a cool zinc bar and good terrace seating (daily, 6 Place Forum). **$ Au Bureau,** on the cathedral square, has average café fare—but it's a good people-watching place to linger over coffee (daily, 9 Place du Cardinal Luçon). The grand old **$$ Brasserie du Boulingrin** serves traditional French cuisine at reasonable prices (closed Sun, 31 Rue de Mars).

If you spend the night, **$$ Grand Hôtel Continental***** has rooms in every size, shape, and price (93 Place Drouet d'Erlon, www.grandhotelcontinental.com); **$ Grand Hôtel du Nord**** is a decent value and surprisingly quiet (75 Place Drouet d'Erlon, www.hotel-nord-reims.com); and **$ La Parenthèse** offers kitchenettes and easy car access (83 Rue Clovis, www.laparenthese.fr).

Giverny

Claude Monet spent his last—and most creative—years cultivating his garden and his art at Giverny (zhee-vayr-nee), the spiritual home of Impressionism. Visiting the Orangerie Museum in Paris before your visit here heightens your appreciation of these gardens.

Getting There

Drivers can get in and out of Giverny in a half-day with ease—it's 50 miles west of Paris. The trip is also doable in a half-day by public transportation with a train/bus connection, but because trains are not frequent, be prepared for a full six-hour excursion.

By Car: From Paris' *périphérique* ring road, follow A-13 toward Rouen, exit at *Sortie 14* to Vernon, and follow *Centre Ville* signs, then signs to *Giverny*. Park right at Monet's house or at one of several nearby lots.

By Tour: Big tour companies run day trips from Paris to Giverny; if interested, ask at your hotel.

By Train: Take the Rouen-bound train from Paris Gare St. Lazare Station to Vernon, about four miles from Giverny (8/day Mon-Sat, 6/day Sun, 45 minutes). Taking a train that leaves Paris at around 8:15 is ideal for this trip.

Arrival in Giverny: The Vernon-Giverny **bus** is timed to meet every train from Paris for the 15-minute run to Giverny (buy ticket from driver, www.giverny.org/transpor). Note return times (timetable at bus stop, on bus, and online).

Taxis wait at the station (€14 one-way, mobile 06 77 49 32 90 or 06 50 12 21 22).

You can rent a **bike** (ask for easy-to-follow map) opposite the train station at the café, L'Arrivée de Giverny, then follow a paved bike path *(piste cyclable)* to Giverny (30 minutes). **Hikers** can follow the same route (about 1.5 hours).

Orientation

All of Giverny's sights and shops string along Rue Claude Monet, which runs in front of Monet's house.

Day Plan: Give yourself a full hour or more to view the picturesque gardens, and another hour to tour the house. Afterwards, pay your respects at Monet's grave, then drop by the Museum of Impressionisms, which has picnic-pleasant gardens in front.

Tourist Information: The TI is located at the intersection of Rue Claude Monet and Rue du Pressoir (daily April-Oct, closed off-season, 80 Rue Claude Monet, tel. 02 32 64 45 01, www.normandie-giverny.fr).

Sights

▲MONET'S GARDEN AND HOUSE

In 1883, middle-aged Claude Monet, his wife Alice, and their eight children settled into this farmhouse. Already a famous artist and happiest at home, Monet would spend 40 years in Giverny and his gardens,

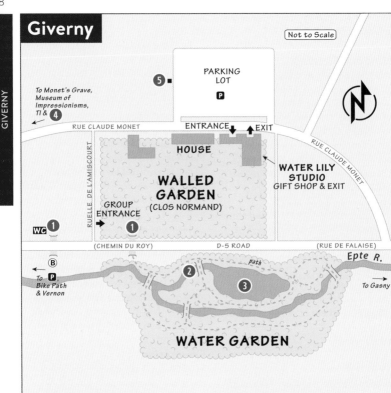

Giverny

Not to Scale

PARKING LOT

To Monet's Grave, Museum of Impressionisms, TI & 4

RUE CLAUDE MONET

ENTRANCE

EXIT

HOUSE

RUE CLAUDE MONET

WATER LILY STUDIO
GIFT SHOP & EXIT

WALLED GARDEN
(CLOS NORMAND)

RUELLE DE L'AMISCOURT

GROUP ENTRANCE

WC

(CHEMIN DU ROY)

D-5 ROAD

(RUE DE FALAISE)

Epte R.

Path

To P, Bike Path & Vernon

To Gasny

WATER GARDEN

1 Pedestrian Tunnels (2)
2 Japanese Bridge
3 Water Lily Pond
4 To Hôtel Baudy
5 Café/Restaurant & Sandwich/Drink Stand

which he memorably painted from every angle, at every time of day, in all kinds of weather.

Cost and Hours: €9.50, €16.50 combo-ticket includes nearby Museum of Impressionisms, daily April-Oct 9:30-18:00, closed Nov-March; tel. 02 32 51 90 31, http://fondation-monet.com.

Crowd-Beating Tips: Minimize crowds by arriving a little before the garden opens, or come after 16:00 and stay until it closes. The busiest months—May and June—are also the best time for blooms. Your best bet is to buy advance tickets online or at any FNAC department store in Paris (which allows you to skip the ticket line and use the group entrance). If you plan to visit the Museum of Impressionisms (described later), go there first and buy a combo-ticket (*billet couplé*).

Monet's kitchen

Visiting the House and Gardens: There are two gardens, split by a busy road (but connected by a pedestrian underpass). For the **Walled Garden,** nearest to the house, Monet laid out symmetrical flowerbeds of lilies, irises, and clematis, split down the middle by a "grand alley" covered with iron trellises of climbing roses. In the **Water Garden,** the Japanese bridge, weeping willows, draped wisteria, and pond full of floating lilies leave artists aching for an easel.

Monet's **home** is worth a wander for the lovely furnishings and the artist's prized collection of Japanese prints. The gift shop at the exit is the actual sky-lighted studio where Monet painted his water-lily masterpieces (displayed at the Orangerie Museum in Paris).

Visting Monet's Grave: Monet's grave is a 15-minute walk from his door. Turn left from his house and walk down Rue Claude Monet; you'll find his grave behind the white Eglise Sainte-Radegonde.

MUSEUM OF IMPRESSIONISMS (MUSEE DES IMPRESSIONNISMES)

This bright, modern museum, dedicated to the history of Impressionism and its legacy, displays rotating exhibits of Impressionist art.

Cost and Hours: €7, daily April-Oct 10:00-18:00, closed Nov-March; tel. 02 32 51 94 00, www.mdig.fr.

Eating

A flowery **café/restaurant** and a **sandwich/drink stand** sit right next to the parking lot across from Monet's home. Rose-colored **Hôtel Baudy,** once a hang-out for American Impressionists, offers a pretty setting for lunch or dinner (81 Rue Claude Monet).

Wisteria drapes the Japanese bridge in Monet's Water Garden.

Normandy

The long coast of Normandy (Normandie) shelters romantic villages, a church with a precious tapestry, the historic D-Day beaches, and the iconic island abbey of Mont St-Michel. Parisians call Normandy "the 21st arrondissement." It's their nearest beach escape.

Despite the peacefulness you sense today, the region's history is filled with war. Normandy was founded by Viking Norsemen who invaded from the north, settled here in the ninth century, and gave the region its name. A couple of hundred years later, William the Conqueror invaded England from Normandy. His victory is commemorated in a remarkable tapestry at Bayeux. A few hundred years after that, Joan of Arc (Jeanne d'Arc) was convicted of heresy and burned at the stake by the English, against whom she rallied France during the Hundred Years' War. And in 1944, Normandy was the site of a WWII battle that changed the course of history.

This large region is ideal for exploring by car. Travelers without a car can rely on taking a combination of trains, buses, and minivan tours.

NORMANDY IN 3 DAYS

You'll want a full day for the D-Day beaches and a half-day each for Honfleur, Bayeux, and Mont St-Michel.

On your first day, if you're driving between Paris and Bayeux, Honfleur makes a good day stop. Spend the night in Bayeux, the best home base for touring the D-Day beaches.

Use your second day to tour the D-Day beaches. Drive to Arromanches, then work your way west and end at Ste-Mère Eglise. Return to Bayeux for the night.

On the third day, see the sights at Bayeux, then travel in the afternoon to Mont St-Michel, which must be seen early or late to avoid the masses of midday tourists (it's best to arrive late in the day and spend the night). Leave the next morning for your next destination—likely the Loire Valley.

With extra time: Drivers coming from Paris could add a visit to Giverny en route and overnight in lovely Honfleur, then continue to Bayeux the next day.

Without a car: Take the train (3 hours) from Paris to Bayeux (skip Honfleur unless you'd like to overnight there). On the second day, take a minivan tour from Bayeux of the D-Day beaches, then return to Bayeux. On the third day, visit Mont St-Michel: Either take a shuttle-van day trip from Bayeux, or take a train-and-bus trip to Mont St-Michel and spend the night.

HONFLEUR

Idyllic little Honfleur (ohn-flur) was a favorite of 19th-century Impressionists, who were captivated by the towns's unusual light—the result of its river-meets-sea setting. Eugène Boudin (boo-dan) lived and painted in Honfleur, drawing Monet and other creative types from Paris. In some ways, modern art was born here.

Gazing at its cozy harbor lined with skinny, soaring houses, it's easy to overlook the town's historic importance. For more than a thousand years, sailors have enjoyed this port's ideal location, where the Seine River greets the English Channel. William the Conqueror received supplies shipped from Honfleur. In 1608, Samuel de Champlain sailed from here to North America, where he discovered the St. Lawrence River and founded Quebec City.

Honfleur escaped the bombs of World War II, and today offers a romantic port enclosed on three sides by sprawling outdoor cafés. Long eclipsed by the gargantuan port of Le Havre just across the Seine, Honfleur happily uses its past as a bar stool...and sits on it.

Orientation

Honfleur is popular—expect crowds on weekends and during summer. All of Honfleur's appealing lanes and activities are within a short stroll of its old port (Vieux Bassin). The Seine River flows just east of the center, the hills of the Côte de Grâce form its western limit, and Rue de la République slices north-south through the center to the port. Honfleur has two can't-miss sights—the harbor and Ste. Catherine Church—and a handful of other intriguing monuments. But really, the town itself is its best sight.

Tourist Information: The TI is in the glassy public library (Mediathéque) on Quai le Paulmier, two blocks from the Vieux Bassin toward Le Havre (July-Aug Mon-Sat 9:30-19:00, Sun 10:00-17:00; Sept-June Mon-Sat 9:30-12:30 & 14:00-18:30, Sun 10:00-12:30 & 14:00-17:00 except closed Sun afternoon Oct-Easter; tel. 02 31 89 23 30, www.ot-honfleur.fr).

Artists have found inspiration in Honfleur for generations.

NORMANDY AT A GLANCE

Honfleur

▲▲**Vieux Bassin** Honfleur's picturesque square harbor, lined with fishing boats, exerting a powerful attraction on artists and travelers alike. **Hours:** Always open. See page 150.

▲▲**Ste. Catherine Church** Church with unusual architecture (like an upside-down boat), with a freestanding bell tower that plays a short video about itself. **Hours:** Daily July-Aug 9:00-18:30, Sept-June 9:00-17:15, shorter hours for tower. See page 151.

▲**Eugène Boudin Museum** Features paintings of Honfleur by a hometown artist who painted outdoors and encouraged Monet to do the same. **Hours:** May-Sept Wed-Mon 10:00-12:00 & 14:00-18:00, closed Tue, shorter hours off-season. See page 151.

▲**Maisons Satie** House of composer Erik Satie, with interactive musical exhibits. **Hours:** May-Sept Wed-Mon 10:00-19:00, Oct-Dec and mid-Feb-April Wed-Mon 11:00-18:00, closed Jan-mid-Feb and Tue year-round. See page 153.

Bayeux

▲▲▲**Bayeux Tapestry** A remarkable 11th-century embroidered report on the pivotal Battle of Hastings, fought between the English and French in 1066 (won by a Norman duke, William now-called Conqueror), well presented in an excellent museum. **Hours:** Daily May-Aug 9:00-19:00, March-April and Sept-Oct 9:00-18:30, Nov-Dec and Feb 9:30-12:30 & 14:00-18:00, closed Jan. See page 160.

▲**Bayeux Cathedral** Huge cathedral, magnificent in size and decoration. **Hours:** Daily July-Aug 8:30-19:00, Sept-June 8:30-18:00. See page 163.

D-Day Beaches

▲▲▲**Port Winston Artificial Harbor** Just off Arromanches, a harbor built by the Allies, from which they launched their amphibious attack and began the liberation of Europe. **Hours:** Always open. See page 172.

▲▲▲**WWII Normandy American Cemetery and Memorial** Above Omaha Beach, the final resting place of 9,387 Americans who gave their lives to liberate Europe. **Hours:** Daily mid-April-mid-Sept 9:00-18:00, mid-Sept-mid-April 9:00-17:00. See page 176.

▲▲▲**Pointe du Hoc** The incredibly steep cliffs and odds faced by US Army Rangers charged with disabling a Nazi gun battery atop the cliffs. **Hours:** Visitors center open daily mid-April-mid-Sept 9:00-18:00, off-season 9:00-17:00. See page 178.

▲▲▲**Utah Beach Landing Museum** Region's best museum on the D-Day beaches, built around a bunker, featuring a terrific film, impressive displays, and views of the beach. **Hours:** Daily June-Sept 9:30-19:00, Oct-Nov and Jan-May 10:00-18:00, closed Dec. See page 180.

▲▲**Arromanches 360° Theater** Archival footage of the D-Day assault presented in a modern format, with an immersive, emotional punch. **Hours:** Daily June-Aug 9:40-18:40, April-May and Sept 10:10-18:10, Oct-mid-Nov 10:10-17:40, shorter hours off-season, closed most of Jan. See page 173.

▲**D-Day Landing Museum** Shows through displays, modes, and film how the artificial harbor at Port Winston in Arromanches was built in just 12 days. **Hours:** Daily May-Aug 9:00-19:00, Sept 9:00-18:00, Oct-Dec and Feb-April 10:00-12:30 & 13:30-17:00, closed Jan. See page 174.

▲**Longues-sur-Mer Gun Battery** At Omaha Beach, the only original coastal artillery guns—built by the Nazis—that remain in place on the D-Day beaches. **Hours:** Always open. See page 175.

▲**Ste-Mère Eglise** First village liberated—with great sacrifices made—by American paratroopers. See page 181.

Mont St-Michel

▲▲**Abbey of Mont St-Michel** Historic abbey atop a dreamy-from-a-distance island off the coast of Normandy. **Hours:** May-mid-July daily 9:00-19:00; mid-July-Aug Mon-Sat 9:00-24:00, Sun 9:00-19:00; Sept-April daily 9:30-18:00. See page 186.

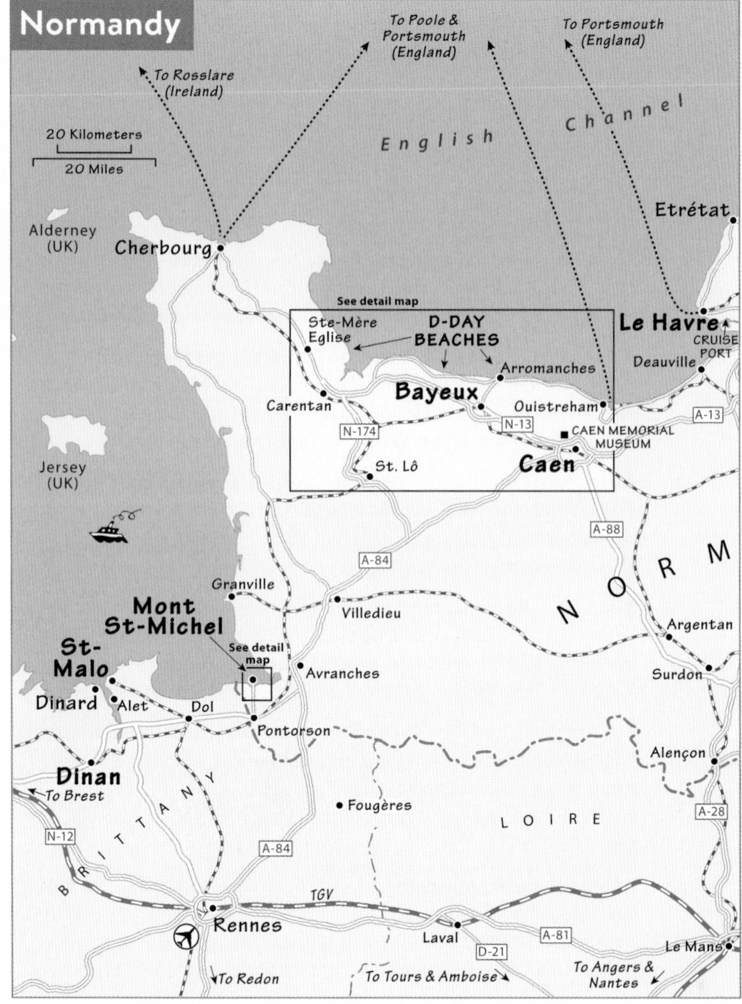

Here you can rent a €3.50 audioguide for a self-guided town walk, or pick up a town map, schedules for buses and trains, and information on the D-Day beaches.

Museum Pass: The €10.20 museum pass, sold at participating museums, more than pays for itself even if you only visit the Eugène Boudin and Maisons Satie museums (www.musees-honfleur.fr).

Market Day: The area around Ste. Catherine Church becomes a colorful open-air market every Saturday (9:00–13:00). A smaller organic-food-only market takes place here on Wednesday mornings, and a flea market takes center stage here the first Sunday of every month and also on Wednesday evenings in summer.

Regional Products: Visit **Produits Regionaux Gribouille** for any Norman delicacy you can dream up. Say *bonjour* to Monsieur Gribouille (gree-boo-ee), and watch your head—his egg-beater collection hangs from above (Mon-Tue and Thu-Fri 9:30-12:45 & 14:00-18:30, Sat

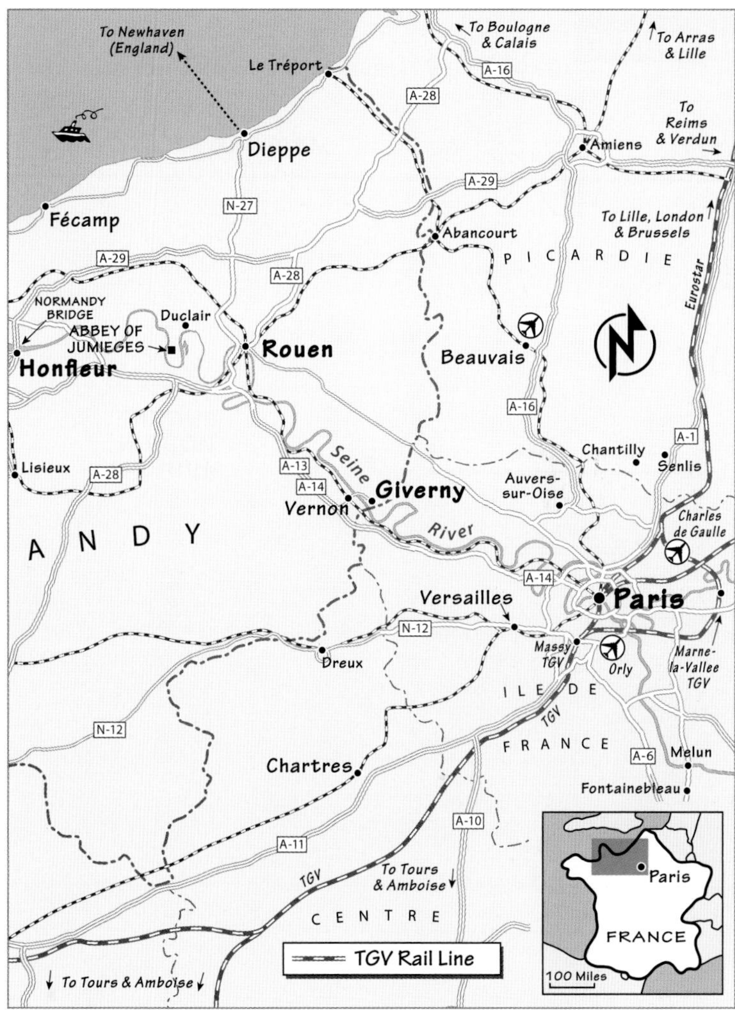

9:30-19:00, Sun 10:00-18:00, closed Wed, 16 Rue de l'Homme de Bois, tel. 02 31 89 29 54).

Taxi: Call mobile 06 08 60 17 98.

Tourist Train: Honfleur's *petit train* toots you up the Côte de Grâce—the hill overlooking the town—and back in about 45 minutes (€6.50, 4/day, more in summer, departs from across gray swivel bridge that leads to Parking du Môle).

Honfleur Walk

For good exercise and a bird's-eye view of Honfleur and the Normandy Bridge, take the steep 20-minute walk (or quick drive) up to the **Côte de Grâce,** worth ▲. It's best in the early morning or at sunset. From Ste. Catherine Church, walk or drive up Rue du Puits, then follow the blue-on-white signs to reach the splendid view over Honfleur at the top of the ramp (benches and information plaque). *Piétons* (walkers) should veer right up La

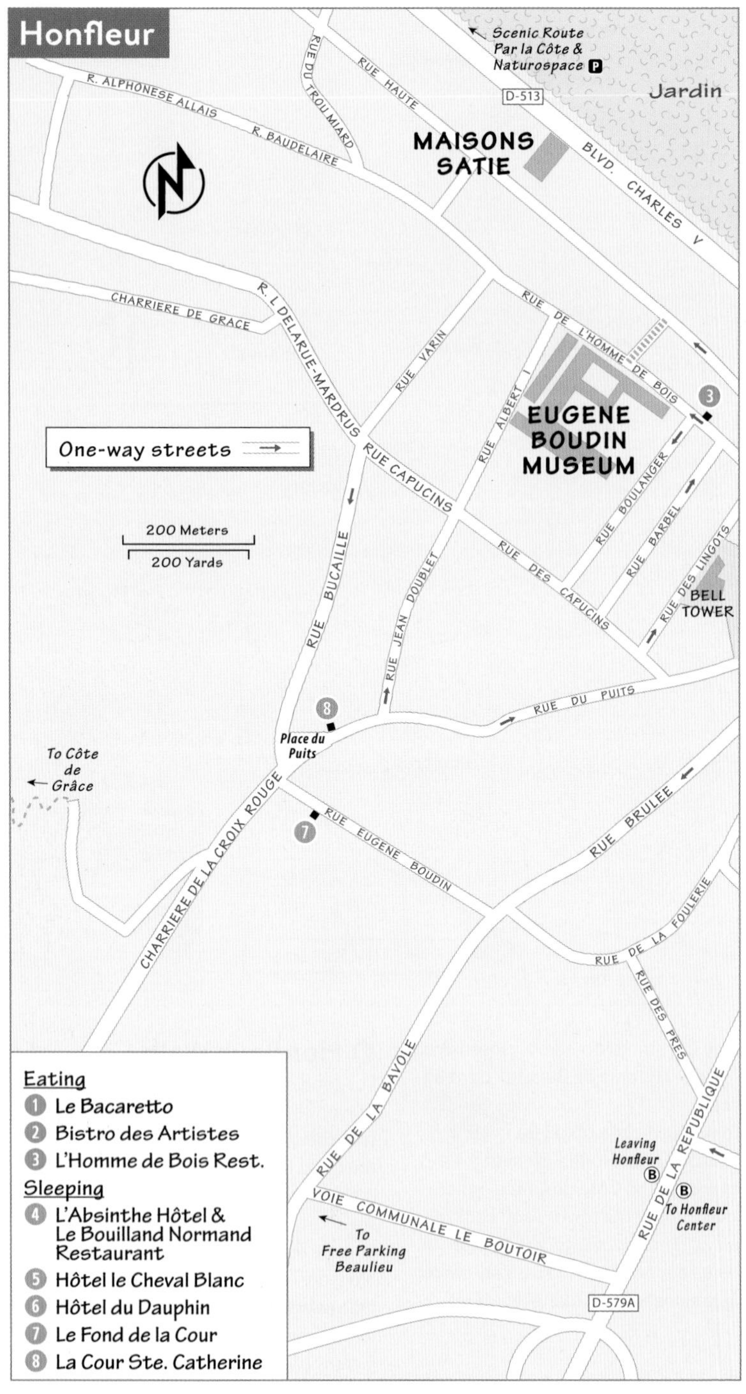
Honfleur
Scenic Route
Par la Côte &
Naturospace
Jardin
D-513
R. ALPHONESE ALLAIS
R. BAUDELAIRE
RUE DU TROU MIARD
RUE HAUTE
MAISONS SATIE
BLVD. CHARLES V
CHARRIERE DE GRACE
R. L DELARUE-MARDRUS
RUE VARIN
RUE ALBERT I
RUE DE L'HOMME DE BOIS
EUGENE BOUDIN MUSEUM
One-way streets
RUE CAPUCINS
RUE BOULANGER
RUE BARBEL
200 Meters
200 Yards
RUE BUCAILLE
RUE JEAN DOUBLET
RUE DES CAPUCINS
RUE DES LINGOTS
BELL TOWER
RUE DU PUITS
Place du Puits
To Côte de Grâce
CHARRIERE DE LA CROIX ROUGE
RUE EUGENE BOUDIN
RUE BRULEE
RUE DE LA FOULERIE
RUE DES PRES
RUE DE LA BAVOLE
RUE DE LA REPUBLIQUE
Leaving Honfleur
To Honfleur Center
VOIE COMMUNALE LE BOUTOIR
To Free Parking Beaulieu
D-579A
Eating
1 Le Bacaretto
2 Bistro des Artistes
3 L'Homme de Bois Rest.
Sleeping
4 L'Absinthe Hôtel & Le Bouilland Normand Restaurant
5 Hôtel le Cheval Blanc
6 Hôtel du Dauphin
7 Le Fond de la Cour
8 La Cour Ste. Catherine

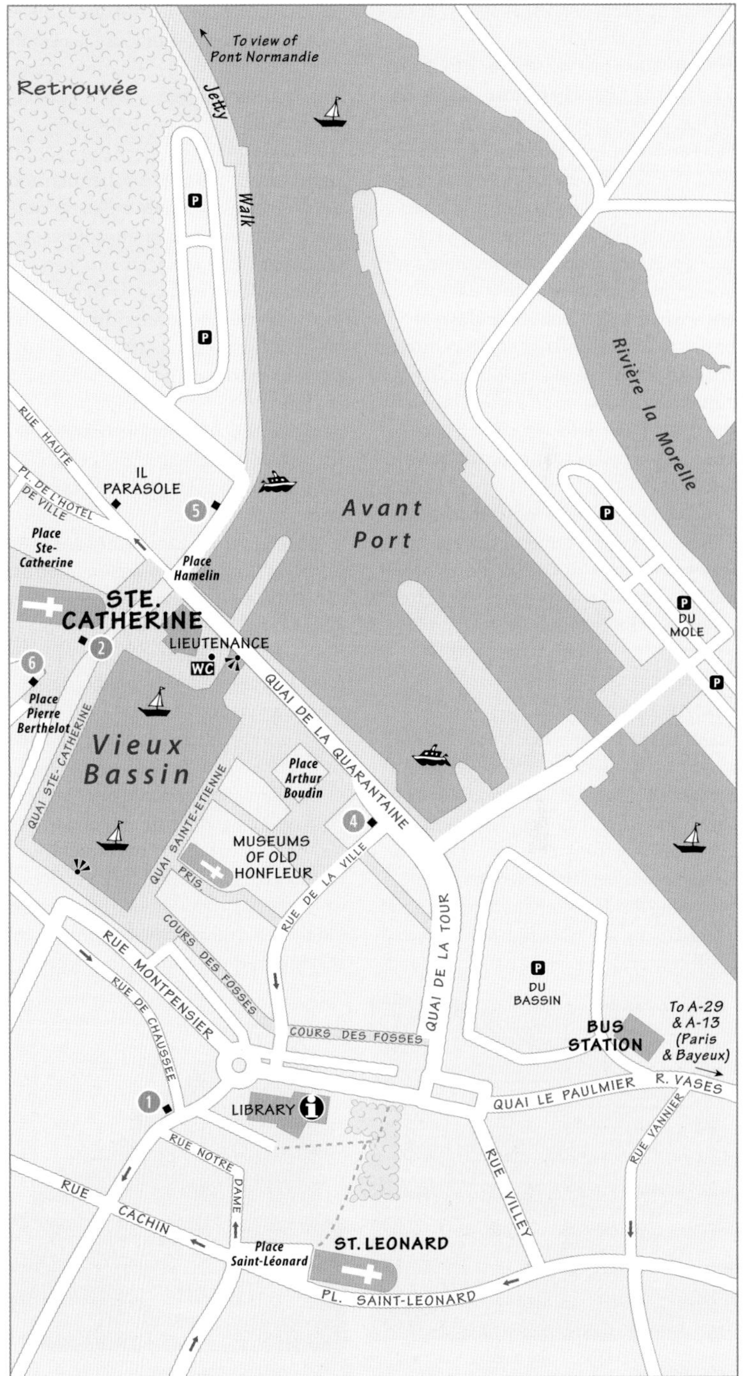
To view of Pont Normandie
Retrouvée
Jetty
Walk
Rivière la Morelle
RUE HAUTE
IL PARASOLE
PL. DE L'HOTEL DE VILLE
Place Ste-Catherine
Place Hamelin
Avant Port
STE. CATHERINE
LIEUTENANCE
WC
DU MOLE
Place Pierre Berthelot
QUAI DE LA QUARANTAINE
Vieux Bassin
QUAI STE-CATHERINE
QUAI SAINTE-ETIENNE
Place Arthur Boudin
MUSEUMS OF OLD HONFLEUR
PRIS.
RUE DE LA VILLE
COURS DES FOSSES
RUE MONTPENSIER
RUE DE CHAUSSEE
QUAI DE LA TOUR
DU BASSIN
BUS STATION
To A-29 & A-13 (Paris & Bayeux)
COURS DES FOSSES
LIBRARY
QUAI LE PAULMIER
R. VASES
RUE VANNIER
RUE NOTRE DAME
RUE VILLEY
RUE CACHIN
Place Saint-Léonard
ST. LEONARD
PL. SAINT-LEONARD

Rampe du Mont Joli; *conducteurs* (drivers) should keep straight.

Continue past the view for about 300 yards to the **Chapel of Notre-Dame de Grâce.** Built in the early 1600s by the mariners and people of Honfleur, the church oozes seafaring mementos. Model boats hang from the ceiling, pictures of boats balance high on the walls, and several stained-glass windows are decorated with images of sailors praying to the Virgin Mary while at sea. Even the holy water basins to the left and right of the entrance are in the shape of seashells. Find the church bells hanging on a wood rack to the right as you leave the church and imagine the racket they could make (daily 8:30-17:15).

Below the chapel, a lookout offers a sweeping view of super-industrial Le Havre, with the Manche (English Channel) to your left and the (just visible) Normandy Bridge to your right.

Sights

▲▲VIEUX BASSIN

Stand near the water facing Honfleur's square harbor, with the merry-go-round across the lock to your left, and survey the town. The word "Honfleur" is Scandinavian, meaning the shelter *(fleur)* of Hon (a Norse settler). This town has been sheltering residents for about a thousand years. During the Hundred Years' War (14th century), the entire harbor was fortified by a big wall with twin gatehouses (the one surviving gatehouse, La Lieutenance, is on your right). A narrow channel allowing boats to pass was protected by a heavy chain.

Those skinny houses on the right side were built for the town's fishermen and designed at a time when buildings were taxed based on their width, not height (and when knee replacements were unheard of). How about a room on the top floor, with no elevator? Imagine moving a piano or a refrigerator into one of these units today. The spire halfway up the left side of the port belongs to Honfleur's oldest church and is now home to the Marine Museum. The port, once crammed with fishing boats, now harbors sleek sailboats.

Walk toward the La Lieutenance gatehouse. In front of the barrel-vaulted arch (once the entry to the town), you can see a bronze bust of Samuel de Champlain—the explorer who sailed with an Honfleur crew 400 years ago to make his discoveries in Canada.

Turn around to see various tour and fishing boats and the masts of the high-flying Normandy Bridge in the distance. Fisherfolk catch flatfish, scallops, and tiny shrimp daily to bring to the Marché au Poisson, located toward the river (look for white metal structures with blue lettering). On the left, you may see fishermen's wives selling *crevettes* (shrimp). You can buy

Vieux Bassin

La Lieutenance gatehouse

them *cuites* (cooked) or *vivantes* (alive and wiggly). They are happy to let you sample one (rip off the cute little head and tail, and pop the middle into your mouth—*délicieuse!*), or buy a cupful for a few euros (daily in season).

You'll probably see artists sitting at easels around the harbor, as Boudin and Monet did. Many consider Honfleur the birthplace of 19th-century Impressionism. This was a time when people began to revere, not fear, the out-of-doors, and started to climb mountains "because they were there." Pretty towns like Honfleur and the nearby coast made perfect subjects to paint—and still are—thanks to what locals called the "unusual luminosity" of the region. And with the advent of trains in the late 1800s, artists could travel to the best light like never before. Artists would set up easels along the harbor to catch the light playing on the line of buildings, slate shingles, timbers, geraniums, clouds, and reflections in the water. Monet came here to visit the artist Boudin, a hometown boy, and the battle cry of the Impressionists—"Out of the studio and into the light!"—was born.

If you're an early riser, you can watch what's left of Honfleur's fishing fleet prepare for the day, and you just might experience that famous luminosity.

▲▲STE. CATHERINE CHURCH (EGLISE STE. CATHERINE)

The unusual wood-shingled exterior suggests that this church has a different story to tell than most. Walk inside. You'd swear that if it were turned over, it would float—the legacy of a community of sailors and fishermen, with loads of talented boat-builders and nary a cathedral architect. When workers put up the first nave in 1466, it soon became apparent that more space was needed—so the second was built in 1497. Because it felt too much like a market hall, they added side aisles. Notice the oak pillars, some full-length and others supported by stone bases. Trees come in different sizes, yet each pillar had to be the same thickness. In the last months of World War II, a bomb fell through the roof—but didn't explode. The pipe organ behind you is popular for concerts, and half of the modern pews are designed to flip so that you can face the music. Take a close look at the many medieval instruments carved into the railing below the organ—a 16th-century combo band in wood.

Ste. Catherine Church

Cost and Hours: Free, daily July-Aug 9:00-18:30, Sept-June 9:00-17:15.

Bell Tower: The church's bell tower was built away from the church to avoid placing too much stress on the wooden church's roof, and to help minimize fire hazards. Historians consider the structure ugly—I like it. Notice the funky shingled chestnut beams that run from its squat base to support the skinny tower, and find the small, faded wooden sculpture of St. Catherine over the door. Go inside to appreciate the ancient wood framing and to see a good 15-minute video describing the bell tower's history. The highlights of the tiny museum are two wooden sculptures from the bows of two Louis XIII-era ships. Until recently the bell ringer lived in the bell tower—notice his fireplace behind the video area (€2, free with ticket to Eugène Boudin Museum, April-Sept Wed-Mon 10:00-12:00 & 14:00-18:00, closed Oct-March and Tue year-round).

▲EUGENE BOUDIN MUSEUM

Eugène Boudin ignited Honfleur's artistic tradition, which still burns today. This

Eugène Boudin (1824-1898)

Born in Honfleur, Boudin was the son of a harbor pilot. As an amateur teenage artist, he found work in an art-supply store that catered to famous artists from Paris (such as Jean-Baptiste-Camille Corot and Jean-François Millet) who came to paint the seaside. Boudin studied art in Paris but kept his hometown roots. Thanks to his Paris connections, Boudin's work was exhibited at the Paris salons.

At age 30, Boudin met the teenage Claude Monet. Monet had grown up in nearby Le Havre and, like Boudin, sketched the world around him—beaches, boats, and small-town life. Boudin encouraged him to don a scarf, set up his easel outdoors, and paint the scene exactly as he saw it. Today, we say: "Well, duh!" But "open-air" painting was unorthodox for artists trained to thoroughly study their subjects in the perfect lighting of a controlled studio setting. Boudin didn't teach Monet as much as give him the courage to follow his artistic instincts.

In the 1860s and 1870s, Boudin spent summers at his farm (St. Siméon) on the outskirts of Honfleur, hosting Monet, Edouard Manet, and other hangers-on. They taught Boudin the Impressionist techniques of using bright colors and building a subject with many individual brushstrokes. Boudin adapted those "strokes" to build subjects with "patches" of color. In 1874, Boudin joined the renegade Impressionists at their "revolutionary" exhibition in Paris.

Boudin, Beach at Trouville

pleasing little museum has three interesting floors with many paintings of Honfleur and the surrounding countryside. The first floor displays Norman folk costumes, the second floor has the Boudin collection, and the third floor houses the Hambourg/Rachet collection and the Katia Granoff room. The museum is in the midst of a multiyear renovation; some sections (or even the entire museum) may be closed, so go with the flow.

Rick's Tip: *As you walk around Honfleur, take time to enjoy today's art, too. The* **best art galleries** *are along the streets between Ste. Catherine Church and the port.*

Cost and Hours: €6, more during special exhibits, covered by museum pass; May-Sept Wed-Mon 10:00-12:00 & 14:00-18:00, closed Tue, shorter hours off-season; €2 English audioguide covers selected works (no English explanations on display—but none needed); elevator, no photos, Rue de l'Homme de Bois, tel. 02 31 89 54 00.

▲MAISONS SATIE

If Honfleur is over-the-top cute, this museum, housed in composer Erik Satie's birthplace, is a burst of witty charm—just like the musical genius it honors. While enjoyable for Satie's fans, it can be a ho-hum experience for those unfamiliar with Satie and his music.

Cost and Hours: €6.10, covered by museum pass; May-Sept Wed-Mon 10:00-19:00, Oct-Dec and mid-Feb-April Wed-Mon 11:00-18:00, closed Jan-mid-Feb and Tue year-round; last entry one hour before closing, includes audioguide, 5-minute walk from harbor at 67 Boulevard Charles V, tel. 02 31 89 11 11, www.musees-honfleur.fr.

Visiting the Museum: As you wander from room to room with your included audioguide, infrared signals transmit bits of Satie's minimalist music, along with a first-person story (in English). As if you're living as an artist in 1920s Paris, you'll drift past winged pears, strangers in the window, and small girls with green eyes. (If you like what you hear...don't move; the infrared transmission is hypersensitive, and the soundtrack switches every few feet.) The finale—performed by you—is the *Laboratory of Emotions* pedal-go-round, a self-propelled carousel where your feet create the music (be sure to pedal softly). For a relaxing break, enjoy the 12-minute movie featuring modern dance springing from *Parade,* Satie's collaboration with Pablo Picasso and Jean Cocteau; the Dadaist *Relâche;* and other works. You'll even hear the boos and whistles that greeted these ballets' debuts (4/hour, French only).

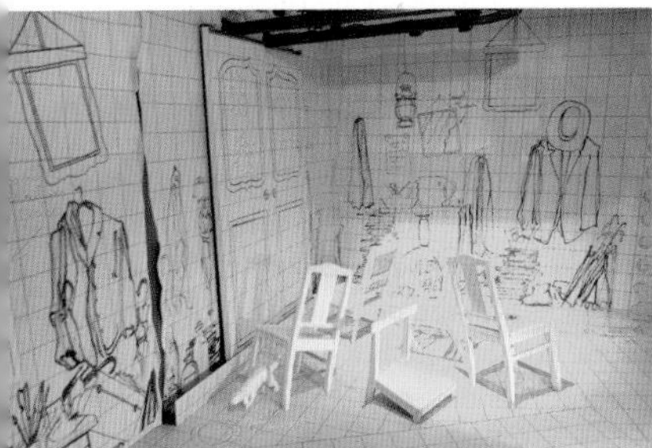

Maisons Satie

Near Honfleur

BOAT EXCURSIONS

Boat trips in and around Honfleur depart from various docks between Hôtel le Cheval Blanc and the opposite end of the outer port (Easter-Oct usually about 11:00-17:00). The tour boat *Calypso* takes good 45-minute spins around Honfleur's harbor (€6, mobile 06 71 64 50 46). Other cruises run to the Normandy Bridge (described next), which, unfortunately, means two boring trips through the locks (€9.50/1.5 hours, choose between *Jolie France,* mobile 06 71 64 50 46, or *Les Vedettes Cauchois* near Hôtel le Cheval Blanc, mobile 06 31 89 21 10).

NORMANDY BRIDGE (PONT DE NORMANDIE)

The 1.25-mile-long Normandy Bridge is the longest cable-stayed bridge in the Western world. This is a key piece of European expressway that links the Atlantic ports from Belgium to Spain (€5.40 toll each way, not worth a detour). View the bridge from Honfleur (better from an excursion boat or my Honfleur Walk described earlier, and best at night, when bridge is floodlit). Also consider visiting the bridge's free Exhibition Hall (daily 8:00-19:00, under tollbooth on Le Havre side). The Seine finishes its winding 500-mile journey here, dropping only 1,500 feet from its source, 450 miles away.

BEACHES

Parisians enjoy basking at the beaches at Deauville and Trouville, about a 20-minute drive southwest of Honfleur.

Eating

Eat seafood or cream sauces here. It's a tough choice between the irresistible waterfront tables of the many look-alike places lining the harbor and the eateries with good reputations elsewhere in town. Trust my dinner suggestions and consider your hotelier's opinion. Call ahead for reservations, particularly on weekends.

$$$ Le Bouilland Normand hides a block off the port on a pleasing square and offers a true Norman experience at reasonable prices. Claire and chef-hubby Bruno provide quality *Normand* cuisine and enjoy serving travelers. Daily specials complement the classic offerings (€22-30 *menus*, closed Wed, dine inside or out, 7 Rue de la Ville, tel. 02 31 89 02 41, www.aubouillonnormand.fr).

Normandy Bridge

Sleep Code

$$$$ Splurge: Over €250
$$$ Pricier: €190-250
$$ Moderate: €130-190
$ Budget: €70-130
¢ Backpacker: Under €70

Hotels are classified based on the average price of a standard double room with bath in high season. Unless otherwise noted, credit cards are accepted, breakfast is not included, hotel staff speak English, and Wi-Fi is available.

Rick's Tip: *If you're in Honfleur on a clear morning,* **enjoy the ambience of breakfast on the port,** *where several cafés offer* petit déjeuner *(€3-7 for continental fare, €7-13 for more elaborate choices). Morning sun and views are best from the high side of the harbor.*

$ Le Bacaretto wine bar-café is run by laid-back Hervé, the antithesis of a wine snob. This relaxed, tiny, wine-soaked place offers a fine selection of wines by the glass at good prices and a small but appealing assortment of appetizers and *plats du jour* that can make a full meal (closed Wed-Thu for lunch and Sun for dinner, 44 Rue de la Chaussée, tel. 02 31 14 83 11).

$$ Bistro des Artistes is a two-woman operation and the joy of locals (call ahead for a window table). Hardworking Anne-Marie cooks from a select repertoire upstairs while her server takes care of business in the pleasant little dining room. Portions are huge and very homemade; order only one course and maybe a dessert (€19-28 *plats*, closed Wed, 30

Normandy's Cuisine Scene

Normandy is known as the land of the four C's: Calvados, Camembert, cider, and *crème*. The region specializes in cream sauces, organ meats (sweetbreads, tripe, and kidneys—the gizzard salads are great), and seafood ***(fruits de mer).*** You'll see *crêperies* offering inexpensive and good-value meals everywhere. A galette is a savory buckwheat crêpe enjoyed as a main course; a crêpe is sweet and eaten for dessert.

Dairy products are big, too. Local cheeses are **Camembert** (mild to very strong; see page 165), **Brillat-Savarin** (buttery), **Livarot** (spicy and pungent), **Pavé d'Auge** (spicy and tangy), and **Pont l'Evêque** (earthy flavor).

What, no local wine? *Oui,* that's right. Here's how to cope. Fresh, white **Muscadet** wines are made nearby (in western Loire); they're cheap and a good match with much of Normandy's cuisine. But Normandy is famous for its many apple-based beverages. You can't miss the powerful **Calvados apple brandy** or the **Bénédictine brandy** (made by local monks). The local dessert, ***trou Normand,*** is apple sorbet swimming in Calvados. The region also produces three kinds of alcoholic apple ciders: ***Cidre*** can be *doux* (sweet), *brut* (dry), or *bouché* (sparkling—and the strongest). You'll also find bottles of **Pommeau,** a tasty blend of apple juice and Calvados (sold in many shops), as well as ***poiré,*** a tasty pear cider. Don't leave Normandy without sampling ***kir Normand,*** a mix of crème de cassis and cider. Be on the lookout for ***Route du Cidre*** signs (with a bright red apple); this tourist trail leads you to small producers of handcrafted cider and brandy.

Restaurants serve only during lunch (11:30-14:00) and dinner (19:00-21:00, later in bigger cities); cafés serve food throughout the day.

Place Berthelot, tel. 02 31 89 95 90).

$$ L'Homme de Bois combines way-cozy ambience with authentic Norman cuisine and good prices (€23 three-course *menu* with few choices, €26-36 *menus* give more choices, daily, a few outside tables, 30 Rue de l'Homme de Bois, tel. 02 31 89 75 27).

Sleeping

Though Honfleur is popular in summer, it's busiest on weekends and holidays (blame Paris). English is widely spoken (blame vacationing Brits). A few moderate accommodations remain, but most hotels are pretty pricey.

Hotels

$$$ L'Absinthe Hôtel*** offers 11 stylish, tastefully restored rooms with king-size beds in two locations. Rooms in the main (reception) section come with wood-beamed decor and Jacuzzi tubs, and share a cozy public lounge with a fireplace (Db-€160-210). Five rooms are located above their next-door restaurant and have views of the modern port and three-star, state-of-the-art comfort (Db-€190,

Db suite-€265; breakfast-€13, air-con in both buildings, private parking-€13/day, 1 Rue de la Ville, tel. 02 31 89 23 23, www.absinthe.fr, reservation@absinthe.fr).

$$$ Hôtel le Cheval Blanc***, a Best Western, is a waterfront splurge with port views from all of its 35 plush and pricey rooms (many with queen-size beds), plus a rare-in-this-town elevator and a spa, but no air-conditioning. Noise can be a problem with windows open (small Db with lesser view-€155, Db with full port view-€180-230, family rooms/suites-€280-435, breakfast-€13, 2 Quai des Passagers, tel. 02 31 81 65 00, www.hotel-honfleur.com, info@hotel-honfleur.com).

$$ Hôtel du Dauphin*** is centrally located, with a colorful lounge/breakfast room, many narrow stairs (normal in Honfleur), and an Escher-esque floor plan. The 30 mostly smallish rooms—some with open-beam ceilings, some with queen- or king-size beds—provide reasonable comfort for the price. If you need a lower floor or bigger bed, request it when you book (Db-€109-165 depending on size of bed and view, Tb-€159, Qb-€165-179, breakfast-€13, Wi-Fi in lobby only, a stone's throw from Ste. Catherine Church at 10 Place Pierre Berthelot, tel. 02 31 89 15 53, www.hoteldudauphin.com, info@hoteldudauphin.com).

Chambres d'Hotes

The TI has a long list of Honfleur's many *chambres d'hôtes* (rooms in private homes), but most are too far from the town center. Those listed here are good values.

$$ At **Le Fond de la Cour,** British expats Amanda and Craig offer a good mix of crisp, modern, and comfortable accommodations around a peaceful courtyard. There's a large cottage that can sleep four, two apartments with small kitchens, and three standard doubles (Db-€145, Tb-€160, price depends on size, extra person-€30, short apartment stays possible, standard rooms include English-style breakfast, apartment dwellers also get free breakfast with this book, free street parking, limited private parking-€10/day, 29 Rue Eugène Boudin, mobile 06 72 20 72 98, www.lefonddelacour.com, amanda.ferguson@orange.fr).

$ La Cour Ste. Catherine, kitty-corner to Le Fond de la Cour, is an enchanting bed-and-breakfast run by the openhearted Madame Giaglis ("call me Liliane") and her big-hearted husband, Monsieur Liliane (a.k.a. Antoine). Their six big, modern rooms—each with firm beds and a separate sitting area—surround a perfectly Norman courtyard with a small terrace, fine plantings, and a cozy lounge area ideal for cool evenings. The rooms are as cheery as the owner—ask about her coffee shop (Db-€120, Db suite-€140, Tb/Qb-€150, extra bed-€30, includes breakfast, small apartments that sleep up to 6 and cottage with kitchen also available, cash only, 200 yards up Rue du Puits from Ste. Catherine Church at #74, tel. 02 31 89 42 40, www.coursaintecatherine.com, coursaintecatherine@orange.fr).

Transportation

Arriving and Departing

BY CAR

Approaching Honfleur, follow *Centre-Ville* signs, then find your hotel (easier said than done) and unload your bags (double-parking is OK for a few minutes). Parking is a headache in Honfleur, especially on summer and holiday weekends. Some hotels offer parking...for a price. Otherwise, your hotelier knows where you can park for free. If you don't mind paying for convenience, check first for a space in the small lot directly in front of the TI (€2/hour, €8/24 hours); if that's full, continue a couple of blocks farther to Parking du Bassin (€2/hour, €14/24 hours). Street parking, metered during the day, is free from 20:00 to 8:00.

BY BUS

There's no direct train service to Honfleur, so you must take a bus to or from a city with rail service. In Honfleur, get off at the small bus station *(gare routière)*, and confirm your departure at the helpful information counter. To reach the TI and old town, turn right as you exit the station and walk five minutes up Quai le Paulmier. The bus stop on Rue de la République may be more convenient for some accommodations (see map on page 148).

Leaving Honfleur: Although train and bus service usually are coordinated, confirm your connection with the helpful staff at Honfleur's bus station (English info desk open Mon-Fri 9:30-12:00 & 13:00-18:00, in summer also Sat-Sun, tel. 02 31 89 28 41, www.busverts.fr). If the station is closed, you can get schedules at the TI.

Bus Routes: The express PrestoBus—line #39—which links Honfleur with Caen and Le Havre is handy, but runs only two or three times a day. Non-express bus routes also connect Honfleur with Le Havre, Caen, Deauville, and Lisieux—all with direct rail service to Paris. Bus #50 runs between Le Havre, Honfleur, and Lisieux; bus #20 connects Le Havre, Honfleur, Deauville, and Caen.

From Honfleur by Bus and Train to: Bayeux (2-3/day, 1.5 hours; first take PrestoBus to Caen, then 20-minute train to Bayeux, more via scenic bus #20 via the coast to Caen); **Paris'** Gare St. Lazare (13/day, 2.5-3.5 hours, start by taking bus to Caen, Lisieux, Deauville, or Le Havre, then train to Paris; buses from Honfleur meet most Paris trains).

BAYEUX

Even without its famous medieval tapestry and proximity to the D-Day beaches, Bayeux would be worth a visit for its enjoyable town center and awe-inspiring cathedral, beautifully illuminated at night. Its location and manageable size (pop. 14,000) makes Bayeux an ideal home base for visiting the area's sights, particularly if you lack a car.

Bayeux was the first city liberated after the D-Day landing. Incredibly, the town was spared the bombs of World War II. After a local chaplain made sure London knew that his city was not a German headquarters and was of no strategic importance, a scheduled bombing raid

Water mill and mill pond, Bayeux

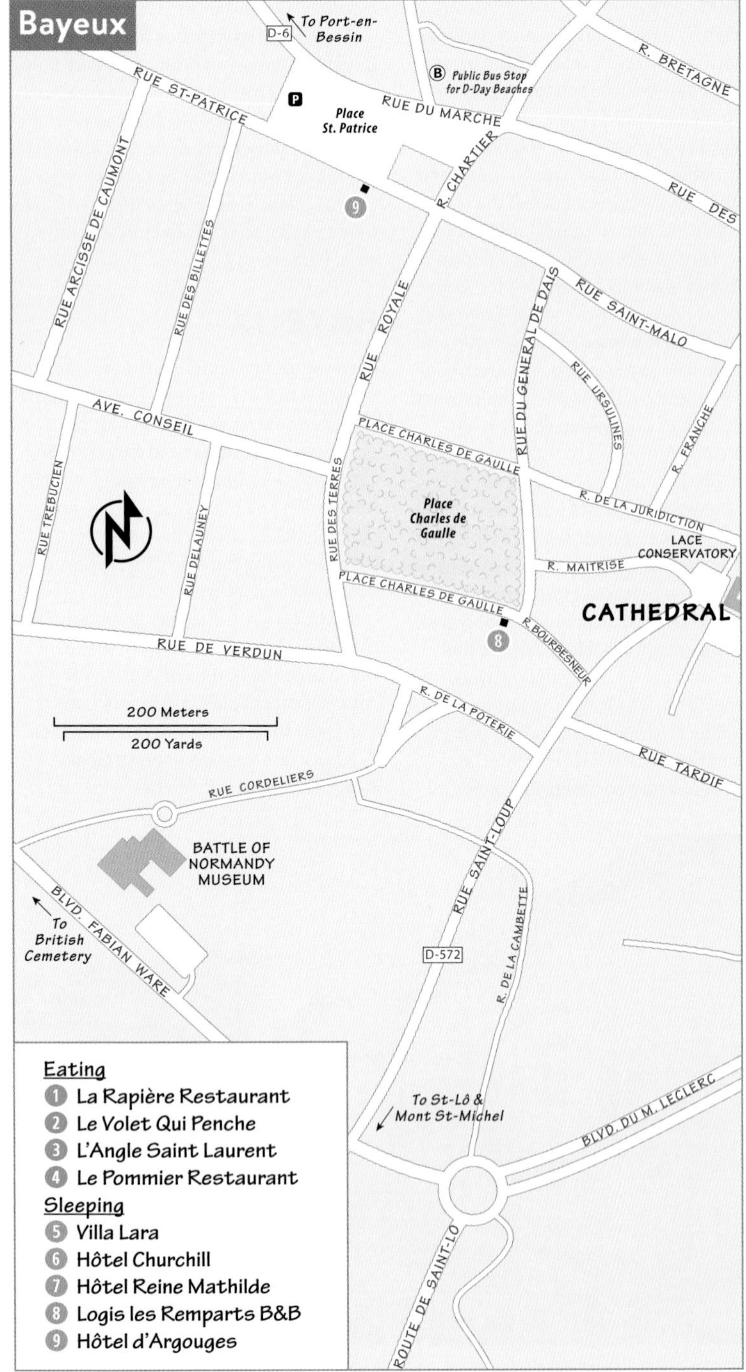
Bayeux
To Port-en-Bessin
D-6
Public Bus Stop for D-Day Beaches
R. BRETAGNE
RUE ST-PATRICE
Place St. Patrice
RUE DU MARCHE
R. CHARTIER
RUE DES
RUE ARCISSE DE CAUMONT
RUE DES BILLETTES
RUE ROYALE
RUE DU GENERAL DE DAIS
RUE SAINT-MALO
RUE URSULINES
R. FRANCHE
AVE. CONSEIL
PLACE CHARLES DE GAULLE
Place Charles de Gaulle
R. DE LA JURIDICTION
LACE CONSERVATORY
R. MAITRISE
RUE TREBUCIEN
RUE DELAUNEY
RUE DES TERRES
CATHEDRAL
R. BOURBESNEUR
RUE DE VERDUN
R. DE LA POTERIE
200 Meters
200 Yards
RUE TARDIF
RUE CORDELIERS
BATTLE OF NORMANDY MUSEUM
RUE SAINT-LOUP
BLVD. FABIAN WARE
To British Cemetery
D-572
R. DE LA CAMBETTE
To St-Lô & Mont St-Michel
BLVD. DU M. LECLERC
ROUTE DE SAINT-LO
Eating
1 La Rapière Restaurant
2 Le Volet Qui Penche
3 L'Angle Saint Laurent
4 Le Pommier Restaurant
Sleeping
5 Villa Lara
6 Hôtel Churchill
7 Hôtel Reine Mathilde
8 Logis les Remparts B&B
9 Hôtel d'Argouges

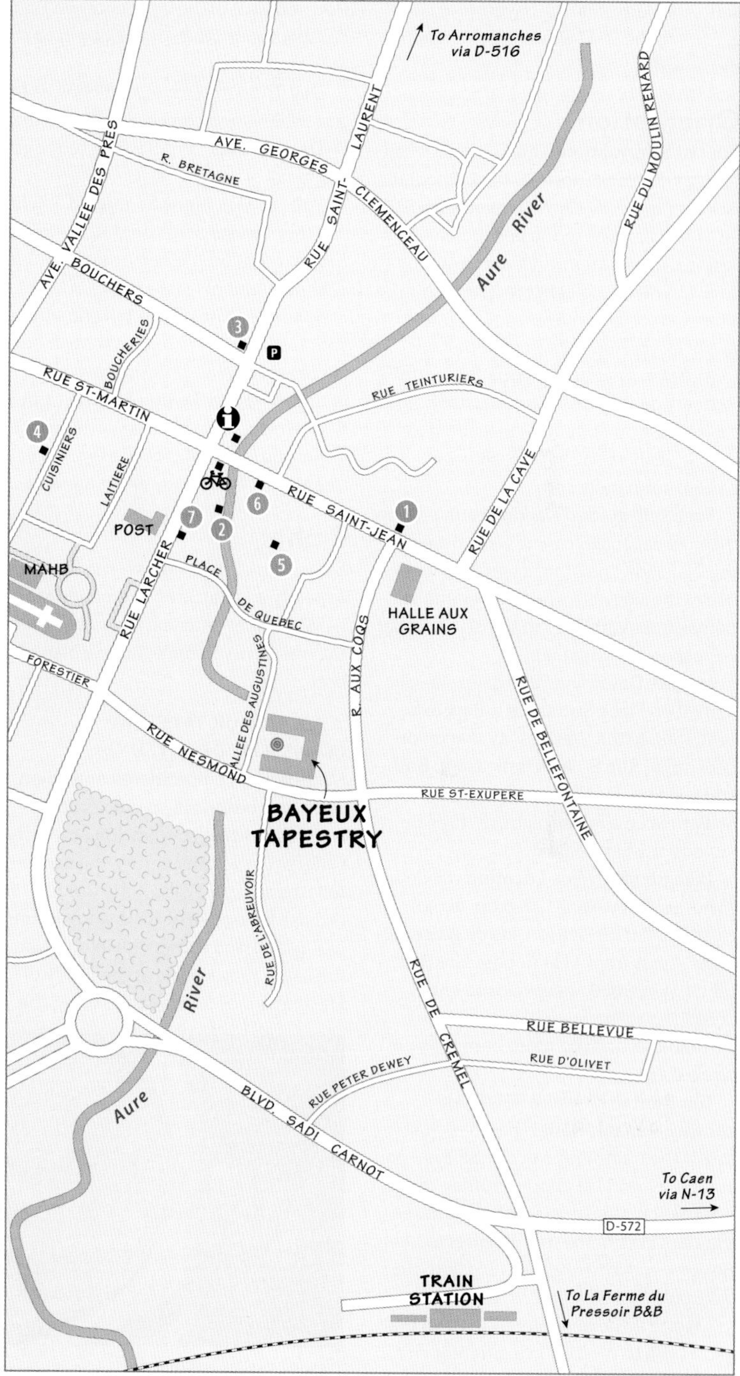

To Arromanches via D-516
AVE. GEORGES CLEMENCEAU
R. BRETAGNE
RUE SAINT-LAURENT
AVE. VALLEE DES PRES
RUE DU MOULIN RENARD
Aure River
BOUCHERS
BOUCHERIES
RUE ST-MARTIN
RUE TEINTURIERS
CUISINIERS
LAITIERE
RUE SAINT-JEAN
RUE DE LA CAVE
POST
MAHB
RUE LARCHER
PLACE DE QUEBEC
HALLE AUX GRAINS
R. AUX COQS
ALLEE DES AUGUSTINES
FORESTIER
RUE NESMOND
RUE DE BELLEFONTAINE
RUE ST-EXUPERE
BAYEUX TAPESTRY
RUE DE L'ABREUVOIR
River
Aure
RUE DE CREMEL
RUE BELLEVUE
RUE D'OLIVET
RUE PETER DEWEY
BLVD. SADI CARNOT
To Caen via N-13
D-572
TRAIN STATION
To La Ferme du Pressoir B&B

was canceled—making Bayeux the closest city to the D-Day landing site not destroyed.

Orientation

Tourist Information: The TI is on a small bridge two blocks north of the cathedral. Ask for the free *D-Day Normandy* booklet, bus schedules to the beaches, and regional information, and inquire about special events and concerts (June-Aug Mon-Sat 9:00-19:00, Sun 9:00-13:00 & 14:00-18:00; April-May and Sept-Oct Mon-Sat 9:30-12:30 & 14:00-18:00, Sun 10:00-13:00 & 14:00-18:00; shorter hours off-season; on Pont St. Jean leading to Rue St. Jean, tel. 02 31 51 28 28, www.bessin-normandie.com).

For a **self-guided walking tour,** pick up the map called *Découvrez Vieux Bayeux* at the TI. Follow the bronze plates embedded in the sidewalk, and look for information plaques with English translations that correspond to your map.

Market Days: The Saturday open-air market on Place St. Patrice is Bayeux's best, though the Wednesday market on pedestrian Rue St. Jean is pleasant. Both end by 13:00. Don't leave your car on Place St. Patrice on a Friday night, as it will be towed early Saturday.

Bike Rental: Vélos Location will deliver to hotels (daily April-Oct 8:00-20:30, closes earlier off-season, inside grocery store across from TI at Impasse de Islet, tel. 02 31 92 89 16, www.velosbayeux.com).

Taxi: Call 02 31 92 92 40 or mobile 06 70 40 07 96.

Car Rental: Bayeux offers a few choices. **Renault Rent** is handiest, just below the train station at the BP gas station. A rental at about €70/day with a 200-kilometer limit is sufficient to see the key sights from Arromanches to Utah Beach—you'll drive about 180 kilometers (16 Boulevard Sadi Carnot, tel. 02 31 51 18 51). **Hertz** is the only agency in town that allows you to drop off in a different city (located west of the city center on Route de Cherbourg, off D-613, tel. 02 31 92 03 26).

Day Trips: You have great choices for great guides and companies that tour the **D-Day beaches** from Bayeux; see page 166 for all of the specifics.

You can visit **Mont St-Michel** as a fine day trip. Two services run shuttle-van day trips to Mont St-Michel (about 1.5 hours each way, plus at least 3 hours at Mont St-Michel): **Hôtel Churchill** (€65/person; available to the public, though hotel clients get a small discount; www.hotel-churchill.fr) and **Bayeux Shuttle** (around €55/person, www.bayeuxshuttle.com). Either trip is a terrific deal, as you'll get a free tour of Normandy along the way.

Sights

Bayeux's main museums—the Bayeux Tapestry and Battle of Normandy Memorial Museum—offer a €12 combo-ticket that will save you money if you plan to see both sights.

▲▲▲BAYEUX TAPESTRY (TAPISSERIE DE BAYEUX)

Made of wool embroidered onto linen cloth, this historically precious document is a mesmerizing 70-yard-long cartoon. Created in the 11th century, this tapestry tells the story of William the Conqueror's rise from duke of Normandy to king of England, and shows his victory over England's King Harold at the Battle of Hastings in 1066. Long and skinny, the

Viewing the Bayeux Tapestry

The Battle of Hastings

Because of this pivotal battle, the most memorable date of the Middle Ages is 1066. England's king, Edward the Confessor, was about to die without an heir. The big question: Who would succeed him—Harold, an English nobleman and the king's brother-in-law, or William, duke of Normandy and the king's cousin? Edward chose William, and sent Harold to Normandy to give William the news. On the journey, Harold was captured. To win his release, he promised he would be loyal to William and not contest the decision. To test his loyalty, William sent Harold to battle for him in Brittany. Harold was successful, and William knighted him. To further test his loyalty, William had Harold swear on the relics of the Bayeux cathedral that when Edward died, he would allow William to ascend the throne. Harold returned to England, Edward died...and Harold grabbed the throne.

William, known as William the Bastard, invaded England to claim the throne. Harold met him in southern England at the town of Hastings, where their forces fought a fierce 14-hour battle. Harold was killed, and his Saxon forces were routed. William—now "the Conqueror"—marched to London, claimed his throne, and became king of England (though he spoke no English) as well as duke of Normandy.

The advent of a Norman king of England muddied the political waters and set in motion 400 years of conflict between England and France—not to be resolved until the end of the Hundred Years' War (1453). The Norman conquest of England brought that country into the European mainstream (but still no euros). The Normans established a strong central English government. Historians speculate that had William not succeeded, England would have remained on the fringe of Europe (like Scandinavia), and French culture (and language) would have prevailed in the New World.

tapestry was designed to hang in the nave of Bayeux's cathedral as a reminder to locals of their ancestor's courage. The terrific museum that houses the tapestry is an unusually good chance to teach your kids about the Middle Ages: Models, mannequins, a movie, and more make it an engaging, fun place to visit.

Cost and Hours: €9, or €12 comboticket, includes excellent audioguide for adults and a special kids' version, daily May-Aug 9:00-19:00, March-April and Sept-Oct 9:00-18:30, Nov-Dec and Feb 9:30-12:30 & 14:00-18:00, closed Jan, last entry 45 minutes before closing, tel. 02 31 51 25 50, www.bayeuxmuseum.com.

Crowd-Beating Tips: To avoid crowds, arrive before 10:00 or late in the day. It's busiest in August, and most crowded from 10:00 to 17:00.

Film: When buying your ticket, ask when they'll show the English version of the 16-minute battle film (runs every 40 minutes, English times also posted at the base of the steps to the theater).

➲ **Self-Guided Tour:** Your visit has three separate parts that tell the basic story of the Battle of Hastings, provide historical context for the event, and explain how the tapestry was made. At a minimum, allow a full hour to appreciate this important artifact.

Your visit starts with the actual **tapestry,** accompanied by an included audioguide that gives a top-notch, fast-moving, 20-minute scene-by-scene narration complete with period music (if you lose your place, find subtitles in Latin). To keep crowds moving from May through September, the audioguide's pause and rewind functions are disabled, though these are helpful to use off-season. Appreciate the fun details—such as the bare legs in scene 4 or Harold's pouting expressions in various frames—and look for references to places you may have visited (like Dinan). Pay strict attention to scene 23, where Harold takes his oath to William; the importance of keeping one's word is the point of the tapestry. Get close and (almost) feel the tapestry's texture.

Next you'll climb upstairs into a room filled with engaging **exhibits,** including a full-size replica of a Viking ship, much like the one William used to cross the Channel (Normans inherited their weaponry and seafaring skills from the Norsemen). You'll also see mannequins (find William looking unmoved with his new crown), a replica of the Domesday Book (an inventory of noblemen's lands as ordered by William), and models of castles (who knew that the Tower of London was a Norman project?). Good explanations outline the events surrounding the invasion and the subsequent creation of the tapestry, and a touchscreen lets you see the back side of the embroidery.

Your visit finishes with a 16-minute **film** that ties it all together one last time (in the cinema upstairs, skippable if you're pressed for time). You'll exit below, through a *formidable* boutique.

Remember, this is Norman propaganda: The English (the bad guys, referred to as *les goddamns,* after a phrase the French kept hearing them say) are shown with mustaches and long hair; the French (*les* good guys) are clean-cut and clean-shaven—with even the backs of their heads shaved for a better helmet fit.

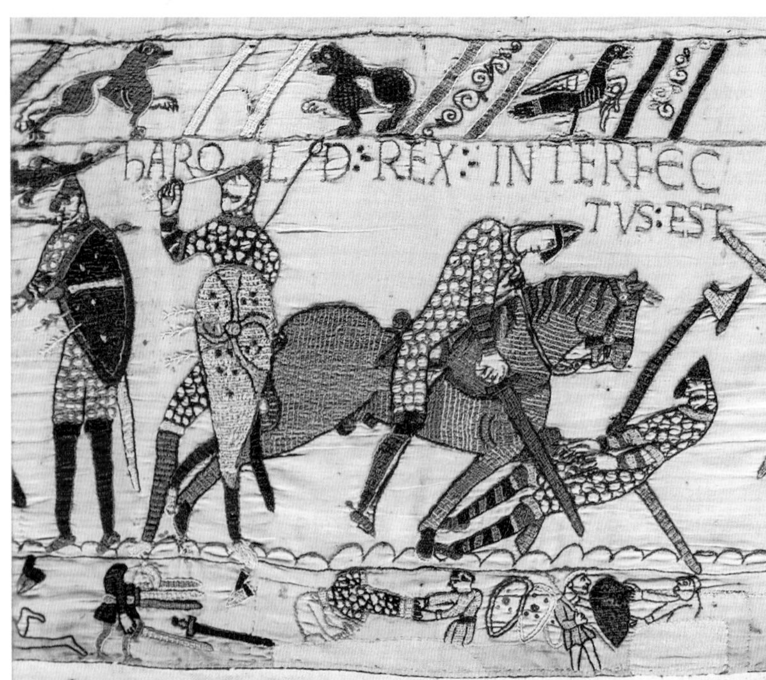

King Harold's death as depicted in the Bayeux Tapestry

▲BAYEUX CATHEDRAL

This massive building, as big as Paris' Notre-Dame, dominates the small town of Bayeux. Make it a point to see the cathedral after dark, when it's beautifully illuminated.

Cost and Hours: Free, daily July-Aug 8:30-19:00, Sept-June 8:30-18:00.

➲ **Self-Guided Tour:** To start your visit, find the small **square** opposite the front entry (information board about the cathedral in rear corner). Notice the two dark towers—originally Romanesque, they were capped later with tall Gothic spires. The cathedral's west facade is structurally Romanesque, but with a decorative Gothic "curtain" added.

Before entering, head just to the left of the cathedral, find the stairs at the top of a walking lane, and crane your neck up. The little rectangular stone house atop the near tower was the **watchman's home,** from which he'd keep an eye out for incoming English troops during the Hundred Years' War...and for Germans five centuries later (it didn't work—the Germans took the town in 1940). Bayeux was liberated on D-Day plus one: June 7. About the only casualty was the German lookout—shot while doing just that from the window of this stone house.

Bayeux Cathedral

Now step inside the cathedral. The magnificent view of the **nave** from the top of the steps shows a mix of Romanesque (ground floor) and soaring Gothic (upper floors). Historians believe the Bayeux tapestry originally hung here. Imagine it hanging halfway up the big Romanesque arches. This section is brightly lit by the huge windows above. Try to visualize this scene with the original, richly colored stained glass in all those upper windows. Rare 13th-century stained-glass bits are in the high central window above the altar; the other stained glass is from the 19th and 20th centuries.

Walk down the nave and notice the areas between the big, round **arches.** That busy zigzag patterning characterizes Norman art in France as well as in England. These 11th-century Romanesque arches are decorated with a manic mix of repeated geometric shapes: half-circles, hash marks, full circles, and diagonal lines. Notice also the creepy faces eyeing you, especially the ring of devil heads three arches up on the right. Yuck.

Information panels in the side aisles give basic facts about the cathedral (in English). More 13th-century Norman Gothic is in the choir (the fancy area behind the central altar). Here, simple Romanesque carvings lie under Gothic arches with characteristic tall, thin lines adding a graceful verticality to the overall feel of the interior.

For maximum 1066 atmosphere, step into the spooky **crypt** (beneath the central altar), which was used originally as a safe spot for the cathedral's relics. The crypt displays two freestanding columns and bulky capitals with fine Romanesque carving. During a reinforcement of the nave, these two columns were replaced. Workers removed the Gothic veneer and discovered their true inner Romanesque beauty. Orange angel-musicians on other columns add color to this somber room.

BATTLE OF NORMANDY MEMORIAL MUSEUM (MUSEE MEMORIAL DE LA BATAILLE DE NORMANDIE)

This museum provides a manageable, if dry, overview of WWII's Battle of Normandy. With its many maps and timelines of the epic battle to liberate northern France, it's aimed at military history buffs. You'll get a good briefing on the Atlantic Wall (the German fortifications stretching along the coast—useful before visiting Longues-sur-Mer), learn why Normandy was selected as the landing site, understand General Charles de Gaulle's contributions to the invasion, and realize the key role played by aviation. You'll also appreciate the challenges faced by doctors, war correspondents, and civil engineers (who had to clean up after the battles—the gargantuan bulldozer on display looks useful).

Cost and Hours: €7, €12 combo-ticket with Bayeux Tapestry, daily May-Sept 9:30-18:30, Oct-Dec and mid-Feb-April 10:00-12:30 & 14:00-18:00, closed Jan-mid-Feb, last entry one hour before closing, on Bayeux's ring road, 20 minutes on foot from center on Boulevard Fabian Ware, free parking, tel. 02 31 51 46 90, www.bayeuxmuseum.com.

Film: A 25-minute film gives a good summary of the Normandy invasion from start to finish (shown in English 3-5 times daily—ask when the next English showing will be).

Nearby: Taking a right out of the museum leads along a footpath to the **Monument to Reporters,** a grassy walkway lined with white roses and stone monuments listing, by year, the names of reporters who have died in the line of duty from 1944 to today. The path continues to the **British Military Cemetery,** decorated with 4,144 simple gravestones marking the final resting places of these fallen soldiers. The memorial's Latin inscription reads, "In 1944, the British came to free the homeland of William the Conqueror." Interestingly, this cemetery has soldiers' graves from all countries involved in the battle of Normandy (even Germany) except the United States, which requires its soldiers to be buried on US property—such as the American Cemetery at Omaha Beach.

Eating

Traffic-free Rue St. Jean is lined with cafés, *crêperies,* and inexpensive dining options.

$$$ La Rapière is a lovely, traditional wood-beamed eatery filled with locals enjoying a refined meal and a rare-these-days cheese platter for your finale. The veal with Camembert sauce is memorable. Reservations are wise (€29-52 *menus,* closed for lunch Mon and Wed and all day Sun, 53 Rue St. Jean, tel. 03 31 21 05 45, www.larapiere.net).

$ Le Volet Qui Penche is a cool, wine-shop-meets-bistro place run by gentle, English-speaking Pierre-Henri. He serves great charcuterie and cheese platters and offers a small selection of à la carte items and wines by the glass but no wine tastings. There is nonstop service until 20:00 most days, making early dinners easy (€10-12 *plat du jour,* salads, *tartines,* closed for lunch Mon and Sat and all day Sun, near the TI at 3 Passage de l'Islet, tel. 03 31 21 98 54).

$$$ L'Angle Saint Laurent is a refined and romantic place run by a husband-and-wife team (lovely Caroline speaks English and manages the restaurant, Sébastien cooks). Come here for a special meal of *Normand* specialties done in a contemporary style. The selection is lim-

Camembert Cheese

This cheap, soft, white, Brie-like cheese is sold all over France (and America) in distinctive, round wooden containers. Camembert has been known for its cheese for 500 years, but local legend has it that today's cheese got its start in the French Revolution, when a priest on the run was taken in by Marie Harel, a Camembert farmer. He repaid the favor by giving her the secret formula from his own hometown—Brie.

From cow to customer, Camembert takes about three weeks to make. High-fat milk from Norman cows is curdled with rennet, ladled into round, five-inch molds, sprinkled with *Penicillium camemberti* bacteria, and left to dry. In the first three days, the cheese goes from the cow's body temperature to room temperature to refrigerator cool (50 degrees).

Two weeks later, the ripened and aged cheese is wrapped in wooden bands and labeled for market. Like wines, Camembert cheese is controlled by government regulations and must bear the "A.O.C." (*Appellation d'Origine Contrôlée*) stamp of approval.

ited, changes often, and is all homemade (€30-40 *menus*, good wine list, closed for lunch Wed and Sat and all day Sun, 2 Rue des Bouchers, tel. 02 31 92 03 01, www.langlesaintlaurent.com).

$$ Le Pommier, with street appeal inside and out, is a good place to sample regional products with clever twists in a relaxed yet refined atmosphere. Owner Thierry mixes old and new in his cuisine and decor and focuses on organic food with no GMOs. His fish and meat dishes are satisfying no matter how he prepares them, and there's a vegetarian *menu* as well—a rarity in meat-loving France (two-course *menu* €21, good three-course *menu* from €25, open daily, 38 Rue des Cuisiniers, tel. 02 31 21 52 10, www.restaurantlepommier.com).

Sleeping

$$$$ Villa Lara**** owns the town's most luxurious accommodations smack in the center of Bayeux. The 28 spacious and well-configured rooms all have brilliant views of the cathedral, and a few have small terraces. Helpful owner Rima and her well-trained staff take wonderful care of their guests (Db-€270-360 depending on size and season, palatial Db suite-€420-460, pricey but excellent breakfast-€23, elevator, exercise room, ice machines, comfortable lounges, free and secure parking, between the tapestry museum and TI at 6 Place de Québec, tel. 02 31 92 00 55, www.hotel-villalara.com, info@hotel-villalara.com).

$$ Hôtel Churchill***, on a traffic-free street across from the TI, could not be more central. Owners Eric and Patricia are great hosts (ask Eric about his professional soccer career). The hotel has 32 plush-and-pricey rooms with wood furnishings, big beds, and convivial public spaces peppered with historic photos of Bayeux's liberation (small Db-€130, bigger Db-€155, deluxe Db or Tb-€187, Qb-€207, 14 Rue St. Jean, tel. 02 31 21 31 80, www.hotel-churchill.fr, info@hotel-churchill.fr).

$ Hôtel Reine Mathilde** is a solid, centrally located value with good service. There are 16 sharp rooms above an easygoing brasserie (Db-€85), and six large rooms with three-star comfort in an annex next door (Db-€125, Tb-€140, Qb-€155, breakfast-€9.50, one block from the TI at 23 Rue Larcher, tel. 02 31 92 08 13, www.hotel-bayeux-reinemathilde.fr, hotel.reinemathilde@orange.fr).

$ Logis les Remparts, run by bubbly Christèle, is a delightful, three-room bed-and-breakfast situated above an atmospheric Calvados cider-tasting shop, near the catedral. The rooms are big, comfortable, and homey—one is a huge, two-room suite (Db-€65-90, Tb-€80-110, cash only for payments under €200, breakfast-€7, a few blocks above the cathedral on the park-like Place Charles de Gaulle at 4 Rue Bourbesneur, tel. 02 31 92 50 40, www.lecornu.fr, info@lecornu.fr).

$ Hôtel d'Argouges*** (dar-goozh) is named for its builder, Lord d'Argouges. This tranquil retreat has a mini château feel with classy public spaces, lovely private gardens, and 28 standard-comfort rooms. The hotel is run by formal Madame Ropartz, who has had every aspect of the hotel renovated (Db-€127, larger Db-€149, Tb-€170, fine family suites-€240, deluxe family suite-€290 for up to 6—works fine for two couples, extra bed-€20, breakfast-€14, no elevator, secure free parking, just off Place St. Patrice at 21 Rue St. Patrice, tel. 02 31 92 88 86, www.hotel-dargouges.com, info@hotel-dargouges.com).

Transportation

Arriving and Departing

BY CAR

Nearing Bayeux, look for the cathedral spires and follow signs for *Centre-Ville*, then signs for the *Tapisserie* (tapestry) or your hotel (individual hotels are well-signed from the ring road—wait for yours to appear). Day-trippers will find pay parking lots in the town center (including at the Hôtel de Ville near the TI, and at Place St. Patrice; €1/hour, 3-hour limit). A few other parking lots are free but require a cardboard clock on your dashboard and are limited to four hours. (These time limits are not enforced from 12:00 to 14:00, allowing you to stretch your stay.) To park longer, you can find free, unlimited lots along the southern ring road (along Boulevard Marechal Leclerc and Boulevard Sadi Carnot).

Drivers connecting Bayeux with Mont St-Michel should use the speedy, free A-84 autoroute.

BY TRAIN AND BUS

Trains and buses share the same station in Bayeux (no bag storage). It's a 15-minute walk from the station to the tapestry, and 15 minutes from the tapestry to Place St. Patrice (and several recommended hotels). To reach the tapestry, the cathedral, and the hotels, cross the major street in front of the station and follow Rue de Cremel toward *l'Hôpital*, then turn left on Rue Nesmond. Find signs to the *Tapisserie* or continue on to the cathedral. Taxis are usually waiting at the station. Allow €8 for a taxi from the train station to any recommended hotel or sight in Bayeux, and €21 to Arromanches (€32 after 19:00 and on Sundays, taxi tel. 02 31 92 92 40 or mobile 06 70 40 07 96).

From Bayeux by Train to: Paris' Gare St. Lazare (9/day, 2.5 hours, some change in Caen), **Amboise** (2/day, 4.5 hours, change in Caen and Tours' St-Pierre-des-Corps), **Honfleur** (2-3/day, 20-minute train to Caen, then 1-hour PrestoBus—line #39—express bus to Honfleur; for bus info, call 02 31 89 28 41, www.busverts.fr), **Pontorson/Mont St-Michel** (2-3/day, 2 hours to Pontorson, then 20-minute bus ride to Mont St-Michel).

D-DAY BEACHES

The 54 miles of Atlantic coast stretching from Utah Beach in the west to Sword Beach in the east are marked with tributes to the courage of the British, Canadian, and American armies that successfully carried out the largest military operation in history: D-Day. (It's called *Jour J* in French.) It was on these serene beaches, at the crack of dawn on June 6, 1944, that the Allies finally gained a foothold in France; from this moment, Nazi Europe was destined to crumble.

The first 24 hours of the invasion will be decisive... The fate of Germany depends on the outcome... For the Allies, as well as Germany, it will be the longest day.

—Field Marshal Erwin Rommel to his aide, April 22, 1944

June 6, 2014, marked the 70th anniversary of the landings. Locals will never forget what the troops and their families sacrificed all those years ago. They talk of the last visits of veterans with heartfelt sorrow; they have adored seeing the old soldiers in their villages and fear losing the firsthand accounts of the battles. This remains particularly friendly soil for Americans—a place where their soldiers are still honored and the image of the US as a force for good remains untarnished.

Orientation

I've listed the D-Day sites from east to west, starting with Arromanches. Many visitors prefer to focus on the American sector (west of Arromanches), rather than the British and Canadian sectors (Arromanches and eastward), which have been overbuilt with resorts, making it harder to envision the events of June 1944. The American sector looks today very much as it would have 70 years ago. For a useful resource on visiting the D-Day beaches, see www.normandiememoire.com.

Rick's Tip: *The free* ***D-Day Normandy: Land of Liberty*** *booklet gives succinct reviews of area D-Day museums and sites with current opening times. It's available at TIs, but you usually need to ask for it (or you can download it yourself from www.normandiememoire.com).*

D-Day Sites in One Day

If you have only one day, spend it entirely on the beaches. If you're traveling by car, begin on the cliffs above Arromanches. From there, visit Port Winston and the D-Day Landing Museum, then continue west to Longues-sur-Mer and tour the German gun battery. Spend your afternoon visiting the American Cemetery and its thought-provoking visitors center, walking on Omaha Beach at Vierville-sur-Mer, and exploring Pointe du Hoc. If you have extra time, spend it at the Utah Beach sites to learn about the paratroopers' role in the invasion. You can return to

Utah Beach memorial

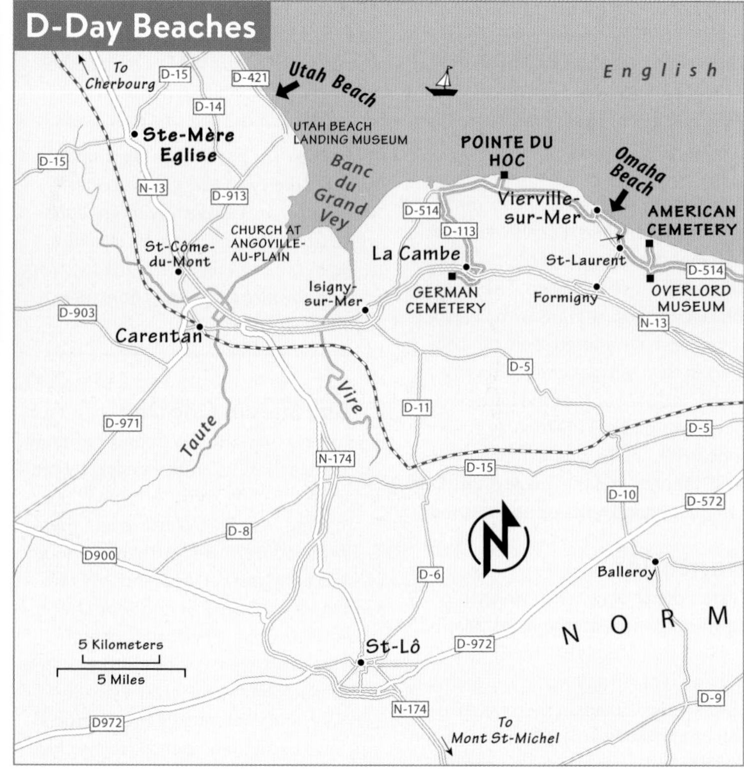

Bayeux or continue on to Mont St-Michel.

Canadians will want to start at the Juno Beach Centre and Canadian Cemetery (in Courseulles-sur-Mer, 10 minutes east of Arromanches).

Getting Around the D-Day Beaches

It's easy for drivers. Without a car, taking a minivan tour is best. Taking a taxi is cheaper than taking a tour, but you'll miss out on having a guide. Public transport is available, but not practical for more than one sight.

By Car

Renting a car for a day is an affordable way to visit the beaches, particularly for three or more people (to rent a car in Bayeux, see page 160).

By Minivan Tour

An army of small companies offers all-day excursions to the D-Day beaches from Bayeux or nearby. Because demand has grown, it seems that anyone with passable English wants to guide. Travelers beware. Anyone can get you around the beaches, but effective teaching of the events is another story. You should expect your guide to deliver coherent history lessons and go with you to all sights (and not orient and disperse you).

The tour companies and guides below are people I trust to take your time seriously. Most deliver riveting commentary about these moving sites. To land one of these top-notch guides, book your tour in advance (3-6 months is best during peak periods), or pray for a last-minute cancellation. While you can save by hiring a

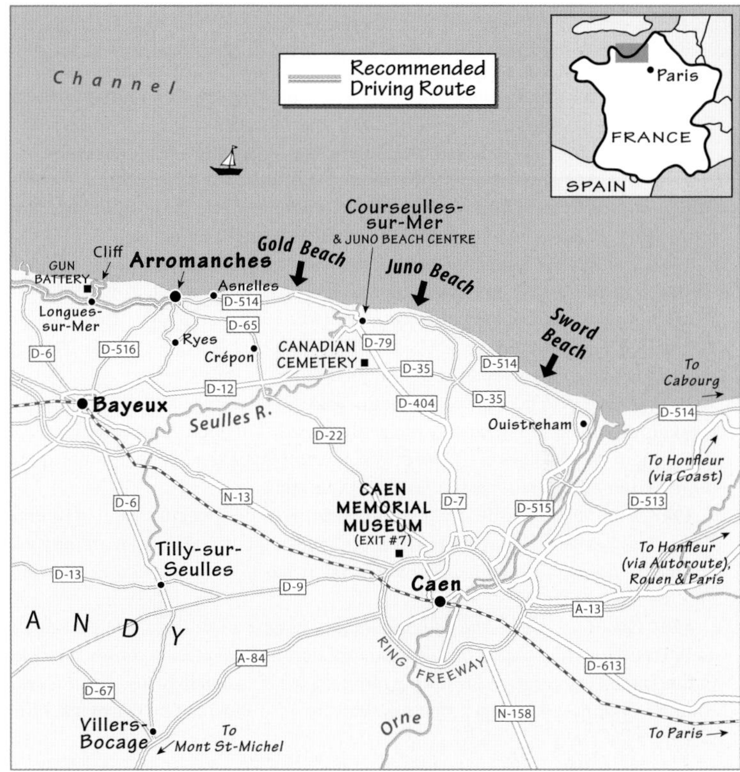

guide who offers half-day tours, a full day on the beaches is right for most. To spend less, look for a guide who will join you in your rental car.

Many tours prefer to pick up in or near Bayeux. Many guides skip Arromanches, preferring to focus on sights farther west. While some companies discourage children, others (including Dale Booth and Sylvain Kast) welcome them.

Bayeux Shuttle, run by British expat Andy Sutherland, works hard to incorporate technology (online sign-ups, GPS info displayed onboard) and great guiding into their tours. It's user-friendly for individuals: The pick-up point is in Bayeux, and you can usually book at the last minute. Check www.bayeuxshuttle.com for their latest offers (and other tours); half-day tours run about €50, while full-day tours are about €95.

Dale Booth, a fine historian and fascinating storyteller, leads tours for up to eight people to the American, Canadian, and British sectors (tel. 02 33 71 53 76, www.dboothnormandytours.com, dboothholidays@sfr.fr).

Normandy Battle Tours are led by easygoing Stuart Robertson, an effective teacher and historian. He also owns a bed-and-breakfast near Ste-Mère Eglise and offers combo accommodation/tour packages (tel. 02 33 41 28 34, www.normandybattletours.com, stuart@normandybattletours.com).

Sylvain Kast has good overall knowledge and many French family connections to the war; he's strong in the American sector and the roles that the Air Force and paratroopers played (mobile 06 17 44 04

The Countdown to D-Day—and Victory

1939 On September 1, Adolf Hitler invades the Free City of Danzig (today's Gdańsk, Poland), sparking World War II.

1940 Germany's "Blitzkrieg" ("lightning war") quickly overwhelms France, Nazis goose-step down Avenue des Champs-Elysées, and the country is divided into Occupied France (the north) and Vichy France (the south, ruled by right-wing French). Just like that, nearly the entire Continent is fascist.

1941 The Allies (Britain, the Soviet Union, and others) peck away at the fringes of "fortress Europe." The Soviets repel Hitler's invasion at Moscow, while the Brits (with American aid) battle German U-boats for control of the seas. On December 7, Japan bombs the US naval base at Pearl Harbor, Hawaii. The US enters the war against Japan and its ally, Germany.

1942 Three crucial battles—at Stalingrad, El-Alamein, and Guadalcanal—weaken the German forces and their ally, Japan. The victorious tank battle at El-Alamein in the deserts of North Africa soon gives the Allies a jumping-off point (Tunis) for the first assault on the Continent.

1943 More than 150,000 Americans and Brits, under the command of George Patton and Bernard "Monty" Montgomery, land in Sicily and begin working their way north through Italy. Meanwhile, Germany has to fend off tenacious Soviets on their eastern front.

1944 On June 6, 1944, the Allies launch "Operation Overlord," better known as D-Day. The Allies amass three million soldiers and six million tons of matériel in England in preparation for the biggest fleet-led invasion in history—across the English Channel to France, then eastward toward Berlin. The Germans, hun-

46, www.d-day-experience-tours.com, sylvainkast@yahoo.fr).

Vanessa Letourneur is highly capable as a guide anywhere in Normandy. She offers top-notch, half-day tours from Bayeux (mobile 06 98 95 89 45, www.normandypanorama.com).

Rick's Tip: *Some guides can get lost in battle minutiae that you don't have time for. Tell your guide what you want to see;* **be specific about your interests.** *Request extra time at the Normandy American Cemetery to see the excellent visitors center.*

Rodolphe Passera speaks fluent English and is a serious student of the Normandy invasion. He works as a guide at the D-Day Landing Museum at Utah Beach. He can join your car or drive you in his Lexus SUV (mobile 06 30 55 63 39, leopardbusinesslanguages@gmail.com).

Cost: These tours are pricey because you're hiring a professional guide and driver/vehicle for the day. All guides charge about the same. A few have regularly scheduled departures available for individual sign-ups (figure on paying about €90/person for a day and €60/person for a half-day). Private groups should expect to pay €500-660 for up to eight people for all day and €250-330 for a half-day. Most tours don't go inside museums (which have good explanations posted in any case), but those that do usually include entry fees—ask. Although many guides offer all-day tours only, these guides may do half-day trips: Bayeux Shuttle, Vanessa Letourneur, and Rodolphe Passera.

kered down in northern France, know an invasion is imminent, but the Allies keep the details top secret. On the night of June 5, more than 180,000 soldiers board ships and planes, not knowing where they are headed until they're under way. Each one carries a note from General Dwight D. Eisenhower: "The tide has turned. The free men of the world are marching together to victory."

At 6:30 on June 6, 1944, Americans spill out of troop transports into the cold waters off a beach in Normandy, code-named Omaha. The weather is bad, seas are rough, and the prep bombing has failed. The soldiers, many seeing their first action, are dazed, confused, and weighed down by heavy packs. Nazi machine guns pin them against the sea. Slowly, they crawl up the beach on their stomachs. More than a thousand die. They hold on until the next wave of transports arrives.

Americans also see action at Utah Beach, while the British and Canadian troops storm Sword, Juno, and Gold. All day long, Allied confusion does battle with German indecision—the Nazis never really counterattack, thinking D-Day is just a ruse, not the main invasion. By day's end, the Allies have taken all five beaches along the Normandy coast and soon begin building two completely artificial harbors, code-named "Mulberry," providing ports for the reconquest of western Europe. The stage is set for a quick and easy end to the war. (Right.)

1945 Having liberated Paris (August 26, 1944), the Allies' march on Berlin from the west bogs down, hit by poor supply lines, bad weather, and the surprising German counterpunch at the Battle of the Bulge. Finally, in the spring, the Americans and Brits cross the Rhine, Soviet soldiers close in on Berlin, Hitler shoots himself, and—after nearly six long years of war—Europe is free.

By Taxi

Taxi minivans shuttle up to seven people between the key sites at reasonable rates, which vary depending on how far you go. Allow €240 for an eight-hour taxi day (€300 on Sun) to visit the top Utah and Omaha Beach sites (without guiding, of course). Figure about €21 each way between Bayeux and Arromanches, €37 between Bayeux and the American Cemetery, and €100 for a 2.5-hour visit to Omaha Beach sites from Bayeux or Arromanches (50 percent surcharge after 19:00 and on Sun, taxi tel. 02 31 92 92 40 or mobile 06 70 40 07 96, www.taxisbayeux.com, taxisbayeux@orange.fr).

Arromanches

This small town—part of Gold Beach (in the British landing zone)—was ground zero for the D-Day invasion. The Allies decided it would be easier to build their own port than to try to take one from the Nazis. And so, almost overnight, Arromanches sprouted the immense harbor, Port Winston, which gave the Allies a foothold in Normandy, allowing them to begin their victorious push to Berlin and end World War II.

The postwar period brought a long decline. Only recently has the population of tiny Arromanches finally returned to its June 5, 1944, numbers. Here you'll find a good museum, an evocative beach and bluff, and a touristy-but-fun little town that offers a pleasant cocktail of war memories, cotton candy, and beachfront trinket shops.

For drivers who want to linger longer, Arromanches makes a fine home base for touring the D-Day beaches. Sit on the seawall after dark and listen to the waves lick the sand while you contemplate the events that took place here 70 years ago.

Orientation

Tourist Information: The service-oriented TI has the *D-Day Normandy* booklet, a free leaflet illustrating the Port Winston harbor, bus schedules, a listing of area hotels and *chambres d'hôtes,* and helpful Mathilde (daily 10:00-12:00 & 14:00-17:00, longer hours in summer—9:30-19:00 in July-Aug, across the parking lot from the D-Day Landing Museum at 2 Avenue Maréchal Joffre, tel. 02 31 22 36 45, www.ot-arromanches.fr). You may find a seasonal branch TI at the parking lot near Arromanches 360.

ATM: An ATM is across from the museum parking lot.

Groceries: The grocery store is a long block above the beach, across from L'Hôtel Ideal de Mountbatten.

Taxi: To get an Arromanches-based taxi, call mobile 06 66 62 00 99.

Parking: The main parking lot by the D-Day Landing Museum costs €1.50 per hour (free 19:00-9:00). For free parking and less traffic, look for the lot between the grocery store and L'Hôtel Ideal de Mountbatten as you enter Arromanches.

WWII Paraphernalia Store: Arromanches Militaria sells all sorts of D-Day relics (daily 10:00-19:00, 11 Boulevard Gilbert Longuet).

Sights

In this section, I've linked Arromanches' D-Day sites with some self-guided commentary.

▲▲▲PORT WINSTON ARTIFICIAL HARBOR

To appreciate the massive undertaking of creating this harbor in a matter of days, you'll view it from two vantage points: from the cliff above and from the town itself. Start on the cliffs, overlooking the site of the impressive WWII harbor.

Getting There: Drive two minutes toward Courseulles-sur-Mer and pay €3 to park in the big, can't-miss-it lot overlooking the sea. Nondrivers—or drivers who'd rather leave their car in Arromanches—can hike 10 minutes up the hill behind the town's D-Day Landing Museum, or take the free white train from the museum to the top of the bluff (runs

Concrete blocks from the Port Winston Artificial Harbor

daily June-Sept, Sat-Sun only Oct-mid-Nov and April-May, none in winter).

➲ **Self-Guided Tour:** This commentary will lead you around the site.

• *Find the circular concrete viewpoint tower overlooking the town and the beaches and prepare for your briefing. Beyond Arromanches to the left is the American sector, with Omaha Beach and then Utah Beach (notice the sheer cliffs between these two sectors); below and to the right lie the British and Canadian sectors.*

Now get this: Along the beaches below, the Allies arrived in the largest amphibious attack ever, launching the liberation of Western Europe. On D-Day +1—June 7, 1944—17 old ships sailed 100 miles across the English Channel under their own steam to Arromanches. Their crews sank them so that each bow faced the next ship's stern, forming a sea barrier. Then 500 tugboats towed 115 football-field-size cement blocks (called "Phoenixes") across the channel. These were also sunk, creating a four-mile-long breakwater 1.5 miles offshore. Finally, engineers set up seven floating steel "pierheads" with extendable legs; they then linked these to shore with four mile-long floating roads made of concrete pontoons. (You can see a segment of pontoon road in the parking lot behind you, by the statue of the Virgin Mary.) Soldiers placed 115 antiaircraft guns on the Phoenixes and pontoons, protecting a port the size of Dover, England. Within just six days of operation, 54,000 vehicles, 326,000 troops, and 110,000 tons of goods had crossed the English Channel. An Allied toehold in Normandy was secure. Eleven months later, Hitler was dead and the war was over.

▲▲ARROMANCHES 360° THEATER

The domed building just off the cliff-top parking lot houses the powerful film *Normandy's 100 Days*. The screens surrounding you show archival footage and photographs of the endeavor to liberate Normandy (works in any language). In addition to honoring the many Allied and German soldiers who died, it gently reminds us that 20,000 French civilians were killed in aerial bombardments. The experience is as loud and slickly produced as anything at the D-Day beaches. It's more emotional and immersive than educational, and for that reason some prefer to see it at the end of their D-Day experience to sum up all they've seen.

Cost and Hours: €5, shows at :10 and :40 past the hour, daily June-Aug 9:40-18:40, April-May and Sept 10:10-18:10, Oct-mid-Nov 10:10-17:40, these are first and last show times, shorter hours off-season, closed most of Jan, tel. 02 31 06 06 45, www.arromanches360.com.

• *Head down to the town's main parking lot (follow signs to Musée du Débarquement) and find the round bulkhead on the seawall, near the D-Day Landing Museum entry. Stand facing the sea.*

The **prefab harbor** was created out there by the British. Since it was Churchill's brainchild, it was named Port Winston. Designed to be temporary (it was used for six months), it was supposed to wash out to sea over time—which is exactly what happened with its twin harbor at Omaha Beach (that one lasted only 12 days, thanks to a terrible storm). If the tide is out, you'll see several rusted floats mired on the sand close in—these supported the pontoon roads. If you stare hard enough at the concrete blocks in the sea to the right, you'll see that one still has what's left of an antiaircraft gun platform on it.

On the hill beyond the museum, you'll spot a Sherman tank, one of 50,000 deployed during the landings. Behind the museum (not viewable from here) is another section of a pontoon road, an antiaircraft gun, and a Higgins boat, which was used to ferry 30 soldiers at a time from naval ships to the beaches. If you can, walk down to the beach and wander among the concrete and rusted litter of the battle—and be thankful that all you hear are birds and surf.

▲D-DAY LANDING MUSEUM (MUSEE DU DEBARQUEMENT)
The D-Day Landing Museum, facing the harbor, makes a worthwhile 30-45-minute visit and is the only way to get a full appreciation of how the artificial harbor was built. While gazing through windows at the site of this amazing endeavor, you can study helpful models, videos, and photographs illustrating the construction and use of the prefabricated harbor. Screens over the model show a virtual reconstruction of Port Winston. Those blimp-like objects tethered to the port prevented German planes from getting too close (though the German air force had been made largely irrelevant by this time). Ponder the remarkable undertaking that resulted in this harbor being built in just 12 days, while battles raged. The essential 15-minute film (up the stairs behind the cashier) uses British newsreel footage to illustrate the construction of the port; a different video (10 minutes, far end of ground floor) recalls D-Day. Ask for times when each film is shown in English, or wait for the announcement.

Cost and Hours: €8, daily May-Aug 9:00-19:00, Sept 9:00-18:00, Oct-Dec and Feb-April 10:00-12:30 & 13:30-17:00, closed Jan, pick up English flier at door, tel. 02 31 22 34 31, www.arromanches-museum.com.

Eating and Sleeping

Arromanches, with its pinwheels and seagulls, has a salty beach-town ambience that makes it a fun overnight stop. Park in the town's main lot at the museum (€1.50/hour, free 19:00-9:00). All of the hotels have restaurants except for the last one, L'Hôtel Ideal de Mountbatten.

$ Hôtel de la Marine*** has a knockout location with point-blank views to the artificial harbor site from most of its 33 comfortable rooms (Db-€116, Tb-€165, Qb-€195, bigger family rooms, includes breakfast, elevator, view restaurant, Quai du Canada, tel. 02 31 22 34 19, www.hotel-de-la-marine.fr, hotel.de.la.marine@wanadoo.fr). Its restaurant allows you to dine or drink in style on the water (*menus* from €19, daily).

$ Hôtel d'Arromanches**, which sits on the main pedestrian drag near the TI, is a good value, with nine mostly small, straightforward rooms, some with water views, all up a tight stairway that feels like a tree house (Db-€70-85, newer "deluxe" Db-€90-99, Tb-€96, breakfast-€10, 2 Rue Colonel René Michel, tel. 02 31 22 36 26, www.hoteldarromanches.fr, reservation@hoteldarromanches.fr). Here you'll find the cheery **Restaurant "Le Pappagall"** (French slang for "parakeet"), with tasty mussels, filling fish *choucroute*, "*les* feesh and cheeps," salads, and a full offering at fair prices (daily in high season, closed Wed and possibly other days off-season). For more of a nightclub scene, head to **Pub Marie Celeste,** around the corner on Rue de la Poste.

$ Le Mulberry** is an intimate place with nine simple rooms and a small restaurant (*menus* from €20, daily). It's a five-minute walk up from the touristy beach, near the town's church, so expect bells to mark the hour until 22:00 (Db-€85-99, Tb-€102-124, breakfast-€9, reception closed 14:00-16:00 and after 19:00, a block below the church at 6 Rue Maurice Lihare, tel. 02 31 22 36 05, www.lemulberry.fr, mail@lemulberry.fr).

$ L'Hôtel Ideal de Mountbatten***, located a long block up from the water, is an eight-room, two-story, motel-esque place with generously sized, stylish, clean, and good-value lodgings, and welcoming owners Sylvie and Laurent (Db-€72-99, Tb-€125-135, breakfast-€10, reception closed 14:00-16:00, easy and free parking, short block below the main post office—La Poste—at 20 Boulevard Gilbert Longuet, tel. 02 31 22 59 70, www.hotelarromancheslideal.fr, contact@hotelarromancheslideal.fr).

American D-Day Sites

The American sector, stretching west of Arromanches, is divided between Omaha and Utah Beaches. Omaha Beach starts just a few miles west of Arromanches and has the most important sites for visitors, including the American Cemetery and—just beyond the beach—Pointe du Hoc. Utah Beach sites are farther away (on the road to Cherbourg), but these were also critical to the ultimate success of the Normandy invasion. The American Airborne sector covers a broad area behind Utah Beach and centers on Ste-Mère Eglise. You'll see memorials sprouting up all around the countryside.

Rick's Tip: *The D-Day landing sites are rural, so you won't find a grocery on every corner.* **Pack ahead if you plan to picnic.**

Omaha Beach

Omaha Beach is the landing zone most familiar to Americans. This well-defended stretch was where US troops saw their biggest losses (dramatized in the movie *Saving Private Ryan*). I've listed several stops going west from Arromanches.

▲LONGUES-SUR-MER GUN BATTERY

Four German casemates (three with guns intact)—built to guard against seaborne attacks—hunker down at the end of a country road. The guns, 300 yards inland, were arranged in a semicircle to maximize the firing range east and west, and are the only original coastal artillery guns remaining in place in the D-Day region. (Much was scrapped after the war, long before people thought of tourism.) This battery, staffed by 194 German soldiers, was more defended than the better-known Pointe du Hoc (described later). The Longues-sur-Mer Gun Battery was a critical link in Hitler's Atlantic Wall defense, which consisted of more than 15,000 structures stretching from Norway to the Pyrenees. The guns could hit targets up to 12 miles away with relatively sharp accuracy if linked to good target information. The Allies had to take them out.

German gun at Longues-sur-Mer

Cost and Hours: Free and always open; on-site TI open April-Oct daily 10:00-13:00 & 14:00-18:00. The TI's €5.70 booklet is helpful, but skip the €5 tour.

Getting There: You'll find the guns 10 minutes west of Arromanches on D-514. Follow *Port en Bessin* signs; once in Longues-sur-Mer, follow *Batterie* signs; turn right at the town's only traffic light.

Visiting the Battery: Enter the third bunker you pass. It took seven soldiers to manage each gun, which could be loaded and fired six times per minute (the shells weighed 40 pounds). Outside, climb above the bunker and find the hooks that were used to secure camouflage netting, making it nigh-impossible for bombers to locate them.

Head down the path between the second and third bunkers until you reach a lone observation bunker (look for the low-lying concrete roof just before the cliffs). This was designed to direct the firing; field telephones connected the bunker to the gun batteries by underground wires. Walk to the observation bunker to appreciate the strategic view over the Channel. From here you can walk along the glorious *Sentier du Littoral* (coastal path) above the cliffs and see Arromanches in the distance, then walk the road back to your car. You can also drive five minutes down to the water on the small road past the site's parking lot.

The WWI Russian cannon near the parking lot's info kiosk looks like a Tinkertoy compared to those up the short trail.

▲▲▲WWII NORMANDY AMERICAN CEMETERY AND MEMORIAL

Soldiers' graves are the greatest preachers of peace.

—Albert Schweitzer

Crowning a bluff just above Omaha Beach and the eye of the D-Day storm, 9,387 brilliant white-marble crosses and Stars of David glow in memory of Americans who gave their lives to free Europe on the beaches below. You'll want to spend at least 1.5 hours at this stirring site.

Cost and Hours: Free, daily mid-April-mid-Sept 9:00-18:00, mid-Sept-mid-April 9:00-17:00, tel. 02 31 51 62 00, www.abmc.gov. Park carefully, as break-ins are a problem. Good WCs and water fountains are at the parking lot. Guided 45-minute tours are offered a few times a day in high season (usually at 11:00 and 14:00—call ahead to confirm times).

Getting There: The cemetery is just east of St-Laurent-sur-Mer and northwest of Bayeux in Colleville-sur-Mer. From route D-514, you'll enter the village of Colleville-sur-Mer; at the big roundabout, you can't miss the signs to the cemetery.

Visiting the Cemetery: Your visit begins at the impressive **visitors center**. Pass security, pick up the handout, sign the register, and allow for time to appreciate the superb displays. On the arrival floor, computer terminals provide access to a database containing the story of each US serviceman who died in Normandy.

Descend one level, where you'll learn about the invasion preparations and the immense logistical challenges they presented. The heart of the center tells the stories of the brave individuals who gave their lives to liberate people they could not know, and shows the few possessions they died with (about 25,000 Americans died in the battle for Normandy). This adds a personal touch to the D-Day landings and prepares visitors for the fields of

American Cemetery at Omaha Beach

On Omaha Beach

You're wasted from a lack of sleep and nervous anticipation. Now you get seasick too, as you're about to land in a small, flat-bottomed boat, cheek-to-jowl with 29 other soldiers. Your water-soaked pack feels like a boulder, and your gun feels even heavier. The boat's front ramp drops open, and you run for your life for 500 yards through water and sand onto this open beach, dodging bullets from above (the landings had to occur at low tide so that mines would be visible).

Omaha Beach witnessed by far the most intense battles of any along the D-Day beaches—although the war planners thought Utah Beach would be more deadly. The hills above were heavily fortified with machine gun and mortar nests. (The aerial, naval, and supporting rocket fire that the Allies poured onto the German defenses failed to put them out of commission.) A single German machine gun could fire 1,200 rounds a minute. That's right—1,200. It's amazing that anyone survived. The highest casualty rates in Normandy occurred here at Omaha Beach, nicknamed "Bloody Omaha." Though there are no accurate figures for D-Day, it is estimated that on the first day of the campaign, the Allies suffered 10,500 casualties (killed, wounded, and missing)—6,000 of whom were Americans. Estimates for Omaha Beach casualties range from 2,500 to 4,800 killed and wounded on that day, many of whom drowned after being wounded. But thanks to an overwhelming effort and huge support from the US and Royal British navies, 34,000 Americans would land on the beach by day's end.

Omaha Beach was littered with obstacles to disrupt the landings. Thousands of metal poles and Czech hedgehogs, miles of barbed wire, and more than six million mines were scattered along these beaches. At least 150,000 tons of metal were taken from the beaches after World War II, and they still didn't get it all. They never will.

white crosses and Stars of David outside. The pressure on these men to succeed in this battle is palpable. There are a manageable number of display cases, a few moving videos (including an interview with Dwight Eisenhower), and a touching 16-minute film with excerpts of letters home from servicemen who now lie at rest in this cemetery (on the half-hour, you can enter late, cushy theater chairs).

A lineup of informational plaques provides a worthwhile and succinct overview of key events from September 1939 to June 5, 1944. Starting with June 6, 1944, the plaques present the progress of the landings in three-hour increments. Amazingly, Omaha Beach was secured within six hours of the landings.

You'll exit the visitors center through the "Sacrifice Gallery," with photos and bios of several people now buried here, as well as some survivors. A voice reads the names of each of the cemetery's permanent residents on a continuous loop.

A path from the visitors center leads to a bluff overlooking the piece of Normandy **beach** called "that embattled shore—portal of freedom." It's quiet and peaceful today, but the horrific carnage of June 6, 1944, is hard to forget. An orientation table looks over the sea. Nearby, steps climb down to the beautiful beach below. A walk on the beach is a powerful experience and a must if you are *sans* both car and tour (be sure to read the "On Omaha Beach" sidebar above; visitors with cars can easily drive to the beach at Vierville-sur-Mer).

In the **cemetery,** you'll find a striking memorial with a soaring statue representing the spirit of American youth. Around the statue, giant reliefs of the Battle of Normandy and the Battle of Europe are etched on the walls. Behind is the semicircular Garden of the Missing, with the names of 1,557 soldiers who were never found. A small metal button next to the name indicates one whose body was eventually found—there aren't many.

Finally, wander through the peaceful and poignant sea of headstones. Notice the names, home states, and dates of death (but no birth dates) inscribed on each. Dog-tag numbers are etched into the lower backs of the crosses. During the campaign, the dead were buried in temporary cemeteries throughout various parts of Normandy. After the war, the families of the soldiers could decide whether their loved ones should remain with their comrades or be brought home (61 percent opted for repatriation).

A disproportionate number of officers are buried here, including General Theodore Roosevelt, Jr., who insisted on joining the invasion despite having a weak heart—he died from a heart attack one month after D-Day (Ted's grave—and his brother Quentin's—lie along the sea, about 150 yards down, in the back-right corner of the second grouping of graves, just after the row 27 marker—look for the gold lettering). Families knew that these officers would want to be buried alongside the men with whom they fought. Also buried here are two of the Niland brothers, now famous from *Saving Private Ryan* (in the middle of the cemetery, just before the circular chapel, turn right down row 15—the row marked by the letter "F"; theirs are the 9th and 10th crosses down).

France has given the US permanent free use of this 172-acre site. It is immaculately maintained by the American Battle Monuments Commission.

▲▲▲POINTE DU HOC

The intense bombing of the beaches by Allied forces is best imagined here, where US Army Rangers scaled impossibly steep cliffs to disable a German gun battery. Pointe du Hoc's bomb-cratered, lunar-like landscape and remaining bunkers make it one of the most evocative of the D-Day sites.

Cost and Hours: Free, daily mid-April-mid-Sept 9:00-18:00, off-season 9:00-17:00, tel. 02 31 51 62 00.

Getting There: It's off route D-514, 20 minutes west of the American Cemetery.

Visiting Pointe du Hoc: Park near the visitors center, where you can get a concise overview of the heroic efforts to take the Pointe. Relax in the cinema for an eight-minute film that offers first-person accounts of this Mission Impossible assault. Then follow the path toward the sea.

Upon entering the site, you'll see an **opening** on your left that's as wide as a manhole cover and about six feet deep. This was a machine gun nest. Three soldiers would be holed up down there—a commander, a gun loader, and the gunner.

Climb to the **viewing platform** ahead and survey the scene. This point of land was the Germans' most heavily fortified position along the D-Day beaches. It held six 155mm guns that were capable of firing up to 13 miles. The farthest part of Omaha Beach is nine miles to the east; Utah Beach is only eight miles to the west. For the American landings to succeed, the Allies had to run the Germans off this cliff. So they bombed it to smithereens, dropping over 1,500 tons of bombs on this one cliff top. That explains the craters. Heavy bombing started in April of 1944, continued into May, and hit its peak on June 6—making this the most intensely bombarded site of the D-Day targets. Even so, only about 5 percent of the bunkers were destroyed. The problem? Multiple direct hits were needed to destroy bunkers like these, which were well-camouflaged, and whose thick, dense walls were heavily reinforced.

Walk around. The battle-scarred **German bunkers** and the cratered landscape remain much as the Rangers left them. You can crawl in and out of the bunkers at your own risk, but picnicking is forbidden—the bunkers are considered gravesites. Notice the six large, round open sites with short rusted poles stuck in a concrete center. Each held a gun (picture the 155mm gun you saw by the Omaha Beach Museum). Destroying these was the Rangers' goal.

Walk to the bunker hanging over the ocean with the stone column at its top. This **memorial** symbolizes the Ranger "Dagger," planted firmly in the ground. Read the inscription, then walk below the sculpture to peer into the narrow slit of the bunker. From here, men would direct the firing of the six anti-ship guns via telephone.

Look over the cliff, and think about the 205 handpicked Rangers who attempted a castle-style assault. They landed to your right, using rocket-propelled grappling hooks connected to 150-foot ropes, and climbed ladders borrowed from London fire departments. With the help of supporting naval fire, the Rangers would take relatively light casualties in the initial attack, partially because the Germans weren't prepared. They regarded their position as nearly impregnable to any attack from the sea.

Timing was critical, though; the Rangers had just 30 minutes before the rising tide would overcome the men below. After finally succeeding in their task, the Rangers found that the guns had been moved—the Germans had put telegraph poles in their place. (Commander Erwin Rommel had directed that all coastal guns not under the cover of roofs be pulled back due to air strikes.) The Rangers eventually found the guns stashed a half-mile inland and destroyed them.

Utah Beach

Utah Beach, added late in the planning for D-Day, proved critical. This was where two US paratrooper units (the 82nd and the 101st Airborne Divisions) dropped behind enemy lines the night before the invasion, as dramatized in *Band of Brothers* and *The Longest Day*. Many landed off-target (such as in Ste-Mère Eglise).

The landscape at Pointe du Hoc is still pocked by WWII bombing craters.

It was essential for the invading forces to succeed here, then push up the peninsula (which had been intentionally flooded by the Nazis) to the port city of Cherbourg. While the brutality on this beach paled in comparison with the carnage on Omaha Beach, many of the paratroopers missed their targets—causing confusion and worse—and the units that landed here faced a three-week battle before finally taking Cherbourg.

These sights are listed in logical order coming from Bayeux or Omaha Beach. For the first two sights, take the Utah Beach exit (D-913) from N-13 and turn right.

▲▲▲UTAH BEACH LANDING MUSEUM (MUSEE DU DEBARQUEMENT)

This is the best museum located on the D-Day beaches, and worth the 45-minute drive from Bayeux. For the Allied landings to succeed, many coordinated tasks had to be accomplished: Paratroopers had to be dropped inland, the resistance had to disable bridges and cut communications, bombers had to deliver payloads on target and on time, the infantry had to land safely on the beaches, and supplies had to follow the infantry closely. This thorough yet manageable museum pieces those many parts together in a series of fascinating exhibits and displays.

Cost and Hours: €8, daily June-Sept 9:30-19:00, Oct-Nov and Jan-May 10:00-18:00, closed Dec, last entry one hour before closing, tel. 02 33 71 53 35, www.utah-beach.com. Guided museum tours are offered (2/day); call ahead for times or ask when you arrive (tours are free, tips appropriate).

Getting There: From Bayeux, travel west toward Cherbourg on N-13 and take the Utah Beach exit (D-913). Turn right at the exit to reach the museum. An American and French flag duo leads to the entry as you approach. You'll park in the *"obligitaire"* lot, then walk the remaining five minutes.

The road leaving the museum, the Route de la Liberté, runs all the way from Utah Beach to Cherbourg, and in the other direction, on to Paris and Berlin, with every kilometer identified with historic road markers. A mile or so before the museum, watch for the relatively new monument with a quote from Richard Winters, the leader of Easy Company in Stephen Ambrose's WWII classic *Band of Brothers*, that helps even pacifists feel

Utah Beach Landing Museum

good about what happened here: "Wars do not make men great, but they do bring out the greatness in good men."

➲ **Self-Guided Tour:** Built around the remains of a concrete German bunker, the museum nestles in the sand dunes on Utah Beach, with floors above and below sea level. Your visit starts with background about the American landings on Utah Beach (20,000 troops landed on the first day alone) and the German defense strategy (Rommel was displeased at what he found two weeks before the invasion). See the outstanding 12-minute film, *Victory in the Sand*, which sets the stage well.

The highlight of the museum is the display of innovative invasion equipment with videos demonstrating how it worked: the remote-controlled Goliath mine, the LVT-2 Water Buffalo and Duck amphibious vehicles, the wooden Higgins landing craft (named for the New Orleans man who invented it), and the best—a fully restored B-26 bomber with its zebra stripes and 11 menacing machine guns, without which the landings would not have been possible (the yellow bomb icons indicate the number of missions a pilot had flown). Enter the simulated briefing room and sense the pilots' nervous energy—would your plane fly *LOW* or *HIGH*? Listen to the many videos as veterans describe how they took the beach and rushed into the interior, including testimony from Easy Company's Richard Winters.

Head upstairs for the stunning grand finale: the large, glassed-in room overlooking the beach. From here, you'll peer over re-created German trenches and feel what it must have felt like to be behind enemy lines. Many German bunkers remain buried in the dunes today. Outside, find the beach access where Americans first broke through Hitler's Atlantic Wall. You can hike up to the small bluff, which is lined with a variety of monuments to the branches of military service that participated in the fight.

To reach the next sight, follow the coastal route (D-421) and signs to Ste-Mère Eglise.

▲STE-MERE EGLISE

This celebrated village lies 15 minutes north of Utah Beach and was the first village to be liberated by the Americans, due largely to its strategic location on the Cotentin Peninsula. The area around Ste-Mère Eglise was the center of action for American paratroopers, whose objective was to land behind enemy lines in support of the American landing at Utah Beach.

For *The Longest Day* movie buffs, Ste-Mère Eglise is a necessary pilgrimage. It was around this village that many paratroopers, facing terrible weather and heavy antiaircraft fire, landed off-target—and many landed in the town. One American paratrooper dangled from the town's church steeple for two hours (a parachute has been reinstalled on the steeple where Private John Steele's became snagged—though not in the correct corner). And though many paratroopers were killed in the first hours of the invasion, the Americans eventually overcame their poor start and managed to take the town (Steele survived his ordeal and the war). They played a critical role in the success of the Utah Beach landings by securing roads and bridges behind enemy lines. Today, the village greets travelers with flag-draped streets and a handful of worthwhile sights.

Drive right to the church and park in the handy €2 lot (or find free parking on

Ste-Mère Eglise

side streets). The **TI** on the square across from the church has loads of information and rents audiovisual guides with GPS, allowing you to discover the town and D-Day sites in the area on your own. It's called the **Open Sky Museum**—but actually it's a three-hour driving tour of the region linking all the D-Day sites together (€8, €250 deposit for GPS unit). The TI may sell a combo-ticket good for the Utah Beach Landing Museum and the Open Sky Museum driving tour (€15, only available at the TI; open July-Aug Mon-Sat 9:00-18:30, Sun 10:00-16:00; Sept and April-June Mon-Sat 9:00-13:00 & 14:00-18:00, Sun 10:00-13:00; shorter hours Oct-March; 6 Rue Eisenhower, tel. 02 33 21 00 33, www.sainte-mere-eglise.info).

MONT ST-MICHEL

Mont St-Michel, among the top four pilgrimage sites in Christendom through the ages, floats like a mirage on the horizon. For more than a thousand years, the distant silhouette of this island abbey sent pilgrims' spirits soaring. Today, it does the same for tourists. Several million visitors—far more tourists than pilgrims—flood the single street of the tiny island each year. Mont St-Michel recently wrapped up a multiyear engineering project to replace the old causeway with a modern bridge, improving water circulation in the bay (see sidebar). With the work finally done, now is a great time to visit.

Orientation

Mont St-Michel is surrounded by a vast mudflat and connected to the mainland by a bridge. Think of the island as having three parts: the fortified abbey soaring above, the petite village squatting in the middle, and the lower-level medieval fortifications. The village has just one main street, on which you'll find all the hotels, restaurants, and trinkets.

Between 11:00 and 16:00, tourists trample the dreamscape (much like pilgrims did 800 years ago). If you're staying overnight, arrive after 16:00 and leave by 11:00 to avoid the worst crowds. The island's main drag is wall-to-wall people from 11:00 to 16:00.

An Island Again

In 1878, a causeway was built that allowed Mont St-Michel's pilgrims to come and go regardless of the tide (and without hip boots). The causeway increased the flow of visitors, but blocked the flow of water around the island. The result: Much of the bay silted up, and Mont St-Michel was no longer an island.

An ambitious project to return the island to its original form was completed in 2015. The first phase, in 2010, saw the construction of a dam (*barrage*) on the Couesnon River, which traps water at high tide and releases it at low tide, flushing the bay and forcing sediment out to the sea. The dam is an attraction in its own right, with informative panels and great views of the abbey from its sleek wood benches. Parking lots at the foot of the island were removed and a huge mainland parking lot was built, with shuttle buses to take visitors to the island. In 2014, workers tore down the old causeway and replaced it with the super-sleek bridge you see today. This allowed water to flow underneath the bridge, and Mont St-Michel became an island once again.

Rick's Tip: *To bypass the tacky souvenir shops and human traffic jam on the main drag, follow my suggested walking routes. Either take the* **gendarmerie shortcut** *or the* **detour path;** *both are described on page 186.*

A ramble on the ramparts offers mud-

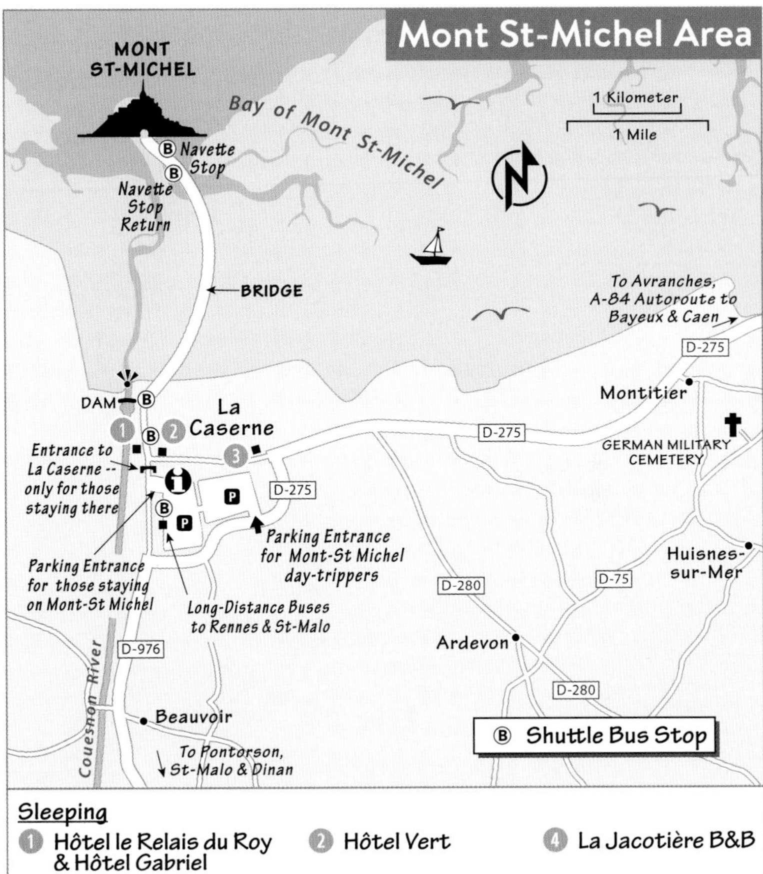

flat views and an escape from the tourist zone. Though several tacky history-in-wax museums tempt visitors, the only worthwhile sights are the abbey at the summit of the island and views from the ramparts and quieter lanes as you descend.

Daytime Mont St-Michel is a touristy gauntlet—worth a stop, but a short one will do. To avoid crowds, arrive late, sleep on the island or nearby on the mainland, and depart early. The tourist tide recedes late each afternoon. On nights from autumn through spring, the island stands serene, its floodlit abbey towering above a sleepy village. The abbey interior is open until midnight from mid-July to the end of August (Mon-Sat only).

On the mainland side of the causeway, the small town of La Caserne consists of a lineup of modern hotels and a handful of shops.

Tourist Information: On the mainland, near the parking lot's shuttle stop, look for the excellent wood-and-glass **visitors center,** which has slick touchscreen monitors describing the various phases of the causeway project, free WCs and luggage lockers, and information about Normandy (daily April-Sept 9:00-19:00, off-season 10:00-18:00). The visitors center can be less crowded than the island's helpful official **TI,**

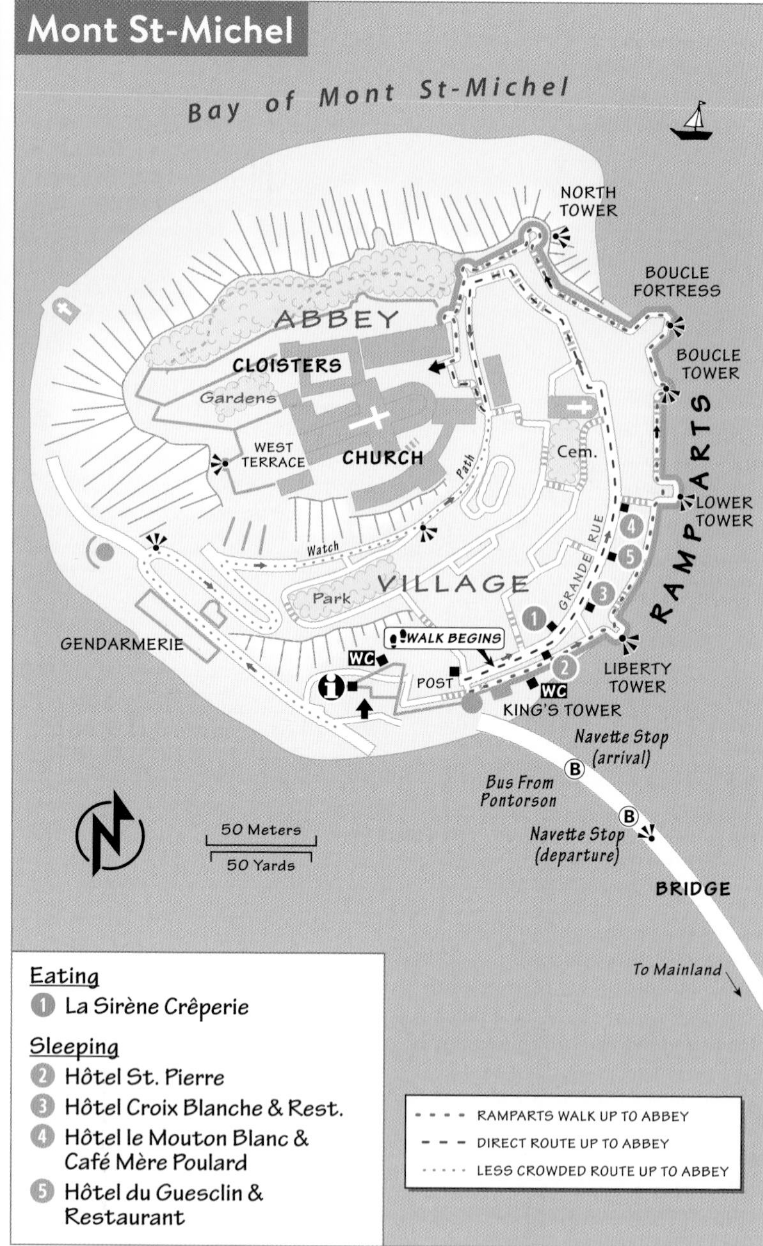

Eating

1. La Sirène Crêperie

Sleeping

2. Hôtel St. Pierre
3. Hôtel Croix Blanche & Rest.
4. Hôtel le Mouton Blanc & Café Mère Poulard
5. Hôtel du Guesclin & Restaurant

which is on your left as you enter Mont St-Michel's gates (daily July-Aug 9:00-19:00, March-June and Sept-Oct 9:00-12:30 & 14:00-18:00, Nov-Feb 10:00-12:30 & 14:00-17:00; tel. 02 33 60 14 30, www.ot-montsaintmichel.com). A post office and ATM are 50 yards beyond the TI.

Rick's Tip: *Because Mont St-Michel faces southwest,* **morning light from the bridge is eye-popping.** *Take a memorable walk before breakfast. And* **don't miss the illuminated island after dark** *(also best from the bridge).*

Either office is a good place to ask about English tour times for the abbey, bus schedules, and the tide table *(Horaires des Marées)*, which is essential if you plan to explore the mudflats.

Tides: The tides here rise above 50 feet—the largest and most dangerous in Europe. High tides *(grandes marées)* lap against the TI door, where you should find tide hours posted.

Taxi: Call 02 33 60 33 23 or 02 33 60 26 89.

Guided Walks: The TI can refer you to companies that run inexpensive guided walks across the bay (with some English).

Sights

These sights are listed in the order by which you approach them from the mainland.

THE BAY OF MONT ST-MICHEL

The vast Bay of Mont St-Michel has long played a key role. Since the sixth century, hermit-monks in search of solitude lived here. The word "hermit" comes from an ancient Greek word meaning "desert." The next best thing to a desert in this part of Europe was the sea. Imagine the desert this bay provided as the first monk climbed the rock to get close to God. Add to that the mythic tide, which sends the surf speeding eight miles in and out with each lunar cycle. Long before the original causeway was built, when Mont St-Michel was an island, pilgrims would approach across the mudflat, aware that the tide swept in "at the speed of a galloping horse" (well, maybe a trotting horse—12 mph, or about 18 feet per second at top speed).

Quicksand was another peril. A short stroll onto the sticky sand helps you imagine how easy it would be to get one or both feet stuck as the tide rolled in. The greater danger for adventurers today is

Mont St-Michel

the thoroughly disorienting fog and the fact that the sea can encircle unwary hikers. (Bring a mobile phone, and if you're stuck, dial 112.) Braving these devilish risks for centuries, pilgrims kept their eyes on the spire crowned by their protector, St. Michael, and eventually reached their spiritual goal.

THE VILLAGE BELOW THE ABBEY

The island's main street (Rue Principale, or "Grande Rue"), lined with shops and hotels leading to the abbey, is grotesquely touristy. It is some consolation to remember that, even in the Middle Ages, this was a commercial gauntlet, with stalls selling souvenir medallions, candles, and fast food. With only 30 full-time residents, the village lives solely for tourists. If you want to avoid crowds and minimize stairs, follow this **shortcut:** keep left as you enter the island, passing under the stone arch of the *gendarmerie*, and follow the cobbled ramp up to the abbey. This is also the easiest route up, thanks to the long ramps. (Others should follow the directions below, which still avoid most crowds.)

After visiting the TI, check the tide warnings (posted on the wall) and pass through the imposing doors. Before the drawbridge, on your left, peek through the door of Restaurant la Mère Poulard. The original Madame Poulard (the maid of an abbey architect who married the village baker) made quick and tasty omelets here (*omelette tradition*). These were popular for pilgrims who, before the causeway (or bridge) was built, needed to beat the tide to get out. They're still a hit with tourists—even at the rip-off price they charge today (they're much cheaper elsewhere). Pop in for a minute just to enjoy the show as old-time-costumed cooks beat eggs.

In the village below the abbey

You could continue the grueling trudge uphill to the abbey with the masses (all island hotel receptions are located on this street). But if the abbey's your goal, bypass the worst crowds and tourist kitsch by following this **detour path:** Climb the first steps on your right after the drawbridge and follow the ramparts in either direction up and up to the abbey. It's quieter if you go right; the ramparts are described on page 190.

Public WCs are next to the island TI at the town entry, after the Mère Poulard Biscuiterie on the right, and partway up the main drag by the tiny St. Pierre church, where you can attend Mass (times posted on the door), opposite Les Terrasses Poulard gift shop.

▲▲ABBEY OF MONT ST-MICHEL

Mont St-Michel has been an important pilgrimage center since A.D. 708, when the bishop of Avranches heard the voice of Archangel Michael saying, "Build here and build high." With the foresight of a saint, Michael reassured the bishop, "If you build it...they will come." Today's abbey is built on the remains of a Romanesque church, which stands on the remains of a Carolingian church. St. Michael, whose gilded statue decorates the top of the spire, was the patron saint of many French kings, making this a favored site for French royalty through the ages. St. Michael was particularly popular in Counter-Reformation times, as the Church employed his warlike image in the fight against Protestant heresy.

This abbey has 1,200 years of history, though much of its story was lost when its archives were taken to St-Lô for safety during World War II—only to be destroyed during the D-Day fighting. As you climb the stairs, imagine the centuries of pilgrims and monks who have worn down the edges of these same stone steps. Keep to the right, as tour groups can clog the left side of the steps.

Cost and Hours: €9; May-mid-July daily 9:00-19:00; mid-July-Aug Mon-Sat 9:00-24:00, Sun 9:00-19:00; Sept-April daily 9:30-18:00; closed Dec 25, Jan 1, and May 1; last entry one hour before closing, mid-July-Aug ticket office closes from 18:00-18:30; www.mont-saint-michel.monuments-nationaux.fr/en. Buy your ticket to the abbey and keep climbing. Mass is held Mon-Sat at 12:00, Sun at 11:15, in the abbey church (www.abbaye-montsaintmichel.com).

Visiting the Abbey: Allow 15 minutes to hike at a steady pace from the island TI. To avoid crowds, arrive by 10:00 or after 16:00 (the place gets really busy by 11:00). On most summer evenings, when the abbey is open until 24:00 and crowds are gone, visits come with music and mood lighting called *Ballades Nocturnes* (€9, none held Sun). It's worth paying a second admission to see the abbey so peaceful (nighttime program starts at 19:00; daytime tickets aren't valid for re-entry, but you can visit before 19:00 and stay on).

Tours: Get an English leaflet and follow my self-guided tour below. The excellent audioguide gives greater detail (€4.50, €6/2 people). You can also take a 1.25-hour English-language guided tour (free but tip requested, 2-4 tours/day, first and last tours usually around 11:00—or 10:45 on Sun—and 15:00, confirm times at TI, meet at top terrace in front of church). The guided tours, which can be good, come with big crowds. You can start a tour, then decide if it works for you—but I'd skip it, instead following my directions, next.

➲ **Self-Guided Tour:** Visit the abbey by following a one-way route. You'll climb to the ticket office, then climb some more. Stop after you pass a public WC, and look back to the church. That boxy Gothic

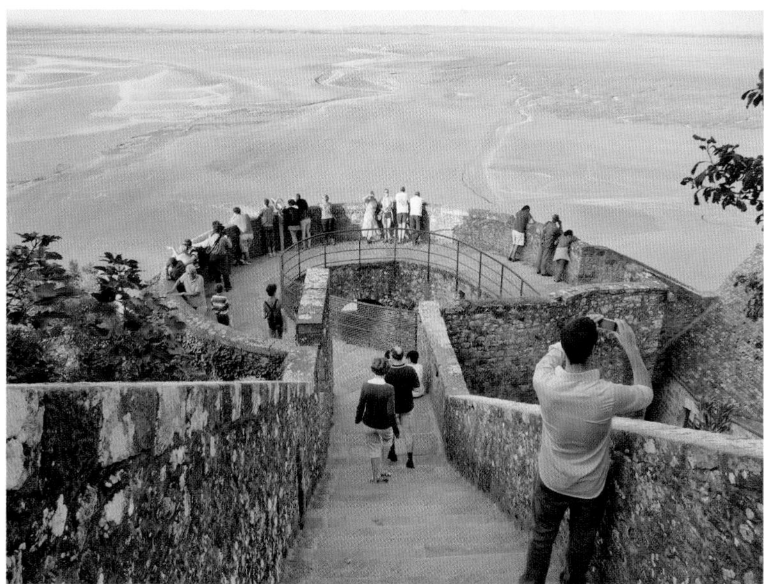

Mudflats surround the abbey at low tide.

structure across the steps is one of six cisterns that provided the abbey with water. Go through the room marked *Accueil*, with interesting models of the abbey through the ages.

• *Emerging on the other side, find your way to the big terrace, walk to the round lookout at the far end, and face the church.*

West Terrace: In 1776, a fire destroyed the west end of the church, leaving this grand view terrace. The original extent of the church is outlined with short walls. In the paving stones, notice the stonecutter numbers, which are generally not exposed like this—a reminder that they were paid by the piece. The buildings of Mont St-Michel are made of granite stones quarried from the Isles of Chausey (visible on a clear day, 20 miles away). Tidal power was ingeniously harnessed to load, unload, and even transport the stones, as barges hitched a ride with each incoming tide.

As you survey the Bay of Mont St-Michel, notice the polder land—farmland reclaimed by Normans in the 19th century with the help of Dutch engineers. The lines of trees mark strips of land used in the process. Today, this reclaimed land is covered by salt-loving plants and grazed by sheep whose salty meat is considered a local treat. You're standing 240 feet above sea level at the summit of what was an island called "the big tomb." The small island just farther out is "the little tomb."

Abbey at Mont St-Michel

The bay stretches from Normandy (on the right as you look to the sea) to Brittany (on the left). The Couesnon River below marks the historic border between the two lands. Brittany and Normandy have long vied for Mont St-Michel. In fact, the river used to pass Mont St-Michel on the other side, making the abbey part of Brittany. Today, it's just barely—but definitively—on Norman soil. The new dam across this river (easy to see from here—it looks like a bridge when its gates are open) was built in 2010. Central to the dam is a system of locking gates that retain water upriver during high tide and release it six hours later, in effect flushing the bay and returning it to a mudflat at low tide.

• *Now enter the...*

Abbey Church: Sit on a pew near the altar, under the little statue of the Archangel Michael (with the spear to defeat dragons and evil, and the scales to evaluate your soul). Monks built the church on the tip of this rock to be as close to heaven as possible. The downside: There wasn't enough level ground to support a sizable abbey and church. The solution: Four immense crypts were built under the church to create a platform to support each of its wings. While most of the church is Romanesque (round arches, 11th century), the light-filled apse behind the altar was built later, when Gothic arches were the rage. In 1421, the crypt that supported the apse collapsed, taking that end of the church with it. Few of the original windows survive (victims of fires, storms, lightning, and the Revolution).

In the chapel to the right of the altar stands a grim-looking statue of the man with the vision to build the abbey

(St. Aubert). Take a spin around the apse and find the suspended pirate-looking ship. Directly in front of the altar, look for the glass-covered manhole (you'll see it again later from another angle).

• *Continue looping around the church, then follow Suite de la Visite signs to enter the...*

Cloisters: A standard feature of an abbey, this was the peaceful zone that connected various rooms, where monks could meditate, read the Bible, and tend their gardens (growing food and herbs for medicine). The great view window is enjoyable today (what's the tide doing?), but it was of no use to the monks. The more secluded a monk could be, the closer he was to God. (A cloister, by definition, is an enclosed place.) Notice how the columns are staggered. This efficient design allowed the cloisters to be supported with less building material (a top priority, given the difficulty of transporting stone this high up). The carvings above the columns feature various plants and heighten the Garden-of-Eden ambience the cloister offered the monks. The statues of various saints, carved among some columns, were de-faced—literally—by French revolutionaries.

Cloister of the abbey church

• *Continue on to the...*

Refectory: This was the dining hall where the monks consumed both food and the word of God in silence—one monk read in a monotone from the Bible during meals (pulpit on the right near the far end). The monks gathered as a family here in one undivided space under one big arch (an impressive engineering feat in its day). The abbot ate at the head table; guests sat at the table in the middle. The clever columns are thin but very deep, allowing maximum light while offering solid support. From 966 until 2001, this was a Benedictine abbey. In 2001, the last three Benedictine monks checked out, and a new order of monks from Paris took over.

• *Stairs lead down one flight to a...*

Round Stone Relief of St. Michael: This scene depicts the legend of Mont St-Michel: The archangel Michael wanted to commemorate a hard-fought victory over the devil with the construction of a monumental abbey on a nearby island. He chose to send his message to the bishop of Avranches (St. Aubert), who saw Michael twice in his dreams. But the bishop did not trust his dreams until the third time, when Michael drove his thumb into the bishop's head, leaving a mark that he could not deny.

• *Continue down the stairs another flight to the...*

Guests' Hall: St. Benedict wrote that guests should be welcomed according to their status. That meant that when kings (or other VIPs) visited, they were wined and dined without a hint of monastic austerity. This room once exploded in color, with gold stars on a blue sky across the ceiling. (This room's decoration was said to be the model for Sainte-Chapelle in Paris.) The floor was composed of glazed red-and-green tiles. The entire space was bathed in glorious sunlight, made divine as it passed through a filter of stained glass. The big double fireplace, kept out of sight by hanging tapestries, served as a kitchen—walk under it and see the light.

• *Hike up the stairs through a chapel to the...*

Hall of the Grand Pillars: Perched on a pointy rock, the huge abbey church had four sturdy crypts like this to prop it up. You're standing under the Gothic portion of the abbey church—this was the crypt that collapsed in 1421. Notice the immensity of the columns (15 feet around) in the new crypt, rebuilt with a determination not to let it fall again. Now look up at the round hole in the ceiling and recognize it as the glass "manhole cover" from the church altar above.

• *To see what kind of crypt collapsed, continue on to the...*

Crypt of St. Martin: This simple 11th-century Romanesque vault has minimal openings, since the walls needed to be solid and fat to support the buildings above. As you leave, notice the thickness of the walls.

• *Next, you'll find the...*

Ossuary (identifiable by its big treadwheel): The monks celebrated death as well as life. This part of the abbey housed the hospital, morgue, and ossuary. Because the abbey graveyard was small, it was routinely emptied, and the bones were stacked here.

During the Revolution, monasticism was abolished. Church property was taken by the atheistic government, and from 1793 to 1863, Mont St-Michel was used as an Alcatraz-type prison. Its first inmates were 300 priests who refused to renounce their vows. (Victor Hugo complained that using such a place as a prison was like keeping a toad in a reliquary.) The big treadwheel—the kind that did heavy lifting for big building projects throughout the Middle Ages—is from the decades when the abbey was a prison. Teams of six prisoners marched two abreast in the wheel—hamster-style—powering two-ton loads of stone and supplies up Mont St-Michel. Spin the rollers of the sled next to the wheel.

From here, you'll pass through a chapel, walk up the Romanesque-arched North-South Stairs, walk through the Promenade of the Monks, go under more Gothic vaults, and finally descend into the vast **Scriptorium Hall** (a.k.a. Knights Hall), where monks decorated illuminated manuscripts. You'll then spiral down to the gift shop, exiting out the back door (follow signs to the *Jardins*).

• *You'll emerge into the rear garden. From here, look up at a miracle of medieval engineering.*

The "Merveille": This was an immense building project—a marvel back in 1220. Three levels of buildings were created: the lower floor for the lower class, the middle floor for VIPs, and the top floor for the clergy. It was a medieval skyscraper, built with the social strata in mind. The vision was even grander—the place where you're standing was to be built up in similar fashion, to support a further expansion of the church. But the money ran out, and the project was abandoned. As you leave the garden, notice the tall narrow windows of the refectory on the top floor.

• *Stairs lead from here back into the village. To avoid the crowds on your descent, turn right when you see the knee-high sign for Musée Historique and find your own route down or, at the same place, follow the Chemin des Ramparts to the left and hike down via the...*

Ramparts: Mont St-Michel is ringed by a fine example of 15th-century fortifications. They were built to defend against a new weapon: the cannon. They were low, rather than tall—to make a smaller target—and connected by protected passageways, which enabled soldiers to zip quickly to whichever zone was under attack. The five-sided Boucle Tower (1481, see map on page 184) was crafted with no blind angles, so defenders could protect it and the nearby walls in all directions. And though the English conquered all of Normandy in the early 15th century, they never took this well-fortified island. Because of its stubborn success against the English in the Hundred Years' War, Mont St-Michel became a symbol of French national identity.

After dark, the island is magically floodlit. Views from the ramparts are sublime. But for the best view, exit the island and walk out on the bridge a few hundred yards.

Eating

The menus at most of the island's restaurants look like carbon copies of one another (with *menus* from €18 to €28, cheap crêpes, and full à la carte choices). Some places have better views or more appealing decor, and a few have outdoor seating with views along the ramparts walk. If it's too cool to sit outside, window-shop the places that face the bay from the ramparts walk and arrive early to land a bay-view table. Unless noted otherwise, the listed restaurants are open daily for lunch and dinner.

Puffy omelets *(omelette montoise,* or *omelette tradition)* are Mont St-Michel's specialty. Also look for mussels (best with crème fraîche), seafood platters, and locally raised lamb *pré-salé* (a salt-water-grass diet gives the meat a unique taste, but beware of impostor lamb from New Zealand—ask where your dinner was raised). Muscadet wine (dry, white, and cheap) from the western Loire valley is made nearby and goes well with most regional dishes.

$ La Sirène Crêperie offers a good island value and a cozy interior (€9 main-course crêpes, open daily for lunch, open for dinner in summer only, closed Fri off-season, enter through gift shop across from Hôtel St. Pierre, tel. 02 33 60 08 60).

$$ Hôtel du Guesclin is the top place for a traditional meal, with white tablecloths and beautiful views of the bay from its inside-only tables (closed Thu, book a window table in advance; tel. 02 33 60 14 10, www.hotelduguesclin.com).

$$ Café Mère Poulard is a stylish three-story café-*crêperie*-restaurant one door up from Hôtel le Mouton Blanc. It's worth considering for its upstairs terrace, which offers the best outside table views up to the abbey (when their umbrellas don't block it).

Sandwiches, pizza by the slice, salads, and drinks are all available to go at shops along the main drag. But you'll find a better selection on the mainland in La Caserne at **Super Marché** next to **Hôtel Vert** (daily 9:00-20:00).

Rick's Tip: *The small lanes above the main street hide* **romantic picnic spots,** *such as the small park at the base of the ancient treadwheel ramp to the upper abbey. Catch late sun by following the ramp that leads through the* gendarmerie *and down behind the island (on the left as you face the main entry to the island).*

Sleeping

Sleep on or near the island so that you can visit Mont St-Michel early and late. What matters is being here before or after the crush of tourists. Sleeping on the island—inside the walls—is a great experience for medieval romantics who don't mind the headaches associated with spending a night here, including average rooms and baggage hassles. To reach a room on the island, you'll need to carry your bags 10 minutes uphill from the *navette* (shuttle) stop. Take only what you need for one night in a smaller bag, but don't leave any luggage visible in your car.

Hotels on the mainland in La Caserne are a good deal cheaper and require less walking—you can park right at your hotel. All are a short walk from the free and frequent shuttle to the island, allowing easy access at any time.

On the Island

Because most visitors day-trip here, finding a room at one of the handful of small hotels on the island is generally no problem (but finding an elevator is). Though some pad their profits by requesting that guests buy dinner from their restaurant, *requiring* it is illegal. Higher-priced rooms generally have bay views. Several hotels are closed from November until Easter.

The following hotels are listed in order of altitude; the first hotels are lowest.

$$$ Hôtel St. Pierre*** and **Hôtel Croix Blanche*****, which share the same owners and reception desk, sit side by side (reception at St. Pierre). Each provides comfortable rooms at inflated prices, some with good views. Both have several family loft rooms (no view Db-€220, view Db-€225, Tb or Qb-€270-300; lower rates for Hôtel Croix Blanche; breakfast-€17, tel. 02 33 60 14 03, www.auberge-saint-pierre.fr, contact@auberge-saint-pierre.fr).

$$ Hôtel le Mouton Blanc** delivers a fair midrange value, with 15 rooms split between two buildings. The main building *(bâtiment principal)* is best, with cozy rooms, wood beams, and decent bathrooms; the more modern "annex" has cramped bathrooms (Db-€145, loft Tb-€160, loft Qb-€195, breakfast-€17, tel. 02 33 60 14 08, www.lemoutonblanc.fr, contact@lemoutonblanc.fr).

$ Hôtel du Guesclin** has the cheapest and best-value rooms I list on the island and is the only family-run hotel left there. Rooms have traditional decor and are perfectly comfortable. Check in at reception one floor up; if no one's there, try the bar on the main-street level (Db-€90-105, Tb-105-130, breakfast-€10, tel. 02 33 60 14 10, www.hotelduguesclin.com, hotel.duguesclin@wanadoo.fr).

On the Mainland

Modern hotels gather in La Caserne on the mainland. These have soulless but cheaper rooms with easy parking (€4 access fee for entering La Caserne) and many tour groups. Call at least a day ahead to get the code that allows you to skip the parking lot and drive to your hotel's front door.

$ Hôtel le Relais du Roy*** houses small but well-configured and plush rooms. Most rooms are on the riverside, with nice countryside views, and many have small balconies allowing "lean-out" views to the abbey (Db-€90-125, bar, restaurant, breakfast-€11, tel. 02 33 60 14 25, www.le-relais-du-roy.com, reservation@le-relais-du-roy.com).

$ Hôtel Gabriel*** has 45 modern rooms, both bright and tight, with flashy colors and fair rates (Db-€110-131, extra person-€21, includes breakfast, tel. 02 33 60 14 13, www.hotelgabriel-montsaintmichel.com, hotelgabriel@le-mont-saint-michel.com).

$ Hôtel Vert** provides 54 motel-esque rooms at good rates (Db-€69-89, extra person-€20, breakfast-€9, tel. 02 33 60 09 33, www.hotelvert-montsaintmichel.com, stmichel@le-mont-saint-michel.com).

Chambres d'Hotes

$ La Jacotière is a few minutes' drive away from Mont St-Michel and within walking distance of the regional bus stop and the shuttle (allowing you to avoid the €12.50 fee to park). Gérald and Alicia, a charming young couple, offer six immaculate rooms and views of the island from the backyard (Db-€85, studio with great view from private patio-€90, extra bed-€20, big family room for up to 4 people-€125, includes breakfast, tel. 02 33 60 22 94, www.lajacotiere.fr, la.jacotiere@wanadoo.fr). Drivers coming from Bayeux should turn off the road just prior to the main parking lot. As the road bends to the left away from the bay, look for a regional-products store standing alone on the right. Take the small lane in front of the store signed *sauf véhicule autorisé*—La Jacotière is the next building.

Transportation

Arriving and Departing

Prepare for lots of walking, particularly if

you arrive by car and are not sleeping on the island or in nearby La Caserne.

BY CAR

If you're staying at a hotel on the island, follow signs for *La Caserne* and enter the parking lot on your right. Parking P3 is for you (€12.50). Those staying in La Caserne can drive right to their hotel, but you need a code number to open a gate blocking the access road (generally €4/entry; get code and directions from your hotelier before you arrive).

Day-trippers are directed to a sea of parking (see map on page 183)—like arriving at an amusement park, you'll have to follow signs to the section that's currently open. To avoid extra walking, take your parking ticket with you and pay at the machines near the TI when you leave (€12.50 flat fee, good for 24 hours but no re-entry privileges, machines accept cash and US credit cards, parking tel. 02 14 13 20 15). If you arrive after 19:00 and stay only for the evening, parking is free. If you arrive after 19:00 and leave before 11:30 in the morning, the fee is €4.30.

From the remote parking lot or *La Caserne* village, you can either walk to the island or take the short ride on the free shuttle (departures every few minutes). The shuttle stops at the parking lot visitors center, near the hotels in the village, near the dam at the start of the bridge, and at the island itself, with ideal views of Mont St-Michel. The return shuttle picks up about a hundred yards farther from the island (look for benches along the road).

BY TRAIN

Bus and train service to Mont St-Michel is a challenge. Depending on where you're coming from, you may find that you're forced to arrive and depart early or late—leaving you with too much or too little time on the island.

The nearest train station is five miles away in Pontorson (called Pontorson-Mont St-Michel). The few trains that stop here are met by a bus waiting to take passengers right to the gates of Mont St-Michel (12 buses/day July-Aug, 8/day Sept-June, fewer on Sun, 20 minutes, tel. 02 14 13 20 15, www.accueilmontsaintmichel.com). Taxis between Pontorson and Mont St-Michel get you to the *navette* (island shuttle) stop and cost about €20 (€25 after 19:00 and on weekends/holidays; tel. 02 33 60 33 23 or 02 33 60 82 70). If you plan to arrive on Saturday night, beware that Sunday train service from Pontorson is almost nonexistent.

From Pontorson by Train to: Bayeux (2-3/day, 2 hours).

From Mont St-Michel to Paris: Most travelers take the regional bus from Mont St-Michel to Rennes and connect directly to the TGV (10/day, allow 4 hours total between Mont St-Michel and Paris' Gare Montparnasse, faster if you connect to the new bullet train from Rennes, route explained in English at www.destination-montstmichel.com). You can also take a short bus ride to Pontorson and catch one of a very few trains from there (3/day, 5.5 hours, transfer in Caen, St-Malo, or Rennes). Flixbus runs direct service from Mont-St-Michel to Paris' Gare de Bercy.

The Loire

As it glides gently east to west, officially separating northern from southern France, the Loire River defines this popular tourist region. The valley's prime location, just south of Paris, has made the Loire a strategic hot potato for more than a thousand years. Today, this region is still the dividing line for the country—for example, weather forecasters say, "north of the Loire...and south of the Loire..."

When a "valley address" became a must-have among 16th-century hunting-crazy royalty, rich Renaissance palaces replaced outdated medieval castles. Hundreds of these castles and palaces are open to visitors, and it's castles that you're here to see (you'll find better villages and cities elsewhere). Old-time aristocratic château-owners, struggling with the cost of upkeep, enjoy financial assistance from the government if they open their mansions to the public.

If you want to sleep in a castle surrounded by a forest, the Loire Valley is the place—you have several choices in all price ranges. Most of my château-hotel recommendations, best for drivers, are located within 15 minutes of Amboise.

Amboise is the best town to use as a home base, with sights of its own and handy access by car and minivan tour to important châteaux. If you'd rather stay in a village, Chenonceaux is a fine choice (its château, Chenonceau, drops the x).

Traveling by car is the easiest way to get around the region, and day rentals are affordable (in Amboise or at the St-Pierre-des-Corps TGV station just outside the city of Tours). Nondrivers based in Amboise can reach well-known châteaux by minivan tour, taxi, or for hardy travelers, by bike.

Frequent bullet trains link the Loire to Paris in less than two hours (with a few direct runs to Charles de Gaulle Airport). Some travelers find the Loire can serve as a good first or last stop on their French odyssey.

THE LOIRE IN 2 DAYS

Two full days are sufficient to sample the best châteaux. Don't go overboard. Two châteaux, possibly three, are the recommended maximum per day.

Sleep in or near Amboise, and visit its sights on your day of arrival. The next day, drive to graceful Chenonceau—arriving early (by 9:00) when crowds are minimal. Spend midday at monumental Chambord, a 30-minute drive from Chenonceau, then stop at Cheverny (where the hunting dogs are fed at 17:00) on your way back.

With more time, head southwest and spend your day touring the château of Villandry.

Drivers following my two-week

THE LOIRE AT A GLANCE

Amboise

▲**Château Royal d'Amboise** For terrific views over Amboise and Leonardo da Vinci memories. **Hours:** Daily April-Oct 9:00-18:00, July-Aug until 19:00, shorter hours off-season. See page 207.

▲**Château Royal d'Amboise Sound-and-Light Show** Late-evening show with costumed performers and light displays, offered in French and in summer. **Hours:** Wed and Sat July 22:30-24:00, Aug 22:00-23:30. See page 210.

▲**Château du Clos-Lucé and Leonardo da Vinci Park** For a chance to see Leonardo da Vinci's final home, and to stroll through gardens decorated with models of his creations. **Hours:** Daily Feb-Oct 9:00-19:00, July-Aug until 20:00, shorter hours off-season. See page 210.

Châteaux Beyond Amboise

▲▲▲**Château de Chenonceau** For sheer elegance arching over the Cher River, and for its lovely gardens. **Hours:** Daily mid-March-mid-Sept 9:00-19:30, July-Aug until 20:00, closes earlier off-season. See page 215.

▲▲▲**Château de Chambord** For its epic grandeur (440 rooms), fun rooftop views, and evocative setting surrounded by a forest. **Hours:** Daily April-Sept 9:00-18:00, Oct-March 9:00-17:00. See page 220.

▲▲**Cheverny** For its intimate feel, lavishly furnished rooms, and daily feeding of the hunting dogs. **Hours:** Daily April-Oct 9:15-18:30, Nov-March 10:00-17:00. See page 223.

▲▲**Chaumont-sur-Loire** For its imposing setting over the Loire River, historic connections to America, and impressive Festival of the Gardens. **Hours:** Daily July-Aug 10:00-19:00, April-June and Sept 10:00-18:30, Oct 10:00-18:00, Nov-March 10:00-17:00. See page 225.

▲▲**Villandry** For the best gardens in the Loire Valley—and possibly all of France. **Hours:** Daily April-Sept 9:00-19:00, March and Oct 9:00-18:00, Nov-Feb 9:00-17:00. See page 228.

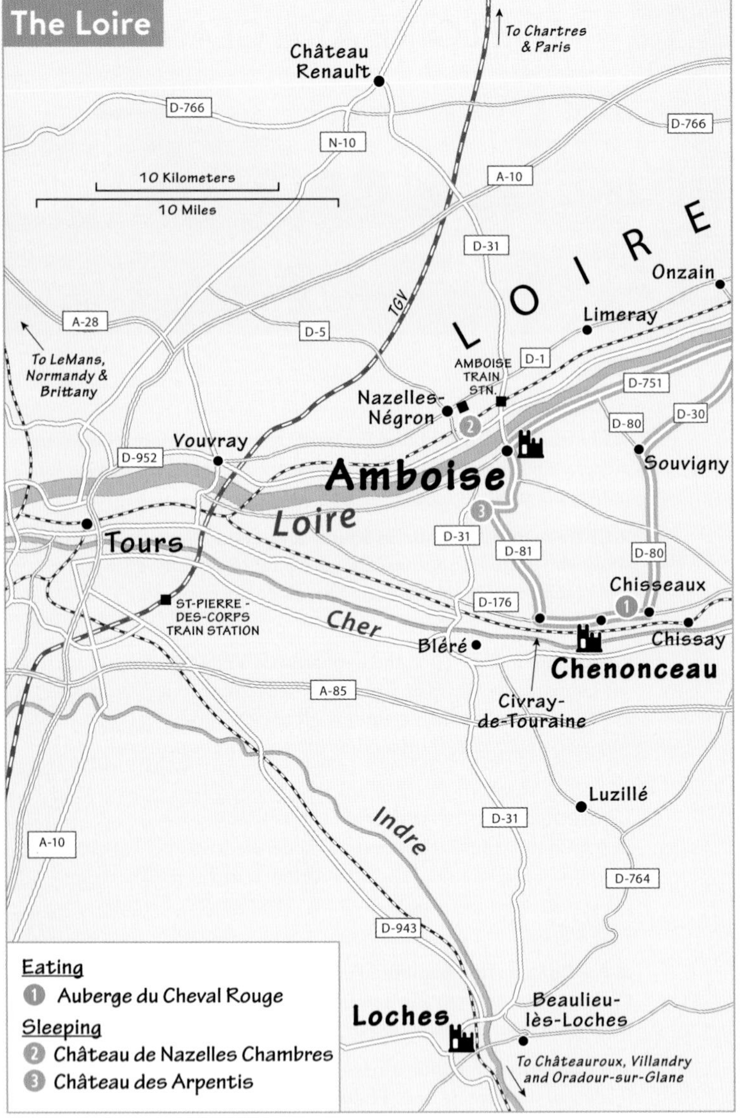
The Loire
To Chartres & Paris
Château Renault
D-766
D-766
N-10
A-10
10 Kilometers
10 Miles
D-31
LOIRE
Onzain
TGV
Limeray
A-28
D-5
To LeMans, Normandy & Brittany
AMBOISE TRAIN STN.
D-1
D-751
Nazelles-Négron
D-30
D-80
Vouvray
Souvigny
D-952
Amboise
Loire
Tours
D-31
D-81
D-80
Chisseaux
ST-PIERRE - DES-CORPS TRAIN STATION
D-176
Cher
Chissay
Bléré
Chenonceau
A-85
Civray-de-Touraine
Luzillé
Indre
D-31
A-10
D-764
D-943
Eating
1 Auberge du Cheval Rouge
Sleeping
2 Château de Nazelles Chambres
3 Château des Arpentis
Loches
Beaulieu-lès-Loches
To Châteauroux, Villandry and Oradour-sur-Glane

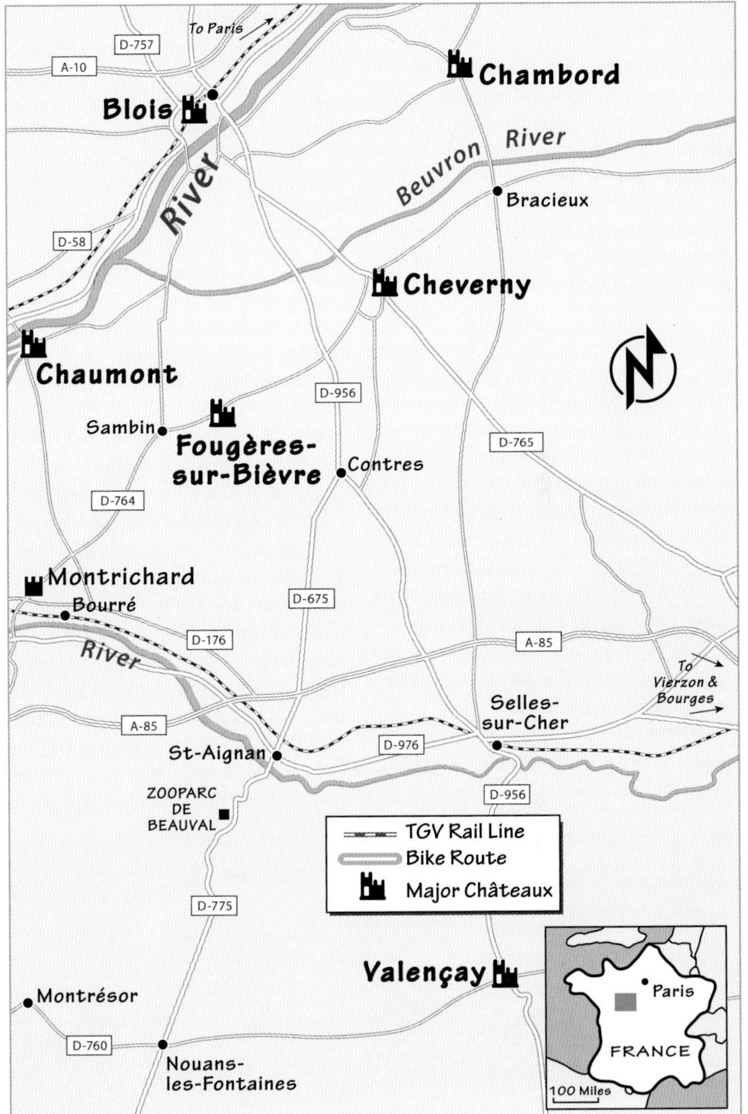

To Paris
D-757
A-10
Chambord
Blois
Beuvron River
Bracieux
River
D-58
Cheverny
Chaumont
D-956
Sambin
Fougères-sur-Bièvre
D-765
Contres
D-764
Montrichard
Bourré
D-675
D-176
A-85
River
To Vierzon & Bourges
Selles-sur-Cher
A-85
St-Aignan
D-976
D-956
ZOOPARC DE BEAUVAL
TGV Rail Line
Bike Route
Major Châteaux
D-775
Valençay
Paris
Montrésor
D-760
FRANCE
Nouans-les-Fontaines
100 Miles

itinerary who are leaving the Loire and heading on to the Dordogne can make an unforgettable stop en route at somber Oradour-sur-Glane (a village destroyed in World War II and turned into a memorial).

AMBOISE

Straddling the widest stretch of the Loire River, Amboise is an inviting town with a pleasing old quarter below its hilltop château. A castle has overlooked the Loire from Amboise since Roman times. Leonardo da Vinci retired here...just one more of his many brilliant ideas.

As the royal residence of François I (r. 1515-1547), Amboise wielded far more importance than you'd imagine from a lazy walk through its pleasant, pedestrian-only commercial zone. In fact, its residents are pretty conservative, giving the town an attitude—as if no one told them they're no longer the second capital of France. The locals keep their wealth to themselves; consequently, many grand mansions hide behind nondescript facades.

With or without a car, Amboise is an ideal small-town home base for exploring the best of château country.

Orientation

Amboise (pop. 14,000) covers ground on both sides of the Loire, with the "Golden Island" (Ile d'Or) in the middle. The train station is on the north side of the Loire, but nearly everything else is on the south (château) side, including the TI. Pedestrian-friendly Rue Nationale parallels the river a few blocks inland and leads from the base of Château d'Amboise through the town center and past the clock tower—once part of the town wall—to the Romanesque Church of St- Denis.

Tourist Information: The information-packed TI is on Quai du Général de Gaulle (April-Oct Mon-Sat 10:00-18:00, Sun 10:00-12:30; Nov-March Mon-Sat 10:00-12:30 & 14:00-17:00, closed Sun; tel. 02 47 57 09 28, www.amboise-valdeloire.com). Pick up the brochures with self-guided walking tours in and around the city, download their free city guide app, and consider purchasing tickets to key area châteaux. Ask about sound-and-light shows in the region (generally summers only). The TI stores bags (€2.50 each), offers free Wi-Fi (for 10 minutes), books local guides, and can reserve a room for you in a hotel or *chambres d'hôte* (€3 fee).

Amboise hugs the bank of the Loire River.

They can also help organize tours to the châteaux with a shuttle bus or minivan service.

Rick's Tip: *The TI sells* **tickets in bundles** *of two or more to sights and châteaux around Amboise, which* **saves on entry fees—and time spent in line.** *You can also get discounted tickets if you take a minivan tour (see below).*

Market Days: Open-air markets are held on Friday (small but local; food only) and Sunday (the big one) in the parking lot behind the TI on the river (both 8:30-13:00).

Regional Products: Galland sells fine food and wine products from the Loire (daily 9:30-19:00, 29 Rue Nationale).

Baggage Storage: Besides the Amboise TI, which stores bags for a fee, most châteaux offer free storage if you've paid admission.

Taxi: There is no taxi station in Amboise, so you must call for one. Try tel. 02 47 57 13 53, tel. 06 12 92 70 46, tel. 02 47 57 30 39, or tel. 06 88 02 44 10 (allow €27 to Chenonceaux, €39 in the evening or on Sun).

Car Rental: It's easiest to rent cars at the St-Pierre-des-Corps train station (TGV service from Paris), a 15-minute drive from Amboise. On the outskirts of Amboise, **Désiré Automobile** rents cars (roughly €55/day for a small car with 100 kilometers/62 miles free, requires credit card for €600 deposit; closed Sun, about a mile downriver from the TI at 105 Avenue de Tours, by Renault garage, tel. 02 47 57 17 92, renault-amboise@orange.fr). Pricier **Europcar** is outside Amboise on Route de Chenonceaux at the Total gas station (about €70/day for a small car, tel. 02 47 57 07 64, reservation tel. 02 47 85 85 85, www.europcar.com). Figure €7 for a taxi from Amboise to either place.

Private Guides: Fabrice Maret is an expert in all things Loire and a great teacher. He lives in Blois but can meet you in Amboise to give an excellent walking tour of the city and its sights, or he'll guide you around the area's châteaux using your rental car (€260/day plus transportation from Blois, tel. 02 54 70 19 59, www.chateauxloire.com, info@chateauxloire.com). Another capable guide is **Charlotte Coignard,** who lives in Tours but can meet you anywhere (mobile 06 34 27 91 94, charlotte.coignard@gmail.com).

Getting from Amboise to the Châteaux

Shuttle services and minivan tours offer affordable transportation to many of the valley's châteaux. Taxis are a pricier option.

By Shuttle Van to Chenonceau, Chambord, and Cheverny: Quart de Tours runs two round-trips per day (high season only) between Amboise and Chenonceau (€16 round-trip, €10 one-way, discount for château, 15-minute trip), and excursion trips from Amboise and Tours to various combinations of the top châteaux, including Chambord and Cheverny (half-day-€37/person, allow 5 hours; full-day-€55/person, allow 7 hours). Book ahead, as seats are limited (mobile 06 30 65 52 01, www.chateaux-tours.com). **Touraine Evasion** runs a van from Amboise that stops at Chambord and Chenonceau; they also have many château options out of Tours (daily in season, none in winter, mobile 06 07 39 13 31, www.tourevasion.com). Check with the Amboise TI for details and pickup locations for both companies.

By Minivan Excursion to Nearby Châteaux: Acco-Dispo runs good half- and all-day English tours from Amboise and Tours to all the major châteaux six days a week (Mon-Sat) for groups of 2-8 people. Costs vary with the itinerary. While on the road, you'll usually get a fun and enthusiastic running commentary—but you're on your own at the sights (discounted tickets available from the driver). Reserve a week ahead by email, or 2-3 days ahead

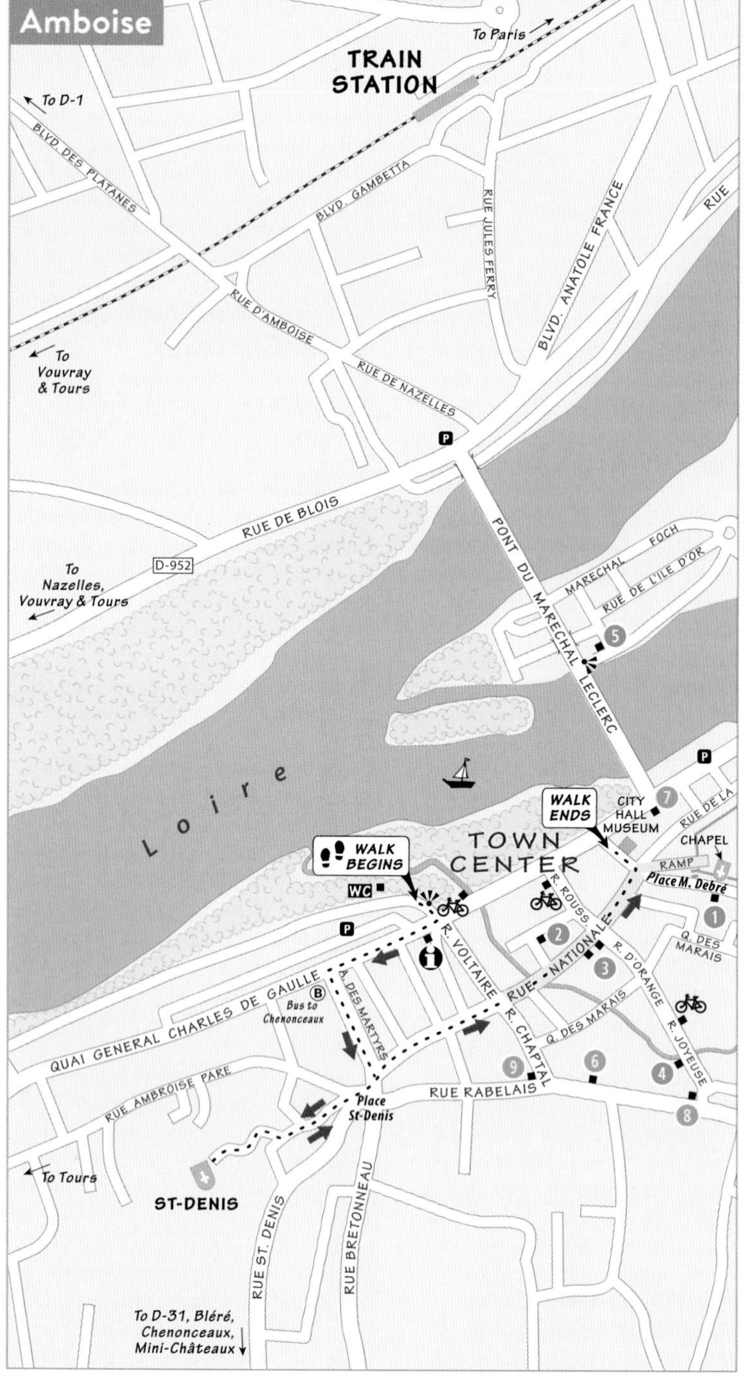
Amboise
To Paris
TRAIN STATION
To D-1
BLVD. DES PLATANES
BLVD. GAMBETTA
RUE JULES FERRY
BLVD. ANATOLE FRANCE
RUE
RUE D'AMBOISE
RUE DE NAZELLES
To Vouvray & Tours
RUE DE BLOIS
D-952
To Nazelles, Vouvray & Tours
PONT DU MARECHAL LECLERC
MARECHAL FOCH
RUE DE L'ILE D'OR
Loire
WALK ENDS
CITY HALL MUSEUM
RUE DE LA
CHAPEL
RAMP
Place M. Debré
TOWN CENTER
WALK BEGINS
WC
R. ROUSS
R. VOLTAIRE
RUE NATIONALE
R. D'ORANGE
Q. DES MARAIS
QUAI GENERAL CHARLES DE GAULLE
Bus to Chenonceaux
A. DES MARTYRS
R. CHAPTAL
Q. DES MARAIS
R. JOYEUSE
RUE AMBROISE PARE
RUE RABELAIS
Place St-Denis
To Tours
ST-DENIS
RUE ST. DENIS
RUE BRETONNEAU
To D-31, Bléré, Chenonceaux, Mini-Châteaux

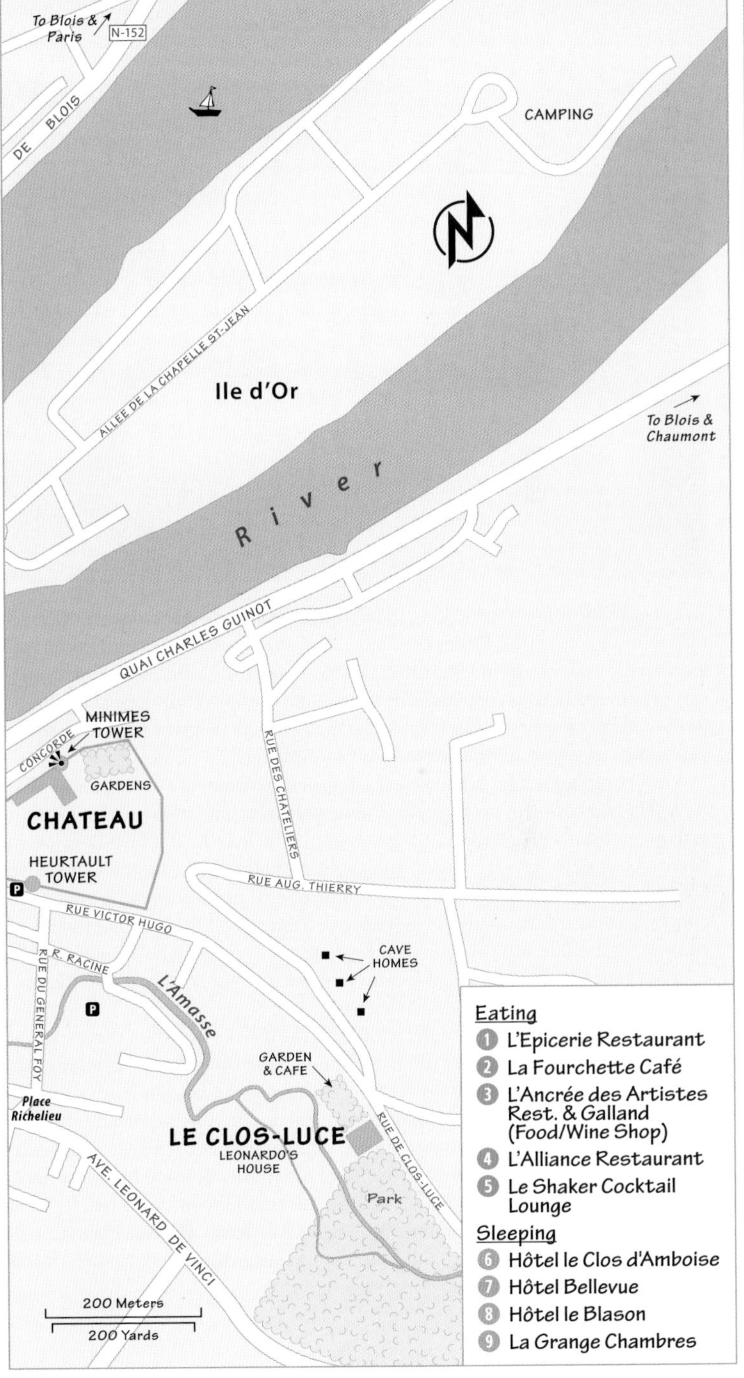

To Blois & Paris
N-152
DE BLOIS
CAMPING
ALLEE DE LA CHAPELLE ST-JEAN
Ile d'Or
To Blois & Chaumont
River
QUAI CHARLES GUINOT
MINIMES TOWER
CONCORDE
GARDENS
CHATEAU
HEURTAULT TOWER
RUE DES CHATELIERS
RUE AUG. THIERRY
RUE VICTOR HUGO
R. RACINE
RUE DU GENERAL FOY
L'Amasse
CAVE HOMES
GARDEN & CAFE
Place Richelieu
LE CLOS-LUCE
LEONARDO'S HOUSE
RUE DE CLOS-LUCE
Park
AVE. LEONARD DE VINCI
200 Meters
200 Yards
Eating
1 L'Epicerie Restaurant
2 La Fourchette Café
3 L'Ancrée des Artistes Rest. & Galland (Food/Wine Shop)
4 L'Alliance Restaurant
5 Le Shaker Cocktail Lounge
Sleeping
6 Hôtel le Clos d'Amboise
7 Hôtel Bellevue
8 Hôtel le Blason
9 La Grange Chambres

Hot-Air Balloon Rides

In France's most popular regions, you'll find hot-air balloon companies eager to take you for a ride (the Loire, Dordogne, and Provence are best suited for ballooning). It's not cheap, but it's unforgettable—a once-in-a-lifetime chance to sail serenely over châteaux, canals, vineyards, Romanesque churches, and villages. Balloons don't go above 3,000 feet and usually fly much lower than that, so you get a bird's-eye view of France's sublime landscapes.

Most companies offer similar deals. Trips range from 45 to 90 minutes of air time; add two hours for preparation, champagne toast, and transport back to your starting point. Deluxe trips add a gourmet picnic, making it a four-hour event. Allow about €210 for a short tour, and about €300 for longer flights. Departures are usually scheduled first thing in the morning or in early evening and are, of course, weather-dependent. If you've booked ahead and the weather turns bad, you can reschedule, but you won't get your money back. Most balloon companies charge about €25 more for a bad-weather refund guarantee; unless your itinerary is very loose, it's a good idea.

Flight season is April through October. Bring a jacket for the breeze, though temperatures in the air won't differ too much from those on the ground. Heat from the propane flames that power the balloon may make your hair stand up—wear a cap. Airsickness is usually not a problem, as the ride is typically slow and even. Baskets have no seating, so count on standing the entire trip. Group size can vary from 4 to 16 passengers. Area TIs have brochures. **France Montgolfières** gets good reviews and offers flights in the areas that I recommend (tel. 02 54 32 20 48, www.france-balloons.com). Others are **Aérocom Montgolfière** (tel. 02 54 33 55 00, www.aerocom.fr) and **Touraine Montgolfière** (tel. 02 47 56 42 05, www.touraine-montgolfiere.fr).

by phone (half-day-€23/person, full-day-€54/person, free hotel pickups in Amboise, mobile 06 82 00 64 51, www.accodispo-tours.com). (Day-trippers from Paris find this service convenient.) Acco-Dispo also runs multiday tours of the Loire and Brittany.

Another minivan option, **Loire Valley Tours** offers all-day itineraries from Amboise and Tours that are fully guided and include admissions, lunch, and wine tasting (about €145/person, tel. 02 54 33 99 80, www.loire-valley-tours.com).

By Train or Bus to Chenonceaux: Amboise and the village of Chenonceaux are connected by train (6/day, 1 hour, transfer at St-Pierre-des-Corps) and less frequent buses (1-2/day, Mon-Sat only, none on Sun, 25 minutes, stop in Amboise is across street from TI, www.tourainefilvert.com).

By Taxi: Most châteaux are too expensive to visit by cab, but a taxi from Amboise to Chenonceau costs about €27 (€39 on Sun and after 19:00).

By Bike: You can rent a bike (leave your passport or a photocopy) at any of these reliable places: **Détours de Loire** (in round building across from TI on Quai du Général de Gaulle, tel. 02 47 30 00 55), **Locacycle** (daily, full-day rentals can be returned the next morning, 2 Rue Jean-Jacques Rousseau, tel. 02 47 57 00 28), or **Cycles le Duc** (good bikes, closed Sun-Mon, 5 Rue Joyeuse, tel. 02 47 57 00 17).

Pick up the free bike-path map (or buy the more detailed map) at the TI or bike shop, or study route options at www.cycling-loire.com. Keep in mind that biking can be strenuous. Travelers with only a day or two may prefer renting a car or sticking to the châteaux easily reached by buses and minivans.

➲ Amboise Walk

This short self-guided walk starts at the banks of the Loire River, winds past the old church of St-Denis, and meanders through the heart of town to a fine little city museum. You'll end near the entrance to Château Royal d'Amboise and Leonardo's house.

Amboise and its Château Royal

• *Climb to the top of the embankment overlooking the river across from the TI.*

Amboise Riverbank: Survey the town, its island, bridge, and castle. If you have a passion for anything French—philosophy, history, food, wine—you'll feel it here, along the Loire. This river, the longest in the country and the natural boundary between northern and southern France, is the last "untamed" river in the country (there are no dams or mechanisms to control periodic flooding). The region's châteaux line up along the Loire and its tributaries, because before trains and trucks, stones for big buildings were best shipped by boat. You may see a few of the traditional flat-bottomed Loire boats moored here. The bridge spanning the river isn't just any bridge. It marks a strategic river crossing and a longtime political border. That's why the first Amboise castle was built here. In the 15th century, this was one of the biggest forts in France.

The half-mile-long "Golden Island" (Ile d'Or) is the only island in the Loire substantial enough to withstand flooding and to have permanent buildings (including a soccer stadium, hostel, and 13th-century church). It was important historically as the place where northern and southern France came together. Truces were made here.

• *Walk downstream paralleling the busy street, Quai du Général Charles de Gaulle, and cross it when you come to the riverfront parking lot with trees and a gazebo. Walk up Avenue des Martyrs de la Résistance (the post office—La Poste—is on the corner) and turn right at Place St-Denis to find the old church standing proudly on a bluff to the right.*

Church of St. Denis (Eglise St-Denis): Ever since ancient Romans erected a Temple of Mars here, this has been a place of worship. According to legend, God sent a bolt of lightning that knocked down the statue of Mars, and Christians took over the spot. The current Romanesque church dates from the 12th century. A cute little statue of St. Denis (above the round arch) greets you as you step in. The delightful carvings capping the columns inside date from Romanesque times. The lovely (but poorly lit) pastel-painted *Deposition* to the right of the choir is restored to its 16th-century brilliance. The medieval stained glass in the windows, likely destroyed in the French Revolution, was replaced with 19th-century glass.

From the steps of the church, look out to the hill-capping Amboise château. For a thousand years, it's been God on this hill and the king on that one. It's interesting to ponder how, throughout French history, the king's power generally trumped the Church's, and how the Church and the king worked to keep people down—setting the stage for the French Revolution.

• *Retrace your steps down from the church and across Place St-Denis, go past Amboise's lone cinema, continue walking straight, and follow Rue Nationale through the heart of town toward the castle.*

Rue Nationale: In France, districts around any castle or church officially classified as historic are preserved. The broad, pedestrianized Rue Nationale, with its narrow intersecting lanes, survives from the 15th century. At that time, when the town spread at the foot of the king's castle, this was the "Champs-Elysées" of Amboise. Supporting the king and his huge entourage was a serious industry. The French king spilled money wherever he stayed.

As you walk along this spine of the town, spot surviving bits of rustic medieval oak in the half-timbered buildings. The homes of wealthy merchants rose from the chaos of this street. Side lanes can be more candid—they often show what's hidden behind modern facades.

Stop when you reach the impressive **clock tower** (Tour de l'Horloge), built into part of the 15th-century town wall. This was once a fortified gate, opening onto the road to the city of Tours. Imagine the hefty wood-and-iron portcullis (fortified door) that dropped from above.

• *At the intersection with Rue François I (where you'll be tempted by the Bigot chocolate shop), turn left a couple of steps to the...*

City Hall Museum (Musée de l'Hôtel de Ville): This free museum is worth a quick peek for its romantic interior, town paintings, and historic etchings (Wed-Mon 10:00-12:30 & 14:00-18:00, closed Tue and off-season). In the room dedicated to Leonardo da Vinci, find his busts and the gripping deathbed painting of him with caring King François I at his side. In the Salle des Rois (Kings' Room), find portraits of Charles VIII (who accidentally killed himself at Amboise's castle) and other kings who called Amboise home; I like to admire their distinct noses.

Upstairs, in the still-functioning city assembly hall (last room), notice how the photo of the current president faces the lady of the Republic. (According to locals, her features change with the taste of the generation, and the bust of France's Lady Liberty is often modeled on famous supermodels of the day.)

• *Your walk ends here, but you can easily continue on to the nearby Château Royal d'Amboise (and beyond that, to Leonardo's last residence): Retrace your steps along Rue François I to Place Michel Debré, at the base of the château. Here, at one of the most touristy spots in the Loire, tourism's importance to the local economy is palpable. Notice the fat, round 15th-century fortified tower, whose interior ramp was built for galloping horses to spiral up to castle level. But to get to the castle without a horse, you'll have to walk up the long ramp.*

Sights

▲CHATEAU ROYAL D'AMBOISE

This historic heap, built mostly in the late 15th century, became the favored royal residence in the Loire under Charles VIII. Charles is famous for accidentally killing himself by walking into a door lintel on his way to a tennis match (seriously). Later, more careful occupants include Louis XII (who moved the royal court to Blois) and François I (who physically brought the Renaissance here in 1516, in the person of Leonardo da Vinci).

Cost and Hours: €11, daily April-Oct 9:00-18:00, July-Aug until 19:00, shorter

Château Royal d'Amboise hovers over the town.

hours off-season, unnecessary audioguide-€4 (kids' version available), Place Michel Debré, tel. 02 47 57 00 98, www.chateau-amboise.com.

➲ **Self-Guided Tour:** After climbing the long ramp to the ticket booth and picking up the free and well-done English brochure, your first stop is the petite **chapel** where Leonardo da Vinci is supposedly buried. This flamboyant little Gothic chapel is where the king began and ended each day in prayer. It comes with two fireplaces "to comfort the king" and two plaques "evoking the final resting place" of Leonardo (one in French, the other in Italian). Where he's actually buried, no one seems to know. Look up at the ceiling to appreciate the lacy design.

Enter the **castle rooms** across from Leonardo's chapel. The three-floor route takes you chronologically from Gothic-style rooms to those from the early Renaissance and on to the 19th century. The first room, **Salle des Gardes,** shows the château's original, much larger size; drawings in the next room give you a better feel for its original look. Some wings added in the 15th and 16th centuries have disappeared. (The little chapel you just saw was once part of the bigger complex.)

You'll pass **council chambers** where the king would meet with his key staff. King **Henry II's bedroom** is livable. The second son of François I, Henry is remembered as the husband of the ambitious and unscrupulous Catherine de' Medici—and for his tragic death in a jousting tournament.

Henry II's bedroom

The rose-colored top-floor rooms are well-furnished from the post-Revolutionary 1800s and demonstrate the continued interest among French nobility in this château. Find the classy portrait of King Louis-Philippe, the last Louis to rule France.

Climb to the top of the **Minimes Tower** for grand views. From here, the strategic value of this site is clear: The visibility is great, and the river below provided a natural defense. The bulky tower climbs 130 feet in five spirals—designed for a mounted soldier in a hurry.

Exit into the **gardens.** Each summer, bleachers are set up for sound-and-light spectacles. Modern art decorating the garden reminds visitors of the inquisitive and scientific Renaissance spirit that Leonardo brought to town. The flags are those of France and Brittany—a reminder that, in a sense, modern France was created at the nearby château of Langeais when Charles VIII (who was born here) married Anne of Brittany, adding her domain to the French kingdom.

To exit, spiral down the **Heurtault Tower** (through the gift shop). As with the castle's other tower, this was designed to accommodate a soldier on horseback. As you gallop down to the exit, notice the cute little characters and scenes left by 15th-century stone carvers. While they needed to behave when decorating churches and palaces, here they could be racier and more spirited.

Leaving the Château: The turnstile puts you on the road to Château du Clos-Lucé (described later; turn left and hike straight for 10 minutes). Along the way, you'll pass **troglodyte houses**—both new and old—carved into the hillside stone (a type called *tuffeau,* a sedimentary rock). Originally, poor people resided here—the dwellings didn't require expensive slate roofing, came with natural insulation, and could be dug essentially for free, as

Châteaux of the Loire: A Brief History

The Loire River's place in history goes back to the very foundation of France. Traditional flat-bottomed boats romantically moored along embankments are a reminder of the age before trains and trucks, when river traffic safely and efficiently transported heavy loads of stone and timber. With prevailing winds sweeping east from the Atlantic, boats headed upriver; on the way back, they flowed downstream with the current.

With this transportation infrastructure providing access to Paris and the region's thick forests—offering plenty of timber, firewood, and hunting terrain—it's no wonder that castles were built here in the Middle Ages. The first stone fortresses went up a thousand years ago; many of the pleasure palaces you see today rose over the ruins of those original keeps.

The Hundred Years' War (roughly 1336 to 1453) was a desperate time for France. Because of a dynastic dispute, the English had a serious claim to the French throne, and by 1415 controlled much of the country, including Paris. French King Charles VII and his court retreated to the Loire Valley. In 1429, the dispirited king was visited by the charismatic Joan of Arc in his refuge at Chinon. She inspired him to get off his duff and send the English packing.

The French kings continued to live in the Loire region for the next two centuries, having grown comfortable with the château culture of the region. The climate was mild, hunting was good, dreamy rivers made nice reflections, and the location was just close enough to Paris—but still far enough away. Charles VII ruled from Chinon, Charles VIII preferred Amboise, Louis XII reigned from Blois, and François I held court in Chambord and Blois.

With peace and stability, there was no need for fortifications. The most famous luxury hunting lodges were built during this period—including Chenonceau, Chambord, Chaumont, Amboise, and Azay-le-Rideau. Kings (François I), writers (Rabelais), poets (Ronsard), and artists (Leonardo da Vinci) made the Loire a cultural hub.

Because French kings ruled effectively only by being constantly on the move among their subjects, many royal châteaux were used infrequently. The entire court and its trappings were portable. A castle kept empty 11 months of the year would come to life when the king came to town. Royal roadies hung tapestries, unfolded chairs, and wrestled with big trunks in the hours before the royal entourage's arrival.

In 1525, François I moved to his newly built super-palace at Fontainebleau, and political power left the Loire. From then on, châteaux were used as vacation retreats, but became refuges for kings again during the French Wars of Religion (1562-1598). Its conclusion marked the end of an active royal presence on the Loire. With the French Revolution in 1789, symbols of the Old Regime, like the fabulous palaces along the Loire, were ransacked. Fast talking saved some châteaux, especially those whose owners had personal relationships with Revolutionary leaders.

Only in the 1840s did the châteaux of the Loire become appreciated for their historic value. In the 19th century, Romantic writers such as Victor Hugo and Alexander Dumas visited and celebrated the châteaux. The Loire Valley and its historic châteaux found a place in our collective hearts and have been treasured to this day.

builders valued the stone quarried in the process. Today wealthy stone-lovers are renovating them into stylish digs worthy of *Better Homes and Caves*. You can see chimneys high above. Unfortunately, none are open to the public.

Rick's Tip: *Many of the major* **châteaux have free apps** *that reproduce their rentable audioguides—check château websites for info. The Amboise TI also offers free city guide apps. Download these apps before you leave home to save time and money when you get here.*

▲CHATEAU ROYAL D'AMBOISE SOUND-AND-LIGHT SHOW

This is considered one of the best shows of its kind in the area. Although it's entirely in French, you can buy the English booklet for €5. Volunteer locals from toddlers to pensioners re-create the life of François I with costumes, juggling, impressive light displays, and fireworks. Dress warmly.

Cost and Hours: Bench-€15, chair-€18, family deals, only about 20 performances a year, 1.5-hour show, Wed and Sat July 22:30-24:00, Aug 22:00-23:30, tel. 02 47 57 14 47, www.renaissance-amboise.com. Buy tickets online or from the ticket window on the ramp to the château (opens at 20:30).

▲CHATEAU DU CLOS-LUCE AND LEONARDO DA VINCI PARK

In 1516, Leonardo da Vinci packed his bags (and several of his favorite paintings, including the *Mona Lisa*) and left an imploding Rome for better wine and working conditions in the Loire Valley. He accepted the position of engineer, architect, and painter to France's Renaissance king, François I. This "House of Light" is the plush palace where Leonardo spent his last three years. (He died on May 2, 1519.) François, only 22 years old, installed the 65-year-old Leonardo here just so he could enjoy his intellectual company.

The house is a kind of fort-château of its own, with a fortified rampart walk and a 16th-century chapel. Two floors of finely decorated rooms are open to the public, but none of the furnishings are original, nor are they particularly compelling (though you can stare face-to-face with a copy of Leonardo's *Mona Lisa*). Come to see well-explained models of Leonardo's inventions, displayed inside the house and out in the huge park.

Leonardo came with disciples who stayed active here, using this house as a kind of workshop and laboratory. The place survived the Revolution because the quick-talking noble who owned it was sympathetic to the cause; he convinced the Revolutionaries that, philosophically, Leonardo would have been on their side.

Cost and Hours: The €14 admission (includes house and park) is worth it for Leonardo fans with two hours to fully appreciate this sight. Skip the garden museum and its €5 supplement. Daily Feb-Oct 9:00-19:00, July-Aug until 20:00; shorter hours off-season, last entry one hour before closing, follow the helpful free English handout, tel. 02 47 57 00 73, www.vinci-closluce.com. A free app in English includes background information and audio tours of the château and grounds.

Getting There: It's a 10-minute walk uphill from Château Royal d'Amboise, past troglodyte homes (see earlier). If you park in the nearby lot, leave nothing of value visible in your car.

Eating: Several garden cafés, including

Château du Clos-Lucé

one just behind the house and others in the park, are reasonably priced and appropriately meditative. For a view over Amboise, choose the terrace *crêperie*.

Visiting the Château and Gardens: Your visit begins with a tour of Leonardo's elegant yet livable Renaissance **home**. This little residence was built in 1450—just within the protective walls of the town—as a guesthouse for the king's château nearby. Today it re-creates (with Renaissance music) the everyday atmosphere Leonardo enjoyed while he lived here, pursuing his passions to the very end. Find the touching sketch in Leonardo's bedroom of François I comforting his genius pal on his deathbed.

The basement level is filled with **sketches** recording the storm patterns of Leonardo's brain and **models** of his remarkable inventions (inspired by nature and built according to his notes). Leonardo was fascinated by water. All he lacked was steam power. It's hard to imagine that this Roman candle of creativity died nearly 500 years ago. Exit into the rose garden, then find another room with 40 small models of his inventions (with handheld English explanations).

Imagine Leonardo's résumé letter to kings of Europe: "I can help your armies by designing tanks, flying machines, wind-up cars, gear systems, extension ladders, and water pumps." The French considered him a futurist who never really implemented his visions.

Your visit finishes with a stroll through the whimsical, expansive, and kid-friendly **park grounds,** with life-size models of Leonardo's inventions (including some that kids can operate), "sound stations" (in English), and translucent replicas of some of his paintings. The models make clear that much of what Leonardo observed and created was based on his intense study of nature.

The Loire's Cuisine Scene

Here in "the garden of France," locally produced food is delicious. Look for seasonal vegetables, such as white and green asparagus, and ***champignons de Paris***—mushrooms grown in local caves, not in the capital. **Pears** and **apples** are preserved *tapées* (dried and beaten flat for easier storage), rehydrated in alcohol, and served in tasty recipes. Loire Valley rivers yield fresh trout ***(truite),*** shad ***(alose)***, and smelt ***(éperlan)***, which are often served fried ***(friture)***. Various dishes highlight ***rillons,*** big chunks of cooked pork, while ***rillettes,*** a stringy pile of *rillons*, make for a cheap, mouthwatering sandwich spread (add a baby pickle, called a ***cornichon***).

Don't be surprised to see **steak, snails, *confit de canard*** (a Dordogne duck specialty), and seafood on menus—the Loire borrows much from neighboring regions. The area's wonderful goat cheeses include **Crottin de Chavignol** (*crottin* means horse dung, which is what this cheese, when aged, resembles), **Saint-Maure de Touraine** (soft and creamy), and **Selles-sur-Cher** (mild). For dessert, try a delicious ***tarte tatin*** (upside-down caramel-apple tart). Regional pastries include ***sablés*** (shortbread cookies) from Sablé-sur-Sarthe.

Restaurants serve food only during lunch (11:30-14:00) and dinner (19:00-21:00, later in bigger cities); bigger cafés offer food throughout the day.

Eating

Amboise is filled with inexpensive and forgettable restaurants, but a handful of places are worth your attention. Some offer a good, end-of-meal cheese platter—a rarity in France these days. The epicenter of the city's dining action is on Place Michel Debré, along Rue Victor Hugo, and across from the château entrance. For an aperitif or after dinner drink, cross the bridge for the best castle views, and consider a relaxing sip at **Le Shaker Cocktail Lounge** (daily from 18:00 until later than you're awake, 3 Quai François Tissard).

$$ L'Epicerie, across from the château exit, serves well-presented traditional cuisine at fair prices. Choose a table outdoors facing the château or in the rustically elegant dining room. The snails are scrumptious (€15 weekday *menu*, €16-25 *plats*, July-Sept daily, Oct-June closed Mon-Tue, reserve ahead, 46 Place Michel Debré, tel. 02 47 57 08 94, www.lepicerie-amboise.com).

$ La Fourchette is Amboise's tiny family diner, with simple decor inside and out. Hardworking chef Christine makes everything fresh in her open kitchen, offering a limited selection at good prices. The place is popular, so call ahead—the morning of the same day is fine (€16-27 *menus*, closed Sun-Mon and Thu evening, on a quiet corner near Rue Nationale at 9 Rue Malebranche, mobile 06 11 78 16 98).

$ L'Ancrée des Artistes is Amboise's reliable and central *crêperie*. It's a young-at-heart place with music to dine by and easygoing servers. Menu items include good meat dishes grilled on stones (*pierres*) and casserole-like *cocottes* (€10 dinner crêpes, €21 three-course crêpe *menus*, daily in July-Aug, off-season closed Sun evening-Mon, 35 Rue Nationale, tel. 02 47 23 18 11).

$$$ L'Alliance, an "alliance" of two chef-brothers and their wives who serve, is a low-key place offering the kind of fresh, delicious French cuisine normally found in more formal restaurants. Here, you'll get quality ingredients prepared with an original twist, not fine decor (*menus* from €31, children's menu, great but pricey cheese tray, closed Tue and Wed for lunch, reservations recommended, 14 Rue Joyeuse, tel. 02 47 30 52 13, www.restaurant-amboise.com).

Sleeping

Amboise is busy in the summer, but there are lots of reasonable hotels and *chambres d'hôtes;* the TI can help with reservations (for a €3 fee).

In the Town Center

$$ Hôtel le Clos d'Amboise**** is a smart urban refuge opening onto beautiful gardens and a small, heated swimming pool. It offers stay-awhile lounges, a lovely rear terrace, and well-designed traditional rooms with warm colors and carpets. Helpful Patricia and Pauline are ever-present (standard Db-€180, bigger Db-€220-240, Db suites-€370, extra person-€20, check website for deals, good buffet breakfast-€15, mini fridges, air-con, elevator, sauna, free parking, 27 Rue Rabelais, tel. 02 47 30 10 20, www.leclosamboise.com, infos@leclosamboise.com).

$$ Hôtel Bellevue*** is a good mid-range bet and centrally located, overlooking the river where the bridge hits the town. The 30 modern rooms are well-appointed, and its stylish bar/bistro, **Lounge B,** has a good selection of local

Sleep Code

$$$$ Splurge: Over €250
$$$ Pricier: €190-250
$$ Moderate: €130-190
$ Budget: €70-130
¢ Backpacker: Under €70

Hotels are classified based on the average price of a standard double room with bath in high season. Unless otherwise noted, credit cards are accepted, breakfast is not included, hotel staff speak English, and Wi-Fi is available.

wines by the glass (standard Db-€75-105, big Db-€120-165, Tb/Qb-€150-180, elevator, 12 Quai Charles Guinot, tel. 02 47 57 02 26, www.hotel-bellevue-amboise.com, contact@hotel-bellevue-amboise.com).

$ Hôtel le Blason**, in a 15th-century, half-timbered building on a busy street, is run by helpful Damien and Bérengère. The basic, tight rooms are clean and come with double-paned windows. There's air-conditioning on the top floor—but these rooms also have sloped ceilings and low beams (Sb-€53, Db-€68, Tb-€81, Qb-€91, quieter rooms in back and on top floor, secure parking-€3/day, 11 Place Richelieu, tel. 02 47 23 22 41, www.leblason.fr, hotel@leblason.fr).

Chambres d'Hôtes

$ La Grange Chambres, in the heart of Amboise, welcomes with an intimate, flowery courtyard and four comfortable rooms, each tastefully restored with modern conveniences and big beds. There's also a common room with a fridge and tables for do-it-yourself dinners (Db-€90, extra person-€25, includes breakfast, credit card to reserve room but pay in cash only, where Rues Châptal and Rabelais meet at 18 Rue Châptal, tel. 02 47 57 57 22, www.la-grange-amboise.com, lagrange-amboise@orange.fr). Adorable Yveline Savin also rents a small two-room cottage (€590/week, 2- to 3-day stays possible) and speaks fluent *franglais.*

Near Amboise

The area around Amboise is peppered with good-value accommodations of every shape, size, and price range. This region offers drivers the best chance to experience château life at affordable rates. For locations, see the map on page 198. Also consider the recommended accommodations in Chenonceaux.

$$$ Château de Pray**** allows you to sleep in a 700-year-old fortified castle with hints of its medieval origins. A few minutes from Amboise, the château's 19 rooms aren't big or luxurious, but they come with character and history—and with tubs in most bathrooms. The lounge is small, but the backyard terrace compensates in agreeable weather. A newer annex offers four contemporary rooms (sleeping up to three each), with lofts, terraces, and castle views. A big pool and the restaurant's vegetable garden lie below the château (small Db in main building-€140-150, bigger Db-€200-265, Db in annex-€170-230, continental breakfast-€17, 3-minute drive upriver from Amboise toward Chaumont on D-751 before the village of Chargé, Rue du Cèdre, tel. 02 47 57 23 67, www.chateaudepray.fr, contact@chateaudepray.fr). The dining room, cut into the hillside rock in the old *orangerie,* is a relaxing place to splurge...and feel good about it (four-course *menus* from €57, reservations required).

$$ At **Château de Nazelles Chambres,** gentle owners Véronique and Olivier Fructus offer six rooms in a 16th-century hillside manor house that comes with a cliff-sculpted pool, manicured gardens, a guest kitchen (picnics are encouraged), views over Amboise, and a classy living room with billiards. The bedrooms in the main building are traditional, while the rooms cut into the hillside come with private terraces and rock-walled bathrooms. They also rent a comfortable two-room cottage with living area, kitchen, and private garden (Db-€115-160, Qb-€260, includes breakfast, cottage-€280-310 for up to 4 guests, extra person-€30, ask for Rick Steves discount if booking direct, 16 Rue Tue-La-Soif, Nazelles-Négron, tel. 02 47 30 53 79, www.chateau-nazelles.com, info@chateau-nazelles.com). From D-952, take D-5 into Nazelles, then turn left on D-1 and quickly veer right onto the little lane between the Town Hall and the post office (La Poste)—don't rely on GPS.

$$$ Château des Arpentis***, a medieval château-hotel centrally located just minutes from Amboise, makes a fun and classy splurge. Flanked by woods and acres of grass, and fronted by a stream and a moat, you'll come as close as you can to château life during the Loire's Golden Age. Rooms are big with tasteful decor—and the pool is even bigger. There's no restaurant, but terrace-table picnics are encouraged. Efficient manager Olivier takes good care of his clients (Db-€170-215, amazing family suites-€355, air-con, elevator, tel. 02 47 23 00 00, www.chateaudesarpentis.com, contact@chateaudesarpentis.com). It's on D-31 just southeast of Amboise; from the roundabout above the Leclerc Market, follow *Autrèche* signs, then look for a small sign on the right next to a tall flagpole.

Transportation

Arriving and Departing

BY CAR

Drivers set their sights on the flag-festooned château that caps the hill. Most recommended accommodations and restaurants either have or can help you locate parking (it's free in the big lot along the river).

BY TRAIN

Amboise's train station is birds-chirping peaceful. You can't store bags here, but you can leave them at the TI. Turn left out of the main station (you may have to cross under the tracks first), make a quick right, and walk down Rue Jules Ferry five minutes to the end, then turn right and cross the long bridge leading over the Loire River to the city center. It's a €7 taxi ride from the station to central Amboise, but taxis seldom wait at the station (see page 201 for taxi phone numbers).

Twenty 15-minute trains link Amboise daily to the regional train hub of St-Pierre-des-Corps (in suburban Tours). There you'll find reasonable connections to distant points (including the TGV to Paris' Gare Montparnasse). Transferring in Paris can be the fastest way to reach many French destinations, even in the south.

From Amboise by Train to: Paris (8/day, 1.5 hours to Gare Montparnasse with change to TGV at St-Pierre-des-Corps, requires TGV reservation; 3/day, 1.75 hours direct to Gare d'Austerlitz, no reservation required; more to Gare d'Austerlitz with transfer in Orléans), **Sarlat-la-Canéda** (3/day, 5-7 hours, change at St-Pierre-des-Corps, then TGV to Libourne, then train to Sarlat), **Pontorson/Mont St-Michel** (1/day, 5.5 hours with transfers at Nantes and Rennes, longer connections through Paris), **Bayeux** (2/day, 4.5 hours, transfer at Tours' St-Pierre-des-Corps and Caen, more with transfer in Paris—arrive at Paris' Gare d'Austerlitz, then Métro to Gare St. Lazare), **Beaune** (1/day, 4.5 hours, transfer at St-Pierre-des-Corps, more with additional transfer at Nevers).

CHENONCEAUX

This one-road, sleepy village—with a knockout château—makes a fine home base for drivers who like a small-town setting. The château itself is wonderfully organized for visitors, making it the most popular in the region (arrive early or late in summer). The gardens are open on summer evenings with mood lighting and music, making the perfect after-dinner activity for those sleeping here. Though Chenonceaux is the name of the town, and Chenonceau (no "x") is the name of the château, they're pronounced the same: shuh-nohn-soh.

Tourist Information: The ignored TI is on the main road from Amboise as you enter the village (July-Aug daily 9:00-19:00, closed for lunch on Sun; Sept-June Mon-Sat 10:00-12:30 & 14:00-18:30, closed Sun; tel. 02 47 23 94 45).

Getting There

By Shuttle Van or Minivan Excursion: Quart de Tours and **Touraine Evasion** run shuttle trips (high season only) from Amboise that pair different châteaux, including Chenonceau and Chambord or Cheverny. Or take a minivan excursion from Amboise. Options are covered on page 201.

By Train or Bus: From Amboise, you can reach Chenonceaux by train (6/day, 1 hour, transfer at St-Pierre-des-Corps); Chenonceaux's unstaffed station sits between the village and château. Buses also connect the two towns (1-2/day, Mon-Sat only, none on Sun, 25 minutes, stops at TI, www.tourainefilvert.com).

Rick's Tip: *The* **tight spaces inside the château are packed** *in high season. Come early (by 9:00) or late (after 17:00).* **Buy advance tickets** *(at area TIs) or from the* **ticket machines** *at the main entry (just follow the prompts; US credit cards work but instructions in English are hit-and-miss—withdraw your card at the prompt "retirez").*

Sights

▲▲▲CHATEAU DE CHENONCEAU

Chenonceau is the toast of the Loire. This 16th-century Renaissance palace arches gracefully over the Cher River and is impeccably maintained, with fresh flower arrangements in the summer and roaring

Château de Chenonceau

log fires in the winter. Plan on a 15-minute walk from the parking lot to the château. Warning: Don't leave any valuables visible in your car.

Cost and Hours: €13, kids under 18-€10, daily mid-March-mid-Sept 9:00-19:30, July-Aug until 20:00, closes earlier off-season, tel. 02 47 23 90 07, www.chenonceau.com.

Chenonceau at Night (Promenade Nocturne): On summer nights, floodlights and period music create a romantic after-dinner cap to your Loire day (gardens only). Just stroll over whenever and for as long as you like (€6, daily July-Aug 21:30-23:30).

Tours: The interior is fascinating—but only if you take advantage of the excellent 20-page **booklet** (included with entry), or rent the wonderful **video/audioguide** (€4.50, choose either the 45-minute condensed tour or the unhurried 60-minute version). There's also an audioguide for kids. Pay for the audioguide when buying your ticket (before entering the château grounds), then pick it up just inside the château's door.

Services: WCs are available by the ticket office and behind the old stables. There's a free bag check.

Eating: An affordable cafeteria is next door to the hospital room. Fancy meals are served in the *orangerie* behind the stables. A cheap *crêperie*/sandwich shop is at the entrance gate. While picnics are not allowed on the grounds, there are picnic tables in a park near the parking lot.

Boat Trips: In summer, the château has rental **rowboats**—an idyllic way to savor graceful château views, but not available when the river is low (€7/30 minutes, July-Aug daily 10:00-19:00, 4 people/boat).

Background: Find a riverside view of the château to get oriented. Although earlier châteaux were built for defensive purposes, Chenonceau was the first great pleasure palace. Nicknamed the "château of the ladies," it housed many famous women over the centuries. The original owner, Thomas Bohier, was away on the king's business so much that his wife, Katherine Briçonnet, made most of the design decisions during construction of the main château (1513-1521).

In 1547, King Henry II gave the château to his mistress, Diane de Poitiers, who added an arched bridge across the river to access the hunting grounds. She enjoyed her lovely retreat until Henry II died (pierced in a jousting tournament in Paris); his vengeful wife, Catherine de' Medici, unceremoniously kicked Diane out (and into the château of Chaumont, described on page 225). Catherine added the three-story structure on Diane's bridge. She died before completing her vision of a matching château on the far side of the river, but not before turning Chenonceau into *the* place to see and be seen by the local aristocracy. (Whenever you see a split coat of arms, it belongs to a woman—half her husband's and half her father's.)

➲ **Self-Guided Tour:** Strut like an aristocrat down the tree-canopied path to the château. (There's a fun plant maze partway up on the left.) You'll cross three moats and two bridges, and pass an old round tower, which predates the main building. Notice the tower's fine limestone veneer, added so the top would better fit the new château.

The main château's original **oak door** greets you with the coats of arms of the first owners. The knocker is high enough to be used by visitors on horseback. The smaller door within the large one could be for two purposes: to slip in after curfew, or to enter during winter without letting out all the heat.

Once inside, you'll tour the château in a clockwise direction (turn left upon entering). Take time to appreciate the beautiful brick floor tiles and lavishly decorated ceilings. As you continue, follow your pamphlet or audioguide, and pay attention to these details:

In the **guard room,** the best-surviving original floor tiles are near the walls—imagine the entire room covered with these tiles. And though the tapestries kept the room cozy, they also functioned to tell news or recent history (to the king's liking, of course). You'll see many more tapestries in this château.

The superbly detailed **chapel** survived the vandalism of the Revolution because the fast-thinking lady of the palace filled it with firewood. Angry masses were supplied with mallets and instructions to smash everything royal or religious. While this room was both, all they saw was stacked wood. The hatch door provided a quick path to the kitchen and an escape boat downstairs. The windows, blown out during World War II, are replacements from the 1950s. Look for graffiti in English left behind by the guards who protected Mary, Queen of Scots (who stayed here after her marriage to King François II).

The centerpiece of the **bedroom of Diane de Poitiers** is a severe portrait of her rival, Catherine de' Medici, at 40 years old. After the queen booted out the mistress, she placed her own portrait over the fireplace, but she never used this bedroom. The 16th-century tapestries are among the finest in France. Each one took an average of 60 worker-years to make. Study the complex compositions of the *Triumph of Charity* (over the bed) and the violent *Triumph of Force.*

At 200 feet long, the three-story **Grand Gallery** spans the river. The upper stories house double-decker ballrooms and a small museum. Notice how differently the slate and limestone of the checkered floor wear after 500 years. Imagine big banquets here. Catherine, a contemporary of Queen Elizabeth I of England, wanted to rule with style. She threw wild parties and employed her ladies to circulate and soak up all the political gossip possible from the well-lubricated Kennedys and Rockefellers of her realm. Parties included impressive fireworks displays and mock naval battles on the river. The niches once held statues—Louis XIV took a liking to them, and consequently, they now decorate the palace at Versailles.

In summer and during holidays, you can take a quick walk outside for more good palace **views:** Cross the bridge, pick up a re-entry ticket, then stroll the other bank of the Cher (across the river from the château). During World War I, the Grand Gallery served as a military hospital, where more than 2,200 soldiers were cared for—picture hundreds of beds lining the gallery. And in World War II, the river you crossed marked the border between the collaborationist Vichy government and Nazi-controlled France. Back then, Chenonceau witnessed many prisoner swaps, and at night, château staff would help resistance fighters and Jews cross in secret. Because the gallery was considered a river crossing, the Germans had their artillery aimed at Chenonceau, ready to destroy the "bridge" to block any Allied advance.

Portrait of Diane de Poitiers

Grand Gallery

Double back through the gallery to find the sensational state-of-the-art (in the 16th century) **kitchen** below. It was built near water (to fight the inevitable kitchen fires) and in the basement; because heat rises, it helped heat the palace. Cross the small bridge (watch your head) to find the stove and landing bay for goods to be ferried in and out.

The staircase leading **upstairs** wowed royal guests. It was the first nonspiral staircase they'd seen...quite a treat in the 16th century. The balcony provides lovely views of the gardens, which originally supplied vegetables and herbs. (Diane built the one to the right; Catherine, the prettier one to your left.) The estate is still full of wild boar and deer—the primary dishes of past centuries. You'll see more lavish bedrooms on this floor. Small side rooms show fascinating old architectural sketches of the château. The walls, 20 feet thick, were honeycombed with the flues of 224 fireplaces and passages for servants to do their pleasure-providing work unseen. There was no need for plumbing. Servants fetched, carried, and dumped everything pipes do today.

On top of the Grand Gallery is the **Medici Gallery,** now a mini-museum for the château. Displays in French and English cover the lives of six women who made their mark on Chenonceau (one of them had a young Jean-Jacques Rousseau, who would later become an influential philosopher, as her personal secretary). There's also a timeline of the top 10 events in the history of the château and a cabinet of curiosities.

To end your visit, escape the hordes by touring the **two gardens** with their postcard-perfect views of the château. The upstream garden hasn't changed since Diane de Poitiers first commissioned it in 1547. Designed in the austere Italian style, the forceful jet in its water fountain was revolutionary in its time. The downstream garden of Catherine de' Medici is more relaxed, with tree roses and lavender gracing its lines in high season.

The remaining sights are best seen after you've toured the château and gardens. The **Military Hospital Room,** located in the château stables, gives an idea of what the Grand Gallery was like when it housed wounded soldiers during World War I (effective English explanations). You can taste the owner's wines in the atmospheric **Cave des Dômes** below. A kids' **play area** lies just past the stables, and a few steps beyond that you can stroll around a **traditional farm.** Imagine the production needed to sustain the château while making your way through the vegetable and flower gardens toward the exit.

Eating

Reserve ahead to dine in formal style at the country-elegant and Michelin-starred **$$$$ Auberge du Bon Laboureur** (€52 and €85 *menus*). **$$$ Hôtel la Roseraie** serves good fixed-price meals in a lovely dining room or on a garden terrace (*menus* from €29, €6 more buys a cheese

Kitchen

Gardens at Chenonceau

Wines of the Loire

Loire wines are overlooked, but there is gold in them thar grapes. The Loire is France's third-largest producer of wine and grows the greatest variety of any region. Four main grapes are grown in the Loire: two reds, gamay and cabernet franc; and two whites, sauvignon blanc and chenin blanc.

The Loire is divided into four subareas; the name of a wine (its *appellation*) generally refers to where its grapes were grown. The Touraine subarea encompasses the wines of Chinon and Amboise. Using 100 percent cabernet franc grapes, growers in Chinon and Bourgeuil are the best producers of reds. Thanks to soil variation and climate differences year in and out, wines made from a single grape have a remarkable range in taste. The best and most expensive white wines are the Sancerres, made on the less-touristed eastern edge of the Loire. Less expensive, but still tasty, are Touraine Sauvignons and the sweeter Vouvray, whose grapes are grown near Amboise. Vouvray is also famous for its light and refreshing sparkling wines (called *vins pétillants*)—locals say the only way to begin any meal in this region is with a glass of it, and I can't disagree (try the *rosé pétillant*). A dry rosé is popular in the Loire in the summer and can be made from a variety of grapes.

You'll pass scattered vineyards as you travel between châteaux, though there's no scenic wine road to speak of (the closest thing is around Bourgueil). It's best to call ahead before visiting a winery.

course, May-Sept daily 19:00-21:00, closed Tue off-season and mid-Nov-mid-March). **$$ Relais Chenonceaux** dishes up savory crêpes, salads, and *plats* at fair prices in a pleasant interior or on its terrace (daily).

The price is right for the basic cuisine at **$ Hostel du Roy** (€9.50 *plat du jour,* €13 *menus,* breakfast-€7.50, daily, 9 Rue du Dr. Bretonneau, tel. 02 47 23 90 17, www.hostelduroy.com, hostelduroy@wanadoo.fr). **$ La Maison des Pages** has some bakery items, sandwiches, cold drinks to go, and just enough groceries for a modest picnic (closed Wed, on the main drag between Hostel du Roy and Hôtel la Roseraie).

For a French treat, book ahead and drive about a mile to Chisseaux and dine at the *très* traditional **$$$ Auberge du Cheval Rouge.** You'll enjoy some of the region's fine cuisine at affordable prices, either inside or on a flower-filled patio (€29-50 *menus,* closed Mon-Tue, 30 Rue Nationale, Chisseaux, tel. 02 47 23 86 67, www.auberge-duchevalrouge.com).

Sleeping

Hotels are a good value in Chenonceaux. You'll find them *tous ensemble* on Rue du Dr. Bretonneau, all with free and secure parking.

$$ Auberge du Bon Laboureur**** turns heads with its ivied facade, lush terraces, and, inside, cozy lounges and bars. The staff acts a tad stiff, but if you get past the formal pleasantries, you have four-star rooms at three-star prices (Db-€134-189, suites-€210-310, breakfast-€18, heated pool, air-con, 6 Rue du Dr. Bretonneau, tel. 02 47 23 90 02, www.bonlaboureur.com, laboureur@wanadoo.fr).

$ Hôtel la Roseraie*** has a flowery terrace, bar, and 22 warmly decorated rooms. Sabine and Jerome run a good show with good prices for three-star comfort, and their big, white Alsatian

Achilles watches over it all (standard Db-€75-92, big Db-€115-138, Tb-€115-150, buffet breakfast-€12.50, queen- or king-size beds, air-con, pool, closed Dec-Feb, 7 Rue du Dr. Bretonneau, tel. 02 47 23 90 09, www.hotel-chenonceau.com, laroseraie-chenonceaux@orange.fr). The traditional dining room and delightful terrace are ideal for a nice dinner, available for guests and nonguests alike who reserve ahead (€29-33 *menus*, daily May-Sept, closed Tue off-season and mid-Nov-mid-March).

$ Relais Chenonceaux**, above a restaurant, greets guests with a nice patio and unimaginative, wood-paneled rooms at fair rates. The coziest—and, in summer, hottest—rooms are on the top floor, but watch your head (Db-€80, Tb-€105, Qb-€120, rental bikes available, tel. 02 47 23 98 11, 10 Rue du Dr. Bretonneau, www.chenonceaux.com, info@chenonceaux.com).

CHATEAU DE CHAMBORD

With its huge scale and prickly silhouette, Château de Chambord, worth ▲▲▲, is the granddaddy of the Loire châteaux. It's surrounded by Europe's largest enclosed forest park, a game preserve defined by a 20-mile-long wall and teeming with wild deer and boar. Chambord (shahm-bor) began as a simple hunting lodge for bored counts and became a monument to the royal sport and duty of hunting. (Apparently, hunting was considered important to keep the animal population under control and the vital forests healthy.)

The château's massive architecture is the star attraction—particularly the mind-boggling double-helix staircase. Six times the size of your average Loire castle, the château has 440 rooms and a fireplace for every day of the year. The château is laid out as a keep in the shape of a Greek cross, with four towers and two wings surrounded by stables. Its four floors are each separated by 46 stairs, creating very high ceilings. The ground floor has reception rooms, the first floor up houses the royal apartments, the second floor up houses temporary exhibits and a hunting museum, and the rooftop offers a hunt-viewing terrace. Special exhibits describing Chambord at key moments in its history help animate the place. Because hunters could see best after autumn leaves fell, Chambord was a winter palace (which helps explain the 365 fireplaces). Only 80 of Chambord's rooms are open to the public—but that's plenty.

Cost and Hours: €11, daily April-Sept 9:00-18:00, Oct-March 9:00-17:00, parking-€4, tel. 02 54 50 40 00, www.chambord.org. There are two ticket offices: one in the village in front of the château, and another (less crowded) inside the actual château.

Rick's Tip: **If you hate crowds, you'll like Chambord.** *Because it's so huge, it's relatively easy to escape the crowds. It helps that there's no one-way, mandatory tour route—you're free to roam like a duke or duchess surveying your domain.*

Getting There: It's a 30-minute drive from Chenonceau. Without a car, take a minivan excursion from Amboise.

Information and Tours: This château requires helpful information to make it come alive. The free handout is a start, and most rooms have adequate English explanations, and for many visitors, this is enough. For more, rent a €5 audioguide (but skip the useless €8 tablet guide).

Services: A TI is by the ticket counter inside the château entry area. The bookshop has a good selection of children's books. Among the collection of shops near the château, you'll find an ATM, local souvenirs, a wine-tasting room, and cafés. There's only one WC at the château itself (in a courtyard corner); otherwise use the pay WC in the village.

Biking Around the Park: Rent a bike on site to explore the park—a network of leafy lanes crisscrossing the vast expanse contained within its 20-mile-long wall.

Views: There are many great views of the château; the best depends on the light. Walk straight out the main entrance 100-200 yards for exquisite looks back to the château. On the opposite (parking lot) side, you can cross the small river in front of the château and turn right for terrific frontal views.

Background: Starting in 1518, François I created this "weekend retreat," employing 1,800 workmen for 15 years. (You'll see his signature salamander symbol everywhere.) François I was an absolute monarch—with an emphasis on absolute. In 32 years of rule (1515-1547), he never once called the Estates-General to session (a rudimentary parliament in *ancien régime* France). This imposing hunting palace was another way to show off his power. Countless guests, like Charles V—the Holy Roman Emperor and most powerful man of the age—were invited to this pleasure palace of French kings...and were wowed.

The grand architectural plan of the château—modeled after an Italian church—feels designed as a place to worship royalty. Each floor of the main structure is essentially the same: four equal arms of a Greek cross branch off of a monumental staircase, which leads up to a cupola. From a practical point of view, the design pushed the usable areas to the four corners. This castle, built while the pope was erecting a new St. Peter's Basilica, is like a secular rival to the Vatican.

Construction started the year Leonardo died, 1519. The architect is unknown, but an eerie Leonardo-esque spirit resides here. The symmetry, balance, and classical proportions combine to reflect a harmonious Renaissance vision that could have been inspired by Leonardo's notebooks.

Typical of royal châteaux, this palace of François I was rarely used. Because any effective king had to be on the road to exercise his power, royal palaces sat empty most of the time. In the 1600s, Louis XIV renovated Chambord, but he

Château de Chambord

visited it only six times (for about two weeks each visit).

➲ **Self-Guided Tour:** This tour covers the highlights, floor by floor.

Ground Floor: This stark level shows off the general plan—four wings, small doors to help heated rooms stay warm, and a massive staircase. In a room just inside the front door, on the left, you can watch a worthwhile 18-minute video—look for a screen on the side wall for viewing with English subtitles.

The attention-grabbing **double-helix staircase** dominates the open vestibules and invites visitors to climb up. Its two spirals are interwoven, so people can climb up and down and never meet. Find the helpful explanation of the staircase posted on the wall. From the staircase, enjoy fine views of the vestibule action, or just marvel at the playful Renaissance capitals carved into its light tuff stone.

First Floor: Here you'll find the most interesting rooms. Starting opposite a big ceramic stove, tour this floor basically clockwise. You'll enter the lavish apartments in the **king's wing** and pass through the grand bedrooms of Louis XIV, his wife Maria Theresa, and, at the far end after the queen's boudoir, François I (follow *Logis de François 1er* signs). These theatrical bedrooms place the royal beds on raised platforms—getting them ready for some nighttime drama. Look for the wooden toilet with removable chamber pot, and notice how the furniture in François' bedroom was designed so it could be easily disassembled and moved with him.

Spiral staircase at Chambord

A highlight of the first floor is the fascinating seven-room **Museum of the Count of Chambord** (Musée du Comte de Chambord). The last of the French Bourbons, Henri d'Artois (a.k.a. the count of Chambord) was next in line to be king when France decided it didn't need one. He was raring to rule—you'll see his coronation outfits and even souvenirs from the coronation that never happened. Check out his boyhood collection of little guns and other weapons. The man who believed he should have become King Henry V lived in exile from the age of 10. Although he opened the palace to the public, he actually visited this château only once, in 1871.

The **chapel** tucked off in a side wing is interesting only for how unimpressive and remotely located it is. It's dwarfed by the mass of this imposing château—clearly designed to trumpet the glories not of God, but of the king of France.

Second Floor: Beneath beautiful coffered ceilings (notice the "F" for François) is a series of ballrooms that once hosted post-hunt parties. Today, a quirky hunting museum with plenty of taxidermy and temporary exhibits occupies these rooms. From here, you'll climb up to the rooftop, but first lean to the center of the staircase and look down its spiral.

Rooftop: A pincushion of spires and chimneys decorates the rooftop viewing terrace. From a distance, the roof—with its frilly forest of stone towers—gives the massive château a deceptive lightness.

From here, ladies could scan the estate grounds, enjoying the spectacle of their ego-pumping men out hunting. On hunt day, a line of beaters would fan out and work inward from the distant walls, flushing wild game to the center, where the king and his buddies waited. The showy lantern tower of the tallest spire glowed with a nighttime torch when the king was in.

Gaze up at the grandiose tip-top of the tallest tower, capped with the king's fleur-de-lis symbol. It's a royal lily—not a cross—that caps this monument to the power of the French king.

Rick's Tip: *Chambord's 45-minute* **Medieval Pageantry on Horseback Show,** *designed for young children, is* **not worth the time or money.**

In the Courtyard: In the far corner, next to the summer café, a door leads to the classy **carriage rooms** and the fascinating **lapidary rooms**. Here you'll come face-to-face with original stonework from the roof, including the graceful lantern cupola, with the original palace-capping fleur-de-lis. Imagine having to hoist that load. The volcanic tuff stone used to build the spires was soft and easy to work, but not very durable—particularly when so exposed to the elements. Several displays explain the ongoing renovations to François' stately pleasure dome.

CHEVERNY

This stately hunting palace, a ▲▲ sight, is one of the more lavishly furnished Loire châteaux. Because the immaculately preserved Cheverny (shuh-vehr-nee) was built and decorated in a relatively short 30 years, from 1604 to 1634, it has a unique architectural harmony and unity of style. The château also has dozens of well-trained hunting dogs, who are fed daily in the afternoon while tourists watch.

From the start, the château has been in the Hurault family; Hurault pride shows in its flawless preservation and intimate feel (it was opened to the public in 1922). The charming viscount and his family still live on the third floor (not open to the public, but you'll see some family photos). Cheverny was spared by the French Revolution; the owners were popular then, as today, even among the village farmers.

The château sits alongside a pleasant

Co-authors Rick Steves and Steve Smith at Cheverny

village, with a small grocery, cafés offering good lunch options, and a few hotels.

Cost and Hours: €10, €14.50 combo-ticket includes Tintin "adventure" rooms, family deals, daily April-Oct 9:15-18:30, Nov-March 10:00-17:00, tel. 02 54 79 96 29, www.chateau-cheverny.fr.

Getting There: Without a car, you can get to Cheverny by shuttle bus or minivan tour from Amboise.

➲ **Self-Guided Tour:** As you walk across the manicured grounds toward the gleaming château, the sound of hungry hounds will follow you. Lined up across the facade are sculpted medallions with portraits of Roman emperors, including Julius Caesar (above the others in the center). As you enter the château, pick up the excellent English self-guided tour brochure, which describes the interior beautifully.

Your visit starts in the lavish **dining room,** decorated with leather walls and a sumptuous ceiling. Next, as you climb the stairs to the private apartments, look out the window and spot the *orangerie* across the gardens. It was here that the *Mona Lisa* was hidden (along with other treasures from the Louvre) during World War II.

On the first floor, turn right from the stairs and tour the I-could-live-here **family apartments** with silky bedrooms, kids' rooms, and an intimate dining room. On the other side of this floor is the impressive **Arms Room** with weapons, a sedan chair, and a snare drum from the count of Chambord (who would have been king, had France wanted one). The **King's Bedchamber** is literally fit for a king. Study the fun ceiling art, especially the "boys will be boys" cupids.

On the top floor peek inside the chapel, before backtracking down to the ground floor. Browse the left wing and find a family tree going back to 1490, a grandfather clock with a second hand that's been ticking for 250 years, and a letter of thanks from George Washington to this family for their help in booting out the English.

Wine Tastings: Opposite the entry at the Château Gate sits a slick wine-tasting room, **La Maison des Vins.** It's run by an association of 32 local vintners. Their mission: to boost the Cheverny reputation for wine (which is fruity, light, dry, and aromatic compared to the heavier, oaky wines made farther downstream). Tasters have two options. In the first, any visitor can have four free tastes from featured bottles of the day, offered with helpful guidance. For most, this is the best approach. Wine aficionados can sample freely among the 96 labels (though there's not enough range in vintage or grape variety to justify this selection) by using modern automated dispensers. Even if just enjoying the free samples, wander among the spouts. Each gives the specs of that wine in English (€6.50 for small tastes of 7 wines, €6-15 bottles, daily 11:00-13:15 & 14:15-19:00, open during lunch in July-Aug, closed in winter, tel. 02 54 79 25 16, www.maisondesvinsdecheverny.fr).

Cheverny's dining room

The hounds of Cheverny

Nearby: Barking dogs remind visitors that the viscount still loves to hunt (he goes twice a week year-round). The **kennel** (200 yards in front of the château, look for *Chenil* signs) is especially interesting when the 70 hounds are fed (daily at 11:30 April-mid-Sept, rest of year on Mon and Wed-Fri). The dogs—half English foxhound and half French Poitou—are bred to have big feet and bigger stamina. They're given food once a day (two pounds each in winter, half that in summer), and the feeding *(la soupe des chiens)* is a fun spectacle that shows off their strict training. Before chow time, the hungry hounds fill the little kennel rooftop and watch the trainer (who knows every dog's name) bring in troughs stacked with delectable raw meat. He opens the gate, and the dogs gather enthusiastically around the food, yelping hysterically. Only when the trainer says to eat can they dig in. You can see the dogs at any time, but the feeding show is fun to plan for.

Also nearby, **Tintin** comic lovers can enter a series of fun rooms designed to take them into a Tintin adventure (called Les Secrets de Moulinsart, €14.50 combo-ticket with castle); hunters can inspect an antler-filled **trophy room**; and gardeners can prowl the château's fine **kitchen and flower gardens** (free, behind the dog kennel).

CHAUMONT-SUR-LOIRE

A castle has been located on this spot since the 11th century; the current version is a ▲▲ sight (▲▲▲ for garden or horse lovers). The first priority at Chaumont (show-mon) was defense. You'll appreciate the strategic location on the long climb up from the village below. Gardeners will appreciate the elaborate Festival of Gardens that unfolds next to the château every year, and modern-art lovers will enjoy how works have been incorporated into the gardens, château, and stables. If it's cold, you'll also appreciate that the château is heated in winter (rare in this region).

Cost and Hours: Château and stables-€11; château open daily July-Aug 10:00-19:00, April-June and Sept 10:00-18:30, Oct 10:00-18:00, Nov-March 10:00-17:00, last entry 45 minutes before closing; audioguide-€4, English handout available, app available in English, tel. 02 54 20 99 22, www.domaine-chaumont.fr.

Festival of Gardens: This annual exhibit, with 25 elaborate gardens arranged around a different theme each year, draws rave reviews from international gardeners. It's as impressive as the Chelsea Flower Show in England, but without the crowds—if you love contemporary garden design, don't miss this (Garden Festival only-€12.50; €4 more for the château and stables; about mid-April to mid-Oct daily 10:00-20:00, special lighting July-Aug 22:00-24:00—keep your day ticket to re-enter for €8.50, tel. 02 54 20 99 22, www.domaine-chaumont.fr). When the festival is on, you'll find several little cafés and reasonable lunch options

A drawbridge leads into the castle of Chaumont-sur-Loire.

scattered about the hamlet (festival ticket not needed). Chaumont also hosts a winter garden festival inside several greenhouses.

Getting There: Chaumont has a river-level entrance (closed in winter) and one up top behind the château (open all year). Drivers should park up top to avoid the hike up. From the river, drive up behind the château (direction: Montrichard), at the first roundabout follow the signs to *Château* and *Festival des Jardins*.

There is no public transport to Chaumont; without a car, your best options are taking a taxi or biking (Chaumont is about 11 level miles from Amboise).

Background: The Chaumont château you see today was built mostly in the 15th and 16th centuries. Catherine de' Medici forced Diane de Poitiers to swap Chenonceau for Chaumont; you'll see tidbits about both women inside.

There's a special connection to America here. Jacques-Donatien Le Ray, a rich financier who owned Chaumont in the 18th century, was a champion of the American Revolution. He used his wealth to finance loans in the early days of the new republic (and even let Benjamin Franklin use one of his homes in Paris rent-free for 9 years). Unfortunately, the US never repaid the loans in full and eventually Le Ray went bankrupt.

Ironically, the American connection saved Chaumont during the French Revolution. Le Ray's son emigrated to New York and became an American citizen, but returned to France when his father deeded the castle to him. During the Revolution, he was able to turn back the crowds set on destroying Chaumont by declaring that he was now an American—and that all Americans were believers in *liberté*, *égalité*, and *fraternité*.

Today's château offers a good look at the best defense design in 1500: on a cliff with a dry moat, big and small drawbridges with classic ramparts, loopholes for archers, and handy holes through which to dump hot oil on attackers.

➲ **Self-Guided Tour:** Your walk through the palace—restored mostly in the 19th century—is described by the English flier you'll pick up when you enter.

Fairy-tale towers of the Château of Chaumont-sur-Loire

As the château has more rooms than period furniture, your tour includes a few modern-art exhibits that fill otherwise empty spaces. The rooms you'll visit first (in the east wing) show the château as it appeared in the 15th and 16th centuries. Your visit ends in the west wing, which features furnishings from the 19th-century owners.

The castle's medieval **entry** is littered with various coats of arms. As you walk in, take a close look at the two drawbridges (a new mechanism allows the main bridge to be opened with the touch of a button). Once inside, the heavy defensive feel is replaced with palatial luxury. Peek into the courtyard—during the more stable mid-1700s, the fourth wing, which had enclosed the courtyard, was taken down to give the terrace its river-valley view.

Entering the château rooms, signs direct you along a one-way loop path *(suite de la visite)* through the château's three wings. Catherine de' Medici, who missed her native Florence, brought a touch of Italy to all her châteaux, and her astrologer (Ruggieri) was so important that he had his own (plush) room—next to hers. **Catherine's bedroom** has a 16th-century throne—look for unicorns holding a shield. The Renaissance-style bed is a reproduction from the 19th century.

The exquisitely tiled **Salle de Conseil** has a grand fireplace designed to keep this conference room warm. The treasury box in the **guard room** is a fine example of 1600s-era locksmithing. The lord's wealth could be locked up here as safely as possible in those days, with a false keyhole, no handles, and even an extra-secure box inside for diamonds.

Next comes the **Diane de Poitiers room,** which doesn't have much to do with Diane but does have a fascinating collection of medallions. Look for the case of ceramic portrait busts dating from 1772, when Le Ray invited the Italian sculptor Jean-Baptiste Nini to work for him. In addition to Marie Antoinette, Voltaire, and Catherine the Great, you'll find several medallions depicting Benjamin Franklin.

A big spiral staircase leads up through

The grounds at Chaumont-sur-Loire

unfurnished rooms and then galleries of contemporary art. After the shock of the 21st century, you go back in time about 150 years to rooms decorated in 19th-century style. The **dining room**'s fanciful limestone fireplace is beautifully carved. Find the food (frog legs, snails, goats for cheese), the maid with the bellows, and even the sculptor with a hammer and chisel at the top (on the left). Your visit ends with a stroll through the 19th-century library, the billiards room, and the living room.

In the **courtyard,** study the entertaining spouts and decor on the walls, and remember that this space was originally enclosed on all sides. Chaumont has one of the best château views of the Loire River—rivaling Amboise for its panoramic tranquility.

The **stables** *(écuries)* were entirely rebuilt in the 1880s. The medallion above the gate reads *pour l'avenir* (for the future), which shows off an impressive commitment to horse technology. Inside, circle clockwise—you can almost hear the clip-clop of horses walking. Notice the deluxe horse stalls, padded with bins and bowls for hay, oats, and water, complete with a strategically placed drainage gutter. The horse kitchen *(cuisine des chevaux)* produced mash twice weekly for the horses, which were named for Greek gods and great châteaux. The "finest tack room in all of France" shows off horse gear. Beyond the covered alcove where the horse and carriage were prepared for the prince, you'll see four carriages parked and ready to go.

The **estate** is set in a 19th-century landscape, with woodlands and a fine lawn. More English than French, it has rolling open terrain, follies such as a water tower, and a brilliantly designed *potager* (vegetable garden) with an imaginative mix of edible and decorative plants. Its trees were imported from throughout the Mediterranean world to be enjoyed—and to fend off any erosion on this strategic bluff.

VILLANDRY

Villandry (vee-lahn-dree) is famous for its extensive gardens, considered to be the best in the Loire Valley, and possibly all of France. Its château is just another Loire palace, but the grounds—arranged in elaborate geometric patterns and immaculately maintained—make it a ▲▲ sight (worth ▲▲▲ for gardeners). Still, if you're visiting anyway, it's worth the extra euros to tour the château as well.

Cost and Hours: €10, €6.50 for gardens only, daily April-Sept 9:00-19:00, March and Oct 9:00-18:00, Nov-Feb 9:00-17:00, unnecessary audioguide-€4, storage lockers, tel. 02 47 50 02 09, www.chateauvillandry.fr. You can stay as late as you like in the gardens, though you must enter before the ticket office closes and exit through the back gate after 19:30. Parking is free and easy between the trees across from the entry (hide valuables in your trunk).

Background: Finished in 1536, Villandry was the last great Renaissance château built on the Loire. It's a pet project of a fabulously wealthy finance minister of François I—Jean le Breton. While serving as ambassador to Italy, Jean picked up a love of Italian Renaissance gardens. When he took over this property, he razed the 12th-century castle (keeping only the old tower), put up his own château, and installed a huge Italian-style garden. The château was purchased in 1906 by the present owner's great-grandfather, and the garden—a careful reconstruction of what the original might have been—is the result of three generations of passionate dedication.

Visiting the Château and Gardens: The excellent English handout included with your admission leads you through the château's 19th-century rooms. They feel so lived-in that you'll wonder if the family just stepped out to get their poodle bathed. The 15-minute *Four Seasons of Villandry* slideshow, with period music and no narration, offers a look at the gardens throughout the year in a relaxing little theater (ask at the ticket window or you may miss it). The literal high point of your château visit is the spiral climb to the top of the keep—the only surviving part of the medieval castle—where you'll find a 360-degree view of the gardens, village, and surrounding countryside. The extra cost for visiting the château seems worth it when you take in the panorama.

The lovingly tended **gardens** are well-described by your handout. Follow its recommended route through the four garden types. The 10-acre Renaissance garden, inspired by the 1530s Italian-style original, is full of symbolism. Even the herb and vegetable sections are put together with artistic flair. The earliest Loire gardens were practical, grown by medieval abbey monks who needed vegetables to feed their community and medicinal herbs to cure their ailments. And those monks liked geometrical patterns. Later Italian influence brought decorative ponds, tunnels, and fountains. Harmonizing the flowers and vegetables was an innovation of 16th-century Loire châteaux. This example is the closest we have to that garden style. Who knew that lentils, chives, and cabbages could look this good?

The 85,000 plants—half of which come from the family greenhouse—are replanted twice a year by 10 full-time gardeners. They use modern organic methods: ladybugs instead of pesticides and a whole lot of hoeing. The place is as manicured as a putting green—just try to find a weed. Stroll under the grapevine trellis, through a good-looking salad zone, and among Anjou pears (from the nearby region of Angers). If all the topiary and straight angles seem too rigid, look for the sun garden in the back of the estate, which has "wilder" perennial borders favored by the Brits. Charts posted throughout identify everything in English.

Bring bread for the piranha-like carp that prowl the fanciful moat. Like the carp swimming around other Loire châteaux, they're so voracious, they'll gather at your feet to frantically eat your spit.

Villandry's gardens are the best in the Loire.

BETWEEN THE LOIRE AND DORDOGNE

ORADOUR-SUR-GLANE

Lost in lush countryside, two hours north of Sarlat-la-Canéda, Oradour-sur-Glane is a powerful experience—worth ▲▲▲. French children know this town well, as most come here on school trips. **Village des Martyrs,** as it is known, was machine-gunned and burned on June 10, 1944, by Nazi troops. With cool attention to detail, the Nazis methodically rounded up the entire population of 642 townspeople, of whom about 200 were children. The women and children were herded into the town church, where they were tear-gassed and machine-gunned as they tried to escape the burning chapel. Oradour's men were tortured and executed. The town was then set on fire, its victims left under a blanket of ashes.

The reason for the mass killings remains unclear today. Some believe that the Nazis wanted revenge for the kidnapping of one of their officers, some believe they wanted to teach locals a lesson for stealing a large amount of gold, and still others believe that the Nazis were simply terrorizing the populace in preparation for the upcoming Allied invasion (this was four days after D-Day). Today, the ghost town, left untouched for 70 years (by order of President Charles de Gaulle), greets every pilgrim who enters with only one English word: Remember.

Cost and Hours: Entering the village is free, but the museum costs €8 (audioguide-€2). Both are open daily mid-May-mid-Sept 9:00-19:00, off-season until 17:00 or 18:00, last visit one hour before closing, tel. 05 55 43 04 30, www.oradour.org. Allow two hours for your visit.

Getting There: Drivers coming from the north should take A-10 to Poitiers, then follow signs toward *Limoges* and turn south at Bellac. Drivers coming from the south will find Oradour-sur-Glane well-signed off the (mostly free) A-20.

➲ **Self-Guided Tour:** Follow *Village des Martyrs* signs to the parking lot and enter at the rust-colored **underground**

Preserved destruction at Oradour-sur-Glane

museum (Centre de la Mémoire). The pricey-for-what-it-offers museum gives a standard timeline of the rise of Hitler and WWII events, shows haunting footage of everyday life in Oradour before the attack, and offers a day-by-day account of the town's destruction. While thorough English explanations are posted, and the 13-minute subtitled movie adds drama, the museum as a whole is skippable for some. At the bookshop, consider picking up a €3 English map to better navigate the site (which has almost no posted information).

From the museum's back door, you pop out at the edge of the ruined village itself. It's shocking just how big and how ruined it is—a harrowing embodiment of the brutality and pointlessness of war.

Join other hushed visitors to walk the length of Oradour's **main street,** past gutted, charred buildings and along lonely streetcar tracks. *Lieu de Supplice* signs show where the townsmen were tormented and murdered. The plaques on the buildings provide the names and occupations of the people who lived there (*laine* means wool, *sabotier* is a maker of wooden shoes, *couturier* is a tailor, *quincaillerie* is a hardware store, *cordonnier* is shoe repair, *menuisier* is a carpenter, and *tissus* are fabrics). You'll pass several cafés and butcher shops, and a hôtel-restaurant. This village was not so different from many you have seen on your trip.

At the end of main street, visit the modest **church,** with its bullet-pocked altar. Then double back through the upper part of the village, bearing right at the long, straight street to the **cemetery.** The names of all who died in the massacre on that June day are etched into the rear wall of the cemetery, around an austere pillar. In front of the pillar, glass cases display ashes of some of the victims. Leaving the cemetery, jog right and cut through the hedges to find the entrance to the easy-to-miss, bunker-like **underground memorial,** where you'll see displays of people's possessions found after the attack: eyeglasses, children's toys, sewing machines, cutlery, pocket watches, and so on.

Nearby: The adorable village of **Mortemart** lies 10 minutes south of Bellac with a good café (closed Mon) wedged between its ancient market hall and low-slung château (a block off the main road, to the right; wander behind for a sweet scene).

Dordogne

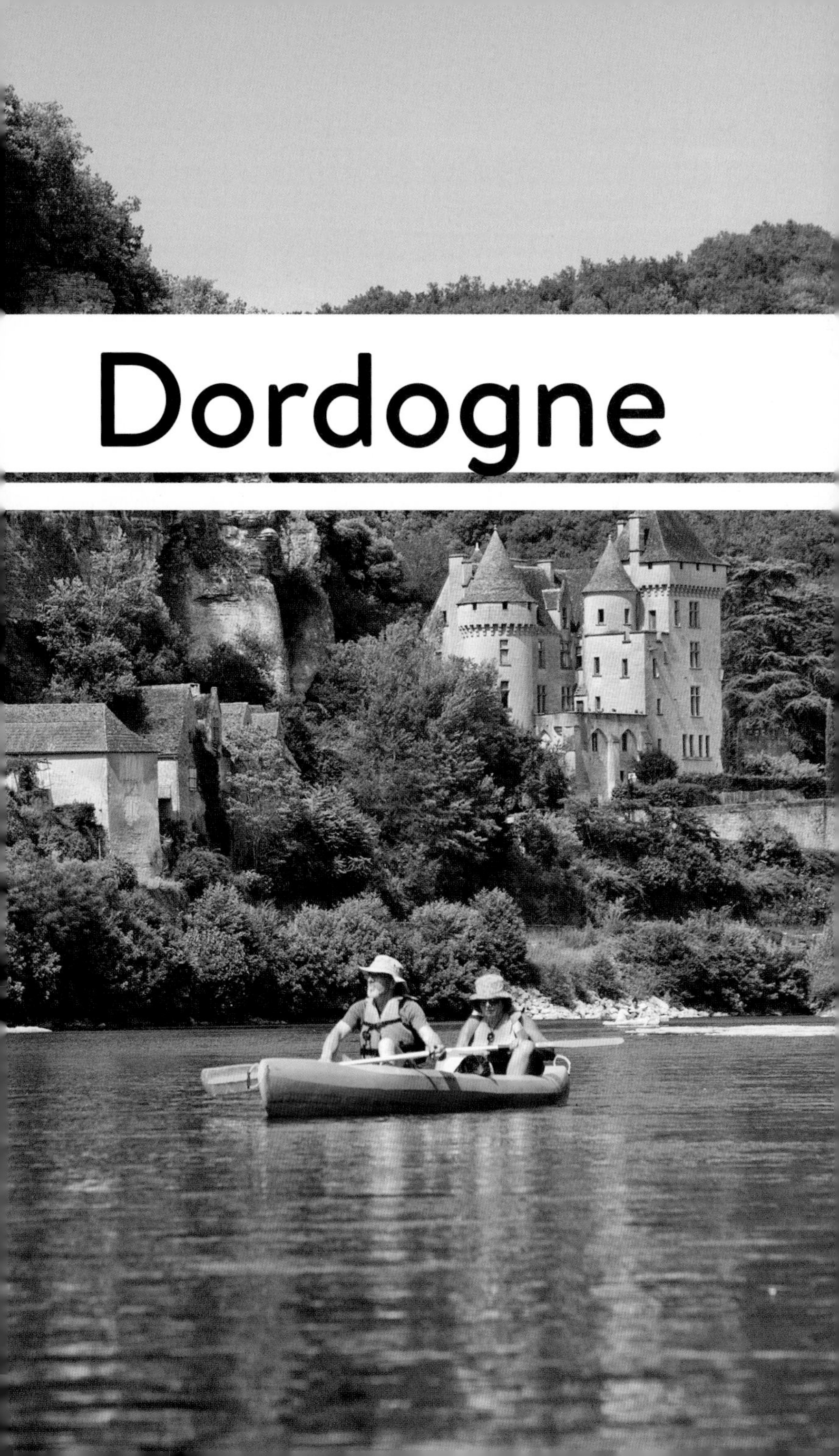

The Dordogne is famous for its prehistoric cave paintings, but also has photogenic villages, thriving market towns, and cliff-topping medieval castles overlooking the Dordogne River.

During much of the on-again, off-again Hundred Years' War, this strategic river—so peaceful today—separated warring Britain and France. Today's Dordogne River carries more travelers than goods, as the region's economy relies heavily on tourism. This region is a joy with a car, and tough without one if you want to visit the caves. Consider renting a car for a day or taking a minivan excursion. Regardless of whether you have a car, renting a canoe is the most fun way to explore the towns along the river.

The best home base for train travelers is the pedestrian-friendly market town of Sarlat-la-Canéda (often shortened to "Sarlat," pronounced sar-lah). Those with a car could consider sleeping in La Roque-Gageac, a beautiful riverside village with good hotels.

If you're serious about visiting the Dordogne's best caves, plan carefully and book ahead when possible (explained on page 262).

THE DORDOGNE IN 2 DAYS

Make your home base in Sarlat. On your first day, enjoy the morning in town (ideally on a market day—Sat or Wed), then take a canoe trip in the afternoon, including stops to explore Castelnaud and Beynac. (If it's not market day in Sarlat, take the canoe trip first, then explore Sarlat.)

Devote the next day to prehistoric cave art—start in Les Eyzies-de-Tayac at the Prehistory Welcome Center and the National Museum of Prehistory. From there your day will depend on the cave(s) you can get an entry for (varies by season, described under each cave later). The Lascaux II replica cave offers an excellent tour that can be reserved; Grotte de Font-de-Gaume is the best cave with original art (though getting in is tricky); and Grotte de Rouffignac makes a good, reliable substitute. With more time, visit a foie gras farm or spend more time in Sarlat.

Without a car, the second day's full list of activities is only possible by taxi or tour.

THE DORDOGNE AT A GLANCE

▲▲▲**Dordogne Canoe Trip** Refreshing way to see (and visit) riverside villages and castles. See page 252.

▲▲▲**La Roque-Gageac** Cute village (known as "La Roque"—The Rock) that looks carved out of the rock between the river and the cliffs. See page 255.

▲▲▲**Beynac** Pretty stone village and home to one of the most imposing castles in France. See page 257.

▲▲▲**Cro-Magnon Caves** World-famous prehistoric paintings and etchings in caves throughout the region. See page 259 for a summary.

▲▲**Sarlat-la-Canéda** Appealing market town and convenient gateway to the region. See page 237.

▲▲**Dordogne Scenic Loop** Lovely route for exploring the scenic river valley by car or bike. See page 249.

▲▲**Domme** Busy village town that merits a stop for its stunning view alone. See page 254.

▲▲**Château de Castelnaud** Medieval castle with displays focusing on warfare. **Hours:** Daily July-Aug 9:00-20:00, April-June and Sept 10:00-19:00, Oct and Feb-March 10:00-18:00, Nov-Jan 14:00-17:00. See page 256.

▲▲**Château de Beynac** Cliff-hanging château overlooking the Dordogne River. **Hours:** Daily May-Oct 10:00-18:30, Nov-April until 17:00 or 17:30. See page 258.

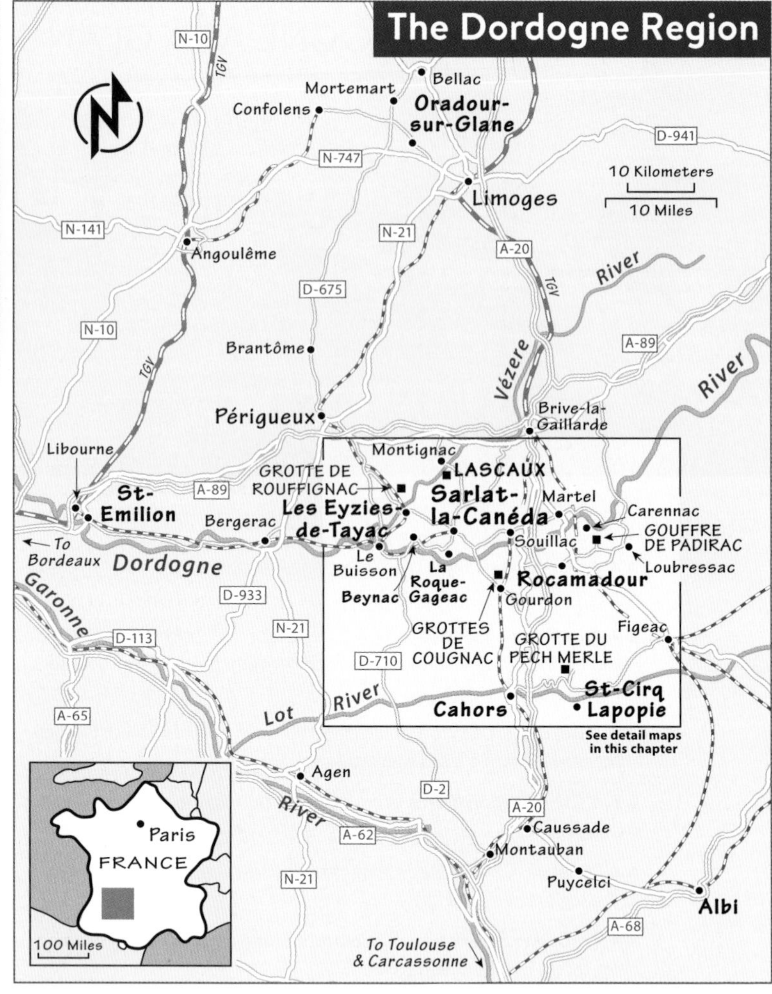

Getting Around the Dordogne

By Car: Roads are small, slow, and scenic. You can rent a car in Sarlat (see page 238). In summer (mid-June–mid-Sept), you'll pay to park in most villages' riverfront lots between 10:00 and 19:00. Leave nothing of value in your car at night.

By Taxi: Taxis are reasonable between Sarlat and the river villages (to Beynac or La Roque-Gageac, allow €27) and pricier to Les Eyzies-de-Tayac (€46 one-way, €88 round-trip); cabbies charge more at night and on Sunday. Christoph and Sarissa (see next) can often pick you up within a few minutes of your call. Helpful Corinne, who runs Beynac-based **Taxi Corinne,** speaks some English (tel. 05 53 29 42 07, mobile 06 72 76 03 32, corinne.brouqui@wanadoo.fr).

By Custom Taxi/Minivan Excursion: Gentle **Christoph** and lively **Sarissa Kusters** speak flawless English and provide top service, whether you need a taxi within Sarlat, a pickup in Paris or Oradour-sur-Glane, or a day-long tour (€40/hour, mobile 06 08 70 61 67, www.taxialacarte.com, taxialacarte@gmail.com).

Rick's Tip: *If you're* **connecting the Dordogne with the Loire region** *by car, the fastest path is via the* **free A-20 autoroute** *(exit at Souillac for Sarlat-la-Canéda and nearby villages). Break up your trip by stopping in Oradour-sur-Glane, an unforgettable WWII memorial.*

Caves and Castles is run by Steve and Judie Burman, a delightful British couple who offer tours of the area's sights, including translation for French-only cave visits (tel. 05 53 50 31 21, www.cavesandcastles.com, cavesandcastles@gmail.com).

By Canoe or Cruise: Canoeing is my favorite way to explore the river's sights and villages. With advance notice, some companies can pick up nondrivers in Sarlat. For options, including cruises, see pages 252 and 256.

By Bike: Cyclists find the Dordogne beautiful but really hilly, with lots of traffic on key roads. You can rent bikes in Sarlat.

By Hot-Air Balloon: The Dordogne is a terrific place to spring for a hot-air balloon trip, taking you high above its gorgeous river and hilly terrain capped with golden-stone castles and villages. Try **Montgolfières du Périgord,** based in La Roque-Gageac; see page 256.

SARLAT-LA-CANEDA

Set serenely amid forested hills, Sarlat is a banquet of a town. While there are no blockbuster sights, Sarlat delivers a seductive tangle of traffic-free, golden cobblestone lanes peppered with beautiful buildings, lined with foie gras shops (geese hate Sarlat), and stuffed with tourists. The town is just the right size, with everything an easy meander from the town center. It's warmly lit at night, ideal for after-dinner strolls. Though undeniably popular with tourists, it's the handiest home base for those without a car.

Sarlat's market is a feast for the senses.

Orientation

Rue de la République slices like an arrow through the circular old town. The action lies east of Rue de la République. Sarlat's smaller half has few shops and many quiet lanes.

Tourist Information: The TI is 50 yards to the right of the Cathedral of St. Sacerdos as you face it (July-Aug Mon-Sat 9:00-19:00, Sun 10:00-12:00 & 14:00-18:00; May-June and Sept closes one hour earlier; April and Oct Mon-Sat 9:00-12:00 & 14:00-18:00, Sun 10:00-13:00 & 14:00-17:00; shorter hours and closed Sun Nov-March; on Rue Tourny, tel. 05 53 31 45 45, www.sarlat-tourisme.com). Their city map with English information is helpful. Ask for information on car, bike, and canoe rental; this and other information can also be downloaded from the TI's website.

The TI also sells tickets for the panoramic elevator ride in the covered market hall (€5, cash only, handy to buy here because you can only pay at the elevator with a chip credit card).

Taxi: Call friendly **Christoph Kusters** (mobile 06 08 70 61 67, www.taxialacarte.com, taxialacarte@gmail.com, also offers regional day trips) or **Taxi Sarlat** (tel. 05 53 59 02 43, mobile 06 80 08 65 05).

Car Rental: Try **Europcar** (Le Pontet, at south end of Avenue Leclerc on roundabout, Place du Maréchal de Lattre de Tassigny, 15-minute walk from center, tel. 05 53 30 30 40).

Cooking Classes: Le Chèvrefeuille offers market tours and cooking classes that focus on Périgord cuisine. Courses are situated in the countryside about a half-hour drive from Sarlat (tel. 05 53 59 47 97, www.lechevrefeuille.com).

➲ Sarlat Walk

This short self-guided walk, rated ▲▲, starts facing the Cathedral of St. Sacerdos (near the TI, where you can buy tickets for the panoramic elevator, which we'll visit on the way). The walk works well in the day, when all of the sights are open—but in some ways, it's even better after dinner, when the gaslit lanes and candlelit restaurants twinkle. (For places that are closed after dark, circle back to the sights that interest you tomorrow.)

• *Start in front of the Cathedral of St. Sacerdos, on the...*

Place du Peyrou: An eighth-century Benedictine abbey once stood where the Cathedral of St. Sacerdos is today. It provided the stability for Sarlat to develop into an important trading city during the Middle Ages. The old Bishop's Palace, built right into the cathedral (on the right, with its top-floor Florentine-style loggia), recalls Sarlat's Italian connection. The Italian bishop was the boyfriend of Catherine de' Medici (queen of France)—a relationship that got him this fine residence. After a short stint here, he split to Paris with lots of local money. And though his departure scandalized the town, it left Sarlat with a heritage of Italian architecture.

Another reason for Sarlat's Italo-flavored urban design was its loyalty to the

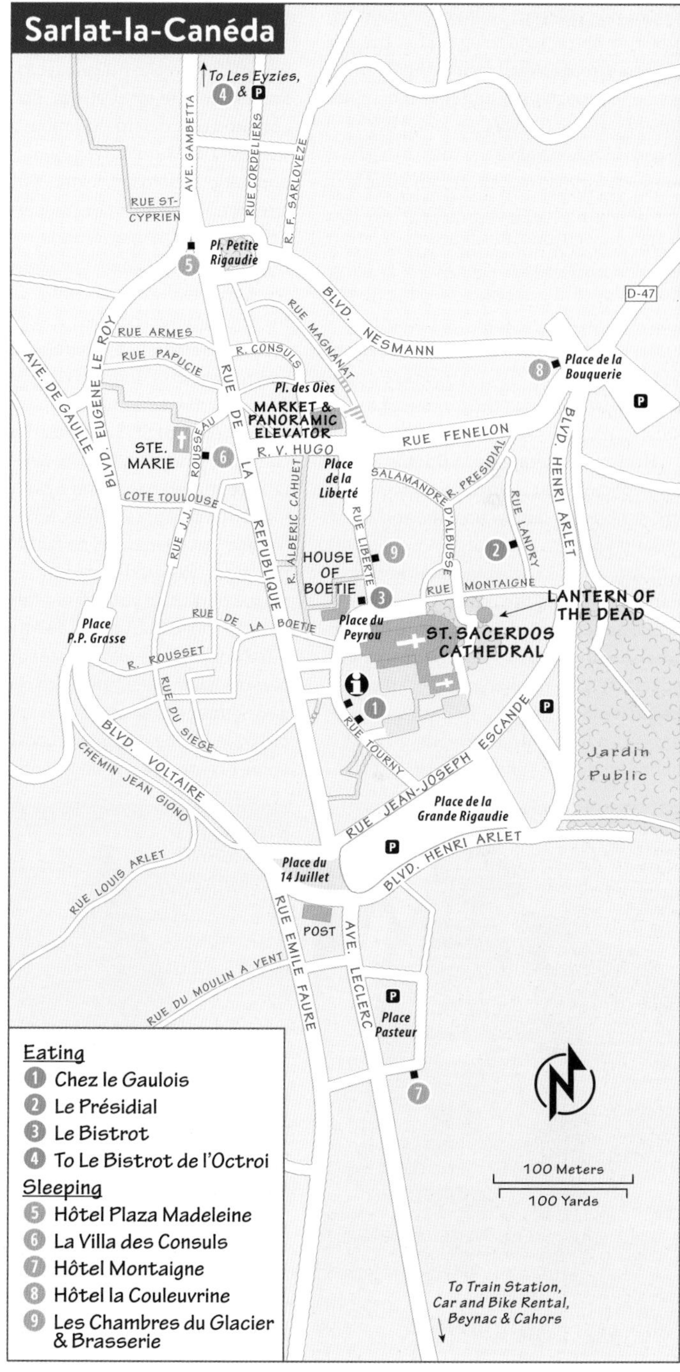
Sarlat-la-Canéda
To Les Eyzies, 4 & P
AVE. GAMBETTA
RUE CORDELIERS
R. F. SARLOVEZE
RUE ST-CYPRIEN
Pl. Petite Rigaudie
5
BLVD. NESMANN
D-47
RUE MAGNANAT
RUE ARMES
RUE PAPUCIE
R. CONSULS
Place de la Bouquerie
8
AVE. DE GAULLE
BLVD. EUGENE LE ROY
RUE DE LA REPUBLIQUE
Pl. des Oies
MARKET & PANORAMIC ELEVATOR
RUE FENELON
BLVD. HENRI ARLET
STE. MARIE
ROUSSEAU
6
R. V. HUGO
Place de la Liberté
SALAMANDRE
R. PRESIDIAL
RUE LANDRY
COTE TOULOUSE
RUE J.-J.
R. ALBERIC CAHUET
RUE LIBERTE
D'ALBUSSE
9
2
HOUSE OF BOETIE
3
RUE MONTAIGNE
LANTERN OF THE DEAD
RUE DE LA BOETIE
Place du Peyrou
Place P.P. Grasse
ST. SACERDOS CATHEDRAL
R. ROUSSET
RUE DU SIEGE
1
RUE TOURNY
RUE JEAN-JOSEPH ESCANDE
P
Jardin Public
BLVD. VOLTAIRE
CHEMIN JEAN GIONO
Place de la Grande Rigaudie
P
BLVD. HENRI ARLET
RUE LOUIS ARLET
Place du 14 Juillet
RUE EMILE FAURE
POST
AVE. LECLERC
RUE DU MOULIN A VENT
P
Place Pasteur
7
Eating
1 Chez le Gaulois
2 Le Présidial
3 Le Bistrot
4 To Le Bistrot de l'Octroi
Sleeping
5 Hôtel Plaza Madeleine
6 La Villa des Consuls
7 Hôtel Montaigne
8 Hôtel la Couleuvrine
9 Les Chambres du Glacier & Brasserie
100 Meters
100 Yards
To Train Station, Car and Bike Rental, Beynac & Cahors

king during wartime. Sarlat's glory century was from about 1450 to 1550, after the Hundred Years' War. Loyal to the French cause—through thick and thin and a century of war—Sarlat was rewarded by the French king, who gave the town lots of money to rebuild itself in stone. Sarlat's new nobility needed fancy houses, complete with ego-boosting features. Many of Sarlat's most impressive buildings date from this prosperous era, when the Renaissance style was in vogue and everyone wanted an architect with an Italian résumé.

Notice the fine Italianate house opposite the cathedral on the far side of the square. It's the...

House of Etienne de la Boëtie: This house was a typical 16th-century merchant's home—family upstairs and open ground floor (its stone arch now filled in) with big, fat sills to display retail goods. Pan up, scanning the crude-but-still-Renaissance carved reliefs. It was a time when anything Italian was trendy (when yokels "stuck a feather in their cap and called it macaroni"). La Boëtie (lah bow-ess-ee), a 16th-century bleeding-heart liberal who spoke and wrote against the rule of tyrannical kings, remains a local favorite.

Notice how the house just to the left arches over the small street. This was a common practice to maximize buildable space in the Middle Ages. Sarlat enjoyed a population boom in the mid-15th century after the Hundred Years' War ended.

• *If you're doing this walk during the day, head into the cathedral now. After hours, skip ahead to the Lantern of the Dead: Face the cathedral, walk around it to the left, up the lane, and through the little door in the wall to the rocket-shaped building on a bluff 30 yards behind the church.*

Cathedral of St. Sacerdos: Though the cathedral's facade has a few well-worn 12th-century carvings, most of it dates from the 18th and 19th centuries. Step inside this historic Sarlat interior. The faithful believed that Mary delivered them from the great plague of 1348, so you'll find a full complement of Virgin Marys here and throughout the town. The Gothic interiors in this part of France are simple, with clean lines and nothing extravagant. The first chapel on the left is the baptistery. Locals would come here to give thanks after they made

House of Etienne de la Boëtie

Lantern of the Dead

the pilgrimage to Lourdes for healing and returned satisfied. The second column on the right side of the nave shows a long list of hometown boys who gave their lives for France in World War I.

• *Exit the cathedral from the right transept (through a padded brown door) into what was once the abbey's cloisters. Snoop through a maze of quiet, interconnecting courtyards, always bearing left. In the final (deserted) courtyard, cut across diagonally to find the easy-to-miss door in the far corner. You'll wind up at the back of the church, where you'll climb steps (above the monks' graveyard) to a bluff. Here you'll find a bullet-shaped building ready for some kind of medieval takeoff, known as the...*

Lantern of the Dead (Lanterne des Morts): Dating from 1147, this is the oldest monument in town. In four horrible days, a quarter of Sarlat's population died in a plague (1,000 out of 4,000). People prayed to St. Bernard of Clairvaux for help. He blessed their bread—and instituted hygiene standards while he was at it, stopping the disease. This tower was built in gratitude.

• *Facing the church, exit downhill and to the right, toward an adorable house with its own tiny tower. Cross one street and keep straight, turn left a block later on Impasse de la Vieille Poste, make a quick right on Rue d'Albusse, and then take a left onto...*

Rue de la Salamandre: The salamander—unfazed by fire or water—was Sarlat's mascot. Befitting its favorite animal, Sarlat was also unfazed by fire (from war) and water (from floods). Walk several steps down this "Street of the Salamander" and find the Gothic-framed doorway just below on your right. Step back and notice the tower that housed the staircase. Staircase towers like this (Sarlat has about 20) date from about 1600 (after the wars of religion between the Catholics and Protestants), when the new nobility needed to show off.

• *Continue downhill, passing under the salamander-capped arch, and pause near (or better, sit down at) the café on the...*

Place de la Liberté: This has been Sarlat's main market square since the Middle Ages, though it was expanded in the 18th century. Sarlat's patriotic Town Hall stands behind you (with a café perfectly situated for people-watching). You can't miss the dark **stone roofs** topping the buildings across the square. They're typical of this region: Called *lauzes* in French, the flat limestone rocks were originally gathered by farmers clearing their fields, then made into cheap, durable roofing material (today few people can afford them). The unusually steep pitch of the *lauzes* roofs—which last up to 300 years—helps distribute the weight of the roof (about 160 pounds per square foot) over a greater area. Although most *lauzes* roofs have been replaced by roofs made from more affordable materials, a great number remain. The small window is critical: It provides air circulation, allowing the lichen that coat the porous stone to grow—sealing gaps between the stones and effectively waterproofing the

Place de la Liberté

View from the panoramic elevator

Foie Gras Facts

Force-feeding geese and ducks has the result of quickly fattening their livers, the principal ingredient of the Dordogne specialty foie gras. The practice is as controversial as bullfighting among animal-rights activists (and their case is well-documented). But, it's fascinating to talk to local farmers and hear the other side of the story. While awful conditions certainly exist in some places, here in the Dordogne, farmers pride themselves on treating their animals in what they consider a humane manner. Here's their take:

French enthusiasts of *la gavage* (as the force-feeding process is called) say the animals are calm, in no pain, and are designed to take in food in this manner because of their massive gullets and expandable livers (used to store fat for long migrations). Geese and ducks do not have a gag reflex, and the linings of their throats are tough (they swallow rocks to store in their gizzards for grinding the food they eat). They can eat lots of food easily, without choking. The lives of Dordogne ducks and geese are at least as comfy as the chickens, cows, and pigs that many people have no problem eating, and they are slaughtered as humanely as any nonhuman can expect in this food-chain existence.

The quality of foie gras depends on a stress-free environment; the birds do best with the same human feeder and a steady flow of good corn. These mostly free-range geese and ducks live six months (most factory-farmed chickens in the US live less than two months, and are plumped with hormones). Their "golden weeks" are the last three or four, when they go into the pen to have their liv-

roof. Without that layer, the stone would crumble after repeated freeze-and-thaw cycles.

• *Walk right, to the "upper" end of the square. The bulky Church of Ste. Marie, right across from you, today serves as Sarlat's...*

Covered Market and Panoramic Elevator: Once a parish church dedicated to St. Marie, with a massive *lauzes* roof and a soaring bell tower, this building was converted into a gunpowder factory and then a post office before becoming today's **indoor market** (daily 8:30-13:00). Marvel at its tall, strangely modern, seven-ton doors, and imagine the effort it took to deliver and install them in the center of this tight-laned town.

On the opposite side of this building (walk through if it's open, or around if it's closed), you'll find the entrance to a modern, glass-sided **panoramic elevator,** which whisks tourists up through the center of the ancient church's bell tower for bird's-eye views over the rooftops. Your elevator operator doubles as a guide, who gives a quick but effective history of Sarlat at the top. If they gather enough English-speakers, the spiel is in English;

ers fattened. With two or three feedings a day, their liver grows from about a quarter-pound to nearly two pounds. A goose with a fattened liver looks like he's waddling around with a full diaper under his feathers. (Signs in the region show geese with this unique shape.)

The varieties of product can be confusing. *Foie gras* means "fattened liver"; *foie gras d'oie* is from a goose, and *foie gras de canard* is from a duck (you'll also see a blend of the two). *Pâté de foie gras* is a "paste" of foie gras combined with other meats, fats, and seasonings (think of liverwurst). Most American consumers get the chance to eat foie gras only in the form of pâtés.

The *foie gras d'oie entier* (a solid chunk of pure goose liver) is the most expensive and prized version of canned foie gras, costing about €18 for 130 grams (about a tuna-can-size tin). The *bloc de foie gras d'oie* is made of chunks of pure goose liver that have been pressed together; it's more easily spreadable (figure €14 for 130 grams). The *medaillons de foie gras d'oie* must be at least 50 percent foie gras (the rest will be a pâté filler, about €8 for 130 grams). A small tin of blended duck-and-goose foie gras costs about €5. Read the label carefully: *elevée en Dordogne/Périgord* means that the animal was raised locally; *produit en Dordogne/Périgord/France* means it was processed here, but could originate elsewhere. It's trendy to label products *artisan conserve*—"conserved artisanally"—but this promises only that the product was canned locally. Airport security may require you to carry these in your checked baggage, not your carry-on.

After a week in the Dordogne, I leave feeling a strong need for foie gras detox.

otherwise, it'll be in French and you'll use the good English handout (feel free to ask questions). Because the elevator is open-air, it doesn't run in the rain (€5, pay using chip credit card—otherwise buy tickets with cash at TI; 5/hour, visit lasts 12 minutes, erratic hours—generally daily in summer 10:00-14:00 & 17:00-21:00, in spring and fall 10:00-13:00 & 14:00-18:00, shorter hours off-season).

• *When you've returned to earth, double back into Place de la Liberté and climb the small lane opposite the market's big doors to meet the "Boy of Sarlat"—a statue marking the best view over Place de la Liberté. Notice the cathedral's tower, with a salamander swinging happily from its spire. Just below you on the stairs are several shops.*

Foie Gras and Beyond: Tourist-pleasing stores like **La Boutique du Badaud** line the streets of Sarlat and are filled with the finest local products. This quiet shop sells it all, from truffles to foie gras to walnut wine to truffle liqueur. They also offer tastings *(dégustations)* of local liquors.

• *Turn left behind the boy statue and trickle like medieval rainwater down the ramp into an inviting square. Here you'll find a little gaggle of geese.*

Place des Oies: Feathers fly when geese are traded on this "Square of the Geese" on market days (Nov-March). Birds have been serious business here since the Middle Ages. Even today, a typical Sarlat menu reads, "duck, duck, goose." Trophy homes surround this cute little square on all sides.

Check out the wealthy merchant's home to the right as you enter the square—the **Manoir de Gisson**—with a tower built big enough to match his ego. The owner was the town counsel, a position that arose as cities like Sarlat outgrew the Middle Ages. Town counsels replaced priests in resolving civil conflicts and performing other civic duties. Touring the interior of the manor shows you how the wealthy lived in Sarlat (study the big poster next to the entry). You'll climb up one of those spiral staircase towers, ogle at several rooms carefully decorated with authentic 16th- to 18th-century furniture, and peek inside the impressive *lauzes* roof. It's fun to gaze out the windows and imagine living here, surrounded by 360 degrees of gorgeous cityscape (€7, daily April-Sept 10:00-18:30, until 19:00 July-Aug, closes earlier off-season, borrow English booklet, tel. 05 53 28 70 55, www.manoirdegisson.com).

Manoir de Gisson

• *Walk to the right along Rue des Consuls. Just before Le Mirandol restaurant, turn right toward a...*

Fourteenth-Century Vault and Fountain: For generations, this was the town's only source of water, protected by the Virgin Mary (find her at the end of the fountain). Opposite the restaurant and fountain, find the wooden doorway (open late June-Aug only) that houses a massive Renaissance stairway. These showy stairways, which replaced more space-efficient spiral ones, required a big house and a bigger income. Impressive.

• *Follow the curve along Rue des Consuls, and enter the straight-as-an-arrow...*

Rue de la République: This "modern" thoroughfare, known as *La Traverse* to locals, dates from the mid-1800s, when blasting big roads through medieval cities was standard operating procedure. It wasn't until 1963 that Sarlat's other streets would become off-limits to cars, thanks to France's forward-thinking minister of culture, André Malraux. The law that bears his name has served to preserve and restore important monuments and neighborhoods throughout France. Eager to protect the country's architectural heritage, private investors, cities, and regions worked together to create traffic-free zones, rebuild crumbling buildings, and make sure that no cables or ugly wiring marred the ambience of towns like this. Without the Malraux Law, Sarlat might well have more "efficient" roads like Rue de la République slicing through its once-charming old town center.

Your tour is over, but make sure you take time for a poetic ramble through the town's quiet side—or, better yet, stroll any of Sarlat's lanes after dark. This is the only town in France illuminated by gas lamps,

Dordogne Markets

The best markets in the region are in Sarlat (Sat and Wed, in that order), but you'll find others throughout the river valley, including Les Eyzies-de-Tayac and Beynac (both Mon). Outdoor markets allow you to meet the farmer. Subtly check out the hands of the person helping customers—if they're not gnarled and rough from working the fields, move on. Here's what to look for:

Strawberries *(fraises):* Available from April to November, they're gorgeous, and they smell even better than they look. Also look for *fraises des bois,* the tiny, sweet, and less visually appealing strawberries found in nearby forests.

Cheeses *(fromages):* The region is famous for its Cabécou goat cheese, though often you'll also find Auvergne cheeses (St. Nectaire and Cantal are the most common) from just east of the Dordogne (usually in big rounds), and Tomme and Brébis (sheep cheeses) from the Pyrenees to the south.

Truffles *(truffes):* Truffle season is our off-season (Nov-Feb), when you'll find them at every market. During summer, the fresh truffles you might see are *truffes d'été,* a less desirable, cheaper, but still tasty species.

Anything with Walnuts *(aux noix): Pain aux noix* is a thick bread loaf chock-full of walnuts. *Moutarde de noix* is walnut mustard. *Confiture de noix* is a walnut spread. *Gâteaux de noix* are tasty cakes.

Goose or Duck Livers and Pâté (foie gras): This spread is made from geese (better) and ducks (still good), or from a mix of the two. You'll see two basic forms: *entier* and *bloc. Entier* is a piece cut right from the product, whereas *bloc* has been blended to make it easier to spread—*mousse* has been whipped for an even creamier consistency.

Confit de Canard: At butcher stands, look for hunks of duck smothered in white fat, just waiting for someone to take them home and cook them up.

Dried Sausages *(saucissons secs):* Long tables are piled high with dried sausages covered in herbs or stuffed with local goodies. Some of the variations include *porc, canard* (duck), *fumé* (smoked), *à l'ail* (garlic), *cendré* (rolled in ashes), *aux myrtilles* (with blueberries), *sanglier* (wild boar), and even *âne* (donkey)—and, of course, *aux noix* (with walnuts).

Olive Oil *(huile d'olive):* You'll find stylish bottles of various olive oils, as well as vegetable oils flavored with truffles, walnuts, chestnuts *(châtaignes),* and hazelnuts *(noisettes)*—good for cooking, salad dressing, and gifts. Pure walnut oil, best on salads, is a local specialty.

Olives and Nuts *(olives et noix):* These interlopers from Provence find their way to every market in France.

Brandies and Liqueurs: Although they're not made here, Armagnac, Cognac, and other southwestern fruit-flavored liquors are often available.

which cause the warm limestone to glow, turning up the romance of Sarlat even higher. Now may also be a good time to find a café and raise a toast to Monsieur Malraux.

Experiences

Markets

Outdoor markets are a big deal in the Dordogne. Some of the best are in Sarlat, which has been an important market town since the Middle Ages. Saturday's market swallows the entire town and is best in the morning (produce and food vendors leave around noon). Come before 8:00 to watch them set up, and, once the market is under way, plant yourself at a well-positioned café to observe the civilized scene. Another market occurs in the same location on Wednesday mornings. On Thursday evenings, a small organic market enlivens the town's lower side (starting at 18:00, best in summer; just south of the old center at Place du 14 Juillet). From November to March, a truffle market takes place on Saturday mornings on Rue Fénelon.

Biking

Sarlat is surrounded by beautiful country lanes that would be ideal for biking were it not for all those hills. Villages along the Dordogne River make good biking destinations, though expect some traffic and some serious ups and downs between Sarlat and the river (bike-rental places can advise quieter routes). A 26-kilometer bike-only lane runs from Sarlat to Souillac, but doesn't connect the river villages I describe.

Liberty Cycle rents bikes and offers short bike tours from Sarlat and Castelnaud (daily, by the canoe rental in Castelnaud, tel. 07 81 24 78 79, www.liberty-cycle.com, guillaume@liberty-cycle.com). **Aquitaine Bike,** run by a British-American couple, can deliver top-quality bikes to your hotel in and near Sarlat in nonsummer months and provides roadside assistance (3-day minimum for most bikes, tours available, tel. 05 53 30 35 17, mobile 06 32 35 56 50, www.aquitainebike.com, aquitainebike@gmail.com). The TI has info on bike rental outside Sarlat.

Eating

Sarlat is stuffed with restaurants that cater to tourists, but you can still dine well and cheaply. The following places have been reliable; Le Présidial is the most formal. If you have a car, consider driving to Beynac (see page 257) or La Roque-Gageac (page 255) for riverfront dining.

$ Chez le Gaulois is a change from the traditional places that line Sarlat's lanes. Pyrenees-raised Olivier and his wife Nora serve a hearty mountain cuisine featuring fondue, raclette, *tartiflette* (roasted potatoes mixed with ham and cheese—comes with a good salad for €14), dinner salads, and thinly sliced ham (Olivier spends all evening slicing away). The *cassolette des légumes* (a ratatouille-like dish) is also tasty (€11). Try *la tarte au figues*—fig tart—for dessert. They have a few sidewalk tables, but the fun is inside and the service is English-fluent. The ceiling is cluttered with ham hocks, and the soundtrack is

The Dordogne's Cuisine Scene

Gourmets flock to this area for its geese, ducks, and wild mushrooms. The geese produce the region's famous foie gras (involuntarily—see sidebar on page 242.) **Foie gras** tastes like butter and is priced like gold. The main duck specialty is ***confit de canard*** (duck meat preserved in its own fat—sounds terrible, but tastes great). ***Magret de canard*** (sautéed duck breast), smoked duck, and anything fried in duck fat also show up on menus.

Pommes de terre sarladaises are mouthwatering, thinly sliced potatoes fried in duck fat and commonly served with *confit de canard.* **Wild truffles** are dirty black tubers that grow underground, generally on the roots of oak trees. Farmers traditionally locate them with sniffing pigs and then charge a fortune for their catch (roughly $250 per pound). Native cheeses are **Cabécou** (a silver-dollar-size, pungent, nutty-flavored goat cheese) and **Echourgnac** (made by local Trappist monks). You'll find walnuts ***(noix)*** in salads, cakes, liqueurs, salad dressings, and more.

Wines to sample are **Bergerac** (red, white, and rosé), Pecharmant (red, must be at least four years old), **Cahors** (a full-bodied red), and **Monbazillac** (sweet dessert wine). The ***vin de noix*** (sweet walnut liqueur) is delightful before dinner.

Restaurants serve only during lunch (11:30-14:00) and dinner (19:00-21:00, later in bigger cities); bigger cafés serve food throughout the day.

jazz. To eat at prime time (12:00 or 19:00), reservations are smart during the high season (daily April-Oct, closed Sun-Mon Nov-March, near the TI at 1 Rue Tourny, tel. 05 53 59 50 64).

$$$ Le Présidial is a lovely place for a refined meal in a historic mansion. The setting is exceptional—you're greeted with beautiful gardens (where you can dine in good weather), and the interior comes with high ceilings, stone walls, and rich wood floors (€19-39 *menus*, closed Sun, 6 Rue Landry, tel. 05 53 28 92 47, www.lepresidial.fr).

$$ Le Bistrot has marvelous outside seating across from the cathedral, plus a cozy interior. The traditional cuisine is served at affordable prices (€18-30 *menus*, daily, 14 Place du Peyrou, tel. 05 53 28 28 40).

$ Brasserie le Glacier offers main-square views from its outdoor tables and good, crowd-pleasing café fare nonstop from 11:00-22:00. Come here for good service (Filomena has the big smile); a big salad for €12 (the *salade paysanne*—peasant salad, with smoked duck—works for me), pizza (€10-12), or *un plat* (€12-16); and a view of the lights warming the town buildings (daily, Place de la Liberté, tel. 05 53 29 99 99, also rents rooms—listed later).

$$ Le Bistro de l'Octroi, overlooking a busy road a few blocks north of the old town, has to provide top cuisine and competitive prices to draw locals—and it does. Quality bistro fare (mostly meat dishes) is served on a generous terrace and within the pleasant interior (€21-36 three-course *menus* offering many options; order two starters if you prefer, daily, 111 Avenue des Selves, tel. 05 53 30 83 40, www.lebistrodeloctroi.fr).

Sleeping

Even with summer crowds, Sarlat is the train traveler's best home base. In July and August, some hotels require half-pension, and hotels in downtown Sarlat book up first.

Sleep Code

$$$$ Splurge: Over €250
$$$ Pricier: €190-250
$$ Moderate: €130-190
$ Budget: €70-130
¢ Backpacker: Under €70

Hotels are classified based on the average price of a standard double room with bath in high season. Unless otherwise noted, credit cards are accepted, breakfast is not included, hotel staff speak English, and Wi-Fi is available.

$$ Hôtel Plaza Madeleine**** is a central and upscale value with formal service, a handsome pub/wine-bar, stylish public spaces, and 39 very sharp rooms with every comfort. You'll find a pool out back, a sauna, and a Jacuzzi—all free for guests (fine standard Db-€130-140, bigger and newer Db-€160-220, extra person-€26, connecting rooms for families, great breakfast buffet-€15, air-con, elevator, garage parking-€15/day, at north end of ring road at 1 Place de la Petite Rigaudie, tel. 05 53 59 10 41, www.plaza-madeleine.com, contact@plaza-madeleine.com).

$ La Villa des Consuls***, a cross between a B&B and a hotel, occupies a 17th-century home buried on Sarlat's quiet side with 13 lovely, spacious rooms with microwave ovens and refrigerators; most also have a kitchen and a living room. The rooms surround a small courtyard and come with wood floors, private decks, and high ceilings. English-fluent owner David prices his rooms to encourage longer stays; these rates are for stays of 2-6 nights (Db-€89-102, big Db/Tb/Qb-€129-169, 10 percent more for 1-night stays, air-con, free use of washers and dryers, garage parking-€10/day, train station pickup-€7, David will help with hauling bags from the street, 3 Rue Jean-Jacques Rousseau, tel. 05 53 31 90 05, www.villaconsuls.fr, villadesconsuls@aol.com).

$ Hôtel Montaigne***, a good value located a block south of the pedestrian zone, is run by the smiling Martinats (mama, papa, and daughter). The 28 rooms are simple, spotless, comfortable, and air-conditioned. Of the hotels I list, this is the one nearest to the train station (Db-€69-90, extra person-€15, two-room family suites-€110-125, good breakfast buffet-€10, air-con, elevator, easy parking nearby, Place Pasteur, tel. 05 53 31 93 88, www.hotelmontaigne.fr, contact@hotelmontaigne.fr).

$ Hôtel la Couleuvrine** offers 27 simple rooms with character at good rates in a historic building with a handy location—across from the launderette and with easy parking (for Sarlat). Families enjoy *les chambres familles* (several in the tower). Some rooms have tight bathrooms, some could use new carpets, and a few have private terraces (Db-€50-85, Db suite-€95, family rooms-€95-115, breakfast-€10, elevator, on ring road at 1 Place de la Bouquerie, tel. 05 53 59 27 80, www.la-couleuvrine.com, contact@la-couleuvrine.com). Half-pension is encouraged during busy periods and in the summer—figure €35 per person beyond the room price for breakfast and a good dinner in the classy restaurant.

$ Les Chambres du Glacier is a *chambres d'hôte* above an outdoor café, in the thick of Sarlat's pedestrian zone—perfect for market days. Kind Monsieur Da Costa and son Bruno offer four cavernous but surprisingly comfortable rooms, with sky-high ceilings, big soundproof windows, polished wood floors, and bathrooms you can get lost in (Db-€85, Tb-€110, Qb-€135, includes breakfast, Place de la Liberté, tel. 05 53 29 99 99, www.chambres-du-glacier-sarlat.com, carlos.da.costa.24@wanadoo.fr).

Transportation

Arriving and Departing

BY CAR

The hilly terrain around Sarlat creates traffic funnels unusual for a town of this size. Metered parking is easy in the center on nonmarket and off-season days (about €4/2 hours, free Mon-Sat 12:00-14:00 & 19:00-9:00 and all day Sun). On market days, avoid the center by parking along Avenue du Général de Gaulle (at the north end of town), or in one of the signed lots on the ring road. The closest parking to the center is metered.

BY TRAIN

Sarlat-la-Canéda's sleepy train station keeps a lonely vigil, without a shop, café, or hotel in sight. It's a mostly downhill, 20-minute walk to the town center (taxis are about €7). To walk into town, turn left out of the station and follow Avenue de la Gare as it curves downhill, then turn right at the bottom, on Avenue Thiers, to reach the town center. Some trains (such as those from Limoges and Cahors) arrive at nearby Souillac, which is connected to Sarlat's train station by an SNCF bus.

Sarlat's TI has train schedules. Souillac and Périgueux are the train hubs for points within the greater region. For all of the following destinations, you could go west on the Libourne/Bordeaux line (transferring in either city, depending on your connection), or east by SNCF bus to Souillac (covered by rail pass, bus leaves from Sarlat train station). I've listed the fastest path in each case. Sarlat train info: tel. 05 53 59 00 21.

Train Connections from Sarlat-la-Canéda to: Les Eyzies-de-Tayac (3-4/day, 1-2.5 hours, transfer in Le Buisson), **Paris** (4/day, 5 hours, change in Bordeaux), **Amboise** (3/day, 5-7 hours, via Libourne, then TGV to Tours' St-Pierre-des-Corps, then local train to Amboise), **Bourges** (4/day, 6-7 hours, 2-4 changes), **Carcassonne** (5/day, 5.5-7 hours, 1-3 changes, some require bus from Sarlat to Souillac).

THE DORDOGNE RIVER VALLEY

The most striking stretch of the Dordogne lies between Carsac and Beynac. Traveling by canoe is the best way to savor the highlights of the valley, though several scenic sights lie off the river and require a car or bike.

Drivers should allow a minimum of a half-day to sample the river valley. Drive slowly to savor the scenery and to stay out of trouble (these are narrow, cliff-hanging roads). The area is picnic-perfect, but buy your supplies before leaving Sarlat; pickings are slim in the villages (though view cafés are abundant). Vitrac (near Sarlat) is the best place to park for a canoe ride down the river. La Roque-Gageac, Beynac, and Domme have good restaurants.

In riverfront villages, you'll pay for parking during the day (about €2-3 for a 3-hour minimum stay, free during midafternoon siesta, pay at meter, then put receipt on your dashboard; cars are checked). Parked cars are catnip to thieves: Take everything out or stow belongings out of sight.

➲ Dordogne Scenic Loop

Follow this self-guided tour, worth ▲▲, to link Sarlat with La Roque-Gageac, Beynac and its château, and Castelnaud before returning to Sarlat after 27 hilly miles. Cyclists can cut seven miles off this distance and still see most of the highlights by following D-704 from Sarlat toward Cahors, then taking the Montfort turnoff (well-signed after the big Leclerc grocery store) and tracking signs to *Montfort*. Once in Montfort, follow the river downstream to La Roque-Gageac.

Key villages along this route are described in detail later in this chapter, under "Dordogne Towns and Sights."

From Sarlat, follow signs on D-704 toward *Cahors*. Not long after leaving

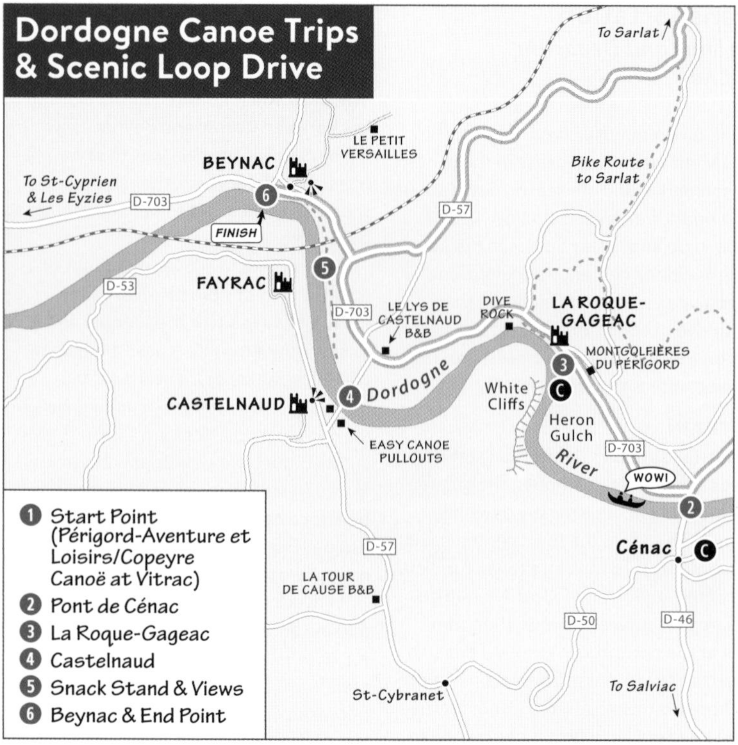

Dordogne Canoe Trips & Scenic Loop Drive

To Sarlat
LE PETIT VERSAILLES
BEYNAC
To St-Cyprien & Les Eyzies
D-703
Bike Route to Sarlat
D-57
FINISH
FAYRAC
D-53
D-703
LE LYS DE CASTELNAUD B&B
DIVE ROCK
LA ROQUE-GAGEAC
MONTGOLFIÈRES DU PÉRIGORD
Dordogne River
White Cliffs
Heron Gulch
CASTELNAUD
EASY CANOE PULLOUTS
D-703
WOW!
Cénac
D-57
LA TOUR DE CAUSE B&B
D-50
D-46
St-Cybranet
To Salviac

1. Start Point (Périgord-Aventure et Loisirs/Copeyre Canoë at Vitrac)
2. Pont de Cénac
3. La Roque-Gageac
4. Castelnaud
5. Snack Stand & Views
6. Beynac & End Point

Sarlat, you'll pass the Rougie foie gras outlet store, then the limestone quarry that gives the houses in this area their lemony color.

In about five minutes, be on the lookout for the little signposted turnoff on the right to the *Eglise de Carsac* (Church of Carsac). Set peacefully among cornfields, with its WWI monument, bonsai-like plane trees, and simple, bulky Romanesque exterior, the **Eglise de Carsac** is part of a vivid rural French scene. Take a break here and enter the church (usually open, English handout). The stone capitals behind the altar are exquisitely medieval. Back outside, the small cornfields nearby are busy growing feed for ducks and geese—locals are appalled that humans would eat the stuff.

From here, continue on, following signs to *Montfort*. About a half-mile west of Carsac, pull over to enjoy the scenic viewpoint (overlooking a bend in the river known as Cingle de Montfort). Across the Dordogne River, fields of walnut trees stretch to distant castles, and the nearby hills are covered in oak trees. This area is nicknamed "black Périgord" for its thick blanket of oaks, which stay leafy through-

Carsac's Romanesque church

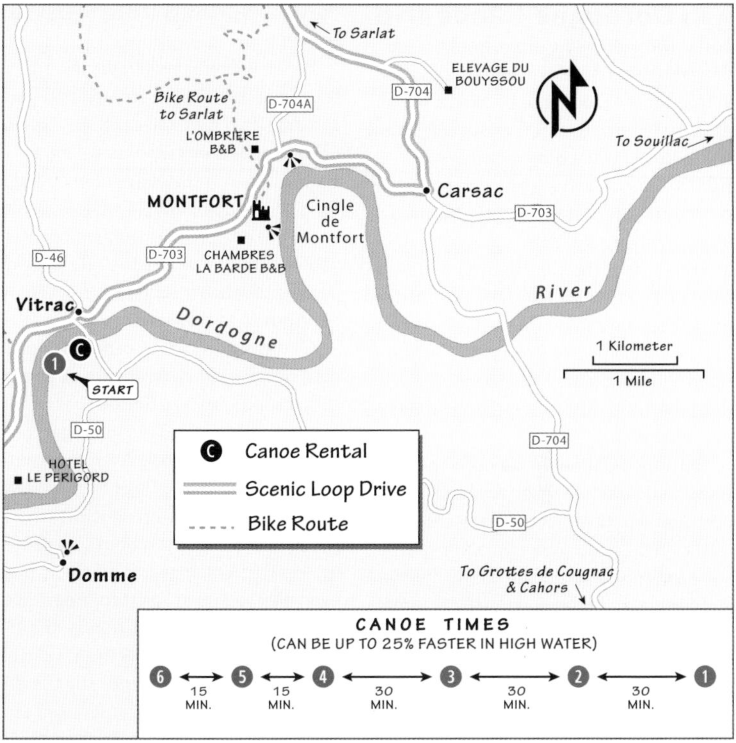

out the winter. The fairy-tale castle you see is **Montfort,** once the medieval home of Simon de Montfort, who led the Cathar Crusades in the early 13th century. Today it's considered mysterious by locals. (It's rumored that the castle is now the home of a brother of the emir of Kuwait.) A plaque on the rock near where you parked honors those who fought Nazi occupiers in this area in 1943.

Château at Montfort

Continue on, passing under Montfort's castle (which you can't tour; its cute little village has a few cafés). If you're combining a canoe trip with this drive, cross the river, following signs to *Domme,* and find my recommended canoe rental on the right side (see "Dordogne Canoe Trip," next).

The touristy *bastide* (fortified village) of **Domme** is well worth a side-trip from Vitrac or La Roque-Gageac for its sensational views (best early in the day). Our driving route continues to the more important riverfront villages of **La Roque-Gageac,** then on to **Castelnaud,** and finally to **Beynac** (all described later in this chapter). From Beynac, it's a quick run back to Sarlat.

▲▲▲Dordogne Canoe Trip

For a vivid, refreshing break from the car or train, explore the riverside castles and villages of the Dordogne by canoe. For an affordable price (a canoe costs only about €18/person for the trip I recommend, from Vitrac to Beynac), you can spend all day on and off the river touring sights. It's a swimmingly good deal.

For the same scenery with no paddling (and no ability to visit villages and castles en route), you can take a boat cruise from La Roque-Gageac or Beynac to Castelnaud and back (€8-9, 50-60 minutes, described in La Roque-Gageac and Beynac sections).

Renting a Canoe (or Kayak): You can rent plastic boats—which are hard, light, and indestructible—from many area outfits in this area. Whether a one-person kayak or a two-person canoe, they're stable enough for beginners. Many rental places will pick you up at an agreed-upon spot (even in Sarlat, provided that your group is big enough, and they aren't too busy). All companies let you put in anytime between 9:30 and 16:00 (start no later than 15:00 to allow time to linger when the mood strikes; they'll pick you up at about 18:00). They all charge about the same and typically accept cash only (€14-18/person for two-person canoes, €17-24 for one-person kayaks). You'll get a life vest and, for about €2 extra, a watertight bucket in which to store your belongings. (The bucket is bigger than you'd need for just a camera, watch, wallet, and cell phone; if that's all you have, bring a resealable plastic baggie or something similar for dry storage.) You must have shoes that stay on your feet; travelers wearing flip-flops will be invited to purchase more appropriate footwear (sold at most boat launches for around €10).

The trip is fun even in light rain (if you don't mind getting wet)—but heavy rains can make the current too fast to handle, so be sure to check on river levels. If you don't see many other canoes in the river, the water is probably too high—ask before you rent.

Beach your boat wherever it works to take a break—it's light enough that you can drag it up high and dry to go explore. (The canoes aren't worth stealing, as they're cheap and clearly color-coded for their parent company.) It's OK if you're a complete novice—the only whitewater you'll encounter will be the rare wake of passing tour boats...and your travel partner frothing at the views.

Of the region's many canoe companies, only **Périgord-Aventure et Loisirs** (also called **Copeyre Canoë**) has a pull-out arrangement in Beynac (to get to their Vitrac put-in base, from the main roundabout in the town of Vitrac, cross the Dordogne, and turn right). You may get a discount with this book (ask about it), and if you arrange it in advance, they'll even pick you up in Sarlat for free and get you to Vitrac (this allows nondrivers a chance to explore the riverfront villages for the price of a canoe trip—tip the driver a few euros for this helpful service; tel. 05 53 28 23 82, mobile 06 83 27 30 06, www.perigordaventureloisirs.com, info@perigordaventureloisirs.com). Allow time to explore Beynac after your river paddle and before the return shuttle trip. Périgord-Aventure also arranges a longer 14-mile trip from Carsac to Beynac, adding the gorgeous Montfort loop *(Cingle de Montfort)*. Ask about their canoe-hike-bike option that starts with the canoe trip

Paddling the Dordogne

to Beynac, continues with a walk along a riverside trail to Castelnaud, and ends with a bike ride back to your starting point in Vitrac (€30, no discounts, reserve in advance, start or end the loop wherever you like).

The Nine-Mile Paddle from Vitrac to Beynac: This is the most interesting, scenic, and handy trip if you're based in or near Sarlat. Vitrac, on the river close to Sarlat, is a good starting point. And, with its mighty castle and pleasant restaurants, Beynac delivers the perfect finale to your journey. Allow 2 hours for this paddle at a relaxed pace in spring and fall, and up to 2.5 hours in summer when the river is usually at its lowest flow.

Here's a rundown of the Vitrac-Beynac adventure: Leave **Vitrac,** paddling at an easy pace through lush, forested land. The fortified hill town of Domme will be dead ahead. Pass through Heron Gulch, and, after about an hour, you'll come to **La Roque-Gageac** (one of two easy and worthwhile stops before Beynac).

Paddle past La Roque-Gageac's wooden docks (with the tour boats) to the stone ramp leading up to the town. Do a 180-degree turn and beach thyself, dragging the boat high and dry. From there you're in La Roque-Gageac's tiny town center (described on page 255), with a TI and plenty of cafés, snacks, and ice-cream options. Enjoy the town before heading back to your canoe and into the water.

When leaving La Roque-Gageac, float backward to enjoy the village view. About 15 minutes farther downstream, you'll approach views of the feudal village and castle of **Castelnaud.** Look for the castle's huge model of medieval catapults silhouetted menacingly against the sky (it's a steep but worthwhile climb to tour this castle—see page 256). About 15 minutes after you first spot the castle, you'll find two grassy pullouts flanking the bridge below the castle, and the bridge arches make terrific frames for castle views. Just past the grass there's a small market and charcuterie with all you need for a picnic. La Plage Café serves good café fare with views (near where you pull out).

Another 15 minutes downstream brings views of **Château de Fayrac** on your left. The lords of Castelnaud built this to spy on Beynac during the Hundred Years' War (1336-1453). It's another 15 minutes to your last stop: **Beynac** (described later).

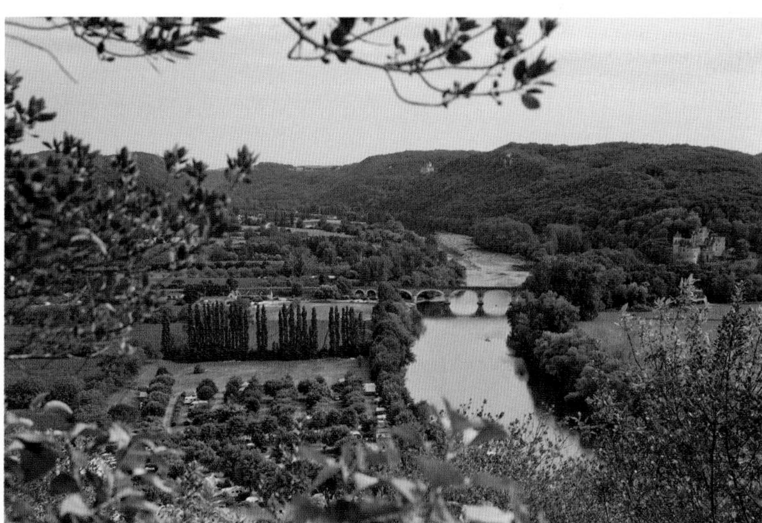

View of the Dordogne River from the castle at Castelnaud

The awesome view of Beynac castle—looming high above the town—gets better and better as you approach. Slow down and enjoy the ride (sometimes there's a snack stand with the same views at the bridge on the right). Keep to the right as you approach the Périgord-Aventure/Copeyre Canoë depot. You'll see the ramp just before the parking lot and wooden dock (where the tour boats generally tie up). Do another 180-degree turn, and beach yourself hard. The office is right there. Return your boat, and explore Beynac.

Other Canoe Options: All along the river you'll see canoe companies, each with stacks of plastic canoes. Depending on their location and relations with places to pull out, each one works best on a particular stretch of the river. All have essentially the same policies. Below Domme in Cénac, **Dordogne Randonnées** has canoes and kayaks for the scenic two-hour stretch to a pullout just past Beynac (to reach their office coming from Sarlat or Beynac, take the first left after crossing the bridge to Cénac, tel. 05 53 28 22 01, randodordogne@wanadoo.fr). In La Roque-Gageac, **Canoe-Dordogne** rents canoes for the worthwhile two-hour float to Château des Milandes, allowing canoers to stop in Beynac along the way (tel. 05 53 29 58 50).

Dordogne Towns and Sights

The towns and sights described next coincide with the Dordogne River Valley scenic loop outlined earlier (see page 249). These villages are a joy to wander before lunch and late in the day. In high season, expect mobs of tourists and traffic in the afternoons. Those with a car can enjoy tranquil rural accommodations at great prices in these cozy villages. I like the comfort they provide and the views they offer.

▲▲*Domme*

This bustling little town, worth a stop for its stunning view, is ideal early in the day. Otherwise, arrive late, when crowds recede and the light is best. If you come for lunch or dinner, show up early enough to savor the cliff-capping setting, and if you come on market day (Thu), expect to hoof it up from a parking lot well below (cars not allowed in old town until the market is over). On other days, follow signs up to *La Bastide de Domme*, and drive right through the narrow gate of the fortified town walls. Park at the pay lot near the view *(Panorama)*. You'll find picnic-perfect benches, cafés, and a view you won't soon forget. While the main street is lined with touristy shops that make the town feel greedy, lose yourself in some of the unusually picturesque back lanes, where roses climb over rustic doorways.

EATING AND SLEEPING

$$$ Hôtel de l'Esplanade delivers the valley's most sensational views from many of its 15 comfortable bedrooms and restaurant tables. If you come for the restaurant (€35-70 *menus*, closed Mon lunch), book ahead for view seating. Both the hotel and the restaurant are traditional, formal, and a bit stiff (Db-€98-140, view Db-€145-165, air-con, tel. 05 53 28 31 41, www.esplanade-perigord.com, esplanade.domme@wanadoo.fr).

Backstreet Domme

▲▲▲*La Roque-Gageac*

Whether you're joyriding, paddling the Dordogne, or taking a hot-air balloon ride, La Roque-Gageac (lah rohk-gah-zhahk) is an essential stop—and a strong contender on all the "cutest towns in France" lists. Called by most simply "La Roque" ("The Rock"), it looks sculpted out of the rock between the river and the cliffs. It also makes a fine base for touring the region.

At the upstream end of town, you'll find plenty of parking, an ATM, the **TI** (April-Sept daily 10:00-13:00 & 14:00-17:00, July-Aug until 18:00, closed off-season, tel. 05 53 29 17 01), a WC, a playground, canoe rental, and *pétanque (boules)* courts that are lively on summer evenings. A small market brightens La Roque-Gageac on Friday mornings in summer. Though busy with day-trippers, the town is peaceful at night.

➲ LA ROQUE-GAGEAC WALK

Stand along the river near the TI and survey La Roque-Gageac: It's a one-street town stretching along the river. The highest stonework (on the far right) was home to the town's earliest inhabitants in the 10th century. High above (about center), 12th-century cave dwellers built a settlement during the era of Norman (Viking) river raids. Long after the Vikings were tamed, French soldiers used this lofty perch as a barracks while fighting against England in the Hundred Years' War. Sturdy concrete supports now reinforce the cave.

Now locate the exotic foliage around the church on the right. Tropical gardens (bamboo, bananas, lemons, cactus, and so on) are a village forte, because limestone absorbs heat.

Those wooden boats on the river are modeled after boats called *gabarres*, originally built here to take prized oak barrels filled with local wine down to Bordeaux. Unable to return against the river current, the boats were routinely taken apart for their lumber. Today, tourists, rather than barrels, fill the boats on river cruises (described later). If you're experiencing a movie-based déjà vu, it's because these actual boats (dolled up, of course) were used by Johnny Depp in the movie *Chocolat*, to the delight of viewers and Juliette Binoche alike.

La Roque-Gageac frequently endures winter floods that would leave you

La Roque-Gageac

(standing where you are now) underwater. When there's a big rain in central France, La Roque-Gageac floods two days later. The first floors of all the riverfront buildings are vacated off-season. The new riverfront wall, finished in 2014, was pushed out into the river, adding 13 feet of width to the street. Notice the openings at sidewalk level allowing water to flow through in heavy rains. Walk on the main drag to get a closer look. A house about five buildings downriver from Hôtel la Belle Etoile shows various high-water marks (*inondation* means "flood"). Looking farther downstream, notice the fanciful castle built in the 19th century by a British aristocrat (whose family still nurtures Joan of Arc dreams in its turrets). The old building just beyond that (downstream end of town) is historic—it's the quarantine house, where lepers and out-of-town visitors who dropped by in times of plague would be kept (after their boats were burned).

Climb into the town by strolling up the cobbled lane to the right of Hôtel la Belle Etoile. Where the stepped path ends, veer right to find the exotic plants and viewpoint (in front of the simple church). From here you can make out Château de Castelnaud downriver, and the village of Domme capping its hill to the left. A left turn at the end of the stepped path takes you to more views and the privately owned Fort Troglodytique (closed to the public). For a terrific medieval fort experience, visit the prehistoric La Roque St-Christophe (described on page 268).

EXPERIENCES

Tour boats cruise from La Roque-Gageac to Castelnaud and back (one-hour cruise-€9, includes audioguide, 2/hour, April-Nov daily, tel. 05 53 29 40 44).

Montgolfières du Périgord offers a variety of **hot-air balloon rides** with well-qualified pilots (one-hour flight-€200/person, departures in good weather generally just after sunrise and just before sunset, tel. 05 53 28 18 58, www.montgolfiere-du-perigord.com, perigordballoons@wanadoo.fr).

EATING AND SLEEPING

Along with Beynac, this is one of the region's most beautiful villages. Park in the lot at the eastern end of town if you're staying in La Roque-Gageac, and take everything of value out of your car.

$$$ Manoir de la Malatrie is a wonderful splurge with five country-classy rooms and one family-ideal apartment with oak-meets-leather public areas, all surrounding a big, heated pool and terraced gardens (begging for a picnic). Your gentle hostess, Ouaffa, manages her place with elegance (Db-€140-160; large modern apartment for two-€140-180, €40/extra person; cheaper in winter, air-con, free parking, barely downstream from the village—10-minute walk to town on trail above road, mobile 06 18 61 61 18, www.chambresdhotes-lamalartrie.com, lamalatire@orange.fr).

$ Hôtel la Belle Etoile**, a well-run hotel-restaurant in the center of La Roque-Gageac, is a terrific value. Hostess Danielle and chef Régis (ray-geez) offer good rooms, most overlooking the river, a nice terrace, and a fine restaurant (no riverview Db-€56, riverview Db-€68-79, gorgeous suite-€140-150, air-con, free parking, closed Dec-March, tel. 05 53 29 51 44, www.belleetoile.fr, hotel.belle-etoile@wanadoo.fr). Régis is the third generation of his family to be chef here and he takes his job seriously. Come for a memorable dinner of classic French cuisine with modern accents in a romantic setting. The *oeufs cocottes* are really good (*menus* from €31, closed for lunch Wed and all day Mon; book a few days ahead).

▲▲*Château de Castelnaud*

This castle may look a tad less mighty than Château de Beynac (down the river), but it packs a powerful medieval punch. The concise English handout escorts you room by room through the castle-museum. The exhibits—which focus on warfare (armor, crossbows, and catapults)—are slicker than Beynac's, but the castle is also more touristy and lacks personality.

Cost and Hours: €9.60, €8.60 before 13:00 in summer; open daily July-Aug 9:00-20:00, April-June and Sept 10:00-19:00, Oct and Feb-March 10:00-18:00, Nov-Jan 14:00-17:00, last entry one hour before closing; daily demonstrations of medieval warfare and guided visits in English mid-July-Aug—call for exact times, tel. 05 53 31 30 00, www.castelnaud.com.

Getting There: From the river, it's a steep 25-minute hike through the village to the castle. Drivers must park in the €3 lot (5-minute walk uphill from there). You can stop at Castelnaud on your canoe trip, or hike an hour from Beynac along a riverside path (though it's tricky to follow in parts—it hugs the river as it passes through campgrounds and farms—determined walkers do fine).

Visiting the Castle: After passing the ticket booth, read your essential handout and follow the *suite de la visite* signs. Start by climbing through the tower. Every room has a story to tell, and many have displays of costumed mannequins, suits of armor, weaponry (including the biggest and most artistic crossbows I've ever seen), and artifacts from the Hundred Years' War. Other rooms show informative videos (with English subtitles)—don't miss the catapult video where you'll learn that the big ones could fire only two shots per hour and required up to 250 men to manage. Kids eat it up, in part thanks to the children's guide with fun puzzles. The upper courtyard has a 150-foot-deep well (drop a pebble). On your way back down, you'll see a sparsely furnished medieval kitchen and an iron forge with an interesting video. The rampart views are as unbeatable as the four siege machines are formidable. A few cafés and fun medieval shops await at the foot of the castle.

Château de Castelnaud

▲▲▲*Beynac*

Four miles downstream from La Roque-Gageac, Beynac (bay-nak) is the other must-see Dordogne village. It's also home to one of the most imposing castles in France.

This well-preserved medieval village winds like a sepia-tone film set, from the castle above to the river below (easy parking at the top avoids the steep climb). The stone village—with cobbled lanes that retain their Occitan (old French) names—is just plain pretty, best late in the afternoon and downright dreamy after dark. For the best light, tour the castle late, or at least walk out to the sensational viewpoint, then have a dinner here.

Orientation: Drivers can **park** at pay lots located on the river, way up at the castle (follow signs to *Château de Beynac*), or halfway between. The same parking ticket works up at the château if you decide against the climb. The **TI** is near the river, across from Hôtel du Château (daily 10:00-13:00 & 14:00-17:00, tel. 05 53 29 43 08). Pick up the *Plan du Village* in English for a simple self-guided walking tour, and get information on hiking and canoes. A few steps down from the TI is the post office with an **ATM** outside. From mid-June to mid-September, a cute little **market** sets up on Monday mornings in the riverfront parking lot. If you need a lift, call Beynac-based **Taxi Corinne** (tel. 05 53 29 42 07, mobile 06 72 76 03 32, corinne.brouqui@wanadoo.fr).

▲▲CHATEAU DE BEYNAC

Beynac's brooding, cliff-clinging château soars 500 feet above the town and the Dordogne River. It's the ultimate for that top-of-the-world, king-of-the-castle feeling. During the Hundred Years' War, the castle of Beynac housed the French, while the British set up camp across the river at Castelnaud. This sparsely furnished castle is best for its valley views, but it still manages to evoke a memorable medieval feel. (These castles never had much furniture in any case.) When buying your ticket, notice the list showing the barons of Beynac *(Beynac et Ses Barons)*—Richard the Lionheart *(Coeur de Lion)* spent 10 years here (€8, daily May-Oct 10:00-18:30, Nov-April until 17:00 or 17:30, last entry 45 minutes before closing, tel. 05 53 29 50 40).

You're free to wander on your own, though occasional tours are available in English. Pick up the English explanations (small fee) or spring for the excellent €5 pamphlet, and don't miss the nearby viewpoint (described next). As you tour the castle, swords, spears, and crossbows keep you honest, and the two stone WCs keep kids entertained. I like the soldiers' party room best—park your sword (in the slots at the end of the table) and hang your crossbow (on the hooks above), *s'il vous plaît*. Authentic-looking wooden stockades were installed for the 1998 filming of the movie *The Messenger: The Story of Joan of Arc*. Circling up through the castle, find your way to the highest crenellated terraces for smashing views. Just down the river, mighty Castelnaud—which seems so imposing from up close—looks like a child's playset.

WALKS AND VIEWPOINTS

A too-busy road separates Beynac from its river, making walks **along the river** unappealing in the village center. Traffic-free lanes climb steeply uphill from the river to the château—the farther you get from the road, the more medieval the village feels. A riverfront trail begins across from Hôtel Bonnet at the eastern end of town and follows the river toward Castelnaud, with great views back toward Beynac and—for able route-finders—a level one-hour hike to the village of Castelnaud. Make time to walk at least a few hundred yards along this trail to enjoy the view to Beynac.

One of the Dordogne's most com-

Château de Beynac and its village

manding views lies a short walk from the castle at the **top of the village** (easy parking). Step just outside the village (on the way between the castle and the upper parking lot) and take the enclosed lane to the right of the little cemetery. Stroll uphill until the view opens up. Castelnaud's castle hangs on the hill in the distance straight ahead. Château de Fayrac (owned by a Texan) is just right of the rail bridge; it was originally constructed by the lords of Castelnaud to keep a closer eye on the castle of Beynac. The Château de Marqueyssac, on a hill to the left, was built by the barons of Beynac to keep a closer eye on the boys at Castelnaud—touché. More than a thousand such castles were erected in the Dordogne alone during the Hundred Years' War. That's right: 1,000 castles in this area alone.

BOAT TRIPS

Boats leave from Beynac's riverside parking lot for relaxing, 50-minute river cruises to Castelnaud and back (€8, nearly hourly, departures Easter-Oct daily 10:00-12:30 & 14:00-18:00, more frequent trips July-Aug, written English explanations, tel. 05 53 28 51 15).

EATING

La Petite Tonnelle, cut into the rock, has a romantic interior and a fine terrace out front. Locals love it for its tasty cuisine served at fair prices, though the service can be very slow. It's a block up from Hôtel du Château (€17-40 *menus,* daily, on the road to the castle, tel. 05 53 29 95 18, www.restaurant-petite-tonnelle.fr).

CRO-MAGNON CAVES

The area around the town of Les Eyzies-de-Tayac—about a 30-minute drive from Sarlat or the Dordogne Valley—has a rich history of prehistoric cave art. The paintings you'll see in this area's caves are famous throughout the world for their remarkably modern-looking technique, beauty, and mystery. Les Eyzies-de-Tayac, near most of the caves, offers two good introductory museums for your visit.

While the cave art here is amazing, it can be a challenge to strategize. Delicate caves come with strict restrictions on visitors, and many are in out of the way locations—making it time-consuming to fit a cave visit into your vacation (allow three hours for a typical visit, including transit time). Certain caves are so restricted that getting in is nigh impossible (Grotte de Font-de-Gaume) and others require long visits, French-only tours, and detours to reach. Others are easier to plan for and worth your time, if you come prepared.

If seeing the very best matters, plan way ahead and try in January to reserve at the best cave: Grotte de Font-de-Gaume. Abri du Cap Blanc is bookable at the Font-de-Gaume office—but it only has carvings, not paintings. Another alternative is Rouffignac—no reservations, but you can often get in without too much of a wait by just showing up. Call ahead to see how busy they are.

Reserve Ahead or Get Up Early: Be clear on which caves take reservations and try to reserve your choice. Other caves are first-come, first-served, which means you must arrive early to secure a ticket, and then find something to do nearby if you have time to kill. How early you need to arrive varies by cave; I've suggested times for caves where you can't make a reservation. July, August, and holiday weekends are busiest, and rainy weather anytime sends sightseers scurrying for the caves. Saturdays are quieter—but Grotte de Font-de-Gaume and Abri du Cap Blanc are closed that day, and from October to April, as is the Prehistory Welcome Center.

Baggage Storage: Photos, daypacks, big purses, and strollers are not allowed. (You can take your camera—without using it—and check the rest at the site.)

Private Guide: Angelika Siméon is a passionate guide/lecturer eager to teach

Cro-Magnon Caves near Sarlat-la-Canéda

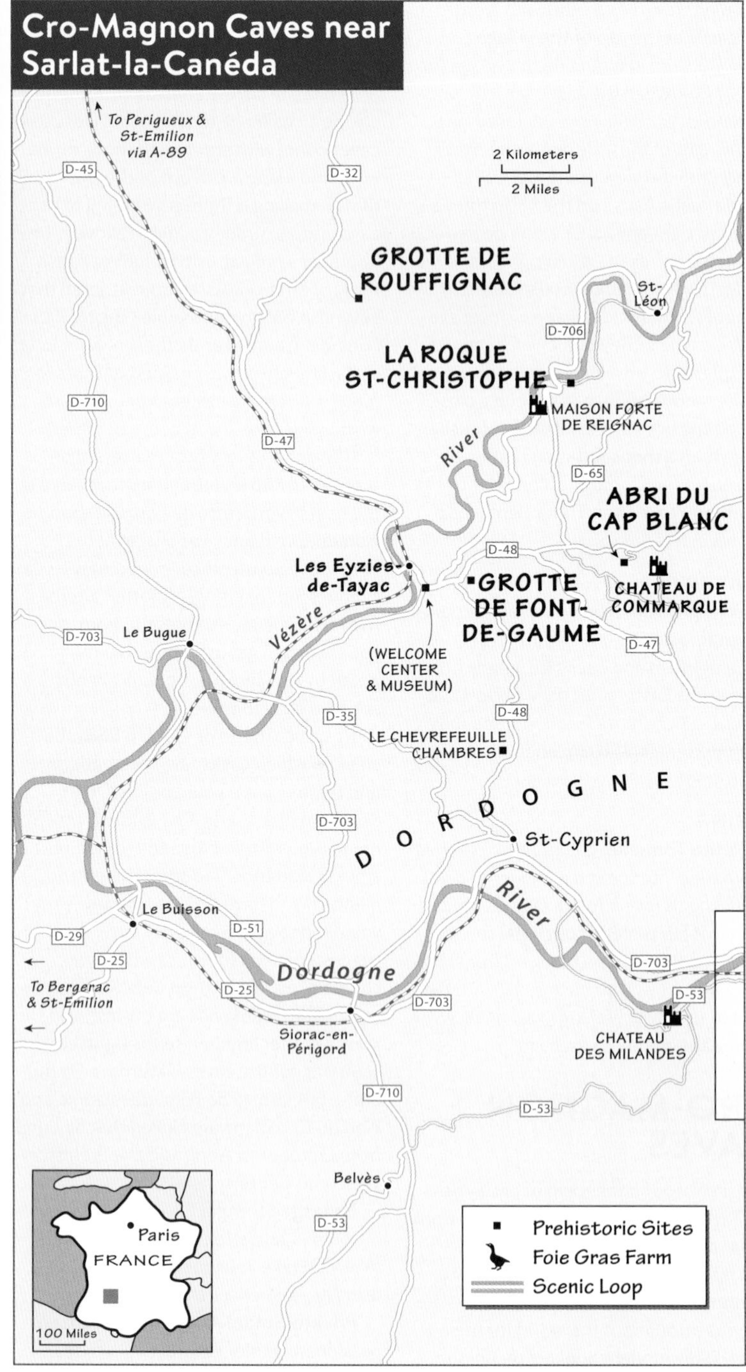
To Perigueux & St-Emilion via A-89
D-45
D-32
2 Kilometers
2 Miles
GROTTE DE ROUFFIGNAC
St-Léon
D-706
LA ROQUE ST-CHRISTOPHE
D-710
MAISON FORTE DE REIGNAC
D-47
River
D-65
ABRI DU CAP BLANC
D-48
Les Eyzies-de-Tayac
GROTTE DE FONT-DE-GAUME
CHATEAU DE COMMARQUE
D-703
Le Bugue
Vézère
(WELCOME CENTER & MUSEUM)
D-47
D-35
D-48
LE CHEVREFEUILLE CHAMBRES
DORDOGNE
D-703
St-Cyprien
River
Le Buisson
D-51
D-29
D-25
D-703
To Bergerac & St-Emilion
Dordogne
D-25
D-703
D-53
Siorac-en-Périgord
CHATEAU DES MILANDES
D-710
D-53
Belvès
D-53
Paris
FRANCE
100 Miles
Prehistoric Sites
Foie Gras Farm
Scenic Loop

To D-6089 & A-89: Périgueux
CHATEAU DE LA FLEUNIE
To A-20: Limoges, Oradour-sur-Glane & Mortemart
Montignac
INTERNATIONAL CENTER FOR CAVE ART
LASCAUX II
D-706
D-65
D-64
D-62
D-60
D-704
St-Geniès
D-48
D-60
Salignac-Eyvigues
D-62
To Souillac & A-20
D-704
D-47
See Greater Sarlat detail map
Sarlat-la-Canéda
To Souillac
VALLEY
D-703
ELEVAGE DU BOUYSSOU
D-704
D-704A
D-57
Dordogne River
BEYNAC
D-46
MONTFORT
Carsac
D-703
La Roque-Gageac
Vitrac
D-703
D-50
CASTELNAUD
Cénac
Domme
D-57
D-50
See Dordogne Canoe Trips detail map
LOT
D-46
D-704
GROTTES DE COUGNAC
To Cahors, "Eastern Dordogne", Grotte du Pech Merle & Lot River Valley
Gourdon

PRFHISTORIC SIGHTS AT A GLANCE

You can reserve ahead only for Lascaux (II and IV), Abri du Cap Blanc, and possibly Font-de-Gaume. For the other caves, it's first-come, first-served.

Les Eyzies-de-Tayac

▲**National Museum of Prehistory** More than 18,000 well-displayed artifacts—good preparation for your cave visit. **Hours:** July-Aug daily 9:30-18:30; June and Sept Wed-Mon 9:30-18:00, closed Tue; Oct-May Wed-Mon 9:30-12:30 & 14:00-17:30, closed Tue. **Reservations:** Not necessary, but reserve if you want a tour. Allow about one hour. See page 266.

Prehistory Welcome Center Your best first stop, providing a free, good intro to the region's important prehistoric sites. **Hours:** May-Sept daily 9:30-18:30; Oct-April Sun-Fri 9:30-17:30, closed Sat. **Reservations:** Not necessary. Allow about 30 minutes to visit. See page 265.

Caves

▲▲▲**Grotte de Font-de-Gaume** France's most impressive prehistoric cave with multicolored paintings open to the public, with strict limits on the number of daily visitors allowed. **Hours:** Mid-May-mid-Sept Sun-Fri 9:30-17:30, mid-Sept-mid-May Sun-Fri 9:30-12:30 & 14:00-17:30, closed Sat year-round. **Reservations:** May be possible—changes year to year—check website for latest. Sans reservation, be in line by 7:00 in summer, by 8:30 in spring and fall, and in winter by 9:00. Required 45-minute tour (likely in French). See page 266.

▲▲**Grotte de Rouffignac** Etchings and paintings of prehistoric creatures such as mammoths in a large cave accessed by a little train. **Hours:** Daily July-Aug 9:00-11:30 & 14:00-18:00, April-June and Sept-Nov 10:00-11:30 & 14:00-17:00, closed Dec-March. **Reservations:** Not available or necessary, arrive by 8:30 in mid-July-Aug, otherwise 30 minutes early. Visit lasts one hour. See page 269.

▲▲**International Center for Cave Art at Lascaux** Exact replicas of the world's most famous cave paintings, and an interactive center on cave art. **Hours:** July-Aug daily 9:00-22:00, night visits possible; April-June and Sept daily 9:30-20:00; Oct-March 10:00-19:00. **Reservations:** Book in advance online, especially in high season. Required 40-minute tour; allow 3 hours total. See page 270.

▲▲**Grottes de Cougnac** Oldest paintings (20,000-25,000 years old) open to public, showing rust-and-black ibex, mammoths, giant deer, and a few humans, on a tour more focused on cave geology than art. **Hours:** July-Aug daily 10:00-18:00; April-June and Sept daily 10:00-11:30 & 14:30-17:00; Oct Mon-Sat 14:00-16:00, closed Sun; closed Nov-March. **Reservations:** Not available. Arrive 10 minutes before it opens in summer. Required 1.25-hour tour (with minimal English explanation). See page 271.

▲**Abri du Cap Blanc** 14,000-year-old carvings that use natural contours of cave to add dimension, but no cave paintings. **Hours:** Mid-May-mid-Sept Sun-Fri 10:00-17:00, mid-Sept-mid-May Sun-Fri 10:00-12:30 & 14:00-17:00, closed Sat year-round, last entry at about 16:15. **Reservations:** Book a tour time by phone or email, or at the Font-de-Gaume ticket office. Required 45-minute tour (usually with some English, usually 6/day); call for times. See page 268.

▲**La Roque St-Christophe** Terraced cliff dwellings where prehistoric people lived, but no cave paintings. **Hours:** Daily April-Sept 10:00-18:30, July-Aug until 20:00, shorter hours off-season. **Reservations:** Not available or necessary. Allow 45 minutes to visit on your own (good English descriptions posted). See page 268.

Cave Art 101

To help you appreciate prehistoric art, my long-time collaborator, Gene Openshaw, offers this background:

From 18,000 to 10,000 B.C., before Stonehenge, before the pyramids, back when mammoths and saber-toothed cats still roamed the earth, prehistoric people painted the walls deep inside limestone caverns in southern France. These are not crude doodles; they're sophisticated, time-consuming engineering projects planned and executed by dedicated artists, supported by a unified and stable culture—the Magdalenians.

The Magdalenians (c. 18,000-10,000 B.C.): These hunter-gatherers of the Upper Paleolithic period (40,000-10,000 B.C.) were driven south by the Second Ice Age. The Magdalenians flourished in southern France for some 8,000 years—long enough to chronicle the evolution and extinction of several animal species. (Consider that Egypt lasted a mere 3,000 years; Rome lasted 1,000; America has made it fewer than 250 so far.)

Physically, the people were Cro-Magnons—fully developed *Homo sapiens* who could blend in to our modern population. We know them by the objects found in their settlements: stone axes, flint arrowheads, bone needles for making clothes, musical instruments, grease lamps, and cave paintings and sculpture. Many objects are beautifully decorated.

The Magdalenians did not live in the caverns they painted (which are cold and difficult to access). But many did live in the shallow cliffside caves that you'll see throughout your Dordogne travels, which were continuously inhabited from prehistoric times until the Middle Ages.

The Paintings: Though there are dozens of caves painted over a span of more than 8,000 years, they're all surprisingly similar. These Stone Age hunters painted the animals they hunted, including bison or bulls (especially at Lascaux

you about the caves and well worth spending a day with. She handles cave reservations and makes it easy and educational (book ahead; €145/half-day, €235/day, tel. 05 53 35 19 30, mobile 06 24 45 96 28, angelika.simeon@wanadoo.fr).

Rick's Tip: *All the prehistoric caves listed here are within* **an hour's drive** *of Sarlat. Public transit is not a viable option.* **If you don't have a car, take a guided tour.**

Les Eyzies-de-Tayac

This single-street town is the touristy hub of a cluster of Cro-Magnon caves, castles, and rivers. It merits a stop for its Prehistory Welcome Center, National Museum of Prehistory, and (if you can get in) the Grotte de Font-de-Gaume cave, a 15-minute walk or 2-minute drive outside of town. Les Eyzies-de-Tayac is world-famous because it's where the original Cro-Magnon man was discovered in 1870. That breakthrough set of bones was found just behind the hotel of Monsieur Magnon—Hôtel le Cro-Magnon, which is in business to this day on the western end of the main street. The name "Cro-Magnon" translates as "Mr. Magnon's Hole."

Orientation: Les Eyzies-de-Tayac's **TI** rents bikes and has free Wi-Fi (July-Aug Mon-Sat 9:30-18:30, Sept-June Mon-Sat

and Grotte de Font-de-Gaume), mammoths (the engravings at Grotte de Rouffignac), and woolly rhinoceroses (at Grotte de Font-de-Gaume). You'll also see some human handprints, along with geometric and abstract designs, such as circles, squiggles, and hash marks.

The animals stand in profile, with unnaturally big bodies and small limbs and heads. The artists engraved them on the wall by laboriously scratching outlines into the rock with a flint blade. A typical animal might be made using several techniques—an engraved outline that follows the natural contour, reinforced with thick outline paint, then colored in. The black outlines are often wavy, suggesting motion. Except for a few friezes showing a conga line of animals running across the cave wall, there is no apparent order or composition. Some paintings are simply superimposed atop others. Some figures are monumental—the bulls at Lascaux are 16 feet high. All are painted high up on walls and ceilings. The "canvas" was huge: Lascaux's main caverns are more than a football field long; Grotte de Font-de-Gaume is 430 feet long; and Grotte de Rouffignac meanders six miles deep.

Dating: It's tricky to determine the exact age of this art. Because much of the actual paint is mineral-based with no organic material, carbon-dating techniques are often ineffective. As different caves feature different animals, prehistorians can deduce which caves are relatively older and younger, since climate change caused various animal species to come and go within certain regions.

Why? No one knows the purpose of the cave paintings. The sites the artists chose were deliberately awe-inspiring, out of the way, and magical. Lit by a light in a dark cavern, the animals appear to flicker to life. Whatever the purpose—religious, aesthetic, or just plain fun—there's no doubt the effect is thrilling.

9:30-12:30 & 14:00-17:00; May-Sept Sun 9:30-12:30, otherwise closed Sun; tel. 05 53 06 97 05, www.tourisme-vezere.com). The train station is a level 500 yards from the town center (turn right from the station to get into town). The street that runs just below the museum is lined with handy lunch eateries.

PREHISTORY WELCOME CENTER (POLE INTERNATIONAL DE LA PREHISTOIRE)

Start your prehistoric explorations at the Pôle International de la Préhistoire (PIP) as you enter town from the east (Sarlat). This glass-and-concrete facility is a helpful resource for planning a visit to the region's important prehistoric sites. The low-slung building houses timelines, slideshows, and exhibits (all in English) that work together to give visitors a primer on the origins of man. Temporary exhibits are near the entrance, with permanent exhibits farther in. The English-speaking staff can provide maps and give suggestions on places to visit. Park here (for free), then walk out the center's back door down a pedestrian-only lane 200 yards to reach the National Museum of Prehistory.

Cost and Hours: Free; May-Sept daily 9:30-18:30; Oct-April Sun-Fri 9:30-17:30, closed Sat; free parking across the street, located east of downtown Les Eyzies-de-Tayac at 30 Rue du Moulin—watch for tall silver *PIP* sign, tel. 05 53 06 06 97, www.pole-prehistoire.com.

▲NATIONAL MUSEUM OF PREHISTORY (MUSEE NATIONAL DE PREHISTOIRE)

This modern museum houses more than 18,000 bones, stones, and crude little doodads that were uncovered locally. It takes you through prehistory—starting 400,000 years ago—and is good preparation for your cave visits. Appropriately located on a cliff inhabited by humans for 35,000 years (above Les Eyzies-de-Tayac's TI), the museum's sleek design helps it blend into the surrounding rock. Inside, exhibits include videos demonstrating scratched designs, painting techniques, and how spearheads were made. You'll also see full-size models of Cro-Magnon people and animals that stare at racks of arrowheads.

Cost and Hours: €8, €6 off-season; July-Aug daily 9:30-18:30; June and Sept Wed-Mon 9:30-18:00, closed Tue; Oct-May Wed-Mon 9:30-12:30 & 14:00-17:30, closed Tue; last entry 45 minutes before closing, tel. 05 53 06 45 65, www.musee-prehistoire-eyzies.fr.

Tours: To get the most out of your visit, consider a private or semiprivate English-language guided tour; for details, call 05 53 06 45 65 or email reservation.prehistoire@culture.gouv.fr.

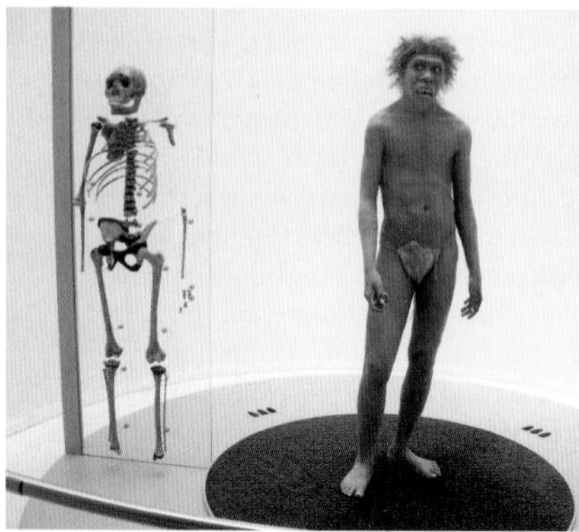

Turkana Boy, *National Museum of Prehistory*

Visiting the Museum: Pick up the museum layout with your ticket. Notice the timeline shown on the stone wall starting a mere 7 million years ago. Then enter, walking in the footsteps of your ancestors, and greet the 10-year-old *Turkana Boy*, whose bone fragments were found in Kenya in 1984 by Richard Leakey and date from 1.5 million years ago.

Spiral up the stairs to the first floor, which sets the stage by describing human evolution and the fundamental importance of tools. You'll also see a life-size recreation of *Megaloceros*—a gigantic deer (with even bigger antlers)—and a skeleton of an oversized steppe bison, both of which appear in some of the area's cave paintings.

The more engaging second floor highlights prehistoric artifacts found in France. Some of the most interesting objects you'll see are displayed in this order: a handheld arrow launcher, a 5,000-year-old flat-bottomed boat (pirogue) made from oak, prehistoric fire pits, amazing cavewoman jewelry (including a necklace labeled *La Parure de St-Germain-la-Rivière*, made of 70 stag teeth—pretty impressive, given that stags only have two teeth each), engravings on stone (find the unflattering yet impressively realistic female figure), a handheld lamp used to light cave interiors *(lampe façonnée)*, and beautiful rock sculptures of horses (much like the sculptures at the cave of Abri du Cap Blanc).

Your visit ends on the cliff edge, with a Fred Flintstone-style photo op on a stone ledge (through the short tunnel) that some of our ancient ancestors once called home.

The Caves

▲▲▲GROTTE DE FONT-DE-GAUME

Even if you're not a connoisseur of Cro-Magnon art, you'll dig this cave—it's France's best prehistoric cave with polychrome paintings still open to the public. The cave was made millions of years ago by the geological activity that created the Pyrenees Mountains. It contains 15,000-year-old paintings of 230 animals, 82 of which are bison.

On a carefully guided and controlled 100-yard walk, you'll see about 20 red-and-black painted bison—often in elegant motion. Some locals knew about the cave long ago, when there was little interest in prehistory, but the paintings were officially discovered in 1901 by the village schoolteacher.

Rick's Tip: *If you can't get a ticket at Grotte de Font-de-Gaume,* **try nearby Abri du Cap Blanc,** *which can be booked at this same office.* **Rouffignac is another safe backup** *(you're already partway there).*

Warning: Access to Font-de-Gaume is extremely restricted. The number of available tickets meets only a fraction of the demand. The site's ticketing and booking processes change regularly. Some years, visits can be booked ahead, while at other times the only option is to get up at dawn and stand in line. Check the website in early January to see if reserved tickets are possible. Otherwise, skip this place unless it's solidly off-season. Lining up for hours is a poor use of your time; other good options exist to see cave art.

Cost and Hours: €7.50, 17 and under free, includes required 45-minute tour; open mid-May-mid-Sept Sun-Fri 9:30-17:30, mid-Sept-mid-May Sun-Fri 9:30-12:30 & 14:00-17:30, closed Sat year-round; last tour departs 1.5 hours before closing, no photography or large bags, tel. 05 53 06 86 00, www.eyzies.monuments-nationaux.fr, fontdegaume@monuments-nationaux.fr—don't expect a fast reply. Those planning to also visit Abri du Cap Blanc (described next) can reserve and buy tickets here.

Getting a Ticket: To preserve the fragile art, tours are limited to six a day, 13 people per tour. The number of daily visitors is strictly regulated. Two tours a day (that's 26 tickets) can be reserved in advance by email or phone; try to reserve as far ahead as possible. Otherwise, tickets for the remaining four tours are doled out in person each morning starting at 9:30. In summer, plan to be in line by 7:00, in spring and fall no later than 8:30, and in the winter arrive by 9:00. (Each person can buy only one ticket, so you can't send

The Dordogne is rich in prehistoric cave sites.

one member of your party ahead for the whole group.) You can drop by the sight at any time during opening hours to get the latest on how early you need to show up to get a ticket. Check in 30 minutes before your tour or you'll lose your place.

Tours: English tours are available but limited; expect to visit with a French guide. Don't fret if you're not on an English tour—it's most important to experience the art itself.

Getting There: The cave is at the corner of D-47 and D-48, about a 2-minute drive (or a 15-minute walk) east of Les Eyzies-de-Tayac (toward Sarlat). There's easy on-site parking. After checking in at the ticket house, walk 400 yards on an uphill path to the cave entrance (where there's a free, safe bag check and a WC).

▲ABRI DU CAP BLANC

This prehistoric cave is a 10-minute drive from Grotte de Font-de-Gaume. Your guide spends the tour in a single stone room explaining the 14,000-year-old carvings. The small museum (with English explanations) helps prepare you for your visit, and a useful English handout describes what the French-speaking guide is talking about. The early artists used the rock's natural contours to add dimension to their sculpture; look for places where they smoothed or roughened the surfaces to add depth. Keep in mind that you'll be seeing carvings, not cave paintings. Impressive as these carvings are, their subtle majesty is lost on some.

Cost and Hours: €7.50, 17 and under free; includes required 45-minute tour, 6 tours/day (35 people each), call for tour times and to reserve. The cave is open mid-May-mid-Sept Sun-Fri 10:00-17:00, mid-Sept-mid-May Sun-Fri 10:00-12:30 & 14:00-17:00, closed Sat year-round, last entry at about 16:15, no photos, tel. 05 53 59 60 30. Tickets and reservations are also available at the Font-de-Gaume cave (fontdegaume@monuments-nationaux.fr).

Getting a Ticket: Like Font-de-Gaume, the reservation process is subject to change. But generally you should be able to book by phone, by email, or in person at the Font-de-Gaume ticket desk.

Getting There: Abri du Cap Blanc is well-signed and is located about four miles after Grotte de Font-de-Gaume on the road to Sarlat. From the parking lot, walk 200 yards down to the entry.

▲LA ROQUE ST-CHRISTOPHE

Five fascinating terraces carved by the Vézère River have provided shelter to people here for 55,000 years. Although the terraces were inhabited in prehistoric times, there's no prehistoric art on display—the exhibit (except for one small cave) is entirely medieval.

Cost and Hours: €8.50, daily April-June and Sept 10:00-18:30, July-Aug until 20:00, shorter hours off-season, last entry 45 minutes before closing, lots of steps.

Getting There: It's five miles north of Les Eyzies-de-Tayac—follow signs to *Montignac;* tel. 05 53 50 70 45, www.roque-st-christophe.com. Park at the free lot across the stream, with picnic tables, a WC, and, adjacent to the babbling brook, a pondside café.

Visiting the Sight: Allow at least 45 minutes. It's simple to visit: Climb through the one-way circuit, which is slippery when damp. Panels show the medieval buildings that once filled this space; don't miss the English translations on the back side. The recorded history goes back to

La Roque St-Christophe

A.D. 976, when people settled here to steer clear of the Viking raiders who sailed up the river. A clever relay of river watch-towers kept an eye out for raiders. When they came, cave dwellers gathered their kids, hauled up their animals (see the big, re-created winch), and pulled up the ladders. Although there's absolutely nothing old here except for the gouged-out rock, you can imagine the entire village in this family-friendly exhibit.

▲▲GROTTE DE ROUFFIGNAC

Rouffignac provides a different experience from other prehistoric caves in this area. Here you'll ride a clunky little train down a giant subterranean riverbed, exploring about half a mile of the six-mile-long gallery. The cave itself was known to locals for decades, but the 13,000-year-old paintings were discovered only in 1956. With some planning, you'll have no trouble getting a ticket.

Cost and Hours: €7, daily July-Aug 9:00-11:30 & 14:00-18:00, April-June and Sept-Nov 10:00-11:30 & 14:00-17:00, closed Dec-March; essential videoguide-€1.50; one-hour guided tours run 2-3/hour, no reservations; tel. 05 53 05 41 71, www.grottederouffignac.fr. Dress warmly. It's crowded only mid-July-Aug—during these months the ticket office opens at 9:00 and closes when tickets are sold out for the day—usually by noon. Arrive by 8:30 in summer and 30 minutes early at other times of year, and you'll be fine. Weekends tend to be quietest, particularly Sat.

Grotte de Rouffignac

Getting There: Grotte de Rouffignac, north of Les Eyzies, is well-signed from the route between Les Eyzies-de-Tayac and Périgueux (don't take the first turnoff, for *Rouffignac*; wait for the *Grotte de Rouffignac* sign); allow 25 minutes from Les Eyzies-de-Tayac.

Visiting the Cave: Your tour will be in French (with highlights described in caveman English), but the videoguide explains it all. Before the tour begins, read your videoguide's background sections and the informative displays in the cave entry area. Once on the tour, it's easy to follow along. Here's the gist of what they're saying on the stops of your train ride:

The cave was created by the underground river. It's entirely natural, but it was much shallower before the train-track bed was excavated. As you travel, imagine the motivation and determination of the painters who crawled more than a half-mile into this dark and mysterious cave. They left behind their art...and the wonder of people who crawled in centuries later to see it all.

You'll ride about five minutes before the first stop. Along the way, you'll see crater-like burrows made by hibernating bears long before the first humans painted here. There are hundreds of them—not because there were so many bears, but because year after year, a few of them would return, preferring to make their own private place to sleep (rather than using some other bear's den). After a long winter nap, bears would have one thing on their mind: Cut those toenails. The walls are scarred with the scratching of bears in need of clippers.

Stop 1: The guide points out bear scratches on the right. On the left, images of woolly mammoths etched into the walls can be seen only when lit from the side (as your guide will demonstrate). As the rock is very soft here, these were simply gouged out by the artists' fingers.

Stop 2: Look for images of finely detailed rhinoceroses outlined in black. Notice how the thicker coloring under their tummies suggests the animals' girth. The rock is harder here, so nothing is engraved. Soon after, your guide will point out graffiti littering the ceiling—made by "modern" visitors who were not aware of the prehistoric drawings around them (with dates going back to the 18th century).

Stop 3: On the left, you'll see woolly mammoths and horses engraved with tools in the harder rock. On the right is the biggest composition of the cave: a herd of 10 peaceful mammoths. A mysterious calcite problem threatens to cover the paintings with ugly white splotches.

Off the Train: When you get off the train, notice how high the original floor was (today's floor was dug out in the 20th century to allow for visitors). Imagine both the prehistoric makers and viewers of this art crawling all the way back here with pretty lousy flashlight-substitutes. The artists lay on their backs while creating these 60 images (unlike at Lascaux, where they built scaffolds).

The ceiling is covered with a remarkable gathering of animals. You'll see a fine 16-foot-long horse, a group of mountain goats, and a grandpa mammoth. Art even decorates the walls far down the big, scary hole. When the group chuckles, it's because the guide is explaining how the mammoth with the fine detail (showing a flap of skin over its anus) helped authenticate the paintings: These paintings couldn't be fakes, because no one knew about this anatomical detail until the preserved remains of an actual mammoth were found in Siberian permafrost in modern times. (The discovery explained the painted skin flap, which had long puzzled French prehistorians.)

▲▲INTERNATIONAL CENTER FOR CAVE ART

The region's—and the world's—most famous cave paintings are at Lascaux, 14 miles north of Sarlat-la-Canéda and Les Eyzies-de-Tayac. The Lascaux caves were discovered accidentally in 1940 by four kids and their dog. From 1948 to 1963, more than a million people climbed through the prehistoric wonderland—but the visitors tracked in fungus on their shoes and changed the temperature and

Lascaux II

humidity with their heavy breathing. In just 15 years, the precious art deteriorated more than during the previous 15,000 years, and the caves were closed.

In 1983, a replica of the cave called Lascaux II was built next to the original—accurate to within one centimeter, reproducing the best 40-yard-long stretch, and showing 90 percent of the paintings found in Lascaux. A brand-new replica, Lascaux IV (reproducing 100 percent of the original cave), opened in 2017. The two replica caves and a good information center are administered by the International Center for Cave Art. Both caves are a constant 56 degrees year-round, so dress warmly.

Given the choice of two cave replicas, I'd pick the new **Lascaux IV** housed in the International Center for Cave Art. Your visit to this dazzling high-tech center, half-buried in the Lascaux hill, includes a 40-minute guided group tour of Lascaux IV.

The center is divided into several sections, the most important being the impressive replica caves that took three years to create. Here the reindeer, horses, and bulls of the original Lascaux cave have been painstakingly reproduced by talented artists, using the same dyes, tools, and techniques their predecessors used 15,000 years ago. Seeing the real thing at one of the other caves is thrilling, but coming to Lascaux and taking one of the scheduled tours is a great introduction to the region's cave art. Although it feels a bit rushed—32 people per tour are hustled through the cave reproduction—the paintings are astonishing. (Forget that these are copies and enjoy being swept away by the prehistoric majesty of it all.) The center's other sections help visitors understand (through an interactive display and a 3-D film that kids appreciate) the role Lascaux played in prehistory, current scientific techniques and research, and the link from cave art to modern art.

Cost and Hours: Lascaux II—€13; Lascaux IV—€16, includes audioguide; July-Aug daily 9:00-22:00, night visits possible; April-June and Sept daily 9:30-20:00; Oct-March 10:00-19:00. Last ticket sold two hours before closing time. Plan to spend three hours here.

Getting Tickets: Reservations are strongly suggested in high season. Book in advance on the Lascaux website at www.lascaux.fr/en, tel. 05 53 50 99 10. Tickets are also sold at the sight.

▲▲GROTTES DE COUGNAC

This cave, south of Sarlat, holds fascinating rock formations and the oldest (20,000-25,000-year-old) paintings open to the public. Family-run and less touristy than other sites, it provides a more intimate look at cave art, as guides take more time to explain the caves and paintings (your guide should give some explanations in English—ask if he or she doesn't). The art is just one small part of the full tour, which focuses heavily on the cave's geology and unique formations—you'll see spaghetti-style stalactites, curtain stalactites, and much more.

Getting There: This is the easiest

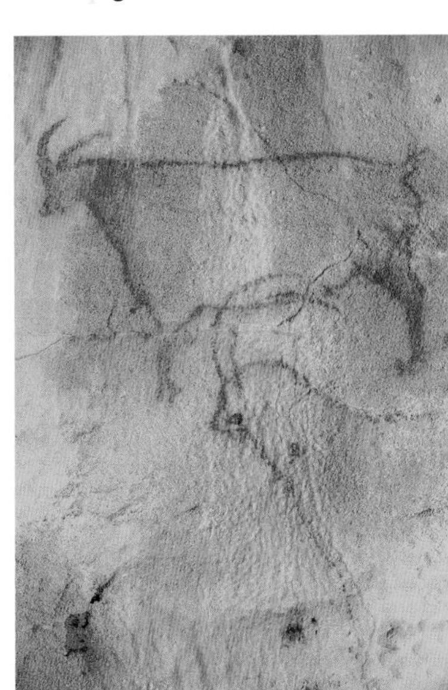

Grottes de Cougnac

cave to visit from Sarlat. It's a 30-minute drive south of the town and two well-signed miles north of Gourdon on D-704. It's a 45-minute drive from Les Eyzies-de-Tayac.

Cost and Hours: €8; these hours correspond to first/last tour times: July-Aug daily 10:00-18:00; April-June and Sept daily 10:00-11:30 & 14:30-17:00; Oct Mon-Sat 14:00-16:00, closed Sun; closed Nov-March; free WCs, beverages sold on-site, tel. 05 65 41 47 54, www.grottesdecougnac.com.

Visiting the Cave: The 1.25-hour tour, likely in French, begins in a cave below the entrance, where the guide explains the geological formations (you'll learn that it takes 70 years for water to make it from the earth's surface into the cave). From this first cave, you'll return to the fresh air and walk eight minutes to a second cave. Inside, you'll twist and twist through forests of stalagmites and stalactites before reaching the grand finale: the paintings you came to see. They are worth the wait. Vivid depictions (about 10) of ibex, mammoths, and giant deer *(Megaloceros)*, as well as a few nifty representations of humans, are outlined in rust or black. The rendering of the giant deer's antlers is exquisite, and many paintings use the cave's form to add depth and movement. The art is subtle—small sketches here and there, rather than the grand canvases of some of the more famous caves—but powerful.

Because access is first-come, first-served (and groups are limited to 25), plan your visit carefully. During busy times (in summer and in bad weather), they're most crowded 11:00-12:00 and 15:00-17:00; try to arrive first thing (ideally 10 minutes before opening). At quieter times, you can usually stop by before 11:00 and get in. Outside of July and August, be careful not to arrive too close to the last tour before lunch (11:30)—if that tour is full, you'll have to wait for the 14:30 departure. English-only tours are possible in peak season; call ahead to ask. You can also buy a €5 English booklet about the site.

BEST OF THE REST

CARCASSONNE

Tucked between the Dordogne and Provence, medieval Carcassonne is a 13th-century world of towers, turrets, and cobblestones. Because it's Europe's ultimate walled fortress city, it's also stuffed with tourists. But early, late, or off-season, a quieter Carcassonne is an evocative playground for any medievalist.

Orientation

Contemporary Carcassonne is neatly divided into two cities: the magnificent, fortified La Cité and the lively Ville Basse (modern lower city). Two bridges, the busy Pont Neuf and the traffic-free Pont Vieux, both with great views, connect the two parts.

Day Plan: Plan your arrival in this popular town carefully, and forget about midday. Get there late in the afternoon, spend the night, and leave no later than 11:00 the next morning to miss most day-trippers. While in town, take my self-guided walk, plus a walk around the walls at night.

Getting There: Carcassonne is accessible by train from Sarlat-la-Canéda (5.5-7 hours), Arles (2.5 hours), Nice (6.5 hours with change), and Paris (5.5 hours), but a car is handy for connecting Carcassonne with the Provence or Dordogne regions.

Arrival in Carcassonne: The **train station** is in the Ville Basse; to get to La Cité, take a taxi, public bus #4 (from Chénier stop on Boulevard Omer Sarraut, at far

The walls of Carcassonne

Carcassonne's La Cité

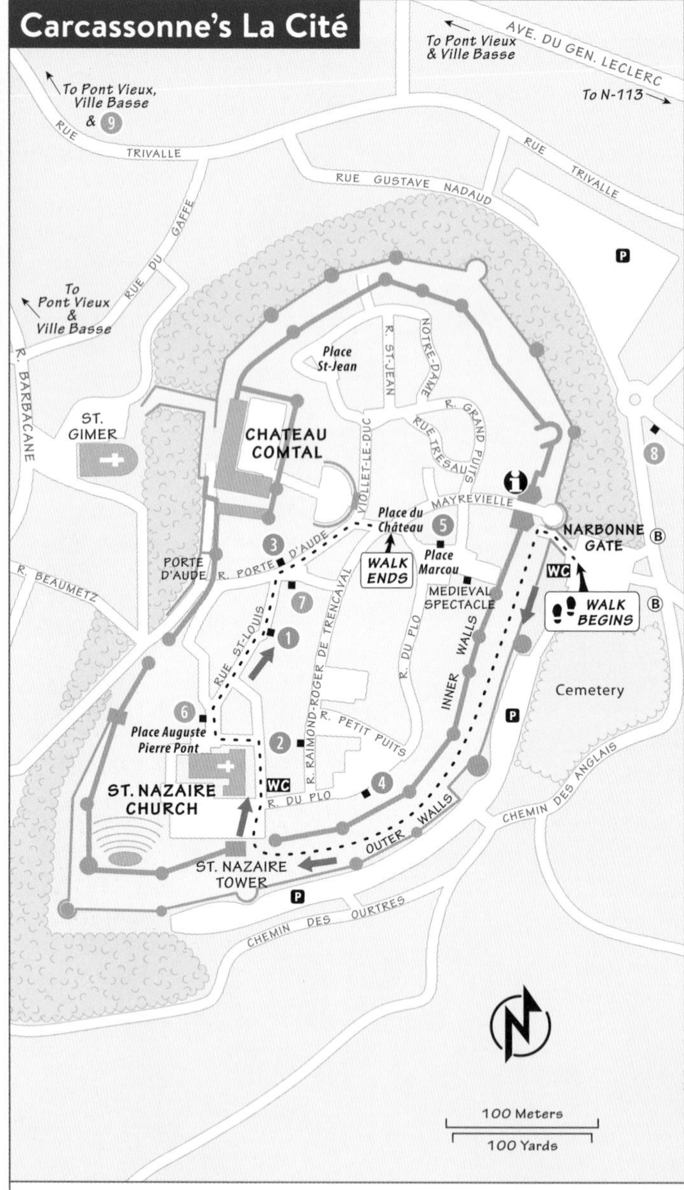

Eating & Nightlife

1. Au Comte Roger Restaurant
2. Auberge des Lices Restaurant
3. Le Jardin de la Tour Rest.
4. Le Bar à Vins Café
5. Place Marcou

Sleeping

6. Hôtel de la Cité
7. Best Western Hôtel le Donjon
8. Hôtel du Château
9. To Hôtel Astoria

edge of park a block from station), or a 30-minute walk. **Drivers** should follow signs to *Centre-Ville*, then *La Cité*. Several huge pay parking lots are clustered around the main Narbonne Gate.

Tourist Information: The most convenient branch is in **La Cité,** to your right as you enter the Narbonne Gate (daily, tel. 04 68 10 24 30, www.carcassonne-tourisme.com). A small TI kiosk is across the canal from the train station.

Market Days: Pleasing Place Carnot in Ville Basse hosts a non-touristy open market (Tue, Thu, and Sat mornings until 13:00; Sat is the biggest).

Carcassonne Walk

This self-guided walk, rated ▲▲▲, introduces you to the city with history and wonder, rather than tour groups and plastic swords. The walk is wonderfully peaceful and scenic early or late in the day.

Start on the asphalt outside La Cité's main entrance, the Narbonne Gate (Porte Narbonnaise).

• *Cross the bridge toward the...*

Narbonne Gate: Pause at the drawbridge and survey this immense fortification. When forces from northern France conquered Carcassonne in the 1200s, it was a strategic prize. Not taking any chances, they evicted the residents, whom they allowed to settle in the lower town (Ville Basse). The drawbridge was made crooked to slow attackers rushing to the main gate and has a similar effect on tourists today.

• *After crossing the drawbridge, walk left between the walls. At the first short set of stairs, climb to the outer-wall walkway and linger while facing the inner walls.*

Wall View: The Romans built Carcassonne's first wall, upon which the bigger medieval wall was constructed. Identify the ancient Roman bits by looking about one-third of the way up and finding the smaller rocks mixed with narrow stripes of red brick (and no arrow slits). The outer wall that you're on wasn't built until the 1300s, more than a thousand years after the Roman walls went up.

Look over the wall and down at the moat below (now mostly used for parking). Like most medieval moats, it was never filled with water (or even alligators). A ditch like this—which was originally even deeper—effectively stopped attacking forces from rolling up against the wall in their mobile towers and spilling into the city.

As you continue your wall walk to higher points, the lack of guardrails is striking. This would never fly in the US, but in France, if you fall, it's your own fault (so be careful).

• *You could keep working your way around the walls, but for this tour, we'll stop at the first entrance possible into La Cité, the...*

Inner Wall Gate: The wall has the same four gates it had in Roman times. Before entering, notice the squat tower on the outer wall—this was a "barbican," placed opposite each inner gate for extra protection. Now breach the walls and enter the square gate—look up to see a slot for the portcullis (the big iron grate) and the frame for a heavy wooden door.

Once safely inside, look back up at the

Carcassonne gate

inner wall tower to view *beaucoup de* narrow arrow slits facing inside La Cité—even if enemies made it past the walls, they still weren't home free.

• *Opposite the tower, work your way around to the entry of...*

St. Nazaire Church (Basilique St. Nazaire): This was a cathedral until the 18th century, when the bishop moved to the lower town. Today, due to the depopulation of the basically dead-except-for-tourism Cité, it's not even a functioning parish church. Step inside. Notice the Romanesque arches of the nave and the delicately vaulted Gothic arches over the altar and transepts. When the lights are off, the interior—lit only by candles and 14th-century stained glass—is evocatively medieval.

• *The ivy-covered building 50 steps in front of the church entrance is...*

Hôtel de la Cité: This luxury hotel sits where the Bishop's Palace did 700 years ago. Today, it's a worthwhile detour to see how the privileged few travel. You're free to wander, so check out the library-cozy bar, then find the rear garden and turn right for super wall views.

• *From the hotel, take the right fork at the medieval flatiron building, and follow Rue St. Louis for several blocks. Merge right onto Rue Port d'Aude, then look for a small castle-view terrace on your left a block up.*

Château Comtal: Originally built in 1125, Carcassonne's third layer of defense was completely redesigned in later reconstructions. From this impressive viewpoint you can see the wooden rampart extensions that once circled the entire city wall. (Notice the empty peg holes to the left of the bridge.) During sieges, these would be covered with wet animal skins as a fire retardant. If you have an interest in Carcassonne's medieval history, Château Comtal is worth a visit, rated ▲ (€8.50, daily April-Sept 10:00-18:30, shorter hours off-season). Or just take a stroll through the tranquil garden moat (free), where you'll see people enjoying a scenic picnic.

• *Fifty yards away, opposite the entrance to the castle, is...*

Place du Château: This busy little square sports a modest statue honoring the man who saved the city from deterioration and neglect in the 19th century. The bronze model circling the base of the statue shows Carcassonne's walls as they looked before the 1855 reconstruction by architect Eugène Viollet-le-Duc.

• *Our walk is finished. If you want, tour the castle. Or, if you turn left at the fountain, you'll pop out in the charming, restaurant-lined Place St-Jean.*

Hôtel de la Cité

Rick's Tip: *You'll find many great* **picnic sites all along the city walls.** *Gather supplies at the shops along the main drag (most open until 19:30), and enjoy a beggar's banquet.*

➲ *Night Walk to Pont Vieux*

Save some post-dinner energy for a don't-miss walk, rated ▲▲▲, around the same walls you visited today. The effect at night is mesmerizing: The embedded lights become torches and unfamiliar voices become the enemy. End at Pont Vieux for a floodlit fantasy. The best route is a partial circumnavigation clockwise between the walls. Start at the Narbonne Gate, and follow my self-guided walk (described earlier) to the Inner Wall Gate. Don't enter La Cité through this gate; instead, continue your walk between the walls (this section is occasionally closed;

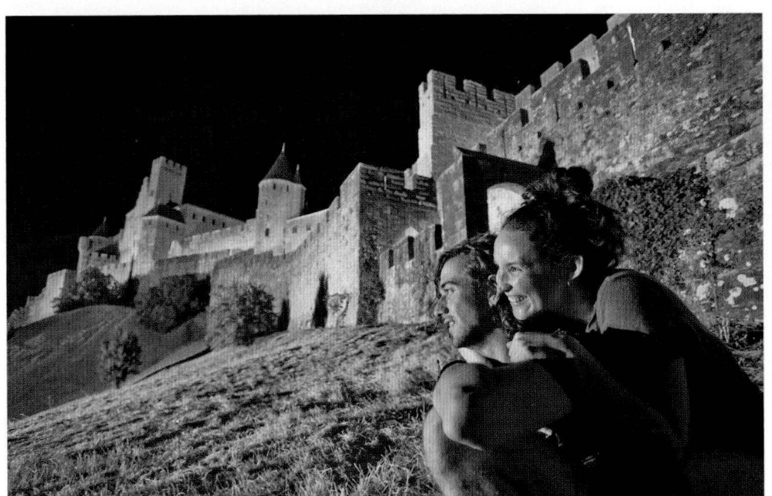

if so, you'll have to make your way through the village and out the rear along Rue de la Porte d'Aude to meet up with the route described from here).

The path narrows as you walk behind Château Comtal. When you come to a ramp leading down (after about five minutes), make a U-turn to the left, just before the path rises back up. This ramp leads down the hill; make a left when you come to the church (St. Gimer), then a right on Rue de la Barbacane (follow the *Centre-Ville* sign). Go straight to reach Pont Vieux and exceptional views of floodlit Carcassonne. Return from the bridge the same way you came, and complete your clockwise walk between the walls back to the Narbonne Gate, or take Rue Trivalle to Rue Gustave Nadaud for a quicker return.

Eating and Nightlife

Elegant **$$$ Comte Roger** serves fresh Mediterranean cuisine (closed Sun-Mon, 14 Rue St. Louis). Good-value **$$ Auberge des Lices** balances price and quality (closed Tue-Wed Sept-June, 3 Rue Raymond Roger Trencavel). Try **$$ Le Jardin de la Tour** for excellent cassoulet (closed Sun-Mon, 11 Rue Porte-d'Aude), or stop by **$ Le Bar à Vins** for a light meal and an enticing selection of open wines (closed Nov-Jan, 6 Rue du Plô).

For relief from all the medieval kitsch, savor a drink in the library-meets-bar ambience at the **Hôtel de la Cité** bar (Place de l'Eglise). To taste the liveliest square, with loads of tourists and strolling musicians, sip a drink or nibble a dessert on **Place Marcou.**

Sleeping

Sleeping inside the walls, you'll enjoy reliable luxury at **$$$$ Hôtel de la Cité******* (Place Auguste-Pierre Pont, www.hoteldelacite.com) and well-appointed rooms at **$$$ Best Western Hôtel le Donjon******(2 Rue Comte Roger, www.hotel-donjon.fr). Outside La Cite, try the comfortable **$$$$ Hôtel du Château****** (2 Rue Camille Saint-Saëns, www.hotelduchateau.net) or well-priced **$ Hôtel Astoria**** (18 Rue Tourtel, www.astoriacarcassonne.com).

GLACES
ARTISANALES
SUR PLACE
OU
À EMPORTER
SALADES
HÔTEL D'ARLATAN
SOL Y SOMBRA
TOM GARCIA
Café
Hôtel d'Arlatan
RESTAURANT
BOISSONS
GLACIER
CAFÉ

Provence

This magnificent region is shaped like a giant wedge of quiche. From its sunburned crust, fanning out along the Mediterranean coast, it stretches north along the Rhône Valley. The splendid recipe *provençale* mixes pastel hills, appealing cities, bountiful vineyards, and sweet, hilltop villages.

The Romans were here in force and left many ruins—some of the best anywhere. Over the centuries, they were followed by seven popes, who resided in a formidable palace in Avignon, and artist Vincent van Gogh, whose work celebrates Provence's sunflowers and starry nights.

A tour of Provence villages is best on your own by car. Public transit is good between cities and decent to some towns, but marginal at best to the smaller towns. For those traveling *sans* car, a variety of minivan tours can help fill in the gaps.

PROVENCE IN 2 DAYS

Make Arles or Avignon your sightseeing base—particularly if you have no car. While Francophiles usually pick urban Avignon, Italophiles prefer smaller Arles.

You'll want one day for sightseeing in Arles and Les Baux. Spend most of the day in Arles—try to time your arrival for Wednesday or Saturday, to enjoy the market. Then visit Les Baux in the late afternoon or early evening. On the second day, allow a half-day for Avignon and a half-day for Pont du Gard.

With another day, measure the pulse of rural Provence and spend at least one night in a smaller town, such as Vaison-la-Romaine. Exploring the Côtes du Rhône wine country takes about a half-day, but you may want to linger.

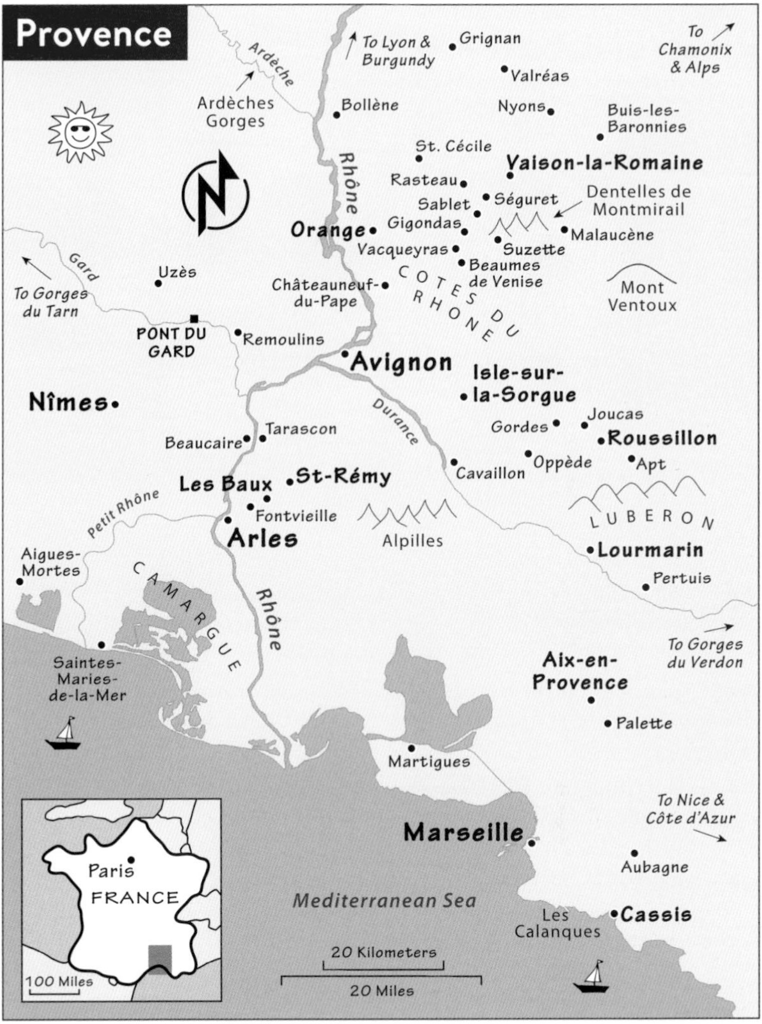

Provence

To Lyon & Burgundy
Grignan
To Chamonix & Alps
Valréas
Ardèche
Ardèches Gorges
Bollène
Nyons
Buis-les-Baronnies
St. Cécile
Rhône
Vaison-la-Romaine
Rasteau
Séguret
Dentelles de Montmirail
Sablet
Orange
Gigondas
Malaucène
Vacqueyras
Suzette
Gard
Uzès
Beaumes de Venise
To Gorges du Tarn
Châteauneuf-du-Pape
COTES DU RHONE
Mont Ventoux
PONT DU GARD
Remoulins
Avignon
Isle-sur-la-Sorgue
Nîmes
Durance
Joucas
Gordes
Tarascon
Beaucaire
Roussillon
Cavaillon
Oppède
Apt
Les Baux
St-Rémy
Petit Rhône
Fontvieille
LUBERON
Arles
Alpilles
Lourmarin
Aigues-Mortes
CAMARGUE
Pertuis
Rhône
To Gorges du Verdon
Saintes-Maries-de-la-Mer
Aix-en-Provence
Palette
Martigues
To Nice & Côte d'Azur
Marseille
Paris
FRANCE
Aubagne
Mediterranean Sea
Les Calanques
Cassis
100 Miles
20 Kilometers
20 Miles

PROVENCE AT A GLANCE

Arles

▲▲**Roman Arena** A big amphitheater, once used by gladiators, that hosts summer "bullgames" and occasional bullfights. **Hours:** Daily May-Sept 9:00-19:00, shorter hours off-season. See page 290.

▲▲**St. Trophime Church** Church with exquisite Romanesque entrance. **Hours:** Daily 9:00-12:00 & 14:00-18:30, until 17:00 Oct-March. See page 294.

▲▲**Ancient History Museum** Filled with models and sculptures, taking you back to Arles' Roman days. **Hours:** Wed-Mon 10:00-18:00, closed Tue. See page 298.

▲**Fondation Van Gogh** Small gallery with works by major contemporary artists paying homage to Van Gogh. **Hours:** Generally daily 11:00-19:00, likely closed Mon off-season. See page 296.

Avignon

▲▲**Palace of the Popes** Fourteenth-century Gothic palace built by the popes who made Avignon their home. **Hours:** Daily March-Oct 9:00-19:00, July-Aug until 20:00, Nov-Feb 9:30-17:45. See page 312.

▲**St. Bénezet Bridge** The "Pont d'Avignon" of nursery-rhyme fame, once connecting the pope's territory to France. **Hours:** Daily March-Oct 9:00-19:00, July-Aug until 20:00, Nov-Feb 9:30-17:45. See page 311.

▲**Jardin du Rochers des Doms** View park overlooking the Rhône River Valley and Avignon's famous broken bridge. **Hours:** Daily from 7:30 until dark. See page 311.

Nearby

▲▲▲**Pont du Gard** Part bridge and part aqueduct, a huge stone structure heralding the greatness of Rome. **Hours:** Aqueduct—daily until 24:00; museum—daily May-Sept 9:00-19:00, until 20:00 July-Aug, until 17:00 Oct-April, closed two weeks in Jan. See page 317.

▲▲▲**Les Baux** Rock-top village sitting in the shadow of its ruined medieval citadel. **Hours:** Village always open; castle—daily Easter-June and Sept 9:00-19:15, July-Aug 9:00-20:15, March and Oct 9:30-18:30, Nov-Feb 10:00-17:00. See page 319.

▲▲▲**Côtes du Rhône Wine Road** A drive through picturesque villages and vineyards, unfurling along a scenic wine-tasting route. See page 326.

Vaison-la-Romaine History-rich town atop a 2,000-year-old Roman site. See page 322.

ARLES

In Roman times, Arles (pronounced "arl") was an important port city. With the first bridge over the Rhône River, it was a key stop on the Roman road from Italy to Spain, the Via Domitia. After reigning as the seat of an important archbishop and a trading center for centuries, the city became a sleepy backwater of little importance in the 1700s. Vincent van Gogh settled here in the late 1800s, but left only a chunk of his ear (now long gone). American bombers destroyed much of Arles in World War II as the townsfolk hid out in its underground Roman galleries. But today Arles thrives again, with its evocative Roman ruins, an eclectic assortment of museums, made-for-ice-cream pedestrian zones, and squares that play hide-and-seek with visitors.

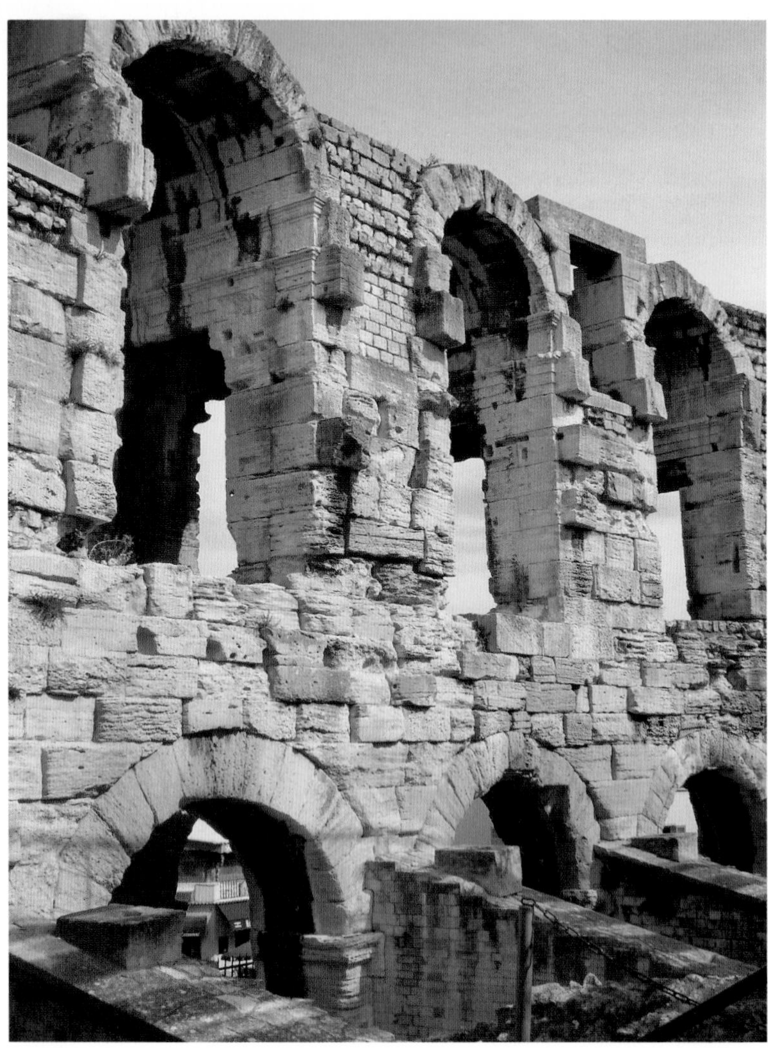

Roman Arena

Workaday Arles is not a wealthy city and, compared to its neighbor Avignon, it feels unpolished and even a little dirty. But to me, that's part of its charm.

Orientation

Though the town is built along the Rhône, it largely ignores the river. Landmarks hide in Arles' medieval tangle of narrow, winding streets. Hotels have good, free city maps, and helpful street-corner signs point you toward sights and hotels.

Tourist Information: The TI is on the ring road Boulevard des Lices, at Esplanade Charles de Gaulle (April-Sept daily 9:00-18:45; Oct-March Mon-Sat 9:00-16:45, Sun 10:00-13:00; tel. 04 90 18 41 20, www.arlestourisme.com).

Sightseeing Pass: A good-value €11 combo-ticket—the **Liberty Passport** (Le Passeport Liberté)—covers any four monuments and the Ancient History Museum (but not the Fondation Van Gogh gallery). Buy the pass at the TI or any included sight. While only the Ancient History Museum is essential, the pass makes the city fun to explore, as you can pop into any sight, even for just a couple of minutes.

Rick's Tip: *In Arles, the* **ancient monuments**—*Roman Arena, Classical Theater, Cryptoporticos, and St. Trophime Cloisters*—**all have the same hours** *(daily May-Sept 9:00-19:00, April and Oct 9:00-18:00, Nov-March 10:00-17:00).*

Baggage Storage and Bike Rental: Hôtel Régence will store your bags for a small fee (daily, closed in winter, 5 Rue Marius Jouveau). They also rent bikes (reserve ahead for electric bikes, one-way rentals within Provence possible).

Car Rental: Avis is at the train station (tel. 04 90 96 82 42). Downtown you'll find **Europcar** (61 Avenue de Stalingrad, tel. 04 90 93 23 24) and **Hertz** (10 Boulevard Emile Combes, nearer Place Voltaire, tel. 04 90 96 75 23).

Local Guide: Charming **Agnes Barrier** offers tours covering Van Gogh and Roman history (€130/3 hours, mobile 06 11 23 03 73, agnes.barrier@hotmail.fr).

Minivan Excursions: Provence Reservation runs day tours to nearby sights (such as Pont du Gard) from Arles, Avignon, and other cities. While the tours provide introductory commentary, there's no guiding at the actual sights. They use eight-seat, air-conditioned minivans (about €60-80/half-day, €100-120/day). Ask about their cheaper big-bus excursions, or consider hiring a van and driver for your private use (plan on €220/half-day, €490/day, tel. 04 90 14 70 00, www.provence-reservation.com).

Arles City Walk

The joy of Arles is how its compact core mixes ancient sights, Van Gogh memories, and a raw and real contemporary scene that can be delightfully covered on foot. All the dimensions of the city come together in this self-guided walk. While workable in the evening, taking this walk during business hours allows you to pop into the sights and shops that give the city its unique character.

Much of the walk focuses on the story of Van Gogh in Arles. We'll also visit ancient sites, including the Roman Arena, Classical Theater, Cryptoporticos, and the cloisters at St. Trophime Church (all covered by the Liberty Passport), along with some of Arles' most characteristic streets and squares.

At the Café Van Gogh

Arles

Arles Walk

1. The Yellow House (Easel)
2. Starry Night over the Rhône (Easel)
3. Rue de la Cavalerie
4. Old Town
5. Arena (Easel) & Roman Arena
6. Alpilles Mountains View
7. Jardin d'Eté (Easel)
8. Classical Theater
9. Republic Square
10. Cryptoporticos
11. St. Trophime Church
12. Rue de la République
13. Espace Van Gogh (Easel)
14. Fondation Van Gogh
15. Rue du Docteur Fanton
16. Forum Square (Place du Forum) & Café at Night (Easel)

Ⓑ Envia Bus Stops

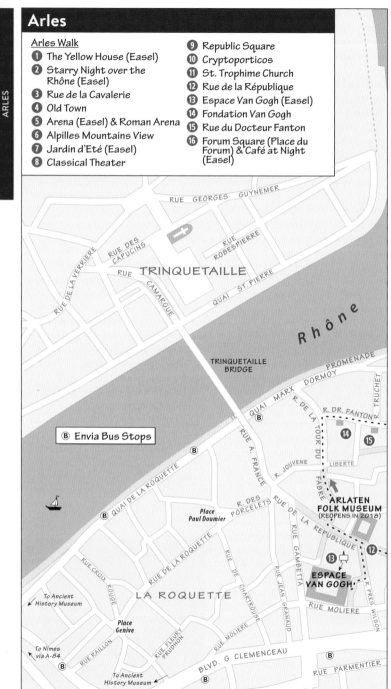

RUE GEORGES GUYNEMER
RUE DES CAPUCINS
RUE ROBESPIERRE
RUE DE LA VERRIERE
TRINQUETAILLE
RUE CAMARGUE
QUAI ST. PIERRE
Rhône
TRINQUETAILLE BRIDGE
PROMENADE
DORMOY
QUAI MARX
R. TRUCHET
R. DR. FANTON
R. DE LA TOUR DU FABRE
RUE A. FRANCE
R. JOUVENE
LIBERTE
ARLATEN FOLK MUSEUM (REOPENS IN 2018)
QUAI DE LA ROQUETTE
R. DES PORCELETS
RUE DE LA REPUBLIQUE
Place Paul Doumier
RUE GAMBETTA
ESPACE VAN GOGH
RUE DE LA ROQUETTE
RUE CROIX ROUGE
RUE DE CHARTROUSE
RUE JEAN GRANAUD
R. PRES. WILSON
RUE MOLIERE
LA ROQUETTE
To Ancient History Museum
Place Genive
RUE MOLIERE
To Nîmes via A-84
RUE RAILLON
RUE FLEURY PRUDHON
BLVD. G CLEMENCEAU
RUE PARMENTIER
To Ancient History Museum

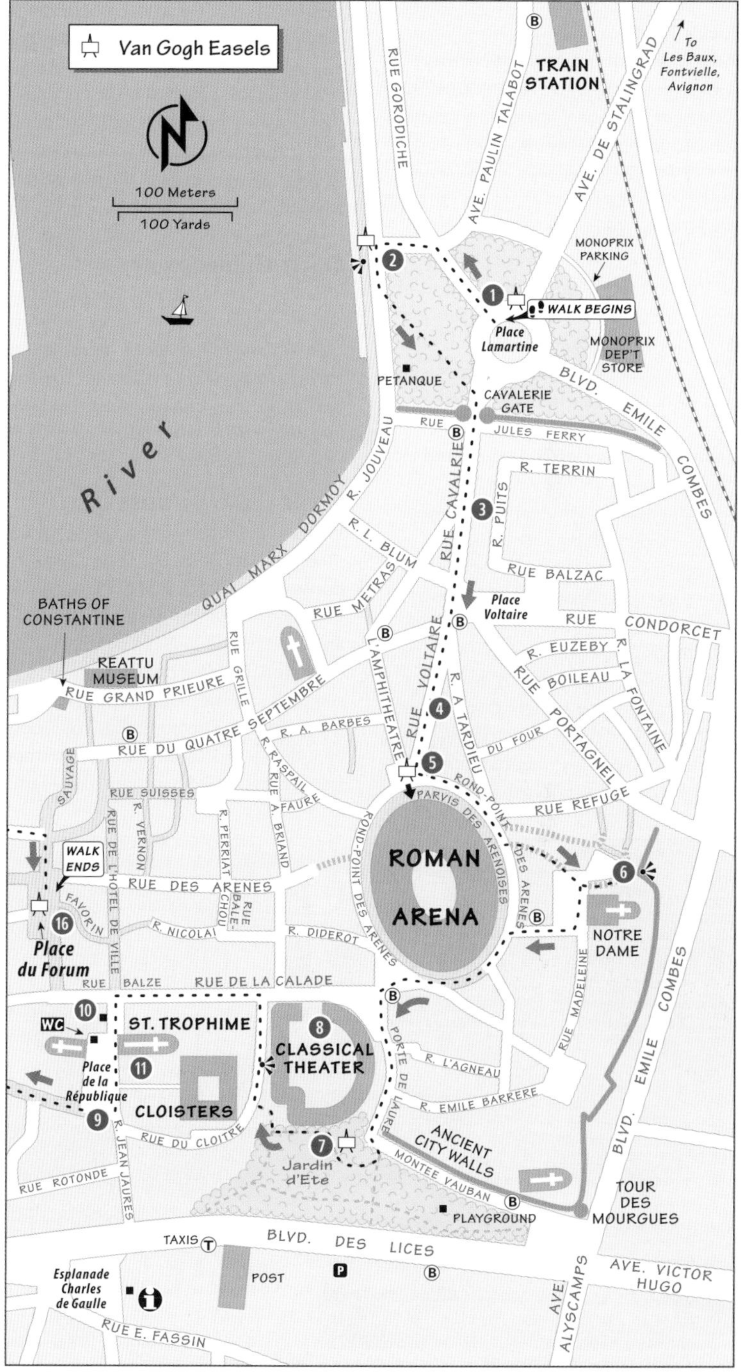
Van Gogh Easels
100 Meters
100 Yards
TRAIN STATION
To Les Baux, Fontvielle, Avignon
RUE GORODICHE
AVE. PAULIN TALABOT
AVE. DE STALINGRAD
MONOPRIX PARKING
WALK BEGINS
Place Lamartine
MONOPRIX DEP'T STORE
PETANQUE
CAVALERIE GATE
BLVD. EMILE COMBES
RUE JULES FERRY
River
R. JOUVEAU
R. TERRIN
R. PUITS
RUE CAVALRIE
QUAI MARX DORMOY
R. L. BLUM
RUE BALZAC
RUE METRAS
Place Voltaire
RUE CONDORCET
R. EUZEBY
R. LA FONTAINE
RUE BOILEAU
RUE PORTAGNEL
BATHS OF CONSTANTINE
REATTU MUSEUM
RUE GRAND PRIEURE
RUE GRILLE
L'AMPHITHEATRE
RUE VOLTAIRE
R. A. TARDIEU
RUE DU QUATRE SEPTEMBRE
R. A. BARBES
DU FOUR
SAUVAGE
R. RASPAIL
RUE A. FAURE
ROND-POINT
PARVIS DES ARENOISES
RUE REFUGE
RUE SUISSES
R. VERNON
R. PERRIAT
RUE A. BRIAND
ROMAN ARENA
WALK ENDS
RUE DE L'HOTEL DE VILLE
RUE DES ARENES
RUE BALECHOU
ROND-POINT DES ARENES
DES ARENES
FAVORIN
R. NICOLAI
R. DIDEROT
NOTRE DAME
Place du Forum
RUE BALZE
RUE DE LA CALADE
RUE MADELEINE
WC
ST. TROPHIME
CLASSICAL THEATER
PORTE DE LAURE
R. L'AGNEAU
Place de la République
CLOISTERS
R. EMILE BARRERE
R. JEAN JAURES
RUE DU CLOITRE
ANCIENT CITY WALLS
Jardin d'Ete
MONTEE VAUBAN
RUE ROTONDE
TOUR DES MOURGUES
PLAYGROUND
TAXIS
BLVD. DES LICES
AVE. VICTOR HUGO
POST
AVE. ALYSCAMPS
Esplanade Charles de Gaulle
RUE E. FASSIN

Rick's Tip: *Before following my self-guided Arles walk,* **visit the Ancient History Museum** *for a helpful overview. Because it's located at the edge of town, drivers should try to stop on their way into Arles.*

Background

The life and artistic times of Dutch artist **Vincent van Gogh** form a big part of Arles' draw, and the city does a fine job of highlighting its Van Gogh connection: Throughout town, about a dozen steel-and-concrete "easels," with photos of the final paintings and the actual view of that painting's subject, provide then-and-now comparisons.

In the dead of winter in 1888, 35-year-old Van Gogh left big-city Paris for Provence, hoping to jump-start his floundering career and social life. He was as inspired as he was lonely. Coming from the gray skies and flat lands of the north, Vincent was bowled over by everything Provençal—the sun, bright colors, rugged landscape, and down-to-earth people. For the next two years he painted furiously, cranking out a masterpiece every few days.

Only a few of the 200-plus paintings that Van Gogh did in the south can be found today in the city that so moved him (you can see a few at the Fondation Van Gogh gallery, which we'll visit on this stroll). But here you can walk the same streets he knew and see the places he painted.

➲*Self-Guided Walk*

• *Start at the north gate of the city, just outside the medieval wall in Place Lamartine (100 yards in front of the medieval gate, with the big Monoprix store across the street to the right, just beyond the roundabout). A four-foot-tall metal panel (or "easel") shows Van Gogh's painting.*

❶ THE YELLOW HOUSE EASEL

Vincent arrived in Arles on February 20, 1888, to a foot of snow. He rented a small house on the north side of Place Lamartine. The house was destroyed in 1944 by an errant bridge-seeking bomb, but the four-story building behind it—where you see the brasserie—still stands (find it in the painting). The house had four rooms, including a small studio and the cramped trapezoid-shaped bedroom made famous

Van Gogh "easels" throughout Arles pair the artist's paintings with actual views.

The Rules of Boules

The game of *boules*—also called *pétanque*—is the horseshoes of France. Invented here in the early 1900s, it's a social yet serious sport, and endlessly entertaining to watch—even more so if you understand the rules.

The game is played with heavy metal balls and a small wooden target ball called a *cochonnet* (piglet). Whoever gets his *boule* closest to the *cochonnet* is awarded points. Teams commonly have specialist players: a *pointeur* and a *tireur*. The pointeur's goal is to lob his balls as close to the target as he can. The tireur's job is to blast away opponents' *boules*.

In teams of two, each player gets three *boules*. The starting team traces a small circle in the dirt (in which players must stand when launching their *boules*), and tosses the *cochonnet* about 30 feet to establish the target. The *boule* must be thrown underhand, and can be rolled, launched sky-high, or rocketed at its target. The first *pointeur* shoots, then the opposing *pointeur* shoots until his *boule* gets closer. Once the second team lands a *boule* nearer the *cochonnet*, the first team goes again. If the other team's *boule* is near the *cochonnet*, the *tireur* will likely attempt to knock it away.

Once all *boules* have been launched, the tally is taken. The team with a *boule* closest to the *cochonnet* wins the round, and they receive a point for each *boule* closer to the target than their opponents' nearest *boule*. The first team to get to 13 points wins. A regulation *boules* field is 10 feet by 43 feet, but the game is played everywhere—just scratch a throwing circle in the sand, toss the *cochonnet*, and you're off.

in paintings. It was painted yellow inside and out, and Vincent named it..."The Yellow House." In the distance, the painting shows the same bridges you see today.

• *Walk directly to the river. You'll pass a monument in honor of two WWII American pilots killed in action during the liberation of Arles, a post celebrating Arles' many sister cities (left), and a big concrete high school (right).*

At the river, find the easel in the wall where ramps lead down.

❷ STARRY NIGHT OVER THE RHONE EASEL

One night, Vincent set up shop along the river and painted the stars boiling above the city skyline. Vincent looked to the night sky for the divine and was the first to paint outside after dark, adapting his straw hat to hold candles (which must have blown the minds of locals back then). The lone couple in the painting pops up again and again in his work. (This painting is not the *Starry Night* you're thinking of—that one was painted later, in another town.)

To his sister Wilhelmina, Vincent wrote, "At present I absolutely want to paint a starry sky. It often seems to me that night is still more richly colored than the day; having hues of the most intense violets, blues, and greens. If only you pay attention to it, you will see that certain stars are lemon yellow, others pink or a green, blue, and forget-me-not brilliance." Vincent painted this scene on his last night in Arles.

• *With your back to the river, angle right through the small park of sycamore trees. Continue into town through the park (past a WC) and through the stumpy 14th-century stone towers where the city gates once stood.*

❸ RUE DE LA CAVALERIE

Van Gogh walked into town the same way. Arles' 19th-century red light district was just east of Rue de la Cavalerie, and the far-from-home Dutchman spent many lonely nights in its bars and brothels. The street still has a certain edgy local color. Belly up to the bar in the down-and-dirty café at Hôtel de Paris for a taste. It's a friendly watering hole with fun paintings of football and bull fighting.

• *Continuing uphill, you'll come to an ornately decorated fountain from 1887: two columns with a mosaic celebrating the high culture of Provence (she's the winged woman who obviously loves music and reading).*

Stay left and keep walking uphill to Place Voltaire, a center of this working-class neighborhood (you'll see the local Communist Party headquarters across on the left).

❹ OLD TOWN

You've left the bombed-out part of town and entered the old town, with buildings predating World War II. The stony white arches of the ancient Roman Arena ahead mark your destination. As you hike up Rue Voltaire, notice the shutters, which contribute to Arles' character. The old town is strictly preserved: These traditional shutters come in a variety of styles but cannot be changed.

• *Keep straight up Rue Voltaire, climb to the Roman Arena, and find the Arena easel at the top of the stairs, to the right.*

❺ ARENA EASEL

All summer long, fueled by sun and alcohol, Vincent painted the town. He loved the bullfights in the arena and sketched the colorful surge of the crowds, spending more time studying the people than watching the bullfights (notice how the bull is barely visible). Vincent had little interest in Arles' antiquity—it was people and nature that fascinated him.

• *Now, let's visit the actual...*

ROMAN ARENA (AMPHITHEATRE)

This well-preserved arena is worth ▲▲ and is still in use today. Nearly 2,000 years ago, gladiators fought wild animals here to the delight of 20,000 screaming fans. Now local daredevils still fight wild animals here—"bullgame" posters around the arena advertise upcoming spectacles (see page 300).

Cost and Hours: €8 combo-ticket with Classical Theater, covered by Liberty Passport; open daily May-Sept 9:00-19:00, April and Oct 9:00-18:00, Nov-March 10:00-17:00, Rond-point des Arènes, tel. 04 90 49 36 86, www.arenes-arles.com.

Visiting the Arena: After passing the ticket kiosk, find the helpful English infor-

Arles' old town

Inside the Roman Arena

mation display that describes the arena's history and renovation, then take a seat in the upper deck. In Roman times, games were free (sponsored by city bigwigs), and fans were seated by social class. More than 30 rows of stone bleachers extended all the way to the top of those vacant arches that circle the arena. All arches were numbered to help distracted fans find their seats. The many passageways you'll see (called vomitoires) allowed for rapid dispersal after the games—fights would break out among frenzied fans if they couldn't leave quickly. During medieval times and until the early 1800s, the arches were bricked up and the stadium became a fortified town—with 200 humble homes crammed within its circular defenses. Parts of three of the medieval towers survive (the one above the ticket booth is open and rewards those who climb it with terrific views).

• *Leaving the arena, walk clockwise around its perimeter, marveling at the ancient stonework. A quarter of the way around, go up the cute stepped lane (Rue Renan, next to Volubilis Restaurant). Take three steps and turn around to study the arena.*

The big stones are Roman. Notice the little medieval stones—more like rubble—filling two upper-level archways. These serve as a reminder of how the arena encircled a jumble of makeshift houses through the Middle Ages. You can even see rooflines and beam holes where the Roman structure provided a solid foundation to lean on.

The well-preserved arena

• *Hike up the pretty lane and continue past the stark and stony church to the highest point in Arles. Take in the view.*

❻ ALPILLES MOUNTAINS VIEW

This view pretty much matches what Vincent, an avid walker, would have seen. Imagine him hauling his easel into those fields under intense sun, leaning against a ferocious wind, struggling to keep his hat on.

Vincent carried his easel as far as the medieval Abbey of Montmajour, that bulky structure three miles straight ahead on the hill. The St. Paul Hospital, where he was eventually treated in St-Rémy, is on the other side of the Alpilles mountains, several miles beyond Montmajour.

• *Continue circling the Roman Arena. At the high point, turn left and walk out Rue de Porte de Laure. (You'll pass the Classical Theater on your right, which we'll see later.) After a couple of blocks, just after the street turns left, go right, down the curved staircase into the park. At bottom of the stairs take the second right (through the gate and into the park) and find the...*

❼ JARDIN D'ETE EASEL

Vincent spent many a sunny day painting the leafy Jardin d'Eté. In another letter to his sister, Vincent wrote, "I don't know whether you can understand that one may make a poem by arranging colors... In a similar manner, the bizarre lines, purposely selected and multiplied, meandering all through the picture may not present a literal image of the garden, but they may present it to our minds as if in a dream."

• *Hike uphill through the park toward the three-story surviving tower of the ancient Roman Theater. At the tower, follow the white metal fence to the left along "the garden of stone"—a collection of ancient carved bits of a once grand Roman theater. Go up four steps and around to the right for a fine view of the...*

How About Them Romans?

Many scholars claim the best-preserved ancient Roman buildings are not in Italy, but in France. These ancient stones will compose an important part of your sightseeing agenda.

Classical Rome endured from about 500 B.C. through A.D. 500—spending about 500 years growing, 200 years peaking, and 300 years declining. Julius Caesar conquered Gaul—which included Provence—during the Gallic Wars (58-51 B.C.), then crossed the Rubicon River in 49 B.C. to incite civil war within the Roman Republic. He erected a temple to Jupiter on the future site of Paris' Notre-Dame Cathedral.

The concept of one-man rule lived on with his grandnephew, Octavian (whom he had also adopted as his son). Octavian took the title "Augustus" and became the first in a line of emperors who would control Rome for the next 500 years. Rome morphed from a Republic into an Empire: a collection of many diverse territories ruled by a single man. At its peak (c. A.D. 117), the Roman Empire had 54 million people; "Rome" didn't just refer to the city, but to all of Western civilization.

Provence, with its strategic location, benefited greatly from Rome's global economy and grew to become an important part of its worldwide empire. After Julius Caesar conquered Gaul, Emperor Augustus Romanized it, building and renovating cities in the image of Rome.

When it came to construction, the Romans' magic building ingredient was concrete. Easier to work than stone, and longer-lasting than wood, concrete served as flooring, roofing, filler, glue, and support. Builders would start with a foundation of brick, then fill it in with poured concrete. They would then cover important structures, such as basilicas, in sheets of expensive marble (held on with nails), or decorate floors and walls with mosaics.

Most cities had a theater, baths, and aqueducts; the most important cities had sports arenas. A typical Roman city (such as Arles) was a garrison town, laid out on a grid plan with two main roads: one running north-south (the *cardus*), the other east-west (the *decumanus*). Approaching the city on your chariot, you'd pass by the cemetery, which was located outside town for hygienic reasons. You'd enter the main gate and speed past warehouses and apartment houses to the town square (forum). Facing the square were the most important temples, dedicated to the patron gods of the city. Nearby, you'd find bathhouses; like today's fitness clubs, these served the almost sacred dedication to personal vigor. Also close by were businesses that catered to the citizens' needs: the marketplace, bakeries, banks, and brothels. Aqueducts brought fresh water for drinking, filling the baths, and delighting the citizens with bubbling fountains.

Some cities in Provence were more urban 2,000 years ago than they are today. For instance, Roman Arles had a population of 100,000—double today's size.

❽ CLASSICAL THEATER (THEATRE ANTIQUE)

This elegant, three-level, first-century B.C. Roman theater once seated 10,000. There was no hillside to provide structural support, so the builders created 27 buttress arches, which radiate out behind the seats. From the outside, it looked much like the adjacent arena.

Cost and Hours: €8 combo-ticket with Roman Arena, covered by Liberty Passport, same hours as Arena.

Visiting the Theater: Start with the 10-minute video outside, which provides helpful background and images that make it easier to put the scattered stones back in place. A large information panel nearby on the grass adds more context.

Walk into the theater and pull up a stone seat in a center aisle. Imagine that for 500 years, ancient Romans gathered here for entertainment. The original structure was much higher, with 33 rows of seats covering three levels to accommodate demand. During the Middle Ages, the old theater became a convenient town quarry—much of St. Trophime Church was built from theater rubble. Precious little of the original theater survives—though it still is used for events, with seating for 2,000 spectators.

• *From the theater, walk downhill on Rue de la Calade. Take the first left into a big square.*

❾ REPUBLIC SQUARE (PLACE DE LA REPUBLIQUE)

This square was called "Place Royale"—until the French Revolution. The obelisk was once the centerpiece of Arles' Roman Circus. The lions at its base are the symbol of the city, whose slogan is (roughly) "the gentle lion." Observe the age-old scene: tourists, peasants, shoppers, pilgrims, children, and street musicians. The City Hall (Hôtel de Ville) has a French Baroque facade, built in the same generation as Versailles. Where there's a City Hall, there's always a free WC (if you win the Revolution, you can pee for free at the mayor's home). Notice the flags: The yellow-and-red of Provence is the same as the yellow-and-red of Catalunya, the region's linguistic cousin in Spain.

• *Today's City Hall sits upon an ancient city center. Inside you'll find the entrance to an ancient cryptoportico (foundation).*

Classical Theater

⑩ CRYPTOPORTICOS (CRYPTOPORTIQUES)

This dark, drippy underworld of Roman arches was constructed to support the upper half of Forum Square. Two thousand years ago, most of this gallery of arches was at or above street level; modern Arles has buried about 20 feet of its history over the millennia. Through the tiny windows high up you would have seen the sandals of Romans on their way to the forum. Other than dark arches and broken bits of forum littering the dirt floor, there's not much down here beyond ancient memories (€3.50, covered by Liberty Passport, same hours as Arena).

• *The highlight of Place de la République is St. Trophime Church. Enjoy its exquisitely carved facade.*

⑪ ST. TROPHIME CHURCH

Named after a third-century bishop of Arles, this church, worth ▲▲, sports the finest Romanesque main entrance I've seen anywhere. The Romanesque and Gothic interior—with tapestries, relics, and a rare painting from the French Revolution when this was a "Temple of Reason"—is worth a visit.

Cost and Hours: Free, daily 9:00-12:00 & 14:00-18:30, until 17:00 Oct-March.

Exterior: Like a Roman triumphal arch, the church **facade** trumpets the promise of Judgment Day. The tympanum (the semicircular area above the door) is filled with Christian symbolism. Christ sits in majesty, surrounded by symbols of the four evangelists: Matthew (the winged man), Mark (the winged lion), Luke (the ox), and John (the eagle). The 12 apostles are lined up below Jesus. It's Judgment Day...some are saved and others aren't. Notice the condemned (on the right)—a chain gang doing a sad bunny-hop over the fires of hell. For them, the tune trumpeted by the three angels above Christ is not a happy one. Below the chain gang, St. Stephen is being stoned to death, with his soul leaving through his mouth and instantly being welcomed by angels. Study the exquisite detail. In an illiterate medieval world, this was colorfully painted, like a neon billboard over the town square. It's full of meaning, and a medieval pilgrim understood it all.

Interior: Just inside the door on the right, a chart locates the interior highlights and helps explain the carvings you just

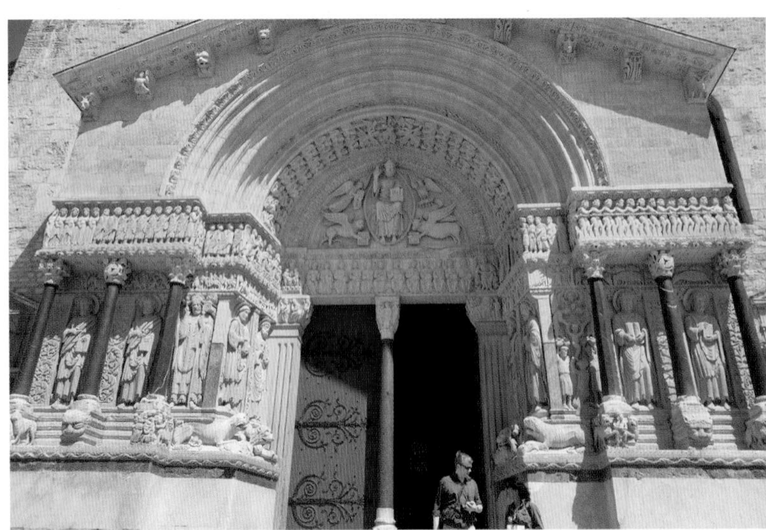

St. Trophime Church

saw on the tympanum. The tall 12th-century Romanesque nave is decorated by a set of tapestries (typical in the Middle Ages) showing scenes from the life of Mary (17th century, from the French town of Aubusson). Circle the church counterclockwise.

Step into the brightly lit **Chapel of Baptism** to view a statue of St. John Paul II under the window. Facing the window, look to the right wall where you'll see a faded painting from 1789. The French Revolution secularized the country and made churches "Temples of Reason." The painting of a triangle with a sunburst is the only example of church decor I've seen from this age.

Amble around the ambulatory toward the **Gothic apse.** Choose which chapel you need or want: If you have the plague or cholera, visit the chapel devoted to St. Roch—notice the testimonial plaques of gratitude on the wall. Some spaces are still available...if you hurry.

Two-thirds of the way around, find the **relic chapel** behind the ornate wrought iron gate, with its fine golden boxes that hold long-venerated bones of obscure saints. These relics generated lots of money for the church from pilgrims through the ages. Pop in a coin to share some light. The next chapel houses the skull of St. Anthony of the Desert.

Several chapels down, look for the early-Christian **sarcophagi** from Roman Arles (dated about A.D. 300). One sarcophagus shows Moses and the Israelites crossing the Red Sea. You'll see Christians wearing togas and praying like evangelicals do today—hands raised. The heads were likely lopped off during the French Revolution.

This church is a stop on the ancient pilgrimage route to Santiago de Compostela in northwest Spain. For 800 years pilgrims on their way to Santiago have paused here...and they still do today. Notice the modern-day pilgrimages advertised on the far right near the church's entry.

• *To reach the adjacent peaceful cloister, leave the church, turn left, then left again through a courtyard.*

ST. TROPHIME CLOISTERS

Worth seeing if you have the Liberty Passport (otherwise €4, same hours as Arena), the cloisters' many small columns were scavenged from the ancient Roman theater. Enjoy the sculpted capitals, the rounded Romanesque arches (12th century), and the pointed Gothic ones (14th century). The pretty vaulted hall exhibits 17th-century tapestries showing scenes from the First Crusade to the Holy Land. There's an instructive video at the base of the stairs. On the second floor, you'll walk along an angled rooftop designed to catch rainwater—notice the slanted gutter that channeled the water into a cistern and the heavy roof slabs covering the tapestry hall below.

• *From Place de la République, exit on the far corner (opposite the church and kitty-corner from where you entered) to stroll a delightful pedestrian street.*

⓬ RUE DE LA REPUBLIQUE

Rue da la République is Arles' primary shopping street. Walk downhill, enjoying the scene and popping into shops that catch your interest.

At the start is **Soulier Bakery.** Inside, you'll be tempted by *fougasse* (bread studded with herbs, olives, and bacon bits), *sablés Provençal* (cookies made with honey and almonds), *tarte lavande* (a sweet almond lavender tart), and big crispy meringues. A few doors down is **Restaurant L'Atelier** (with two prized Michelin stars), **L'Occitane en Provence** (local perfumes), **Puyricard Chocolate** (with enticing €1 treats and *calisson,* a sweet/bitter almond delight), as well as local design and antique shops. The fragile spiral columns on the right (just before the tourist-pleasing Lavender Boutique on the corner) show what 400 years of weather can do to decorative stonework.

• *Take the first left onto Rue Président*

Wilson. Just after the butcher shop, turn right to find ***Hôtel Dieu,*** *a hospital made famous by one of its patients: Vincent van Gogh.*

⓭ ESPACE VAN GOGH EASEL

In December 1888, shortly after his famous ear-cutting incident (see *Café at Night* easel, described later), Vincent was admitted into the local hospital—today's Espace Van Gogh cultural center (free, only the courtyard is open to the public). It surrounds a flowery courtyard that the artist loved and painted when he was being treated for blood loss, hallucinations, and severe depression that left him bedridden for a month. The citizens of Arles circulated a petition demanding that the mad Dutchman be kept under medical supervision. Félix Rey, Vincent's kind doctor, worked out a compromise: The artist could leave during the day so that he could continue painting, but he had to sleep at the hospital at night. Look through the postcards sold in the courtyard and find a painting of Vincent's ward showing nuns attending to patients in a gray hall *(Ward of Arles Hospital).*

• *Return to Rue de la République. Take a left and continue two blocks downhill. Take the second right up Rue Tour de Fabre and follow signs to Fondation Van Gogh. After a few steps, you'll pass* ***La Main Qui Pense*** *(The Hand That Thinks), a pottery workshop. A couple blocks farther, at the no right turn sign, turn right onto Rue du Docteur Fanton. On your immediate right is the...*

⓮ FONDATION VAN GOGH

This art foundation, worth ▲, delivers a refreshing stop for modern-art lovers and Van Gogh fans, with two temporary exhibits per year in which contemporary artists pay homage to Vincent through thought-provoking interpretations of his works. You'll also see at least one original work by Van Gogh (painted during his time in the region).

Cost and Hours: €9, daily 11:00-19:00 except closed between exhibits and likely Mon off-season—check website for current hours, audioguide-€3, Hôtel Leautaud de Donines, 35 Rue du Docteur Fanton, tel. 04 90 49 94 04, www.fondation-vincentvangogh-arles.org.

• *Continue down Rue du Docteur Fanton toward the river.*

⓯ RUE DU DOCTEUR FANTON

A string of recommended restaurants is on the left. On the right is **Crèche Municipale.** Open workdays, this is a free government-funded daycare where parents can drop off their infants up to two years old. The notion: No worker should face financial hardship in order to receive quality childcare. At the next corner is the recommended **Soleileis,** Arles' top ice cream shop.

At the strawberry-and-vanilla ice cream cone, turn right and step into **Bar El Paseo** at 4 Rue des Thermes. The main museum-like room is absolutely full of bull—including the mounted heads of three big ones who died in the local arena and a big black-and-white photo of Arles'

Fondation Van Gogh

A café on Forum Square

arena packed to capacity. Senora Leal—whose family is famous for its bullfighters—has wallpapered the place with photos and bullfighting memorabilia, and serves good Spanish Rioja wine and sangria.

• *A few steps farther is...*

⓰ FORUM SQUARE (PLACE DU FORUM)

Named for the Roman forum that once stood here, Forum Square, worth ▲, was the political and religious center of Roman Arles. Still lively, this café-crammed square is a local watering hole and popular for a *pastis* (anise-based aperitif). The bistros on the square can put together a passable salad or *plat du jour*—and when you sprinkle on the ambience, that's €14 well spent.

At the corner of Grand Hôtel Nord-Pinus, a plaque shows how the Romans built a foundation of galleries to level the main square and to compensate for Arles' slope down to the river. The two columns are all that survive from the upper story of the entry to the forum. Steps leading to the entrance are buried—the Roman street level was about 20 feet below you.

The statue on the square is of **Frédéric Mistral** (1830-1914). This popular poet, who wrote in the local dialect rather than in French, was a champion of Provençal culture. After receiving the Nobel Prize in Literature in 1904, Mistral used his prize money to preserve and display the folk identity of Provence. He founded a regional folk museum at a time when France was rapidly centralizing and regions like Provence were losing their unique identities. (The fierce, local mistral wind—literally "master"—has nothing to do with his name.)

• *Nearby, facing the brightly painted yellow café, find your final Van Gogh easel.*

CAFE AT NIGHT EASEL

In October 1888, lonely Vincent—who dreamed of making Arles a magnet for fellow artists—persuaded his friend Paul Gauguin to come south. He decorated Gauguin's room with several humble canvases of sunflowers (now some of the world's priciest paintings). Their plan was for Gauguin to be the "dean" of a new art school in Arles, and Vincent its instructor-in-chief. At first, the two got along well. They spent days side by side, rendering the same subject in their distinct styles. At night, they hit the bars and brothels. Van Gogh's well-known *Café at Night* captures the glow of an absinthe buzz at Café la Nuit on Place du Forum.

After two months together, the two artists clashed over art and personality differences (Vincent was a slob around the house, whereas Gauguin was meticulous). The night of December 23, they were drinking absinthe at the café when Vincent suddenly went ballistic. He threw his glass at Gauguin. Gauguin left. Walking through Place Victor Hugo, Gauguin heard footsteps behind him and turned to see Vincent coming at him, brandishing a razor. Gauguin quickly fled town. The local paper reported what happened next: "At 11:30 p.m., Vincent van Gogh, painter from Holland, appeared at the brothel at no. 1, asked for Rachel, and gave her his cut-off earlobe, saying, 'Treasure this precious object.' Then he vanished." He woke up the next morning at home with his head wrapped in a bloody towel and his earlobe missing. Was Vincent emulating a successful matador, whose prize is cutting off the bull's ear?

The **bright-yellow café**—called Café la Nuit—was the subject of one of Vincent van Gogh's most famous works in Arles. Although his painting showed the café in a brilliant yellow from the glow of gas lamps, the facade was bare limestone, just like the other cafés on this square. The café is now a tourist trap painted by its current owners to match Van Gogh's version...and to cash in on the Vincent-crazed hordes who pay too much to eat or drink here.

In spring 1889, the bipolar genius (a modern diagnosis) checked himself into the St. Paul Monastery and Hospital in St-Rémy-de-Provence. He spent a year there, thriving in the care of nurturing doctors and nuns. Painting was part of his therapy, so they gave him a studio to work in, and he produced more than 100 paintings. Alcohol-free and institutionalized, he did some of his wildest work. With thick, swirling brushstrokes and surreal colors, he made his placid surroundings throb with restless energy.

Eventually, Vincent's torment became unbearable. In the spring of 1890, he left Provence to be cared for by a sympathetic doctor in Auvers-sur-Oise, just north of Paris. On July 27, he wandered into a field and shot himself. He died two days later.

• *With this walk, you have seen the best of Arles. It's time to enjoy a drink on the Place du Forum and savor the essence of Provence.*

On the Outskirts

▲▲ANCIENT HISTORY MUSEUM (MUSEE DE L'ARLES ET DE LA PROVENCE ANTIQUES)

The Ancient History Museum provides valuable background on Arles' Roman history. Begin your town visit here before delving into the city's sights (drivers should stop on the way into town).

Located on the site of the Roman chariot racecourse (the arc of which is built into the parking lot), this air-conditioned, all-on-one-floor museum is just west of central Arles along the river. Models and original sculptures re-create the Roman city, making workaday life and culture easier to imagine.

Cost and Hours: €8, covered by Liberty Passport; open Wed-Mon 10:00-18:00, closed Tue; Presqu'île du Cirque Romain, tel. 04 13 31 51 03, www.arles-antique.cg13.fr.

Getting There: Drivers entering the city will see signs for the museum. If you're coming from the city center, take the free **Envia minibus** (stops at the train station and along Rue du 4 Septembre, then along the river—see map on page 302; 2/hour Mon-Sat, none Sun). If you're walking from the city center (allow 20 minutes), turn left at the river and take the scruffy riverside path under two bridges to the big, modern blue building. Approach-

Model of Arles' Classical Theater

ing the museum, you'll pass the verdant Hortus Garden—designed to recall the Roman circus and chariot racecourse that were located here. A **taxi** ride costs €11.

Visiting the Museum: The permanent collection is housed in a large hall flooded with natural light. You'll tour it counterclockwise: models of the ancient city and its major landmarks, a Roman boat (with a fine video in a tiny theater at the end of the hall), statues, mosaics, and sarcophagi. Read what English you can find, but—as much of the exhibit is in French only—here's a rundown on what you'll see.

A wall **map** of the region during the Roman era greets visitors and shows the geographic importance of Arles: Three important Roman trade routes—vias Domitia, Grippa, and Aurelia—all converged on or near Arles.

After a small exhibit on pre-Roman Arles you'll come to fascinating **models** of the Roman city and the impressive Roman structures in (and near) Arles. These breathe life into the buildings as they looked 2,000 years ago. Start with the model of Roman Arles and ponder the city's splendor over 2,000 years ago when Arles' population was double that of today. Find the forum—still the center of town today, though only two columns survive (the smaller section of the forum is where today's Place du Forum is built).

At the museum's center stands the original **statue** of Julius Caesar that once graced Arles' ancient theater stage wall. From there find individual models of the major buildings shown in the city model: the elaborately elegant forum; the floating wooden bridge that gave Arles a strategic advantage (over the widest, and therefore slowest, part of the river); the theater (with its magnificent stage wall); the arena (with its movable stadium cover to shelter spectators from sun or rain); and the hydraulic mill of Barbegal (with its 16 waterwheels powered by water cascading down a hillside).

Don't miss the large model of the **chariot racecourse.** Part of the original racecourse was just outside the windows, and though long gone, it likely resembled Rome's Circus Maximus.

A wing (to the right) is dedicated to the museum's newest and most exciting exhibit: a **Gallo-Roman vessel** and much of its cargo. This almost-100-foot-long Roman barge was hauled out of the Rhône in 2010, along with some 280 amphorae and 3,000 ceramic artifacts. It was typical of flat-bottomed barges used to shuttle goods between Arles and ports along the Mediterranean (vessels were manually towed upriver).

Continuing your counterclockwise circle of the museum, you'll see displays of pottery, jewelry, metal, and glass artifacts, as well as well-crafted mosaic floors that illustrate how Roman Arles was a city of art and culture. The many **statues** are all original, except for the greatest—the *Venus of Arles,* which Louis XIV took a liking to and had moved to Versailles.

Experiences

▲▲MARKETS

Provençal market days offer France's most colorful and tantalizing outdoor shopping. On Wednesday and Saturday mornings, Arles' ring road erupts into an open-air festival of fish, flowers, produce...and everything Provençal. The main event is on Saturday, with vendors jamming the ring road from Boulevard Emile Combes to the east, along Boulevard des Lices

Wednesday and Saturday are market days.

near the TI (the heart of the market), and continuing down Boulevard Georges Clemenceau to the west. Wednesday's market runs only along Boulevard Emile Combes, between Place Lamartine and Avenue Victor Hugo; the segment nearest Place Lamartine is all about food, and the upper half features clothing, tablecloths, purses, and so on. On the first Wednesday of the month, a flea market doubles the size of the usual Wednesday market along Boulevard des Lices near the main TI. Both markets are open until about 12:30.

▲▲BULLGAMES (*COURSES CAMARGUAISES*)

The nonviolent *courses camarguaises* (bullgames) held in Arles are more sporting than bloody bullfights (though traditional Spanish-style bullfights still take place on occasion). Spectators occupy the same seats that fans have used for nearly 2,000 years. The bulls of Arles (who, locals insist, "die of old age") are promoted in posters even more boldly than their human foes. In the bullgame, a ribbon *(cocarde)* is laced between the bull's horns. The *razeteur,* with a special hook, has 15 minutes to snare the ribbon. Local businessmen encourage a *razeteur* (dressed in white, with a red cummerbund) by shouting out how much money they'll pay for the *cocarde*. If the bull pulls a good stunt, the band plays the famous "Toreador" song from *Carmen*. The following day, newspapers report on the games, including how many *Carmens* the bull earned.

Three classes of bullgames—determined by the experience of the *razeteurs*—are advertised in posters: The *course de protection* is for rookies. The *trophée de l'Avenir* comes with more experience. And the *trophée des As* features top professionals. During Easter *(Féria du Pâques)* and the fall rice-harvest festival *(Féria du Riz),* the arena hosts traditional Spanish bullfights (look for *corrida*) with outfits, swords, spikes, and the whole gory shebang. (Nearby villages also stage *courses camarguaises* in small wooden bullrings nearly every weekend; TIs have the latest schedule.)

Cost and Hours: Arles' bullgame tickets usually run €7-20; bullfights are pricier (€36-100). Schedules for bullgames vary (usually July-Aug on Wed and Fri)—ask at the TI or check online at www.arenes-arles.com.

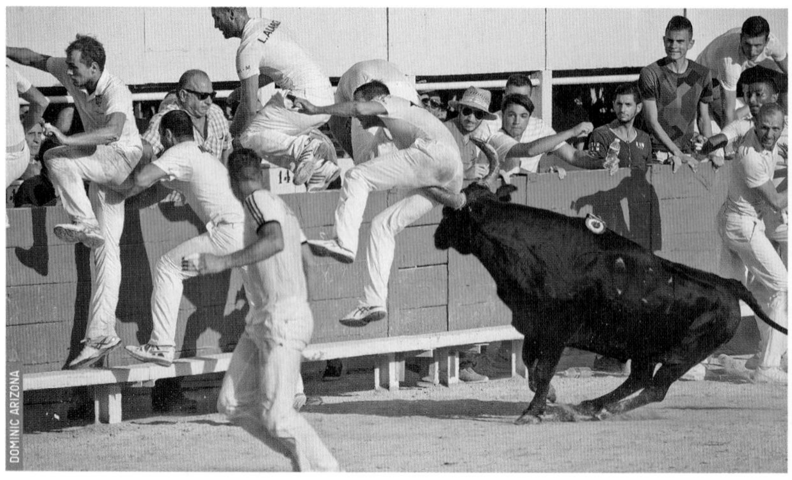

DOMINIC ARIZONA

Bulls are not harmed in Provençal-style "bullgames."

Provence's Cuisine Scene

The extravagant use of garlic, olive oil, herbs, and tomatoes makes Provence's cuisine France's liveliest. To sample it, order anything *à la provençale*. Among the area's specialties are **ratatouille** (a mixture of vegetables in a thick, herb-flavored tomato sauce), **aioli** (a rich, garlicky mayonnaise spread over vegetables, potatoes, fish, or whatever), **tapenade** (a paste of pureed olives, capers, anchovies, herbs, and sometimes tuna), ***soupe au pistou*** (thin yet flavorful vegetable soup with a sauce of basil, garlic, and cheese), and ***soupe à l'ail*** (garlic soup, called ***aigo bouido*** in the local dialect). Look for ***riz de Camargue*** (reddish, chewy, nutty-tasting rice) and ***taureau*** (bull's meat). The native goat cheeses are **Banon de Banon** or **Banon à la Feuille** (wrapped in chestnut leaves) and spicy **Picodon**. Don't miss the region's prized **Cavaillon melons** (cantaloupes) or its delicious cherries and apricots, which are often turned into jams and candied fruits.

Wines of Provence: Provence produces some of France's great wines at relatively reasonable prices. Look for wines from **Gigondas, Rasteau, Cairanne, Beaumes-de-Venise, Vacqueyras,** and **Châteauneuf-du-Pape.** For the cheapest but still tasty wines, look for labels showing **Côtes du Rhône Villages** or **Côtes de Provence.** If you like rosé, you'll be in heaven. **Rosés from Tavel** are considered among the best in Provence. For reds, splurge for Châteauneuf-du-Pape or Gigondas, and for a fine aperitif wine or a dessert wine, try the **Muscat** from **Beaumes-de-Venise.**

Eating

You can dine well in Arles on a modest budget (most of my listings have *menus* for under €25). Sunday is a quiet night for restaurants, though eateries on Place du Forum are open. For groceries, consider the big, Monoprix supermarket/department store on Place Lamartine (closed Sun).

Rick's Tip: *Cafés on the Place du Forum deliver great atmosphere and fair prices, but mediocre food.* **Avoid the garish yellow tourist trap Café la Nuit.** *For serious cuisine, wander away from the square.*

On Rue du Docteur Fanton

$$ Les Filles du 16 is a warm, affordable place to enjoy a fresh salad (€11), or a fine two- or three-course dinner (€21-27). The choices are limited, so check the selection before sitting down. The *taureau* (bull's meat) in a tasty sauce is a good choice (closed Sat-Sun, 16 Rue du Docteur Fanton, tel. 04 90 93 77 36).

$$ Le Plaza buzzes with happy diners and is run by a young couple (Stéphane cooks while Graziela serves). It features delicious Provençal cuisine at good prices (€23 *menus*, closed Wed Oct-March, 28 Rue du Docteur Fanton, tel. 04 90 96 33 15).

$$$ Le Galoubet is a popular local spot,

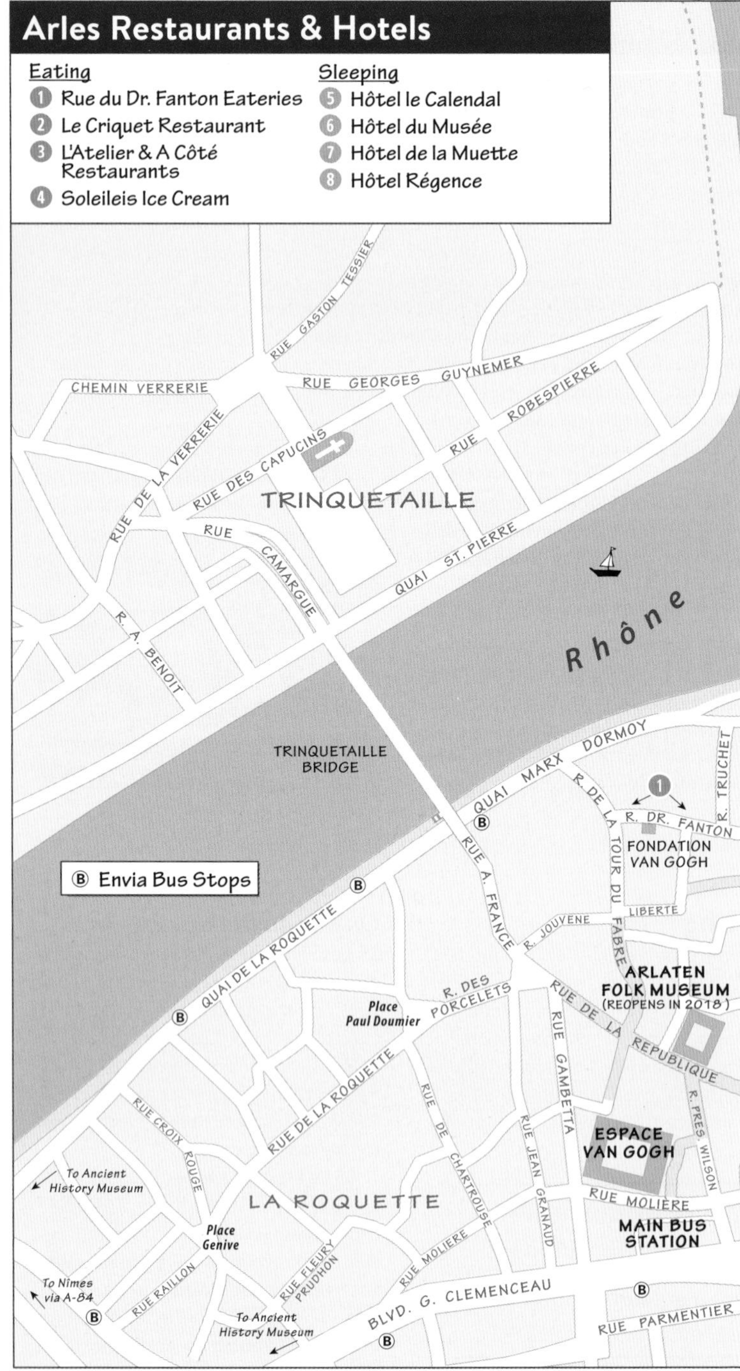
Arles Restaurants & Hotels
Eating
1 Rue du Dr. Fanton Eateries
2 Le Criquet Restaurant
3 L'Atelier & A Côté Restaurants
4 Soleileis Ice Cream
Sleeping
5 Hôtel le Calendal
6 Hôtel du Musée
7 Hôtel de la Muette
8 Hôtel Régence
RUE GASTON TESSIER
CHEMIN VERRERIE
RUE GEORGES GUYNEMER
RUE ROBESPIERRE
RUE DE LA VERRERIE
RUE DES CAPUCINS
TRINQUETAILLE
RUE CAMARGUE
QUAI ST. PIERRE
R. A. BENOIT
Rhône
TRINQUETAILLE BRIDGE
QUAI MARX DORMOY
R. TRUCHET
R. DE LA TOUR DU FABRE
R. DR. FANTON
FONDATION VAN GOGH
Envia Bus Stops
RUE A. FRANCE
LIBERTE
R. JOUVENE
QUAI DE LA ROQUETTE
ARLATEN FOLK MUSEUM
(REOPENS IN 2018)
R. DES PORCELETS
Place Paul Doumier
RUE DE LA REPUBLIQUE
RUE GAMBETTA
RUE DE LA ROQUETTE
RUE CROIX ROUGE
RUE DE CHARTROUSE
RUE JEAN GRANAUD
R. PRES. WILSON
ESPACE VAN GOGH
To Ancient History Museum
LA ROQUETTE
RUE MOLIERE
MAIN BUS STATION
Place Genive
RUE FLEURY PRUDHON
RUE MOLIERE
To Nîmes via A-84
RUE RAILLON
BLVD. G. CLEMENCEAU
To Ancient History Museum
RUE PARMENTIER

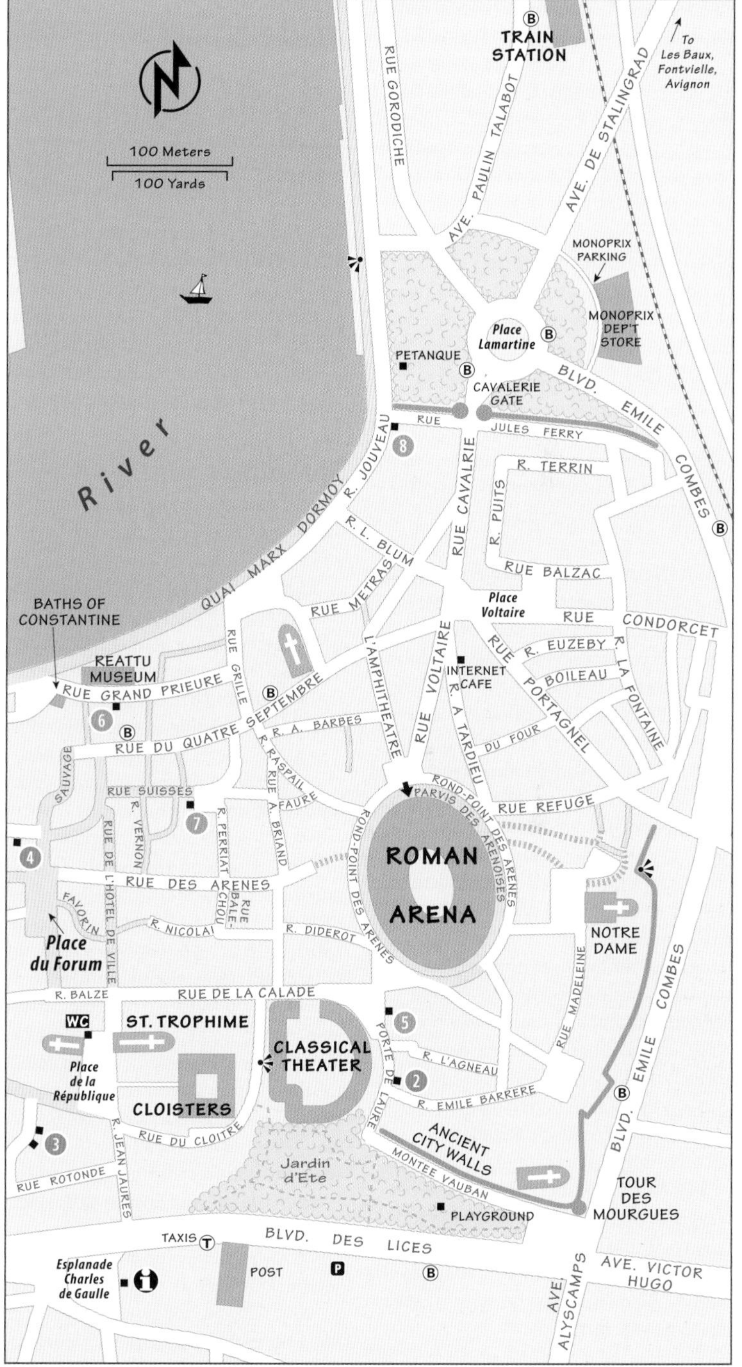
100 Meters
100 Yards
River
TRAIN STATION
To Les Baux, Fontvielle, Avignon
RUE GORODICHE
AVE. PAULIN TALABOT
AVE. DE STALINGRAD
MONOPRIX PARKING
MONOPRIX DEP'T STORE
Place Lamartine
PETANQUE
CAVALERIE GATE
BLVD. EMILE COMBES
RUE JULES FERRY
R. TERRIN
R. PUITS
RUE CAVALRIE
RUE BALZAC
R. JOUVEAU
QUAI MARX DORMOY
R. L. BLUM
RUE METRAS
Place Voltaire
RUE CONDORCET
BATHS OF CONSTANTINE
REATTU MUSEUM
RUE GRAND PRIEURE
RUE GRILLE
RUE DU QUATRE SEPTEMBRE
L'AMPHITHEATRE
RUE VOLTAIRE
INTERNET CAFE
RUE PORTAGNEL
R. EUZEBY
BOILEAU
R. LA FONTAINE
R. A. BARBES
R. A. TARDIEU
DU FOUR
SAUVAGE
RUE SUISSES
R. RASPAIL
RUE A. FAURE
ROND-POINT DES ARENES
PARVIS DES ARENOISES
RUE REFUGE
R. VERNON
R. PERRIAT
R. A. BRIAND
ROMAN ARENA
RUE DE L'HOTEL DE VILLE
RUE DES ARENES
RUE BALECHOU
FAVORIN
R. NICOLAI
R. DIDEROT
NOTRE DAME
Place du Forum
R. BALZE
RUE DE LA CALADE
RUE MADELEINE
WC
ST. TROPHIME
CLASSICAL THEATER
PORTE DE LAURE
R. L'AGNEAU
Place de la République
CLOISTERS
R. EMILE BARRERE
RUE DU CLOITRE
ANCIENT CITY WALLS
MONTEE VAUBAN
Jardin d'Ete
R. JEAN JAURES
RUE ROTONDE
PLAYGROUND
TOUR DES MOURGUES
TAXIS
BLVD. DES LICES
Esplanade Charles de Gaulle
POST
AVE. ALYSCAMPS
AVE. VICTOR HUGO

blending a warm interior, traditional French cuisine, and service with a smile, thanks to owner Frank. It's the most expensive of the places I list on this street and the least flexible, serving a €32 *menu* only. If it's cold, a roaring fire keeps you toasty (closed Sun-Mon, great fries and desserts, 18 Rue du Docteur Fanton, tel. 04 90 93 18 11).

Near the Roman Arena

$$ Le Criquet, a sweet little eatery two blocks above the arena, serves Provençal classics with joy at good prices. If you're really hungry, try the €25 *bourride*—a creamy fish soup thickened with aioli and garlic and stuffed with mussels, clams, calamari, and more (good €24-28 *menus*, indoor and outdoor dining, 21 Rue Porte de Laure, tel. 04 90 96 80 51).

A Gastronomic Dining Experience

One of France's most recognized chefs, Jean-Luc Rabanel, runs two different places 50 yards from Place de la République (at 7 Rue des Carmes). They sit side by side, both offering indoor and terrace seating.

$$$$ L'Atelier, a destination restaurant with two Michelin stars, attracts people from great distances to happily pay €125 for dinner and €65 for lunch. There is no menu, just a parade of delicious taste sensations served in artsy dishes. Don't plan on a quick dinner, and don't come for a traditional setting: Everything is enthusiastically contemporary. You'll probably see or hear the famous chef with his long salt-and-pepper hair and a deep voice. Friendly servers will hold your hand through this palate-widening experience (closed Mon-Tue, book ahead, tel. 04 90 91 07 69, www.rabanel.com).

$$$ A Côté, next door, offers a wine bar/bistro ambience and the chef's top-quality cuisine for much less money. There is a limited selection of wines by the glass (open daily, tel. 04 90 47 61 13, www.bistro-acote.com).

Sleep Code

$$$$ Splurge: Over €250
$$$ Pricier: €190-250
$$ Moderate: €130-190
$ Budget: €70-130
¢ Backpacker: Under €70

Hotels are classified based on the average price of a standard double room with bath in high season. Unless otherwise noted, credit cards are accepted, breakfast is not included, hotel staff speak English, and Wi-Fi is available.

Sleeping

Hotels are a great value here. Many are air-conditioned, though few have elevators.

$$ Hôtel le Calendal*** is a thoughtfully managed place ideally located between the Roman Arena and Classical Theater. The hotel opens to the street with airy lounges and a lovely palm-shaded courtyard, providing an enjoyable refuge. The rooms sport Provençal decor and come in random shapes and sizes (standard Db-€119, larger or balcony Db-€139-159, family rooms available, breakfast buffet-€12, air-con, reserve ahead for parking-€8/day, café/sandwich bar open daily, just above arena at 5 Rue Porte de Laure, tel. 04 90 96 11 89, www.lecalendal.com, contact@lecalendal.com).

$ Hôtel du Musée** is a quiet, affordable manor-home hideaway tucked deep in Arles (if driving, ask for access code to street barrier so you can drop off your bags). This delightful place comes with 28 wood-floored rooms, a flowery courtyard, and comfortable lounges. Lighthearted Claude and English-speaking Laurence are good hosts (Sb-€65, Db-€70-90, family rooms available, buffet breakfast-€8.50, no elevator, garage parking-€10/day, follow signs to *Réattu Museum* to 11 Rue du Grand Prieuré, tel.

04 90 93 88 88, www.hoteldumusee.com, contact@hoteldumusee.com).

$ Hôtel de la Muette**, run by Brigitte and Alain, is located in a quiet corner of Arles. Rooms come with stone walls, tiled floors, and pebble showers (Db-€81, family rooms available, direct booking discount for Rick Steves readers, buffet breakfast-€9, no elevator, private garage-€10/day, 15 Rue des Suisses, tel. 04 90 96 15 39, www.hotel-muette.com, hotel.muette@wanadoo.fr).

Rick's Tip: *An international photo event* **jams hotels in Arles the second weekend of July,** *while the twice-yearly Féria* **draws crowds over Easter and in mid-September.**

$ Hôtel Régence**, a top budget deal, has a riverfront location, comfortable Provençal rooms, safe parking, and a location near the train station. Gentle Valérie and Eric speak English (Db-€60-75, family rooms available, choose river-view or quieter courtyard rooms, good buffet breakfast-€6, no elevator but only two floors, garage parking-€7/day; from Place Lamartine, turn right after passing between towers to reach 5 Rue Marius Jouveau; tel. 04 90 96 39 85, www.hotel-regence.com, contact@hotel-regence.com).

Transportation

Getting Around Arles

In this flat city, everything's within **walking** distance. Only the Ancient History Museum requires a healthy walk (20 minutes). The elevated riverside promenade provides Rhône views and a direct route to the Ancient History Museum (to the southwest) and the train station (to the northeast). Keep your head up for *Starry Night* memories, but eyes down for doggie droppings.

Arles' **taxis** charge a set fee of about €11, but nothing except the Ancient History Museum is worth a taxi ride. To call a cab, dial 04 90 96 52 76 or 04 90 96 90 03.

The free **Envia minibus** circles the town, useful for access to the train station, hotels, and the Ancient History Museum (2/hour, Mon-Sat 7:00-19:00, none Sun).

Arriving and Departing

Compare train and bus schedules: For some nearby destinations the bus may be the better choice, and it's usually cheaper.

BY TRAIN

The train station is on the river, a 10-minute walk from the town center. There's no baggage storage at the station, but you can walk 10 minutes to stow it at Hôtel Régence (see "Orientation," earlier).

To reach the town center or Ancient History Museum from the train station, wait for the free **Envia minibus** at the glass shelter facing away from the station (cross the street and veer left, 2/hour Mon-Sat 7:00-19:00, none Sun). The bus makes a counterclockwise loop around Arles, stopping near most of my recommended hotels (see map on page 302 for stops). **Taxis** usually wait in front of the station.

Train Connections from Arles to: Paris (11/day, 2 direct TGVs—4 hours, 9 more with transfer in Avignon—5 hours), **Avignon Centre-Ville** (roughly hourly, 20 minutes; 5-minute shuttle train from Avignon Centre-Ville connects to Avignon TGV Station), **Carcassonne** (4/day direct, 2.5 hours, more with transfer in Narbonne, direct trains may require reservations), **Beaune** (10/day, 5 hours), **Nice** (11/day, 4 hours, most require transfer in Marseille).

BY BUS

Arles' bus station is on Boulevard Georges Clémenceau. Most buses to regional destinations depart from here and most cost only €1.50. Get schedules at the TI or from the bus company (tel. 08 10 00 13 26, www.lepilote.com).

Bus Connections from Arles Train Station to Avignon TGV Station: The direct SNCF bus is easier than the train (€9, 9/day, 1 hour, included with rail pass).

Bus Connections from Arles to Les Baux: Bus #57 connects Arles to Les Baux (6/day daily July-Aug, Sat-Sun only in May-June and Sept, none Oct-April; 35 minutes to Les Baux, then runs to Avignon).

BY CAR

For most hotels, first follow signs to *Centre-Ville*, then *Gare SNCF* (train station). You'll come to a big roundabout (Place Lamartine) with a Monoprix department store to the right. You can park along the city wall (except on Tue night when tow trucks clear things out for the Wed market); the hotels I list are no more than a 15-minute walk from here. Fearless drivers can plunge into the narrow streets between the two stumpy towers via Rue de la Calade, and follow signs to their hotel. Theft is a problem—leave nothing in your car, and trust your hotelier's advice on where to park.

Most hotels have metered parking nearby (free Mon-Sat 12:00-14:00 & 19:00-9:00, and all day Sun; some meters limited to 2.5 hours). If you can't find a space near your hotel, Parking des Lices (Arles' only parking garage), near the TI on Boulevard des Lices, is a good fallback.

AVIGNON

Famous for its nursery rhyme, medieval bridge, and brooding Palace of the Popes, contemporary Avignon (ah-veen-yohn) bustles and prospers behind its mighty walls. For nearly 100 years (1309-1403) Avignon was the capital of Christendom, home to seven popes. (And, for a difficult period after that—during the Great Schism when there were two competing popes—Avignon was "the other Rome.") During this time, it grew from a quiet village into a thriving city.

Today, with its large student population and fashionable shops, Avignon is an intriguing blend of medieval history, youthful energy, and urban sophistication. Street performers entertain the international throngs who fill Avignon's ubiquitous cafés and trendy boutiques. And each July the city goes crazy during its huge theater festival (with about 2,000 performances, big crowds, higher prices, and hotels booked up long in advance). Clean, lively, and popular with tourists, Avignon is more impressive for its outdoor ambience than for its museums and monuments.

Orientation

Cours Jean Jaurès, which turns into Rue de la République, runs straight from the Centre-Ville train station to Place de l'Horloge and the Palace of the Popes, splitting Avignon in two. The larger eastern half is where the action is. Climb to the Jardin du Rochers des Doms for the town's best view, tour the pope's immense palace, lose yourself in Avignon's back streets, and find a shady square to call home.

Tourist Information: The TI is helpful, with lots of information about the city and the region (April-Oct Mon-Sat 9:00-18:00, Sun 10:00-17:00, daily until 19:00 in July, shorter hours off-season; between the train station and the old town at 41 Cours Jean Jaurès, tel. 04 32 74 32 74, www.avignon-tourisme.com).

Sightseeing Pass: At the TI, pick up the free **Avignon Passion Pass** (for up to 5 family members). Get it stamped at your first sight to receive discounts at the others. The pass comes with the Avignon "Passion" map and guide, which includes several good (but tricky-to-follow) walking tours. The TI also has bike maps for good rides in the area, including the Ile de la Barthelasse.

Bike Rental: Rent pedal and electric bikes and scooters near the train station at **Provence Bike** (April-Oct 9:00-18:30, 7 Avenue St. Ruf, tel. 04 90 27 92 61, www.provence-bike.com). You'll enjoy riding on the Ile de la Barthelasse (the TI has bike maps).

Car Rental: The TGV Station has

counters for all the big companies; only Avis is at the Centre-Ville Station.

Local Guides: Imagine Tours focuses on cultural excursions adapted to your interests. Guides will meet you at your hotel or the departure point of your choice (€190/half-day, €315/day, prices for up to 4 people starting from near Avignon or Arles, mobile 06 89 22 19 87, www.imagine-tours.net, imagine.tours@gmail.com). The **Avignon Gourmet Walking Tour** is a wonderful experience if you like to eat; charming Aurelie meets small groups daily (except Sun and Mon) at the TI at 9:15 for a well-designed three-hour, eight-stop walk. Book in advance on her website (€55/person, 2-8 people per group, tel. 06 35 32 08 96, www.avignongourmetours.com).

Tourist Train: The little train leaves regularly from in front of the Palace of the Popes and offers a decent overview of the city, including the Jardin du Rochers des Doms and St. Bénezet Bridge (€7, 2/hour, 40 minutes, English commentary, mid-March-mid-Oct daily 10:00-18:00, July-Aug until 19:00).

Minivan Excursions: Provence Reservation offers day tours by minivan or bus to nearby sights (such as lavender fields) from Avignon, Arles, and more. Tours from Avignon run year-round and cover a great variety of destinations; tours from other cities run April through September only and are more limited in scope. You'll get comfortable transportation but not guiding; you're on your own at the sights (about €60-80/half-day, €100-120/day for minivan tours, less for their big-bus tours, tel. 04 90 14 70 00, www.provence-reservation.com).

➔ Avignon Walk

This self-guided walk, worth ▲▲, offers a fine overview of the city and its major sights.

• *Start your tour where the Romans did, on Place de l'Horloge, in front of City Hall (Hôtel de Ville).*

PLACE DE L'HORLOGE

In ancient Roman times this was the forum, and in medieval times it was the market square. The square is named for the clock tower (now hiding behind the more recently built City Hall), which, in its day, was a humanist statement. In medieval France, the only bells in town rang

Place de l'Horloge

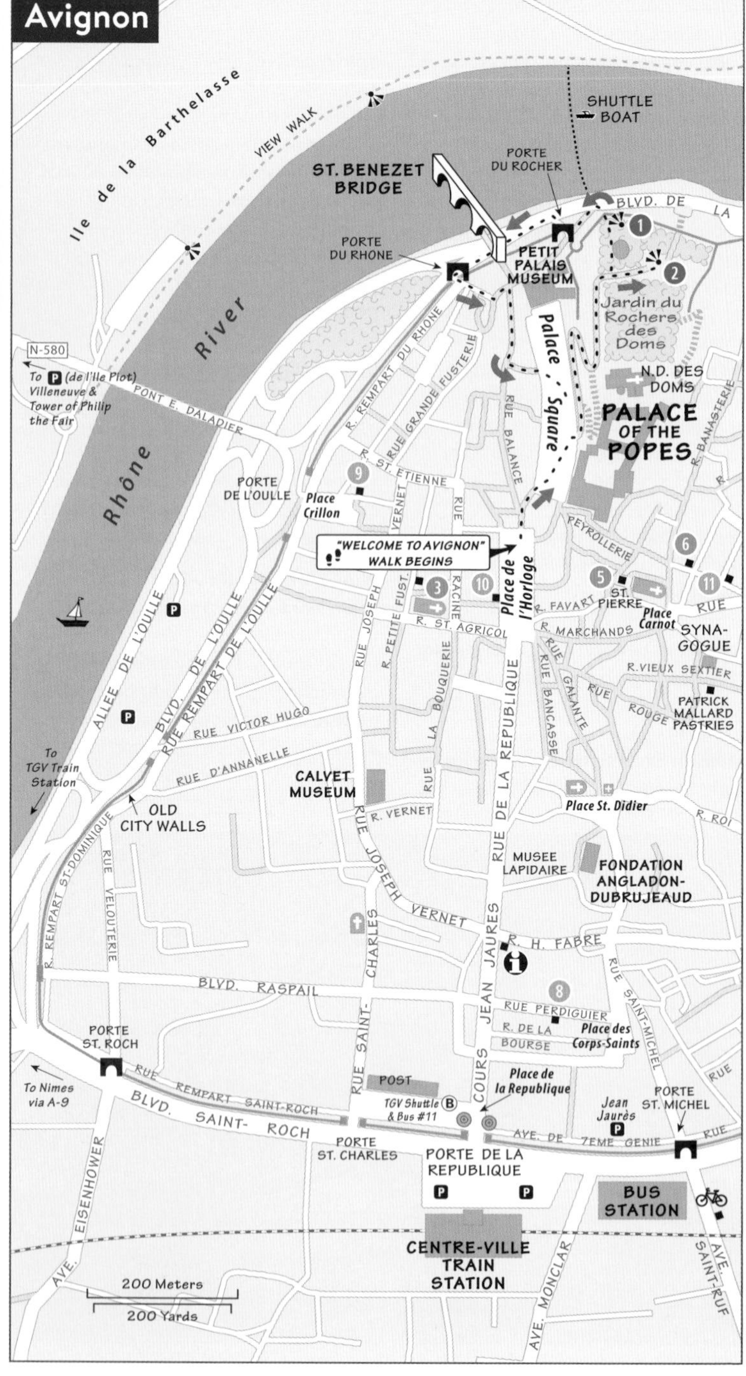
Avignon
Ile de la Barthelasse
VIEW WALK
SHUTTLE BOAT
ST. BENEZET BRIDGE
PORTE DU ROCHER
BLVD. DE LA
PORTE DU RHONE
PETIT PALAIS MUSEUM
Jardin du Rochers des Doms
N.D. DES DOMS
PALACE OF THE POPES
Palace Square
Rhône River
N-580
To P (de l'Ile Piot) Villeneuve & Tower of Philip the Fair
PONT E. DALADIER
R. REMPART DU RHONE
RUE GRANDE FUSTERIE
RUE BALANCE
R. BANASTERIE
R. ST. ETIENNE
PORTE DE L'OULLE
Place Crillon
VERNET
RUE RACINE
PEYROLLERIE
"WELCOME TO AVIGNON" WALK BEGINS
Place de l'Horloge
ST. PIERRE
Place Carnot
R. FAVART
RUE
SYNAGOGUE
R. ST. AGRICOL
R. MARCHANDS
R. PETITE FUST.
RUE JOSEPH
RUE LA BOUQUERIE
RUE DE LA REPUBLIQUE
RUE GALANTE
RUE BANCASSE
R. VIEUX SEXTIER
RUE ROUGE
PATRICK MALLARD PASTRIES
ALLEE DE L'OULLE
BLVD. DE L'OULLE
RUE REMPART DE L'OULLE
RUE VICTOR HUGO
RUE D'ANNANELLE
CALVET MUSEUM
Place St. Didier
R. ROI
To TGV Train Station
OLD CITY WALLS
R. VERNET
RUE JOSEPH VERNET
R. REMPART ST-DOMINIQUE
RUE VELOUTERIE
MUSEE LAPIDAIRE
FONDATION ANGLADON-DUBRUJEAUD
R. H. FABRE
RUE SAINT-MICHEL
RUE SAINT-CHARLES
COURS JEAN JAURES
BLVD. RASPAIL
RUE PERDIGUIER
R. DE LA BOURSE
Place des Corps-Saints
PORTE ST. ROCH
To Nimes via A-9
RUE REMPART SAINT-ROCH
POST
Place de la Republique
BLVD. SAINT-ROCH
TGV Shuttle & Bus #11
Jean Jaurès
PORTE ST. MICHEL
RUE
AVE. DE 7EME GENIE
PORTE ST. CHARLES
PORTE DE LA REPUBLIQUE
BUS STATION
CENTRE-VILLE TRAIN STATION
AVE. EISENHOWER
AVE. MONCLAR
AVE. SAINT-RUF
200 Meters
200 Yards

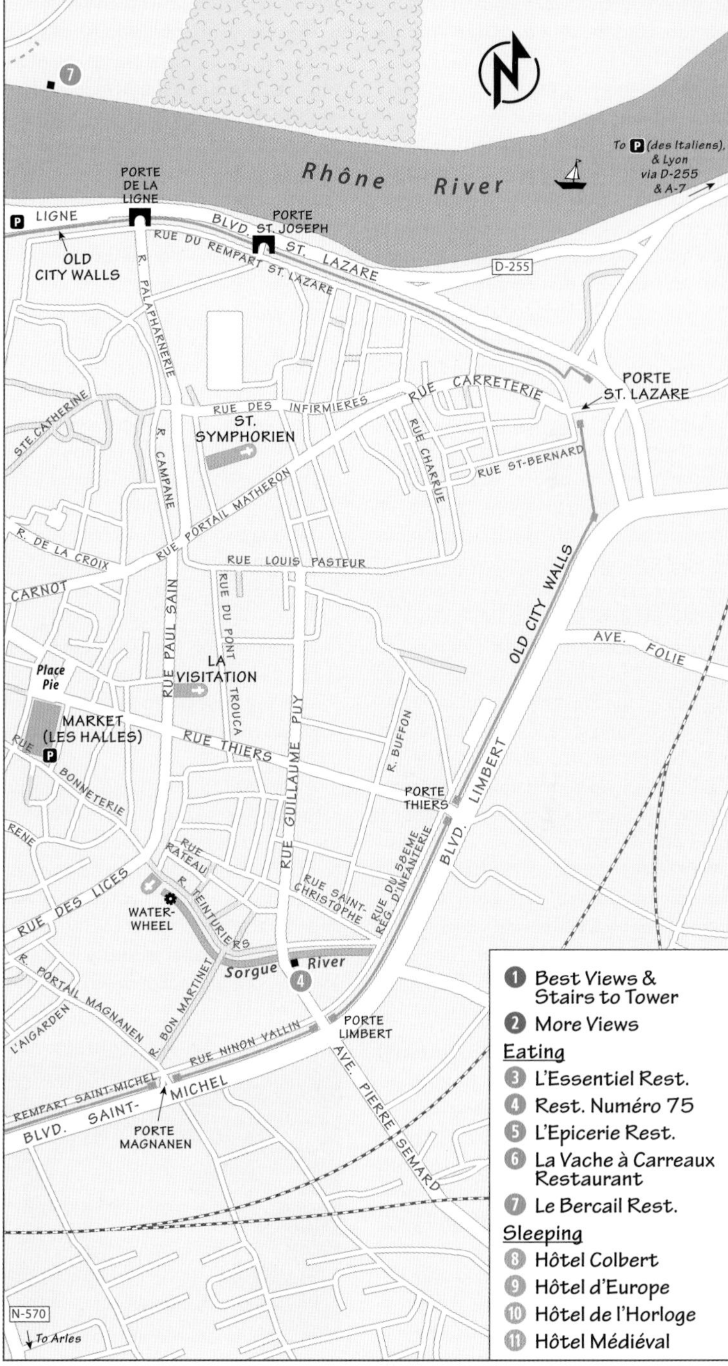

Rhône River
To P (des Italiens), & Lyon via D-255 & A-7
PORTE DE LA LIGNE
LIGNE
OLD CITY WALLS
PORTE ST. JOSEPH
BLVD. ST. LAZARE
RUE DU REMPART ST. LAZARE
D-255
R. PALAPHARNERIE
PORTE ST. LAZARE
RUE CARRETERIE
RUE DES INFIRMIERES
ST. SYMPHORIEN
STE. CATHERINE
RUE CHARRUE
RUE ST-BERNARD
R. CAMPANE
RUE PORTAIL MATHERON
R. DE LA CROIX
CARNOT
RUE LOUIS PASTEUR
OLD CITY WALLS
RUE PAUL SAIN
RUE DU PONT
LA VISITATION
TROUCA
AVE. FOLIE
Place Pie
MARKET (LES HALLES)
RUE BONNETERIE
RUE THIERS
RUE GUILLAUME PUY
R. BUFFON
PORTE THIERS
BLVD. LIMBERT
RENE
RUE RATEAU
R. TEINTURIERS
RUE SAINT-CHRISTOPHE
RUE DU 58EME REG. D'INFANTERIE
RUE DES LICES
WATER-WHEEL
Sorgue River
R. PORTAIL MAGNANEN
L'AIGARDEN
R. BON MARTINET
RUE NINON VALLIN
PORTE LIMBERT
AVE. PIERRE SEMARD
REMPART SAINT-MICHEL
BLVD. SAINT-MICHEL
PORTE MAGNANEN
N-570
To Arles
1 Best Views & Stairs to Tower
2 More Views
Eating
3 L'Essentiel Rest.
4 Rest. Numéro 75
5 L'Epicerie Rest.
6 La Vache à Carreaux Restaurant
7 Le Bercail Rest.
Sleeping
8 Hôtel Colbert
9 Hôtel d'Europe
10 Hôtel de l'Horloge
11 Hôtel Médiéval

from the church tower to indicate not the hours but the calls to prayer. With the dawn of the modern age, secular clock towers like this rang out the hours as people organized their lives.

Taking humanism a step further, the City Hall (Hôtel de Ville), built after the French Revolution, obstructed the view of the old clock tower while celebrating a new era. The slogan "liberty, equality, and brotherhood" is a reminder that the people supersede the king and the church. And today, judging from the square's jammed cafés and restaurants, it's the people who do rule.

The square's present popularity arrived with the trains in 1854. Facing City Hall, look left down the main drag, Rue de la République. When the trains came to Avignon, proud city fathers wanted a direct, impressive way to link the new station to the heart of the city—so they plowed over homes to create Rue de la République and widened Place de l'Horloge. This main drag's Parisian feel is intentional—it was built not in the Provençal manner, but in the Haussmann style that is so dominant in Paris (characterized by broad, straight boulevards lined with stately buildings). Today, this Champs-Elysées of Avignon is lined with department stores and banks.

• *Walk slightly uphill past the Neo-Renaissance facade of the theater and the carousel (public WCs behind). Look back to see the late Gothic bell tower. Then veer right at the Hôtel des Palais des Papes and continue into...*

PALACE SQUARE (PLACE DU PALAIS)

Pull up a concrete stump just past the café. Nicknamed *bites* (slang for penis), these effectively keep cars from double-parking in areas designed for people. Many of the metal ones slide up and down by remote control to let privileged cars come and go.

Now take in the scene. This grand square is lined with the Palace of the Popes, the Petit Palais, and the cathedral. In the 1300s, the entire headquarters of the Roman Catholic Church was moved to Avignon. The Church bought Avignon and gave it a complete makeover. Along with clearing out vast spaces like this square and building a three-acre palace, the Church erected more than three miles of protective wall (with 39 towers), "appropriate" housing for cardinals (read: mansions), and residences for its entire bureaucracy. The city was Europe's largest construction zone. Avignon's population grew from 6,000 to 25,000 in short order. (Today, 13,000 people live within the walls.) The limits of pre-papal Avignon are outlined on your city map: Rues Joseph Vernet, Henri Fabre, des Lices, and Philonarde all follow the route of the city's earlier defensive wall (about half the diameter of today's wall).

The imposing facade behind you, across the square from the Palace of the Popes' main entry, was "the papal mint," which served as the finance department for the Holy See. The Petit Palais (Little Palace) seals the uphill end of the square and was built for a cardinal; today it houses medieval paintings (museum described next).

Avignon's 12th-century Romanesque cathedral, just to the left of the Palace of the Popes, has been the seat of the local bishop for more than a thousand years. Predating the Church's purchase of Avignon by 200 years, its simplicity reflects Avignon's pre-papal modesty. The gilded Mary was added in 1854 when the Vatican

Palace Square

established the doctrine of her Immaculate Conception (born without the stain of original sin).

• *You can visit the massive* ***Palace of the Popes*** *(described on page 312) now, but it's better to visit it at the end of this walk.*

Now is a good time to take in the...

PETIT PALAIS MUSEUM (MUSEE DU PETIT PALAIS)

This former cardinal's palace now displays the Church's collection of (mostly) art. The information is only in French, but a visit here before going to the Palace of the Popes helps furnish and populate that otherwise barren building. You'll see bits of statues and tombs—an inventory of the destruction of exquisite Church art wrought by the French Revolution (which tackled established French society with Taliban-esque fervor). Then come many rooms filled with religious Italian paintings, organized in chronological order from early Gothic to late Renaissance.

Cost and Hours: €6, Wed-Mon 10:00-13:00 & 14:00-18:00, closed Tue, at north end of Palace Square, tel. 04 90 86 44 58, www.petit-palais.org.

• *From Palace Square, head up to the cathedral (enjoy the viewpoint overlooking the square), and zig-zag up the ramps to the top of a rocky hill where Avignon was first settled. Atop the hill is an inviting café and pond in a park—our next stop. At the far side is a viewpoint high above the river from where you can see Avignon's beloved broken bridge.*

Petit Palais Museum

▲JARDIN DU ROCHERS DES DOMS

Enjoy the view from this bluff. On a clear day, the tallest peak you see, with its white limestone cap, is Mont Ventoux ("Windy Mountain"). Below and just to the right, you'll spot free passenger ferries shuttling across the river to Ile de la Barthelasse, an island nature-preserve where Avignon can breathe. Tucked amid the trees on the island side of the river is a fun, recommended restaurant, Le Bercail, a local favorite. To the left in the distance is the TGV rail bridge.

The Rhône River marked the border of Vatican territory in medieval times. Fort St. André (across the river on the hill) was across the border, in the kingdom of France. The fort was built in 1360, shortly after the pope moved to Avignon, to counter the papal incursion into this part of Europe. Avignon's famous bridge was a key border crossing, with towers on either end—one was French, and the other was the pope's. The French one, across the river, is the Tower of Philip the Fair.

• *Take the walkway down to the left and find the stairs (closed at dusk) leading down to the tower. You'll catch glimpses of the...*

RAMPARTS

The only bit of the rampart you can walk on is accessed from St. Bénezet Bridge (pay to enter—see next). Just after the papacy took control of Avignon, the walls were extended to take in the convents and monasteries that had been outside the city. What you see today was partially restored in the 19th century.

• *When you leave the tower on street level, exit the walls, then turn left along the wall to the old bridge. Pass under the bridge to find its entrance shortly after.*

▲ST. BENEZET BRIDGE (PONT ST. BENEZET)

This bridge, whose construction and location were inspired by a shepherd's religious vision, is the "Pont d'Avignon" of nursery-rhyme fame. The ditty (which you've probably been humming all day) dates back to the 15th century: *Sur le Pont d'Avignon, on y danse, on y danse, sur le Pont d'Avignon, on y danse tous en rond* ("On the bridge of Avignon, we will dance, we will dance, on the bridge of Avignon, we will dance all in a circle").

And the bridge was a big deal even outside of its kiddie-tune fame. Built between 1171 and 1185, it was strategic—one of only three bridges crossing the mighty Rhône in the Middle Ages, important to pilgrims, merchants, and armies. It was damaged several times by floods and subsequently rebuilt. In 1668 most of it was knocked out for the last time by a disastrous icy flood. The townsfolk decided not to rebuild this time, and for more than a century, Avignon had no bridge across the Rhône. While only 4 arches survive today, the original bridge was huge: Imagine a 22-arch, 3,000-foot-long bridge extending from Vatican territory across the island to the lonely Tower of Philip the Fair, which marked the beginning of France (see displays of the bridge's original length).

Cost and Hours: €5, includes audioguide, €13.50 combo-ticket includes Palace of the Popes, daily March-Oct 9:00-19:00, July-Aug until 20:00, Nov-Feb 9:30-17:45, last entry one hour before closing; tel. 04 90 27 51 16.

• *To get to the Palace of the Popes from here, leave via the riverfront exit, turn left, then turn left again back into the walls. Walk to the end of the short street, then turn right following signs to Palais des Papes. Next, look for brown signs leading left under the passageway, then stay the course up the narrow steps to Palace Square.*

▲▲PALACE OF THE POPES (PALAIS DES PAPES)

In 1309 a French pope was elected (Pope Clément V). His Holiness decided that dangerous Italy was no place for a pope, so he moved the whole operation to Avignon for a secure rule under a supportive French king. The Catholic Church literally bought Avignon (then a two-bit town), and popes resided here until 1403. Meanwhile, Italians demanded a Roman pope, so from 1378 on, there were twin popes—one in Rome and one in Avignon—causing a schism in the Catholic Church that

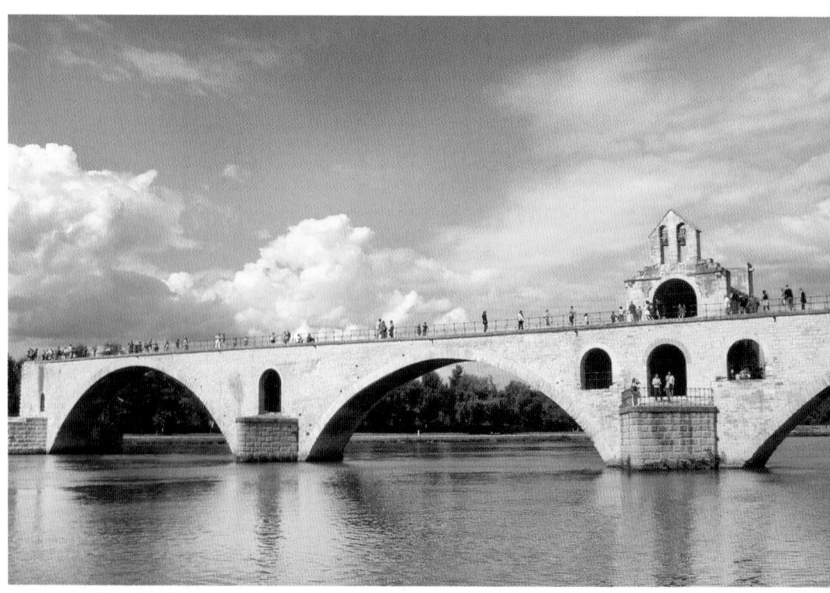

St. Bénezet Bridge

wasn't fully resolved until 1417.

Cost and Hours: €11, €13.50 combo-ticket includes St. Bénezet Bridge, daily March-Oct 9:00-19:00, July-Aug until 20:00, Nov-Feb 9:30-17:45, last entry one hour before closing; thorough and essential audioguide-€2; tel. 04 90 27 50 00, www.palais-des-papes.com.

Visiting the Palace: You'll follow a one-way route. A big room near the start functions as "the museum," with artifacts (such as cool 14th-century arrowheads) and a good intro video.

The palace was built stark and strong, before the popes knew how long they'd be staying (and before the affluence and fanciness of the Renaissance and Baroque ages). This was the most fortified palace of the time (remember, the pope left Rome to be more secure). With 10-foot-thick walls, it was a symbol of power. There are huge ceremonial rooms (rarely used) and more intimate living quarters. The bedroom comes with the original wall paintings, a decorated wooden ceiling, and fine tiled floor. And there's one big "chapel" (twice the size of the adjacent cathedral) that, while simple, is majestic in its pure French Gothic lines.

This largest surviving Gothic palace in Europe was built to accommodate 500 people as the administrative center of the Holy See and home of the pope. Seven popes ruled from here, making this the center of Christianity for nearly 100 years. The last pope checked out in 1403, but the Church owned Avignon until the French Revolution in 1791. During this interim period, the palace still housed Church authorities. Avignon residents, many of whom had come from Rome, spoke Italian for a century after the pope left, making the town a cultural oddity within France.

The palace is pretty empty today—nothing portable survived both the pope's return to Rome and the French Revolution. You can climb the tower (Tour de la Gâche) for grand views. The artillery room is now a gift shop, channeling all visitors on a full tour of knickknacks for sale.

• *You'll exit at the rear of the palace. To return to Palace Square, make two rights after exiting the palace.*

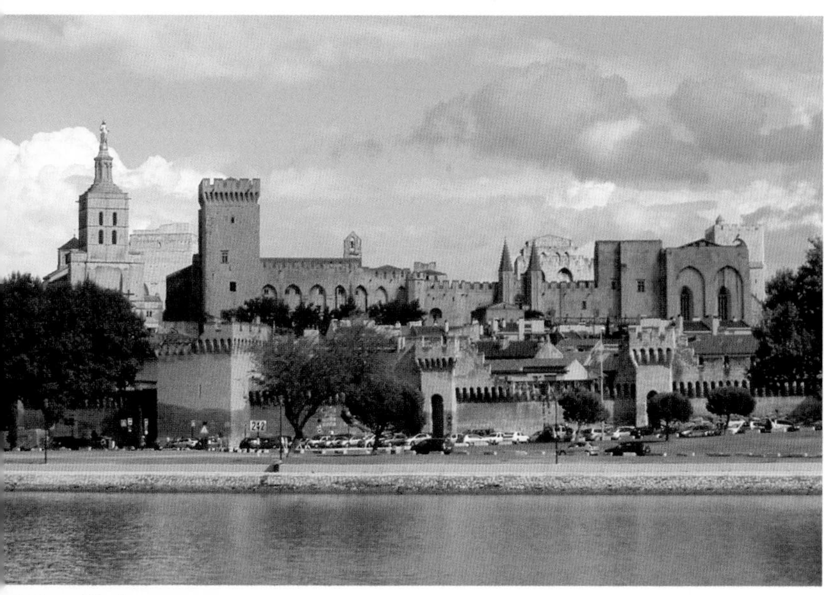

Palace of the Popes

Experiences

Ile de la Barthelasse Saunter

A free shuttle boat, the *Navette Fluviale*, plies back and forth across the Rhône River to Ile de la Barthelasse. This peaceful island offers grassy walks, bike rides, and the recommended riverside restaurant Le Bercail. For great views, walk the riverside path to Daladier Bridge, and then cross back over the bridge into town.

Cost and Hours: Free; 3 boats/hour depart from near St. Bénezet Bridge, daily April-June and Sept 10:00-12:30 & 14:00-18:00, July-Aug 11:00-21:00; Oct-March weekends and Wed afternoons only.

Rick's Tip: *If you stay on the island for dinner, check the schedule to make sure you* **don't miss the last return boat.**

Eating

Avignon offers a good range of restaurants and settings, from lively squares to atmospheric streets. Skip the overpriced, underwhelming restaurants on Place de l'Horloge and find a more intimate location for your dinner. At the finer places, reservations are generally smart (especially on weekends).

Fine Dining

$$$$ L'Essentiel is where locals go for a fine meal. The setting is classy-contemporary inside, the back terrace is romantic, the wine list is extensive, the cuisine is classic French, and gentle owner Dominique makes timid diners feel at ease (€31-45 *menus*, closed Sun-Mon, inside and outdoor seating, 2 Rue Petite Fusterie, tel. 04 90 85 87 12, www.restaurantlessentiel.com).

$$$ Restaurant Numéro 75 is worth the walk. It fills the Pernod mansion (of *pastis* liquor fame) with a romantic, chandeliered, Old World dining hall that extends to a leafy, gravelly courtyard. They serve delightful lunch salads, fish is a forte, and the French cuisine is beautifully presented (€32 lunch *menu*, dinner *menus*: €29 two-course and €37 three-course, closed Sun, 75 Rue Guillaume Puy, tel. 04 90 27 16 00, www.numero75.com).

Dining on a Moderate Budget

$$$ L'Epicerie sits alone under green awnings on the romantic Place St-Pierre and is ideal for dinner outside (or in the small but cozy interior). The cuisine is as delicious as the setting (€10 starters, €24 *plats*, daily, 10 Place St-Pierre, tel. 04 90 82 74 22).

$$ La Vache à Carreaux venerates cheese and wine while offering a range of choices from its big chalkboard. It's a young, lively place, with colorful decor, easygoing service (thanks to owner Jean-Charles), and a reasonable wine list (€12 starters, €12-16 *plats*, €5 wines by the glass, daily, just off atmospheric Place des Châtaignes at 14 Rue de la Peyrolerie, tel. 04 90 80 09 05).

Across the Rhône

$$$ Le Bercail offers a fun opportunity to get out of town (barely) and take in *le fresh air* with a terrific riverfront view of Avignon, all while enjoying big portions of Provençal cooking (*menus* from €28, daily April-Oct, serves late, reservations recommended, tel. 04 90 82 20 22). Take the free shuttle boat (located near St.

Bénezet Bridge) to the Ile de la Barthelasse, turn right, and walk five minutes. As the boat usually stops running at about 18:00 (except in July-Aug, when it runs until 21:00), you can either taxi back or walk 25 minutes along the pleasant riverside path and over Daladier Bridge.

Sleeping

Hotel values are better in Arles, though I've found some pretty good deals in Avignon. Drivers should ask about parking discounts through hotels.

Rick's Tip: *During the* **July theater festival,** *rooms are few in Avignon—you must book long ahead and pay inflated prices.* **It's better to stay in Arles.**

Near Centre-Ville Station

$ Hôtel Colbert** is on a quiet lane, with a dozen spacious rooms gathered on four floors around a skinny spiral staircase (no elevator). Patrice decorates each room with a colorful (occasionally erotic) flair. There are warm public spaces and a sweet little patio (Sb-€74, small Db-€82, bigger Db-€100, some tight bathrooms, rooms off the patio can be musty, closed Nov-mid-March, 7 Rue Agricol Perdiguier, tel. 04 90 86 20 20, www.lecolbert-hotel.com, contact@avignon-hotel-colbert.com).

Near Place de l'Horloge

$$$ Hôtel d'Europe*****, with Avignon's most prestigious address, lets peasants sleep royally—but only if they land one of the 13 reasonable "classique" rooms. Enter through a shady courtyard, linger in the lounges, and savor every comfort. The hotel is located on the handsome Place Crillon, near the river (standard "classique" Db-€230, large Db-€390-590, view suites-€1,100, breakfast-€22, garage parking-€20/day, near Daladier Bridge at 12 Place Crillon, tel. 04 90 14 76 76, www.heurope.com, reservations@heurope.com).

$$ Hôtel de l'Horloge**** is as central as it gets—on Place de l'Horloge. It offers 66 unimaginative but comfortable rooms at fair rates, some with terraces and views of the city and the Palace of the Popes (standard Db-€140-170, bigger Db with terrace-€180-225, elaborate €18 buffet breakfast/brunch, 1 Rue Félicien David, tel. 04 90 16 42 00, www.hotel-avignon-horloge.com, hotel.horloge@hotels-ocre-azur.com).

$ Hôtel Médiéval**, burrowed deep a few blocks from the Church of St. Pierre, was built as a cardinal's home. This stone mansion's grand staircase leads to 35 comfortable, pastel rooms (Sb-€65, Db-€75-102, family rooms available, no elevator, 5 blocks east of Place de l'Horloge, behind Church of St. Pierre at 15 Rue Petite Saunerie, tel. 04 90 86 11 06, www.hotelmedieval.com, hotel.medieval@wanadoo.fr, run by helpful Régis).

Transportation

Getting Around Avignon

Avignon's walled city is compact, and all the major sights can be visited on foot. The streets are cobbled, so wear comfortable shoes.

Arriving and Departing

BY TRAIN

Avignon has two train stations: Centre-Ville and TGV. While most TGV trains serve only the TGV Station, some also stop at Centre-Ville— check your ticket and verify your station in advance.

Centre-Ville Station *(Gare Avignon Centre-Ville)*: This station gets all non-TGV trains and a few TGV trains. To reach the town center, cross the busy street in front of the station and walk through the city walls onto Cours Jean Jaurès (the TI is three blocks down).

Train Connections from Centre-Ville Station to: **Arles** (roughly hourly, 20 minutes, less frequent in the afternoon), **Carcassonne** (8/day, 7 with transfer in Narbonne or Nîmes, 3 hours).

TGV Station *(Gare TGV)*: On the outskirts of town, this station has a summer-only TI (short hours), but no baggage storage. Car rental, buses, and taxis are outside the north exit *(sortie nord)*. To reach the city center, take the **shuttle train** from platform A or B to Centre-Ville Station (€1.60, 2/hour, 5 minutes, buy ticket from machine on platform or at desk in main hall). A **taxi** ride between the TGV station and downtown Avignon costs about €15.

If you're connecting from the TGV Station to other points, you'll find **buses** to Arles' Centre-Ville train station at the second bus shelter (€9, 9/day, 1 hour, included with rail pass, schedule posted on shelter and available at info booths inside station). If you're **driving** a rental car directly to Arles or Les Baux, leave the station following signs to *Avignon Sud*, then *La Rocade*. You'll soon see exits to Arles (best for Les Baux, too).

Train Connections from TGV Station to: **Nice** (10/day, most by TGV, 4 hours, many require transfer in Marseille), Paris' Gare de Lyon (10/day direct, 2.5 hours; more connections with transfer, 3-4 hours), Paris' **Charles de Gaulle airport** (7/day, 3.25 hours).

BY BUS

The efficient bus station *(gare routière)* is 100 yards to the right as you leave the Centre-Ville train station, beyond and below Hôtel Ibis (info desk open Mon-Fri 8:00-19:30, Sat 10:00-12:30 & 13:30-18:00, closed Sun, tel. 04 90 82 07 35). Nearly all buses leave from this station (a few leave from the ring road outside the station—ask, buy tickets on bus, small bills only). Service is reduced or nonexistent on Sundays and holidays. Make sure to verify your destination with the driver.

Bus Connections from Avignon to: Pont du Gard (3/day, 50 minutes, departs from bus station), **Arles** (9/day, 1 hour, leaves from TGV Station), **Vaison-la-Romaine** and **Séguret** (3-6/day during the school year—*période scolaire*, 3/day otherwise; 1/day from TGV Station; 1.5 hours, all buses pass through Orange—faster to take train to Orange, and transfer to bus there).

BY CAR

Drivers entering Avignon follow *Centre-Ville* and *Gare SNCF* (train station) signs. You'll find central pay lots in the garage next to the Centre-Ville train station and at the Parking Jean Jaurès under the ramparts across from the station (enter the old city through the Porte St-Michel gate). Hotels have advice for overnight parking, and some offer parking deals.

Two free parking lots have complimentary shuttle buses to the center except on Sunday (follow *P Gratuit* signs): **Parking de l'Ile Piot** is across Daladier Bridge (Pont Daladier) on Ile de la Barthelasse, with shuttles to Place Crillon; **Parking des Italiens** is along the river east of the Palace of the Popes, with shuttles to Place Carnot (allow 30 minutes to walk from either to the center). Street parking is free in the *bleu* zones 12:00-14:00 and 19:00-9:00. (Hint: If you put €2 in the meter anytime between 19:00 and 9:00, you're good until 14:00.)

No matter where you park, leave nothing of value in your car.

NEAR ARLES AND AVIGNON

It's a short hop from Arles or Avignon to splendid scenery, Roman sights, warm stone villages, and world-class wine. See the great Roman Pont du Gard aqueduct; explore the ghost town that is ancient Les Baux; and spend time in pleasant Vaison-la-Romaine, a handy hub for the sunny Côtes du Rhône wine road.

Pont du Gard

Throughout the ancient world, aqueducts were like flags of stone that heralded the greatness of Rome. A visit to ▲▲▲ Pont du Gard still works to proclaim the wonders of that age. This impressively preserved Roman aqueduct was built in about 19 B.C., and while most of it is on or below the ground, at Pont du Gard it spans a canyon on a massive bridge over the Gardon River—one of the most remarkable surviving Roman ruins anywhere. The 30-mile aqueduct supported a small canal that, by dropping one inch for every 350 feet, supplied nine million gallons of water per day (about 100 gallons per second) to Nîmes—one of ancient Europe's largest cities. Allow about four or five hours for visiting Pont du Gard (including transportation time from Avignon).

Cost and Hours: €18/car (regardless of number of passengers), otherwise €7/person; aqueduct—daily until 24:00; museum—daily May-Sept 9:00-19:00,

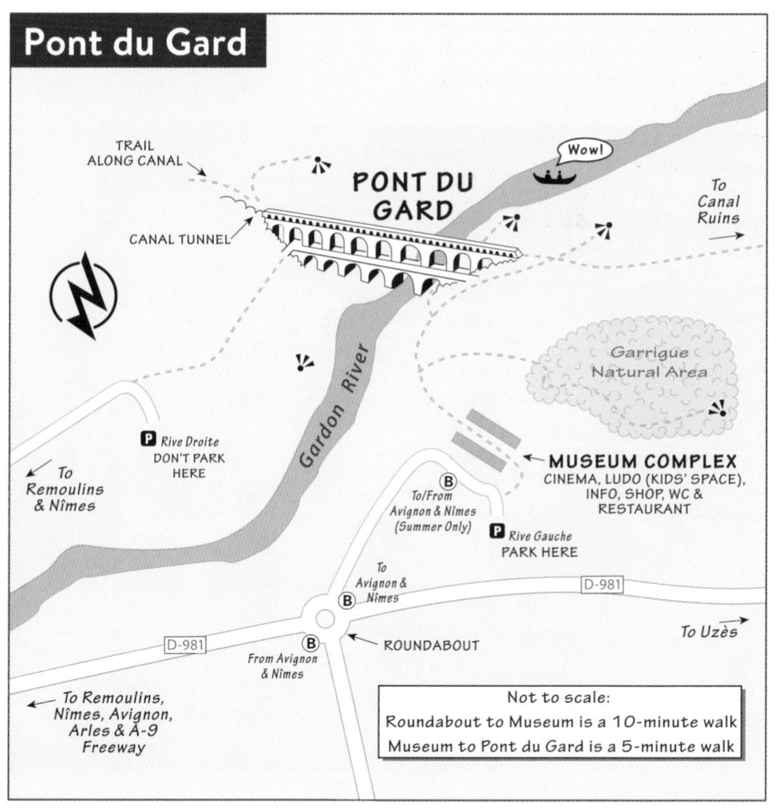

until 20:00 July-Aug, until 17:00 Oct-April, closed two weeks in Jan.

After Hours: The aqueduct is illuminated on summer evenings, and after the museum closes, you'll pay only €10 per carload to enter.

Getting There: The aqueduct is a 30-minute **drive** due west of Avignon (via N-100), and 45 minutes northwest of Arles (via Tarascon on D-6113). It's also reachable from Avignon by **bus** (3/day, 50 minutes), **taxi** (about €60), or **minivan tour** (Provence Reservation, also runs tours from Arles; see page 285).

Information: Tel. 04 66 37 59 99, www.pontdugard.fr.

Tours: In July and August, six tours a day go through the water channel at the top of the aqueduct (€4, check times posted at the museum and entry, no reservations are taken—limited to 33 people).

Canoe Rental: Floating under Pont du Gard by canoe is an unforgettable experience. **Collias Canoes** will pick you up at Pont du Gard (or elsewhere, if pre-arranged) and shuttle you to the town of Collias. You'll float down the river to the nearby town of Remoulins, where they'll pick you up and take you back to Pont du Gard (€21/person, €12/child under 12, usually 2 hours, though you can take as long as you like, reserve the day before in July-Aug, tel. 04 66 22 85 54).

Rick's Tip: *Pont du Gard is perhaps best enjoyed on your back and in the water—* **bring a swimsuit and flip-flops** *for the rocks. The best Pont du Gard viewpoints are up steep hills with uneven footing—* **bring good shoes, too.**

Visiting the Aqueduct: There are two riversides to Pont du Gard—the Left Bank (Rive Gauche) and Right Bank (Rive Droite). Park on the Rive Gauche, where you'll find the ticket booth and TI. You'll see the aqueduct in two parts: first the

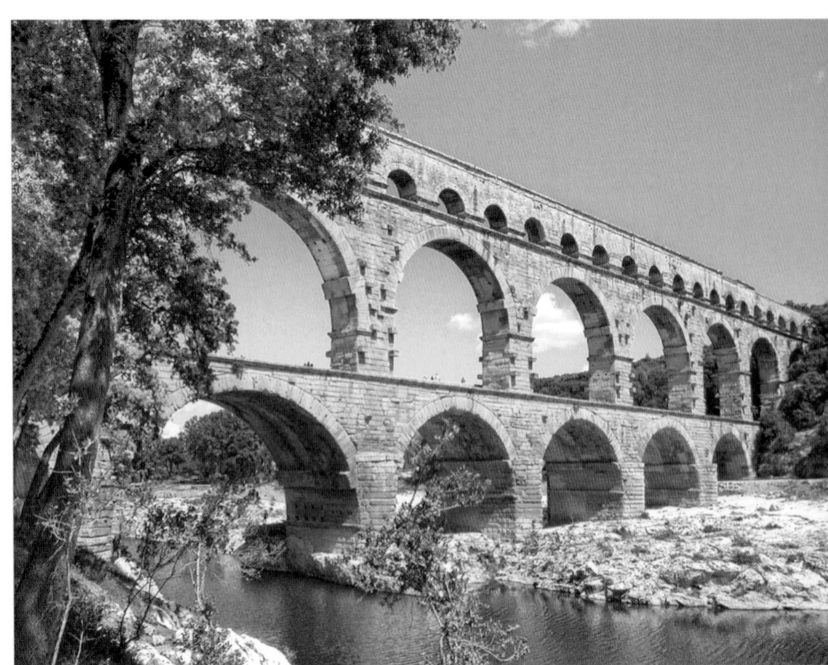

Pont du Gard

fine ▲ museum complex, then the actual river gorge spanned by the ancient bridge.

In the state-of-the-art **museum** (well-presented in English), you'll enter to the sound of water and understand the critical role fresh water played in the Roman "art of living." You'll see copies of lead pipes, faucets, and siphons; walk through a mock rock quarry; and learn how they moved those huge rocks into place and how those massive arches were made. A wooden model shows how Roman engineers determined the proper slope. While actual artifacts from the aqueduct are few, the exhibit shows the immensity of the undertaking as well as the payoff. Imagine the jubilation when this extravagant supply of water finally tumbled into Nîmes.

A park-like path leads to the **aqueduct.** Until a few years ago, this was an actual road—adjacent to the aqueduct—that had spanned the river since 1743. Before you cross the bridge, walk to the riverside viewpoint: Pass under the bridge and aqueduct and hike about 300 feet along the riverbank to the concrete steps leading down to a grand view of the world's second-highest standing Roman structure.

Ninety percent of the aqueduct is on or under the ground, but a few river canyons like this required bridges—and this was the biggest bridge in the whole 30-mile-long aqueduct. The arches are twice the width of standard aqueducts, and the main arch is the largest the Romans ever built—80 feet across (the width of the river). The bridge is about 160 feet high and was originally about 1,200 feet long.

A stone lid hides a four-foot-wide, six-foot-tall chamber lined with waterproof mortar that carried the stream for more than 400 years. For 150 years, this system provided Nîmes with good drinking water.

Hike over the bridge for a closer look and the best views. Steps lead up a high trail (marked *view point/panorama*) to a superb vista (go right at the top; best views are soon after the trail starts descending).

Les Baux

Tucked between Arles and Avignon, the hilltop town of Les Baux crowns the rugged Alpilles mountains. Many of the ancient walls of its striking castle still stand, a testament to the proud past of this village—now more a museum than a living town.

Orientation

Les Baux is actually two visits in one: castle ruins perched on an almost lunar landscape, and a medieval town below.

Day Plan: It's mobbed with tourists most of the day, but Les Baux rewards those who arrive by 9:00 or after 17:30. Savor the castle, then tour—or blitz—the lower streets on your way out. The lower town's polished-stone gauntlet of boutiques is a Provençal dream come true for shoppers.

Rick's Tip: *From Arles you can* **ride a rental bike to Les Baux** *(25 miles round-trip). It's a darn steep climb going into Les Baux, so consider busing up there (regional buses have bike racks) and gliding back.*

Getting There: Les Baux is a 20-minute **drive** from Arles: Follow signs for *Avignon*, then *Les Baux*. From Arles, Cartreize **bus #57** runs to Les Baux (daily July-Aug, Sat-Sun only in May-June and Sept, no service Oct-April, 6/day, 35 min-

A demonstration at Les Baux

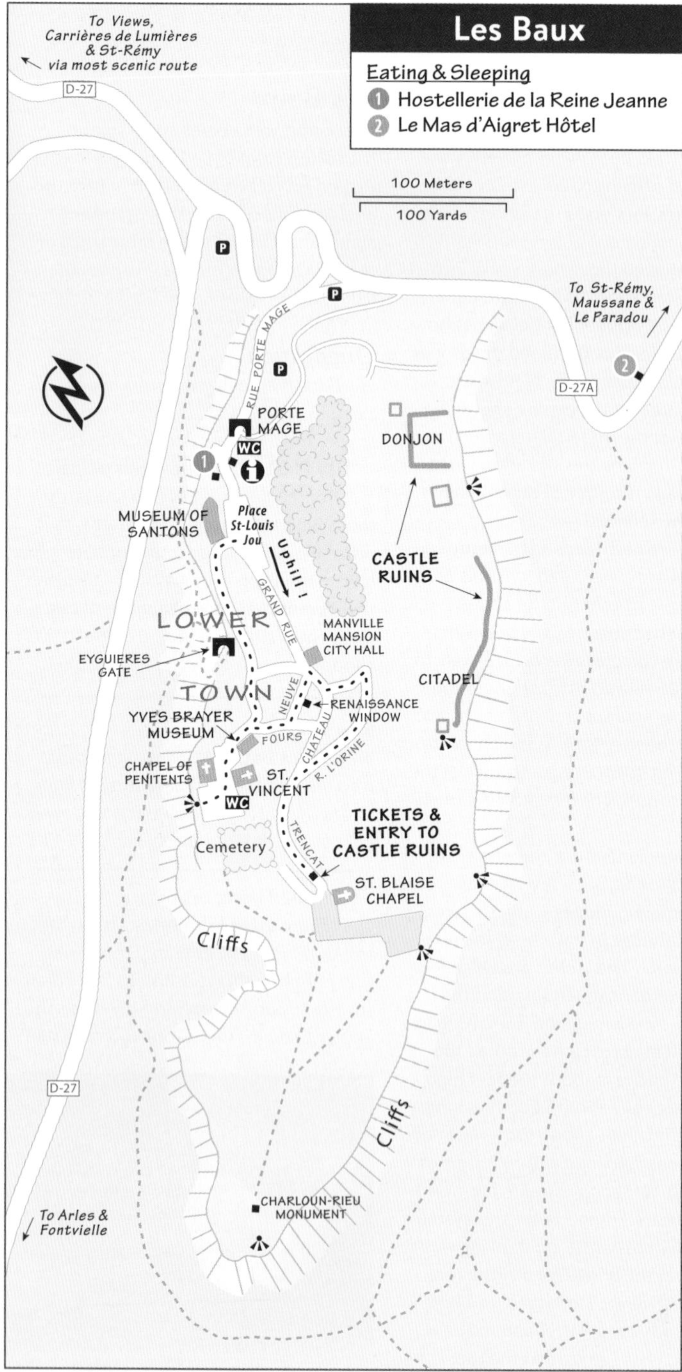
Les Baux
Eating & Sleeping
1 Hostellerie de la Reine Jeanne
2 Le Mas d'Aigret Hôtel
100 Meters
100 Yards
To Views, Carrières de Lumières & St-Rémy via most scenic route
D-27
To St-Rémy, Maussane & Le Paradou
D-27A
RUE PORTE MAGE
PORTE MAGE
WC
DONJON
MUSEUM OF SANTONS
Place St-Louis Jou
Uphill!
CASTLE RUINS
GRAND RUE
LOWER TOWN
MANVILLE MANSION CITY HALL
EYGUIERES GATE
CITADEL
NEUVE
RENAISSANCE WINDOW
YVES BRAYER MUSEUM
FOURS
CHATEAU
R. L'ORINE
CHAPEL OF PENITENTS
ST. VINCENT
TRENCAT
TICKETS & ENTRY TO CASTLE RUINS
Cemetery
ST. BLAISE CHAPEL
Cliffs
Cliffs
CHARLOUN-RIEU MONUMENT
To Arles & Fontvielle

utes, www.lepilote.com). The best option for many is a **minivan tour** from Arles or Avignon; consider Provence Reservation tours (see page 285).

Arrival in Les Baux: Drivers will find pay lots near the entrance to the village. Or park for free at the Carrières de Lumières (described later) and walk along the road to Les Baux. The cobbled street into town and up the main drag leads directly to the castle—just keep going uphill (10-minute walk).

Tourist Information: The TI is immediately on the left as you enter the village (daily April-Oct, closed Sun off-season).

Sights

▲▲▲THE CASTLE RUINS (CHATEAU DES BAUX)

The sun-bleached ruins of the stone fortress of Les Baux are carved into, out of, and on top of a rock 650 feet above the valley floor. Here you can imagine the struggles of a strong community of people who lived a rough-and-tumble life—more interested in top-notch fortifications than dramatic views.

In the 11th century, Les Baux was a powerhouse in southern France, controlling about 80 towns. The lords of Baux fought the counts of Barcelona for control of Provence...and eventually lost. Later, Les Baux struggled with the French kings, who destroyed the fortress in 1483 and again in 1632. The once-powerful town of 4,000 was forever crushed.

Cost and Hours: €8, €10 if there's entertainment (see next), €15 comboticket with Carrières de Lumières (described later), includes excellent audioguide, daily Easter-June and Sept 9:00-19:15, July-Aug 9:00-20:15, March and Oct 9:30-18:30, Nov-Feb 10:00-17:00, tel. 04 90 54 55 56, www.chateau-baux-provence.com.

Rick's Tip: Château des Baux *closes at the end of the day, but once you're inside, you can* **stay as long as you like.** *You're welcome to bring a picnic (no food sold inside) and live out your medieval fantasies, all night long.*

View from the Château des Baux

Entertainment: Every day from April through September, the castle presents medieval pageantry, tournaments, demonstrations, and jousting matches. Pick up a schedule as you enter (or check online).

Visiting the Castle: As you walk on the windblown spur (*baux* in French), you'll pass kid-thrilling medieval siege weaponry (go ahead, try the battering ram). Good displays help reconstruct the place. Imagine 4,000 people living up here. Notice the water-catchment system (a slanted field that caught rainwater and drained it into cisterns—necessary during a siege) and find the reservoir cut into the rock below the castle's highest point. Look for post holes throughout the stone walls that reveal where beams once supported floors. For the most sensational views, climb to the blustery top of the citadel. Hang on. The mistral wind just might blow you away.

▲LOWER TOWN

After your castle visit, you can shop and eat your way back through the lower town. Or, escape some of the crowds by dropping in at these minor but worthwhile sights as you descend. The 15th-century **City Hall** offers art exhibits under its cool vaults; the enjoyable Musée Yves Brayer lets you peruse three floors of Van Gogh-like Expressionist paintings; the 12th-century Romanesque **St. Vincent Church** was built short and wide to fit the terrain; and the free and fun **Museum of Santons** displays a collection of *santons* ("little saints"), popular folk figurines that decorate local Christmas mangers.

Castle ruins at Les Baux

▲CARRIERES DE LUMIERES (QUARRIES OF LIGHT)

A 10-minute walk from Les Baux, this colossal quarry-cave with immense vertical walls offers a mesmerizing sound-and-slide experience. The show lasts 40 minutes and runs continuously. Dress warmly, as the cave is cool.

Cost and Hours: €11, €16 combo-ticket with Les Baux castle ruins, daily April-Sept 9:30-19:30, March and Oct-Dec 10:00-18:00, closed Jan-Feb, tel. 04 90 54 47 37, www.carrieres-lumieres.com.

Eating and Sleeping

In the **lower town**, you'll find quiet view cafés such as **$ Hostellerie de la Reine Jeanne****, which also offers **$** good-value rooms (just inside the town gate, www.la-reinejeanne.com). A plusher overnight option is **$$ Le Mas d'Aigret*****, a 10-minute walk east of Les Baux on D-27 (www.masdaigret.com).

Vaison-la-Romaine

With quick access to vineyards and villages, this lively little town of 6,000 sits north of Avignon and makes a good base for exploring the Côtes du Rhône wine region. You get two villages for the price of one: The "modern" lower city has Roman ruins and a bustling main square—café-lined Place Montfort. The car-free medieval hill town looms above, with meandering cobbled lanes and a ruined castle with a fine view.

Le Mistral

Provence lives with its vicious mistral winds, which blow 30 to 60 miles per hour, about 100 days of the year. The mistral clears people off the streets and turns lively cities into ghost towns. You'll likely spend a few hours or days taking refuge.

When the mistral blows, you can't escape. Author Peter Mayle said it could blow the ears off a donkey (I'd include the tail). According to the natives, it ruins crops, shutters, and roofs (look for stones holding tiles in place on many homes). They'll also tell you that this pernicious wind has driven many people crazy (including young Vincent van Gogh).

The mistral starts above the Alps and Massif Central mountains, then gathers steam as it heads south, funneling through the Rhône Valley before exhausting itself when it hits the Mediterranean. And though this wind rattles shutters everywhere in the Riviera and Provence, it's strongest over the Rhône Valley...so Avignon, Arles, and the Côtes du Rhône villages bear its brunt. While wiping the dust from your eyes, remember the good news: The mistral brings clear skies.

Orientation

The city is split in two by the Ouvèze River. The town's Roman Bridge connects the lower town (Ville-Basse) with the hill-capping upper town (Ville-Haute).

Getting There: Bus service connects Avignon and Vaison-la-Romaine, usually via Orange (3-6/day, 1.5 hour; 1 express bus/day, 1 hour). Vaison-la-Romaine is about a 40-minute **drive** from Avignon.

Arrival in Vaison-la-Romaine: If you're riding the bus, tell the driver you want to go to the *Office de Tourisme.* From the bus stop, walk five minutes down Avenue Général de Gaulle to reach the TI. Drivers should follow signs to *Centre-Ville,* then *Office de Tourisme;* parking is free across from the TI and at most places in town.

Tourist Information: The superb TI is in the lower city, between the two Roman ruin sites, at Place du Chanoine Sautel (daily but closed Sun off-season, tel. 04 90 36 02 11, www.vaison-ventoux-tourisme.com).

Private Guide: For historic town walks, try **Anna-Marie Melard** (tel. 04 90 36 50 48) or **Janet Henderson** (www.provencehistorytours.com).

Cooking Classes: Charming Barbara Schuerenberg offers reasonably priced cooking classes from her view home (€80, cash only, includes lunch, www.cuisinedeprovence.com).

Sights

ROMAN RUINS

Ancient Vaison-la-Romaine had a treaty that gave it a preferred "federated" relationship with Rome. This, along with a healthy farming economy (olives and vineyards), made it a prosperous place, as a close look at its sprawling ruins demonstrates.

Cost and Hours: €8; daily April-May 9:30-18:00, June-Sept until 18:30, shorter hours off-season, closed Jan-Feb; videoguide-€3 or download free app, tel. 04 90 36 50 48, www.vaison-la-romaine.com.

Visiting the Ruins: Vaison-la-Romaine's Roman ruins are split by a modern road into two sites: Puymin and La Villasse. Each is well-presented, thanks to the videoguide and information panels, offering a good look at life during the Roman Empire. What you can see is only a small fraction of the ancient town's extent—most is still buried under today's city.

Visit **Puymin** first. Nearest the entry are the scant but impressive ruins of a sprawling mansion. Find the faint remains of a colorful frescoed wall. Climb the hill

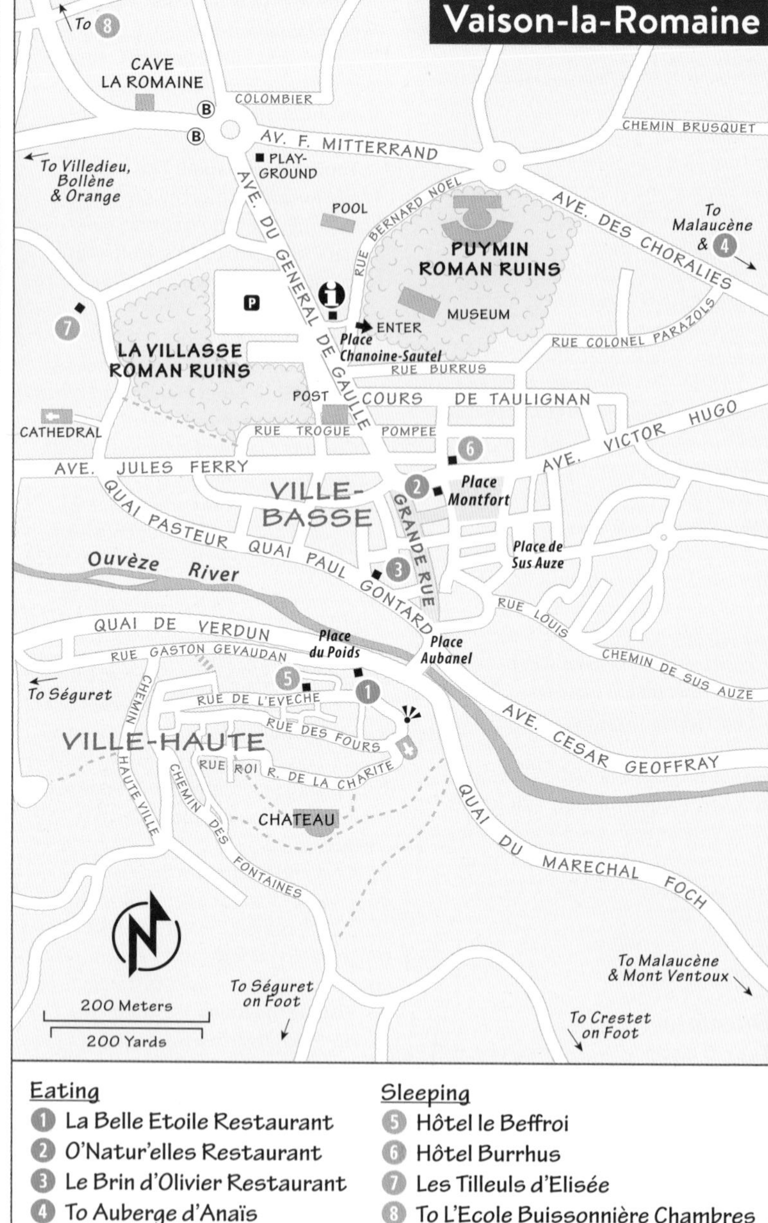

Eating

1. La Belle Etoile Restaurant
2. O'Natur'elles Restaurant
3. Le Brin d'Olivier Restaurant
4. To Auberge d'Anaïs

Sleeping

5. Hôtel le Beffroi
6. Hôtel Burrhus
7. Les Tilleuls d'Elisée
8. To L'Ecole Buissonnière Chambres

to the good little **museum** (pick up your videoguide here). Be sure to see the **3-D film** that takes you inside the home of a wealthy Vaison resident and explores daily life some 2,000 years ago. Behind the museum is a still well-used, 6,000-seat theater, with just enough seats for the whole town (of yesterday and today).

Back across the modern road in **La Villasse,** you'll explore a "street of shops" and the foundations of more houses. You'll also see a few wells, used before Vaison's two aqueducts were built.

LOWER TOWN (VILLE-BASSE)

Vaison-la-Romaine's modern town centers on café-friendly Place Montfort. A 10-minute walk below Place Montfort, the stout **Notre-Dame de Nazareth Cathedral** is a good example of Provençal Romanesque dating from the 11th century, with an evocative cloister and fine stone carvings (free, daily, closed Oct-March). The pedestrian-only Grand Rue is a lively shopping street leading to the small river gorge and the **Roman Bridge,** a sturdy, no-nonsense vault cut by the Romans into the canyon rock 2,000 years ago.

UPPER TOWN (VILLE-HAUTE)

Although there's nothing of particular importance to see in the fortified medieval old town atop the hill, the cobbled lanes and enchanting fountains make you want to break out a sketchpad. Vaison-la-Romaine was ruled by a prince-bishop starting in the fourth century. He came under attack by the Count of Toulouse in the 12th century. Anticipating a struggle, the prince-bishop abandoned the lower town and built a castle on this rocky outcrop (about 1195). Over time, the townspeople followed, vacating the lower town and building their homes at the base of the château behind the upper town's fortified wall.

To reach the upper town, hike up from the Roman Bridge through the medieval gate, under the lone tower crowned by an 18th-century wrought-iron bell cage. The château is closed, but a steep, uneven trail to its base rewards hikers with a sweeping view.

Vaison-la-Romaine's ancient theater

▲HIKING AND BIKING

The hills above Vaison-la-Romaine are picture-perfect for hikers and bikers. The TI has good information on your options, and can direct you to bike-rental shops. For destinations, consider the quiet hill town of Crestet, cute little Séguret, or delightful Villedieu.

Eating

$$ La Belle Etoile is where locals go for fresh, good-value meals (closed Thu, 5 Rue du Pont Romain). **$$ O'Natur'elles** is ideal for vegetarians; the all-organic dishes can be served with or without meat (reservations smart, closed Tue eve, tel. 04 90 65 81 67). Romantic **$$$ Le Patio** has soft lighting and good food (closed Wed eve and Sat lunch, 4 Rue du Ventoux). With a car, drive 10 minutes east from town to **$$ Auberge d'Anaïs** for a true Provençal experience—ask for a table *sur la terrasse* (closed Sun eve and Mon, on the road to St-Marcellin, tel. 04 90 36 20 06).

Sleeping

In the upper town, try the cozy **$$ Hôtel le Beffroi***** (www.le-beffroi.com); in the lower town, two good choices are **$ Hôtel Burrhus**** (1 Place Montfort, www.burrhus.com) and **$ Les Tilleuls d'Elisée** (1 Avenue Jules Mazen, www.vaisonchambres.info). Drivers will enjoy a stay at **$ L'Ecole Buissonnière Chambres,** a restored farmhouse 10 minutes north of town (cash only, between Villedieu and Buisson on D-75, www.buissonniere-provence.com).

Rick's Tip: *Sleep in Vaison-la-Romaine on Monday night, and you'll wake to an amazing* **Tuesday market,** *one of France's best. But be* **careful where you park:** *Avoid anyplace signed* Stationnement Interdit le Mardi *(parking forbidden on Tuesday), or you won't find your car where you left it.*

Côtes du Rhône Wine Road

To experience the best of the Côtes du Rhône vineyards and villages, take this half-day ▲▲▲ loop around the rugged Dentelles de Montmirail mountain peaks (figure about 40 miles total; see map on facing page). You'll experience the finest this region has to offer: natural beauty, glowing limestone villages, inviting wineries, and rolling hills of vineyards.

Start just south of Vaison-la-Romaine in little **Séguret.** This town is best for a visit early or late, when it's quieter. Explore the village (ideal for a morning coffee break), then drive up and up to the **Domaine de Mourchon** winery. From here, return to Vaison-la-Romaine and follow signs toward *Carpentras/Malaucène*, pass through Crestet, then follow signs leading up to *Le Village* (D-76).

After ambling the quiet village of **Crestet,** follow signs to *Malaucène* and turn right on D-90 (direction: Suzette) just before the gas station. The D-90 route is the scenic highlight of this loop, which follows the back side of the Dentelles de Montmirail past mountain views, remote villages, and beautifully situated wineries (**Domaine de Coyeux** is best).

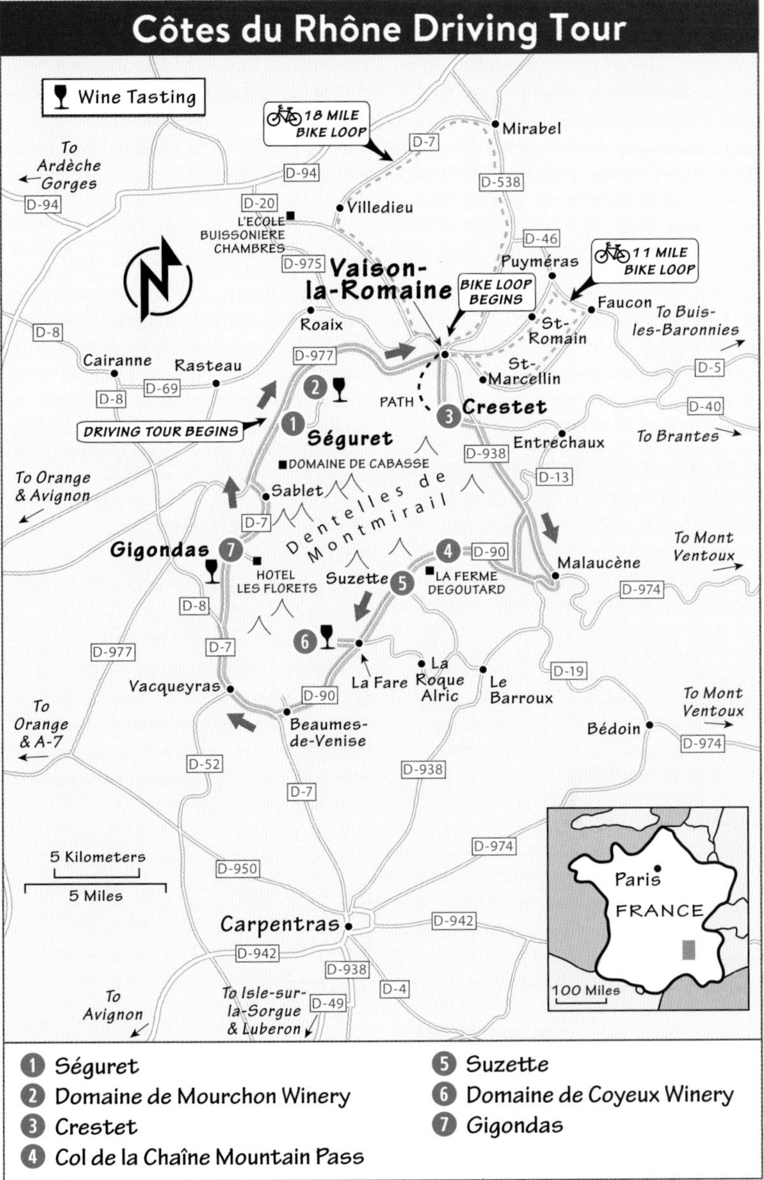

Take your time for this drive: You'll pass trailheads, scenic pullouts, and good picnic spots. Consider lunch along the way.

D-90 ends in Beaumes de Venise. Follow signs back toward *Vaison-la-Romaine* to **Gigondas** and explore this village.

Self-Guided Tour

1 SEGURET

Séguret's name comes from the Latin word *securitas* (meaning "security"). The bulky entry arch came with a massive gate, which drilled in the message of the village's name. In the Middle Ages, Séguret was patrolled 24/7—they never took their *securitas* for granted. Walk through the arch. To appreciate how the homes' outer walls provided security in those days, drop down the first passage on your right (near the fountain). These exit passages, or *poternes,* were needed in periods of peace to allow the town to expand below. Wander deep. Rue Calade leads up to the unusual 12th-century St. Denis church for views (the circular village you see below is Sablet). Make your way down to the main drag and a café, and return to parking along Rue des Poternes.

❷ DOMAINE DE MOURCHON WINERY

This high-flying winery blends state-of-the-art technology with traditional winemaking methods (a shiny ring of stainless-steel vats holds grapes grown on land plowed by horses). Free and informative English tours of the vineyards are usually offered (wines-€8-33/bottle; winery open Mon-Sat 9:00-18:00, Sun by appointment only; from Easter-Sept, call to verify; tel. 04 90 46 70 30, www.domainedemourchon.com).

❸ CRESTET

This village—founded after the fall of the Roman Empire, when people banded together in high places like this for protection from marauding barbarians—followed the usual hill-town evolution. The outer walls of the village did double duty as ramparts and house walls. The castle above (from about A.D. 850) provided a final safe haven when the village was attacked.

Wander the peaceful lanes and appreciate the amount of work it took to put these stones in place. Notice the elaborate water channels. Crestet was served by 18 cisterns in the Middle Ages. The peaceful (usually closed) church has a beautiful stained-glass window behind the altar. Imagine hundreds of people living here and animals roaming everywhere. Get to the top of town. Signs from the top of the village lead to the footpath to Vaison-la-Romaine. The café-restaurant **Le Panoramic,** at the top of old **Crestet,** must have Provence's greatest view tables (closed Dec-March).

The village of Séguret

❹ COL DE LA CHAINE MOUNTAIN PASS

Get out of your car at the pass (elevation: about 1,500 feet) and enjoy the breezy views. Wander about. The peaks in the distance—thrusting up like the back of a stegosaurus or a bad haircut (you decide)—are the Dentelles de Montmirail, a small range running just nine miles basically north to south and reaching 2,400 feet in elevation.

Now turn around and face Mont Ventoux. Are there clouds on the horizon? You're looking into the eyes of the Alps (behind Ventoux), and those "foothills" help keep Provence sunny.

❺ SUZETTE

Tiny Suzette floats on its hilltop, with a small 12th-century chapel, one café, a handful of residents, and the gaggle of houses where they live. Park in Suzette's lot, below, then find the big orientation board above the lot. Look out to the broad shoulders of Mont Ventoux. At 6,000 feet, it always seems to have some clouds hanging around. If it's clear, the top looks like it's snow-covered; if you drive up there, you'll see it's actually white stone.

6 DOMAINE DE COYEUX WINERY

A private road winds up and up to this impossibly beautiful setting, with the best views of the Dentelles I've found. Olive trees frame the final approach, and *Le Caveau* signs lead to a modern tasting room (you may need to ring the buzzer). This stop is for serious wine lovers—skip it if you only want a quick taste or are not interested in buying (wines-€8-16/bottle; winery generally open daily 10:00-12:00 & 14:00-18:00, except closed Sun off-season and no midday closure July-Aug; tel. 04 90 12 42 42, http://domainedecoyeux.com/en, some English spoken).

7 GIGONDAS

This town produces some of the region's best reds and is ideally situated for hiking, mountain biking, and driving into the mountains. The **TI** has lists of wineries, rental bikes, and tips for good hikes or drives (Mon-Sat 10:00-12:30 & 14:00-18:00, closed Sun, Place du Portail, tel. 04 90 65 85 46, www.gigondas-dm.fr). Take a short walk through the village lanes above the TI—the church is an easy destination with good views over the heart of the Côtes du Rhône vineyards.

You'll find several good tasting opportunities on the main square; **Le Caveau de Gigondas** is the best (daily 10:00-12:00 & 14:00-18:30, near TI, www.caveaudugigondas.com). The restaurant at **Hôtel les Florets,** serving classic French cuisine with Provençal accents, is well worth it—particularly if you dine on the magnificent terrace (closed Wed, service can be slow).

A *Wine tasting in the Côtes du Rhône*
B *Vineyards of Domaine de Coyeux*
C *Côtes du Rhône vineyards*
D *Café in Suzette*

The French Riviera

A hundred years ago, celebrities from London to Moscow flocked to the French Riviera to socialize, gamble, and escape the dreary weather at home. Today, budget vacationers and heat-seeking Europeans fill belle époque resorts at France's most sought-after fun-in-the-sun destination.

Some of the Continent's most stunning scenery and intriguing museums lie along this strip of land—as do millions of sun-worshipping tourists. The Riviera's gateway is urban Nice, with world-class museums, a splendid beachfront promenade, a seductive old town, the best selection of hotels in all price ranges, and good nightlife options.

This sunny sliver of land is well served by public transportation, making day trips by train or bus almost effortless. If you drive here, expect traffic—although you'll be rewarded with sensational views on the coastal routes. If you head east from Nice, you'll find little Villefranche-sur-Mer staring across the bay at exclusive Cap Ferrat. Farther along, Monaco offers a royal welcome and a fairytale past. To the west, Antibes has a thriving port and silky sand beaches. Wherever you choose to spend your days, evenings everywhere on the Riviera are radiant—made for a promenade and outdoor dining.

THE FRENCH RIVIERA IN 2 DAYS

My favorite home bases are Nice, Villefranche-sur-Mer, and Antibes. Nice, with convenient train and bus connections to most regional sights, is the most practical base for train travelers. Villefranche-sur-Mer is the romantic's choice, with a peaceful setting and small-town warmth, while midsize Antibes has the best beaches and works best for drivers.

Allow a full day for Nice: Spend your morning sifting through the old city (called Vieux Nice; take my Old Nice Walk) and ascend the elevator up Castle Hill for fine views. Devote the afternoon to the museums (Chagall is best, closed Tue) and strolling the Promenade des Anglais, taking my self-guided walk (best before or after dinner, but anytime is fine).

Save most of your second day for Monaco (tour Monaco-Ville, have lunch, and drop by the famous Monte Carlo casino), then consider a late afternoon or dinner in Villefranche-sur-Mer. With more time, explore Antibes' fine Picasso Museum and sandy old town. Or stop by lush Cap Ferrat, filled with mansions, gardens, and beaches.

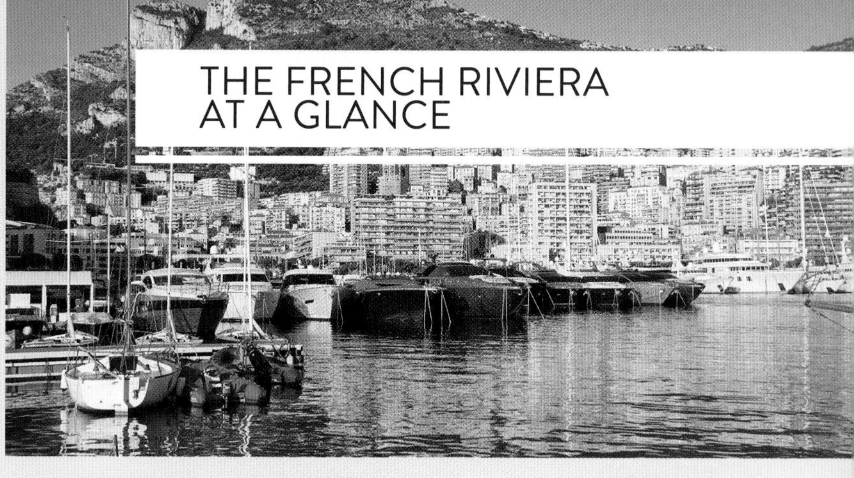

THE FRENCH RIVIERA AT A GLANCE

Nice

▲▲▲**Promenade des Anglais Walk** Nice's sunstruck seafront promenade. **Hours:** Always open. See page 336.

▲▲▲**Chagall Museum** The world's largest collection of Marc Chagall's work, popular even with people who don't like modern art. **Hours:** May-Oct Wed-Mon 10:00-18:00, Nov-April until 17:00, closed Tue year-round. See page 344.

▲▲**Old Nice Walk** Exploring the enjoyable old city, with its charming French-Italian cultural blend. **Hours:** Always open. See page 341.

▲**Matisse Museum** Modest collection of Henri Matisse's paintings, sketches, and paper cutouts. **Hours:** Wed-Mon 10:00-18:00, closed Tue. See page 346.

▲**Russian Cathedral** Finest Orthodox church outside Russia. **Hours:** Mon 13:30-17:00, Tue-Sun 10:00-17:00. See page 347.

▲**Castle Hill** Site of an ancient fort boasting great views. **Hours:** Park closes at 20:00 in summer, earlier off-season. See page 347.

Nearby

▲▲▲**Villefranche-sur-Mer** Romantic Italianate beach town with a serene setting, yacht-filled harbor, and small-town ambience. See page 359.

▲▲▲**Monaco** Tiny independent municipality known for its classy casino and Grand Prix car race. See page 365.

▲▲**Cap Ferrat** Exclusive, woodsy peninsula with a family-friendly beach and tourable Rothschild mansion. See page 363.

▲▲**Antibes** Laid-back beach town with a medieval center, worthwhile Picasso Museum (closed Mon), sandy beaches, and view-strewn hikes. See page 371.

NICE

Nice (sounds like "niece"), with its spectacular Alps-to-Mediterranean surroundings, is the big-city highlight of the Riviera. Its traffic-free old town mixes Italian and French flavors to create a spicy Mediterranean dressing, while its big squares, broad seaside walkways, and long beaches invite lounging and people-watching. Nice may be nice, but it's hot and jammed in July and August—reserve ahead and get a room with air-conditioning.

Orientation

The main points of interest lie between the beach and the train tracks (about 15 blocks apart). The city revolves around its grand Place Masséna, where pedestrian-friendly Avenue Jean Médecin meets Vieux (Old) Nice and the Albert I parkway (with quick access to the beaches). It's a 20-minute walk (or about €12 by taxi) from the train station to the beach, and a 20-minute stroll along the promenade from the fancy Hôtel Negresco to the heart of Vieux Nice.

Everything you'll want to see in Nice is either within walking distance, or a short bike, bus, or tram ride away. A 10-minute ride on the smooth-as-silk tram through the center of the city connects the train station, Place Masséna, Vieux Nice, and the port (from nearby Place Garibaldi).

Tourist Information: Nice has several helpful TIs (tel. 08 92 70 74 07, www.nicetourisme.com), including branches at the **airport** (daily 9:00-18:00, April-Sept until 20:00), the **train station** (summer, daily 8:00-20:00, rest of year Mon-Sat 9:00-19:00, Sun 10:00-17:00), at 5 **Promenade des Anglais** (daily 9:00-18:00, July-Aug until 20:00), and on the north side of **Place Masséna** (May-mid-Sept only, daily 10:00-17:00). Ask for day-trip information, including details on boat excursions, and train and bus schedules.

Theft Alert: Nice has its share of pickpockets (especially at the train station, on the tram, and trolling the beach). Stick to main streets in Vieux Nice after dark.

SNCF Boutique: A French rail ticket office is a half-block west of Avenue Jean Médecin at 2 Rue de la Liberté (Mon-Fri 10:00-17:50, closed Sat-Sun).

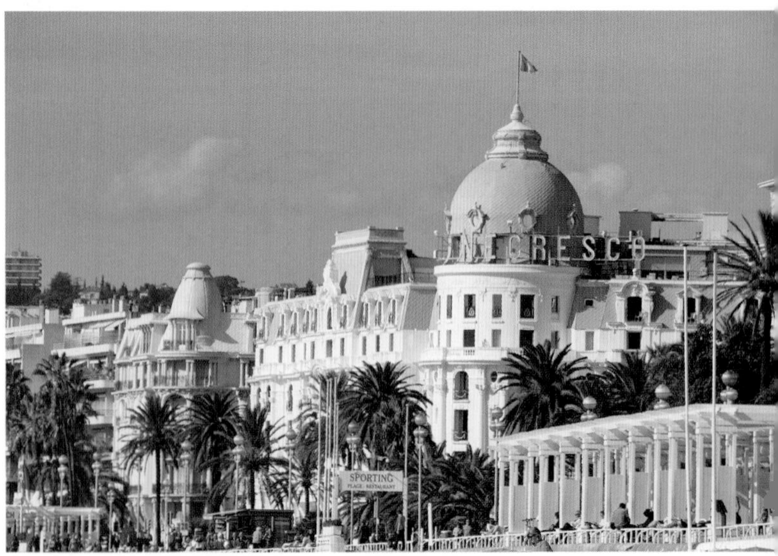

Nice's historic Hôtel Negresco overlooks the Promenade des Anglais.

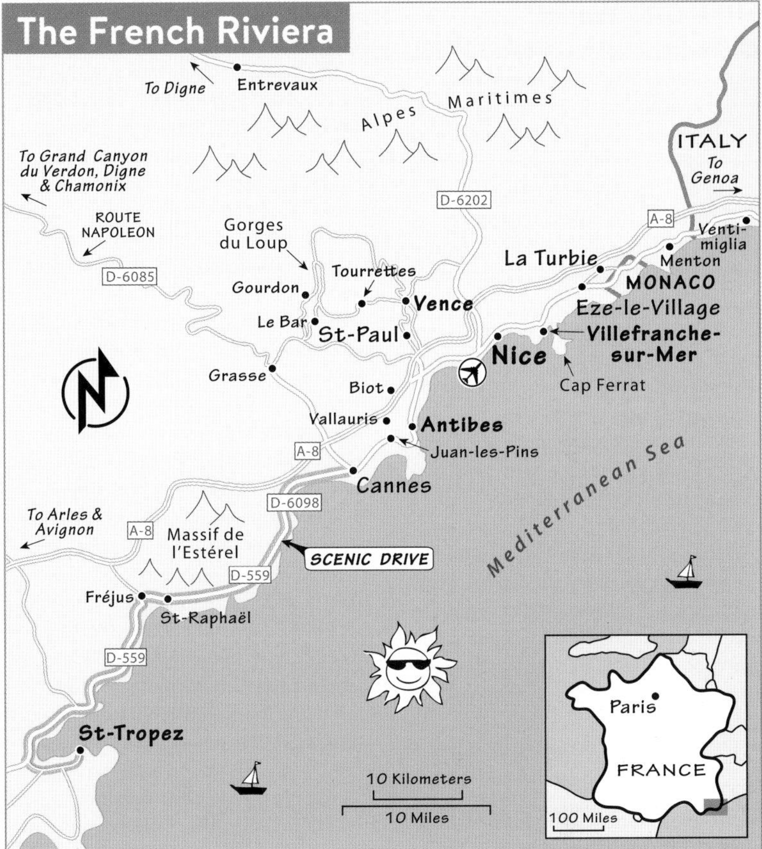

Renting a Bike (and Other Wheels): Holiday Bikes has multiple locations, including one across from the train station, and they have electric bikes (www.loca-bike.fr). **Roller Station** is well-situated near the sea and rents bikes, rollerblades, skateboards, and Razor-style scooters (bikes-€5/hour, €10/half-day, €15/day, leave ID as deposit, open daily, next to yellow awnings of Pailin's Asian restaurant at 49 Quai des Etats-Unis, tel. 04 93 62 99 05).

Private Guide: Consider **Pascale Rucker,** an art-loving guide who teaches with the joy and wonder of a flower child (€160/half-day, €260/day, tel. 06 16 24 29 52, pascalerucker@gmail.com).

Minivan Tours: These two energetic and delightful women have comfortable minibuses and enjoy taking couples and small groups anywhere in the region: **Sylvie Di Cristo** (€600/day, €350/half-day for up to 8 people, mobile 06 09 88 83 83, www.frenchrivieraguides.net, dicristosylvie@gmail.com) and **Ingrid Schmucker** (€490/day for 4 people or €550/day for 5-7 people, €180/half-day or €285/day if you don't need transportation, tel. 06 14 83 03 33, www.kultours.fr, info@kultours.fr). The TI and most hotels have information on more economic shared minivan excursions from Nice (roughly €50-70/person per half-day, €80-120/person per day).

Nice City Walks

➲ *Promenade des Anglais Walk*

This leisurely, level self-guided walk, worth ▲▲▲, is a straight line along this much-strolled beachfront. It begins near the landmark Hôtel Negresco and ends just before Castle Hill. While this one-mile section is enjoyable at any time, the first half makes a great pre- or post-dinner stroll (perhaps with a dinner on the beach). If you plan to extend this stroll to Castle Hill, try to time it so you end up on top of the hill at sunset. Allow one hour at a promenade pace to reach the elevator up to Castle Hill.

Biking the Promenade: To rev up the pace of your promenade, rent a bike and glide along the coast in either or both directions (about 30 minutes each way; for rental info, see page 335). The path to the **west** stops just before the airport at perhaps the most scenic *boules* courts in France. If you take the path heading **east,** you'll round Castle Hill to the harbor of Nice, with a chance to survey some fancy yachts.

• *Start your walk at the pink-domed...*

HOTEL NEGRESCO

Nice's finest hotel is also a historic monument, offering up the city's most expensive beds and a museum-like interior. While the hotel is off-limits to nonguests, the doorman explained to me that shoppers and drinkers are "guests" as much as people actually sleeping there. So if you say you're going in for a drink (at their pricey Le Bar du Negresco) or to shop, you may be allowed in.

Biking the promenade

The huge ballroom (walk straight until you see the big chandelier) is the **Salon Royal.** The chandelier hanging from its Eiffel-built dome is made of 16,000 pieces of crystal. It was built in France for the Russian czar's Moscow palace...but thanks to the Bolshevik Revolution in 1917, he couldn't take delivery. Bronze portrait busts of Czar Alexander III and his wife, Maria Feodorovna—who returned to her native Denmark after the revolution—are to the right, facing the shops. Circle the interior and then the perimeter to enjoy both historic and modern art. Fine portraits include Emperor Napoleon III and wife, Empress Eugénie (who acquired Nice for France from Italy in 1860), and Jeanne Augier (who owns the hotel).

If you wonder why such a grand hotel has such an understated entry, it's because today's front door was originally the back door. In the 19th century, elegant people stayed out of the sun, and any posh hotel that cared about its clientele would design its entry on the shady north side. If you walk around to the back you'll see a grand but unused front door.

• *Across the street from Hôtel Negresco is...*

VILLA MASSENA

When Nice became part of France, France invested heavily in what it expected to be the country's new high society retreat—an elite resort akin to Russia's Sochi on the Black Sea. The government built this fine palace for the military hero of the Napoleonic age, Jean-Andre Masséna and his family. Take a moment to stroll around the lovely garden (free, daily 10:00-18:00).

• *From Villa Masséna, head for the beach and begin your Promenade des Anglais stroll. But first, grab a blue chair and gaze out to the...*

BAY OF ANGELS (BAIE DES ANGES)

Face the water. The body of Nice's patron saint, Réparate, was supposedly escorted into this bay by angels in the fourth century. To your right is where you might have been escorted into France—Nice's airport, built on a massive landfill. The tip of land beyond the runway is Cap d'Antibes. Until 1860, Antibes and Nice were in different countries—Antibes was French, but Nice was a protectorate of the Italian kingdom of Savoy-Piedmont, a.k.a. the Kingdom of Sardinia. During that period, the Var River—just west of Nice—was the geographic border between these two peoples. In 1850 the people here spoke Italian and ate pasta. As Italy was uniting, the region was given a choice: Join the new country of Italy or join France (which was enjoying prosperous times under the rule of Napoleon III). The vast majority voted in 1860 to go French...and *voilà!* (In reality, the Italian king needed France's support in helping Italian regions controlled by Austria break away to join the emerging union of Italian states. Italy's price for France's support against Austria: Nice.)

The lower green hill to your left is Castle Hill. Farther left lie Villefranche-sur-Mer and Cap Ferrat (marked by the tower at land's end, and home to lots of millionaires), then Monaco (which you can't see, with more millionaires), then Italy. Behind you are the foothills of the Alps, which trap threatening clouds, ensuring that the Côte d'Azur enjoys sunshine more than 300 days each year.

• *With the sea on your right, begin strolling.*

THE PROMENADE

Nearby sit two fine belle époque establishments: the West End and Westminster hotels, both boasting English names to help those original guests feel at home (the West End is now part of the Best Western group...to help American guests feel at home). These hotels symbolize Nice's arrival as a tourist mecca in the 19th century, when the combination of leisure time and a stable economy allowed visitors to find the sun even in winter.

As you walk, be careful to avoid the green bike lane. You'll pass a number of separate rocky beaches. You can go local and rent gear—about €15 for a *chaise longue* (long chair) and a *transat* (mattress), €5 for an umbrella, and €4 for a towel. You'll also pass several beach restaurants. Some of these eateries serve breakfast, all serve lunch, some do dinner, and a few have beachy bars...tailor-made for a break from this walk. (Plage Beau

The Bay of Angels epitomizes the beauty of the French Riviera.

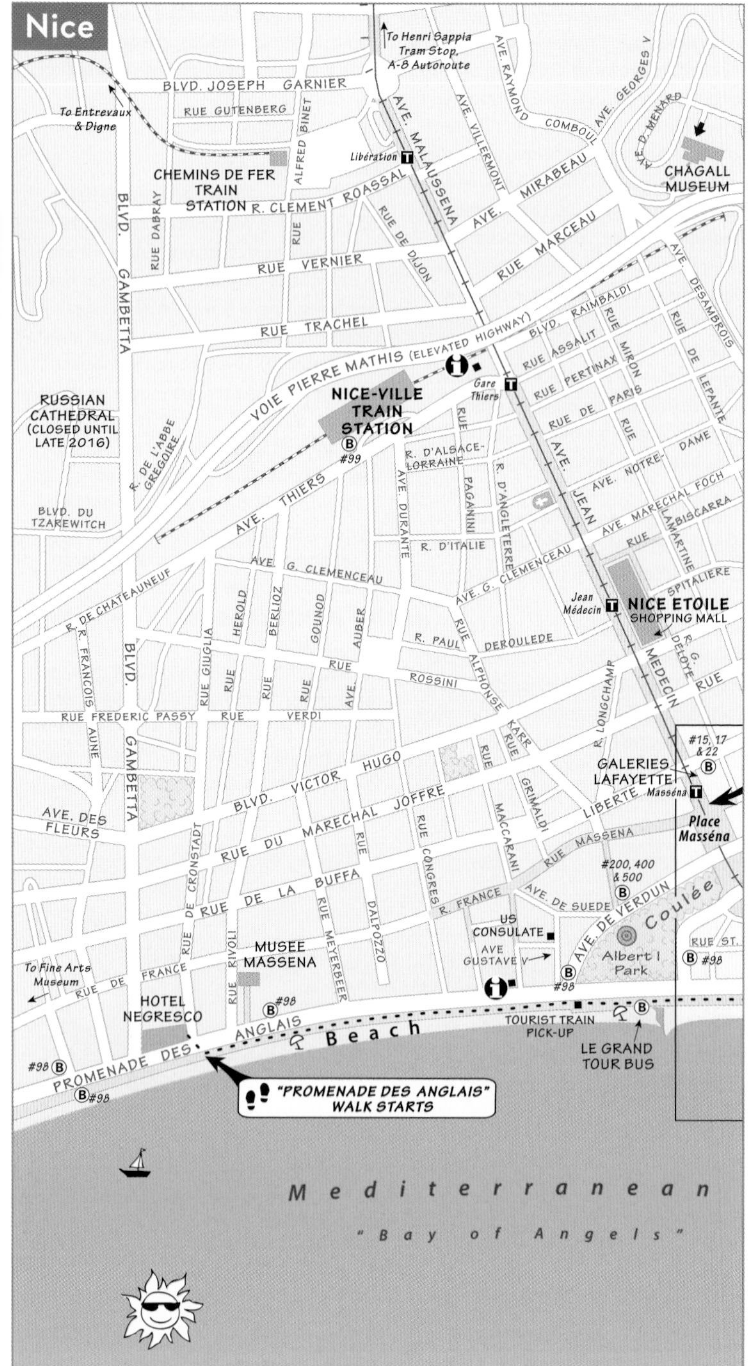
Nice
To Henri Sappia Tram Stop, A-8 Autoroute
To Entrevaux & Digne
BLVD. JOSEPH GARNIER
RUE GUTENBERG
ALFRED BINET
CHEMINS DE FER TRAIN STATION
Libération
AVE. MALAUSSENA
AVE. VILLERMONT
AVE. RAYMOND COMBOUL
AVE. GEORGES V
AVE. D. MENARD
CHAGALL MUSEUM
AVE. MIRABEAU
R. CLEMENT ROASSAL
RUE DE DIJON
RUE DABRAY
BLVD. GAMBETTA
RUE VERNIER
RUE MARCEAU
RUE TRACHEL
VOIE PIERRE MATHIS (ELEVATED HIGHWAY)
BLVD. RAIMBALDI
AVE. DESAMBROIS
RUE ASSALIT
RUE PERTINAX
RUE MIRON
RUE DE PARIS
RUE DE LEPANTE
Gare Thiers
NICE-VILLE TRAIN STATION
#99
RUSSIAN CATHEDRAL (CLOSED UNTIL LATE 2016)
R. DE L'ABBE GREGOIRE
R. D'ALSACE-LORRAINE
AVE. NOTRE-DAME
AVE. JEAN MEDECIN
AVE. THIERS
AVE. DURANTE
PAGANINI
R. D'ANGLETERRE
AVE. MARECHAL FOCH
RUE BISCARRA
RUE LAMARTINE
BLVD. DU TZAREWITCH
R. D'ITALIE
AVE. G. CLEMENCEAU
SPITALIERE
R. DE CHATEAUNEUF
Jean Médecin
NICE ETOILE SHOPPING MALL
HEROLD
BERLIOZ
GOUNOD
AUBER
R. PAUL DEROULEDE
RUE ALPHONSE KARR
R. G. DELOYE
R. FRANCOIS AUNE
RUE GIUGLIA
RUE ROSSINI
RUE VERDI
RUE FREDERIC PASSY
R. LONGCHAMP
#15, 17 & 22
GALERIES LAFAYETTE
Masséna
Place Masséna
BLVD. VICTOR HUGO
LIBERTE
AVE. DES FLEURS
RUE DU MARECHAL JOFFRE
RUE GRIMALDI
MACCARANI
RUE CONGRES
RUE MASSENA
RUE DE CRONSTADT
RUE DE LA BUFFA
#200, 400 & 500
R. FRANCE
AVE. DE SUEDE
AVE. DE VERDUN
Coulée
RUE MEYERBEER
DALPOZZO
RUE RIVOLI
MUSEE MASSENA
US CONSULATE
AVE GUSTAVE V
Albert I Park
RUE ST.
#98
To Fine Arts Museum
RUE DE FRANCE
HOTEL NEGRESCO
PROMENADE DES ANGLAIS
Beach
TOURIST TRAIN PICK-UP
LE GRAND TOUR BUS
"PROMENADE DES ANGLAIS" WALK STARTS
Mediterranean
"Bay of Angels"

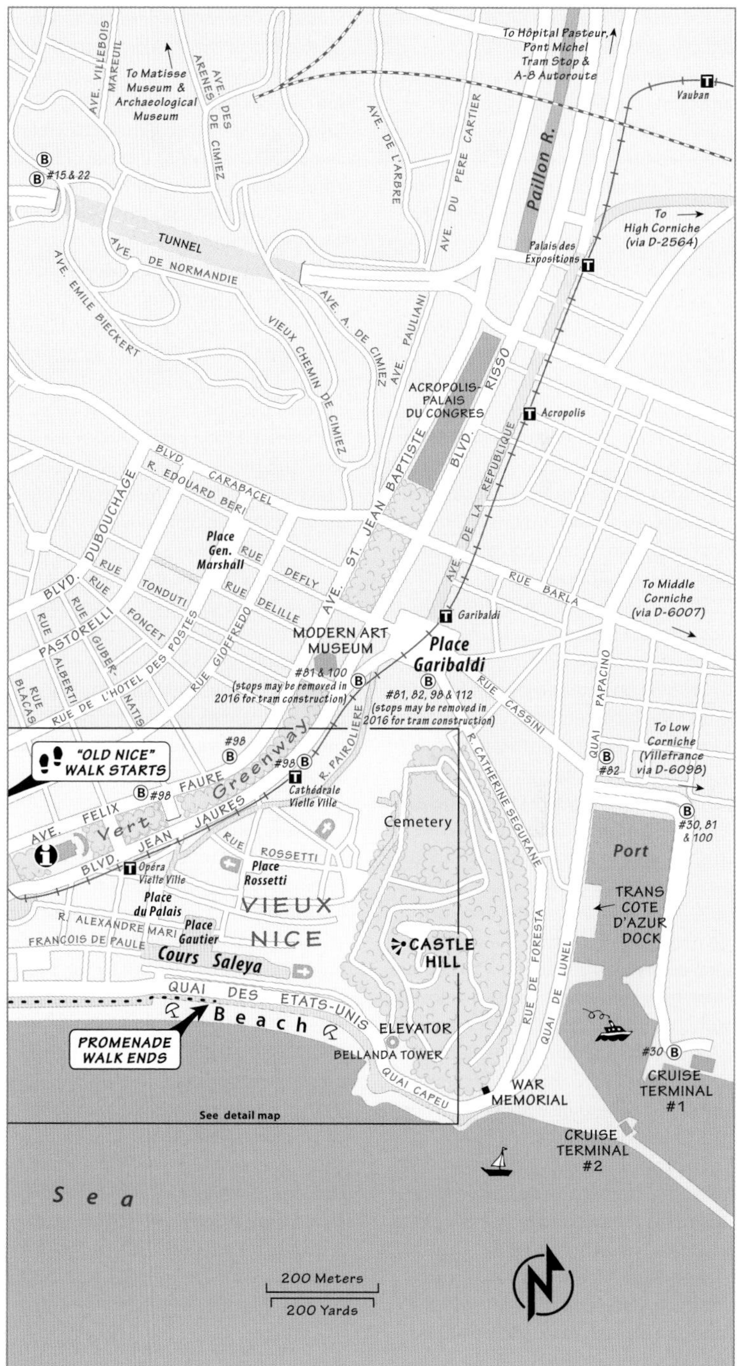
To Matisse Museum & Archaeological Museum
To Hôpital Pasteur, Pont Michel Tram Stop & A-8 Autoroute
Vauban
Paillon R.
To High Corniche (via D-2564)
Palais des Expositions
TUNNEL
AVE. DE NORMANDIE
AVE. EMILE BIECKERT
AVE. A. DE CIMIEZ
VIEUX CHEMIN DE CIMIEZ
AVE. PAULIANI
AVE. DU PERE CARTIER
AVE. DE L'ARBRE
AVE. DES ARENES DE CIMIEZ
AVE. VILLEBOIS MAREUIL
ACROPOLIS-PALAIS DU CONGRES
Acropolis
BLVD. RISSO
AVE. ST. JEAN BAPTISTE
AVE. DE LA REPUBLIQUE
BLVD. CARABACEL
R. EDOUARD BERI
BLVD. DUBOUCHAGE
Place Gen. Marshall
RUE DEFLY
RUE TONDUTI
RUE DELILLE
RUE BARLA
To Middle Corniche (via D-6007)
Garibaldi
MODERN ART MUSEUM
Place Garibaldi
#81 & 100 (stops may be removed in 2016 for tram construction)
#81, 82, 98 & 112 (stops may be removed in 2016 for tram construction)
RUE CASSINI
QUAI PAPACINO
To Low Corniche (Villefrance via D-6098)
#82
#30, 81 & 100
RUE PASTORELLI
RUE FONCET
RUE GUBERNATIS
RUE ALBERTI
RUE BLACAS
RUE DE L'HOTEL DES POSTES
RUE GIOFFREDO
#98
"OLD NICE" WALK STARTS
AVE. FELIX FAURE
Vert Greenway
BLVD. JEAN JAURES
R. PAIROLIERE
Cathédrale Vielle Ville
R. CATHERINE SEGURANE
Cemetery
Port
RUE ROSSETTI
Place Rossetti
Opéra Vielle Ville
Place du Palais
R. ALEXANDRE MARI
FRANCOIS DE PAULE
Place Gautier
VIEUX NICE
Cours Saleya
CASTLE HILL
TRANS COTE D'AZUR DOCK
RUE DE FORESTA
QUAI DE LUNEL
QUAI DES ETATS-UNIS
Beach
PROMENADE WALK ENDS
ELEVATOR
BELLANDA TOWER
QUAI CAPEU
WAR MEMORIAL
#30
CRUISE TERMINAL #1
CRUISE TERMINAL #2
See detail map
Sea
200 Meters
200 Yards

Rivage, farther along on Quai des Etats-Unis, is cool for a drink.)

Even a hundred years ago, there was sufficient tourism in Nice to justify building its first casino (a leisure activity imported from Venice). Part of an elegant casino, La Jetée Promenade stood on those white-covered pilings (with flags flapping) just offshore, until the Germans destroyed it during World War II. When La Jetée was thriving, it took gamblers two full days to get to the Riviera by train from Paris.

Although La Jetée Promenade is gone, you can still see the striking 1927 Art Nouveau facade of the **Palais de la Méditerranée,** a grand casino, hotel, and theater. It became one of the grandest casinos in Europe, and today it is one of France's most exclusive hotels, though the casino feels cheap and cheesy.

The unappealing Casino Ruhl (with the most detested facade on the strip) disfigures the next block. Anyone can drop in for some one-armed-bandit fun, but to play the tables at night, you'll need to dress up and bring your passport.

Albert I Park is named for the Belgian king who enjoyed wintering here—these were his private gardens. While the English came first, the Belgians and Russians were also big fans of 19th-century Nice. That tall statue at the edge of the park commemorates the 100-year anniversary of Nice's union with France. The happy statue features two beloved women embracing the idea of union (Marianne, the symbol of the Republic of France, and Catherine Ségurane, a 16th-century heroine who helped Nice against Saracen pirates).

The park is a long, winding greenbelt called the Promenade du Paillon. The Paillon River flows under the park on its way to the sea. This is the historical divide between Old Nice and the new town. Continue along, past the vintage belle époque carousel. You're now on Quai des Etats-Unis ("Quay of the United States"). This name was given as a tip-of-the-cap to the Americans for finally entering World War I in 1917. Check out the laid-back couches at the Plage Beau Rivage lounge. The big, blue chair statue celebrates the inviting symbol of this venerable walk and kicks off what I consider the best stretch of beach—quieter and with less traffic.

The tall, rusted **steel girders** reaching for the sky were erected in 2010 to celebrate the 150th anniversary of Nice's union with France. (The seven beams represent the seven valleys of the Nice region.) Designed by the same artist who created the popular Arc of the Riviera sculpture in the parkway near Place Masséna, this "art" infuriates many locals as an ugly waste of money.

The elegant back side of Nice's opera house faces the sea. In front of it, a tiny bronze Statue of Liberty reminds all that this stretch of seafront promenade is named for the USA.

The long, low building lining the walk on the left once served the city's fishermen. Behind its gates bustles the Cours Saleya Market—long the heart and soul of Old Nice.

Ahead, on the right, find the three-foot-tall white **metal winch.** It's a reminder that before tourism, hardworking fishing boats lined the beach rather than vacationing tourists. The boats were hauled in through the surf by winches like this and tied to the iron rings on either side.

• *Your walk is over. From here you have several great options: Continue 10 minutes along the coast to the* ***port,*** *around the foot of Castle Hill (fine views of the entire promenade and a monumental war memorial carved into the hillside); hike or ride the free elevator up to* ***Castle Hill*** *(see page 347); head into the* ***old town*** *(you can follow my "Old Nice Walk," next); or grab a blue chair or piece of* ***beach*** *and just be on vacation—Riviera style.*

Rick's Tip: *To make life tolerable on the rocks, swimmers should buy a pair of the cheap plastic* **beach shoes** *sold at many shops.* **Go Sport** *at #13 on Place Masséna is a good bet (open daily).*

Old Nice Walk

This self-guided walk through Nice's old town, from Place Masséna to Place Rossetti, gives you a helpful introduction to the city's bicultural heritage and its most interesting neighborhoods. Allow about an hour at a leisurely pace for this level walk, rated ▲▲. It's best done in the morning (while the outdoor market thrives), and preferably not on a Sunday, when things are quiet. This ramble is also a joy at night, when fountains glow and pedestrians control the streets.

• *Start where Avenue Jean Médecin hits the people-friendly Place Masséna—the successful result of a long, expensive city upgrade and the new center of Nice.*

PLACE MASSENA

The grand Place Masséna is Nice's drawing room, where old meets new, and where the tramway bends between Vieux (Old) Nice and the train station. The square's black-and-white pavement feels like an elegant outdoor ballroom, with the sleek tram waltzing across its dance floor. While once congested with cars, the square today is frequented only by these trams, which swoosh silently by every couple of minutes. The men on pedestals sitting high above are modern-art additions that arrived with the tram. For a mood-altering experience, return after dark and watch the illuminated figures float yoga-like above. Place Masséna is at its sophisticated best after the sun goes down.

This vast square dates from 1848 and pays tribute to Jean-André Masséna, a French military leader during the Revolutionary and Napoleonic wars. Not just another pretty face in a long lineup of French military heroes, he's considered among the greatest commanders in history—anywhere, anytime. Napoleon called him "the greatest name of my military Empire."

Standing in the center of the square, face the sea and start a clockwise spin tour: The towering **modern swoosh sculpture** in the park is meant to represent the arc of the bay. To the right stretches modern Nice, born with the arrival of tourism in the 1800s. **Avenue Jean Médecin,** Nice's main street, cuts from here through the new town to the train station. In the distance you can see the tracks, the freeway, and the Alps beyond that. Once crammed with cars, buses, and delivery vehicles, Avenue Jean Médecin was turned into a walking and cycling nirvana in 2007. Businesses flourish in the welcoming environment of generous sidewalks and no traffic.

Appreciate the city's Italian heritage—it feels as much like Venice as Paris. The portico flanking Avenue Jean Médecin is Italian, not French. The rich colors of the buildings reflect the taste of previous Italian rulers.

Turn to your right and look east to see the **Promenade du Paillon,** a green parkway that stretches from the sea to Place Masséna. Notice the fountain—its surprise geysers delight children by day and its fine lighting enhances romance at night. Beyond the fountain stands a

Promenade du Paillon

bronze statue of the square's namesake, Masséna. And the hills beyond that separate Nice from Villefranche-sur-Mer.

Turn farther to the right to see the old town, with its jumbled facades below Castle Hill. The **statue of Apollo** holds a beach towel as if to say, "It's beer o'clock, let's go."

• *Walk past Apollo with the beach towel into the old town. After a block down Rue de l'Opéra, turn left onto Rue St. François de Paule (or you can detour right one block to the* ***Molinard*** *perfume shop at #20, which has a free one-room museum and offers create-your-own-perfume sessions for a price; see www.molinard.com).*

RUE ST. FRANÇOIS DE PAULE

This colorful street leads into the heart of Vieux Nice. On the left is Hôtel de Ville (City Hall). Peer into the **Alziari olive oil shop** (at #14 on the right). Dating from 1868, the shop produces top-quality stone-ground olive oil. The proud and charming owner, Gilles Piot, claims that stone wheels create less acidity, since metal grinding builds up heat (see photo in back over the door). Locals fill their own containers from the huge vats.

La Couqueto (at #8) is a colorful shop filled with Provençal handicrafts, including lovely folk characters *(santons)*.

Across the street is Nice's grand **opera house.** Imagine this opulent jewel back in the 19th century. With all the fancy big-city folks wintering here, this rough-edged town needed some high-class entertainment. And Victorians needed an alternative to those "devilish" gambling houses. (Queen Victoria, so disgusted at casinos, would actually close the drapes on her train window when passing Monte Carlo.) The four statues on top represent theater, dance, music, and party poopers.

On the left (at #7), **Pâtisserie Auer's** grand old storefront tempts you with chocolates and candied fruits. It's changed little over the centuries. The writing on the window says, "Since 1820 from father to son." The gold royal shields on the back wall remind shoppers that Queen Victoria indulged her sweet tooth here.

• *Continue on, sifting your way through a cluttered block of tacky souvenir shops to the big market square.*

COURS SALEYA

Named for its broad exposure to the sun *(soleil)*, Cours Saleya is a commotion of color, sights, smells, and people. It's been Nice's main market square since the Middle Ages (flower market all day Tue-Sun, produce market Tue-Sun until 13:00, antiques on Mon). While you're greeted by the ugly mouth of an underground parking lot, much of this square itself was a parking lot until 1980, when the mayor of Nice had this solution dug.

The first section is devoted to the Riviera's largest flower market. In operation since the 19th century, this market offers

Cours Saleya Market

A movable art gallery

plants and flowers that grow effortlessly and ubiquitously in this climate, including these favorites: carnations, roses, and jasmine. Locals know the season by what's on sale (mimosas in February, violets in March, and so on). Until the recent rise in imported flowers, this region supplied all of France with flowers. Still, fresh flowers are cheap here, the best value in this notoriously expensive city. The Riviera's three big industries are tourism, flowers, and perfume (made from these flowers... take a whiff).

Rick's Tip: *The* **Cours Saleya** *produce and flower market is replaced by antique stalls* **on Mondays.**

The boisterous produce section trumpets the season with mushrooms, strawberries, white asparagus, zucchini flowers, and more—whatever's fresh gets top billing.

The market opens up at Place Pierre Gautier. It's also called Plassa dou Gouvernou—you'll see bilingual street signs here that include the old Niçois language, an Italian dialect. This is where farmers set up stalls to sell their produce and herbs directly.

Look up to the **hill** that dominates to the east. In the Middle Ages, a massive castle stood there with soldiers at the ready. Over time, the city grew down to where you are now. With the river guarding one side and the sea the other, this mountain fortress seemed strong—until Louis XIV leveled it in 1706. Nice's medieval seawall ran along the line of two-story buildings where you're standing.

Now, look across Place Pierre Gautier to the large "palace." The **Ducal Palace** was where the kings of Sardinia, the city's Italian rulers until 1860, resided when in Nice. (For centuries, Nice was under the rule of the Italian capital of Torino.) Today, the palace is the police headquarters. The land upon which the Cours Saleya sits was once the duke's gardens and didn't become a market until Nice's union with France.

• *Continue down Cours Saleya. The fine golden building that seals the end of the square is where Henri Matisse spent 17 years. I imagine he was inspired by his view. The* ***Café les Ponchettes*** *is perfectly positioned for you to enjoy the view, too, if you want a coffee break. At the café, turn onto...*

RUE DE LA POISSONNERIE

Look up at the first floor of the first building on your right. **Adam and Eve** are squaring off, each holding a zucchini-like gourd. This scene represents the annual rapprochement in Nice to make up for the sin of too much fun during Carnival (Mardi Gras, the pre-Lenten festival). Residents of Nice have partied hard during Carnival for more than 700 years.

Next, check out the small **Baroque church** (Notre-Dame de l'Annonciation) dedicated to St. Rita, the patron saint of desperate causes and desperate people. She holds a special place in locals' hearts, making this the most popular church in Nice. Drop in for a peek at the dazzling Baroque interior. Inside, the first chapel on the right is dedicated to St. Erasmus, protector of mariners.

• *Turn right on the next street, where you'll pass Vieux Nice's most happening bar* ***(Distilleries Ideales).*** *Pause at the next corner and simply study the classic Old Nice scene. Now turn left on Rue Droite and enter an area that feels like Little Naples.*

RUE DROITE

In the Middle Ages, this straight, skinny street provided the most direct route from river to sea within the old walled town. Pass the recommended restaurant L'Acchiardo. Notice stepped lanes leading uphill to the castle. Stop at **Espuno's bakery** (at Place du Jésus) and say "*Bonjour*, what's cooking?" to Natalie from England and her husband Fabrice, who's from here. Notice the firewood stacked behind the oven. Try the house specialty, *tourte aux blettes*—a tart stuffed with

Swiss chard, apples, pine nuts, and raisins.

Pop into the Jesuit **Eglise St-Jacques** for an explosion of Baroque exuberance hidden behind that plain facade.

The balconies of the large mansion on the left mark the **Palais Lascaris** (c. 1647), home of one of Nice's most prestigious families. Today it is a museum with an impressive collection of antique musical instruments—harps, guitars, violins, and violas—along with elaborate tapestries and a few well-furnished rooms. The palace has four levels: The ground floor was used for storage, the first floor was devoted to reception rooms (and musical events), the owners lived a floor above that, and the servants lived at the top. Look up and make faces back at the guys under the balconies.

• *Turn left on the Rue de la Loge, then left again on Rue Benoît Bunico.*

In the 18th century, Rue Benoît served as a **ghetto** for Nice's Jews. At sunset, gates would seal the street at either end, locking people in until daylight. To identify Jews as non-Christians, the men were forced to wear yellow stars and the women wore yellow scarves. The white columns across from #19 mark what was the synagogue until 1848, when revolution ended the notion of ghettos in France.

• *Around the corner and downhill on Rue Benoît Bunico find...*

PLACE ROSSETTI

The most Italian of Nice's piazzas, Place Rossetti comes alive after dark—in part because of the **Fenocchio gelato shop,** popular for its many innovative flavors.

Check out the **Cathedral of St. Réparate**—an unassuming building for a big-city cathedral. It was relocated here in the 1500s, when Castle Hill was temporarily converted to military use. The name comes from Nice's patron saint, a teenage virgin named Réparate, whose martyred body floated to Nice in the fourth century accompanied by angels.

• *This is the end of our walk. From here you can hike up* ***Castle Hill*** *(from Place Rossetti, take Rue Rossetti uphill; see page 347). Or you can have ice cream and browse the colorful lanes of Old Nice. Or you can grab Apollo and hit the beach.*

Sights

Some of Nice's top attractions—the Promenade des Anglais, the beach, and the old town—are covered in my self-guided walks. But Nice offers other worthwhile sights as well.

The Chagall and Matisse museums are a long walk northeast of the city center. If you want to visit both, combine them in one trip, because they're in the same direction and served by the same bus line (#15 Mon-Sat, #22 Sun). From Place Masséna, the Chagall Museum is a 10-minute bus ride, and the Matisse Museum is a few stops beyond that.

▲▲▲CHAGALL MUSEUM (MUSEE NATIONAL MARC CHAGALL)

Even if you don't get modern art, this museum—with the world's largest collection of Marc Chagall's work in captivity—

Eglise St-Jacques

Place Rossetti

is a delight. After World War II, Chagall returned from the United States to settle in Vence, not far from Nice. Between 1954 and 1967 he painted a cycle of 17 large murals designed for, and donated to, this museum. These paintings, inspired by the biblical books of Genesis, Exodus, and the Song of Songs, make up the "nave," or core, of what Chagall called the "House of Brotherhood."

Rick's Tip: *Both the* **Chagall** *and* **Matisse museums** *are* **closed on Tuesdays.**

Cost and Hours: €8, €1-2 more with special exhibits, includes audioguide, May-Oct Wed-Mon 10:00-18:00, Nov-April until 17:00, closed Tue year-round, Avenue Docteur Ménard, tel. 04 93 53 87 20, http://en.musees-nationaux-alpesmaritimes.fr. An idyllic café awaits in the corner of the garden.

Getting There: Taxis to and from the city center cost €12. Buses connect the museum with downtown Nice and the train station. From downtown, catch bus #15 (6/hour, 10 minutes) from the east end of the Galeries Lafayette department store, near the Masséna tram stop, on Rue Sacha Guitry; on Sunday catch #22 from the same stop. Exit the bus at the stop called Musée Chagall on Boulevard de Cimiez.

Visiting the Museum: This small museum consists of six rooms: two rooms (the main hall and Song of Songs room) with the 17 murals, two rooms for special exhibits, an auditorium with stained-glass windows, and a mosaic-lined pond.

In the **main hall** you'll find the core of the collection (Genesis and Exodus scenes). Each painting is a lighter-than-air collage of images that draws from Chagall's Russian folk-village youth, his Jewish heritage, biblical themes, and his feeling that he existed somewhere between heaven and earth. He believed that the Bible was a synonym for nature, and that color and biblical themes were key for understanding God's love for his creation. Chagall's brilliant blues and reds celebrate nature, as do his spiritual and folk themes. Notice the focus on couples. To Chagall, humans loving each other mirrored God's love of creation.

The adjacent **octagonal room** houses five paintings inspired by the Old Testament Song of Songs. Chagall was one of the few "serious" 20th-century artists to portray unabashed love. Where the Bible uses the metaphor of earthly, physical, sexual love to describe God's love for humans, Chagall uses unearthly colors and a mystical ambience to celebrate human love. These red-toned canvases are hard to interpret on a literal level, but they capture the rosy spirit of a man in love with life.

The **auditorium** is worth a peaceful moment to enjoy three Chagall stained-glass windows depicting the seven days of creation. This is also where you'll find a wonderful film (52 minutes) on Chagall, which plays at the top of each hour.

Chagall Museum

Chagall, Song of Songs IV

The Riviera's Art Scene

The list of artists who have painted the Riviera reads like a *Who's Who* of 20th-century art. Henri Matisse, Marc Chagall, Georges Braque, Raoul Dufy, Fernand Léger, and Pablo Picasso all lived and worked here—and raved about the region's wonderful light. Their simple, semiabstract, and—most important—colorful works reflect the pleasurable atmosphere of the Riviera. You'll experience the same landscapes they painted in this bright, sun-drenched region, punctuated with views of the "azure sea." Try to imagine the Riviera with a fraction of the people and development you see today.

The Riviera's collection of museums allows art lovers to appreciate these masters' works while immersed in the same sun and culture that inspired them. The designs of many of the museums blend artworks with surrounding views, gardens, and fountains, thus highlighting that modern art is not only stimulating, but sometimes simply beautiful.

Leaving the Museum: From here, you can return to downtown Nice or the train-station area, or go to the Matisse Museum. For the bus back to downtown Nice, turn right out of the museum, then make another right down Boulevard de Cimiez, and ride bus #15 or #22 heading downhill. To continue on to the Matisse Museum, catch #15 or #22 using the uphill stop located across the street. To walk to the train-station area from the museum takes about 20 minutes.

▲MATISSE MUSEUM (MUSEE MATISSE)

This small and neglected little museum, which fills an old mansion in a park surrounded by scant Roman ruins, contains a sampling of works from the various periods of Henri Matisse's artistic career. The museum offers an introduction to the artist's many styles and materials, both shaped by Mediterranean light and by fellow Côte d'Azur artists Picasso and Renoir.

Matisse, the master of leaving things out, could suggest a woman's body with a single curvy line—letting the viewer's mind fill in the rest. Ignoring traditional 3-D perspective, he expressed his passion for life through simplified but recognizable scenes in which dark outlines and saturated, bright blocks of color create an overall decorative pattern. As you tour the museum, look for Matisse's favorite motifs—including fruit, flowers, wallpaper, and sunny rooms—often with a window opening onto a sparkling landscape. Another favorite subject is the *odalisque* (harem concubine), usually shown

Matisse "cutout" painting

sprawled in a seductive pose and with a simplified, masklike face. You'll also see a few souvenirs from his foreign travels, which influenced much of his work.

Cost and Hours: €10, Wed-Mon 10:00-18:00, closed Tue, 164 Avenue des Arènes de Cimiez, tel. 04 93 81 08 08, www.musee-matisse-nice.org.

Getting There: Take a cab (€15 from Promenade des Anglais). Alternatively, hop bus #15 Mon-Sat or #22 on Sun (6/hour, 15 minutes, board from east end of Galeries Lafayette department store, near Masséna tram stop, on Rue Sacha Guitry—see map on page 350). Get off at the Arènes-Matisse bus stop (look for the crumbling Roman arena), then walk 50 yards into the park to find the pink villa.

Leaving the Museum: Turn left from the museum into the park, exiting at the Archaeological Museum. The bus stop across the street is for bus #20, which heads to the port. For buses #15 and #22 (frequent service to downtown and the Chagall Museum), turn right, passing the stop above, walk to the small roundabout, and find the shelter (facing downhill).

Russian Cathedral

▲RUSSIAN CATHEDRAL (CATHEDRALE RUSSE)

Nice's Russian Orthodox church—claimed by some to be the finest outside Russia—is worth a visit.

Five hundred rich Russian families wintered in Nice in the late 19th century, and they needed a worthy Orthodox house of worship. Czar Nicholas I's widow provided the land and Czar Nicholas II gave this church to the Russian community in 1912. (A few years later, Russian comrades who *didn't* winter on the Riviera assassinated him.) Here in the land of olives and anchovies, these proud onion domes seem odd. But, I imagine, so did those old Russians.

Pick up an English info sheet on your way in. The one-room interior is filled with icons and candles, and traditional Russian music adds to the ambience. The park around the church makes a fine setting for picnics.

Cost and Hours: Free; Mon 13:30-17:00, Tue-Sun 10:00-17:00; services Sat at 17:00, Sun at 10:00; no tourist visits during services, no shorts allowed, 17 Boulevard du Tzarewitch, tel. 04 93 96 88 02, www.sobor.fr.

▲CASTLE HILL (COLLINE DU CHATEAU)

This hill—in an otherwise flat city center—offers sensational views over Nice, the port (to the east, created for trade and military use in the 15th century), the foothills of the Alps, and the Mediterranean. The views are best early, at sunset, or whenever the weather's clear.

Nice was founded on this hill. Its residents were crammed onto the hilltop until the 12th century, as it was too risky to live in the flatlands below. Today you'll find a playground, a café, and a cemetery—but no castle—on Castle Hill.

Cost and Hours: Park is free and closes at 20:00 in summer, earlier off-season.

Getting There: You can get to the top by foot or by elevator (free, daily 10:00-19:00, until 20:00 in summer, next to beachfront Hôtel Suisse).

See the Promenade des Anglais Walk on page 336 for a pleasant stroll that ends near Castle Hill.

Leaving Castle Hill: After enjoying the views and hilltop fun, you can walk via the cemetery directly down into Vieux Nice (just follow the signs), descend to the beach (via the elevator or a stepped lane next to it), or hike down the back side to Nice's port (departure point for boat trips and buses to Monaco and Villefranche-sur-Mer).

Experiences

Mediterranean Cruise

To see Nice from the water, hop aboard a one-hour ▲**Trans Côte d'Azur cruise.** You'll travel on a comfortable yacht-size vessel to Cap Ferrat and past Villefranche-sur-Mer, then return to Nice with a final lap along Promenade des Anglais.

Guides play Robin Leach (in French and English), pointing out mansions owned by famous people, including Elton John, Sean Connery, and Microsoft co-founder Paul Allen (€18; April-Oct Tue-Sun 2/day, usually at 11:00 and 15:00, no boats Mon or in off-season; verify schedule, arrive 30 minutes early to get best seats; boats leave from Nice's port—Bassin des Amiraux, tel. 04 92 98 71 30, www.trans-cote-azur.com).

The view from Castle Hill is worth the climb.

Nightlife

While you should choose your neighborhoods with caution, the city is a delight after dark. Promenade des Anglais, Cours Saleya, the old town, and Rue Masséna are all safe and worth an evening walk. Nice's bars play host to a happening late-night scene, filled with jazz, rock, and trolling singles.

Most activity focuses on Vieux Nice. Rue de la Préfecture and Place du Palais are ground zero for bar life, though Place Rossetti and Rue Droite are also good targets. **Distilleries Ideales** is a good place to start or end your evening, with a lively international crowd, a *Pirates of the Caribbean* interior, and a *Cheers* vibe (15 beers on tap, happy hour 18:00-21:00, where Rue de la Poissonnerie and Rue Barillerie meet). **Wayne's Bar** is a happening spot for the younger, English-speaking backpacker crowd (15 Rue Préfecture). Along the Promenade des Anglais, the plush bar at **Hôtel Negresco** is fancy-cigar old English.

Eating

For the most energy and variety, I'd eat in Vieux Nice. If Vieux Nice is too far, I've listed good places handier to your hotel. Promenade des Anglais is ideal for picnic dinners on warm, languid evenings or a meal at a beachside restaurant. For a more romantic (and expensive) meal, head for nearby Villefranche-sur-Mer (see page 359). Avoid the fun-to-peruse but terribly touristy eateries lining Rue Masséna.

In Vieux Nice

$$$ Le Safari is a fair option for Niçois cuisine and outdoor dining on Cours Saleya. The place, convivial and rustic with a mix of modern art inside, is packed with locals and tourists, and staffed with hurried waiters (€18-30 *plats,* open daily, 1 Cours Saleya, tel. 04 93 80 18 44, www.

The Riviera's Cuisine Scene

While many of the same dishes served in Provence are available throughout the Riviera (see page 301), there are differences, especially if you look for anything Italian or from the sea. When dining on the Riviera, I expect views and ambience more than top-quality cuisine.

La salade niçoise is where most Riviera meals start. A true specialty from Nice, the classic version is a base of green salad with boiled potatoes, tomatoes, anchovies, olives, hard-boiled eggs, and lots of tuna. This is my go-to salad for a tasty, healthy, and fast lunch. I like to spend a couple of extra euros and eat it in an elegant, atmospheric place with a view.

For lunch on the go, look for a ***pan bagnat*** (like a *salade niçoise* stuffed into a hollowed-out soft roll). Other tasty bread treats include ***pissaladière*** (bread dough topped with onions, olives, and anchovies), ***fougasse*** (a spindly, lace-like bread sometimes flavored with nuts, herbs, olives, or ham), and ***socca*** (a thin chickpea crêpe, seasoned with pepper and olive oil and often served in a paper cone by street vendors).

Bouillabaisse is the Riviera's most famous dish; you'll find it in any seafront village or city. It's a spicy fish stew based on recipes handed down from sailors in Marseille. This dish often requires a minimum order of two and can cost up to €40-60 per person.

Those on a budget can enjoy other seafood soups and stews. Far less pricey than bouillabaisse and worth trying is the local ***soupe de poisson*** (fish soup). It's a creamy soup flavored like bouillabaisse, with anise and orange, and served with croutons and *rouille* sauce (but has no chunks of fish).

The Riviera specializes in all sorts of fish and shellfish. Options include ***fruits de mer,*** or platters of seafood (including tiny shellfish, from which you get the edible part only by sucking really hard), herb-infused mussels, stuffed sardines, squid (slowly simmered with tomatoes and herbs), and tuna *(thon)*. The popular ***loup flambé au fenouil*** is grilled sea bass, flavored with fennel and torched with *pastis* prior to serving.

Do as everyone else does, and drink **wines** from Provence. **Bandol** (red) and **Cassis** (white) are popular and from a region nearly on the Riviera. The only wines made in the Riviera are **Bellet** rosé and white, the latter often found in fish-shaped bottles.

restaurantsafari.fr).

$$ L'Acchiardo is a homey eatery that mixes loyal clientele with hungry tourists. As soon as you sit down you know this is a treat. The simple, hearty Niçois cuisine is served by Monsieur Acchiardo and his good-looking sons. The small plaque under the menu outside says the restaurant has been run by father and son since 1927 (€9 starters, €16 *plats,* €7 desserts, closed Sat-Sun, indoor seating only, 38 Rue Droite, tel. 04 93 85 51 16).

$$ Bistrot D'Antoine has street appeal. It's a warm, popular, vine-draped option whose menu emphasizes Niçois cuisine and good grilled selections. The food is delicious and the prices are reasonable. Call a day ahead to reserve a table—the upstairs room is quieter (€10 starters, €17 *plats*, €7 desserts, closed Sun-Mon, 27

Vieux Nice Restaurants & Hotels

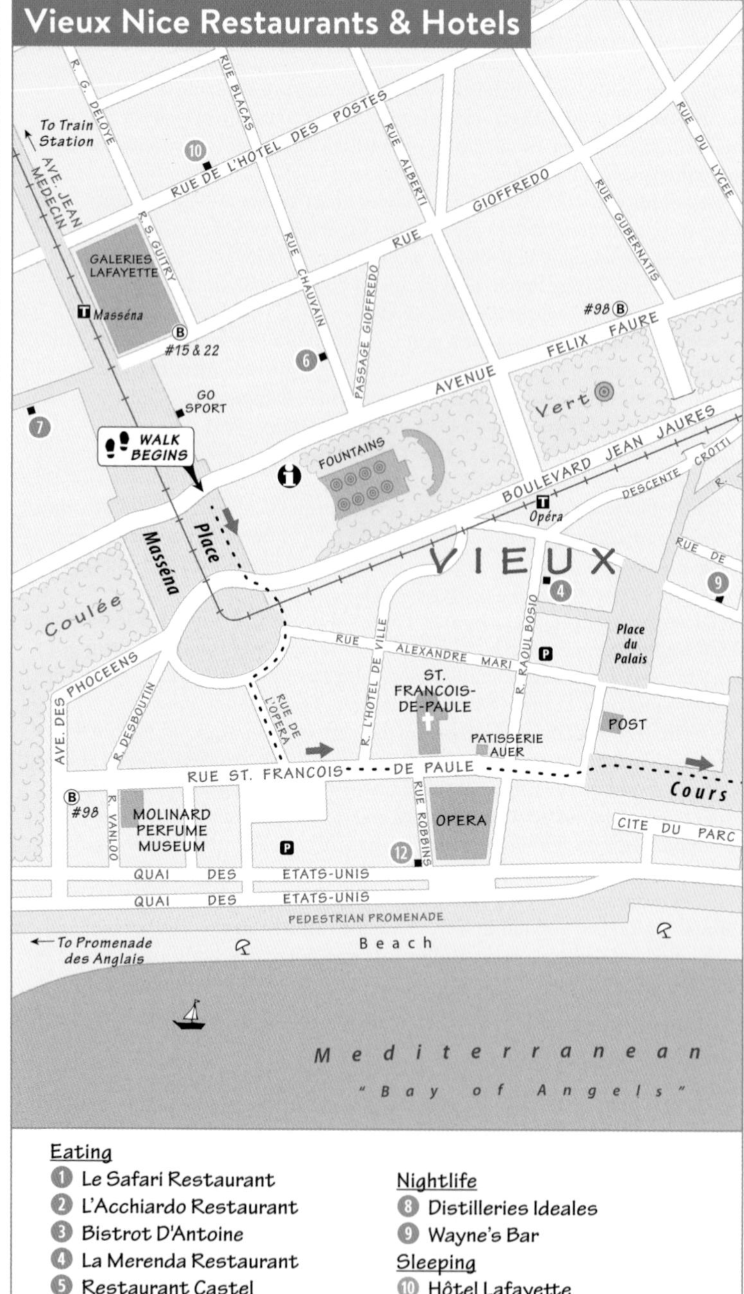

Eating

1. Le Safari Restaurant
2. L'Acchiardo Restaurant
3. Bistrot D'Antoine
4. La Merenda Restaurant
5. Restaurant Castel
6. Le Luna Rossa Restaurant
7. La Maison de Marie Restaurant

Nightlife

8. Distilleries Ideales
9. Wayne's Bar

Sleeping

10. Hôtel Lafayette
11. Hôtel la Perouse
12. Hôtel Mercure Marché aux Fleurs

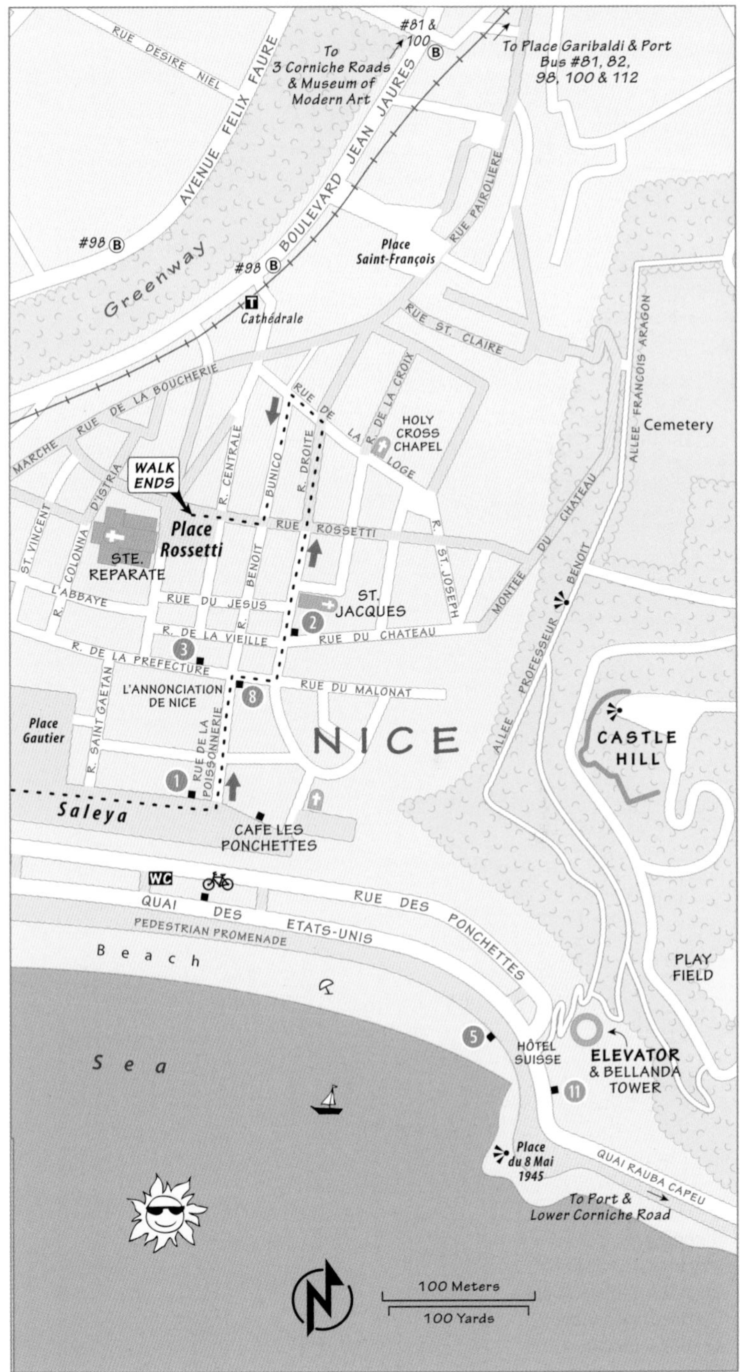

RUE DESIRE NIEL
AVENUE FELIX FAURE
To 3 Corniche Roads & Museum of Modern Art
#81 & 100
BOULEVARD JEAN JAURES
To Place Garibaldi & Port Bus #81, 82, 98, 100 & 112
RUE PAIROLIERE
Place Saint-François
#98
Greenway
Cathédrale
RUE ST. CLAIRE
ALLEE FRANCOIS ARAGON
Cemetery
MARCHE RUE DE LA BOUCHERIE
RUE DE LA LOGE
R. DE LA CROIX
HOLY CROSS CHAPEL
WALK ENDS
R. CENTRALE
BUNICO
R. DROITE
Place Rossetti
RUE ROSSETTI
R. ST. JOSEPH
MONTEE DU CHATEAU
ST. VINCENT
COLONNA D'ISTRIA
STE. REPARATE
BENOIT
L'ABBAYE
RUE DU JESUS
ST. JACQUES
R. DE LA VIEILLE
RUE DU CHATEAU
R. DE LA PREFECTURE
ALLEE PROFESSEUR BENOIT
L'ANNONCIATION DE NICE
RUE DU MALONAT
Place Gautier
R. SAINT GAETAN
RUE DE LA POISSONNERIE
NICE
CASTLE HILL
Saleya
CAFE LES PONCHETTES
WC
QUAI DES ETATS-UNIS
RUE DES PONCHETTES
PEDESTRIAN PROMENADE
Beach
PLAY FIELD
Sea
HÔTEL SUISSE
ELEVATOR & BELLANDA TOWER
Place du 8 Mai 1945
QUAI RAUBA CAPEU
To Port & Lower Corniche Road
100 Meters
100 Yards

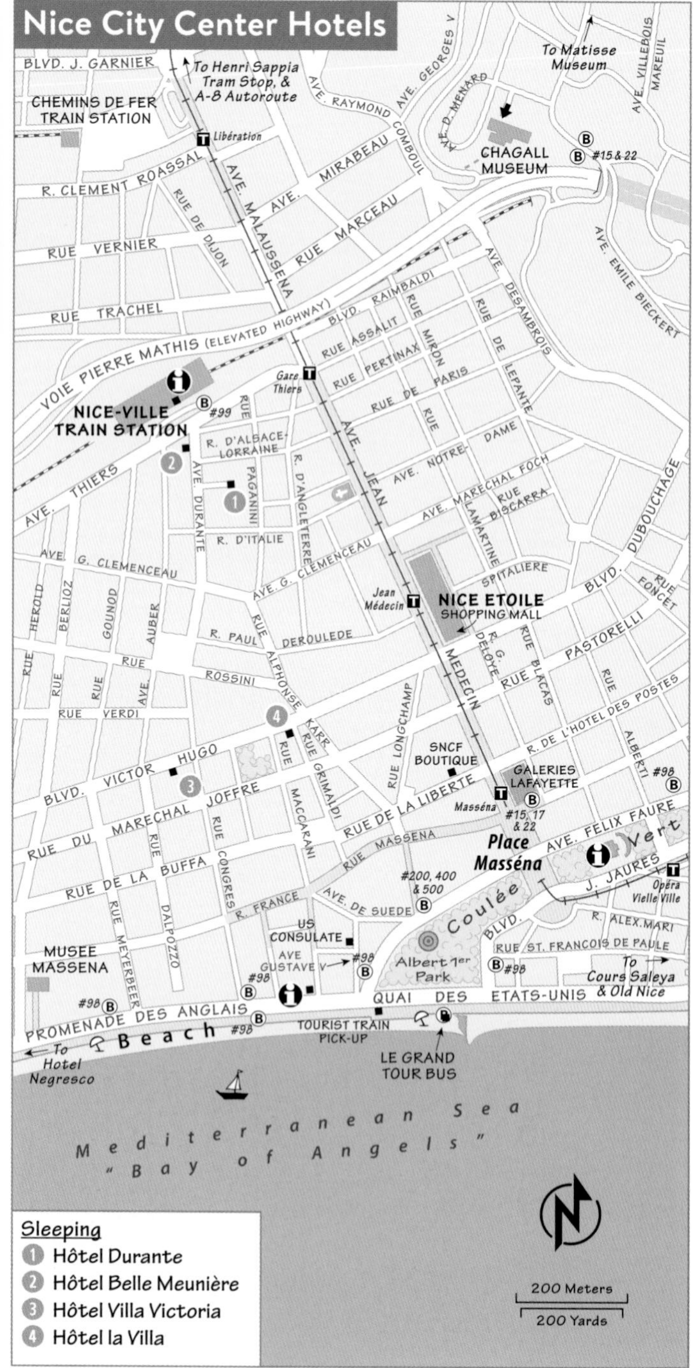
Nice City Center Hotels
To Henri Sappia Tram Stop, & A-8 Autoroute
CHEMINS DE FER TRAIN STATION
To Matisse Museum
CHAGALL MUSEUM
#15 & 22
NICE-VILLE TRAIN STATION
#99
NICE ETOILE SHOPPING MALL
SNCF BOUTIQUE
GALERIES LAFAYETTE
#15, 17 & 22
Place Masséna
#200, 400 & 500
US CONSULATE
MUSEE MASSENA
Albert 1er Park
To Cours Saleya & Old Nice
TOURIST TRAIN PICK-UP
LE GRAND TOUR BUS
To Hotel Negresco
Mediterranean Sea
"Bay of Angels"
200 Meters
200 Yards
Sleeping
1 Hôtel Durante
2 Hôtel Belle Meunière
3 Hôtel Villa Victoria
4 Hôtel la Villa

Rue de la Préfecture, tel. 04 93 85 29 57).

$$ La Merenda is a shoebox where you'll sit on small stools and dine on simple, home-style dishes in a communal environment. The menu changes with the season, but the hardworking owner, Dominique, does not. This place fills fast, so arrive early, or better yet, drop by during the day to reserve—they have two seatings at 19:00 and 21:00 (€10 starters, €14 *plats,* €6 desserts, closed Sat-Sun, cash only, 4 Rue Raoul Bosio, no telephone, www.lamerenda.net).

On the Beach

$$$ Restaurant Castel is a fine eat-on-the-beach option, thanks to its location at the very east end of Nice, under Castle Hill. The city vanishes as you step down to the beach. The food is creative and nicely presented, and the tables feel classy, even at the edge of the sand. Arrive for the sunset and you'll have an unforgettable meal (€19 salads and pastas, €20-25 daily plates, open for dinner mid-May-Aug, lunch April-Sept, 8 Quai des Etats-Unis, tel. 04 93 85 22 66, www.castelplage.com). Sunbathers can rent beach chairs and have drinks and meals served literally on the beach (lounge chairs €16/half-day, €19/day).

In the City Center

For a more contemporary slice of France, try one of these spots around the Nice Etoile shopping mall.

Rick's Tip: *Nice's* **dinner scene converges on Cours Saleya,** *which is entertaining enough in itself to make the generally mediocre food a good deal. It's a fun spot to compare tans and mussels—and worth wandering through even if you eat elsewhere.*

$$ Le Luna Rossa is a small neighborhood eatery serving delicious French-Italian dishes. Owner Christine welcomes diners with attentive service and reasonable prices. Dine inside (classy tables) or outside on a sidewalk terrace (€10 starters, €14-27 *plats,* closed Sun-Mon, just north of parkway at 3 Rue Chauvain, tel. 04 93 85 55 66).

Pick an outdoor table in Nice and try the socca *(thin chickpea crêpe).*

$$ La Maison de Marie is a surprisingly high-quality refuge off Nice's touristy restaurant row—Rue Masséna. The interior tables are as appealing as those in the courtyard, but expect some smokers outside. The €24 *menu* is a good value (€12-18 starters, €20-30 *plats,* open daily, 5 Rue Masséna, tel. 04 93 82 15 93).

Sleeping

Don't look for charm in Nice. I prefer to stay in the new town—a 10-minute walk from the old town—for modern, clean, and air-conditioned rooms. For parking, ask your hotelier, or see page 358.

Sleep Code

$$$$ Splurge: Over €250
$$$ Pricier: €190-250
$$ Moderate: €130-190
$ Budget: €70-130
¢ Backpacker: Under €70

Hotels are classified based on the average price of a standard double room with bath in high season. Unless otherwise noted, credit cards are accepted, breakfast is not included, hotel staff speak English, and Wi-Fi is available.

In the City Center

The train station area offers Nice's cheapest sleeps, but the neighborhood can feel seedy after dark. The cheapest places are older, well-worn, and come with some street noise. Places closer to Boulevard Victor Hugo are more expensive and in a more comfortable area.

Rick's Tip: *The Riviera is famous for staging major* **events.** *Stay away unless you're actually participating, as you'll only experience room shortages, higher prices, and traffic jams. The three biggies are the* **Nice Carnival** *(Feb-March, www.nicecarnaval.com),* **Cannes Film Festival** *(mid-May, www.festival-cannes.com), and* **Grand Prix of Monaco** *(late May, www.acm.mc). To accommodate the busy schedules of the rich and famous (and really mess up a lot of normal people), the film festival and car race often overlap.*

$ Hôtel Durante*** feels Mediterranean—a happy, orange building with rooms wrapped around a flowery courtyard. All but two of its quiet rooms overlook the well-maintained patio. The rooms are good enough (mostly modern decor), the price is right enough, and the parking is free—book well ahead (Sb-€85-115, Db-€100-130, Tb-€155-185, Qb-€190-220, breakfast-€10, 16 Avenue Durante, tel. 04 93 88 84 40, www.hotel-durante.com, info@hotel-durante.com).

$$ Hôtel Lafayette***, located a block behind the Galeries Lafayette department store, is a modest, homey place with 17 mostly spacious and good-value rooms (some with thin walls, some traffic noise, all one floor up from the street). It's family-run by Kiril and George (standard Db-€105-130, spacious Db-€120-150, Tb-€130-180, preferential direct booking rates for Rick Steves readers, breakfast-€12, no elevator, 32 Rue de l'Hôtel des Postes—see map on page 350, tel. 04 93 85 17 84, www.hotellafayettenice.com, info@hotellafayettenice.com).

$ Hôtel Belle Meunière*, in an old mansion built for Napoleon III's mistress, attracts budget-minded travelers of all ages with cheap beds and private rooms a block below the train station. Creaky but well-kept, the place has adequate rooms, thin mattresses, and charismatic Mademoiselle Marie-Pierre presiding with her perfect English (bunk in 4-bed dorm-€28 with private bath, less with shared bath; Db-€60-86, Tb-€86-100, Qb-€118-135, breakfast-€6 or free if you book direct, no air-con, no elevator, laundry service, limited parking-€9/day, 21 Avenue Durante, tel. 04 93 88 66

15, www.bellemeuniere.com, hotel.belle.meuniere@cegetel.net).

In or near Vieux Nice

These Vieux Nice hotels are either on the sea or within an easy walk of it. For locations, see the map on page 350.

$$$$ Hôtel la Perouse****, built into the rock of Castle Hill at the east end of the bay, is a fine splurge. This refuge-hotel is top-to-bottom flawless in every detail—from its elegant rooms (satin curtains, velour headboards) and attentive staff to its rooftop terrace with Jacuzzi, sleek pool, and lovely garden restaurant (€40 *menus*). Sleep here to be spoiled and escape the big city (garden-view Db-€300-400, seaview Db-€420-580, good family options and Web deals, 11 Quai Rauba Capeu, tel. 04 93 62 34 63, www.hotel-la-perouse.com, lp@hotel-la-perouse.com).

$$ Hôtel Mercure Marché aux Fleurs**** is ideally situated near the sea and Cours Saleya. Rooms are tastefully designed and prices can be reasonable—check their website for deals (standard Db-€180, superior Db-€225-260 and worth the extra euros, smaller seaview room-€50 extra, 91 Quai des Etats-Unis, tel. 04 93 85 74 19, www.hotelmercure.com, h0962@accor.com).

Near the Promenade des Anglais

These hotels are close to the beach (and mostly far from Vieux Nice).

$$$ Hôtel Villa Victoria**** is managed by cheery Marlena, who welcomes travelers into this spotless, classy old building that has an open, attractive lobby overlooking a sprawling garden-courtyard. Rooms are comfortable and well-kept, with space to stretch out (streetside Db-€170-200, gardenside Db-€175-225, Tb-€190-240, suites-€210, breakfast-€15, parking-€18/day, 33 Boulevard Victor Hugo, tel. 04 93 88 39 60, www.villa-victoria.com, contact@villa-victoria.com).

$$ Hôtel la Villa*** is a well-run hotel with 47 rooms, contemporary decor in its light-filled public spaces, and a small front terrace (standard Db-€100-160, larger Db-€200, good breakfast-€12, 19 bis Boulevard Victor Hugo, tel. 04 93 87 15 00, www.hotels-la-villa.com, contact@hotel-villa-nice-centre.com).

Transportation

Getting Around Nice

BY PUBLIC TRANSPORTATION

Although you can walk to most attractions, smart travelers make good use of the buses and tram.

Tickets: Both buses and trams are covered by the same €1.50 single-ride ticket, or you can pay €10 for a 10-ride ticket that can be shared (each use good for 74 minutes in one direction, including transfers between bus and tram). The €5 all-day pass is valid on city buses and trams, as well as buses to some nearby destinations (including Villefranche-sur-Mer and Cap Ferrat, but not buses to the airport). You must validate your ticket on every bus or tram trip. Buy single tickets from the bus driver or from the ticket machines on tram platforms (coins only—press the button twice at the end to get your ticket). Passes and 10-ride tickets are also available from machines at tram stops. Info: www.lignesdazur.com.

Buses: The bus is handy for reaching the Chagall and Matisse museums (for specifics, see museum listings under "Sights"), and the Russian Cathedral. Route diagrams inside the buses identify each stop. For more on riding buses in Nice and throughout the Riviera, see page 357.

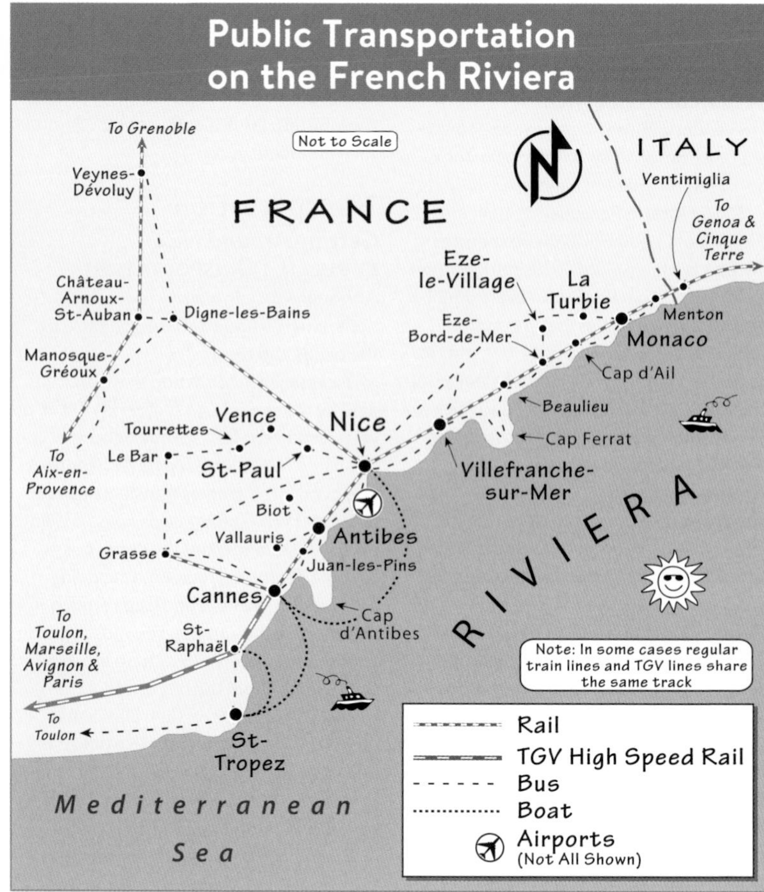

Trams: Nice has a single modern and efficient L-shaped tram line. Trams run every few minutes along Avenue Jean Médecin and Boulevard Jean Jaurès, and connect the main train station with Place Masséna and Old Nice (Opéra stop), the port (Place Garibaldi stop), and buses east along the coast (Vauban stop). Boarding the tram in the direction of Hôpital Pasteur takes you toward the beach and Vieux Nice (direction: Henri Sappia goes the other way). Tram info: http://tramway.nice.fr.

BY TAXI

While pricey, cabs can be useful for getting to Nice's less-central sights. Cabbies normally pick up only at taxi stands *(tête de station)*, or you can call 04 93 13 78 78.

Getting Around the Riviera from Nice

Nice is perfectly situated for exploring the Riviera. Trains and buses do a good job of linking towns along the coast, with bonus views along many routes. Have coins handy. Ticket machines don't take US credit cards or euro bills; smaller train stations may be unstaffed; and bus drivers can't make change for large bills.

BY BUS

Buses are an amazing deal in the Riviera, whether you're riding just within Nice or to Villefranche-sur-Mer, Cap Ferrat, Monaco, or Antibes. The €1.50 single-ride ticket allows transfers between the buses of the Lignes d'Azur (the region's main bus company, www.lignesdazur.com) and the TAM (Transports Alpes-Maritimes); if you board a TAM bus and need a transfer, ask for *un ticket correspondance*. The €5 all-day ticket good on Nice's city buses and tramway also covers buses serving Villefranche and Cap Ferrat. The maps throughout this chapter indicate the locations of the handiest bus stops.

Rick's Tip: *I follow this general rule of thumb when riding a Nice-area bus with an* **all-day bus pass:** *If the bus number has one or two digits, it's covered with the pass; with three digits, it's not.*

Bus Connections Heading East to: **Villefranche-sur-Mer** (#100, 3-4/hour, 20 minutes; or #81, 2-3/hour, 20 minutes), **St-Jean-Cap-Ferrat** (#81, 2-3/hour, 30 minutes), **Monaco** (#100, 3-4/hour, 45 minutes). Due to work on the tram system, eastbound buses may stop only at the port (Le Port stop) when you visit. Ask at the TI if a closer bus stop is now available.

Bus Connections Heading West to: **Antibes** (#200, 4/hour Mon-Sat, 2/hour Sun, 1.5 hours). Use the Albert I/Verdun stop on Avenue de Verdun, a 10-minute walk along the parkway west of Place Masséna.

BY TRAIN

Speedy trains link the Riviera's beachfront destinations. The train is a bit more expensive than the bus (Nice to Monaco by train is about €4), but there's no quicker way to move about the Riviera (http://en.voyages-sncf.com). Never board a train without a ticket or valid pass—fare inspectors accept no excuses. The minimum fine is €70. See below under "Arriving and Departing" for specific trip information.

BY CAR

This is France's most challenging region to drive in. Beautifully distracting vistas (natural and human), loads of Sunday-driver tourists, and every hour being lush-hour in the summer make for a dangerous combination. Parking can be exasperating. Bring lots of coins and patience.

Rick's Tip: *The Riviera is awash with* **scenic roads.** *To sample one of its most beautiful and thrilling drives, take the coastal* **Middle Corniche road** *from Nice to Monaco. You'll find breathtaking views over the Mediterranean and several scenic pullouts.*

BY BOAT

Trans Côte d'Azur offers boat service from Nice to Monaco seasonally (reservations required, tel. 04 92 98 71 30, www.trans-cote-azur.com). They also run one-hour round-trip cruises along the coast to Cap Ferrat (see page 363).

Arriving and Departing

BY TRAIN

All trains stop at Nice's main station, called Nice-Ville (you don't want the suburban Nice Riquier Station). The TI is straight out the main doors. Nice's single tram line zips you to the center in a few minutes (exit left as you leave the station, departs every few minutes, direction: Hôpital Pasteur). To walk to the beach, Promenade des Anglais, or many of my recommended hotels, cross Avenue Thiers in front of the station, go down the steps by Hôtel Interlaken, and continue down Avenue Durante.

Train Connections from Nice to: **Antibes** (2/hour, 20 minutes), **Villefranche-sur-Mer** (2/hour, 10 minutes), **Monaco** (2/hour, 20 minutes), **Arles** (11/day, 4 hours, most require transfer in Marseille or Avignon), **Avignon** (10/day, most by TGV, 4 hours, many require transfer in Marseille), **Paris'** Gare de Lyon (hourly, 6 hours, may require change; 11-hour night train goes to Paris' Gare d'Austerlitz), **Chamonix** (4/day, 10 hours, many change in St-Gervais and Lyon), **Beaune** (7/day, 7 hours, 1-2 transfers). Most long-distance train connections to other French cities require a change in Marseille.

BY CAR

To reach the city center on the autoroute from the west, take the first Nice exit (for the airport—called *Côte d'Azur, Central*) and follow signs for *Nice Centre* and *Promenade des Anglais.* Hoteliers know where to park (allow €18-30/day; some hotels offer deals but space is limited—book ahead). The parking garage at the Nice Etoile shopping center on Avenue Jean Médecin is near many recommended hotels (ticket booth on third floor, about €26/day, 18:00-8:00). Other centrally located garages have similar rates. All on-street parking is metered (9:00-18:00), but usually free on Sunday.

You can avoid driving in the center—and park for free during the day (no overnight parking)—by ditching your car at a parking lot at a remote tram or bus stop. Look for blue-on-white *Parcazur* signs (find locations at www.lignesdazur.com), and ride the bus or tram into town (must buy round-trip tram or bus ticket and keep it with you because you'll need it later to exit the parking lot; for details on riding the tram, see "Getting Around Nice," earlier). As lots are unguarded, don't leave anything in your car.

BY PLANE

Nice's easy-to-navigate airport (Aéroport de Nice Côte d'Azur, airport code: NCE) is literally on the Mediterranean, with landfill runways a 30-minute drive west of the city center. The two terminals are connected by shuttle buses *(navettes).* Both terminals have TIs, banks, ATMs, and buses to Nice (tel. 04 89 88 98 28, www.nice.aeroport.fr).

A **taxi into the city center** is expensive considering the short distance (figure €35 to Nice hotels, €60 to Villefranche-sur-Mer, €70 to Antibes, small fee for bags). Nice's airport taxis are notorious for overcharging. Before riding, confirm that your fare into town is roughly €35 (or €40 at night or on Sun). Don't pay much more. It's always a good idea to ask for a receipt *(reçu).*

Airport shuttles work better for trips from your hotel to the airport, since they offer a fixed price (figure €30 for one person, and only a little more for additional people). Your hotel can arrange this. Try **Nice Airport Shuttle** (1-2 people-€32, additional person-€14, mobile 06 60 33 20 54, www.nice-airport-shuttle.com) or **Med-Tour** (tel. 04 93 82 92 58, mobile 06 73 82 04 10, www.med-tour.com).

Two **bus lines** connect the airport with the city center. **Bus #99** (airport express) runs to Nice's main train station (€6, 2/hour, 8:00-21:00, 30 minutes, drops you within a 10-minute walk of many recommended hotels). To take this bus *to* the airport, catch it right in front of the train station (departs on the half-hour). **Bus #98** runs along Promenade des Anglais and along the edge of Vieux Nice (€6, 3/hour, from the airport 6:00-23:00, to the airport until 21:00, 30 minutes).

For all buses, buy tickets from the driver. To reach the bus-information office and stops at Terminal 1, turn left after passing customs and exit the doors at the far end. Buses serving Terminal 2 stop across the street from the airport exit (info kiosk and ticket sales to the right as you exit).

Getting from the Airport to Nearby Destinations: To reach **Villefranche-sur-Mer,** take bus #98 (described above) to Place Garibaldi; from there, use the same ticket to transfer to bus #81 or #100 (you may need to walk to the port to catch eastbound buses in 2016, due to work on the tram system). To get to **Antibes,** take bus #250 from either terminal (about 2/hour, 40 minutes, €10). Express bus #110 runs from the airport directly to **Monaco** (2/hour, 50 minutes, €20).

NEAR NICE

Day-trip possibilities from Nice are easy and exciting. Villefranche-sur-Mer has a serene setting and small-town warmth. Woodsy Cap Ferrat boasts belle époque mansions and a family-friendly beach. Glitzy little Monaco offers a fancy casino and royal flair. Antibes has sandy beaches, a Picasso museum, and good walking trails. Quick and easy public transportation gets you where you want to go (see "Getting Around the Riviera from Nice" on page 356 for details).

Villefranche-sur-Mer

Villefranche-sur-Mer, just east of Nice, is a romantic's top Riviera choice. Come here for an upscale Mediterranean atmosphere, narrow cobbled streets tumbling into a mellow waterfront, and fancy yachts bobbing in the harbor. Pebbly beaches and a handful of interesting sights keep visitors just busy enough.

Orientation

Tiny and easy-to-cover, Villefranche-sur-Mer snuggles around its harbor.

Day Plan: My self-guided walk laces together everything of importance in town. Your biggest decision will be choosing between a beachfront dinner or an ice-cream-licking village stroll.

Getting There: From Nice, **trains** run to Villefranche twice an hour (10 minutes); **bus #81** or **#100** will also get you there (2-4/hour, 20 minutes). From Nice's port, **drivers** should follow signs for *Menton, Monaco,* and *Basse Corniche.*

Arrival in Villefranche: The train station is just above the beach, a short stroll from the old town. Bus riders can get off at the Octroi stop and walk downhill past the TI to town. Drivers will find pay lots just below the TI or on the water (at Parking Wilson).

Rick's Tip: **Skip the useless white tourist train,** *which goes nowhere interesting.*

Tourist Information: The main TI is off the road that runs between Nice and Monaco, located in a park—Jardin François Binon—below the Nice/Monaco

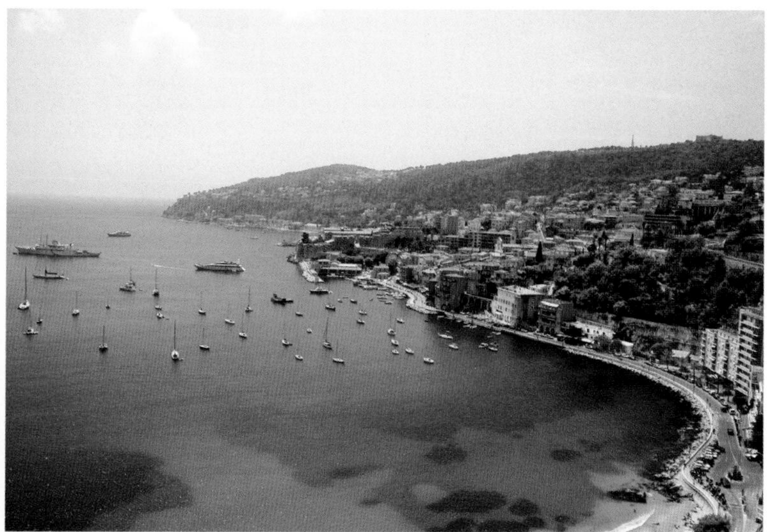

The beautiful deep-water bay at Villefranche-sur-Mer attracts every kind of boat.

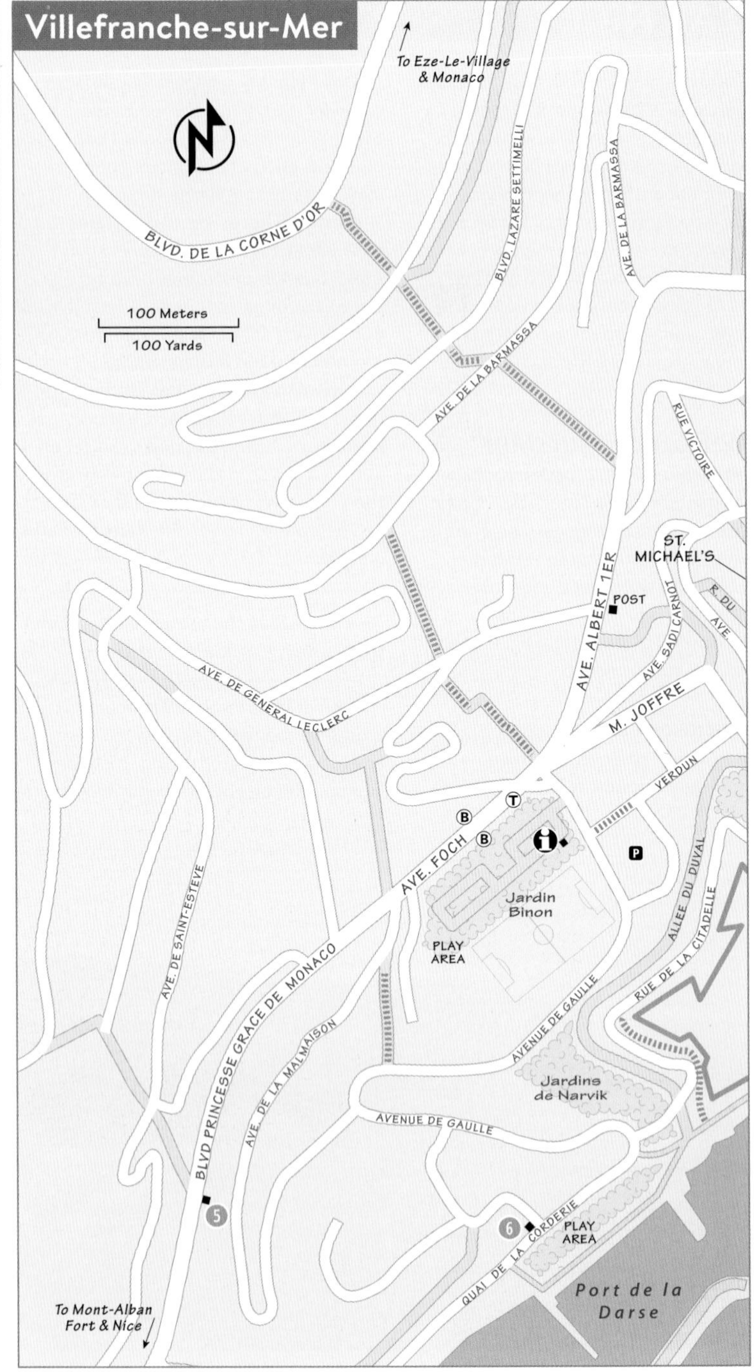
Villefranche-sur-Mer
To Eze-Le-Village & Monaco
BLVD. DE LA CORNE D'OR
BLVD. LAZARE SETTIMELLI
AVE. DE LA BARMASSA
100 Meters
100 Yards
AVE. DE LA BARMASSA
RUE VICTOIRE
ST. MICHAEL'S
AVE. ALBERT 1ER
POST
AVE. SADI CARNOT
R. DU
AVE.
AVE. DE GENERAL LECLERC
M. JOFFRE
VERDUN
AVE. FOCH
Jardin Binon
PLAY AREA
ALLEE DU DUVAL
RUE DE LA CITADELLE
AVE. DE SAINT-ESTEVE
BLVD PRINCESSE GRACE DE MONACO
AVE. DE LA MALMAISON
AVENUE DE GAULLE
Jardins de Narvik
AVENUE DE GAULLE
QUAI DE LA CORDERIE
PLAY AREA
Port de la Darse
To Mont-Alban Fort & Nice

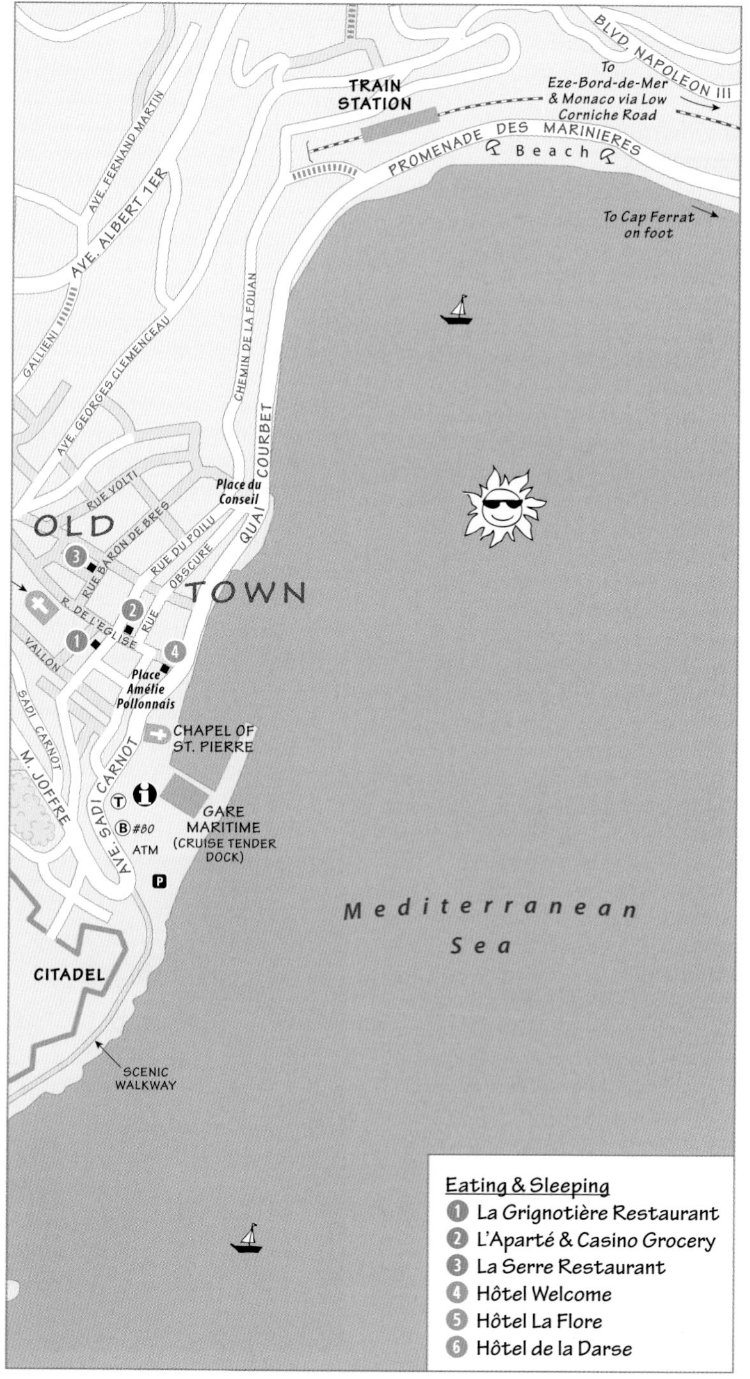
BLVD. NAPOLEON III
To Eze-Bord-de-Mer & Monaco via Low Corniche Road
TRAIN STATION
PROMENADE DES MARINIERES
Beach
To Cap Ferrat on foot
AVE. FERNAND MARTIN
AVE. ALBERT 1ER
GALLIENI
AVE. GEORGES CLEMENCEAU
CHEMIN DE LA FOUAN
QUAI COURBET
Place du Conseil
RUE VOLTI
OLD TOWN
RUE BARON DE BRES
RUE DU POILU
RUE OBSCURE
R. DE L'EGLISE
VALLON
SADI CARNOT
M. JOFFRE
Place Amélie Pollonnais
CHAPEL OF ST. PIERRE
AVE. SADI CARNOT
#80
ATM
GARE MARITIME (CRUISE TENDER DOCK)
CITADEL
SCENIC WALKWAY
Mediterranean Sea
Eating & Sleeping
1 La Grignotière Restaurant
2 L'Aparté & Casino Grocery
3 La Serre Restaurant
4 Hôtel Welcome
5 Hôtel La Flore
6 Hôtel de la Darse

Octroi bus stop (daily in season, closed Sun off-season, tel. 04 93 01 73 68, www.villefranche-sur-mer.com).

➲ *Villefranche-sur-Mer Town Walk*

This quick self-guided stroll starts at the waterfront and finishes at the citadel.

• *Go to the end of the little pier directly in front of Hôtel Welcome, where we'll start with a spin tour (spin to the right) to get oriented.*

The Harbor: At 2,000 feet, this is the deepest natural harbor on the Riviera and was the region's most important port until Nice built its own in the 18th century. Look out to sea. Cap Ferrat, the hill across the bay, is a landscaped paradise where the 1 percent of the 1 percent compete for the best view. Geologically, Cap Ferrat is the southern tip of the Alps. The range emerges from the sea here and arcs all across Europe, over 700 miles, to Vienna. The Rothschild's pink mansion, Villa Ephrussi (slightly left of center, hugging the top) is the most worthwhile sight to visit on the Cap (see page 364).

Up on the hill, the 16th-century citadel is marked by flags. The yellow fisherman's chapel (with the little-toe bell tower) has an interior painted by the writer/artist Jean Cocteau. Hôtel Welcome offers the balconies of dreams. Up the lane is the baroque facade of St. Michael's Church. The promenade, lined by fancy fish restaurants, leads to the town beach. Fifty yards above the beach stands the train station and above that, supported by arches, is the Low Corniche road, which leads to Monaco.

• *Walk left 30 yards past the last couple of boats surviving from the town's once important fishing community to a small bronze bust of Jean Cocteau. Step up to the little chapel he painted.*

Chapel of St. Pierre (Chapelle Cocteau): This chapel is the town's cultural highlight (open Wed-Mon 10:00-12:00 & 15:00-19:00, usually closed Tue). Cocteau, who decorated the place, was a Parisian transplant who adored little Villefranche-sur-Mer and whose career was distinguished by his work as an artist, poet, novelist, playwright, and filmmaker. Influenced by his pals Marcel Proust, André Gide, Edith Piaf, and Pablo Picasso, Cocteau was a leader among the 20th-century avant-garde.

• *From the chapel, stroll the harbor promenade 100 yards past Restaurant La Mère Germaine. Just past the restaurant, a lane (signed Vieille Ville) leads up into the old town. Walk a few steps until you reach a long tunnel-like street.*

Rue Obscure, the Old Town, and St. Michael's Church: Here, under these 13th-century vaults, you're in another age. Before the long stepped lane (which we'll climb later), turn right and walk to the end of Rue Obscure (which means "dark street"). At the end, wind up to the sunlight past a tiny fountain at Place du Conseil, and a few steps beyond that to a viewpoint overlooking the beach. Then stroll back past the fountain and gently downhill. At Place des Deux Canons, turn right and climb the stepped lanes, and then take your first left (at a restaurant) to St. Michael's Church, facing a delightful square (Place de l'Eglise) with a single

Chapel of St. Pierre

magnolia tree. The church features an 18th-century organ, a particularly engaging crucifix at the high altar, and a fine statue of a recumbent Christ—carved, they say, from a fig tree by a galley slave in the 1600s.

• *Leaving St. Michael's, go downhill halfway to the water, where you hit the main commercial street. Go right on Rue du Poilu to Place de la République. Head through the square and angle left, up the hill to the...*

Citadel: The town's mammoth castle, with walls sloping thickly at the base, was built in the 1500s, the so-called "Age of Black Powder." With the advent of gunpowder, stout cannonball-deflecting walls became a necessity for any effective fortification.

• *That concludes our introductory walk.*

Experiences

BOAT RIDES (*PROMENADES EN MER*)

To view this beautiful coastline from the sea, take a quick sightseeing cruise (€12 for one-hour trip around Cap Ferrat, €20 for two-hour cruise as far as Monaco, departures from harbor across from Hôtel Welcome, June-Sept Wed and Sat, also Thu in July-Aug, no trips Oct-May, reservations a must, tel. 04 93 76 65 65, www.amv-sirenes.com).

HIKE TO MONT-ALBAN FORT

This fort, with a remarkable setting on the high ridge that separates Nice and Villefranche-sur-Mer, is a good destination for hikers (also accessible by car; info at TI). From the TI, walk on the main road toward Nice about 200 yards past Hôtel Versailles. Look for wooden trail signs labeled *Escalier de Verre* and climb about 45 minutes as the trail makes long switchbacks through the woods up to the ridge. Find your way to Mont-Alban Fort (interior closed to tourists) and its view terrace.

Waterfront tables line Villefranche's harbor.

MARKETS

A fun bric-a-brac market enlivens Villefranche-sur-Mer on Sundays (on Place Amélie Pollonnais by Hôtel Welcome, and in Jardin François Binon by the TI). On Saturday and Wednesday mornings, a small food market sets up in Jardin François Binon.

Eating and Sleeping

$$$ La Grignotière serves generous and tasty *plats* (closed Wed off-season, 3 Rue du Poilu). **$$$ L'Aparté** is where locals go for fresh cuisine and a special experience (closed Mon, 1 Rue Obscure). **$ La Serre** serves well-priced dinners (open evenings only, 16 Rue de May). Picnickers can raid the handy **Casino grocery** (closed Sun afternoon and all day Wed, 12 Rue du Poilu).

Overnighters will find seaview rooms at **$$$ Hôtel Welcome****** (3 Quai Amiral Courbet, www.welcomehotel.com); **$$ Hôtel La Flore***** (5 Boulevard Princesse Grace de Monaco, www.hotel-la-flore.fr), and **$ Hôtel de la Darse**** (32 Avenue du Général de Gaulle, www.hoteldeladarse.com).

Cap Ferrat

Exclusive Cap Ferrat is a peaceful eddy off the busy Nice-Monaco route. If you owned a house here, some of the richest people on the planet would be your neighbors. Take a leisurely tour of the Villa Ephrussi de Rothschild mansion and gardens, then enjoy the late afternoon on the beach at Plage de Passable.

Getting There: Take **Bus #81** (direction: *Le Port/Cap Ferrat*); for the Villa Ephrussi or the beach, get off at the

Passable stop (the return bus is direction: *Nice*). **Warning:** Late-afternoon buses back to Villefranche-sur-Mer or Nice can be jammed (worse on weekends), potentially leaving passengers stranded at stops for long periods.

Cap Ferrat is quick by **car** (take the Low Corniche) or **taxi** (allow €25 one-way from Villefranche-sur-Mer, €50 from Nice).

Tourist Information: The main TI is near the Villa Ephrussi (Mon-Fri 9:00-16:00, closed Sat-Sun, 59 Avenue Denis Séméria, bus #81 stops here). A smaller TI is in the sleepy village of St-Jean-Cap-Ferrat (closed Sun, 5 Avenue Denis Séméria, tel. 04 93 76 08 90, office-tourisme@saintjeancapferrat.fr).

Rick's Tip: *Cap Ferrat is perfect for a walk; you'll find* **well-maintained, mostly level foot trails** *covering most of its length. The TIs in Villefranche-sur-Mer and on the Cap have maps with walking paths marked.*

Sights

▲VILLA EPHRUSSI DE ROTHSCHILD

In what seems like the ultimate in Riviera extravagance, Venice, Versailles, and the Côte d'Azur come together in the pastel-pink Villa Ephrussi. Rising above Cap Ferrat, this 1905 mansion has views west to Villefranche-sur-Mer and east to Beaulieu-sur-Mer.

Cost and Hours: Palace and gardens-€13, includes audioguide; mid-Feb-Oct daily 10:00-18:00, July-Aug until 19:00, shorter hours off-season; tel. 04 93 01 33 09, www.villa-ephrussi.com.

Villa Ephrussi de Rothschild

Visiting the Villa: Pick up the audioguide and garden map as you enter, then start with the well-furnished belle époque **interior.** Upstairs, an 18-minute film covers the life of rich and eccentric Beatrice, Baroness de Rothschild, the French banking heiress who built and furnished the place. Don't miss the view over the gardens from the terrace.

As you stroll through the rooms, you'll pass royal furnishings and personal possessions, including the baroness's porcelain collection and her bathroom case for cruises. An appropriately classy **garden-tearoom** serves drinks and lunches with a view (12:00-17:30).

Behind the mansion are literally ship-shape gardens, inspired by Beatrice's many ocean-liner trips. The seven lush gardens are re-created from locations all over the world. Highlights include the Jardin Exotique's wild cactus, the rose garden at the far end, and the view back to the house from the "Temple of Love" gazebo.

PLAGE DE PASSABLE

Located below the Villa Ephrussi is a pebbly little beach with great views, popular with families. One half is public (free, with snack bar, shower, and WC), and the other is run by a small restaurant (€22 includes changing locker, lounge chair, and shower; they have 260 "beds," but still reserve ahead in summer or on weekends as this is a prime spot, tel. 04 93 76 06 17). If you were ever to do the French Riviera rent-a-beach ritual, this would be the place.

Getting There: Bus #81 stops just above the beach (Passable stop). Drivers can park curbside or in a pay lot near the beach.

Eating: Plage de Passable is a great place for dinner. Arrive before sunset, then watch as darkness descends and lights flicker over Villefranche-sur-Mer's heavenly setting. **Restaurant de la Plage de Passable** is your chance to dine on the beach with romance and class while enjoying terrific views and the sounds of children still at play (€12-16 starters, €18-30 *plats*, open daily late May-early Sept, always make a reservation, tel. 04 93 76 06 17, www.plage-de-passable.com).

Monaco

The minuscule principality of Monaco (less than a square mile) is a special place—it's home to one of the world's most famous auto races and one of its fanciest casinos. The glamorous 1956 marriage of the American actress Grace Kelly to Prince Rainier added to Monaco's mystique. Don't look for anything too deep in this glittering little land of luxury; the majority of its 36,000 residents have relocated here mainly to avoid paying income tax. Yet despite high prices, wall-to-wall daytime tourists, and a Disney-esque atmosphere, Monaco is a Riviera must for many a traveler.

Orientation

All of Monaco's major sights except the casino are in Monaco-Ville, packed within a few cheerfully tidy blocks. The famous casino is in the Monte Carlo neighborhood.

Day Plan: The surgical-strike plan is to start with my self-guided walk in Monaco-Ville, and then finish by gambling away whatever you have left in the Monte Carlo Casino.

Getting There: Ride **bus #100** (3-4/hour) from Nice (45 minutes) or Villefranche-sur-Mer (20 minutes). Trains run twice an hour (20 minutes from Nice, 10 minutes from Villefranche). Monaco's traffic isn't worth the fight for drivers—leave the car behind and ride the train or bus into town.

Arrival in Monaco: Bus riders wanting to start with the self-guided walk should disembark at the *Place d'Armes* stop at the base of Monaco-Ville; casino-goers should wait for the *Monte Carlo-Casino* stop.

From the train station, for Monaco-Ville, take the exit marked *Sortie Fontvieille/Le Rocher*, which leads through a long tunnel to Place d'Armes. For the casino, follow *Sortie Port* and *Accès Port* signs until you pop out at the port. From here, it's a 20-minute walk to the casino (up Avenue d'Ostende to your left), or a short trip via bus (#1 or #2, find stops across the busy street).

Getting Around Monaco: City buses #1 and #2 link all areas with frequent service (single ticket-€2, 6 tickets-€10, day pass-€5, pay driver or buy from curbside machines). You can split a six-ride ticket with your travel partners.

Tourist Information: The main TI is at the top of the park above the casino (Mon-Sat 9:00-19:00, Sun 11:00-13:00, 2 Boulevard des Moulins, tel. 00-377/92 16 61 16 or 00-377/92 16 61 66, www.visitmonaco.com). Another TI is at the train station (Tue-Sat 9:00-18:00, also open Sun-Mon in July-Aug, closed 12:00-14:00 off-season).

Rick's Tip: *If you want an official memento of your Monaco visit, you can get your* **passport stamped** *at the main TI.*

➲ *Monaco-Ville Walk*

This self-guided walk connects many of the main sights with a tight little loop, starting from the palace square, Monaco-Ville's sightseeing center.

• *If you're walking up from the Place d'Armes stop for bus #100, a well-marked lane leads directly to the palace.*

PALACE SQUARE (PLACE DU PALAIS)

This square is the best place to get oriented to Monaco. Facing the palace, go to the right and look out over the city (er... principality). This rock gave birth to the little pastel Hong Kong look-alike in 1215, and it's managed to remain an independent country for most of its 800 years.

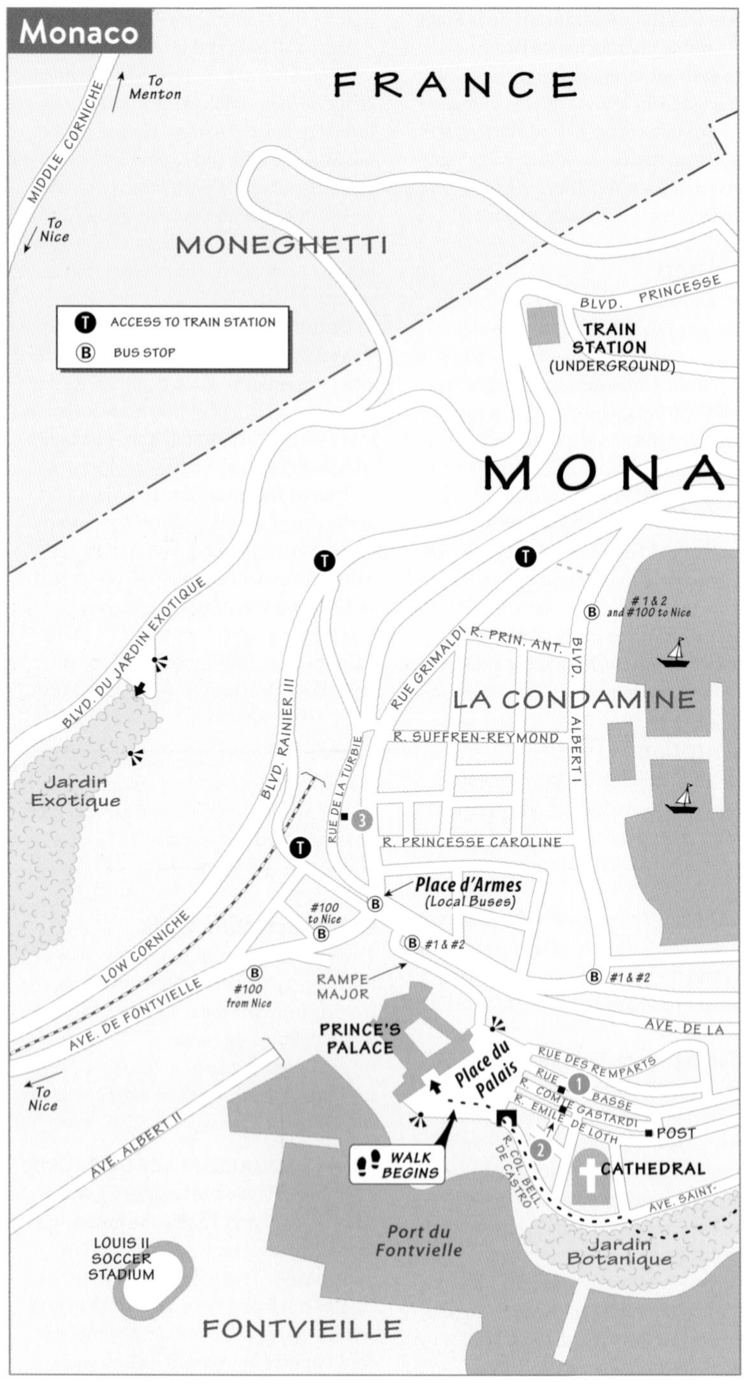
Monaco
FRANCE
To Menton
MIDDLE CORNICHE
To Nice
MONEGHETTI
ACCESS TO TRAIN STATION
BUS STOP
BLVD. PRINCESSE
TRAIN STATION (UNDERGROUND)
MONA
#1 & 2 and #100 to Nice
BLVD. DU JARDIN EXOTIQUE
RUE GRIMALDI
R. PRIN. ANT.
BLVD. ALBERT I
LA CONDAMINE
BLVD. RAINIER III
RUE DE LA TURBIE
R. SUFFREN-REYMOND
Jardin Exotique
R. PRINCESSE CAROLINE
Place d'Armes (Local Buses)
#100 to Nice
#1 & #2
LOW CORNICHE
RAMPE MAJOR
#100 from Nice
AVE. DE FONTVIELLE
#1 & #2
PRINCE'S PALACE
AVE. DE LA
Place du Palais
RUE DES REMPARTS
RUE BASSE
R. COMTE GASTARDI
R. EMILE DE LOTH
POST
To Nice
AVE. ALBERT II
WALK BEGINS
R. COL. BELL. DE CASTRO
CATHEDRAL
AVE. SAINT-
Port du Fontvielle
Jardin Botanique
LOUIS II SOCCER STADIUM
FONTVIEILLE

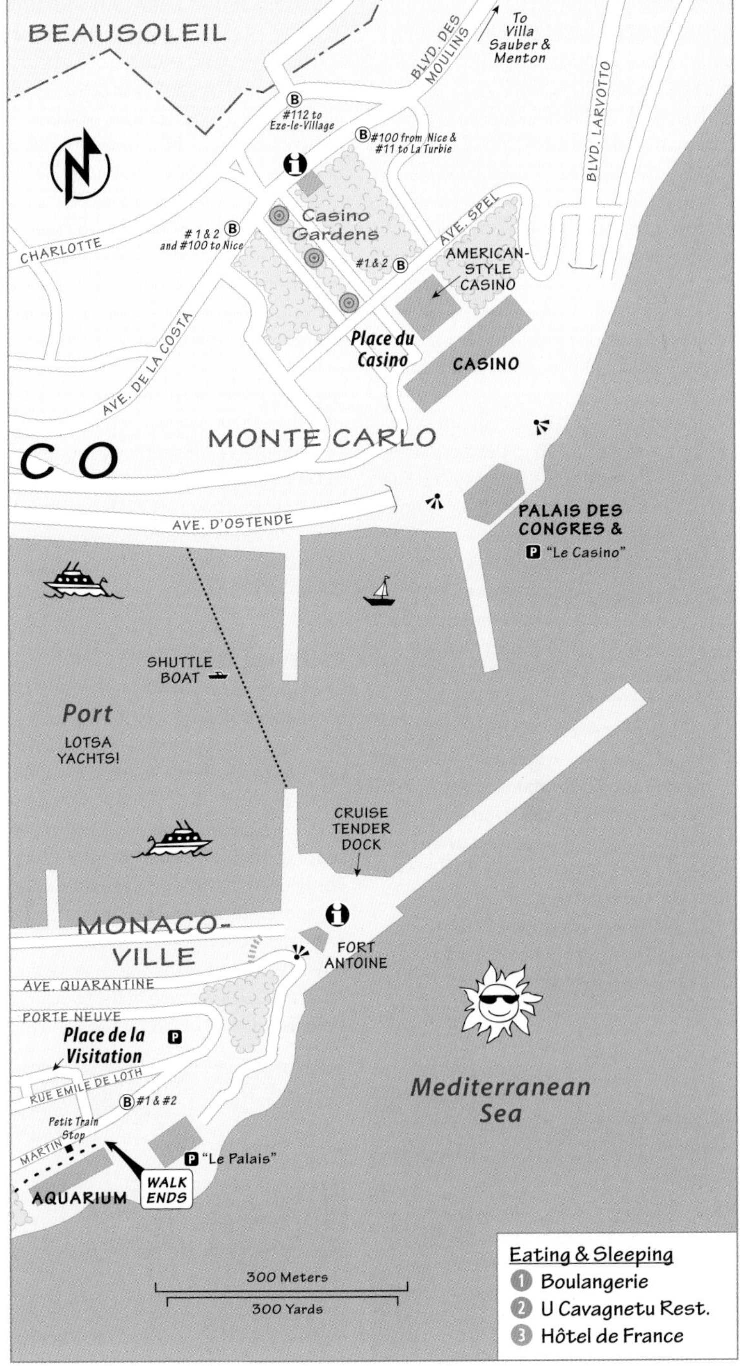

BEAUSOLEIL
BLVD. DES MOULINS
To Villa Sauber & Menton
BLVD. LARVOTTO
#112 to Eze-le-Village
#100 from Nice & #11 to La Turbie
Casino Gardens
#1 & 2 and #100 to Nice
CHARLOTTE
AVE. SPEL
#1 & 2
AMERICAN-STYLE CASINO
AVE. DE LA COSTA
Place du Casino
CASINO
MONTE CARLO
C O
AVE. D'OSTENDE
PALAIS DES CONGRES &
"Le Casino"
SHUTTLE BOAT
Port
LOTSA YACHTS!
CRUISE TENDER DOCK
MONACO-VILLE
FORT ANTOINE
AVE. QUARANTINE
PORTE NEUVE
Place de la Visitation
RUE EMILE DE LOTH
#1 & #2
Petit Train Stop
MARTIN
"Le Palais"
WALK ENDS
AQUARIUM
Mediterranean Sea
300 Meters
300 Yards
Eating & Sleeping
1 Boulangerie
2 U Cavagnetu Rest.
3 Hôtel de France

Looking beyond the glitzy port, notice the faded green roof above and to the right: It belongs to the casino that put Monaco on the map in the 1800s.

The modern buildings just past the casino mark the eastern limit of Monaco. The famous Grand Prix runs along the port and then up the ramp to the casino (at top speeds of 180 mph). Italy is so close, you can almost smell the pesto. Just beyond the casino is France again (which flanks Monaco on both sides)—you could walk one-way from France to France, passing through Monaco in about 60 minutes.

The odd statue of a woman with a fishing net is dedicated to the glorious reign of **Prince Albert I** (1889-1922). The son of Charles III (who built the casino), Albert I was a true Renaissance man. He had a Jacques Cousteau-like fascination with the sea (and built Monaco's famous aquarium) and was a determined pacifist who made many attempts to dissuade Germany's Kaiser Wilhelm II from becoming involved in World War I.

• *As you head toward the palace, you'll find a statue of a monk grasping a sword nearby.*

Meet **François Grimaldi,** a renegade Italian dressed as a monk, who captured Monaco in 1297 and began the dynasty that still rules the principality. The current ruler, Prince Albert, is his great-great-great...grandson, which gives Monaco's royal family the distinction of being the longest-lasting dynasty in Europe.

• *Now walk to the...*

PRINCE'S PALACE (PALAIS PRINCIER)

A medieval castle sat where the palace is today. Its strategic setting has had a lot to do with Monaco's ability to resist attackers. Today, Prince Albert and his wife live in the palace, while poor Princesses Stephanie and Caroline live down the street. The palace guards protect the prince 24/7 and still stage a **Changing of the Guard** ceremony with all the pageantry of an important nation (daily at 11:55, fun to watch but jam-packed, arrive by 11:30). Audioguide tours take you through part of the prince's lavish palace in 30 minutes. The rooms are well-furnished and impressive, but interesting only if you haven't seen a château lately (€8, includes audioguide, €19 combo-ticket also covers Oceanographic Museum and Aquarium; April-Oct daily 10:00-18:00, closed Nov-March, www.palais.mc).

• *Head to the west end of the palace square. Below the cannonballs is the district known as...*

FONTVIEILLE

Monaco's newest, reclaimed-from-the-sea area has seen much of Monaco's post-WWII growth (notice the lushly planted building tops). Prince Rainier continued—some say, was obsessed with—Monaco's economic growth, creating landfills (and topping them with apartments such as in Fontvieille), flashy ports, more beaches, a big sports stadium marked by tall arches, and a rail station.

• *With your back to the palace, leave the square through the arch at the far right (Rue Colonel Bellando de Castro) and find the...*

Monaco's classy port

Palace Square

CATHEDRAL OF MONACO (CATHEDRALE DE MONACO)

The somber but beautifully lit cathedral, rebuilt in 1878, shows that Monaco cared for more than just its new casino. It's where centuries of Grimaldis are buried, and where Princess Grace and Prince Rainier were married. Inside, circle slowly behind the altar (counterclockwise). The second tomb is that of Albert I, who did much to put Monaco on the world stage. The second-to-last tomb—inscribed "*Gratia Patricia, MCMLXXXII*"—is where Princess Grace was buried in 1982. Prince Rainier's tomb lies next to Princess Grace's (daily 8:30-19:15).

• *As you leave the cathedral, find the 1956 wedding photo of Princess Grace and Prince Rainier, then dip into the immaculately maintained* ***Jardin Botanique,*** *with more fine views. In the gardens, turn left. Eventually you'll find the impressive building housing the...*

Rick's Tip: *If you're into* **stamps,** *drop by the* **post office,** *where postcard writers with panache can see—or buy—impressive Monegasque stamps (closed Sun, on Place de la Mairie, a few blocks from the Oceanographic Museum and Aquarium).*

OCEANOGRAPHIC MUSEUM AND AQUARIUM (MUSEE OCEANOGRAPHIQUE)

Prince Albert I built this cliff-hanging aquarium in 1910 as a monument to his enthusiasm for things from the sea. The aquarium, which Jacques Cousteau captained for 32 years, has 2,000 different specimens, representing 250 species. You'll find Mediterranean fish and colorful tropical species. Rotating exhibits occupy the entry floor. Upstairs, the fancy Albert I Hall houses a museum that's filled with ship models, whale skeletons, and oceanographic instruments. Take the elevator to the rooftop terrace view café (€14, €19 combo-ticket includes Prince's Palace;

A *Changing of the guard*
B *Cathedral of Monaco*
C *Fontvieille harbor*
D *Oceanographic Museum*

daily April-Sept 10:00-19:00, July-Aug until 19:30, Oct-March until 18:00, www.oceano.mc).

• *Our walk is over. The red-brick steps across from the aquarium lead up to stops for buses #1 and #2, both of which run to the casino and the train station.*

Rick's Tip: *For a* **cheap and scenic loop ride** *through Monaco, ride bus #2 from one end to the other and back (25 minutes each way). You need two tickets (€2 each) and have to get off the bus at the last stop and then get on again.*

Experiences

▲MONTE CARLO CASINO (CASINO DE MONTE-CARLO)

Monte Carlo, which means "Charles' Hill" in Spanish, is named for the prince who presided over Monaco's 19th-century makeover. In the mid-1800s, olive groves stood here. Then, with the construction of a casino and spas, and easy road and train access, one of Europe's poorest countries was on the Grand Tour map—*the* place for the vacationing aristocracy to play. Today, Monaco has the world's highest per-capita income.

The Monte Carlo casino is intended to make you feel comfortable while losing your retirement nest egg. Charles Garnier designed the place (with an opera house inside) in 1878, in part to thank the prince for his financial help in completing Paris' Opéra Garnier (which the architect also designed).

The **first rooms** (Salle Renaissance, Salon de l'Europe, and Salle des Amériques) have European and English roulette, black-jack, craps, and slot machines. The more glamorous **private game rooms** (Salons Touzet, Salle Medecin, and Terrasse Salle Blanche) have those same games, plus Trente et Quarante, Ultimate Texas Hold 'Em poker, and Punto Banco—a version of baccarat.

Cost and Hours: Hours and entry fees are shuffled regularly. Plan on €10 to enter at any hour, whether you gamble or not. Public areas are open daily 9:00-12:30 (no gambling). Guided tours may be available, or take an English brochure and tour on your own. From 14:00 to very late the gaming rooms are open to appropriately

Lush gardens lead to Monte Carlo Casino.

attired humans over 18 (bring your passport as proof, www.montecarlocasinos.com).

Dress Code: Before 14:00, shorts are allowed in the atrium area, though you'll need decent attire to go any farther. After 14:00, shorts are off-limits everywhere, and tennis shoes are not permitted. Men should wear a jacket and slacks, and women should dress up a bit as well.

Take the Money and Run: The stop for buses returning to Nice and Villefranche-sur-Mer and for local buses #1 and #2 is on Avenue de la Costa, at the top of the park above the casino (at the small shopping mall). To reach the train station from the casino, take bus #1 or #2 from this stop, or walk about 15 minutes down Avenue d'Ostende toward the port, and follow signs to *Gare SNCF*.

Eating and Sleeping

In Monaco-Ville, you'll find massive *pan bagnat*, quiche, and sandwiches at the yellow-bannered **$ Boulangerie,** a block off Place du Palais (8 Rue Basse). At **$$ U Cavagnetu,** just a block from Albert's palace, you'll dine cheaply on specialties from Monaco (14 Rue Comte Félix Gastaldi).

Centrally located and comfortable, **$$ Hôtel de France**** is reasonably priced—for Monaco (6 Rue de la Turbie, www.monte-carlo.mc/france).

Antibes

Rising above the blue Mediterranean south and west of Nice, Antibes is charming in a sandy-sophisticated way. Besides offering wide, pleasant beaches, it's the launching point for several scenic hikes along the rocky coast.

Orientation

Day Plan: Visitors can browse Europe's biggest yacht harbor, snooze on a sandy beach, loiter through the charming old town, and hike along a sea-swept trail. The town's cultural claim to fame, the Picasso Museum, shows off its appealing collection in a fine old building.

Getting There: Trains and buses run from Nice to Antibes, but the train is the better choice—it's faster and won't get you stuck in traffic (2/hour, 20 minutes).

Arrival in Antibes: To walk from the train station to the port, the old town, and

Antibes' Plage de la Gravette

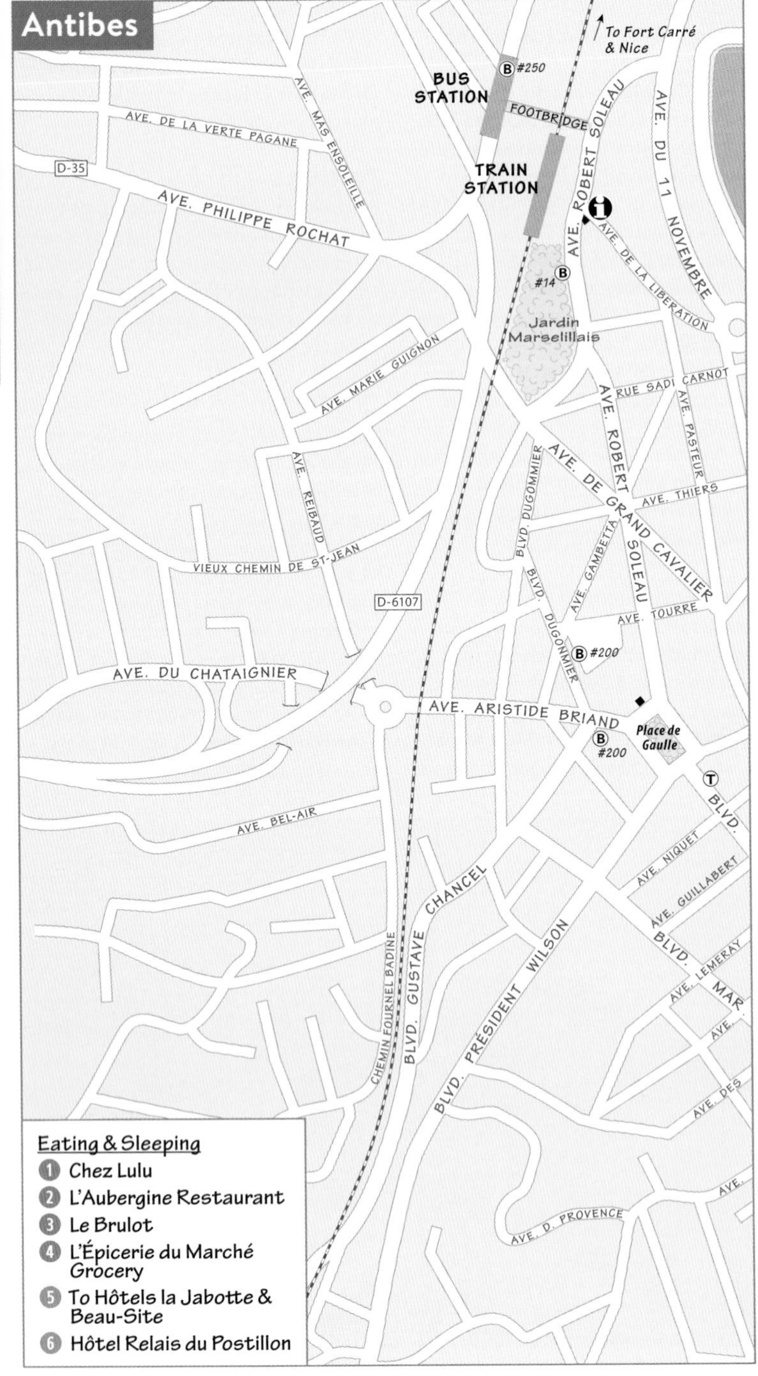

Eating & Sleeping

1. Chez Lulu
2. L'Aubergine Restaurant
3. Le Brulot
4. L'Épicerie du Marché Grocery
5. To Hôtels la Jabotte & Beau-Site
6. Hôtel Relais du Postillon

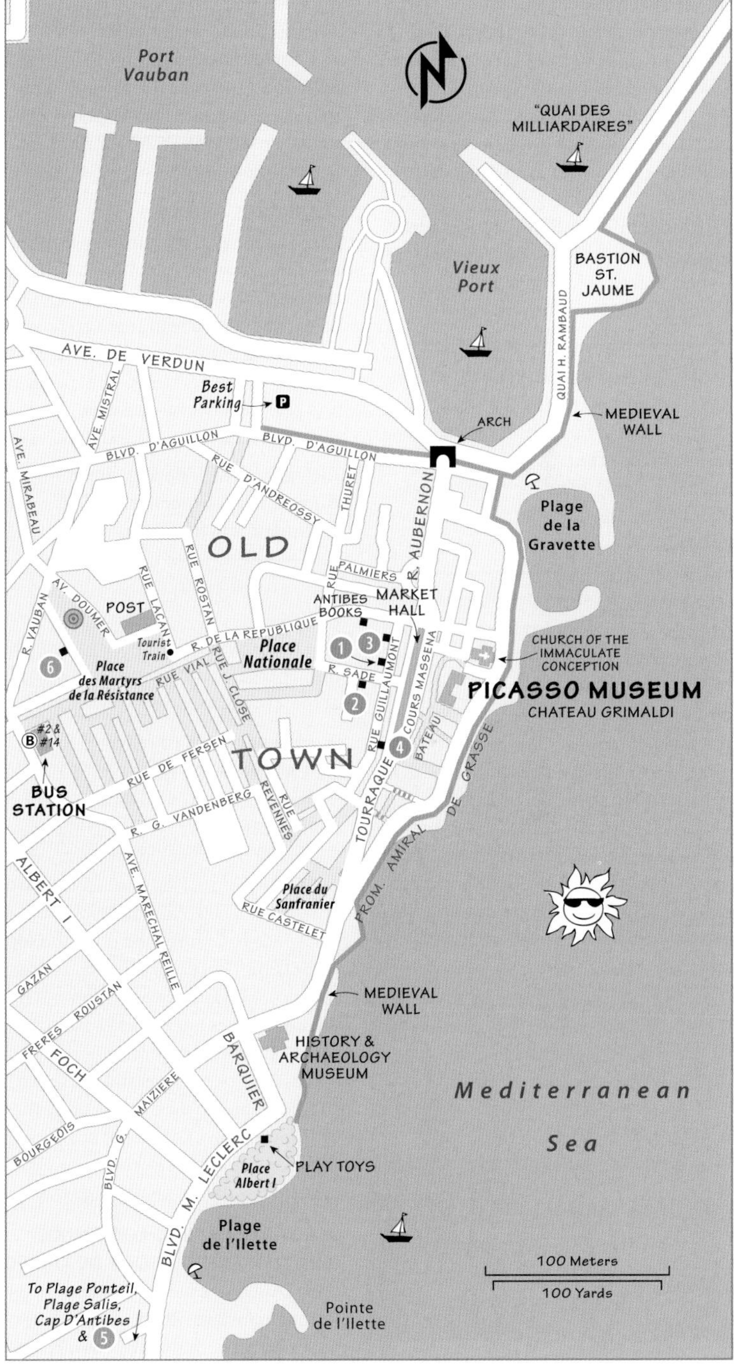
Port Vauban
"QUAI DES MILLIARDAIRES"
Vieux Port
BASTION ST. JAUME
QUAI H. RAMBAUD
AVE. DE VERDUN
Best Parking
ARCH
MEDIEVAL WALL
AVE. MISTRAL
BLVD. D'AGUILLON
RUE D'ANDREOSSY
THURET
R. AUBERNON
AVE. MIRABEAU
Plage de la Gravette
OLD
RUE ROSTAN
RUE LACAN
RUE PALMIERS
AV. DOUMER
POST
R. VAUBAN
ANTIBES BOOKS
MARKET HALL
R. DE LA REPUBLIQUE
Tourist Train
Place Nationale
CHURCH OF THE IMMACULATE CONCEPTION
Place des Martyrs de la Résistance
RUE VIAL
RUE J. CLOSE
R. SADE
RUE GUILLAUMONT
COURS MASSENA
PICASSO MUSEUM
CHATEAU GRIMALDI
#2 & #14
RUE DE FERSEN
TOWN
BATEAU
BUS STATION
R. G. VANDENBERG
RUE REVENNES
TOURRAQUE
PROM. AMIRAL DE GRASSE
ALBERT I
AVE. MARECHAL REILLE
Place du Sanfranier
RUE CASTELET
GAZAN
FRERES ROUSTAN
MEDIEVAL WALL
FOCH
HISTORY & ARCHAEOLOGY MUSEUM
BARQUIER
MAIZIERE
Mediterranean Sea
BOURGEOIS
BLVD. G.
BLVD. M. LECLERC
Place Albert I
PLAY TOYS
Plage de l'Ilette
100 Meters
100 Yards
To Plage Ponteil, Plage Salis, Cap D'Antibes & 5
Pointe de l'Ilette

the Picasso Museum (15 minutes), cross the street in front of the station, skirting left of the café, and follow Avenue de la Libération downhill as it bends left. At the end of the street, head right along the port. Day-trippers arriving by car should follow signs to *Centre-Ville,* then *Port Vauban.*

Tourist Information: The TI is a few blocks from the train station at 42 Avenue Robert Soleau (open daily, tel. 04 22 10 60 10, www.antibesjuanlespins.com).

Rick's Tip: *Antibes'* **market hall,** *on Cours Masséna, bustling under a 19th-century canopy, changes throughout the day: flowers and produce until 13:30 (daily but closed Mon Sept-May), handicrafts most afternoons (Thu-Sun), and outdoor dining in the evenings.*

Sights

▲▲PICASSO MUSEUM (MUSEE PICASSO)

Sitting serenely where the old town meets the sea, this compact three-floor museum offers a manageable collection of Picasso's paintings, sketches, and ceramics. Picasso lived in this castle (the former Château Grimaldi) for several months in 1946, when he cranked out an amazing amount of art. Most of the paintings you'll see here are from this short but prolific stretch of his long career. The resulting collection (donated by Picasso) put Antibes on the tourist map.

Terrace at the Picasso Museum

Cost and Hours: €6; mid-June-mid-Sept Tue-Sun 10:00-18:00, mid-Sept-mid-June Tue-Sun 10:00-12:00 & 14:00-18:00, closed Mon year-round; tel. 04 92 90 54 20, www.antibes-juanlespins.com.

▲BEACHES (*PLAGES*)

Good beaches stretch from the south end of Antibes toward Cap d'Antibes. They're busy but manageable in summer and on weekends, with cheap snack stands and good views of the old town. The closest beach is at the port (Plage de la Gravette) and seems calm in any season.

Rick's Tip: *Locals* **don't swim in July and August,** *as the warming sea brings swarms of* **stinging jellyfish.** *Ask before you dip.*

Hikes

The two hikes below are easy to combine by bus, bike, or car. For bus schedules, ask at the TI or consult www.envibus.fr.

▲▲CHAPELLE ET PHARE DE LA GAROUPE HIKE

The exceptional territorial views—best in the morning—from this lighthouse viewpoint more than merit the 20-minute uphill climb from Plage de la Salis. An orientation table explains that you can see from Nice to Cannes and up to the Alps.

Getting There: Take Envibus bus #2 or #14 to the Plage de la Salis stop and find the trail a block ahead (a few blocks after Maupassant Apartments; where the road curves left, follow signs and the rough, cobbled Chemin du Calvaire up to the lighthouse tower). By car or bike, follow signs for *Cap d'Antibes,* then look for *Chapelle et Phare de la Garoupe* signs.

▲▲CAP D'ANTIBES LOOP HIKE (SENTIER TOURISTIQUE DE TIREPOIL)

Cap d'Antibes is filled with exclusive villas and mansions. Roads are just lanes, bounded on both sides by the high and greedy walls of some of the most expensive real estate in France. But all the money in the world can't buy you the beach in France, so a thin strip of rocky coastline forms a two-mile long, park-like zone with an extremely scenic, mostly paved but often rocky trail (Sentier Touristique de Tirepoil).

At a fast clip you can walk the entire circle in just over an hour. Don't do the hike without the tourist map (available at hotels or the TI). While you can do it in either direction (or in partial segments), I prefer a counterclockwise loop.

Rick's Tip: *You can tour star-shaped* **Fort Carré,** *on the headland overlooking the harbor, but there's little to see inside. It's only worth a visit for* **fantastic views** *over Antibes.*

Getting There: Ride Envibus bus #2 from Antibes for about 15 minutes to the La Fontaine stop at Rond-Point A. Meiland (next to Hôtel Beau-Site). By car or bike, follow signs to *Cap d'Antibes,* then to *Plage de la Garoupe,* and park there. The trail begins at the far-right end of Plage de la Garoupe.

Eating and Sleeping

$$ Chez Lulu is a fun family dining adventure (arrive early, opens at 19:00, closed Sun-Mon, 5 Rue Frédéric Isnard). Intimate **$$ L'Aubergine** delivers fine cuisine at fair prices (opens at 18:30, closed Wed, 7 Rue Sade). **$$ Le Brulot** is known for its meats cooked on an open fire (closed Sun, 2 Rue Frédéric Isnard). Romantics on a shoestring can drop by the handy **L'Épicerie du Marché** and assemble a picnic dinner to enjoy on the beach or ramparts (3 Cours Masséna).

$$ Hôtel la Jabotte** is a cozy boutique hotel (13 Avenue Max Maurey, www.jabotte.com). The comfortable **$$ Hôtel Beau-Site***** is a good-value option, a 10-minute drive from town (141 Boulevard Kennedy, www.hotelbeausite.net). **$ Hôtel Relais du Postillon**** has cute rooms at good rates (8 Rue Championnet, www.relaisdupostillon.com).

Cap d'Antibes' seaside walk

Burgundy

If you're looking for quintessential French culture, you'll find it in Burgundy. This is a calm, cultivated, and serene region, where nature is as sophisticated as its people. Its luscious landscapes are crisscrossed with canals and dotted with quiet farming villages. Both the soil and the farmers who work it are venerated. Its rolling hills give birth to superior wine and fine cuisine.

The town of Beaune is the transportation funnel for eastern France and makes a convenient stopover for travelers (car or train), with easy access north to Paris or Alsace (Colmar), east to the Alps (Chamonix), and south to Provence. Burgundy's lovely tree-lined roads are a joyride for drivers; navigate using the excellent, free map of the region available at all TIs. Without a car, take a bike, minibus tour, or short taxi ride to get from Beaune into the countryside.

BURGUNDY IN 1 DAY

Stay in Beaune. With one day, spend the morning in Beaune and the afternoon exploring the surrounding vineyards and wine villages. If you have a car, or good legs and a bike, the best way to spend your afternoon is by following one of the scenic vineyard drives outlined in this chapter.

BEAUNE

You'll feel comfortable right away in this prosperous, popular, and perfectly French little wine capital, where life centers on the production and consumption of Burgundy's prestigious Côte d'Or (Gold Coast) vintages.

Beaune's real charm is the town itself, which is especially vibrant on Saturday, when colorful market stands fill the main square, Place de la Halle. The one must-see sight is the medieval hospital—Hôtel Dieu des Hospices de Beaune. Stroll the squares and pedestrian lanes to enjoy the town's ambience. Try a wine-tasting in town, or bike or drive through nearby vineyards.

Orientation

Beaune's ring road (with a bike path) follows the foundations of its medieval walls. All roads and activities converge on the town's two squares, Place de la Halle and Place Carnot.

Tourist Information: The main TI is located on the ring road, across from the post office (look for the *Porte Marie de Bourgogne* sign above the doorway, daily June-Sept 9:00-19:00, April-May and Oct until 18:30, shorter hours off-season and closes earlier Sun year-round, tel. 03 80 26 21 30, www.beaune-tourisme.fr). A small TI annex ("Point-I") is housed in the market hall, across from Hôtel Dieu.

BURGUNDY AT A GLANCE

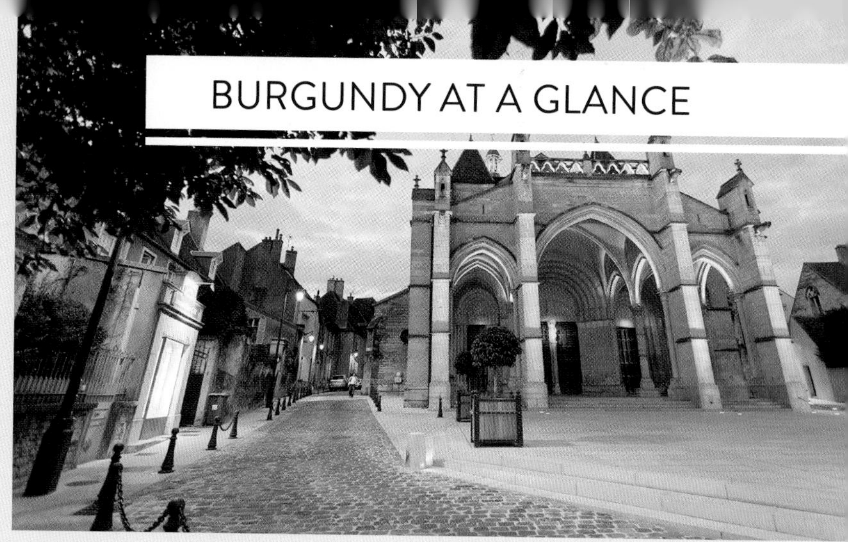

In Beaune

▲▲▲**Hôtel Dieu des Hospices de Beaune** Colorfully decorated medieval charity hospital that's now a fine museum. **Hours:** Daily April-mid-Nov 9:00-18:30, shorter hours off-season. See page 382.

Museum of the Wine of Burgundy Folk museum featuring the history of the vine. **Hours:** April-Sept Wed-Mon 10:00-13:00 & 14:00-18:00, shorter hours off-season, closed Tue year-round and Dec-Feb. See page 385.

Vineyard Loops near Beaune

▲▲**South Vineyard Loop** Beautiful route from Beaune to Château de la Rochepot with plenty of tasting opportunities—best by car. See page 389.

▲**North Vineyard Loop** This route connects wine villages from Beaune to Savigny-lès-Beaune—good by car or bike. See page 393.

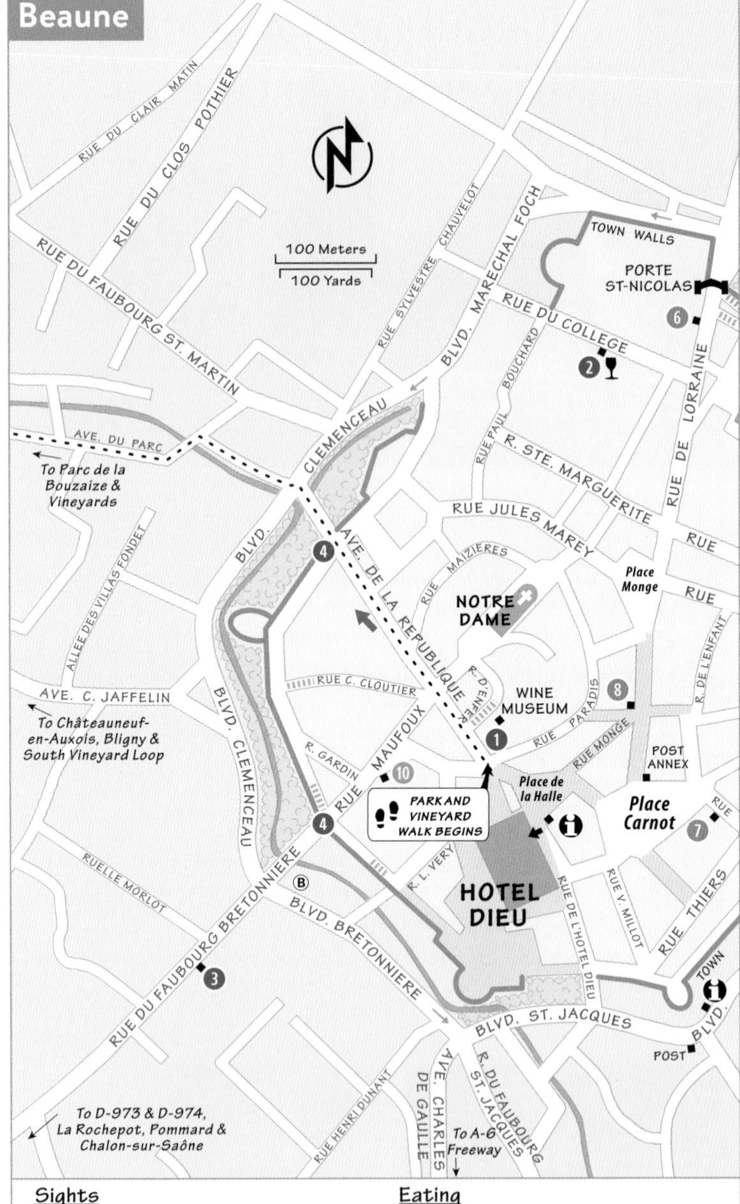

Sights

1. Museum of the Wine of Burgundy
2. Patriarche Père et Fils Wine Tasting
3. The Mustard Mill
4. Access to Ramparts Walk (4)

Eating

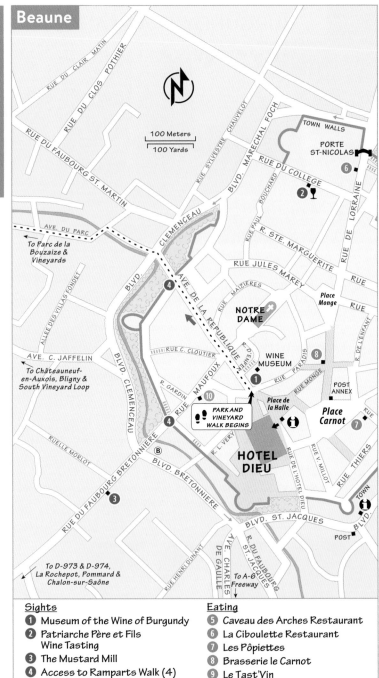

5. Caveau des Arches Restaurant
6. La Ciboulette Restaurant
7. Les Pôpiettes
8. Brasserie le Carnot
9. Le Tast'Vin

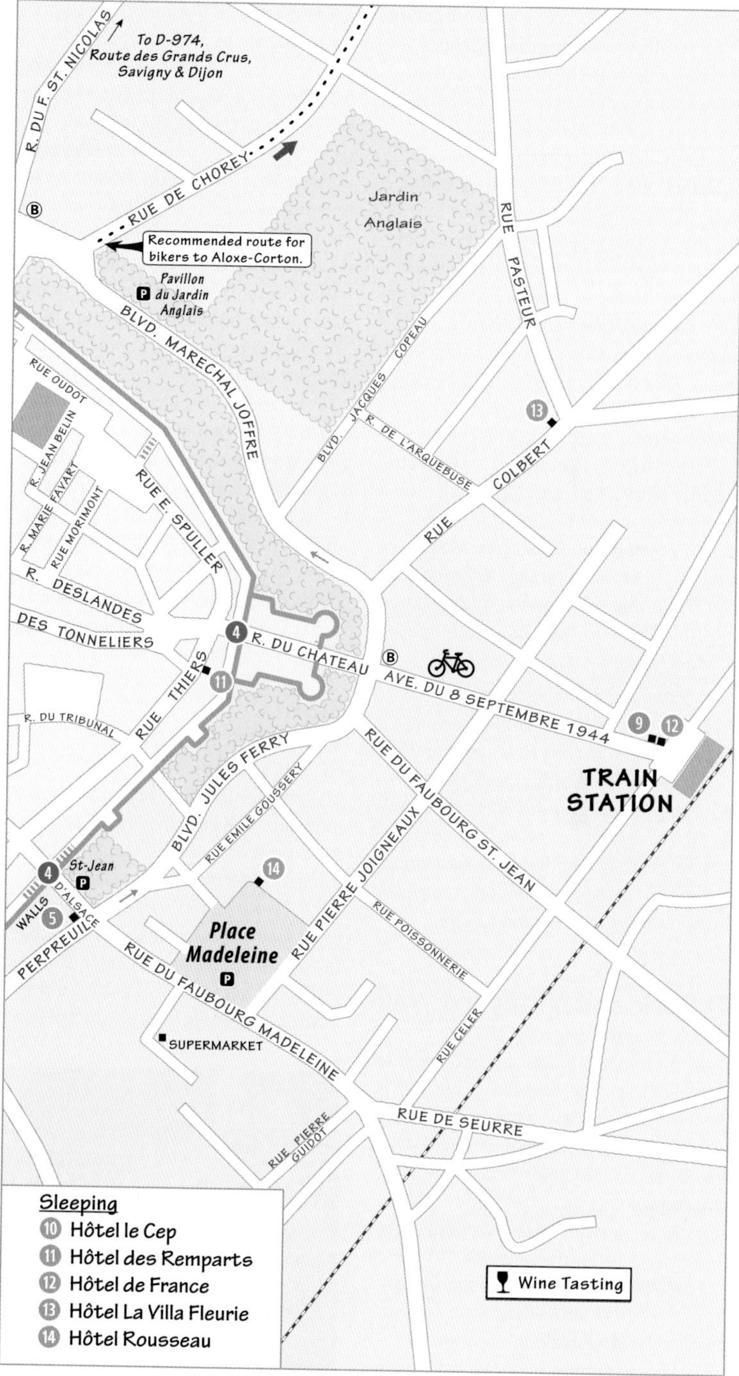
To D-974, Route des Grands Crus, Savigny & Dijon
R. DU F. ST. NICOLAS
RUE DE CHOREY
Recommended route for bikers to Aloxe-Corton.
Jardin Anglais
Pavillon du Jardin Anglais
RUE PASTEUR
BLVD. MARECHAL JOFFRE
BLVD. JACQUES COPEAU
R. DE L'ARQUEBUSE
RUE COLBERT
RUE OUDOT
R. JEAN BELIN
R. MARIE FAVART
RUE MORIMONT
RUE E. SPULLER
R. DESLANDES
DES TONNELIERS
R. DU CHATEAU
AVE. DU 8 SEPTEMBRE 1944
RUE THIERS
R. DU TRIBUNAL
BLVD. JULES FERRY
RUE EMILE GOUSSERY
RUE DU FAUBOURG ST. JEAN
RUE PIERRE JOIGNEAUX
TRAIN STATION
St-Jean
D'ALSACE
WALLS
PERPREUIL
Place Madeleine
RUE DU FAUBOURG MADELEINE
RUE POISSONNERIE
RUE CELER
SUPERMARKET
RUE DE SEURRE
RUE PIERRE GUIDOT
Sleeping
10 Hôtel le Cep
11 Hôtel des Remparts
12 Hôtel de France
13 Hôtel La Villa Fleurie
14 Hôtel Rousseau
Wine Tasting

Tours: Florian Garcenot at **Bourgogne Evasion** offers walking or biking tours into the vineyards (from €20/half-day walk, 6 people minimum; €32/half-day bike tour, mobile 06 64 68 83 57, www.burgundybiketour.com).

Safari Wine Tours offers daily van tours of the villages and vineyards around Beaune (€40-58, tour #2 is best for beginners; tel. 03 80 24 79 12, www.burgundy-tourism-safaritours.com, or call TI to reserve). **Chemins de Bourgogne** has three itinerary choices and an SUV to get you off the beaten path (€52-60/half-day, €120/day, mobile 06 60 43 68 86, www.chemins-de-bourgogne.com).

For private vineyard tours, try **Colette Barbier** (€280/half-day, €440/day, mobile 06 80 57 47 40, www.burgundy-guide.com) or **Stephanie Jones** (prices are per person, 2-person minimum: €105/half-day, €200/day, mention this guide for best rate, mobile 06 10 18 04 12, www.burgundywinetours.fr).

Rick's Tip: *Pedaling a* **rental bike** *from Beaune takes you within minutes into the world-famous vineyards of the Côte d'Or.* **Bourgogne Randonnées** *offers excellent rental bikes of all types, as well as maps and itineraries (daily, near Beaune train station at 7 Avenue du 8 Septembre, tel. 03 80 22 06 03, www.bourgogne-randonnees.fr).*

➔ Park and Vineyard Walk

Stroll across the ring road, through a pleasant Impressionist-like park, and into Beaune's beautiful vineyards. This walk is ideal for those lacking a car, families (good play toys in park), and vine enthusiasts. The vine-covered landscape is criss-crossed with narrow lanes and stubby stone walls and provides memorable early-morning and sunset views.

Follow Avenue de la République west from the center, cross the ring road, and parallel the stream along a few grassy blocks for about five minutes, then angle right into the serene park (Parc de la Bouzaize, opens at 8:00 and closes a bit before sunset). Walk through the park with the pond to your right and pop out at the right rear (northwest) corner (find the small opening past the house-like building in the park). Turn left on the small road, and enter the Côte de Beaune vineyards. Find the big poster showing how the land is sliced and diced among different plots (called *clos*, for "enclosure"). Each *clos* is named; look for the stone marker identifying the area behind the poster as Clos Les Teurons (*1er cru*).

Poke about Clos Les Teurons, noticing the rocky soil (wine grapes need to struggle). As you wander, keep in mind that subtle differences of soil and drainage between adjacent plots of land can be enough to create very different-tasting wines—from grapes grown only feet apart. *Vive la différence.* A perfectly situated picnic table awaits under that lone tree up Chemin des Tilleuls.

Sights

▲▲▲HOTEL DIEU DES HOSPICES DE BEAUNE

This medieval charity hospital is now a museum. The Hundred Years' War and the plague devastated Beaune, leaving three-quarters of its population destitute. Nicholas Rolin, chancellor of Burgundy (enriched, in part, by his power to collect taxes), had to do something for "his people" (or, more likely, was getting old and wanted to close out his life on a philan-

thropic note). So, in 1443, Rolin paid to build this place. It was completed in just eight years and served as a hospital until 1971, when the last patient checked out. You'll notice Hospices de Beaune on wine labels in fine shops—they are Burgundy's largest landowner of precious vineyards, thanks to donations made by patients over the centuries (and still happening today). Besides its magnificently decorated exterior, the Hôtel Dieu is famous for Rogier van der Weyden's superb *Last Judgment* altarpiece, which Rolin commissioned.

Cost and Hours: €7.50, includes audioguide, daily April-mid-Nov 9:00-18:30, mid-Nov-March 9:00-11:30 & 14:00-17:30, last entry one hour before closing, on Place de la Halle, www.hospices-de-beaune.com.

➲ SELF-GUIDED TOUR

Tour the rooms, which circle the courtyard, in a clockwise direction (following *Sens de la Visite* signs). To start your visit, enter the courtyard.

Courtyard of Honor: Honor meant power, and this was all about showing off. The exterior of the hospital and the town side of the courtyard are intentionally solemn, so as not to attract pesky brigands and looters. The dazzling inner courtyard features a colorful glazed-tile roof in a style recognized in France as typically "Burgundian." The sturdy tiles, which last 300 years, are fired three times: once to harden, again to burn in the color, and finally for the glaze.

Paupers' Ward: This grandest room of the hospital was the ward for the poorest patients. Rolin, who believed every patient deserved dignity, provided each patient with a pewter jug, mug, bowl, and plate. A painting on an easel in this room shows patients being treated right here in 1949, 500 years after the hospital's founding. During epidemics, there were two to a bed.

Chapel: The hospice was not a place of hope. People came here to die. Care was more for the soul than the body. The stained glass shows Nicolas Rolin (lower left) and his wife, Guigone (lower right), dressed as a nun to show her devotion. Notice the action on Golgotha. As Jesus is crucified, the souls of the two criminals crucified with him (portrayed as miniature naked humans) are being snatched

Hôtel Dieu des Hospices de Beaune

up—one by an angel and the other by a red devil. At the bottom, Mary cradles the dead body of Christ.

St. Hugue Ward: In the 17th century, this smaller ward was established for wealthy patients (who could afford Cadillac insurance plans). They were more likely to survive, and the decor displays themes of hope, rather than resignation: The series of Baroque paintings lining the walls shows the biblical miracles that Jesus performed.

St. Nicolas Room: Originally divided into smaller rooms used for "surgery" (a.k.a. bloodletting and amputation), this room now holds a model of the steep roof support and more tools of the doctoring trade (amputation saws, pans for bloodletting, and so on).

Kitchen: The kitchen display shows a 16th-century rotisserie. When fully wound, the cute robot would crank away, and the spit would spin slowly for 45 minutes. The 19th-century stove provided hot running water, which spewed from the beaks of swans.

Pharmacy: The nuns grew herbs out back, and strange and wondrous concoctions were mixed, cooked, and then stored in pottery jars. The biggest jar (by the window in the second room) was for *theriaca* ("panacea," or cure-all). The most commonly used medicine back then, it was a syrup of herbs, wine, and opium.

St. Louis Ward: A maternity ward until 1969, this room is lined with fine 16th- and 17th-century tapestries illustrating mostly Old Testament stories. Dukes traveled with tapestries to cozy up the humble places they stayed in while on the road.

Rogier van der Weyden's *Last Judgment*: This exquisite painting, the treasure of the Hôtel Dieu, was commissioned by Rolin in 1450 for the altar of the Paupers' Ward. He spared no cost, hiring the leading Flemish artist of his time. The entire altarpiece survives. The back side (on right wall) was sliced off so everything could be viewed at the same time. The painting is full of symbolism. Christ presides over Judgment Day. The lily is mercy, the sword is judgment, the rainbow promises salvation, and the jeweled globe at Jesus' feet symbolizes the universality of Christianity's message.

The intricate detail, painted with a three-haired brush, is typical of Flemish art from this period. While Renaissance

St. Hugue Ward was for wealthy patients.

artists employed mathematical tricks of perspective, these artists captured a sense of reality by painting minute detail upon detail.

Except for Sundays and holidays, the painting was kept closed and people saw only the panels that now hang on the right wall: Nicolas and Guigone piously at the feet of St. Sebastian—invoked to fight the plague—and St. Anthony, whom patients called upon for help in combating burning skin diseases.

COLLEGIALE NOTRE-DAME

Built in the 12th and 13th centuries, during the transition from Romanesque to Gothic architecture, Beaune's cathedral features a mix of both styles: Its foundation is decidedly Romanesque (notice the small windows and thick walls of the apse), while much of the rest is Gothic.

Enter the second chapel on the left to see the vivid remains of frescoes depicting the life of Lazarus, and then, behind the altar, find five 15th-century tapestries illustrating the life of the Virgin Mary.

Cost and Hours: Free, tapestries on view June-Sept Wed-Mon 10:00-13:00 & 14:00-18:00, closed Tue; April-May and Oct-Nov on view Fri-Sun only; tapestries not on view Dec-March.

MUSEUM OF THE WINE OF BURGUNDY (MUSEE DU VIN DE BOURGOGNE)

From this well-organized, detailed wine museum, it's clear that the history and culture of Burgundy and its wine were fermented in the same bottle. Wander into the free courtyard for a look at the striking palace, antique wine presses, and a concrete model of Beaune's 15th-century street plan. Inside the museum, you'll see a model of the region's topography, along with tools and scenes of Burgundian wine history.

Cost and Hours: €5.80, April-Sept Wed-Mon 10:00-13:00 & 14:00-18:00, Oct-Nov and March 11:00-18:00, closed Tue year-round and Dec-Feb; in Hôtel des Ducs on Rue d'Enfer, www.musees-bourgogne.org.

Rick's Tip: *It costs about €15 per bottle to* **ship a case of wine home,** *though you'll save about 20 percent on the VAT tax—so expensive wines are worth the shipping cost. The simplest solution for bringing six or so bottles back is to pack them very well and check the box on the plane with you.*

WINE TASTING IN BEAUNE

There are several good places to learn about Burgundy wines without leaving Beaune. **Patriarche Père et Fils** is home to the region's largest and most impressive wine cellar, where you can tour their underground passages and taste 13 Burgundian classics (€16, daily 9:30-11:30 & 14:00-17:30, 5 Rue du Collège, tel. 03 80 24 53 78, www.patriarche.com). Or you can try the informative classes in the comfortable wine bar/classroom at **Sensation Vin** (reserve ahead, €35 for 1.5-hour class,

Van der Weyden, Last Judgment

Medieval wine cellar

Burgundy's Wines

Burgundy is why France is famous for wine. You'll find great fruity reds, dry whites, and crisp rosés. The three key grapes are chardonnay (dry white wines), pinot noir (medium-bodied red wines), and gamay (light, fruity red wines, such as Beaujolais). Sixty percent of the wines are white, thanks to the white-only impact of the Chablis and Mâcon regions.

The Romans brought winemaking knowledge with them to Burgundy more than 2,000 years ago, but it was medieval monks who perfected the art a thousand years later. They determined that pinot noir and chardonnay grapes grew best with the soil and climate in this region, a lesson that is followed to the letter by winemakers today. The French Revolution put capitalists in charge of the vineyards (no longer a monkish labor of love), which led to quantity over quality and a loss of Burgundy's esteemed status. Phylloxera insects destroyed most of Burgundy's vines in the late 1800s, and forced growers to rethink how and where to best cultivate grapes in Burgundy. This led to a return of the monks' approach, with the veneration of pinot noir and chardonnay grapes, a focus on quality over quantity, and a big reduction in the land area devoted to vines.

In Burgundy, location is everything, and winery names take a back seat to the place where the grape is grown. Every village produces its own distinctive wine, from Chablis to Meursault to Chassagne-Montrachet. Road maps read like wine lists. If the village has a hyphenated name, the second half usually comes from the town's most important vineyard (such as Gevrey-Chambertin, Aloxe-Corton, and Vosne-Romanée).

Burgundy wines are divided into four classifications: From top to bottom you'll find *grand cru*, *premier cru* (or *1er cru*), *village*, and *Bourgogne*. Each level allows buyers to better pinpoint the quality and origin of the grapes in their wine. With *Bourgogne* wines, the grapes can come from anywhere in Burgundy; *village* identifies the exact village where they were grown; and *grand cru* and *premier cru* locate the actual plots of land. As you drop from top to bottom, production increases—there is far more *Bourgogne* made than *grand cru*. In general, the less wine a vine produces, the higher the quality.

daily, 1 Rue d'Enfer, tel. 03 80 22 17 57, www.sensation-vin.com). Ask about their tastings-in-the-vineyards class.

THE MUSTARD MILL (LA MOUTARDERIE FALLOT)

The last of the independent mustard mills in Burgundy opens its doors for guided tours in French (with a little English). They offer two tours: one with a focus on production and another that highlights the history of mustard. The tours are long yet informative—you'll learn why Burgundy was the birthplace of mustard (it's about wine juice), and where they get their grains today (Canada).

Cost and Hours: €10, daily at 10:00 and 11:30, also several in the afternoon in summer, call to reserve or book online, as space is limited; free mustard tasting—daily 9:30-18:00, except closed Sun afternoon year-round and lunchtime in winter; across ring road in the appropriately yellow building at 31 Rue du Faubourg Bretonnière, tel. 03 80 22 10 10, www.fallot.com.

Eating

$$$ Caveau des Arches is a reliable choice if you want to dine on Burgundian specialties at fair prices in romantic stone cellars (€25 *menu* with the classics, €33 *menu* with greater choices, €52 gourmand *menu*, portions can be small, closed Sun-Mon and in Aug, where the ring road crosses Rue d'Alsace—which leads to Place Madeleine—at 10 Boulevard Perpreuil, tel. 03 80 22 10 37, www.caveau-des-arches.com).

$$ La Ciboulette, intimate and family-run with petite Hélèna as your hostess, offers reliable cuisine that mixes traditional Burgundian flavors with creative dishes and lovely presentation. It's worth the longer walk—and you can do your laundry next door while you dine (€20 and €38 *menus*, indoor seating only, closed Mon-Tue; from Place Carnot, walk out Rue Carnot to 69 Rue Lorraine; tel. 03 80 24 70 72).

$$$ Les Pôpiettes is a lively place and popular with locals and foodies, with a communal table on one side, booths on the other, and a cheery ambience. The chef-owner produces an eclectic blend of delicious and inventive--though limited in choice--cuisine, such as risotto and snails (inside dining only, closed Tue-Wed, 10 Rue d'Alsace, tel. 03 80 21 91 81).

$$ Brasserie le Carnot is a perennially popular café with good interior seating and better exterior tables in the thick of the pedestrian zone. It serves pizza, salads, pasta dishes (all about €14) as well as the usual café offerings (open daily, where Rue Carnot and Rue Monge meet, tel. 03 80 22 32 93).

$$ Le Tast'Vin, across from the train station at the recommended Hôtel de France, has a good-value menu and fun cheeseburgers with Burgundian cheese (closed Sat and Mon for lunch and all day Sun, 35 Avenue du 8 Septembre, tel. 03 80 24 10 34).

Burgundy's Cuisine Scene

Arrive hungry. Considered by many to be France's best, Burgundy's cuisine is peasant cooking elevated to an art.

Several classic dishes were born in Burgundy: ***escargots de Bourgogne*** (snails served sizzling hot in garlic butter), ***bœuf bourguignon*** (beef simmered for hours in red wine with onions and mushrooms), **coq au vin** (rooster stewed in red wine), and ***œufs en meurette*** (poached eggs in a red wine sauce, often served on a large crouton), as well as the famous **Dijon mustards.** Look also for delicious ***jambon persillé*** (cold ham layered in a garlic-parsley gelatin), ***pain d'épices*** (spice bread), and ***gougères*** (light, puffy cheese pastries). Those white cows (called Charolais) dotting the green pastures make France's best steak and *bœuf bourguignon.*

Native cheeses are **Epoisses** and **Langres** (both mushy and great) and my favorite, **Montrachet** (a tasty goat cheese). **Crème de cassis** (black currant liqueur) is another Burgundian specialty; look for it in desserts and snazzy drinks (try a *kir*).

Remember, restaurants serve only during lunch (11:30-14:00) and dinner (19:00-21:00, later in bigger cities); some cafés serve food throughout the day.

Sleeping

$$$ Hôtel le Cep**** is *the* venerable place to stay in Beaune, if you have the means. Buried in the town center, this historic building comes with fine public spaces inside and out, and 65 gorgeous wood-beamed, traditionally decorated rooms in all sizes (standard Sb-€153, Db-€193, deluxe with king-size beds Db-€273, family rooms available, breakfast-€21, air-con, fitness center, parking-€19/day, 27 Rue Maufoux, tel. 03 80 22 35 48, www.hotel-cep-beaune.com, resa@hotel-cep-beaune.com).

$$ Hôtel des Remparts*** is a peaceful oasis in a rustic manor house built around a calming courtyard. It features faded Old World comfort, many rooms with beamed ceilings, big beds, and a few good family suites (standard Db-€130, Db suite-€180, ask about Rick Steves discount, air-con, laundry service, bike rental, garage-€10/day, just inside ring road between train station and main square at 48 Rue Thiers, tel. 03 80 24 94 94, www.hotel-remparts-beaune.com, hotel.des.remparts@wanadoo.fr, run by the formal Epaillys).

$ Hôtel de France*** is a good place that's easy for train travelers and drivers. It comes with standard rooms with air-conditioning, and fun, English-speaking owners Nicolas and Virginie (Sb-€60, Db-€86, Tb-€100, Qb-€115, bar, good bistro, garage parking-€11/day, 35 Avenue du 8 Septembre, tel. 03 80 24 10 34, www.hoteldefrance-beaune.com, contact@hoteldefrance-beaune.com).

$ Hôtel La Villa Fleurie, an adorable 10-room refuge, is a great value and run well by affable Madame Chartier. First-floor-up rooms are wood-floored, plush, and *très* traditional; second-floor rooms are carpeted and cozy. Most rooms have queen-size beds, and all rooms have big bathrooms (small Db-€77, bigger Db-€87, nifty Tb/Qb loft-€127-137, breakfast-€9, community fridge, easy and free parking, a 15-minute walk from the center at 19 Place Colbert, tel. 03 80 22 66 00, www.lavillafleurie.fr, contact@lavillafleurie.fr). From Beaune's ring road, turn right in front of the Bichot winery.

¢ Hôtel Rousseau is a good-value, no-frills, frumpy, old manor house that turns its back on Beaune's sophistication. Cheerful, quirky, and elusive owner Madame Rousseau—who has run the place since 1959—her pet birds, and the quiet garden will make you smile, and the tranquility will help you sleep. The cheapest rooms are a godsend for budget travelers. Check-ins after 19:00 and morning departures before 7:30 must be arranged in advance (S-€39, D-€50, D with toilet-€60, Db-€66, T with toilet-€70, Tb-€75, Qb-€110, showers down the hall, includes breakfast, cash only, no air-con, no Wi-Fi, reservations preferred by email, free and easy parking, 11 Place Madeleine, tel. 03 80 22 13 59, hotelrousseaubeaune@orange.fr).

Sleep Code

$$$$ Splurge: Over €250
$$$ Pricier: €190-250
$$ Moderate: €130-190
$ Budget: €70-130
¢ Backpacker: Under €70

Hotels are classified based on the average price of a standard double room with bath in high season. Unless otherwise noted, credit cards are accepted, breakfast is not included, hotel staff speak English, and Wi-Fi is available.

Transportation

Arriving and Departing

BY CAR

Driving provides the ultimate flexibility for touring the vineyards. To reach the center of Beaune, follow *Centre-Ville/Place de la Madeleine* signs and park for free in Place Madeleine. If the lot is full—which it often is—spaces usually open up before long. The free Parking du Jardin Anglais, at the north end of the ring road, usually has spaces (even during Saturday market day), and there are some free parking spots all along the ring road. Parking inside Beaune's ring road is metered 9:00-12:30 and 14:00-19:00; there's a convenient parking garage next to the main TI on the ring road.

BY TRAIN

Trains link Beaune with Dijon to the north and Lyon to the south. To reach the city center from the train station (no baggage storage), walk straight out of the station up Avenue du 8 Septembre, cross the busy ring road, and continue up Rue du Château. Follow it as it angles left and pass the mural, veering right onto Rue des Tonneliers. A left on Rue de l'Enfant leads to Beaune's pedestrian zone and Place Carnot.

Train Connections from Beaune to: Paris' Gare de Lyon (nearly hourly, 2.5 hours, most require reservation and easy change in Dijon; more via Dijon to Paris' Gare de Bercy, no reservation required, 3.5 hours), **Colmar** (10/day, 2.5-4 hours via TGV between Dijon and Mulhouse, reserve well ahead, changes in Dijon and Mulhouse or Belfort), **Arles** (10/day, 4.5-5 hours, 9 with transfer in Lyon and Nîmes or Avignon), **Chamonix** (7/day, 7 hours, change in Lyon and St-Gervais, some require additional changes), **Amboise** (1/day, 4.5 hours, transfer at St-Pierre-des-Corps; also possible with changes at St-Pierre-des-Corps and Nevers).

NEAR BEAUNE

VINEYARD LOOPS

These two vineyard loops near Beaune combine great scenery with some of my favorite wine destinations. Certain sections are doable by bike depending on your bike-fitness and determination.

If time is tight and you have a car, drive the beautiful **"South Vineyard Loop"** to Château de la Rochepot (with off-the-beaten-path villages and ample tasting opportunities). This is a tough ride on a bike (unless it's electric), so most bikers will prefer doing just the first section of this route (ideally to Puligny-Montrachet and back—an easy, level ride).

My **"North Vineyard Loop"** takes you to Savigny-lès-Beaune and is good by car or by bike (manageable hills and distances).

Along these routes, I avoid famous wine châteaux and look for smaller, more personal places. Although you can drop in unannounced at a *caveau* representing multiple wineries, at private wineries it's best to call ahead and arrange an appointment (ask your hotelier for help). Remember that at free tastings, you're expected to buy at least a bottle or two (unless you're on a group tour).

Before heading out, read the section on Burgundy's wines (page 386). You'll almost certainly see workers tending the vines. In winter, plants are pruned way back (determining the yield during grape harvest in the fall). Starting in spring, plants are trimmed to get rid of extraneous growth, allowing just the right amount of sun to reach the grapes. The arrival date of good weather in spring determines the date of harvest (100 days later).

South Vineyard Loop

▲▲ *Beaune to Château de la Rochepot*

Take this pretty, peaceful route to glide through several of Burgundy's most reputed vineyards—and end up at Burgundy's most romantic castle, Château de la Rochepot. Read ahead and note

South Vineyard Loop

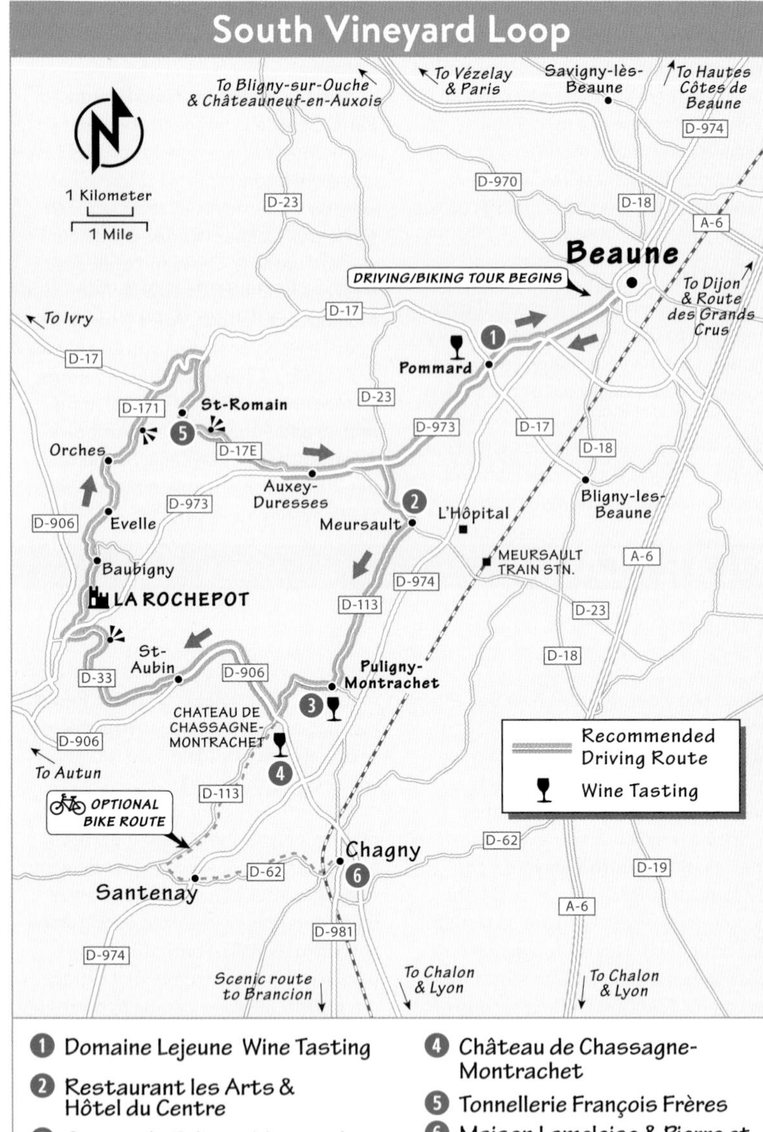

1. Domaine Lejeune Wine Tasting
2. Restaurant les Arts & Hôtel du Centre
3. Caveau de Puligny-Montrachet; Le Montrachet & L'Estaminet des Meix Restaurants
4. Château de Chassagne-Montrachet
5. Tonnellerie François Frères
6. Maison Lameloise & Pierre et Jean Restaurants

the open hours of wineries and sights along the route (you can do this loop in reverse). There are wonderful picnic spots along the way; you'll find my favorite one just before entering Puligny-Montrachet from the north (past the first picnic spot by 100 yards, closer to the hills).

Bikers can follow the first part of this route to Puligny-Montrachet, along Burgundy's best bike path (which connects the wine villages of Pommard, Volnay, Meursault, and Puligny-Montrachet for a level, 18-mile loop; allow two hours round-trip). All but power riders should avoid the hills to La Rochepot.

➲ SELF-GUIDED TOUR

Drivers leave Beaune's ring road, following signs for *Chalon-sur-Saône* (often abbreviated "Chalon-s/ S.," first turnoff after Auxerre exit), then follow signs to *Pommard/Autun*. Cyclists take the vineyard bike path by leaving the ring road toward Auxerre, and turning left at the signal after Lycée Viticole de Beaune (look for bike-route icons).

Whether on a bike or in a car, when you come to Pommard, you'll pass many wine-tasting opportunities, including **Domaine Lejeune** (Mon-Sat 9:00-12:00 & 14:00-18:00, OK to stop by but better to call ahead, behind the church, tel. 03 80 22 90 88, www.domaine-lejeune.fr).

South of Pommard, the road gradually climbs past Volnay and terrific views; bikers take their own parallel path, following bike icons. From here, follow signs into **Meursault.** The village has a fine square, bakeries, grocery shops, and good restaurants; try **Restaurant les Arts** (closed Mon eve and Tue) or **Hôtel du Centre** (open daily).

Follow *Toutes Directions* (and D-974) around the village, turn right on D-113, and follow signs for *Puligny-Montrachet*. You'll pass through low-slung vineyards south of Meursault, then enter **Puligny-Montrachet** (with good picnic spots on the right as you enter). At the big roundabout with a bronze sculpture of vineyard workers, find the **Caveau de Puligny-Montrachet.** This user-friendly spot has a convivial wine-bar-like tasting room, a smart outdoor terrace, and no pressure to buy (about €20 for 6 wines, can ship to US; March-Oct daily 9:30-19:00, sometimes closes at lunch; Nov-Feb Tue-Sun 10:00-12:00 & 15:00-18:00, closed Mon;

Vineyards line the roads between Beaune and the Château de la Rochepot.

tel. 03 80 21 96 78, www.caveau-puligny.com).

A block straight out the door of the *caveau* leads to a small grocery and the town's big square (Place des Marronniers), with **Hôtel-Restaurant Le Montrachet** (daily) and **Café de l'Estaminet des Meix** (closed Mon eve and Tue).

Go back to the roundabout and follow signs to *Chassagne-Montrachet* and *St. Aubin*, leading through more manicured vineyards. To tour the elegant cellars of the upscale, well-signed **Château de Chassagne-Montrachet,** turn left on D-906, and you'll see it soon to the right (€17 includes tour, allow at least an hour, daily 10:00-18:00, best to call ahead, tel. 03 80 21 98 57, www.chateaudechassagnemontrachet.com).

From here, cyclists can double back to Beaune or continue on the bike path to Santenay, then along the canal to **Chagny**, with the recommended **Maison Lameloise restaurant,** which has Michelin's top three-star rating—book well ahead if you're tempted to summit the pinnacle of French cuisine (daily, 36 Place d'Armes, tel. 03 85 87 65 65, www.lameloise.fr). Their nearby bistro **Pierre et Jean** has a simpler menu for less money (2 Rue de la Poste). Cyclists can take the train from Chagny back to Beaune (2/hour, 10 minutes).

Drivers should continue on to the splendid ▲ **Château de la Rochepot** by making a hard right on D-906 to St-Aubin and following *La Rochepot* signs onto D-33. After heading over the hills and through the vineyards of the Hautes-Côtes (upper slopes), you'll come to a drop-dead view of the castle (stop mandatory). Turn right when you reach La Rochepot, and follow *Le Château* signs to the castle.

Construction of this pint-sized, very Burgundian castle began during the end of the Middle Ages—when castles were built to defend—and was completed during the Renaissance, when castles became luxury homes. So it's neither a purely defensive structure (as in the Dordogne) nor a palace (as in the Loire)—it's a bit of both (€4.75 to visit on your own, €9.50 includes 25-minute guided tour, usually possible between 15:00-16:30 only; open May-Sept Wed-Sun 10:00-12:00 & 14:00-17:30, closed Mon-Tue and off-season; www.larochepot.com).

Château de la Rochepot

After visiting the castle, turn right from its parking lot and mosey through Baubigny, Evelles, and rock-solid Orches. After Orches, climb to the top of Burgundy's world—keeping straight on D-17, you'll pass several **exceptional lookouts** on your right. Get out of your car and wander cliffside for a postcard-perfect Burgundian image. The village of St-Romain swirls below, and if it's really clear, look for Mont Blanc on the eastern horizon.

Next drive down to lovely little **St-Romain,** passing Burgundy's most important wine-barrel maker, **Tonnellerie Francois Frères** (it's above the village in the modern building on the left, and closed to the public). Inside, well-stoked fires heat the oak staves to make them flexible, and sweaty workers use heavy hammers to pound iron rings around the barrels, as they've done since medieval times.

Next, follow signs for *Auxey-Duresses*, and then *Beaune* for a scenic finale to your journey.

North Vineyard Loop

▲ *Beaune to Savigny-lès-Beaune*

For an easy and rewarding spin by car—or ideally by bike—through waves of vineyards that smother traditional villages, follow this relatively level 12-mile loop from Beaune. Including stops, allow a half-day by bike or 1.5 hours by car. The route laces together three renowned wine villages—Aloxe-Corton, Pernand-Vergelesses, and Savigny-lès-Beaune—connecting you with Burgundian nature and village wine culture. Those wanting a little more should take the beautiful and short extension to Magny-les-Villers. Bring water and snacks, as there is precious little available until the end of this route. There's a dreamy picnic spot with shade on the small road halfway between Aloxe-Corton and Pernand-Vergelesses. Your tour concludes in Savigny-lès-Beaune, where you'll find a café-pizzeria, wine tastings, a small grocery, and a unique château.

➲ SELF-GUIDED TOUR

This loop drive/pedal starts in Beaune.

• *From Beaune's ring road,* ***drivers*** *take D-974 north toward Dijon. Soon, follow signs for Savigny-lès-Beaune, leading left at the signal and then quickly right. On the outskirts of town you'll cross over the freeway, then veer right, following the second signs you see to Pernand-Vergelesses (D-18). Turn right at the first sign to Aloxe-Corton, and glide into the town. Make a hard left at the stop sign and climb uphill to find a small parking area with several recommended wine tastings close by.*

Bikers *follow a different route leaving Beaune. From Beaune's ring road, turn right on Rue de Chorey after passing the public pool (just before D-974 to Dijon), following signs for Grigny. Continue to follow signs towards Gigny into Chorey-les-Beaune. In Chorey-les Beaune, veer left onto Rue Pavelot, pass through two stop signs, then follow the lane as it curves left. Cross busy D-974, go straight up the tree-lined road, then make a hard left at the stop sign and climb uphill into...*

Aloxe-Corton: This tiny town, with a world-class reputation among wine enthusiasts, is packed with top tasting opportunities (but no cafés). Choose from these three wineries: Easygoing **Domaines d'Aloxe-Corton** charges a small tasting fee, which is waived if you buy two bottles (usually closed Tue-Wed, tel. 03 80 26 49 85, http://aloxe.corton.free.fr). English-owned **Mischief and Mayhem** offers tastings by appointment

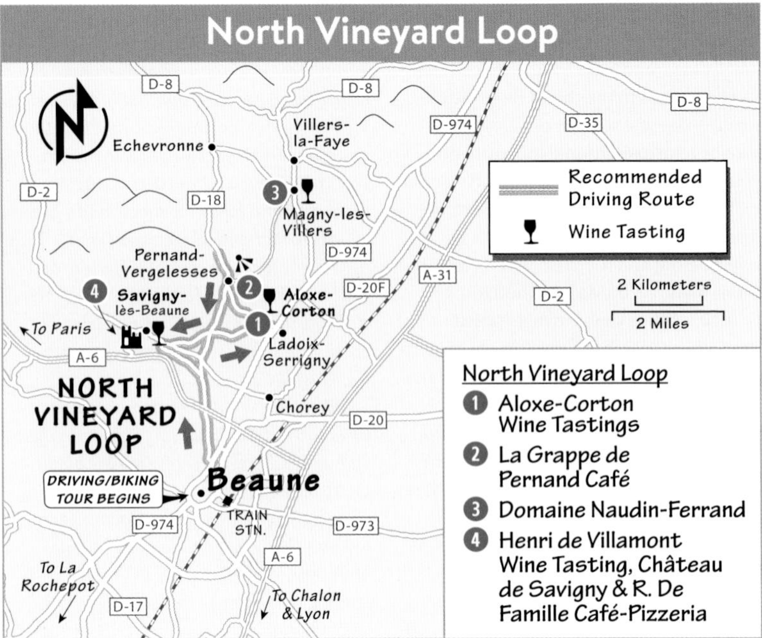

only (a few blocks below the church on D-115d to Ladoix-Serrigny at 10 Impasse du Puits, mobile 06 30 01 23 76, www.mischiefandmayhem.com). Also reserve ahead for the more upscale **Domaine de Senard** (Tue-Sat 10:00-11:30 & 14:30-17:30, closed Sun-Mon, 1 Rue des Chaumes, tel. 03 80 26 41 65, www.domainesenard.com, table@domainesenard.com).

• *Leave Aloxe-Corton and head up the hill on Rue des Chaumes, following signs for Pernand-Vergelesses (you'll pass a picture-perfect picnic spot). At the T-intersection with D-18, most bikers will want to turn left and pick up the directions for leaving Pernand-Vergelesses (below). Otherwise, turn right and head into...*

Pernand-Vergelesses: As you enter the village, look for a cute little café called **La Grappe de Pernand** (closed Mon-Tue, tel. 03 80 21 59 46).

Drivers and strong bikers should consider two worthwhile detours from Pernand-Vergelesses: Climbing well above the village leads to one of the best vineyard panoramas in Burgundy. To get there, enter Pernand-Vergelesses, look for a small roundabout and head up, turning right on Rue du Creux St. Germain, and then continue straight and up along Rue Copeau. Curve up past the church until you see small *Panorama* signs. Drivers and bikers wanting to extend their ride can also follow signs (after passing the church, en route to the panorama) to **Magny-les-Villers** and take a gorgeous and hilly wine lane for about two miles to one of my favorite wineries, **Domaine Naudin-Ferrand** (tastings by appointment only, Mon-Fri 9:00-12:00 & 13:30-17:30, Sat 14:00-18:00, closed Sun, Rue du Meix-Grenot, carefully track the faded signs, tel. 03 80 62 91 50, www.naudin-ferrand.com, info@naudin-ferrand.com).

• *Leaving Pernand-Vergelesses, bikers and drivers both follow the main road (D-18) back toward Beaune, and turn right into the vineyards on the first lane (about 400 yards from Pernand-Vergelesses). Keep left at the first fork and rise gently to lovely views. Drop down and turn right when you come to a T, then joyride along the vine service lanes (bikers should watch for loose gravel). To reach Savigny-lès-Beaune, keep going until you see a 5T sign. Turn left just before the sign, then take the first right, and right again when you reach the T-intersection at the bottom. Merge onto the larger road; you'll soon come to a three-way intersection in...*

Savigny-lès-Beaune: The left fork leads back to Beaune, the middle fork leads to Centre-Ville, and the road to the right leads to a good free wine tasting at the big-time enterprise **Henri de Villamont** (hours vary but generally Mon-Fri, call to confirm or to book a visit, Rue du Dr. Guyot, tel. 03 80 21 52 13, www.hdv.fr). Follow the middle fork to find the medieval four-towered **Château de Savigny,** with its amazing collection of sports cars, motorcycles, and fighter jets (daily, www.chateau-savigny.com) and the **R. De Famille** café-pizzeria (closed Mon).

• *From Savigny-lès-Beaune, drive or pedal back into Beaune. To avoid busy D-18 back to Beaune, bikers could turn left towards Pernand-Vergelesses when leaving Savigny, and immediately right on D-2a to reach Chorey-les-Beaune before heading back to Beaune.*

BEST OF THE REST

Two enticing destinations are within striking distance of Beaune. Head southeast to reach Chamonix and the French Alps, where you can skip along alpine ridges, glide over mountain meadows, or meander riverside paths. Or turn northeast to Colmar, in the Alsace region, to experience the small-town, Germanic warmth of one of Europe's most enchanting cities.

If you're following my two-week itinerary, but want to add stops in Chamonix, Beaune, and Colmar, add them after Nice. Autoroutes are easy for drivers, who will savor some remarkable views en route to the French Alps.

By public transit, it'll involve some long train rides: Take the train from Nice to Chamonix (10 hours), and after visiting Chamonix, train to Beaune (6-7 hours), then Colmar (2.5-4 hours), then end in Paris (3.5 hours) to fly home. If you don't visit Colmar, train from Beaune to Paris (2.5-3.5 hours). Remember that any TGV trip requires reservations.

Chamonix

Showered with snow-dipped peaks, graced with glaciers, and blanketed with hiking trails, the resort of Chamonix is France's best base for alpine exploration. Near where Switzerland, Italy, and France come together to "high five" the sky, Chamonix sits at the base of Mont Blanc, with about 10,000 residents and nearly as many mountain lifts (well, almost). Chamonix's purpose in life has always been to dazzle visitors with some of Europe's top alpine thrills.

Orientation

The frothy Arve River splits Chamonix in two. The thriving pedestrian zone, above and west of the river along Rues du Docteur Paccard and Joseph Vallot, forms Chamonix's core.

Day Plan: If you have one sunny day, spend it this way: Start with Europe's ultimate cable-car ride, the Aiguille du Midi. Ride the lift up, then take another lift over the Alps to the Italian border (Helbronner Point). Double back and get off at Plan de l'Aiguille. From there, hike to Montenvers and the Mer de Glace glacier, then take the train down to Chamonix. End your day with a well-deserved drink and dinner at a view café in town.

Getting There: Trains link Chamonix with **Nice** (4/day, 10 hours), **Arles** (5/day, 7-8 hours), and **Beaune** (7/day, 6-7 hours); these routes generally involve transfers in St-Gervais and Lyon. Chamonix is also connected with **Paris'** Gare de Lyon (7/day, 5-7 hours, some change in Switzerland).

Arrival in Chamonix: From the train station, walk straight up Avenue Michel Croz. In three blocks, you'll reach the town center; turn left at the big clock, then right for the TI. Most **parking** is metered and well-signed; from mid-July to late August, traffic is a mess in Chamonix, and finding parking is messier—arrive before 10:00 to get a spot.

Tourist Information: Stop by the TI in the center of town to pick up a "panorama" map of the valley lifts, buy a hiking map *(Carte des Sentiers),* and ask about weather, snow levels, and hours of lifts and trains (daily, closed Sun off-season, 85 Place du Triangle de l'Amitié, tel. 04 50 53 00 24, www.chamonix.com).

Sights

For the latest information and to confirm schedules for all the lifts and trains described below, ask at the TI or check www.compagniedumontblanc.com. To lace together lifts and hikes, ride the free shuttle bus that runs along the Chamonix valley floor (schedules at TI or www.chamonix.montblancbus.com/en).

▲▲▲AIGUILLE DU MIDI GONDOLA

The Aiguille du Midi is easily the valley's (and, arguably, Europe's) most spectacular and popular lift. If the weather's clear, the price doesn't matter. Take an early lift and have breakfast above 12,000 feet. Bring sunglasses (bright snow abounds up high) and be sure your camera has enough battery power.

Rick's Tip: *From* **July to August, reserve the Aiguille du Midi lift in advance,** *either at the information booth next to the lift, online at www.montblancnaturalresort.com.*

Cost: From Chamonix to Aiguille du Midi round-trip-€60 (one-way-€49); from Chamonix to Helbronner Point round-trip-€84. If you get off at Plan de l'Aiguille and hike to Montenvers, use your round-tip ticket for the train back to Chamonix. Tickets for the lift from Aiguille du Midi to Helbronner Point are sold at both base and summit lift stations for the same price (about €30 round-trip, must show passport).

Chamonix with Mont Blanc in the background

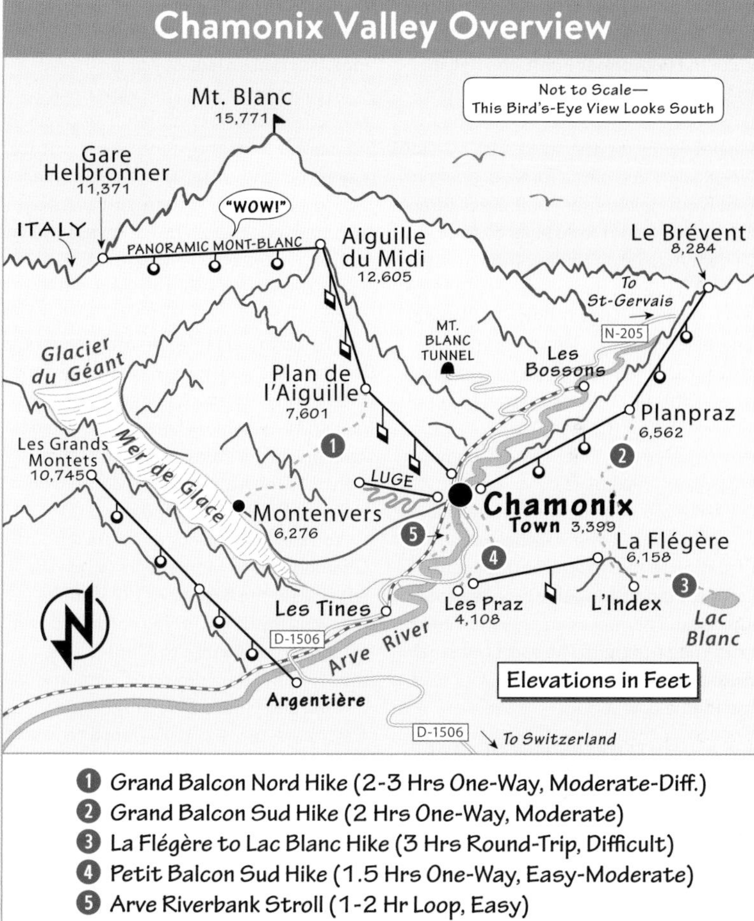

Hours: Lifts are weather- and crowd-dependent, but generally run daily starting at 6:30 or 7:30. Gondolas run every 10 minutes during busy times; the last return from Aiguille du Midi is generally one hour after the last ascent (which is 15:30-17:00, depending on the season).

Visiting the Aiguille du Midi: Pile into the *téléphérique* (gondola) and soar to the tip of Aiguille du Midi, a rock needle 12,600 feet above sea level. Get a spot on the right side for glacier views. Chamonix shrinks as trees fly by, soon replaced by whizzing rocks, ice, and snow. Change gondolas at Plan de l'Aiguille to reach Aiguille du Midi. No matter how sunny it is, it's cold, the air is thin, and people are giddy with delight. If you're not too winded, join the locals in the halfway-to-heaven tango.

At Aiguille du Midi, you have several options: Ride the free **elevator** through the rock to the summit of this pinnacle; explore more than 150 yards of **tunnels** *(galeries)* that lead to an enclosed view room and a worthwhile exhibit on mountain climbing; or eat at the view cafeteria or restaurant.

Next, get into the little red *télécabine* (called Panoramic Mont Blanc) and sail south to **Helbronner Point,** the Italian border station (typically open late June–early Sept). In a gondola for four, you'll dangle silently for 40 minutes as you glide over glaciers and past a forest of peaks to Italy. From Helbronner Point, you'll turn around and return to Aiguille du Midi.

From Aiguille du Midi, you can ride all the way back to Chamonix; or—way, way better—get off halfway down at **Plan de l'Aiguille,** where you'll find a scenic café with outdoor tables and paragliders jumping off cliffs. But the best reason to get off here is to follow the wonderful trail to the Mer de Glace (for details, see "Chamonix Area Hikes," next page).

Even if you don't do the hike, take a 35-minute round-trip walk below the lift station to the ignored and peaceful **Refuge-Plan de l'Aiguille** for a reasonable meal. This makes an easy mini-hike for hurried travelers. The short but steep climb back up to the lift will be your exercise for the day.

▲▲▲ MONTENVERS/MER DE GLACE

A cute cogwheel train runs between Gare de Montenvers (near Chamonix's main train station) and Montenvers, which overlooks the receding glacier called Mer de Glace ("Sea of Ice"). At eight miles long, it's France's largest glacier.

In Montenvers, find the **view deck** across from the train station. The glacier is impressive from above and below—its **ice cave** is beneath you. Take the free, small gondola down and prepare to walk about 460 steps each way. The ice cave, a hypnotizing shade of blue-green, is actually a long tunnel dug about 75 yards into the glacier.

The **Terminal Neige du Montenvers,** a few minutes' walk toward Chamonix from the view deck, offers a full-service restaurant and view tables (fair prices, limited selection). The little museum upstairs describes the history of the Montenvers train (no English, but good exhibits).

You can take the cogwheel train from Chamonix up to Montenvers (sit on the left side for the best views), or if you're following my day plan, you can hike down from Plan de l'Aiguille to Montenvers, then take the train down to Chamonix.

Cost and Hours: One-way on train-€25, round-trip-€31, daily from 8:30, last trip down at 16:30, 2-3/hour, 20 minutes, confirm times with TI or call 04 50 53 12 54.

Riding the gondola to Aiguille du Midi

Rick's Tip: *If you're spending two or more days in the Chamonix valley, consider a* **Multipass,** *which allows unlimited access to lifts and trains (except the Helbronner gondola) and lets you bypass lines (€60/1 day, €73/2 days, €84/3 days; buy online at www.montblancnaturalresort.com, at participating lift stations, and at some hotels).*

▲▲▲GONDOLA LIFTS TO LE BREVENT AND LA FLEGERE

Though Aiguille du Midi gives a more spectacular ride, the Le Brévent and La Flégère lifts (*téléphériques*) offer worthwhile hiking and viewing options, with unobstructed panoramas across to the Mont Blanc range and fewer crowds. The Le Brévent lift is in Chamonix; the La Flégère lift (with hikes to Planpraz and Lac Blanc) is in nearby Les Praz. The lifts are connected by a scenic hike or by bus along the valley floor; both have sensational view cafés.

Cost and Hours: Chamonix-Planpraz-Le Brévent round-trip-€31, daily in summer 8:15-18:00, tel. 04 50 53 13 18. **Les Praz-La Flégère** round-trip-€17, daily in summer 8:00-17:30.

Chamonix Area Hikes

A good first stop for hiking advice is the full-service **Maison de la Montagne** across from the TI. On the second floor, the **Office de Haute-Montagne** (High Mountain Office) can help you plan your hikes. Always ask about trail conditions, as many trails can be covered with snow into June (open daily, tel. 04 50 53 22 08, www.chamoniarde.com).

For your hike, pack sunglasses, sunscreen, rain gear, water, snacks, and maybe light gloves. Wear good shoes and layer your clothing; mountain weather can change in a moment.

▲▲ PLAN DE L'AIGUILLE TO MONTENVERS-MER DE GLACE (GRAND BALCON NORD)

This is the most efficient way to incorporate a high-country hike into your ride

Mer de Glace

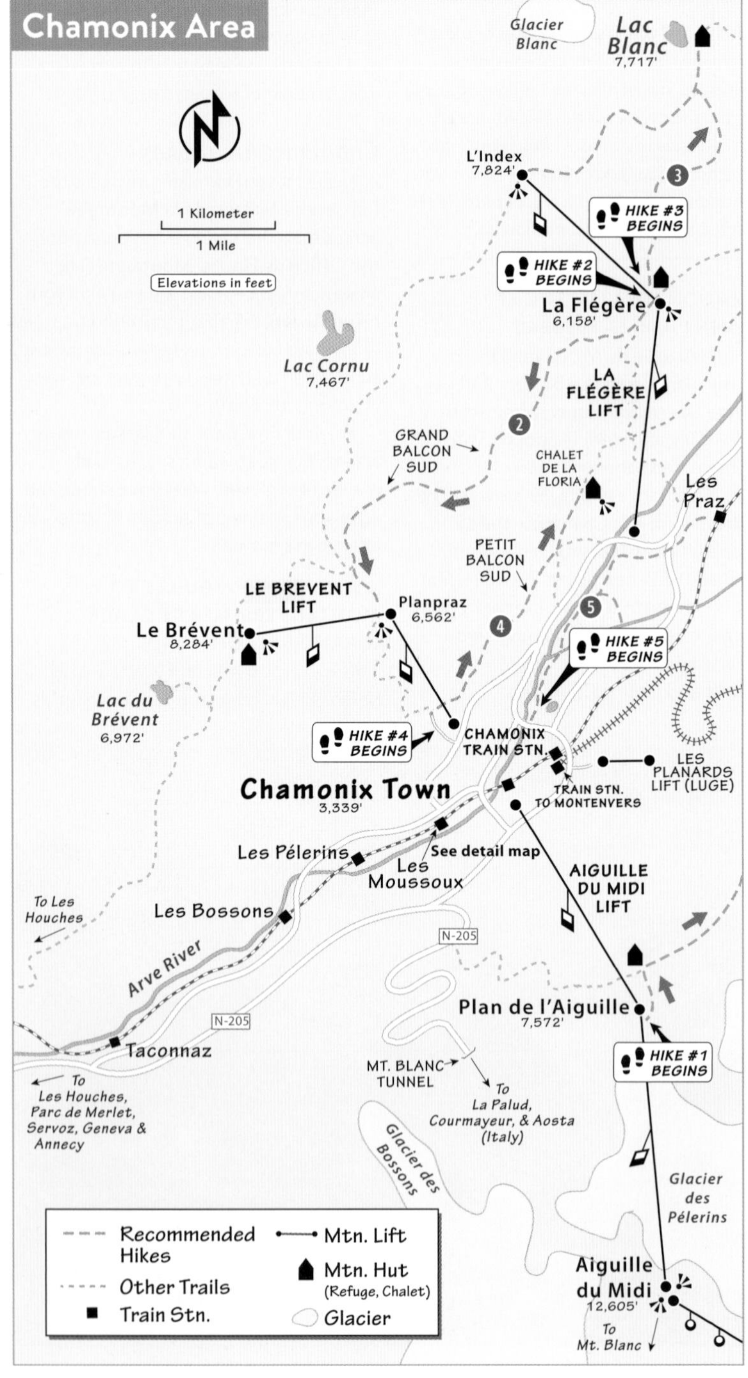
Chamonix Area
1 Kilometer
1 Mile
Elevations in feet
Glacier Blanc
Lac Blanc
7,717'
L'Index
7,824'
HIKE #3 BEGINS
HIKE #2 BEGINS
La Flégère
6,158'
Lac Cornu
7,467'
LA FLÉGÈRE LIFT
GRAND BALCON SUD
CHALET DE LA FLORIA
Les Praz
PETIT BALCON SUD
LE BREVENT LIFT
Planpraz
6,562'
Le Brévent
8,284'
HIKE #5 BEGINS
Lac du Brévent
6,972'
HIKE #4 BEGINS
CHAMONIX TRAIN STN.
LES PLANARDS LIFT (LUGE)
Chamonix Town
3,339'
TRAIN STN. TO MONTENVERS
Les Pélerins
See detail map
Les Moussoux
AIGUILLE DU MIDI LIFT
To Les Houches
Les Bossons
N-205
Arve River
Plan de l'Aiguille
7,572'
N-205
Taconnaz
HIKE #1 BEGINS
MT. BLANC TUNNEL
To La Palud, Courmayeur, & Aosta (Italy)
To Les Houches, Parc de Merlet, Servoz, Geneva & Annecy
Glacier des Bossons
Glacier des Pélerins
Recommended Hikes
Other Trails
Train Stn.
Mtn. Lift
Mtn. Hut (Refuge, Chalet)
Glacier
Aiguille du Midi
12,605'
To Mt. Blanc

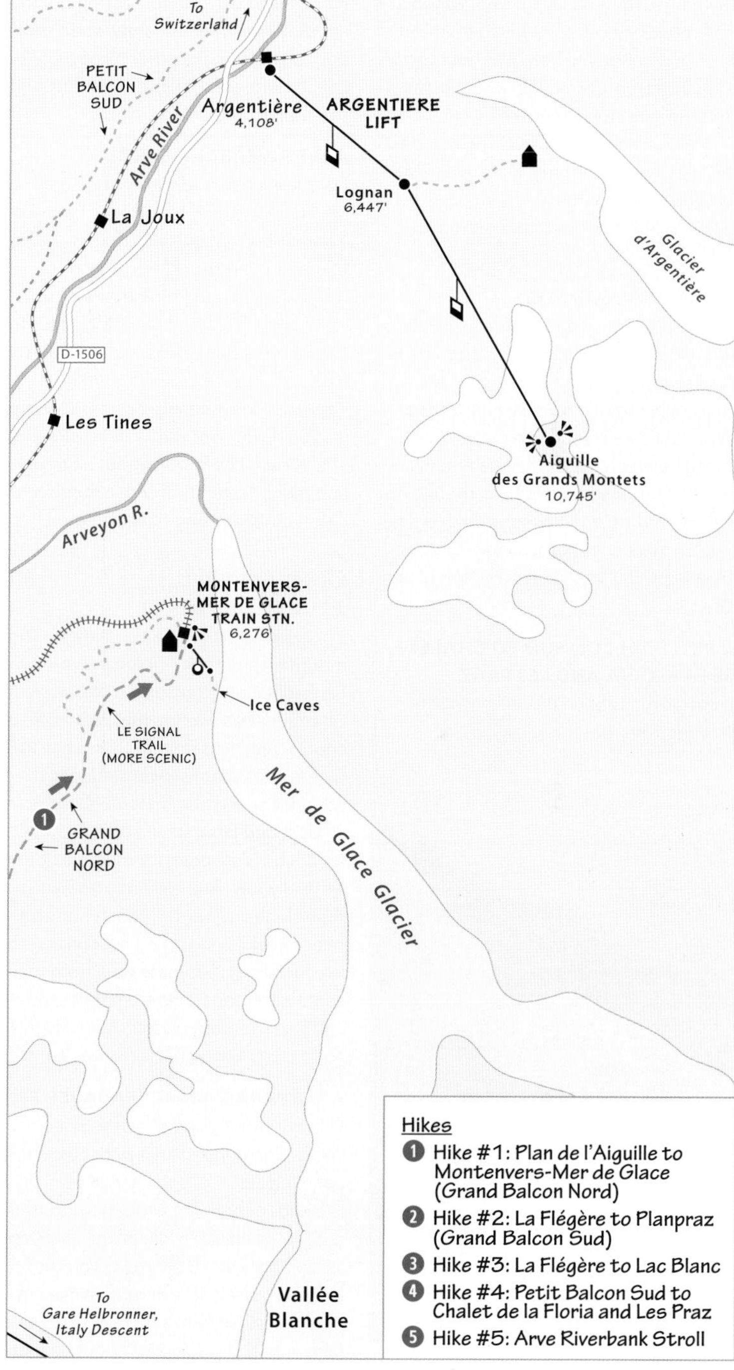
To
Switzerland
PETIT
BALCON
SUD
Argentière
4,108'
ARGENTIERE
LIFT
Arve River
Lognan
6,447'
La Joux
Glacier
d'Argentière
D-1506
Les Tines
Aiguille
des Grands Montets
10,745'
Arveyon R.
MONTENVERS-
MER DE GLACE
TRAIN STN.
6,276'
Ice Caves
LE SIGNAL
TRAIL
(MORE SCENIC)
1
GRAND
BALCON
NORD
Mer de Glace Glacier
To
Gare Helbronner,
Italy Descent
Vallée
Blanche
Hikes
1 Hike #1: Plan de l'Aiguille to
Montenvers-Mer de Glace
(Grand Balcon Nord)
2 Hike #2: La Flégère to Planpraz
(Grand Balcon Sud)
3 Hike #3: La Flégère to Lac Blanc
4 Hike #4: Petit Balcon Sud to
Chalet de la Floria and Les Praz
5 Hike #5: Arve Riverbank Stroll

down from the Aiguille du Midi gondola—while checking out a world-class glacier to boot. The well-used trail rises but mostly falls, and is moderately difficult. Some stretches are steep and strenuous, with uneven footing and slippery rocks. Note the last train time from Montenvers-Mer de Glace back to Chamonix, or you'll be hiking another 1.5 hours straight down.

▲▲ LA FLEGERE TO PLANPRAZ (GRAND BALCON SUD)

This lovely hike undulates for 2.5 hours above the Chamonix valley, with staggering views of Mont Blanc and countless other peaks, glaciers, and wildflowers. There's just 370 feet of difference in elevation between the La Flégère and Planpraz lift stations—so this hike, though not without its ups and downs, is doable. The trail is a mix of dirt paths, ankle-twisting rocky sections, and short stretches of service roads.

▲ PETIT BALCON SUD TO CHALET DE LA FLORIA AND LES PRAZ

This trail runs above the valley on the Brévent side from the village of Les Houches to Argentière, passing Chamonix about halfway, and is handy when snow or poor weather make other hikes problematic. No lifts are required—just firm thighs to climb up and down.

ARVE RIVERBANK STROLL

For a level, forested-valley stroll, follow the Arve River toward Les Praz. At Chamonix's Hôtel Alpina, follow the path upstream past the middle school, red-clay tennis courts, and find the green arrow to Les Praz. You'll cross a few bridges to the left, turn right along the rushing Arve River, and then follow Promenade des Econtres. Several trails loop through these woods; if you continue walking straight, you'll reach Les Praz in about an hour—an appealing destination with a number of cafés and a pleasing village green.

Other Activities

▲LUGE (LUGE D'ETE)

Thrill-seekers can ride a chairlift up the mountain and then scream down a twisty, banked, slalom course on a plastic sled. Chamonix has two roughly parallel luge courses, each just longer than a half-mile: One is marked for slower sledders, the other for speed demons.

Cost and Hours: One ride-€5.50, €7.50 for double sled, deals for multiple rides; generally July-Aug daily 10:00-18:30, mid-April-June and Sept-Oct Sat-Sun and select weekdays 13:30-18:00, check website for hours; 15-minute walk from town center, over the tracks from train station and past Montenvers train station; tel. 04 50 53 08 97, www.chamonixparc.com.

▲▲▲PARAGLIDING (PARAPENTE)

When it's sunny and clear, the skies above Chamonix sparkle with colorful parachute-like sails that circle the valley like birds of prey. For €100-110 plus the cost of the lift up to Planpraz (Le Brévent ski area) or Plan de l'Aiguille, you can launch yourself off a mountain in a tandem paraglider with a trained, experienced pilot and fly like a bird for about 20 minutes (true thrill-seekers can launch from Aiguille du Midi, €240, 40-minute ride). Most pilots will meet you at the lift station in Chamonix (usually from Le Brévent side, as it has the most reliable conditions). **Sean Potts** is English (no language barrier) and easy to work with (info@fly-chamonix.com). You can also try **Summits Parapente** (smart to reserve a day ahead, open year-round, tel. 04 50 53 50 14, mobile 06 84 01 26 00, www.summits.fr).

Eating and Sleeping

$$ La Boccalatte Brasserie serves good-value meals in a casual interior and on a big, easygoing terrace (59 Avenue de l'Aiguille du Midi). **$$$$ La Calèche** presents delicious regional dishes (18 Rue du Docteur Paccard), while **$$$ La Flambée** cooks up everything from burgers to pizza to fondue to steaks (closed Mon, 232 Avenue Michel Croz). **$$ Bistrot des Sports** serves budget meals in the back of their lively bar (176 Rue Joseph Vallot).

To spend the night, consider the gorgeous **$$$$ Hôtel Hermitage****** (63 Chemin du Cé, www.hermitage-paccard.com), the family-friendly **$$$ Hôtel l'Oustalet***** (330 Rue du Lyret, www.hotel-oustalet.com), or the comfortable **$$ Hôtel de l'Arve***** (60 Impasse des Anémones, www.hotelarve-chamonix.com).

Colmar

With its steep pitched roofs, pastel stucco, and aged timbers, Colmar feels made for wonder-struck tourists. Antiques shops welcome browsers, homeowners fuss over their geraniums, and hoteliers hurry down the sleepy streets to pick up fresh croissants in time for breakfast. Located near the German border, Colmar has a hybrid culture: Natives who curse do so bilingually, and the local cuisine features both sauerkraut and escargot.

Orientation

There isn't a straight street in Colmar—count on getting lost. Thankfully, most streets are pedestrian-only, and it's a lovely town to be lost in. Navigate by church steeples and the helpful signs that seem to pop up whenever you need them.

Day Plan: Take my self-guided Old Town walk (later), which delivers you to the Unterlinden Museum, home to the amazing *Isenheim Altarpiece*. In the afternoon, drivers could explore the Route du Vin (Wine Road).

Getting There: Colmar is linked by train with **Beaune** (10/day, 2.5-4 hours, fastest by TGV via Mulhouse, reserve well ahead, possible changes in Mulhouse or Belfort and Dijon), **Reims** (TGV: 10/day, 3 hours, most change in Strasbourg), and **Paris'** Gare de l'Est (nearly hourly, 3.5 hours, some change in Strasbourg).

Arrival in Colmar: The town center is Place Unterlinden, a 20-minute walk from the train station (from the station, turn left onto Avenue de la République, and keep walking). For a faster trip, take any Trace bus from the station to the Théâtre stop, next to the Unterlinden Museum (pay driver, www.trace-colmar.fr). By car, follow signs for *Centre-Ville*, then *Place*

Colmar

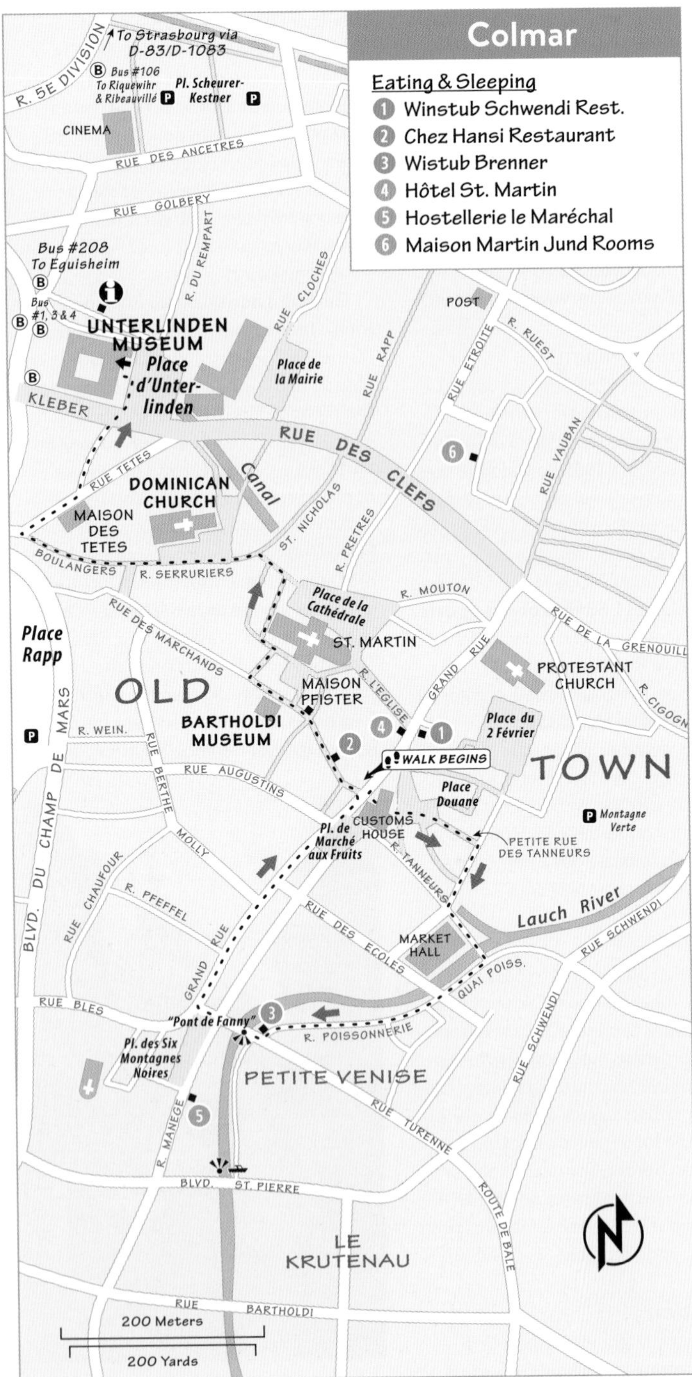
Colmar
Eating & Sleeping
1 Winstub Schwendi Rest.
2 Chez Hansi Restaurant
3 Wistub Brenner
4 Hôtel St. Martin
5 Hostellerie le Maréchal
6 Maison Martin Jund Rooms
To Strasbourg via D-83/D-1083
R. 5E DIVISION
Bus #106 To Riquewihr & Ribeauvillé
Pl. Scheurer-Kestner
CINEMA
RUE DES ANCETRES
RUE GOLBERY
Bus #208 To Eguisheim
Bus #1, 3 & 4
R. DU REMPART
RUE CLOCHES
UNTERLINDEN MUSEUM
Place d'Unterlinden
Place de la Mairie
RUE RAPP
POST
R. RUEST
RUE ETROITE
KLEBER
RUE DES CLEFS
Canal
RUE VAUBAN
RUE TETES
DOMINICAN CHURCH
MAISON DES TETES
ST. NICHOLAS
R. PRETRES
BOULANGERS
R. SERRURIERS
Place de la Cathédrale
R. MOUTON
RUE DE LA GRENOUILL
RUE DES MARCHANDS
ST. MARTIN
Place Rapp
GRAND RUE
PROTESTANT CHURCH
R. L'EGLISE
R. CIGOGN
OLD
MAISON PFISTER
BARTHOLDI MUSEUM
Place du 2 Février
R. WEIN.
BLVD. DU CHAMP DE MARS
RUE BERTHE
WALK BEGINS
TOWN
RUE AUGUSTINS
Place Douane
Montagne Verte
CUSTOMS HOUSE
Pl. de Marché aux Fruits
PETITE RUE DES TANNEURS
MOLLY
R. TANNEURS
RUE CHAUFOUR
R. PFEFFEL
Lauch River
RUE DES ECOLES
RUE SCHWENDI
MARKET HALL
QUAI POISS.
GRAND RUE
RUE BLES
"Pont de Fanny"
R. POISSONNERIE
Pl. des Six Montagnes Noires
PETITE VENISE
R. MANEGE
RUE TURENNE
ROUTE DE BALE
BLVD. ST. PIERRE
LE KRUTENAU
RUE BARTHOLDI
200 Meters
200 Yards

Rapp. Parking is available at a huge garage under Place Rapp.

Tourist Information: The TI is next to the Unterlinden Museum on Place Unterlinden (daily, but closed Sun off-season, tel. 03 89 20 68 92, www.tourisme-colmar.com).

Private Guide: Muriel Brun is a good choice (tel. 03 89 79 70 92, muriel.h.brun@calixo.net).

Market Days: The vintage market hall hosts a market nearly daily (*marché couvert*; Tue-Sat 8:00-18:00). The Saturday morning market on Place St. Joseph is where locals go for fresh produce and cheese (over the train tracks, 15 minutes on foot from the center).

➲ *Colmar Old Town Walk*

This self-guided walk—good by day, romantic by night—is a handy way to link the city's most worthwhile sights in about an hour (more if you enter sights). Supplement my commentary by reading the sidewalk information plaques that describe points of interest in the old town.

• *Start in front of the Customs House (where Rue des Marchands hits Grand Rue). Face the old...*

Customs House (Koïfhus): Colmar is so attractive today because of its trading wealth. And that's what its Customs House is all about. The city was an economic powerhouse in the 15th, 16th, and 17th centuries because of its privileged status as a leading member of the Decapolis, a trading league of 10 Alsatian cities founded in 1354.

This "Alsatian Big Ten" enjoyed special tax and trade privileges, the right to build fortified walls, and to run their internal affairs. As "Imperial" cities, they were ruled directly by the Holy Roman Emperor rather than via one of his lesser princes. The towns of the Decapolis enjoyed this status until the 17th century.

Delegates of the Decapolis would meet here to sort out trade issues, much like the European Union does in nearby Strasbourg today. Note the plaque above the door with the double eagle of the Holy Roman Emperor—a sign that this was an Imperial city.

Walk under the archway to Place de l'Ancienne Douane and face the Frédéric-Auguste Bartholdi statue of General Lazarus von Schwendi—arm raised (Statue of Liberty-style) and

Customs House

clutching a bundle of pinot gris grapes. He's the man who brought the grape from Hungary to Alsace.

• *Follow the statue's left elbow and walk down Petite Rue des Tanneurs (not the larger "Rue des Tanneurs"). The half-timbered commotion of higgledy-piggledy rooftops on the downhill side of the fountain marks the...*

Tanners' Quarter: These vertical 17th- and 18th-century rooftops competed for space in the sun to dry their freshly tanned hides, while the nearby river channel flushed the waste products. Notice the openings just below the roofs where hides would be hung out to dry. At the street's end, carry on a few steps, and then turn back. Stinky tanners' quarters were always at the edge of town. You've stepped outside the old center and are looking back at the city's first defensive wall. The oldest and lowest stones you see are from 1230, now built into the row of houses.

• *Walk with the old walls on your right, then take the first left along the stream.*

Old Market Hall: On your right is Colmar's historic (c. 1865) market hall. Here, locals buy fish, produce, and other products. You'll find terrific picnic fixings and produce, sandwiches and bakery items, wine tastings, and clean WCs. Several stands are run like cafés, and there's even a bar (Tue-Sat 8:00-18:00, closed Sun-Mon).

• *Back on the street, cross the canal and turn right on Quai de la Poissonnerie ("Wharf of the Fish Market"), and you'll enter...*

Petite Venise: This neighborhood, a collection of Colmar's most colorful houses lining a small canal, lies between the town's first wall (built to defend against arrows) and its later wall (built in the age of gunpowder). Medieval towns needed water. If they weren't on a river, they'd often redirect parts of nearby rivers to power their mills and quench their thirst. Colmar's river was canalized this way for medieval industry.

• *Walk along the flower-box-lined canal to the end of Rue de la Poissonnerie.*

Half-Timbered Houses: As you stroll, notice the picturesque houses. The pastel colors are just from this generation—designed to pump up the cuteness of Colmar for tourists. But the houses themselves are historic and real as can be.

Houses of the rich were made of stone, while budget builders made half-timbered

Petite Venise

structures. When the rich moved here in the 18th century, they disguised the cheap wattle and daub with a thick layer of plaster. To them, the half-timbers looked cheap...and German. To be French was *à la mode* and that meant no half-timbers. Today, in the 21st century, half-timbered has become charming, so the current owners have peeled away the plaster to reveal the old beams.

At the end of Rue de la Poissonnerie, on your right, is "Pont de Fanny," a bridge so popular with tourists for its fine views that you see lots of fannies lined up along the railing. Walk to the center of the bridge, and enjoy the scene. To the right you'll see examples of the flat-bottomed gondolas used to transport goods on the small river. Today, they give tourists sleepy, scenic, 30-minute canal tours. (The better tour departs from the dock at Boulevard St. Pierre in Petite Venise; €6, departures every 10 minutes, daily 10:00-12:00 & 13:30-18:30).

• *Cross the bridge and take the second right on Grande Rue. Walk for several blocks to the Customs House (green-tiled roof) and land back where you started. With your back to the Customs House, walk uphill along Rue des Marchands ("Merchants Street"), and you'll soon come face-to-face with the...*

Maison Pfister (Pfister House): This richly decorated merchant's house dates from 1537. Here, the owner displayed his wealth for all to enjoy (and to envy). The external spiral-staircase turret, a fine loggia on the top floor, and the bay windows were pricey add-ons. The painted walls illustrate the city elites' taste for Renaissance humanism.

Stand outside facing the Pfister House for a little review. Find the four main styles of Colmar architecture: the Gothic church (right), local medieval half-timbered structures, Renaissance (that's Mr. Pfister's place), and (behind you) the urbane and elegant shutters and ironwork of Paris from the 19th century.

A short block farther up the street on the left is the ▲ **Bartholdi Museum,** located in the home of Frédéric-Auguste Bartholdi, the sculptor of America's Statue of Liberty (€5, closed Tue and Jan-Feb, get the good audioguide, www.musee-bartholdi.fr).

• *A passage opposite the museum (on the right) leads you through the old guards' house to...*

Church of St. Martin: The city's cathedral-like church was erected in 1235 after Colmar became an Imperial city and needed a bigger place of worship. Colmar's ruler at the time was Burgundian, so the church has a Burgundian-style tiled roof.

Walk left, under expressive gargoyles, to the west portal. Facing the front of the church, notice that the relief over the main door depicts not your typical Last Judgment scene, but the Three Kings who visited Baby Jesus. The Magi, whose remains are nearby in the Rhine city of Cologne, Germany, are popular in this region. The church's interior is dark, but it holds a few finely carved and beautifully painted altarpieces.

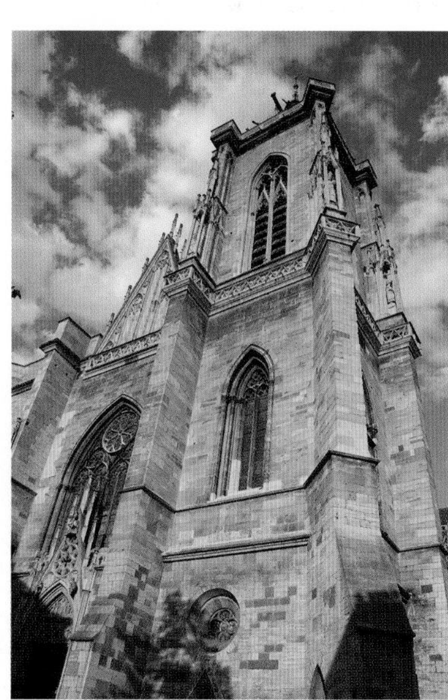

Church of St. Martin

• Walk past the church, go left around Café Jupiler, and wander up Rue des Serruriers ("Locksmiths Street") to the...

Dominican Church: Compare the Church of St. Martin's ornate exterior with this simple ▲▲▲ Dominican structure (closed Tue). While the churches were built at the same time, they make different statements. The "High Church" of the 13th century was fancy and corrupt. The Dominican order was all about austerity. It was a time of crisis in the Roman Catholic Church. Monastic orders (as well as heretical movements like the Cathars in southern France) preached a simpler faith and way of life. In the style of St. Dominic and St. Francis, they tried to get Rome back on a Christ-like track. Inside, this church houses a mesmerizing medieval masterpiece—Martin Schongauer's angelically beautiful *Virgin in the Rosebush* (1473).

• Continuing past the Dominican Church, Rue des Serruriers becomes Rue des Boulangers ("Bakers Street"). Stop at #16.

Skyscrapers and Biscuits: The towering six-story house at #16, dating from the 16th century, was one of Colmar's tallest buildings from that age. Notice how it contrasts with the string of buildings to the right, which are lower, French-style structures—likely built after a fire cleared out older, higher buildings.

As this is Bakers Street, check out the one right here at #16. Maison Alsacienne de Biscuiterie sells traditional, home-baked *biscuits* (cookies) including Christmas delights year-round.

• Turn right on Rue des Têtes (notice the beautiful swan sign over the pharmacie at the corner). Walk a block to the fancy old house festooned with heads (on the right).

Maison des Têtes ("House of Heads"): Colmar's other famous merchant's house, built in 1609 by a big-shot winemaker (see the grapes hanging from the wrought-iron sign and the happy man at the tip-top), is playfully decorated with about 100 faces and masks. On the ground floor, the guy in the window's center has pig feet.

Look four doors to the right to see a 1947 bakery sign (above the big pretzel), which shows the *boulangerie* basics in Alsace: croissant, *Kugelhopf*, and baguette. Notice the colors of the French flag, indicating that this house supported French rule.

Isenheim Altarpiece

• *Angle down Rue de l'Eau ("Water Street") for a shortcut to the TI and the Unterlinden Museum, with its namesake linden trees lining the front yard. Your walk ends here, at the doorstep of Colmar's top museum.*

Unterlinden Museum: This museum, rated ▲▲▲, fills a 13th-century former convent with exhibits ranging from Roman artifacts to medieval winemaking, and from traditional wedding dresses to paintings from the High Middle Ages.

Its undisputed highlight is Matthias Grünewald's gripping *Isenheim Altarpiece.* Designed to help people in a medieval hospital endure horrible skin diseases—long before the age of painkillers—it's one of the most powerful paintings ever produced. Germans know this painting like Americans know the *Mona Lisa*. It's actually a series of three paintings on hinges that pivot like shutters (study the little models—look for one with English explanations). After you witness the agony and suffering of the Crucifixion, look on the other side of the panel to appreciate the rocketing joy of the Resurrection (€13, Wed-Mon 10:00-18:00, Thu until 20:00, closed Tue, www.musee-unterlinden.com).

Route du Vin

France's smallest wine region is long (75 miles) and skinny (just over a mile wide on average). Peppering the landscape are villages full of quaint half-timbered architecture corralled within medieval walls and welcoming wineries featuring crisp, dry white wines.

Drivers and energetic bikers (bikes rentable at Colmar's train station) can pick up a detailed map of the wine road (Route du Vin) at any area TI. Be advised that after seeing two or three towns, they start looking the same. Two villages work well for most. Distances are short; you can lace together what you like. Focus on towns within easy striking range of Colmar. The most picturesque are Eguisheim, Kaysersberg (Mon morning market), Hunawihr, Ribeauvillé (Sat morning market), and the *très* popular Riquewihr.

Eating and Sleeping

$ Winstub Schwendi has a fun, German pub energy and hearty Swiss *Rösti* plates (3 Grand Rue). **$$$ Chez Hansi** is where Colmarians go for a traditional Alsace meal (closed Wed-Thu, 23 Rue des Marchands). **$$ Wistub Brenner** is perhaps your best mix of economy, quality cooking, and characteristic ambience (1 Rue Turenne).

Family-run **$$ Hôtel St. Martin***** is near the old Customs House (38 Grand Rue, www.hotel-saint-martin.com), and characteristic **$$ Hostellerie le Maréchal****** is in the heart of Petite Venise (4 Place des Six Montagnes Noires, www.le-marechal.com). **¢ Maison Martin Jund** has my favorite budget beds in town (12 Rue de l'Ange, www.martinjund.com).

France: Past and Present

French History in an Escargot Shell

About the time of Christ, Romans "Latinized" the land of the **Gauls.** With the fifth-century fall of Rome, the barbarian Franks and Burgundians invaded. Today's France evolved from this unique mix of Latin and Celtic cultures.

While France wallowed with the rest of Europe in medieval darkness, it got a head start in its development as a nation-state. In 507, Clovis, the king of the **Franks,** established Paris as the capital of his Christian Merovingian dynasty. Clovis and the Franks would eventually become Louis and the French. The Frankish military leader Charles Martel stopped the spread of Islam by beating the North African Moors at the Battle of Tours. And **Charlemagne** ("Charles the Great"), the most important of the "Dark Age" Frankish kings, was crowned Holy Roman Emperor by the pope in 800. Charlemagne presided over the "Carolingian Renaissance" and effectively ruled an empire that was vast for its time.

The Treaty of Verdun (843), which divided Charlemagne's empire among his grandsons, marks what could be considered the birth of Europe. For the first time, a treaty was signed in vernacular languages (French and German), rather than in Latin. This split established a Franco-Germanic divide, and heralded an age of fragmentation. While petty princes took the reigns, the Frankish king ruled only Ile-de-France, a small region around Paris.

Vikings, or Norsemen, settled in what became Normandy. Later, in 1066, these **"Normans"** invaded England. The Norman king, William the Conqueror, consolidated his English domain, accelerating the formation of modern England. But his rule also muddied the political waters between England and France, kicking off a centuries-long struggle between the two nations.

In the 12th century, **Eleanor of Aquitaine** (a separate country in southwest France) married Louis VII, King of France, bringing Aquitaine under French rule.

They divorced, and she married Henry of Normandy (soon to be Henry II of England). This marital union gave England control of a huge swath of land from the English Channel to the Pyrenees. For 300 years, France and England would struggle over control of Aquitaine. Any enemy of the French king would find a natural ally in the English king.

In 1328, the French king, Charles IV, died without a son. The English king, Edward III (Charles IV's nephew), was interested in the throne, but the French resisted. This quandary pitted France, the biggest and richest country in Europe, against England, which had the biggest army. They fought from 1337 to 1453 in what was modestly called the **Hundred Years' War.**

Regional powers from within France actually sided with England. Burgundy took Paris, captured the royal family, and recognized the English king as heir to the French throne. England controlled France from the Loire north, and things looked bleak for the French king.

Enter **Joan of Arc,** a 16-year-old peasant girl driven by religious voices. France's national heroine left home to support Charles VII, the dauphin (boy prince, heir to the throne but too young to rule). Joan rallied the French, ultimately inspiring them to throw out the English. In 1430, Joan was captured by the Burgundians, who sold her to the English, who convicted her of heresy and burned her at the stake in Rouen. But the inspiration of Joan of Arc lived on, and by 1453 English holdings on the Continent had dwindled to the port of Calais.

By 1500, a strong, centralized France had emerged, with borders similar to today's. Its kings (from the Renaissance François I through the Henrys and all those Louises) were model **divine monarchs,** setting the standards for absolute rule in Europe.

Outrage over the power plays and spending sprees of the kings—coupled with the modern thinking of the Enlightenment (whose leaders were the French *philosophes*)—led to the **French Revolution** (1789). In France, it was the end of the *ancien régime*, as well as its notion that some are born to rule, while others are born to be ruled.

The excesses of the Revolution in turn led to the rise of **Napoleon,** who ruled the French empire as a dictator. Eventually, *his* excesses ushered him into a South Atlantic exile, and after another half-century of monarchy and empire, the French settled on a compromise role for their leader. The modern French "king" is ruled by a constitution. Rather than dress in leotards and powdered wigs, France's president goes to work in a suit and carries a briefcase.

The **20th century** spelled the end of France's reign as a military and political superpower. Devastating wars with Germany in 1870, 1914, and 1940—and the loss of her colonial holdings—left France with not quite enough land, people, or production to be a top player on a global scale. But the 21st century may see France rise again: Paris is a cultural capital of Europe, and France—under the EU banner—is a key player in integrating Europe as a single, unified economic power. And when Europe is a superpower, Paris may yet be its capital.

Top French Notables in History

Madame and Monsieur Cro-Magnon: Prehistoric hunter-gatherers who moved to France (c. 30,000 B.C.), painted cave walls at Lascaux and Font-de-Gaume, and eventually settled down as farmers (c. 10,000 B.C.).

Vercingétorix (72 B.C.-46 B.C.): This long-haired warrior rallied the Gauls against Julius Caesar's invading Roman legions (52 B.C.). Defeated by Caesar, France fell under Roman domination, resulting in 500 years of peace and prosperity.

Charlemagne (742-814): For Christmas in 800, the pope gave King Charlemagne the title of Emperor, thus uniting much of Europe under the leadership of the Franks ("France"). Charlemagne stabilized France amid centuries of barbarian invasions.

Eleanor of Aquitaine (c. 1122-1204): The sophisticated ex-wife of the King of France married the King of England, creating an uneasy union between the two countries. During her lifetime, French culture was spread across Europe by roving troubadours, theological scholars, and skilled architects pioneering "the French style"—a.k.a. Gothic.

Joan of Arc (1412-1431): When France and England fought the Hundred Years' War to settle who would rule (1337-1453), teenager Joan of Arc—guided by voices in her head—rallied the French troops. Though Joan was captured and burned as a heretic, the French eventually drove England out of their country for good, establishing the current borders.

François I (1494-1547): This Renaissance king ruled a united, modern nation, making it a cultural center that hosted the Italian Leonardo da Vinci. François set the tone for future absolute monarchs.

Louis XIV (1638-1715): Charismatic and cunning, the "Sun King" ruled Europe's richest, most populous, most powerful nation-state. Every educated European spoke French, dressed in Louis-style leotards and powdered wigs, and built Versailles-like palaces. Though Louis ruled as an absolute monarch, his reign also fostered the arts and philosophy, sowing the seeds of democracy and revolution.

Marie-Antoinette (1755-1793): As the wife of Louis XVI, she came to symbolize (probably unfairly) the decadence of France's ruling class. When revolution broke out (1789), she was arrested, imprisoned, and executed.

Napoleon Bonaparte (1769-1821): This daring young military man became a hero during the Revolution, fighting Europe's royalty. He went on to conquer much of the Continent, become leader of France, and eventually rule as a dictator with the title of emperor. In 1815, an allied Europe defeated and exiled Napoleon, reinstating the French monarchy.

Claude Monet (1840-1926): Monet's Impressionist paintings captured the soft-focus beauty of the belle époque—middle-class men and women enjoying drinks in cafés, walks in gardens, and picnics along the Seine.

Charles de Gaulle (1890-1970): A career military man, de Gaulle helped France survive occupation by Nazi Germany during World War II with his rousing radio broadcasts and unbending faith in his countrymen. He left politics in the postwar period, but after France's divisive wars in Vietnam and Algeria, he came to the rescue, becoming president of the Fifth Republic in 1959.

France Today

Today, the main political issue in France is—like everywhere—the economy. Initially, France weathered the 2008 downturn better than the US, because it was less invested in risky home loans and the volatile stock market. But now France, along with the rest of Europe, has been struggling. The challenge for French leadership is to address its economic problems while maintaining the high level of social services that the French people expect from their government.

Ironically, while France's economy may be one of the world's largest, the French remain skeptical about the virtues of capitalism and the work ethic. The French believe that the economy should support social good, not vice versa. This has produced a cradle-to-grave social security system of which the French are proud. France's poverty rate is half of that in the US, proof to the French that they are on the right track. On the other hand, France is routinely plagued with strikes, demonstrations, and slowdowns as workers try to preserve their hard-earned rights in the face of a competitive global economy.

The French political scene is complex and fascinating. France is governed by a president (currently Emmanuel Macron), elected by popular vote every five years. The president then selects the prime minister, who in turn chooses the cabinet ministers. Collectively, this executive branch is known as the *gouvernement.* The parliament consists of a Senate (348 seats) and the Assemblée Nationale (577 seats).

In France, compromise and coalition-building are essential to keeping power. Unlike America's two-party system, France has a half-dozen major political parties, plus more on the fringes. A simple majority is rare. Even the biggest parties rarely get more than a third of the votes.

In recent years the French political scene has become as polarized as in the United States, although terrorist attacks brought some unity. These attacks shocked a nation unaccustomed to terrorism on its soil. The government's challenge: to respond with sufficient intensity to deter would-be terrorists without infringing on the rights of its Muslim population.

Another ongoing issue that French leaders must work together to address is immigration, which is shifting the country's ethnic and cultural makeup in ways that challenge French society. Ten percent of France's population is of North African descent, mainly immigrants from former colonies. The increased number of Muslims raises cultural questions in this heavily Catholic society that institutes official state secularism. The French have (quite controversially) made it illegal for women to wear a full, face-covering veil *(niqāb)* in public. They continue to debate whether banning the veil enforces democracy—or squelches diversity.

Practicalities

TOURIST INFORMATION

The French national tourist office is a wealth of information (http://us.rendezvousenfrance.com), with particularly good resources for special-interest travel. Paris' official TI website, www.parisinfo.com, offers practical information on hotels, special events, museums, children's activities, fashion, nightlife, and more.

In France, a good first stop in every town is the tourist information office (abbreviated **TI** in this book). Prepare a list of questions and a proposed plan to double-check. Pick up a city map, confirm opening hours of sights, and get the latest info on public transit (including bus and train schedules), walking tours, special events, and nightlife.

TRAVEL TIPS

Time Zones: France, like most of continental Europe, is generally six/nine hours ahead of the East/West Coasts of the US. The exceptions are the beginning and end of Daylight Saving Time: Europe "springs forward" the last Sunday in March (two weeks after most of North America), and "falls back" the last Sunday in October (one week before North America). For a handy online time converter, see www.

timeanddate.com/worldclock.

Business Hours: You'll find much of France closed weekdays from noon to 14:00 (lunch is sacred). On Sunday, most businesses are closed (family is sacred); on Mondays, some businesses are closed until 14:00 and possibly all day. Saturdays are virtually weekdays, with earlier closing hours at some shops. Banks are generally open on Saturday and closed on Sunday and possibly Monday.

Discounts: This book lists only the full adult price for sights. However, many sights offer discounts for youths (up to age 18), students (with proper identification cards, www.isic.org), families, and seniors (loosely defined as retirees or those willing to call themselves seniors). Always ask—though some discounts are only available for citizens of the European Union.

Online Translation Tips: The Google Translate app converts spoken English into most European languages (and vice versa) and can also translate text it "reads" with your mobile device's camera. To translate websites, use Google's Chrome browser (www.google.com/chrome) or paste the URL of the site into the translation window at www.google.com/translate.

HELP!

Emergency and Medical Help

Dial 112 for any emergency. For English-speaking police, call 17. To summon an ambulance, call 15. Or ask at your hotel for help—they'll know the nearest medical and emergency services. If you get a minor ailment, do as the locals do and go to a pharmacist for advice.

Theft or Loss

To replace a passport, you'll need to go in person to an embassy or consulate (listed below). If your credit and debit cards disappear, cancel and replace them. If your things are lost or stolen, file a police report, either on the spot or within a day or two; you'll need it to submit an insurance claim for rail passes or travel gear, and it can help with replacing your

Avoiding Theft

Pickpockets are common, but fortunately, violent crime is rare. Thieves don't want to hurt you; they just want your money and gadgets.

My recommendations: Stay alert and wear a money belt (tucked under your clothes) to keep your cash, debit card, credit card, and passport secure; carry only the money you need for the day in your front pocket.

Treat any disturbance (e.g., a stranger bumps into you, spills something on you, or tries to get your attention for an odd reason) as a smoke screen for theft. Be on guard waiting in line at sights, at train stations, and while boarding and leaving crowded buses and subways. Thieves target tourists overloaded with bags or distracted with smartphones.

When paying for something, be aware of how much cash you're handing over (state the denomination of the bill when paying a cabbie) and count your change. For tips on using cash machines smartly, read "Security Tips" under "Cash" on page 416. For advice on avoiding big-city scams and pickpockets, read page 43 of the Paris chapter.

There's no need to be scared; just be smart and prepared.

passport or credit and debit cards. For more information, see www.ricksteves.com/help.

Damage Control for Lost Cards

If you lose your credit, debit, or ATM card, you can stop people from using your card by reporting the loss immediately to your card company. Call these 24-hour US numbers collect: Visa (tel. 303/967-1096), MasterCard (tel. 636/722-7111), and American Express (tel. 336/393-1111). In France, to make a collect call to the US, dial 08 00 90 06 24, then say "operator" for an English-speaking operator. Visa's and MasterCard's websites list European toll-free numbers by country.

If you report your loss within two days, you typically won't be responsible for any unauthorized transactions on your account, although many banks charge a liability fee of $50. You can generally receive a temporary replacement card within two or three business days in Europe.

Embassies and Consulates

US Embassy in Paris: Tel. 01 43 12 22 22 (4 Avenue Gabriel, http://france.usembassy.gov)

US Consulate in Marseille: Tel. 01 43 12 48 85 (Place Varian Fry, https://fr.usembassy.gov/embassy-consulates/marseille).

Canadian Embassy in Paris: Tel. 01 44 43 29 02 (35 Avenue Montaigne, Mo: Franklin D. Roosevelt, www.amb-canada.fr)

Canadian Consulate in Nice: Tel. 04 93 92 93 22 (10 Rue Lamartine, nice@international.gc.ca)

MONEY

This section offers advice on how to pay for purchases on your trip (including getting cash from ATMs and paying with plastic), VAT (sales tax) refunds, and tipping.

What to Bring

Bring both a credit card and a debit card. You'll use the debit card at cash machines (ATMs) to withdraw local cash for most purchases, and the credit card to pay for larger items. Some travelers carry a third card, as a backup, in case one gets demagnetized or eaten by a rogue machine.

For an emergency stash, carry €200 in hard cash in €20-50 bills (dollars can be hard to change in France). If you're the careful type, consider getting €200 from your local bank before leaving; otherwise withdraw euros from a cash machine at the airport upon arriving in France.

Cash

Cash is just as desirable in Europe as it is at home. Small businesses (mom-and-pop cafés, shops, etc.) prefer that you pay your bills with cash. Some vendors will charge you extra for using a credit card, some won't accept foreign credit cards, and some won't take any credit cards at all. Cash is the best—and sometimes only—way to pay for cheap food, bus fare, taxis, and local guides.

Throughout Europe, ATMs are the standard way for travelers to get cash. They work just like they do at home. To withdraw money from an ATM (known as a *distributeur* in France; dee-stree-bew-tur), you'll need a debit card plus a four-digit PIN code. Although you can use a credit card to withdraw cash at an ATM, this comes with high bank fees and only makes sense in an emergency.

Security Tips: Shield the keypad when entering your PIN code. When possible, use ATMs located outside banks—a thief is less likely to target a cash machine near

Exchange Rate

1 euro (€) = about $1.20

To convert prices in euros to dollars, add about 20 percent: €20=about $24, €50=about $60. (Check www.oanda.com for the latest exchange rates.) Just like the dollar, one euro is broken down into 100 cents. You'll find coins ranging from €0.01 to €2, and bills from €5 to €500 (bills over €50 are rarely used).

surveillance cameras, and if you have trouble with the transaction, you can go inside for help.

Don't use an ATM if anything on the front of the machine looks loose or damaged (a sign that someone may have attached a "skimming" device to capture account information). If a cash machine eats your card, check for a thin plastic insert with a tongue hanging out (thieves use these devices to extract cards).

Stay away from "independent" ATMs such as Travelex, Euronet, YourCash, Cardpoint, and Cashzone, which charge huge commissions and have terrible exchange rates, and may try to trick users with "dynamic currency conversion" (see page 418).

If you want to monitor your accounts online during your trip to detect any unauthorized transactions, be sure to use a secure connection (see page 433).

Credit and Debit Cards

For purchases, Visa and MasterCard are more commonly accepted than American Express. Just like at home, credit or debit cards work easily at larger hotels, restaurants, and shops. I typically use my debit card to withdraw cash to pay for most purchases.

I use my credit card sparingly: to book hotel reservations, to buy advance tickets for events or sights, to cover major expenses (such as car rentals or plane tickets), and to pay for things online or near the end of my trip (to avoid another visit to the ATM). While you could instead use a debit card for these purchases, a credit card offers a greater degree of fraud protection.

Ask Your Credit- or Debit-Card Company: Before your trip, contact the company that issued your debit or credit cards.

Confirm that your **card will work overseas,** and alert them that you'll be using it in Europe; otherwise, they may deny transactions if they perceive unusual spending patterns.

Ask for the specifics on transaction **fees.** When you use your credit or debit card, you'll typically be charged additional "international transaction" fees of up to 3 percent. If your card's fees seem high, consider getting a different card just for your trip: Capital One (www.capitalone.com) and most credit unions have low-to-no international fees.

Verify your daily ATM **withdrawal limit,** and if necessary, ask your bank to adjust it. I prefer a high limit that allows me to take out more cash at each ATM

stop and save on bank fees; some travelers prefer to set a lower limit in case their card is stolen. Note that foreign banks also set maximum withdrawal amounts for their ATMs.

Get your bank's emergency **phone number** in the US (but not its 800 number, which isn't accessible from overseas) to call collect if you have a problem.

Ask for your credit card's **PIN** in case you need to make an emergency cash withdrawal or encounter Europe's chip-and-PIN system; the bank won't tell you your PIN over the phone, so allow time for it to be mailed to you.

Magnetic-Stripe versus Chip-and-PIN Credit Cards: Europeans use chip-and-PIN credit cards that are embedded with an electronic security chip and require a four-digit PIN. Your American-style card (with just the old-fashioned magnetic stripe) will work fine in most places. But it probably won't work at unattended payment machines, such as those at train and subway stations, toll plazas, parking garages, bike-rental kiosks, and gas pumps. If you have problems, try entering your card's PIN, look for a machine that takes cash, or find a clerk who can process the transaction manually.

Major US banks are beginning to offer credit cards with chips. Many of these are not true chip-and-PIN cards, but instead are "chip-and-signature" cards, for which your signature verifies your identity. These cards should work for live transactions and at some payment machines, but won't work for offline transactions such as at unattended gas pumps. If you're concerned, ask if your bank offers a true chip-and-PIN card. Andrews Federal Credit Union (www.andrewsfcu.org) and the State Department Federal Credit Union (www.sdfcu.org) offer these cards and are open to all US residents.

No matter what kind of card you have, it pays to carry euros; remember, you can always use an ATM to withdraw cash with your magnetic-stripe debit card.

Dynamic Currency Conversion: If merchants or hoteliers offer to convert your purchase price into dollars (called dynamic currency conversion, or DCC), refuse this "service." You'll pay even more in fees for the expensive convenience of seeing your transaction in dollars.

Tipping

Tipping in France isn't as automatic and generous as it is in the US. For special service, tips are appreciated, but not expected. As in the US, the right amount depends on your resources and the circumstances, but some general guidelines apply.

Restaurants: At cafés and restaurants, a service charge is included in the price of what you order, and it's unnecessary to tip extra, though you can for superb service.

For details on tipping in restaurants, see page 422.

Taxis: Round up your fare a bit (for instance, if the fare is €13, pay €14). If the cabbie hauls your bags and zips you to the airport to help you catch your flight, you might want to toss in a little more. But if you feel like you're being driven in circles or otherwise ripped off, skip the tip.

Services: In general, if someone in the service industry does a super job for you, a small tip of a euro or two is appropriate...but not required. If you're not sure whether (or how much) to tip for a service, ask a local for advice.

Getting a VAT Refund

Wrapped into the purchase price of your French souvenirs is a Value-Added Tax (VAT) of about 20 percent. You're entitled to get most of that tax back if you purchase more than €175 worth of goods at a store that participates in the VAT-refund scheme. Typically, you must ring up the minimum at a single retailer—you can't add up your purchases from various shops to reach the required amount.

If the merchant ships the goods to your home, the tax will be subtracted from your purchase price. Otherwise, you'll need to:

Get the paperwork. Have the merchant completely fill out the necessary refund document, called a *bordereau de détaxe*. You'll have to present your passport. Get the paperwork done before you leave the store to ensure you'll have everything you need (including your original sales receipt).

Get your stamp at the border or airport. Process your VAT document at your last stop in the European Union (the airport or border) with the customs agent who deals with VAT refunds. Arrive an additional hour before you need to check in for your flight to allow time to find the customs office and wait in line. It's best to keep your purchases in your carry-on. If they're too large or dangerous to carry on (such as knives), pack them in your checked bags and alert the check-in agent. You'll be sent (with your tagged bag) to a customs desk outside security; someone will examine your bag, stamp your paperwork, and put your bag on the belt. You're not supposed to use your purchased goods before you leave. If you show up at customs wearing your chic new beret, officials might look the other way—or deny you a refund.

Collect your refund. You'll need to return your stamped document to the retailer or its representative. Many merchants work with a service—such as Global Blue or Premier Tax Free—that has offices at major airports, ports, or border crossings. These services, which extract a 4 percent fee, can refund your money immediately in cash or credit your card. If the retailer handles VAT refunds directly, it's up to you to contact the merchant for your refund. You can mail the documents from home or from your point of departure. You'll then have to wait—it can take months.

Customs for American Shoppers

You are allowed to take home $800 worth of items per person duty-free, once every 31 days. You can take home many processed and packaged foods: vacuum-packed cheeses, dried herbs, jams, baked goods, candy, chocolate, oil, vinegar, mustard, and honey. Fresh fruits and vegetables and most meats are not allowed, with exceptions for some canned items.

You can bring home one liter of alcohol duty-free. It can be packed securely in your checked luggage, along with any other liquid-containing items. But if you want to pack alcohol (or liquid-packed foods) in your carry-on bag for your flight home, buy it at a duty-free shop at the airport.

For details on allowable goods, customs rules, and duty rates, visit http://help.cbp.gov.

SIGHTSEEING

Sightseeing can be hard work. Use these tips to make your visits to France's finest sights meaningful, fun, efficient, and painless.

Plan Ahead

Set up an itinerary that allows you to fit in all your must-see sights. Most places keep stable hours, but you can confirm the latest at the TI or by checking museum websites. Many museums are closed or have reduced hours at least a few days a year, especially on major holidays. In summer, some sights may stay open late. Off-season, many museums have shorter hours. Whenever you go, don't put off visiting a must-see sight—you never know if a place will close unexpectedly for a holiday, strike, or restoration.

Several cities, including Paris, offer sightseeing passes that cover many (but not all) museums. For most people, the Paris Museum Pass is a great deal. But to evaluate any pass, do the math: Add up the entry costs of the sights you want to see to figure out if the pass will save you money. An added bonus is that passes allow you to bypass the long ticket-buying lines at popular sights; that alone can make a pass worthwhile.

Sometimes you can avoid lines by making reservations for an entry time (for example, at the Eiffel Tower or Picasso Museum in Paris). At some popular places (such as Monet's garden at Giverny), you can get in more quickly by buying your ticket or pass at a less-crowded sight nearby (Giverny's Museum of Impressionisms). If you haven't reserved ahead, taking a guided tour can help you skip lines at some sights, such as the palace at Versailles. Specifics appear in the chapters.

If you can't reserve ahead for a popular sight, try going very early or very late. When available, evening visits are usually peaceful, with fewer crowds.

Study up. To get the most out of the sight descriptions in this book, read them before you visit. That said, every sight or museum offers more than what is covered in this book. Use the information in this book as an introduction—not the final word.

At Sights

Here's what you can typically expect:

Entering: Be warned that you may not be allowed to enter if you arrive 30 to 60 minutes before closing time. And guards start ushering people out well before the actual closing time, so don't save the best for last.

Some important sights have a security check, where you must open your bag or send it through a metal detector. Some sights require you to check daypacks and coats. (If you'd rather not check your daypack, try carrying it tucked under your arm like a purse as you enter.)

Photography: If the museum's photo policy isn't clearly posted, ask a guard. Generally, taking photos without a flash or tripod is allowed.

Temporary Exhibits: Museums may show special exhibits in addition to their permanent collection. Some exhibits are included in the entry price, while others come at an extra cost (which you may have to pay even if you don't visit the exhibit).

Expect Changes: Artwork can be on tour, on loan, out sick, or shifted at the whim of the curator. Pick up a floor plan

as you enter, and ask museum staff if you can't find a particular item. Say the title or artist's name, or point to the photograph in this book and ask for its location by saying, "*Où est?*" (oo ay).

Audioguides and Apps: Many sights rent audioguides, which generally offer dry-but-useful recorded descriptions (sometimes included with admission). If you bring your own earbuds, you can enjoy better sound. Increasingly, sights offer apps—often free—that you can download to your mobile device (check their websites). I've produced free, downloadable audio tours for some of France's major sights; these are indicated in this book with the 🎧 symbol. For more on my audio tours, see page 30.

Before Leaving: At the gift shop, scan the postcard rack or thumb through a guidebook to be sure that you haven't overlooked something that you'd like to see.

EATING

The French eat long and well. Relaxed and tree-shaded lunches with a chilled rosé, three-hour dinners, and endless hours of sitting in outdoor cafés are the norm. Here, celebrated restaurateurs are as famous as great athletes, and mamas hope their babies will grow up to be great chefs. Cafés, cuisine, and wines should become a highlight of any French adventure: It's sightseeing for your palate. Even if the rest of you is sleeping in a cheap hotel, let your taste buds travel first-class in France. (They can go coach in Britain.)

You can eat well without going broke—but choose carefully: You're just as likely to blow a small fortune on a mediocre meal as you are to dine wonderfully for €20. In bigger cities, lunches are a particularly good value, as most restaurants offer the same quality and similar selections for far less than at dinner. To save money, make lunch your main meal, then have a lighter evening meal at a café.

Breakfast

Most hotels offer an optional breakfast for about €8-15. A few hotels serve a classic continental breakfast, called *petit déjeuner*. Traditionally, this consisted of a café au lait, hot chocolate, or tea; a roll with butter and marmalade; and a croissant. But these days most hotels put out a buffet breakfast (cereal, yogurt, fruit, cheese, croissants, juice, and hard-boiled eggs).

If all you want is coffee or tea and a croissant, the corner café offers more atmosphere and is less expensive (though you get more coffee at your hotel).

Picnics and Food to Go

Whether going all out on a perfect French picnic or simply grabbing a sandwich to eat on an atmospheric square, dining with the village or city as your backdrop can be one of your most memorable meals.

Picnics

Great for lunch or dinner, French picnics can be first-class affairs and adventures in high cuisine. Be daring. Try the smelly cheeses, ugly pâtés, sissy quiches, and minuscule yogurts. Shopkeepers are accustomed to selling small quantities of produce. Get a succulent salad-to-go, and ask for a plastic fork. If you need a knife or corkscrew, borrow one from your hotelier (but don't picnic in your room, as French hoteliers uniformly detest this). Though drinking wine in public places is taboo in the US, it's *pas de problème* in France.

Visit several small stores to put together a complete meal. Shop early, as many shops close from 12:00 or 13:00 to 15:00 for their lunch break. Say "*Bonjour*" as you enter, then point to what you want and say, "*S'il vous plaît.*" Another option is to visit open-air markets *(marchés)*, which are fun and photogenic, but shut down around 13:00 (many are listed in this book; local TIs have complete lists).

To-Go Food

Throughout France you'll find plenty

of to-go options at *crêperies*, bakeries, and small stands. Baguette sandwiches, quiches, and pizza-like items are tasty, filling, and budget-friendly (about €4-5).

Sandwiches: Anything served *à la provençale* has marinated peppers, tomatoes, and eggplant. A sandwich *à la italienne* is grilled. Common sandwiches are *fromage* (cheese), *jambon* (ham), *pain salé* or *fougasse* (salty bits of bacon, cheese, or olives), *poulet* (chicken), *saucisson* (thinly sliced sausage), and *thon* (tuna). The word crudités, as in *jambon* crudités, means that your ham sandwich comes with tomatoes, lettuce, cucumbers, and mayonnaise. *Beurre* is butter.

Quiche: Typical quiches are *lorraine* (ham and cheese), *fromage* (cheese only), *aux oignons* (with onions), *aux poireaux* (with leeks—my favorite), *aux champignons* (with mushrooms), *au saumon* (salmon), and *au thon* (tuna).

Crêpes: The quintessentially French thin pancake called a crêpe (rhymes with "step," not "grape") is filling, usually inexpensive, and generally quick. They come either *sucrée* (sweet) or *salée* (savory). Standard toppings include cheese *(fromage)*, ham *(jambon)*, egg *(oeuf)*, mushrooms *(champignons)*, chocolate, Nutella, jam *(confiture)*, whipped cream *(chantilly)*, apple jam *(compote de pommes)*, chestnut cream *(crème de marrons)*, and Grand Marnier.

Dining in France

To get the most out of dining, slow down. Allow enough time, engage the waiter, and enjoy the experience as much as the food itself.

French waiters probably won't overwhelm you with friendliness. To get a waiter's attention, try to make meaningful eye contact. If this doesn't work, raise your hand and simply say, "*S'il vous plaît*"—"please."

This phrase should also work when you want to ask for the check. In French eateries, a waiter will rarely bring you the check unless you request it. If you're in a hurry, ask for the bill when your server comes to clear your plates or checks to see if you want dessert or coffee.

Note that all café and restaurant interiors are smoke-free. Today the only smokers you'll find are at outside tables, which—unfortunately—may be exactly where you want to sit.

For a list of common French dishes that you'll see on menus, see page 424. For specific suggestions on what to sample in each region, see the "Cuisine Scene" sections throughout the book.

Tipping: At cafés and restaurants, a 12-15 percent service charge is always included in the price of what you order *(service compris or prix net)*, but you won't see it listed on your bill. France pays servers a decent wage; because of this, most locals never tip. If you feel the service was exceptional, you could tip up to 5 percent extra. If you want the waiter to keep the change when you pay, say "*C'est bon*" (say bohn), meaning "It's good." When using a credit card, leave your tip in cash—credit-card receipts don't even have space to add a tip. But never feel guilty if you don't leave a tip.

Cafés and Brasseries

French cafés and brasseries provide user-friendly meals and a relief from sightseeing overload. They're not necessarily cheaper than many restaurants and bistros, and famous cafés on popular squares can be pricey affairs. Their key advantage is flexibility: They offer long serving hours,

and you're welcome to order just a salad, a sandwich, or a bowl of soup, even for dinner. It's also fine to split starters and desserts, though not main courses.

Cafés and brasseries usually open by 7:00, and some cafés and all brasseries serve food throughout the day, making them the best option for a late lunch or an early dinner. Note that many cafés in smaller towns close their kitchens from about 14:00 until 18:00.

Check the price list first, which by law must be posted prominently (if you don't see one, go elsewhere). There are two sets of prices: You'll pay more for the same drink if you're seated at a table *(salle)* than if you're seated or standing at the bar or counter *(comptoir)*.

Ordering: A salad, crêpe, quiche, or omelet is a fairly cheap way to fill up. Each can be made with various extras, such as ham, cheese, mushrooms, and so on.

Sandwiches, generally served day and night, are inexpensive, but most are very plain (*boulangeries* serve better ones). To get more than a piece of ham *(jambon)* on a baguette, order a *sandwich jambon crudités*, which means it's garnished with veggies. Popular sandwiches are the *croque monsieur* (grilled ham-and-cheese) and *croque madame* (*monsieur* with a fried egg on top).

Salads are typically large and often can be ordered with warm ingredients mixed in, such as melted goat cheese, fried gizzards, or roasted potatoes.

The daily special—*plat du jour,* or just *plat*—is your fast, hearty, and garnished hot plate for about €12-20. At most cafés, feel free to order only *entrées* (which in French means the starter course); many people find these lighter and more interesting than a main course. A vegetarian can enjoy a tasty, filling meal by ordering two *entrées*.

Restaurants

Restaurants open for dinner around 19:00 and are most crowded about 20:30 (or 21:00 in cities). The early bird gets the table. Last seating is usually about 21:00 (22:00 in cities and on the French Riviera).

Tune in to the quiet, relaxed pace of French dining. The French don't do dinner and a movie on date nights; they just do dinner. The table is yours for the night.

If a restaurant serves lunch, it generally begins at 12:00 and goes until around 14:00, with last orders taken at about 13:30. If you're hungry when restaurants are closed (late afternoon), go to a *boulangerie*, brasserie, or café (see previous section). Remember that even the fanciest places usually have affordable lunch *menus* (often called *formules* or *plat de midi*), allowing you to sample the same gourmet cooking for generally about half the cost of dinner.

Ordering: In French restaurants, you can choose something off the menu (called the *carte*), or you can order a multicourse, fixed-price meal (confusingly called a *menu*). Or, if available, you can get one of the special dishes of the day *(plat du jour)*.

Two people can split an *entrée* or a big

salad (since small-size dinner salads are usually not offered á la carte) and then each get a *plat principal*. At restaurants, it's considered inappropriate for two diners to share one main course. If all you want is a salad or soup, go to a café or brasserie.

Fixed-price *menus*, which usually include two or three courses, are generally a good value and will help you pace your meal like the locals. With a three-course *menu* you'll choose a starter of soup, appetizer, or salad; select from three or four main courses with vegetables; and then finish up with a cheese course and/or a choice of desserts.

French Cuisine

The following list of items should help you navigate a typical French menu. Galloping gourmets should bring a menu translator. The *Rick Steves' French Phrase Book & Dictionary*, with a menu decoder, works well for most travelers.

First Course (Entrée)

Crudités: A mix of raw and lightly cooked fresh vegetables, usually including grated carrots, celery root, tomatoes, and beets, often with a hefty dose of vinaigrette dressing

Escargots: Snails cooked in parsley-garlic butter

Foie gras: Rich and buttery in consistency—and hefty in price—this pâté is made from the swollen livers of force-fed geese (or ducks, in *foie gras de canard*).

Huîtres: Oysters, served raw any month, are particularly popular at Christmas and on New Year's Eve, when every café seems to have overflowing baskets in their window.

Œuf mayo: A simple hard-boiled egg topped with a dollop of flavorful mayonnaise

Pâtés* and *terrines: Slowly cooked ground meat (usually pork, though game, poultry liver, and rabbit are also common) that is highly seasoned and served in slices with mustard and cornichons (little pickles). Pâtés are smoother than the similarly prepared but chunkier *terrines*.

Soupe à l'oignon: Hot, salty, and filling, French onion soup is a beef broth served with a baked cheese-and-bread crust over the top.

Salads (Salades)

With the exception of a *salade mixte* (simple green salad, often difficult to find), the French get creative with their *salades*. Here are some classics:

Salade au chèvre chaud: Mixed green salad topped with warm goat cheese on small pieces of toast

Salade aux gésiers: Salad with chicken gizzards, and often slices of duck

Salade composée: "Composed" of any number of ingredients, including *lardons* (bacon), Comté (Swiss-style cheese), Roquefort (blue cheese), *œuf* (egg), *noix* (walnuts), and/or *jambon* (ham)

Salade niçoise: Greens topped with green beans, boiled potatoes, tomatoes, anchovies, olives, hard-boiled eggs, and lots of tuna

Salade paysanne: Potatoes *(pommes de terre),* walnuts *(noix),* tomatoes, ham, and egg

Main Course (Plat Principal)

Duck, lamb, and rabbit are popular in France, and each is prepared in a variety of ways. You'll also encounter various stew-like dishes that vary by region. The most common regional specialties are described here.

Bifteck: Steak—also referred to as *pavé* (thick hunk of prime steak), *bavette* (skirt steak), *faux filet* (sirloin), or *entrecôte* (rib steak), often served with a sauce (*au poivre* is a pepper sauce, *une sauce roquefort* is blue cheese). Because steak is usually better in North America, I generally avoid it in France.The French version of rare, *saignant* (seh-nyahn), means "bloody" and is close to raw. What they consider medium, *à point* (ah pwan), is what an American would call rare. Their term for well-done, or *bien cuit* (bee-yehn kwee), would translate as medium for Americans.

Bœuf bourguignon: A classy beef stew cooked slowly in red wine and served with onions, potatoes, and mushrooms (specialty of Burgundy)

Confit de canard: Duck that has been preserved in its own fat, then cooked in its fat, and often served with potatoes (cooked in the same fat)—not for dieters (Dordogne)

Coq au vin: Rooster marinated ever so slowly in red wine, then cooked until it melts in your mouth (Burgundy)

Daube: Stew made with beef or lamb

Escalope normande: Turkey or veal in a cream sauce (Normandy)

Gigot d'agneau: Leg of lamb, often grilled and served with white beans (Provence)

Poulet rôti: Roasted chicken on the bone

Saumon and truite: Salmon, usually from the North Sea, most commonly served with a sorrel *(oseille)* sauce. Trout *(truite)* is also fairly routine on menus.

Tartare: Very lean, freshly ground, raw hamburger served with capers and raw onions, and topped with a raw egg yolk

Cheese Course (Le Fromage)

In France the cheese course is served just before (or instead of) dessert. Some restaurants will offer a cheese platter, from which you select a few different kinds. A good platter has at least four cheeses: a hard cheese (such as Cantal), a flowery cheese (such as Brie or Camembert), a blue or Roquefort cheese, and a goat cheese. If you'd like to sample several types of cheese, say, "*Un assortiment, s'il vous plaît*" (uhn ah-sor-tee-mahn see voo play).

Dessert (Le Dessert)

Baba au rhum: Pound cake drenched in rum, served with whipped cream

Café gourmand: A sampler of small desserts

Crème brûlée: Rich, creamy, caramelized custard

Crème caramel: Flan in a caramel sauce

Fondant au chocolat: Molten chocolate cake with a runny center

Fromage blanc: Fresh, creamy cheese served with sugar or herbs

Glace: Ice cream

Ile flottante: Islands of meringue floating on a pond of custard sauce

Mousse au chocolat: Chocolate mousse

French Wine Tasting 101

France is peppered with wineries and wine-tasting opportunities. For some visitors, trying to make sense of the vast range of French wines can be overwhelming, particularly when faced with a no-nonsense winemaker or sommelier. Take a deep breath, do your best to follow my guidance, and don't linger where you don't feel welcome.

Visit several private wineries or stop by a *cave cooperative* or a *caveau*—an excellent opportunity to taste wines from a number of local vintners in a single, less intimidating setting. (Throughout this book, I've tried to identify which vineyards are most accepting of wine novices.) You'll have a better experience if you call ahead to a winery to let them know you're coming—even if they are open all day, it's good form to announce your visit (ask your hotelier for help. Avoid visiting places between noon and 14:00—many wineries are closed then, and those that aren't are staffed by people who would rather be at lunch.

Whereas many Americans like a big, full-bodied wine, most French prefer subtler flavors. They judge a wine by how well it pairs with a meal. The French like to sample younger wines, buying bottles at cheaper prices and stashing them in their cellars.

Remember that the vintner is hoping you'll buy at least a bottle or two. If you don't buy, you may be asked to pay a small fee for the tasting.

French Wine Lingo

Here are some phrases to get you started when wine tasting:

Hello, sir/madam.
Bonjour, monsieur/madame.
(bohn-zhoor, muhs-yur/mah-dahm)

Profiterole: Cream puff filled with vanilla ice cream, smothered in warm chocolate sauce

Riz au lait: Rice pudding

Sorbet: Fruity ice, sometimes laced with brandy

Tarte: Open-face pie, often fruit

Tarte tatin: Caramelized, upside-down apple pie

Beverages

Water and Soft Drinks

The French are willing to pay for bottled water *(l'eau minérale)* with their meal because they prefer the taste over tap water. Badoit is my favorite carbonated water *(l'eau gazeuse)*. To get a free pitcher of tap water, ask for *une carafe d'eau*.

In France *limonade* is Sprite or 7-Up. Kids love the local orange drink, Orangina, a carbonated orange juice with pulp. They also like *sirop à l'eau*, flavored syrup mixed with bottled water.

Coffee and Tea

The French define various types of espresso drinks by how much milk is added. To the French, milk is a delicate form of nutrition: You need it in the morning, but as the day goes on, too much can upset your digestion. Therefore, the amount of milk that's added to coffee decreases as the day goes on. A café au

We would like to taste a few wines.
Nous voudrions déguster quelques vins.
(noo voo-dree-ohn day-goo-stay kehl-kuh van)

We would like a wine that is ____ and ____.
Nous voudrions un vin ____ et ____.
(noo voo-dree-ohn uhn van ____ ay ____)

Fill in the blanks with your favorites from this list:

English	French	Pronunciation
red	*rouge*	roozh
white	*blanc*	blahn
rosé	*rosé*	roh-zay
light	*léger*	lay-zhay
full-bodied	*robuste*	roh-bewst
fruity	*fruité*	frwee-tay
sweet	*doux*	doo
tannic	*tannique*	tah-neek
ready to drink (mature)	*prêt à boire*	preh tah bwar
oaky	*goût du fût de la chêne*	goo duh foo duh lah sheh-nuh
sparkling	*pétillant*	pay-tee-yahn

lait is exclusively for breakfast time, and a *café crème* is appropriate through midday.

Café (kah-fay): Shot of espresso

Café allongé, a.k.a. café longue (kah-fay ah-lohn-zhay; kah-fay lohn): Espresso topped up with hot water—like an Americano

Noisette (nwah-zeht): Espresso with a dollop of milk

Café au lait (kah-fay oh lay): Espresso mixed with lots of warm milk

Café crème (kah-fay krehm): Espresso with a sizable pour of steamed milk

Grand crème (grahn krehm): Double shot of espresso with steamed milk

Décafféiné (day-kah-fee-nay): Decaf—available for any of the above

Thé nature (tay nah-toor): Plain tea

Thé au lait (tay oh lay): Tea with milk

Thé citron (tay see-trohn): Tea with lemon

Infusion (an-few-see-yohn): Herbal tea

Alcoholic Beverages

Be aware that the legal drinking age is 16 for beer and wine and 18 for the hard stuff—at restaurants it's *normale* for wine to be served with dinner to teens.

Wine: Wines are often listed in a separate *carte des vins.* House wine at the bar is generally cheap and good (about €3-6/glass). At a restaurant, a bottle or carafe of house wine costs €8-20. To order inexpensive wine at a restaurant, ask for table wine in a pitcher (only available when seated and when ordering food), rather than a bottle. Finer restaurants usually offer only bottles of wine.

Here are some useful wine terms:

Vin du pays (van duh pay): Table wine

Verre de vin rouge (vehr duh van roozh): Glass of red wine

Verre de vin blanc (vehr duh van blahn): Glass of white wine

Pichet (pee-shay): Pitcher

Demi-pichet (duh-mee pee-shay): Half-carafe

Quart (kar): Quarter-carafe (ideal for one)

Beer: Local *bière* costs about €5 at a restaurant and is cheaper on tap *(une pression)* than in the bottle *(bouteille)*. France's better beers are Alsatian; try Kronenbourg or the heavier Pelfort (one of your author's favorites).

Aperitifs: For a refreshing before-dinner drink, order a *kir* (pronounced "keer")—a thumb's level of *crème de cassis* (black currant liqueur) topped with white wine. *Pastis*, the standard southern France aperitif, is a sweet anise (licorice) drink that comes on the rocks with a glass of water. Cut it to taste with lots of water.

SLEEPING

I favor hotels and restaurants that are handy to your sightseeing activities. Rather than list hotels scattered throughout a city, I choose hotels in my favorite neighborhoods.

Book your accommodations well in advance, especially if you want to stay at one of my top listings or if you'll be traveling during busy times. Reserving ahead is particularly important for Paris—the sooner, the better. Wherever you're staying, be ready for crowds during holiday periods (see page 449 for a list of major holidays and festivals in France). For tips on making reservations, see page 431.

The Good and Bad of Online Reviews

User-generated travel review websites—such as TripAdvisor, Booking.com, and Yelp—give you access to actual reports—good and bad—from travelers who have experienced the hotel, restaurant, tour, or attraction.

While these sites try hard to weed out bogus users, I've seen hotels "bribe" guests (for example, offer a free breakfast) in exchange for a positive review. Nor can you always give credence to negative reviews: Different people have different expectations.

A user-generated review is based on the experience of one person, who likely stayed at one hotel and ate at a few restaurants, and doesn't have much of a basis for comparison. A guidebook is the work of a trained researcher who visited many alternatives to assess their relative value. When I've checked out top-rated TripAdvisor listings in various towns, I've found that some are gems but just as many are duds.

Guidebooks and review websites both have their place, and in many ways, they're complementary. If a hotel or restaurant is well-reviewed in a guidebook, and also gets good ratings on one of these sites, it's likely a winner.

Rates and Deals

I've described my recommended accommodations using a Sleep Code (see sidebar). The prices I list are for one-night stays in peak season, do not include breakfast (unless noted), and assume you're booking directly with the hotel, not through a hotel-booking website or TI.

Sleep Code

$$$$ Splurge: Most rooms over €250
$$$ Pricier: €190-250
$$ Moderate: €130-190
$ Budget: €70-130
¢ Backpacker: Under €70

Hotels are classified based on the average price of a standard double room with bath in high season. Unless otherwise noted, credit cards are accepted, breakfast is not included, hotel staff speak basic English, and free Wi-Fi is available.

Abbreviations

I use the following code to describe accommodations in this book. When a price range is given for a type of room (such as double rooms listed for €100-150), it means the price fluctuates with the season, size of room, or length of stay; expect to pay the upper end for peak-season stays, especially in resort areas.

S = Single room (or price for one person in a double)
D = Double with bathroom down the hall. "Double beds" can be two twins sheeted together and are big enough for nonromantic couples.
T = Triple (generally a double bed with a single).
Q = Quad (usually two double beds; adding an extra child's bed to a T is usually cheaper).
b = Private bathroom with toilet and shower or tub.
* = French hotel rating system, ranging from zero to five stars

According to this code, a couple staying at a "Db-€140" hotel would pay a total of €140 for a double room with a private bathroom.

Hotels in France must charge a daily tax (*taxe du séjour*) of about €1-2 per person per day. Some hotels include it in the listed prices, but most add it to your bill.

Booking services extract a commission from the hotel, which logically closes the door on special deals. Book direct.

My recommended hotels each have a website (often with a built-in booking form) and an email address; you can expect a response in English within a day and often sooner.

If you're on a budget, it's smart to email several hotels to ask for their best price. Comparison-shop and make your choice. In general, prices can soften if you do any of the following: offer to pay cash, stay at least three nights, or mention this book.

Types of Accommodations

Hotels

The French have a simple hotel rating system based on amenities and rated by stars (indicated in this book by asterisks, from * through *****). The number of stars does not always reflect room size or guarantee quality. One- and two-star hotels are less expensive, but some three-star (and even a few four-star hotels) offer good value, justifying the extra cost. Most French hotels now have queen-size beds—to confirm, ask, "*Avez-vous des lits de cent-soixante?*" (ah-vay-voo day lee duh

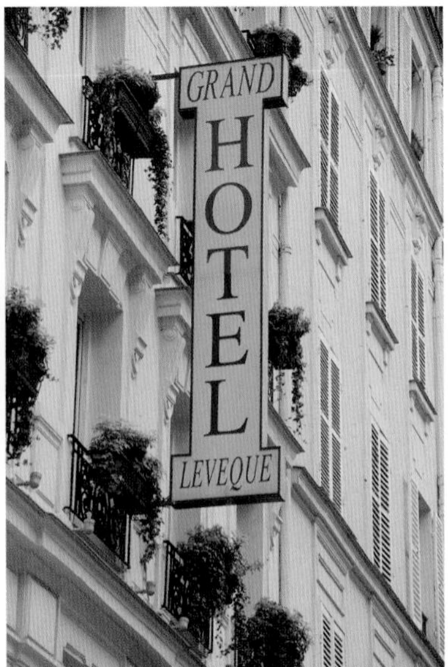

sahn-swah-sahnt). Some hotels push two twins together under king-size sheets and blankets to make *le king* size. If you'll take either twins or a double, ask for a generic *une chambre pour deux* (room for two) to avoid being needlessly turned away.

Hotel lobbies, halls, and breakfast rooms are off-limits to smokers, though they can light up in their rooms. Still, I seldom smell any smoke in my rooms. Some hotels have nonsmoking rooms or floors—ask.

Most hotels offer some kind of breakfast (see page 421), but it's rarely included in the room rates—pay attention when comparing rates between hotels. While hotels hope you'll buy their breakfast, it's optional unless otherwise noted; to save money, head to a bakery or café instead.

Some hoteliers, especially in resort towns, strongly encourage their peak-season guests to take *demi-pension* (half-pension)—that is, breakfast and either lunch or dinner. By law, they can't require you to take half-pension unless you are staying three or more nights, but, in practice, some do during summer.

If you're arriving in the morning, your room probably won't be ready. Drop your bag safely at the hotel and dive right into sightseeing.

Hoteliers can be a great help and source of advice. Most know their city well, and can assist you with everything from public transit and airport connections to calling an English-speaking doctor.

Even at the best places, mechanical breakdowns occur: air-conditioning malfunctions, sinks leak, hot water turns cold, and toilets gurgle and smell. Report your concerns clearly and calmly at the front desk. For more complicated problems, don't expect instant results.

To guard against theft in your room, keep valuables out of sight. Some rooms come with a safe, and other hotels have safes at the front desk. I've never bothered using one.

Checkout can pose problems if surprise charges pop up on your bill. If you settle your bill the afternoon before you leave, you'll have time to discuss and address any points of contention (before 19:00, when the night shift usually arrives).

Above all, keep a positive attitude. Remember, you're on vacation. If your hotel is a disappointment, spend more time out enjoying the place you came to see.

Modern Hotel Chains: France is littered with ultramodern chain hotels (Ibis, Kyriad, Mercure, and Novotel, to name a few), providing drivers with low-stress accommodations, often located just outside town. Though hardly quaint, these can be a good value (look for deals on their websites), particularly when they're centrally located.

Bed & Breakfasts

B&Bs (*chambres d'hôtes,* abbreviated "CH") generally are found in smaller towns and rural areas. They're usually family-run and a great deal, offering double the cultural intimacy for less than most hotel rooms. While you may lose some hotel conveniences—such as lounges, in-room

Making Hotel Reservations

Reserve your rooms several months in advance—or as soon as you've pinned down your travel dates. Note that some national holidays merit your making reservations far in advance (see page 449).

Requesting a Reservation: It's easiest to book your room through the hotel's website. (For the best rates, always use the hotel's official site and not a booking agency's site.) If there's no reservation form, or for complicated requests, send an email. Most recommended hotels take reservations in English.

The hotelier wants to know:

- the number and type of rooms you need
- the number of nights you'll stay
- your date of arrival (use the European style for writing dates: day/month/year)
- your date of departure
- any special needs (such as bathroom in the room or down the hall, cheapest room, twin beds vs. double bed)

Mention any discounts—for Rick Steves readers or otherwise—when you make the reservation.

Confirming a Reservation: Most places will request a credit-card number to hold your room. If they don't have a secure online reservation form—look for the *https*—you can email it (I do), but it's safer to share that confidential info via a phone call or two emails (splitting your number between them).

Canceling a Reservation: If you must cancel, it's courteous—and smart—to do so with as much notice as possible, especially for smaller family-run places. Be warned that cancellation policies can be strict; read the fine print or ask about these before you book. Internet deals may require prepayment, with no refunds for cancellations.

Reconfirming a Reservation: Always call or email to reconfirm your room reservation a few days in advance. For smaller hotels, I call again on my day of arrival to tell my host what time I expect to get there (especially important if arriving late—after 17:00).

Phoning: For tips on how to call hotels overseas, see page 435.

From: rick@ricksteves.com
Sent: Today
To: info@hotelcentral.com
Subject: Reservation request for 19-22 July

Dear Hotel Central,
I would like to reserve a room for 2 people for 3 nights, arriving 19 July and departing 22 July. If possible, I would like a quiet room with a double bed and private bathroom inside the room.

Please let me know if you have a room available and the price.

Thank you!
Rick Steves

phones, daily bed-sheet changes, and credit-card payments—I happily make the trade-off for the personal touch and lower rates. Though your hosts may not speak English, they will almost always be enthusiastic and pleasant.

Hostels

A hostel *(auberge de jeunesse)* provides cheap dorm beds and sometimes has a few double rooms and family rooms. Travelers of any age are welcome. Most hostels offer kitchen facilities, guest computers, Wi-Fi, and a self-service laundry. Most provide all bedding, including sheets.

There are two kinds of hostels. **Independent hostels** tend to be easygoing, colorful, and informal (no membership required); try www.hostelworld.com, www.hostelz.com, or www.hostels.com. **Official hostels** are part of Hostelling International (HI), share an online booking site (www.hihostels.com), and typically require that you either have a membership card or pay extra per night.

Other Accommodation Options

Renting an apartment, house, or villa can be a fun and cost-effective way to go local. Websites such as Booking.com, Airbnb, VRBO, and FlipKey let you browse properties and correspond directly with European property owners or managers. Airbnb and Roomorama also list rooms in private homes. Beds range from air-mattress-in-living-room basic to plush-B&B-suite posh.

For information on *gîtes*—countryside homes for rent—visit www.gites-de-france.com (with the most rentals) or www.gite.com. If you want a place to sleep that's free, try Couchsurfing.org.

STAYING CONNECTED

Staying connected in Europe gets easier and cheaper every year. The simplest solution is to bring your own device—mobile phone, tablet, or laptop—and use it just as you would at home (following the tips below, such as connecting to free Wi-Fi whenever possible). Another option is to buy a European SIM card for your mobile phone—either your US phone or one you buy in Europe. Or you can travel without a mobile device and use public phones and computers to connect. Each of these options is described below, and you'll find even more details at www.ricksteves.com/phoning.

Using Your Mobile Device in Europe

Roaming with your mobile device in Europe doesn't have to be expensive. These budget tips and options will keep your costs in check.

Use free Wi-Fi whenever possible. Unless you have an unlimited-data plan, you're best off saving most of your online tasks for Wi-Fi (pronounced *wee-fee* in French). You can access the Internet, send texts, and even make voice calls over Wi-Fi.

Many cafés—including Starbucks and McDonald's—have hotspots for customers; look for signs offering it and ask for the Wi-Fi password when you buy something. You'll also often find Wi-Fi at TIs, city squares, major museums, public-transit hubs, airports, and aboard trains and buses.

Sign up for an international plan. Most providers offer a global calling plan that cuts the per-minute cost of phone calls and texts, and a flat-fee data plan that includes a certain amount of megabytes. Your normal plan may already include international coverage (T-Mobile's does).

Before your trip, call your provider or

Tips on Internet Security

Using the Internet while traveling brings added security risks, whether you're accessing the Internet with your own device or at a public terminal using a shared network.

First, make sure that your device is running the latest version of its operating system and security software. Next, ensure that your device is password- or passcode-protected so thieves can't access your information if your device is stolen. For extra security, set passwords on apps that access key info (such as email or Facebook).

On the road, use only legitimate Wi-Fi hotspots. Ask the hotel or café staff for the specific name of their Wi-Fi network, and make sure you log on to that exact one. Hackers sometimes create a bogus hotspot with a similar or vague name (such as "Hotel Europa Free Wi-Fi"). The best Wi-Fi networks require entering a password.

Be especially cautious when checking your online banking, credit-card statements, or other personal-finance accounts. Internet security experts advise against accessing these sites while traveling. Even if you're using your own mobile device at a password-protected hotspot, any hacker who's logged on to the same network may be able see what you're doing. If you do need to log on to a banking website, use a hard-wired connection (such as an Ethernet cable in your hotel room) or a cellular network, which is safer than Wi-Fi.

Never share your credit-card number (or any other sensitive information) online unless you know that the site is secure. A secure site displays a little padlock icon, and the URL begins with *https* (instead of the usual *http*).

check online to confirm that your phone will work in Europe, and research your provider's international rates. A day or two before you leave, activate the plan by calling your provider or logging on to your mobile phone account. Remember to cancel your plan (if necessary) when your trip's over.

Minimize the use of your cellular network. When you can't find Wi-Fi, you can use your cellular network—convenient but slower and potentially expensive—to connect to the Internet, text, or make voice calls. When you're done, avoid further charges by manually switching off "data roaming" or "cellular data" (in your device's Settings menu; if you don't know how to switch it off, ask your service provider or Google it). Another way to make sure you're not accidentally using data roaming is to put your device in "airplane" or "flight" mode (which also disables phone calls and texts, as well as data), and then turn on Wi-Fi as needed.

Don't use your cellular network for bandwidth-gobbling tasks, such as Skyping, downloading apps, and watching YouTube—save these for when you're on Wi-Fi. A navigation app such as Google Maps can take lots of data, so use this sparingly.

Limit automatic updates. By default, your device is constantly checking for a data connection and updating apps. It's smart to disable these features so they'll only update when you're on Wi-Fi, and to change your device's email settings from "auto-retrieve" to "manual."

It's also a good idea to keep track of your data usage. On your device's menu, look for "cellular data usage" or "mobile data" and reset the counter at the start of your trip.

Use calling/messaging apps for cheaper calls and texts. Certain calling and messaging services let you make voice/video calls and send texts for free or cheap. With an app installed on your phone, tablet, or laptop, you can log on to a Wi-Fi network and contact friends or family members who use the same service.

With apps like Google+ Hangouts, Whats App, Viber, Facebook Messenger, and iMessage, you can **text** for free. Skype, Viber, FaceTime, and Google+ Hangouts let you make free **voice and video calls.** With some of these services (if you buy credit in advance), you can call any mobile phone or landline worldwide for just pennies per minute.

Using a European SIM Card

This option works well for those wanting to make voice calls at cheap local rates or needing faster connection speeds than their US carrier provides. Either buy a basic cell phone in Europe (as little as $40 from mobile-phone shops anywhere), or bring an "unlocked" US phone. With an unlocked phone, you can replace the original SIM card (the microchip that stores info about the phone) with one that will work with a European provider.

In Europe, buy a European SIM card. Inserted into your phone, this card gives you a European phone number—and European rates. SIM cards are sold at mobile-phone shops, department-store electronics counters, newsstands, and vending machines. Costing about $5-10, they usually include about that much prepaid calling credit, with no contract and no commitment. A SIM card that also includes data costs (including roaming) will cost $20-40 more for one month of data within the country in which you bought it. To get the best rates, buy a new SIM card whenever you arrive in a new country.

I like to buy SIM cards at a mobile-phone shop where there's a clerk to help explain the options and brands. Certain brands—including Lebara and Lycamobile, both of which operate in multiple European countries—are reliable and economical. Ask the clerk to help you insert your SIM card, set it up, and show you how to use it. In some countries you'll be required to register the SIM card with your passport as an antiterrorism measure (which may mean you can't use the phone for the first hour or two).

Find out how to check your credit balance. When you run out of credit, you can top it up at newsstands, tobacco shops, mobile-phone stores, or many other businesses (look for your SIM card's logo in the window), or online.

Phoning Cheat Sheet

Here are instructions for dialing, along with examples of how to call one of my recommended hotels in Paris (tel. 01-45-51-63-02).

Calling from the US to Europe: Dial 011 (US access code), country code (33 for France), and phone number.* To call my recommended hotel in Paris, I dial 011-33-1-45-51-63-02.

Calling from Europe to the US: Dial 00 (Europe access code), country code (1 for US), area code, and phone number. To call my office in Edmonds, Washington, I dial 00-1-425-771-8303.

Calling country to country within Europe: Dial 00, country code, and phone number.* To call the Paris hotel from Spain, I dial 00-33-1-45-51-63-02.

Calling within France: Dial the entire phone number. To call the Paris hotel from Nice, I dial 01-45-51-63-02 (France doesn't use area codes).

Calling with a mobile phone: The "+" sign on your mobile phone automatically selects the access code you need (for a "+" sign, press and hold "0").* To call the Paris hotel from the US or Europe, I dial +33-01-45-51-63-02.

For more dialing help, see www.howtocallabroad.com.

**If the European phone number starts with zero, drop it when calling from another country (except Italian numbers, which retain the zero).*

Country	Country Code
Austria	43
Belgium	32
Croatia	385
Czech Republic	420
Denmark	45
England	44
France	33
Germany	49
Greece	30

Country	Country Code
Hungary	36
Ireland/N Ireland	353/44
Italy	39
Netherlands	31
Norway	47
Portugal	351
Scotland	44
Spain	34
Switzerland	41

Public Phones and Computers

It's easy to travel in Europe without a mobile device. You can check email or browse websites using public computers and Internet cafés, and make calls from your hotel room.

Phones in your **hotel room** can be inexpensive for local calls and calls made with cheap international phone cards *(carte international),* sold at many newsstands, street kiosks, tobacco shops, and train stations. You'll either get a prepaid card with a toll-free number and a scratch-to-reveal PIN code, or a code printed on a receipt; to make a call, dial the free (usually 4-digit) access number. If that doesn't work, dial the toll-free number, follow the prompts, enter the code, then dial your number.

Most hotels charge a fee for placing local and "toll-free" calls, as well as long-distance or international calls—ask for the rates before you dial. Since you're never charged for receiving calls, it's better to have someone from the US call you in your room.

It's always possible to find **public computers:** at your hotel (many have one in their lobby for guests to use), or at an Internet café or library (ask your hotelier or the TI for the nearest location). If typing on a European keyboard, use the "Alt Gr" key to the right of the space bar to insert the extra symbol that appears on some keys. To type an @ symbol on French keyboards, press the "Alt Gr" and "à/0" key. If you can't locate a special character, simply copy it from a Web page and paste it into your email message.

Mail

You can mail one package per day to yourself worth up to $200 duty-free from Europe to the US (mark it "personal purchases"). If you're sending a gift to someone, mark it "unsolicited gift." For details, visit www.cbp.gov and search for "Know Before You Go."

The French postal service works fine, but for quick transatlantic delivery (in either direction), consider services such as DHL (www.dhl.com). One convenient, if expensive, way to send packages home is to use the post office's Colissimo XL postage-paid mailing box. It costs €50-90 to ship boxes weighing 5-7 kilos (about 11-15 pounds).

TRANSPORTATION

France's bigger cities are well connected by train, and a snap to visit by public transportation. Arriving by train in the middle of town makes hotel-hunting and sightseeing easy. But in France, many of your destinations are likely to be small, remote places far from a station, such as Mont St-Michel, the D-Day beaches, Loire châteaux, Dordogne caves, and villages in Provence and Burgundy. For these far-flung spots, a car is a good way to go. Those without a car should consider signing on for one of the excellent minibus tours I recommend in these regions.

Trains

France's SNCF rail system (short for Société Nationale Chemins de Fer) sets the pace in Europe. Its super TGV (tay zhay vay; Train à Grande Vitesse) system has inspired bullet trains throughout the world. The TGV, which requires a reservation, runs at 170-220 mph. The TGV has changed commuting patterns throughout France by putting most of the country within day-trip distance of Paris.

Rick's Tip: *Going on strike* (en grève) *is a popular pastime in France.* **Train strikes** *generally last no longer than a day or two, and you can usually plan around them. Your hotelier will know the latest (or can find out).*

Any staffed train station has schedule information, can make reservations, and can sell tickets for any destination. For more on train travel, including figuring out the smartest rail pass options for your trip, see www.ricksteves.com/rail.

Schedules

Schedules change by season, weekday, and weekend. Verify train times shown in this book—check www.bahn.com (Germany's excellent all-Europe schedule site), or check locally at train stations. The

French Train Terms and Abbreviations

SNCF (Société Nationale Chemins de Fer): The Amtrak of France, operating all national train lines

TGV (Train à Grande Vitesse): SNCF's high-speed trains that connect major cities (reservations required)

Intercité: These trains are the next best to the TGV for speed and comfort.

TER (Transport Express Régional): Trains serving smaller stops within a single region, such as TER Provence (Provence-only trains)

Paris Region

RATP (Réseau Autonome de Transports Parisiens): Subways and buses in Paris

Le Métro: Subway lines serving central Paris

Suburban trains, formerly RER: Commuter rail and subway system linking central Paris with suburban destinations

Transilien: Trains serving the Ile-de-France region around Paris (covered by rail passes)

French rail website is www.sncf.com; for online sales, go to http://en.voyages-sncf.com. If you'll be traveling on one or two long-distance trains without a rail pass, it's worth looking online, as advance-purchase discounts can be a great deal.

Bigger stations may have helpful information agents roaming the station and at *Accueil* offices or booths.

Rail Passes

Long-distance travelers may save money with a **France Rail Pass,** sold only outside Europe. The **saverpass** version gives two or more people traveling together a 15 percent discount. A **Global Pass** can be a good deal if you're traveling throughout Europe. A cheaper version, the **Select Pass,** allows you to tailor a pass to your trip if you're visiting four adjacent countries directly connected by rail (or ferry).

Note that France's TGV trains require advance seat reservations, which are limited for passholders. Reserving these fast trains at least several weeks in advance is recommended (for strategies, see "Reservations," later).

Buying Tickets

Online: Buy well ahead for any TGV you cannot afford to miss. Tickets go on sale 90 to 120 days in advance, with a wide range of prices on any one route. The cheapest tickets sell out early and reservations for rail-pass holders also go particularly fast.

To buy the cheapest advance-discount tickets (50 percent less than full fare), visit http://en.voyages-sncf.com, 3-4 months ahead of your travel date. Otherwise, US customers can order through a US agency, such as at www.ricksteves.com/rail or Capitaine Train (www.capitainetrain.com).

In France: You can buy train tickets in person at SNCF Boutiques or at any train station, either from a staffed ticket window or from a machine—but the machines probably won't accept your

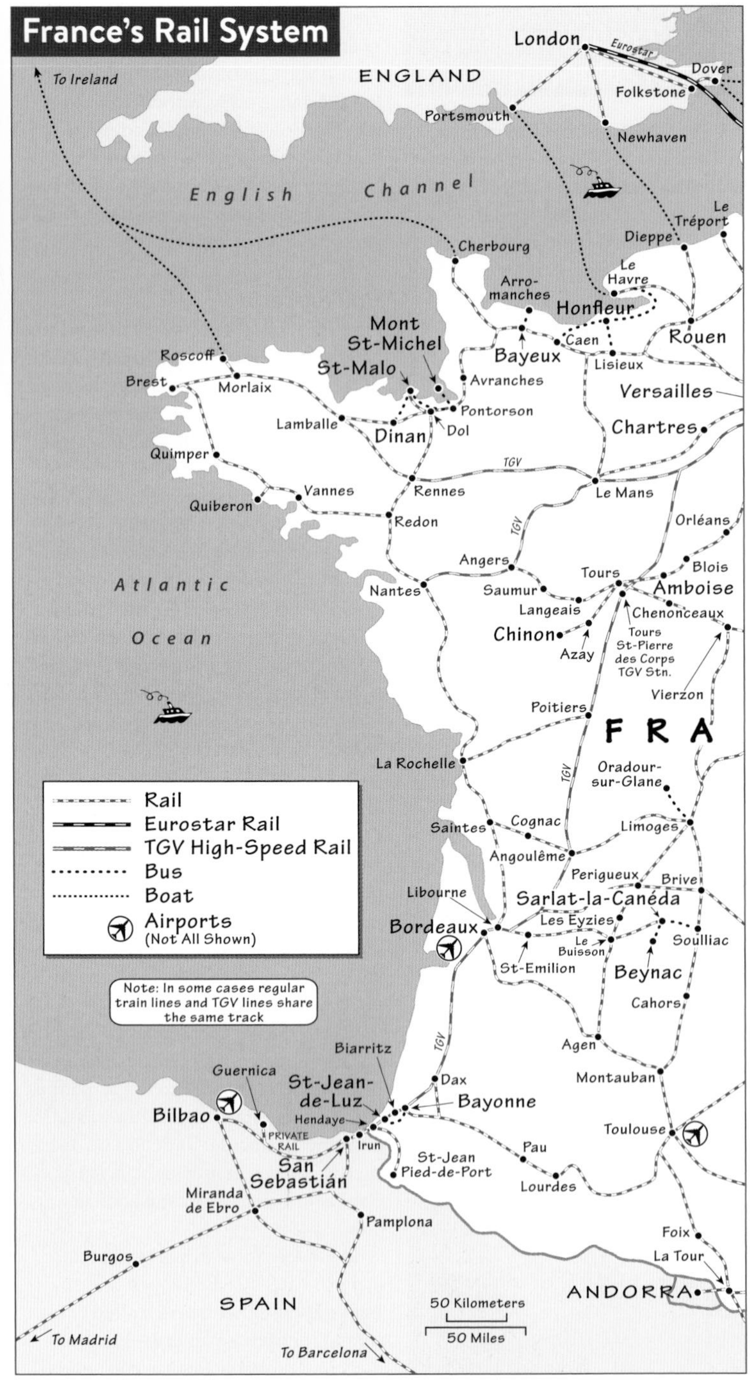
France's Rail System
To Ireland
London
Eurostar
ENGLAND
Dover
Folkstone
Portsmouth
Newhaven
English Channel
Le Tréport
Dieppe
Cherbourg
Le Havre
Arro-manches
Honfleur
Rouen
Mont St-Michel
Caen
Bayeux
Lisieux
Roscoff
St-Malo
Avranches
Brest
Morlaix
Versailles
Pontorson
Lamballe
Dinan
Dol
Chartres
Quimper
TGV
Vannes
Rennes
Le Mans
Quiberon
Redon
Orléans
Angers
Blois
Tours
Atlantic Ocean
Nantes
Saumur
Amboise
Langeais
Chenonceaux
Chinon
Azay
Tours St-Pierre des Corps TGV Stn.
Vierzon
Poitiers
FRA
La Rochelle
Oradour-sur-Glane
Rail
Eurostar Rail
TGV High-Speed Rail
Bus
Boat
Airports (Not All Shown)
Saintes
Cognac
Limoges
Angoulême
Perigueux
Brive
Libourne
Sarlat-la-Canéda
Bordeaux
Les Eyzies
Le Buisson
Soulliac
St-Emilion
Beynac
Note: In some cases regular train lines and TGV lines share the same track
Cahors
Agen
Biarritz
Guernica
St-Jean-de-Luz
Dax
Montauban
Bilbao
Hendaye
Bayonne
PRIVATE RAIL
Irun
Toulouse
San Sebastián
St-Jean Pied-de-Port
Pau
Lourdes
Miranda de Ebro
Pamplona
Foix
Burgos
La Tour
SPAIN
ANDORRA
50 Kilometers
50 Miles
To Madrid
To Barcelona

To Amsterdam
To Hamburg & Munich
NETH.
Ostende
Antwerp
Bruges
Gent
Calais
Ypres
BELGIUM
Brussels
Cologne
Liège
Aachen
GERMANY
Lille
Eurostar
Boulogne
To Berlin
Koblenz
Frankfurt
Amiens
Haute-Picardie TGV Stn.
Aulnoye
LUX.
Trier
Eurostar
Beauvais
Laon
Luxembourg
Mannheim
De Gaulle
Epernay
Reims
Verdun
Saarbrucken
Metz
Marne la Vallée TGV Stn.
Meuse TGV Stn.
TGV
Paris
Massy TGV
Champagne-Ardennes TGV Stn.
Nancy
TGV
Oos
Baden Baden
Orly
Melun
Fontainebleau
Strasbourg
Kehl
Turckheim
GERMANY
TGV
TGV
Colmar
Freiburg
Semur-en-Auxois
Culmont
Mulhouse
Basel
Montbard
Belfort
Zürich
Dijon
Bescançon
Beaune
Dôle
Nevers
TGV
Bern
Le Creusot TGV Stn.
Chagny
SWITZERLAND
N C E
Chalon
Frasne
St-Germain
Lausanne
Interlaken
Cluny
Montreux
Vichy
Mâcon TGV Stn.
Geneva
Geneva (Eaux-Vives Stn.)
Bourg
Clermont-Ferrand
Mâcon
Martigny
Satolas
St. Gervais
Chamonix
Stresa
Como
Annecy
Lyon
Aix-les-Bains
Chambéry
Aosta
Arvant
St-Etienne
Pre St-Didier
Bourg St-M.
Milan
St-Georges
Le Puy
Grenoble
Figeac
Modane
ITALY
Torino
TGV
To Cinque Terre, Pisa & Rome
Genoa
Millau
Vaison-la-Romaine
Veynes
Albi
Alès
Orange
Avignon
Digne
Pont du Gard
Isle-sur-la-Sorgue
Monaco
Avig. TGV
Nîmes
St-Rémy
Ventimiglia
St-Paul
Aix TGV Stn.
Arles
Cannes
Nice
Les Baux
Aix-en-Provence
Carcassonne
Antibes
Béziers
Marseille
TGV
St-Raphael
Narbonne
Cassis
Toulon
St-Tropez
TGV
Perpignan
Collioure
Port Bou
Mediterranean Sea
CORSICA (FRANCE)
To Barcelona

Railpasses

A Eurail **France Pass** lets you travel by train in France for three to eight days (consecutively or not) within a one-month period. Discounted rates are offered for two or more people traveling together.

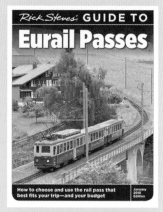

Rick Steves' GUIDE TO
Eurail Passes
How to choose and use the rail pass that best fits your trip—and your budget
January 2018 Edition

France can also be included in a Eurail **Select Pass,** which allows travel in two to four neighboring countries over two months, and it's covered (along with most of Europe) by the classic Eurail **Global Pass.**

Rail passes are sold only outside Europe (through travel agents or Rick Steves' Europe). For more on the ins and outs of rail passes, including prices, download my **free guide to Eurail Passes** (www.ricksteves.com/rail-guide) or go to www.ricksteves.com/rail.

If you're taking just a couple of train rides, look into buying individual **point-to-point tickets,** which may save you money over a pass. Use this map to add up approximate pay-as-you-go fares for your itinerary, and compare that to the price of a rail pass. Keep in mind that significant discounts on point-to-point tickets may be available with advance purchase.

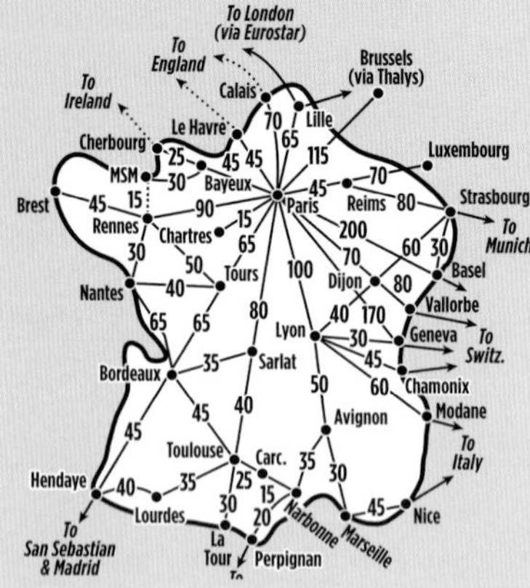

Map shows approximate costs, in US$, for one-way, second-class tickets on faster trains.

American credit card, so be prepared with euro coins.

Reservations

Reservations are required for any TGV train, *couchettes* (sleeping berths) on night trains, and some other trains where indicated in timetables. You can reserve any train at any station up to three days before your departure or through SNCF Boutiques. If you're buying a point-to-point ticket for a TGV train, you'll reserve your seat when you purchase your ticket. Seat reservations cost anywhere from €3 to €26.

It's wise to book well ahead for any TGV, especially on the busy Paris-Avignon-Nice line. If the TGV trains you want are fully booked, ask about TER trains serving the same destination, as these don't require reservations.

Rail-pass holders can book TGV reservations at French stations up to three days before departure; reservations, if still available, can be booked anytime as etickets at www.raileurope.com. Given the difficulty of getting TGV reservations with a rail pass, make those reservations online before you leave home or consider buying separate, advance-discount tickets for key TGV trips (and exclude those legs from your rail pass).

If you're taking an overnight train and need a *couchette,* it can be booked in advance through a US agent (such as www.raileurope.com).

Validating Tickets, Reservations, and Rail Passes

You're required to validate (*composter,* kohm-poh-stay) all train tickets and reservations before boarding any SNCF train. Look for a yellow machine near the platform or waiting area to stamp your ticket or reservation.

If you have a rail pass, activate it at a ticket window before using it the first time (don't stamp it in the machine). If you're traveling with a pass and have a reservation for a certain trip, you must activate the reservation by stamping it. If you have a rail flexipass, write the date on your pass each day you travel (before or immediately after boarding your first train).

Buses

Regional buses work well for many destinations not served by trains. Buses are almost always comfortable and air-conditioned. Bus stations *(gare routière)* are usually located next to train stations. Train stations usually have bus information where train-to-bus connections are important—and vice versa for bus companies.

Most bus company websites are in French only. Here are some key phrases you'll see: *horaires* (schedules), *en semaine* (Monday through Saturday), *dimanche* (Sunday), *jours fériés* (holidays), *année* (bus runs all year on the days listed), *vac* (runs only during summer vacations), *scol/scolaire* (runs only when school is in session), *ligne* (route or bus line), and *réseau* (network—usually all routes).

Renting a Car

If you're renting a car in France, bring your driver's license. Rental companies require you to be at least 21 years old and to have held your license for one year. Drivers under the age of 25 may incur a young-driver surcharge, and some rental companies do not rent to anyone 75 or older. If you're considered too young or old, look into leasing (covered later), which has less-stringent age restrictions.

Research car rentals before you go. It's cheaper to arrange car rentals from the US. Consider several companies to compare rates. Most of the major US rental agencies (including Avis, Budget, Enterprise, Hertz, and Thrifty) have offices throughout Europe. Also consider the two major Europe-based agencies, Europcar and Sixt, and the French agency, ADA (www.ada.fr). It can sometimes be cheaper to use a consolidator, such as

Auto Europe (www.autoeurope.com), or Kemwel (www.kemwel.com).

Always read the fine print carefully for add-on charges—such as one-way drop-off fees, airport surcharges, or mandatory insurance policies—that aren't included in the "total price."

For the best deal, rent by the week with unlimited mileage. I normally rent the smallest, least-expensive model with a stick shift (generally cheaper than an automatic). If you need an automatic, request one in advance; be aware that these cars are usually larger models. Roads and parking spaces are narrow in France, so you'll do yourself a favor by renting the smallest car that meets your needs.

Figure on paying roughly $250 for a one-week rental during busy seasons. Allow extra for supplemental insurance, fuel, tolls, and parking. For trips of three weeks or more, leasing can save you money on insurance and taxes.

Picking Up Your Car: Big companies have offices in most cities, but small local rental companies can be cheaper.

Compare pick-up costs (downtown can be less expensive than the airport or train station) and explore drop-off options. Always check the hours of the location you choose: Many rental offices close from midday Saturday until Monday morning and, in smaller towns, at lunchtime.

When selecting a location, don't trust the agency's description of "downtown" or "city center." In some cases, a "downtown" branch can be on the outskirts of the city—a long, costly taxi ride from the center. Before choosing, plug the addresses into a mapping website. You may find that the "train station" location is handier. But returning a car at a big-city train station or downtown agency can be tricky; get precise details on the car drop-off location and hours, and allow ample time to find it.

When you pick up the rental car, check it thoroughly and make sure any damage is noted on your rental agreement. Find out how your car's lights, turn signals, wipers, radio, and fuel cap function, and know what kind of fuel the car takes (diesel vs. unleaded). When you return the car, make sure the agent verifies its condition with you. Some drivers take pictures of the returned vehicle as proof of its condition.

Car Insurance Options

When you rent a car, you are liable for a very high deductible, sometimes equal to the entire value of the car. Limit your financial risk with one of these options: Buy Collision Damage Waiver (CDW) coverage with a low or zero deductible from the car-rental company, get coverage through your credit card (free, if your card automatically includes zero-deductible coverage), or get collision insurance as part of a larger travel-insurance policy.

Basic **CDW** reduces your liability, but does not eliminate it. When you pick up the car, you'll be offered the chance to

"buy down" the deductible to zero (for an additional $10–30/day; this is sometimes called "super CDW" or "zero-deductible coverage").

If you opt for **credit-card coverage,** there's a catch. You'll technically have to decline all coverage offered by the car-rental company, which means they can place a hold on your card for up to the full value of the car. In case of damage, it can be time-consuming to resolve the charges with your credit-card company. Before you decide on this option, quiz your credit-card company about how it works.

If you're already purchasing a **travel-insurance policy** for your trip, adding collision coverage is an option. For example, Travel Guard (www.travelguard.com) sells affordable renter's collision insurance as an add-on to its other policies.

For more on car-rental insurance, see www.ricksteves.com/cdw.

Leasing

For trips of three weeks or more, consider leasing, which automatically includes zero-deductible collision and theft insurance. Leasing provides you a brand-new car with unlimited mileage and a 24-hour emergency assistance program. You can lease for as little as 21 days to as long as five and a half months. Car leases must be arranged from the US. Reliable companies offering 21-day lease packages include **Auto France** (www.autofrance.net), **Idea Merge** (www.ideamerge.com), and **Kemwel** (www.kemwel.com).

Driving

It's a pleasure to explore France by car, but you need to know the rules.

Road Rules: Seat belts are mandatory for all, and children under age 10 must be in the back seat (hefty fine if caught *sans* belt). In city and town centers, traffic merging from the right (even from tiny side streets) may have the right-of-way *(priorité à droite)*. So even when you're driving on a major road, pay attention to cars merging from the right. In contrast, cars entering the many suburban roundabouts must yield *(cédez le passage)*.

Be aware of typical European road rules; for example, many countries require headlights to be turned on at all times (in France, they must be used whenever visibility is poor), and it's generally illegal to drive while using your mobile phone without a hands-free device. In Europe, you're not allowed to turn right on a red light, unless a sign or signal specifically authorizes it, and on expressways it's illegal to pass drivers on the right. U-turns are prohibited throughout France. Ask your car-rental company about these rules, or check the US State Department website (www.travel.state.gov, search for your country in the "Learn about your destination" box, then click on "Travel and Transportation").

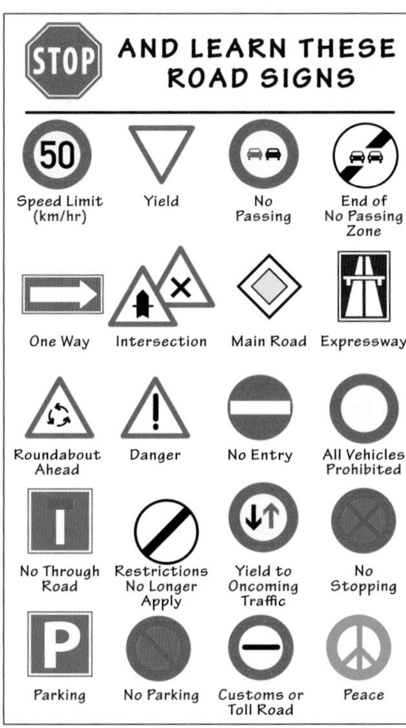

Speed Limits: Because speed limits are by road type, they typically aren't posted, so it's best to memorize them:

- Two-lane D and N routes outside cities and towns: 90 km/hour
- Two-lane roads in villages: 50 km/hour (unless posted at 30 km/hour)
- Divided highways outside cities and towns: 110 km/hour
- Autoroutes: 130 km/hour (unless otherwise posted)

Road speeds are monitored regularly with cameras—a mere two kilometers over the limit yields a pricey ticket. The good news is that signs warn drivers a few hundred yards before the camera and show the proper speed. Look for a sign with a radar graphic that says *Pour votre sécurité, contrôles automatiques.*

Navigation Maps and Apps: A big, detailed regional road map (buy one at a newsstand, gas station, or bookstore) and a semiskilled navigator are helpful.

When driving in Europe, you can use the mapping app on your phone as long as you have an international data plan. Without a data plan (or to conserve data), you can rely on offline maps (via a mapping app or by downloading Google maps). As an alternative, you could rent a GPS device or bring your own GPS device from home (but you'll need to buy and download European maps before your trip).

A number of well-designed offline mapping apps offer much of the convenience of online maps without any costly data demands. City Maps 2Go is popular; OffMaps and Navfree also have good, zoomable offline maps—similar to Google Maps—for much of Europe.

Drinking and Driving: The French are serious about curbing drunk driving. All motorists, including those in rental cars, are required to have a self-test Breathalyzer on hand so they can tell if they're over the legal blood-alcohol limit (0.05mg/ml—which is lower than in the US—drinker beware). When you pick up your rental car, ask if it has a kit or where to get one.

How to Pay Tolls on Autoroutes

For American drivers, getting through the toll payment stations on France's autoroutes is mostly about knowing which lanes to avoid—and having cash on hand. Skip lanes marked with a lowercase "*t*"—they're reserved for cars using the automatic Télépéage payment system. A pictograph of a credit card (usually a blue sign) means credit or debit cards only: Your US card won't work unless you have a chip-and-PIN card. Look instead for green arrows above the tollbooth and/or icons showing bills or coins, which indicate booths accepting cash (booths often allow more than one payment method). Slow down as you approach tollbooths to study your options, and pull off to the side if you aren't positive of the lane to choose.

Exits are entirely automated (if you have a problem at the tollbooth, press the red button for help). Have smaller bills ready (payment machines won't accept €50 bills). Shorter autoroute sections have periodic tollbooths, where you can pay by dropping coins into a basket (change is given for bills, but keep a good supply of coins handy to avoid waiting for an attendant).

To figure out how much cash to have on hand for tolls for your route, use the planning tool at ViaMichelin.com.

Pulling to the Side of the Road: All rental cars are equipped with a yellow safety vest and triangle. You must wear the vest and display the triangle whenever you pull over on the side of the road (say, to fix a flat tire). If you don't, you could be fined.

Fuel: Gas *(essence)* is expensive—about $8 per gallon. Diesel *(gazole)* costs less—about $7 per gallon. Know what type of fuel your car takes before you fill up. Gas is most expensive on autoroutes and cheapest at big supermarkets. Your US credit and debit cards without a security chip won't work at self-serve pumps—so you'll need to find gas stations with attendants, or get a chip-and-PIN card before your trip (see page 418).

Plan ahead for Sundays, as most gas stations in town are closed. I fill my tank every Saturday. If stuck, use an autoroute on Sunday, where the gas stations are always staffed.

Autoroutes and Tolls: Autoroute tolls are pricey, but they save enough time, gas, and nausea to justify the cost. Mix high-speed "autorouting" with scenic country-road rambling.

You'll usually take a ticket when entering an autoroute and pay when you leave. Cash is your best payment option (for more on paying tolls, see the sidebar).

Autoroute gas stations are open even on Sundays and usually come with well-stocked minimarts, clean restrooms, sandwiches, maps, local products, cheap vending-machine coffee, and sometimes Wi-Fi. Many have small cafés or more elaborate cafeterias with reasonable prices. For more information, see www.autoroutes.fr.

Highways: Roads are classified into departmental (D), national (N), and autoroutes (A). D routes (usually yellow lines on maps) are often slower but the most scenic. N routes and important D routes (red lines) are the fastest after autoroutes (orange lines on maps). Green road signs are for national routes; blue are for autoroutes. Note that some key roads in France are undergoing letter designation and number changes (mostly N roads converting to D roads). If you're using an older map, the actual route name may differ from what's on your map. Navigate by destination rather than road name...or buy a new map. There are plenty of good facilities, gas stations (most closed Sun), and rest stops along most French roads.

Parking: Finding a parking place can be a headache in larger cities. Ask your hotelier for ideas, and pay to park at well-patrolled lots (blue *P* signs direct you to parking lots in French cities). Parking garages require that you take a ticket with you and pay at a machine (called a *caisse*) on your way back to the car. US credit cards won't work in these machines, but euro coins will (some accept bills, too). If you don't have enough coins to pay the fee, find the garage's *accueil* office, where the attendant can help or direct you to a nearby shop where you can change bills into coins.

Curbside metered parking also works. Look for a small machine selling time (called an *horodateur,* usually one per block), plug in a few coins (€1.50-2 buys about an hour, varies by city), push the button, get a receipt showing the amount of time you have, and display it inside your windshield. (Avoid spaces outlined in blue, as they require a special permit.) For cheap overnight parking until the next afternoon, buy three hours' worth of time after 19:00. This gets you until noon the next day, after which two more hours are

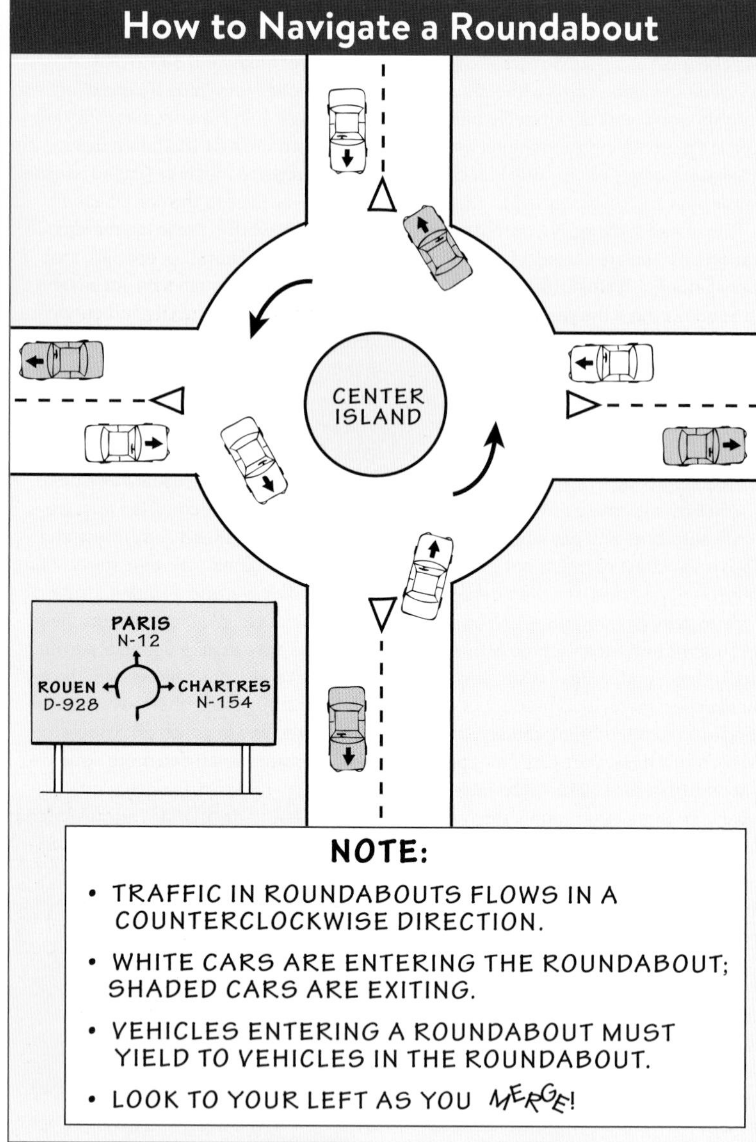

usually free (12:00-14:00), so you're good until 14:00.

How to Navigate a Roundabout
CENTER ISLAND
PARIS
N-12
ROUEN
D-928
CHARTRES
N-154
NOTE:
• TRAFFIC IN ROUNDABOUTS FLOWS IN A COUNTERCLOCKWISE DIRECTION.
• WHITE CARS ARE ENTERING THE ROUNDABOUT; SHADED CARS ARE EXITING.
• VEHICLES ENTERING A ROUNDABOUT MUST YIELD TO VEHICLES IN THE ROUNDABOUT.
• LOOK TO YOUR LEFT AS YOU MERGE!

Theft: Theft is a problem, particularly in southern France. Thieves easily recognize rental cars and assume they are filled with a tourist's gear. Try to make your car look locally owned by hiding the "tourist-owned" rental-company decals and putting a French newspaper in your back window. Be sure all of your valuables are out of sight and locked in the trunk—or, even better, with you or in your room.

Driving Tips

France is riddled with **roundabouts**—navigating them is an art. The key is to know your direction and be ready for your turnoff. If you miss it, take another lap (or two).

At intersections and roundabouts, French **road signs** use the name of the next destination for directions—the highway number is usually missing. That next destination could be a major city, or it could be the next minor town up the road. It's a good idea to check your map ahead of time and get familiar with the names of towns and cities along your route—and even major cities on the same road beyond your destination.

When **navigating into cities,** approach intersections cautiously, stow the map, and follow the signs to *Centre-Ville* (city center).

When **leaving** or just passing through cities, follow the signs for *Toutes Directions* or *Autres Directions* (meaning "anywhere else") until you see a sign for your specific destination. A *suivre* sign—for example, "*Pont du Gard, suivre Nîmes*"—is telling you to follow signs for one destination (Nîmes) to reach a different, usually smaller one (Pont du Gard).

Driving on any roads but autoroutes will take longer than you think, so allow **plenty of time** for slower traffic (tractors, trucks, and hard-to-decipher signs all deserve blame). First-timers should estimate how long they think a drive will take...then double it. I pretend that kilometers are miles (for distances) and base my time estimates accordingly.

On **autoroutes,** keep to the right lanes to let fast drivers by, and be careful when merging into a left lane, as cars can be coming at high speeds.

Keep a stash of **coins** handy for parking and small autoroute tolls.

Flights

The best comparison search engine for both international and intra-European flights is www.kayak.com. For inexpensive flights within Europe, try www.skyscanner.com or www.hipmunk.com; for inexpensive international flights, try www.vayama.com.

Flying to Europe: Start looking for international flights 4-5 months before your trip, especially for peak-season travel. Off-season tickets can be purchased a month or so in advance. Depending on your itinerary, it can be efficient to fly into one city and out of another. If your flight requires a connection in Europe, see our hints on navigating Europe's top hub airports at www.ricksteves.com/hub-airports.

Flying within Europe: If you're visiting one or more French cities on a longer European trip—or linking up far-flung French cities (such as Paris and Nice)—a flight can save both time and money. When comparing your options, factor in the time it takes to get to the airport and how early you'll need to arrive to check in.

These days you can fly within Europe on major airlines affordably for around $100 a flight. If you go instead with a budget airline such as Ryanair (www.ryanair.com), be aware of the potential drawbacks and restrictions: nonrefundable and nonchangeable tickets, minimal or nonexistent customer service, pricey and time-consuming treks to secondary airports, and stingy baggage allowances with steep overage fees. If you're traveling with lots of luggage, a cheap flight can quickly become a bad deal. To avoid unpleasant surprises, read the small print before you book.

Flying to the US: Because security is extra tight for flights to the US, be sure to give yourself plenty of time at the airport. It's also important to charge your electronic devices before you board because security checks may require you to turn them on (see www.tsa.gov for latest rules).

Resources from Rick Steves

Begin Your Trip at www.RickSteves.com

My mobile-friendly **website** is *the* place to explore Europe. You'll find thousands of fun articles, videos, photos, and radio interviews; a wealth of money-saving tips for planning your dream trip; my travel talks and blog; and guidebook updates (www.ricksteves.com/update).

Our **Travel Forum** is an immense collection of message boards, where our travel-savvy community answers questions and shares personal travel experiences—and our well-traveled staff chimes in when they can help.

Our **online Travel Store** offers bags and accessories designed to help you travel smarter and lighter. These include my popular bags (which I live out of four months a year), money belts, totes, toiletries kits, adapters, guidebooks, planning maps, and more.

Choosing the right **rail pass** for your trip can drive you nutty. Our website will help you find the perfect fit for your itinerary and your budget: We offer easy, one-stop shopping for rail passes, seat reservations, and point-to-point tickets.

Guidebooks, TV Shows, Audio Europe, and Tours

Books: *Rick Steves Best of France* is just one of many books in my series on European travel, which includes country and city guidebooks, Snapshot guides (excerpted chapters from my country guides), Pocket Guides (full-color little books on big cities, including Paris), and my budget-travel skills handbook, *Rick Steves Europe Through the Back Door*. My phrase books—including one for French—are practical and budget-oriented. A more complete list of my titles appears near the end of this book.

TV Shows: My public television series, *Rick Steves' Europe,* covers Europe from top to bottom with over 100 half-hour episodes. To watch full episodes online for free, see www.ricksteves.com/tv. Or to raise your travel I.Q. with video versions of our popular classes (including my talks on travel skills, packing smart, most European countries, and European art), see www.ricksteves.com/travel-talks.

Audio: My weekly public radio show, *Travel with Rick Steves,* features interviews with travel experts from around the world. A complete archive is available at www.soundcloud.com/rick-steves, and much of this audio content is available for free, along with my audio tours of Europe's (and France's) top sights, through my free **Rick Steves Audio Europe** app (see page 30).

Rick Steves AUDIO EUROPE

Small Group Tours: Want to travel with greater efficiency and less stress? We offer **tours** with more than 40 itineraries reaching the best destinations in this book...and beyond. You'll find European adventures to fit every vacation length, and you'll enjoy great guides and a fun but small group of travel partners. For all the details, and to get our tour catalog, visit www.ricksteves.com or call us at 425/608-4217.

HOLIDAYS AND FESTIVALS

This list includes selected festivals in major cities, plus national holidays observed throughout France. Many sights and banks close on national holidays—keep this in mind when planning your itinerary. Before planning a trip around a festival, verify its dates by checking with the festival's website or France's national tourism website (www.franceguide.com). Hotels get booked up on Easter weekend, Labor Day, Ascension Day, Pentecost, Bastille Day, and the winter holidays.

Here is a sampling of events and holidays:

Jan 1	New Year's Day
Feb-March	Carnival (Mardi Gras) parades and fireworks, Nice (www.nicecarnaval.com)
March or April	Easter Sunday/Monday
May 1	Labor Day
May 5	Ascension
May 8	VE (Victory in Europe) Day
Mid-May	Monaco Grand Prix auto race (www.grand-prix-monaco.com)
May or June	Pentecost Sunday/Monday
June 6	Anniversary of D-Day Landing, Normandy
July	Nice Jazz Festival (www.nicejazzfestival.fr); Avignon Festival, theater, dance, music (www.festival-avignon.com); Beaune International Music Festival; "Jazz à Juan" International Jazz Festival, Antibes/Juan-les-Pins (www.jazzajuan.com); Jousting matches and medieval festivities, Carcassonne; Colmar International Music Festival (www.festival-colmar.com)
July	Tour de France (www.letour.fr)
July 14	Bastille Day (fireworks, dancing, and revelry all over France)
Aug 15	Assumption
Sept	Jazz at La Villette Festival, Paris (www.jazzalavillette.com); Fall Arts Festival (Fête d'Automne), Paris; Wine harvest festivals in many towns
Early-Mid-Oct	Grape Harvest Festival in Montmartre, Paris (www.fetedesvendangesdemontmartre.com)
Nov 1	All Saints' Day
Nov 11	Armistice Day
Late Nov	Wine Auction and Festival (Les Trois Glorieuses), Beaune
Late Nov-Dec 24	Christmas Markets in Colmar and Sarlat-la-Canéda
Dec 25	Christmas Day
Dec 31	New Year's Eve

CONVERSIONS AND CLIMATE

Numbers and Stumblers

- Europeans write a few of their numbers differently than we do: 1 = 1, 4 = 4, 7 = 7.
- In Europe, dates appear as day/month/year; Christmas is 25/12.
- Commas are decimal points and decimals are commas. A dollar and a half is $1,50, one thousand is 1.000.
- When counting with fingers, start with your thumb. If you hold up your first finger to request one item, you'll probably get two.
- What Americans call the second floor of a building is the first floor in Europe.
- On escalators and moving sidewalks, Europeans keep the left "lane" open for passing. Keep to the right.

Clothing and Shoe Sizes

Shoppers can use these US-to-European comparisons as general guidelines, but note that no conversion is perfect. For info on VAT refunds, see page 419.

Women: For clothing or shoe sizes, add 30 (US shirt size 10 = European size 40; US shoe size 8 = European size 38-39).

Men: For shirts, multiply by 2 and add about 8 (US size 15 = European size 38). For jackets and suits, add 10. For shoes, add 32-34.

Children: For clothing, subtract 1-2 sizes for small children and subtract 4 for juniors. For shoes up to size 13, add 16-18, and for sizes 1 and up, add 30-32.

Metric Conversions

A **kilogram** equals 1,000 grams and about 2.2 pounds. One hundred **grams** (a common unit of sale at markets) is about a quarter-pound.

One **liter** is about a quart, or almost four to a gallon.

A **kilometer** is six-tenths of a mile. To convert kilometers to miles, cut the kilometers in half and add back 10 percent of the original (120 km: 60 + 12 = 72 miles). One **meter** is 39 inches.

Using the **Celsius** scale, 0°C equals 32°F. To roughly convert Celsius to Fahrenheit, double the number and add 30. For weather, 28°C is 82°F—perfect. For health, 37°C is just right. At a launderette, 30°C is cold, 40°C is warm (default setting), and 60°C is hot.

France's Climate

First line, average daily high; second line, average daily low; third line, average days without rain. For more detailed weather statistics for destinations in this book (as well as the rest of the world), check www.wunderground.com.

Paris

J	F	M	A	M	J	J	A	S	O	N	D
43°	45°	54°	60°	68°	73°	76°	75°	70°	60°	50°	44°
34°	34°	39°	43°	49°	55°	58°	58°	53°	46°	40°	36°
14	14	19	17	19	18	19	18	17	18	15	15

Nice

J	F	M	A	M	J	J	A	S	O	N	D
50°	53°	59°	64°	71°	79°	84°	83°	77°	68°	58°	52°
35°	36°	41°	46°	52°	58°	63°	63°	58°	51°	43°	37°
23	22	24	23	23	26	29	26	24	23	21	21

Packing Checklist

Clothing

- ❑ 5 shirts: long- & short-sleeve
- ❑ 2 pairs pants or skirt
- ❑ 1 pair shorts or capris
- ❑ 5 pairs underwear & socks
- ❑ 1 pair walking shoes
- ❑ Sweater or fleece top
- ❑ Rainproof jacket with hood
- ❑ Tie or scarf
- ❑ Swimsuit
- ❑ Sleepwear

Money

- ❑ Debit card
- ❑ Credit card(s)
- ❑ Hard cash ($20 bills)
- ❑ Money belt or neck wallet

Documents & Travel Info

- ❑ Passport
- ❑ Airline reservations
- ❑ Rail pass/train reservations
- ❑ Car-rental voucher
- ❑ Driver's license
- ❑ Student ID, hostel card, etc.
- ❑ Photocopies of all the above
- ❑ Hotel confirmations
- ❑ Insurance details
- ❑ Guidebooks & maps
- ❑ Notepad & pen
- ❑ Journal

Toiletries Kit

- ❑ Toiletries
- ❑ Medicines & vitamins
- ❑ First-aid kit
- ❑ Glasses/contacts/sunglasses (with prescriptions)
- ❑ Earplugs
- ❑ Packet of tissues (for WC)

Miscellaneous

- ❑ Daypack
- ❑ Sealable plastic baggies
- ❑ Laundry soap
- ❑ Clothesline
- ❑ Sewing kit
- ❑ Travel alarm/watch

Electronics

- ❑ Smartphone or mobile phone
- ❑ Camera & related gear
- ❑ Tablet/ereader/media player
- ❑ Laptop & flash drive
- ❑ Earbuds or headphones
- ❑ Chargers
- ❑ Plug adapters

Optional Extras

- ❑ Flipflops or slippers
- ❑ Mini-umbrella or poncho
- ❑ Travel hairdryer
- ❑ Belt
- ❑ Hat (for sun or cold)
- ❑ Picnic supplies
- ❑ Water bottle
- ❑ Fold-up tote bag
- ❑ Small flashlight
- ❑ Small binoculars
- ❑ Small towel or washcloth
- ❑ Inflatable pillow
- ❑ Tiny lock
- ❑ Address list (to mail postcards)
- ❑ Postcards/photos from home
- ❑ Extra passport photos
- ❑ Good book

French Survival Phrases

When using the phonetics, try to nasalize the n sound.

English	French	Pronunciation
Good day.	*Bonjour.*	bohn-zhoor
Mrs. / Mr.	*Madame / Monsieur*	mah-dahm / muhs-yur
Do you speak English?	*Parlez-vous anglais?*	par-lay-voo ahn-glay
Yes. / No.	*Oui. / Non.*	wee / nohn
I understand.	*Je comprends.*	zhuh kohn-prahn
I don't understand.	*Je ne comprends pas.*	zhuh nuh kohn-prahn pah
Please.	*S'il vous plaît.*	see voo play
Thank you.	*Merci.*	mehr-see
I'm sorry.	*Désolé.*	day-zoh-lay
Excuse me.	*Pardon.*	par-dohn
(No) problem.	*(Pas de) problème.*	(pah duh) proh-blehm
It's good.	*C'est bon.*	say bohn
Goodbye.	*Au revoir.*	oh vwahr
one / two	*un / deux*	uhn / duh
three / four	*trois / quatre*	twah / kah-truh
five / six	*cinq / six*	sank / sees
seven / eight	*sept / huit*	seht / weet
nine / ten	*neuf / dix*	nuhf / dees
How much is it?	*Combien?*	kohn-bee-an
Write it?	*Ecrivez?*	ay-kree-vay
Is it free?	*C'est gratuit?*	say grah-twee
Included?	*Inclus?*	an-klew
Where can I buy / find...?	*Où puis-je acheter / trouver...?*	oo pwee-zhuh ah-shuh-tay / troo-vay
I'd like / We'd like...	*Je voudrais / Nous voudrions...*	zhuh voo-dray / noo voo-dree-ohn
...a room.	*...une chambre.*	ewn shahn-bruh
...a ticket to ____.	*...un billet pour ____.*	uhn bee-yay poor ____
Is it possible?	*C'est possible?*	say poh-see-bluh
Where is...?	*Où est...?*	oo ay
...the train station	*...la gare*	lah gar
...the bus station	*...la gare routière*	lah gar root-yehr
...tourist information	*...l'office du tourisme*	loh-fees dew too-reez-muh
Where are the toilets?	*Où sont les toilettes?*	oo sohn lay twah-leht
men	*hommes*	ohm
women	*dames*	dahm
left / right	*à gauche / à droite*	ah gohsh / ah dwaht
straight	*tout droit*	too dwah
When does this open / close?	*Ça ouvre / ferme à quelle heure?*	sah oo-vruh / fehrm ah kehl ur
At what time?	*À quelle heure?*	ah kehl ur
Just a moment.	*Un moment.*	uhn moh-mahn
now / soon / later	*maintenant / bientôt / plus tard*	man-tuh-nahn / bee-an-toh / plew tar
today / tomorrow	*aujourd'hui / demain*	oh-zhoor-dwee / duh-man

For more user-friendly French phrases, check out *Rick Steves' French Phrase Book and Dictionary* or *Rick Steves' French, Italian & German Phrase Book.*

In a French Restaurant

English	French	Pronunciation
I'd like / We'd like...	*Je voudrais / Nous voudrions...*	zhuh voo-dray / noo voo-dree-ohn
...to reserve...	*...réserver...*	ray-zehr-vay
...a table for one / two.	*...une table pour un / deux.*	ewn tah-bluh poor uhn / duh
Is this seat free?	*C'est libre?*	say lee-bruh
The menu (in English), please.	*La carte (en anglais), s'il vous plaît.*	lah kart (ahn ahn-glay) see voo play
service (not) included	*service (non) compris*	sehr-vees (nohn) kohn-pree
to go	*à emporter*	ah ahn-por-tay
with / without	*avec / sans*	ah-vehk / sahn
and / or	*et / ou*	ay / oo
special of the day	*plat du jour*	plah dew zhoor
specialty of the house	*spécialité de la maison*	spay-see-ah-lee-tay duh lah may-zohn
appetizers	*hors d'oeuvre*	or duh-vruh
first course (soup, salad)	*entrée*	ahn-tray
main course (meat, fish)	*plat principal*	plah pran-see-pahl
bread	*pain*	pan
cheese	*fromage*	froh-mahzh
sandwich	*sandwich*	sahnd-weech
soup	*soupe*	soop
salad	*salade*	sah-lahd
meat	*viande*	vee-ahnd
chicken	*poulet*	poo-lay
fish	*poisson*	pwah-sohn
seafood	*fruits de mer*	frwee duh mehr
fruit	*fruit*	frwee
vegetables	*légumes*	lay-gewm
dessert	*dessert*	day-sehr
mineral water	*eau minérale*	oh mee-nay-rahl
tap water	*l'eau du robinet*	loh dew roh-bee-nay
milk	*lait*	lay
(orange) juice	*jus (d'orange)*	zhew (doh-rahnzh)
coffee / tea	*café / thé*	kah-fay / tay
wine	*vin*	van
red / white	*rouge / blanc*	roozh / blahn
glass / bottle	*verre / bouteille*	vehr / boo-tay
beer	*bière*	bee-ehr
Cheers!	*Santé!*	sahn-tay
More. / Another.	*Plus. / Un autre.*	plew / uhn oh-truh
The same.	*La même chose.*	lah mehm shohz
The bill, please.	*L'addition, s'il vous plaît.*	lah-dee-see-ohn see voo play
Do you accept credit cards?	*Vous prenez les cartes?*	voo pruh-nay lay kart
tip	*pourboire*	poor-bwahr
Delicious!	*Délicieux!*	day-lee-see-uh

INDEX

C

D

N

O

P

Q

R

S

T

U

V

W

Y

MAP INDEX

ricksteves.com

your travel dreams into affordable reality

Radio Interviews

Enjoy ready access to Rick's vast library of radio interviews covering travel tips and cultural insights that relate specifically to your Europe travel plans.

Travel Forums

Learn, ask, share! Our online community of savvy travelers is a great resource for first-time travelers to Europe, as well as seasoned pros. You'll find forums on each country, plus travel tips and restaurant/hotel reviews. You can even ask one of our well-traveled staff to chime in with an opinion.

Travel News

Subscribe to our free Travel News e-newsletter, and get monthly updates from Rick on what's happening in Europe.

Audio Europe™

Rick's Free Travel App

Get your FREE Rick Steves Audio Europe™ app to enjoy…

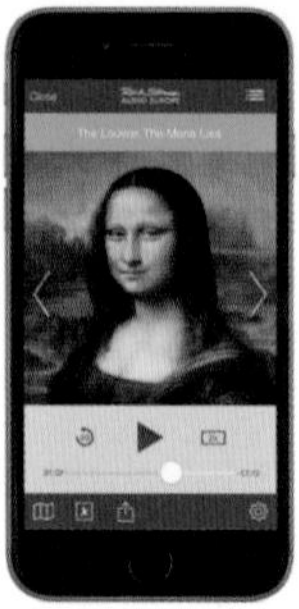

- Dozens of self-guided tours of Europe's top museums, sights and historic walks
- Hundreds of tracks filled with cultural insights and sightseeing tips from Rick's radio interviews
- All organized into handy geographic playlists
- For Apple and Android

With Rick whispering in your ear, Europe gets even better.

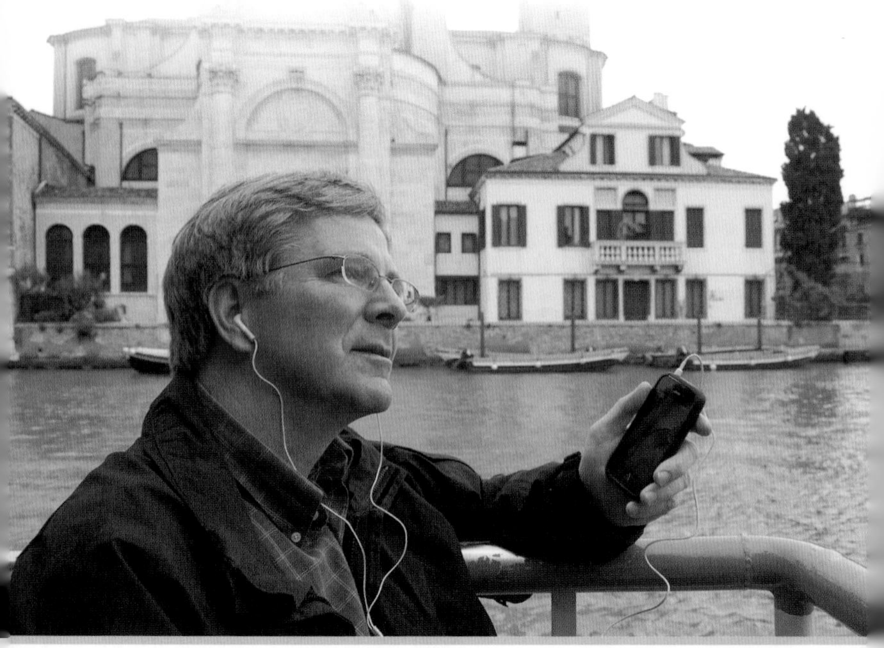

Find out more at ricksteves.com

Rick Steves has

Experience maximum Europe

Save time and energy
This guidebook is your independent-travel toolkit. But for all it delivers, it's still up to you to devote the time and energy it takes to manage the preparation and logistics that are essential for a happy trip. If that's a hassle, there's a solution.

Rick Steves Tours
A Rick Steves tour takes you to Europe's most

great tours, too!

with minimum stress

interesting places with great guides and small groups of 28 or less. We follow Rick's favorite itineraries, ride in comfy buses, stay in family-run hotels, and bring you intimately close to the Europe you've traveled so far to see. Most importantly, we take away the logistical headaches so you can focus on the fun.

Join the fun

This year we'll take thousands of free-spirited travelers—nearly half of them repeat customers—along with us on four dozen different itineraries, from Ireland to Italy to Athens.

Is a Rick Steves tour the right fit for your travel dreams? Find out at ricksteves.com, where you can also request Rick's latest tour catalog.

Europe is best experienced with happy travel partners. We hope you can join us.

See our itineraries at ricksteves.com

A Guide for Every Trip

BEST OF GUIDES

Full-color easy-to-scan format, focusing on Europe's most popular destinations and sights.

Best of England
Best of Europe
Best of France
Best of Germany
Best of Ireland
Best of Italy
Best of Spain

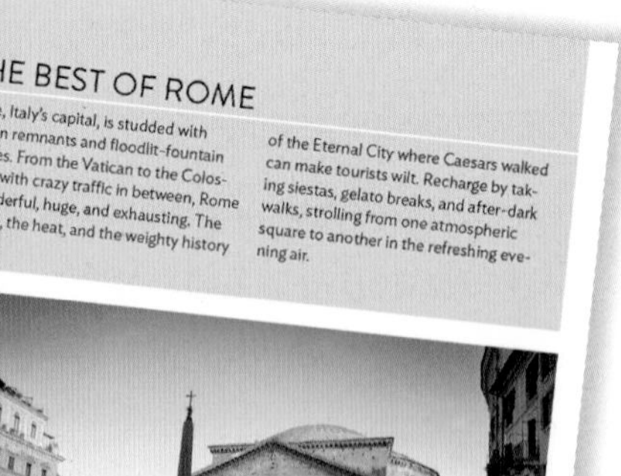

HE BEST OF ROME

e, Italy's capital, is studded with
an remnants and floodlit-fountain
es. From the Vatican to the Colos-
, with crazy traffic in between, Rome
derful, huge, and exhausting. The
s, the heat, and the weighty history
of the Eternal City where Caesars walked
can make tourists wilt. Recharge by taking siestas, gelato breaks, and after-dark
walks, strolling from one atmospheric
square to another in the refreshing evening air.

ed **Pantheon**—which
est dome until the
rly 2,000 years old
ay over 1,500).
of Athens in the **Vat-**
dies the humanistic
nce.
gladiators fought
nother, entertaining
s Rome **ristorante.**
ds at **St. Peter's**

COMPREHENSIVE GUIDES

City, country, and regional guides with detailed coverage for a multi-week trip exploring the most iconic sights and venturing off the beaten track.

Amsterdam & the Netherlands
Barcelona
Belgium: Bruges, Brussels, Antwerp & Ghent
Berlin
Budapest
Croatia & Slovenia
Eastern Europe
England
Florence & Tuscany
France
Germany
Great Britain
Greece: Athens & the Peloponnese
Iceland
Ireland
Istanbul
Italy
London
Paris
Portugal
Prague & the Czech Republic
Provence & the French Riviera
Rome
Scandinavia
Scotland
Spain
Switzerland
Venice
Vienna, Salzburg & Tirol

Rick Steves guidebooks are published by Avalon Travel, an imprint of Perseus Books, a Hachette Book Group compa

POCKET GUIDES

Compact, full-color city guides with the essentials for shorter trips.

Amsterdam
Athens
Barcelona
Florence
Italy's Cinque Terre
London
Munich & Salzburg
Paris
Prague
Rome
Venice
Vienna

SNAPSHOT GUIDES

Focused single-destination coverage.

Basque Country: Spain & France
Copenhagen & the Best of Denmark
Dublin
Dubrovnik
Edinburgh
Hill Towns of Central Italy
Krakow, Warsaw & Gdansk
Lisbon
Loire Valley
Madrid & Toledo
Milan & the Italian Lakes District
Naples & the Amalfi Coast
Normandy
Northern Ireland
Norway
Reykjavik
Sevilla, Granada & Southern Spain
St. Petersburg, Helsinki & Tallinn
Stockholm

CRUISE PORTS GUIDES

Reference for cruise ports of call.

Mediterranean Cruise Ports
Northern European Cruise Ports

Complete your library with...

TRAVEL SKILLS & CULTURE

Study up on travel skills before visiting "Europe through the back door" or gain insight on European history and culture.

Europe 101
European Christmas
European Easter
European Festivals
Europe Through the Back Door
Postcards from Europe
Travel as a Political Act

PHRASE BOOKS & DICTIONARIES

French
French, Italian & German
German
Italian
Portuguese
Spanish

PLANNING MAPS

Britain, Ireland & London
Europe
France & Paris
Germany, Austria & Switzerland
Ireland
Italy
Spain & Portugal

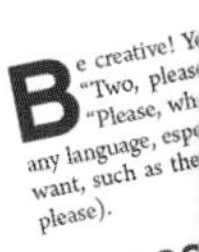

PHOTO CREDITS

Dominic Arizona Bonuccelli (www.azphoto.com): 1 top center, 2 top center, 2 bottom right, 3 center, 3 bottom right, 6, 9 left, 9 right, 10 center right, 11 bottom left, 11 bottom rght, 11 top, 14 bottom right, 17 top, 19 top right, 19 bottom, 20 top, 20 bottom, 22 top left, 22 center, 23 bottom left, 25, 28, 38, 39 top left, 43 left, 43 right, 48 right, 54, 58, 59, 60, 61 top, 73, 80, 81, 82, 86, 87 right, 97, 107, 112, 117, 132, 138, 140, 157, 160, 164, 167, 179, 197, 200, 212, 217 left, 232, 253, 273, 277, 283 left, 283 top right, 285, 292, 300, 319, 326, 342 right, 348, 355, 379 top, 382, 383, 384, 385 right, 393, 410, 414, 418 left, 420, 426, 427, 428

1 bottom © Sborisov | Dreamstime.com, 1 top left © Olga Filipchenko | Dreamstime.com, 2 bottom left © Stevanzz | Dreamstime.com, 11 top © Sborisov | Dreamstime.com, 11 center right © Ixuskmitl | Dreamstime.com, 13 bottom © Sergiyn | Dreamstime.com, 16 center right © Cecoffman | Dreamstime.com, 18 top right © Milosk50 | Dreamstime.com, 18 bottom © Stevanzz | Dreamstime.com, 21 top © Arsty | Dreamstime.com, 21 center right © Arthurr | Dreamstime.com, 23 bottom right © Vichie81 | Dreamstime.com, 32 © Xantana | Dreamstime.com, 51 © Rexbibendi5527 | Dreamstime.com, 55 left © Pivariz | Dreamstime.com, 56 © Eugenesergeev | Dreamstime.com, 72© Sdecoret | Dreamstime.com, 121 © Dreamstime.com, 134 left © Jorisvo | Dreamstime.com, 150 left © Fabieng333 | Dreamstime.com, 154 © Vwalakte | Dreamstime.com, 155 © Philippehalle | Dreamstime.com, 180 © Peregrine | Dreamstime.com, 185 © Zwawol | Dreamstime.com, 204 © Radu Razvan Gheorghe | Dreamstime.com, 278 © Milosk50 | Dreamstime.com, 282 © Photoprofi30 | Dreamstime.com, 296 left © David May | Dreamstime.com, 307 © Uli Danner | Dreamstime.com, 311 © Typhoonski | Dreamstime.com, 330 © Pixattitude | Dreamstime.com, 341 © Rostislav Glinsky | Dreamstime.com, 344 left © Andrewhowson42 | Dreamstime.com, 344 right © Marekusz | Dreamstime.com, 362 © Raeleigh | Dreamstime.com, 368 right © Serrnovik | Dreamstime.com, 369 top middle © Veniamin Kraskov | Dreamstime.com, 369 bottom © Garincha | Dreamstime.com, 376 © Natursports | Dreamstime.com

17 bottom left © Hemis / Alamy Stock Photo, 87 left © Hemis / Alamy Stock Photo, 153 © David Jones / Alamy Stock Photo, 271 © Hemis / Alamy Stock Photo

Public Domain via Wikimedia Commons: 11 bottom right, 129 center right, 152, 162, 269

Additional photography by Ben Cameron, Rich Earl, Tom Griffin, Cameron Hewitt, Suzanne Kotz, Michealanne Jerome, Andrea Johnson, Lauren Mills, Pat O'Connor, Gene Openshaw, Michael Potter, Carol Ries, Steve Smith, Robyn Stencil, Rick Steves, Gretchen Strauch, Laura VanDeventer

Avalon Travel
Hachette Book Group
1700 Fourth Street
Berkeley, CA 94710

Printed in China by RR Donnelley

Second Edition
First printing July 2018

ISBN 978-1-63121-804-0

For the latest on Rick's talks, guidebooks, Europe tours, public radio show, free audio tours, and public television series, contact Rick Steves' Europe, 130 Fourth Avenue North, Edmonds, WA 98020, 425/771-8303, www.ricksteves.com, rick@ricksteves.com.

RICK STEVES' EUROPE
Special Publications Manager: Risa Laib
Managing Editor: Jennifer Madison Davis
Project Editor: Suzanne Kotz
Editorial & Production Assistant: Jessica Shaw
Graphic Content Director: Sandra Hundacker
Maps & Graphics: David C. Hoerlein, Lauren Mills, Mary Rostad

AVALON TRAVEL
Editorial Director: Kevin McLain
Senior Editor and Series Manager: Madhu Prasher
Editor: Jamie Andrade
Editor: Sierra Machado
Copy Editor: Naomi Adler Dancis
Proofreader: Patrick Collins
Indexer: Stephen Callahan
Interior Design & Layout: Tabitha Lahr
Cover Design: Kimberly Glyder Design
Maps & Graphics: Kat Bennett

PHOTO CREDITS
Front Cover Photos: top, left: Macarons © Nejron | Dreamstime.com; top, middle: Lavender field. Lavender field in Valensole, Provence © Felinda | Dreamstime.com; top, right: Gargoyle on the roof of Notre-Dame, Paris © Ben Renard-wiart | Dreamstime.com. Bottom: Chateau de Chenonceau © Scaliger | Dreamstime.com
Back Cover Photos: Left: Louvre Museum in Paris © Ilxuskmitl | Dreamstime.com; middle: Red wine © rostislavsedlacek | 123RF; right: Colmar © Hai Huy Ton That | Dreamstime.com

Let's Keep on Travelin'

Your trip doesn't need to end.

Follow Rick on social media!